BURKE'S
FAMILY INDEX

BURKE'S SERIES

Founded by John Burke 1826
Editor: Hugh Montgomery-Massingberd

BURKE'S
FAMILY
INDEX

LONDON

Burke's Peerage Limited

MCMLXXVI

DISTRIBUTED IN NORTH AMERICA BY **ARCO** PUBLISHING CO INC
NEW YORK

ISBN 0 85011 022 X

R
929.2

This book has been printed and bound by John G Eccles Printers Ltd, Inverness for the Publishers, Burke's Peerage Ltd (Registered Office: 42 Curzon Street, London W1. Publishing and Editorial Offices: 56 Walton Street, London SW3)

MADE AND PRINTED IN GREAT BRITAIN

Distributed in North America by Arco Publishing Company Inc, 219 Park Avenue South, New York, NY 10003, USA

Contents

Preface

WHEN EMBARKING on genealogical research one of the first things to establish is what has been recorded in print about a particular family. Up until now there has not been a reliable and comprehensive guide to the 20,000 different family entries featured in *Burke's* unique range of genealogical and heraldic publications since 1826. The 150th anniversary of the first edition of John Burke's *Peerage and Baronetage* seemed a highly appropriate occasion on which to fill the gap by producing this invaluable new work, *Burke's Family Index*. To describe one's own book as "invaluable" in the PREFACE may appear to be in questionable taste, but we speak from experience as genealogists, having already found the *Family Index* of the utmost usefulness ourselves since the first proofs arrived from the printer. We trust that all genealogists, amateur and professional, will derive a real service from this source of reference, which surely fulfils a long-felt want.

The main text of the book lists surnames (with every variation treated separately, the compound surnames appearing under the last) in alphabetical sequence, with single references to the most recent accounts of the various entries recorded under those names in *Burke's* publications, together with the year of the particular edition. An explanation of how to use the *Family Index* is given in the GUIDE TO THE READER on page xxxi. In effect, the *Family Index* is a guide to the most complete and up-to-date version of a family's narrative pedigree. It is, therefore, much more than just a pure, pedestrian "Index" which sets out each duplicated reference in edition after edition, thereby wasting the reader's time, but rather an interpretative exercise which is the product of an expert editorial team's exhaustive researches in the labyrinthine series of *Burke's* works.

Those who associate *Burke's* with only, say, the *Peerage*, the *Landed Gentry* and the *General Armory*, may be surprised to read the 13 pages of BIBLIOGRAPHY in this book. We thought it would be a good opportunity to set the record straight and we are greatly indebted to Rosemary Pinches for her contribution in which she has managed to unravel the far from straightforward material, so as to achieve an admirably clear and indeed definitive check-list of all the *Burke's* publications. Mrs Pinches is, of course, known to all genealogists and armorists as the proprietor of Heraldry Today, the booksellers, and one could describe her as the *doyenne* of her trade, if *doyenne* did not sound so inappropriate a word for such an attractive and vigorous personality.

The large majority of the editions of *Burke's* works referred to in the *Family Index* are not actually in print (the list facing the title page gives the current books available for sale by the publishers), but we are happy to announce a photocopying service whereby we can supply a photocopy of an entry from an out-of-print edition on receipt of an order giving us the detailed reference and accompanied by £3.00 (the current rate for each entry). In conjunction with the professional body, the Association of Genealogists and Record Agents, we are also pleased to arrange for private genealogical research to be undertaken. Correspondence concerning these services should be addressed to Burke's Peerage Ltd, 56 Walton Street, London SW3.

The expert editorial team, mentioned earlier, which compiled the *Family Index*, was made up of our Assistant Editor Charles Kidd, our editorial assistants Suzanna Osman Jones and Camilla Binny, and our Contributing Editors from outside the office, David Williamson and Hugo Vickers. We are most grateful to them for their hard work and to the others who assisted in this deceptively large task.

In celebration of our 150th anniversary there follows a brief history of *Burke's* At a time when interest in family and social history is spreading significantly — perhaps the search for stability in an unstable world and the sense of identity and continuity of line to be found in genealogy are important factors here — we are enthusiastically seeking a wider audience by making our books educational and entertaining, as well as serious and scholarly. Without neglecting our traditional aristocratic fields, we also hope to till new ground objectively.

HUGH MONTGOMERY-MASSINGBERD
Editorial Director Burke's Peerage Ltd
June 1976

SIR BERNARD BURKE, CB, LLD, Ulster King of Arms, son of the founder of *Burke's*

150 Years of Burke's

THE POPULAR confusion between *Burke's* and *Debrett* (a fundamentally different publication) may well be caused by the name of Burke being commonplace and the (French) name of Debrett being distinctive. There are, after all, a bevy of Burkes: Edmund Burke; Burke and Wills; Burke and Hare; Burkes Club (which although associated with one of Burke's Peerage Ltd's present directors, the Earl of Lichfield, is not connected with the firm); even the obscene cockney epithet. The last-mentioned has led to the tired old jokes about "all the burkes in *Burke's Peerage*"; and to a Peter Cook/ Dudley Moore dialogue about this burke who had the idea of asking people for a lot of information about themselves and then flogging it back to them. (In the interests of historical accuracy it should be pointed out that the rhyming slang epithet is actually spelt "berk", short for Berkeley Hunt).

Our Burkes were a remarkable dynasty of genealogists and heralds, which over a century (1826-1930) created and controlled a unique range of reference works. The next two pages are devoted to an account of that dynasty and of the editors who have carried on their work. The history of the Burke family has been suitably rendered in the narrative style of setting out a pedigree, which, perfected over 150 years, has become *Burke's* trademark and indeed a universally recognised model for all written pedigrees, as opposed to the tabular variety.

The series was founded by John Burke, but he was soon overshadowed by his second son Bernard, who really established the books as a world famous institution. Sir Bernard had a long and colourful reign over the Series and also produced a stream of books of a more general nature. He loved a flowery phrase and, if not a charlatan, took on too much and was undoubtedly uncritical to a degree. Genealogy should be the scholarly, scientific and objective pursuit of truth, but in the nineteenth century it became almost irredeemably tainted with the stigma of snobbery. *Burke's* was in the van of those trying to satisfy the craving for bogus medieval romanticism and some lamentable exercises in "Gothick phantasy" were perpetrated. A brilliantly mounted campaign led by Horace Round and other scholars exposed the myths, and as a result the reputation of *Burke's* as an objective record was rebuilt under the guidance of Sir Bernard's son, Sir Henry Farnham Burke, Garter Principal King of Arms (a distinction denied his father). The books were produced from an attic at the College of

Continued on p.xii

BURKE OF BURKE'S PEERAGE

Lineage — The Burkes descend from DOMINICK BURKE, of Clondagoff Castle, co Galway (*b* 1664), who claimed descent from the De Burghs of Clanricarde through the Burkes of Meelick and Tintrim. For a full account of the family *see* BURKE'S *Landed Gentry* 18th Edn Volume I (1965) *pp* 99-101. Dominick Burke's grandson, JOHN BURKE, Offr Spanish Service, *m* 2ndly, Lucinda, eldest dau of Oliver Plunkett, of Bettyfield, co Roscommon (of the family of St Oliver Plunkett, titular Primate of Ireland and canonised martyr), and by her had issue (with two daus),

    1 JOSEPH, ancestor of the BURKES *of Auberies* (*see* BURKE'S *LGi*). (His only child, John French Burke was author of *The Domestic Manners and Institutions of the Romans*).

    2 PETER, *of whom presently.*

The yr son,

PETER BURKE, of Elm Hall, co Tipperary, JP co Tipperary and King's co, *b* 1756, *m* 1st 1 July 1785, Anne (*d* 18 Feb 1818), 2nd dau and co-heiress of Matthew Dowdall, MD, of Mullingar, by his wife Bridget, sister of Bartholomew Barnewall (*see* BURKE'S *Peerage*, BARNEWALL, Bt), and had issue (with a dau),

    1 JOHN, *of whom presently.*

    2 Joseph, of Elm Hall, co Tipperary, JP, Barrister-at-law, Assist Poor Law Commr 1839, *b* 1788, *m* 31 Jan 1856, Sarah, 2nd dau of Jeremiah John Murphy, QC, a Master in Chancery in Ireland, by his wife Maria, eldest dau of Michael Balfe, of South Park, co Roscommon (*see* BURKE'S *Irish Family Records*), and *dsp* 13 Dec 1864.

Mr Peter Burke *m* 2ndly 26 July 1820, Clarinda (*d* 15 April 1851), eldest dau of Redmond Dolphin, JP, of Corr, co Galway, and *d* 13 Jan 1836. The elder son,

JOHN BURKE, of London, author of the *Peerage and Baronetage, Official Kalendar, Extinct Peerages, Portrait Gallery, Landed Gentry, Extinct Baronetcies, Knightage, General Armory, Heraldic Illustrations, The Patrician, Royal Families*, etc, *b* 12 Nov 1786, *m* 6 May 1807, Mary (*d* 17 Nov 1846), 2nd dau of Bernard O'Reilly, of Ballymorris, co Longford, and *d* 27 March 1848, having had issue (with two sons and one dau who predeceased him *unm*, and one surv dau, who also *dunm*),

    1 Peter Joseph, QC, of Elm Hall, Serjeant-at-law for co Palatine of Lancaster, author of *Royal Register, The Criminal Law, A Treatise on the Law of Copyright, The Three Statutes, The Wisdom and Genius of Edmund Burke, Celebrated Trials, An Exploratory Analysis, Supplement to Godson, The Law of International Copyright, The Patent Law, The Romance of the Forum, The Public and Domestic Life of Edmund Burke, The Copyright Law and the Press, Celebrated Naval and Military Trials*, etc, *b* 7 May 1811; *dunm* 26 March 1881.

    2 (JOHN) BERNARD (Sir), *of whom presently.*

The yr surv son,

SIR (JOHN) BERNARD BURKE, Kt Bach (1854), CB (1868), LLD, MRIA, of Dublin, Barrister-at-law, Middle Temple, Ulster King of Arms and Registrar and Kt attendant on the Order of St Patrick 1853-92, Keeper of State Papers of Ireland 1867-92, a Gov and Trustee of Nat Gallery of Ireland, editor of the *Peerage and Baronetage, Extinct Peerages, Landed Gentry, Extinct Baronetcies, Knightage, General Armory, Heraldic Illustrations, The Patrician, Royal Families*, etc, author of *The House of Gwysoney, Roll of Battle Abbey, Historic Lands, Anecdotes of the Aristocracy, Heraldic Register, Visitation of Seats and Arms, Family Romance, Orders of Knighthood, Pedigree and Arms of the Glovers, Royal Descents, Vicissitudes of Families, Selection of Arms, Rise of Great Families, Sovereigns of England, Book of Precedence, Colonial Gentry*, etc, *b* 5 Jan 1814, *educ* in London and France, *m* 8 Jan 1856, Barbara Frances (*d* 15 Jan 1887), yr dau of James MacEvoy, of Tobertynan, co Meath, and Frankford, co Longford (*see*

BURKE'S *Irish Family Records*, DE STACPOOLE), and *d* 12 Dec 1892, having had issue (with a dau who *dunm*),

1 HENRY FARNHAM (Sir), *of whom presently.*

2 Bernard Louis, Athlone Pursuivant of Arms, *b* 17 May 1861; *dunm* 5 July 1892.

3 Harlowen Joseph, *b* 3 March 1863; *dunm* 13 Nov 1888.

4 Ashworth Peter, Capt R Irish Rifles, ADC to Lord Lieut of Ireland, editor of the *Peerage and Baronetage, Landed Gentry, Colonial Gentry, Landed Gentry of Ireland*, etc, author of *Family Records*, etc, *b* 8 Sept 1864; *dunm* 6 Aug 1919.

5 Edward Plunkett, Capt KOR Lancaster Regt, *b* 1 July 1866, *m* 19 March 1892, Christina Mary *d* 9 Sept 1931), dau of Matthew Peter D'Arcy, DL, MP, of Kilcroney, co Wicklow, and *d* 17 March 1899, leaving issue, two sons Major Edward Bernard Mary Burke, MBE, *m* with issue; and Henry Joseph Burke, S Staffs Regt, *ka* in World War I, *unm*).

6 John Edward, Athlone Pursuivant of Arms, *b* 19 March 1868; *dunm* 9 March 1909.

7 Arthur Meredyth, FSA, Major RA, served in World War I, author of *The Prominent Families of the USA, Key to the Ancient Parish Registers, Indexes to Ancient Testamentary Records of Westminster, Memorials of St Margaret's Westminster*, etc, *b* 17 Aug 1872, *m* 9 Jan 1900, Gertrude (*d* 23 Feb 1959), 1st dau of James Francis Caulfield, of The Elms, Didsbury, Manchester, and *d* 7 April 1920, having had issue, two sons (Brig Brian Arthur Burke, DSO, *dunm*; and Desmond Peter Meredyth Burke, Headmaster Clayesmore Sch) and two daus one *d* an inf).

The eldest son,

SIR HENRY FARNHAM BURKE KCVO (1919) (CVO 1902), CB (1911), FSA, Rouge Croix Pursuivant of Arms 1880-87, Somerset Herald 1887-1911, Dep Ulster King of Arms 1889-93, Norroy King of Arms 1911-19, Garter Prin King of Arms 1919-30, Registrar Coll of Arms 1904-11, Inspr of Regtl Colours of Brit and Ind Armies 1904-29, Geneologist of Order of St Patrick 1889, Order of Bath 1913-30 and Order of St John 1919-30, KGStJ, editor of the *Peerage and Baronetage*, etc, author of *Roman Catholic Families, Pedigree of the Family of Darwin, Pedigree and Quarterings of De Trafford, Examples of Irish Book Plates, Theydon Mount, Historical Record of the Coronation 1902, Historical Record of the Coronation 1911*, etc, *b* 12 June 1859, *educ* Beaumont, *m* 23 April 1885, Helena Mary Ray (Lady Farnham Burke — addl prefix surname of FARNHAM assumed by Deed Poll 1931) (*d* 1 April 1955), only dau of Henry Pollard Palmer, of Oaklands, Eccles, Lancs, and *d* 21 Aug 1930, having had issue, one son (Capt John Bernard Mary Burke, MC, Gren Guards, *m*, and *d* of wounds in World War I, leaving issue, a son (Patrick Henry) Anthony Burke, *m* twice, and was *k* in the hunting field leaving issue (by his 1st *m*), two sons and three daus) and one dau (Lady Bellew — *see* BURKE'S *Peerage).*

Burke's Editors not of the Family

A. C. Fox-Davies: *Landed Gentry of Ireland* 1912; *Landed Gentry* 1914

A. Winton Thorpe: *Peerage and Baronetage* 1921; *Landed Gentry* 1921; *Handbook to the Order of the British Empire* 1921

A. T. Butler: *Peerage and Baronetage* 1923-34; *Landed Gentry* 1925

E. M. Swinhoe: *Peerage and Baronetage* 1935-37

Harry Pirie-Gordon of Buthlaw: *Landed Gentry* 1937

Baron de Spon: (Caretaker) Editor *Burke's* Series 1941-46

L. G. Pine: Managing Editor *Burke's* Series 1946-60

Peter Townend: Editor *Burke's* Series 1960-72

Hugh Montgomery-Massingberd: Executive Editor *Burke's* Series from 1971; Editorial Director from 1972

Arms — an appropriate venue as the original object of the Series was to make public some of the pedigrees recorded there. The links between *Burke's* and the armorial authority have always been strong: the present Board includes John Brooke-Little, Richmond Herald and we publish Sir Anthony Wagner's *Records and Collections of the College of Arms*. The Burke family's connexion with the Series ended on Sir Henry Farnham Burke's death in 1930.

After that, the ownership of the copyright passed through some rather murky water — at one stage the *Peerage* was owned by Mallaby-Deeley, the "50 Shilling Tailor" and the *Landed Gentry* by Maundy Gregory, the notorious titles broker — though happily the contents of the book were not adversely affected. The various titles were reunited under the one imprint in the American-owned Shaw's Reference Series (this did *not* include "Shaw's Ladies Directory"), later incorporated in the Mercury House Group, which eventually sold its controlling interest to the Holdway Group, owned by the Norman family, in 1973.

By this time major expansion plans for the Series had been launched comprising numerous new works covering British and World Royalty; the Peerage and Baronetage (extant and extinct); the histories of distinguished families of America (Presidential and others), British Isles (divided into volumes for each country with *Family Records* replacing the *Landed Gentry* as a title), Commonwealth, Ethnic Groups and Europe; Genealogy; Heraldry; Country Houses; Social History (personal reminiscences under the title *In Living Memory*), etc. Many of the "new" ideas were merely adaptations of old *Burke's* books, though some of the projects were completely original. Continuity and change could be said to be the general theme.

A logical policy has evolved of only producing new editions of all the genealogical works (including the *Peerage*) once a generation, *i.e.* every 15-20 years. A "grand scheme" is envisaged in which 40 different books are to be produced on a 20 year cycle (at the rate of roughly two a year). Inspired by Sir Iain Moncreiffe of that Ilk, the aim is to clothe the skeleton of genealogy with the flesh and blood of family history, while preserving and improving the scholarship. The current staff of *Burke's* — contrary to what some may expect, half-a-dozen young people, still in their twenties, housed in an informal set of rooms in Chelsea — with a formidable band of freelance contributors and sympathetic supporters, believe that amidst the exciting prospects for the next 150 years can be seen a future for the past.

A Bibliography of Burke's 1826-1976

Rosemary Pinches

BURKE — or more commonly *Burke's* — is probably the best known name in peerage, genealogical and heraldic books. The combined number of books produced by the family is prodigious, of which *Burke's Peerage* is the most famous.

This Bibliography lists all the books issued by the Burke family, and those who have carried on their work after them. Most of their publications went through many editions, and quite often the same book has been offered with a new date, or the same edition with a new supplement, making the sorting out of the various editions more difficult than usual.

I have arranged the titles in chronological order of the first edition of each work, so that all editions of any one title have been kept together. Each title has been given in full when the work is first introduced and when there is a change of title or editor, but where the title is exactly the same as the previous edition, it has been abbreviated. Where the editor of a book is known, but his name has not appeared therein, he has been shown in parentheses.

The first of the *Burke* publications was *A General and Heraldic Dictionary of the Peerage and Baronetage*, edited by John Burke in 1826. It gained popularity in its early days, particularly because it was arranged in alphabetical order and was therefore much easier to refer to than previous peerage books which had been in order of precedence. Also, it included in one alphabet the Peerages of Ireland and Scotland as well as England, and in 1833 illustrations of arms were added at the head of each pedigree. By the 1840s, when the page size had been enlarged, the format of the book was very much as we know it today, when it has been through one hundred and five editions.

In 1840 both the *Peerage* and the *Extinct Peerage* had very attractive coloured lithographed additional title pages, but this was soon discontinued. In 1921 the Portraits of Royalty were introduced into the *Peerage*, and in 1938 and 1939 colour plates of arms, which were discontinued after the war.

The first appearance of the name of John Burke's son, John Bernard Burke, as co-editor was in the first edition of the *Extinct Baronetcies* in 1838, when he was twenty-four. He was the second son, his elder brother, Peter, being a Queen's Counsel, and a writer, mainly, of legal works. After his *Criminal Law* and *Treatise on the*

Law of Copyright, his *Celebrated Trials connected with the Aristocracy*
came out in the same year, 1849, as his brother John Bernard's
Anecdotes of the Aristocracy, and it would be interesting to know
which brother had the idea of bringing out this type of book first.

As a review in the *British Army Despatch* said in 1849, referring to
Anecdotes of the Aristocracy:

"Hitherto the talents of the author of the volumes before us have been directed
towards elucidating the hidden treasures of genealogical history. In the present
instance he has abandoned, as it were, the rugged highways of antiquity for more
flowery paths abounding in legend and romance".

I doubt if even Sir Bernard really compared himself to Boccacio,
as did *The Britannia* reviewing the same work, but this type of book
must have been very popular as editions and similar titles multiplied,
such as: *The Romance of the Aristocracy*; *Romantic Records of the
Distinguished Families*; and *Family Romance or Episodes in the
Domestic Annals of the Aristocracy*.

Of the same genre, *Vicissitudes of Families* went through more
editions and series than the others, and often took the most space on
the advertisement pages of Burke's other works. As the title implies,
the stories in it were of the fall of titled and important families —
obviously of appeal to human nature!

In 1853, John Bernard Burke was appointed Ulster King of Arms
and in 1854 he was knighted, after which his name usually appeared
as Sir Bernard Burke. He was by far the most prolific writer and
editor of the Burke family, and, after his father's death in 1848, his
name stood alone on all the works. He issued new editions of his
father's books, and the first work to be produced as a new title by him
alone was *The Roll of Battle Abbey* in 1848, with *The Historic Lands*
following swiftly in the same year.

Burke's Landed Gentry, only slightly less well known than the
Peerage, was first issued under the title — rather strange sounding to
our ears today — *A Genealogical and Heraldic History of the
Commoners of Great Britain and Ireland*. Volume I first appeared in
1833, and between that date and 1838, when volume IV was published,
the first three volumes were reprinted several times. 1843 was the first
publication under the *Landed Gentry* title, and, here again, the
volumes can be found variously dated and re-issued. This edition was
the only one to produce an index to all persons in the whole work,
including those who married into the families, which ran to 311 pages
by itself. It was reprinted for the 1853 edition, or more probably was
never allowed to go out of print, being found variously dated over a
period of ten years.

It was rather a habit of the Burke family, and particularly of Sir
Bernard, to re-issue the same book, perhaps with a new supplement or

addenda, with a new edition number or a new date. That this caused
annoyance to his contemporaries is illustrated from a letter in Sir
Bernard's hand, which I have pasted into a copy of the *Supplement* to
the fifth edition of the *Landed Gentry*, addressed to George Marshall,
the well known author and genealogist. It is from Dublin Castle,
where Ulster's office was housed, and dated 5 April 1876:

"My dear Marshall,
    I know that the Publishers make it a law of the Medes and the Persians to
require the whole book to be purchased; and, as I have nothing to do with the
proceeds of the sale, I have no voice in the matter. Luckily I have a spare copy of
the Supplement for your kind acceptance.
    Most gladly do I avail myself of your obliging offer as to the Arms of Hall and
Marshall. Enclosed are the pages of the old edition containing those names, and
you will do me a great favour if you will add and amend.
    The Genealogist has just reached me and is full of interest.
                                                    Yours ever Sincerely
                                                    J. Bernard Burke.
                                                    Ulster".

The *Supplement* was not, of course, normally issued separately,
but presumably Sir Bernard kept a few with which to placate irate
purchasers who did not want to buy the whole book again for the sake
of the Supplement.

The illustrations of arms which had been included in *Burke's
Commoners*, dropped out of the early editions of the *Landed Gentry*,
and *Burke's Heraldic Illustrations* was advertised as containing

"the Shields of Arms of the Chief Families in the Kingdom, beautifully engraved
on copper, in illustration and completion of 'THE HISTORY OF THE LANDED
GENTRY'."

An *Illuminated Supplement to the Heraldic Illustrations* was
issued in 1851, and again in 1856, with magnificent colour plates, but
presumably the idea did not catch on as no further editions followed
and the illustrations of arms were back in the *Landed Gentry* again in
the next century, although A. C. Fox-Davies regretted, in his Preface
to the 1914 edition, that he had not been able to illustrate all the
arms. The only editions of the *Landed Gentry* to have colour plates
were 1939 and 1952. In 1939 also an American Supplement was
introduced, which was issued separately as *Burke's Distinguished
Families of America*, and now as *Burke's American Families*.

Mention must be made of *Burke's General Armory*, probably the
most often referred to book on heraldry. The Preface to the 1878
edition claims that it included "some 60,000 coats of Arms" and a
Supplement was added to this in later editions. The blazons of arms,
arranged in alphabetical order of surnames, constitute one of the
largest printed collections of the arms of any one country in the world
and is a remarkable work. Although the criticism is sometimes

levelled against it that it is not of official authority and can lead people astray by making them think that they must be entitled to the arms given against their surname, it is not the fault of the editors if the book is misused.

Sir Bernard had one daughter and seven sons, of whom his eldest son, Henry Farnham Burke, succeeded where his father had failed in becoming Garter King of Arms, in 1919. It was, however, in 1887, the same year that he was made Somerset Herald, when his first publication, in conjunction with J. J. Howard, came out. This was *Genealogical Collections illustrating the History of Roman Catholic Families of England*. He did not enter much into the editing of any of the perennial *Burke's* publications, although the Prefaces of the 1897 and 1898 editions of the *Peerage* were signed "H.F.B." He produced eight further works, two of them Historical Records of the two subsequent Coronations. That of King Edward VII and Queen Alexandra was a very large and elaborate volume with fine colour illustrations by Byam Shaw.

Although Sir Bernard died in 1892, his name did not, and many subsequent editions of the *Peerage* and the *Landed Gentry* have been described as "by" him and "edited" by the Editor of the time. His fourth son, Ashworth Peter Burke, carried on with the editing of the *Peerage* and the *Landed Gentry*, although his name did not appear on these until 1900, in which year a photogravure portrait of the late Sir Bernard appeared for the only time.

In the meantime, the only edition of the *Colonial Gentry* had appeared, volume I edited by Sir Bernard in 1891 and volume II by Ashworth P. Burke in 1895. This, in the same format as the *Landed Gentry*, contains pedigrees mainly of families of Australia, New Zealand, Canada and the West Indies.

It was this new editor who first separated out the *Landed Gentry of Ireland* from the rest. Following in his father's footsteps, he initiated an Irish Supplement to the 1898 edition of the *Landed Gentry* which was reprinted alone in 1899 as the *Landed Gentry of Ireland*. Only three further editions have ever been published, and the new *Burke's Irish Family Records* (1976), has taken its place.

The seventh son of Sir Bernard, Arthur Meredyth Burke, was the only other son to put his name to a publication, and his best known work was the *Key to the Ancient Parish Registers of England and Wales*, 1908, re-issued with a supplement in 1909 and reprinted twice in America since the war. He never edited the *Peerage* or *Landed Gentry*.

The First World War did not stop the publication of *Burke's Peerage* until after the 1917 edition. There was then a gap until 1921, as not only the shortages and upheaval of the war had to be contended with, but also the death of the editor, Ashworth P. Burke. For the first time an editor for the *Peerage* had to be brought in who was not a member of the Burke family, and A. Winton Thorpe edited the 1921 edition only. He also edited the 1921 edition of the *Landed Gentry*, although here he had been preceded by another non-member of the family, A. C. Fox-Davies, who had edited it in 1914 (and the *Landed Gentry of Ireland* in 1912).

After a year's gap, Alfred T. Butler took over in 1923. At this time he was Sir Henry Farnham Burke's secretary and right-hand man at the College of Arms, so the editorship cannot be said to have moved far from the family. He continued to edit with Miss E. M. Swinhoe's help after Sir Henry's death in 1930, but in 1935 the name of Swinhoe appears alone, and in 1938 and 1939 no Editor is named, although an office headed by Mr Smallshaw actually undertook the work.

After 1939, no edition of the *Peerage* was published, except for the slim *War Gazette* in 1940, until 1949, when Leslie G. Pine took up the editorship. From then until now it has been issued every three or four years instead of annually (the last three editions edited by Peter Townend), of which the most recent was 1970, with a reprint in 1975 without the Royal Family or Knightage but with a Supplement. The present and future policy of the *Burke's* Series under its current Editor Hugh Montgomery-Massingberd is dealt with elsewhere in this book.

It is interesting that such a large number of the *Burke* books are still valuable reference works, and many have been reprinted since the last war, both here and in the United States of America. It is very satisfying that in the year of the 150th anniversary of its founding, *Burke's* publications should be as active as ever, both in continuing with the old favourites and introducing new titles.

BURKE'S PEERAGE

Burke, John: *A General and Heraldic Dictionary of the Peerage and Baronetage of the United Kingdom for MDCCCXXVI. Exhibiting, under strict alphabetical arrangement, The Present State of those exalted Ranks, with their Armorial Bearings, Mottoes, etc., And deducing the Lineage of each House from the Founder of its Honors. With an Appendix, comprising the Prelates, the Surnames of Peers, Titles by courtesy of their eldest sons, Names of Heirs Presumptive, etc. etc.* Has been seen bound with 76 pages of illustrations of arms (*see next item*) and without   **1826**

Burke, John: *A General and Heraldic Dictionary of the Peerage and Baronetage of the British Empire. Exhibiting, under strict alphabetical arrangement, The Present State of those Exalted Personages, with their Armorial Bearings, Mottoes, etc. And deducing the genealogical line of each house from the earliest period; With an Appendix* . . . A New and enlarged edition. Bound with *The Armorial Bearings of the Peers and Baronets of the United Kingdom, Disposed in strict alphabetical order* (91 pages of illustrations of arms)   **1828**

Burke, John: *A General and Heraldic Dictionary of the Peerage and Baronetage of the British Empire. Exhibiting, under strict alphabetical arrangement, The Present State of these Exalted Ranks, with their Armorial Bearings* . . . Third edition, considerably augmented. Bound with *The Amorial Bearings of the Peers* . . . 91 pages of illustrations of arms, plus 2 pages of additional illustrations. The Preface is dated April 1829   **1830**

Burke, John: *A General and Heraldic Dictionary of the Peerage and Baronetage of the British Empire.* Fourth edition, two volumes   **1832**

Burke, John: *A General and Heraldic Dictionary of the Peerage and Baronetage of the British Empire.* Fourth edition, corrected to MDCCCXXXIII, two volumes. Preface "to the Former edition" dated 1832   **1833**

Burke, John: *A Genealogical and Heraldic Dictionary of the Peerage and Baronetage of the British Empire.* Fifth edition   **1837**

Burke, John: *A Genealogical and Heraldic Dictionary of the Peerage and Baronetage* . . . Sixth edition   **1839**

Burke, John: *A Genealogical and Heraldic Dictionary of the Peerage and Baronetage* . . . Sixth edition. A Reprint of the 1839 edition, with extra correcting sheets   **1840**

Burke, John: *A Genealogical and Heraldic Dictionary of the Peerage and Baronetage* . . . Seventh edition   **1841**

Burke, John: *A Genealogical and Heraldic Dictionary of the Peerage and Baronetage* . . . Seventh edition. A Reprint of the 1841 edition, with extra Correcting Sheets   **1842**

Burke, John: *A Genealogical and Heraldic Dictionary of the Peerage and Baronetage* . . . Eighth edition   **1845**

Burke, John and John Bernard: *A Genealogical and Heraldic Dictionary of the Peerage and Baronetage* . . . Ninth edition   **1847**

Burke, John and John Bernard: *A Genealogical and Heraldic Dictionary of the Peerage and Baronetage* . . . Tenth edition   **1848**

Burke, John B.: *A Genealogical and Heraldic Dictionary of the Peerage and Baronetage* . . . Eleventh edition   **1849**

Burke, John B.: *A Genealogical and Heraldic Dictionary of the Peerage and Baronetage* . . . Twelfth edition   **1850**

Burke, John B.: *A Genealogical and Heraldic Dictionary of the Peerage and Baronetage* . . . Thirteenth edition   **1851**

Burke, John B.: *A Genealogical and Heraldic Dictionary of the Peerage and Baronetage* . . . Fourteenth edition   **1852**

Burke, John B.: *A Genealogical and Heraldic Dictionary of the Peerage and Baronetage* . . . Fifteenth edition   **1853**

Burke, Sir J. Bernard: *A Genealogical and Heraldic Dictionary of the Peerage and Baronetage* . . . Sixteenth edition   **1854**

Burke, Sir Bernard: *A Genealogical and Heraldic Dictionary of the Peerage and Baronetage* . . . Seventeenth edition   1855

Burke, Sir Bernard: *A Genealogical and Heraldic Dictionary of the Peerage and Baronetage* . . . Eighteenth edition   1856

Burke, Sir Bernard: *A Genealogical and Heraldic Dictionary of the Peerage and Baronetage* . . . Nineteenth edition   1857

Burke, Sir Bernard: *A Genealogical and Heraldic Dictionary of the Peerage and Baronetage* . . . Twentieth edition   1858

Burke, Sir Bernard: *A Genealogical and Heraldic Dictionary of the Peerage and Baronetage* . . . Twenty-first edition   1859

Burke, Sir Bernard: *A Genealogical and Heraldic Dictionary of the Peerage and Baronetage* . . . Twenty-second edition   1860

Burke, Sir Bernard: *A Genealogical and Heraldic Dictionary of the Peerage and Baronetage* . . . Twenty-third edition   1861

Burke, Sir Bernard: *A Genealogical and Heraldic Dictionary of the Peerage and Baronetage* . . . Twenty-fourth edition   1862

Burke, Sir Bernard: *A Genealogical and Heraldic Dictionary of the Peerage and Baronetage* . . . Twenty-fifth edition   1863

Burke, Sir Bernard: *A Genealogical and Heraldic Dictionary of the Peerage and Baronetage* . . . Twenty-sixth edition   1864

Burke, Sir Bernard: *A Genealogical and Heraldic Dictionary of the Peerage and Baronetage* . . . Twenty-seventh edition   1865

Burke, Sir Bernard: *A Genealogical and Heraldic Dictionary of the Peerage and Baronetage* . . . Twenty-eighth edition   1866

Burke, Sir Bernard: *A Genealogical and Heraldic Dictionary of the Peerage and Baronetage* . . . Twenty-ninth edition   1867

Burke, Sir Bernard: *A Genealogical and Heraldic Dictionary of the Peerage and Baronetage* . . . Thirtieth edition   1868

Burke, Sir Bernard: *A Genealogical and Heraldic Dictionary of the Peerage and Baronetage* . . . Thirty-first edition   1869

Burke, Sir Bernard: *A Genealogical and Heraldic Dictionary of the Peerage and Baronetage* . . . Thirty-second edition   1870

Burke, Sir Bernard: *A Genealogical and Heraldic Dictionary of the Peerage and Baronetage* . . . Thirty-third edition   1871

Burke, Sir Bernard: *A Genealogical and Heraldic Dictionary of the Peerage and Baronetage* . . . Thirty-fourth edition   1872

Burke, Sir Bernard: *A Genealogical and Heraldic Dictionary of the Peerage and Baronetage* . . . Thirty-fifth edition   1873

Burke, Sir Bernard: *A Genealogical and Heraldic Dictionary of the Peerage and Baronetage* . . . Thirty-sixth edition   1874

Burke, Sir Bernard: *A Genealogical and Heraldic Dictionary of the Peerage and Baronetage* . . . Thirty-seventh edition   1875

Burke, Sir Bernard: *A Genealogical and Heraldic Dictionary of the Peerage and Baronetage* . . . Thirty-eighth edition   1876

Burke, Sir Bernard: *A Genealogical and Heraldic Dictionary of the Peerage and Baronetage* . . . Thirty-ninth edition   1877

Burke, Sir Bernard: *A Genealogical and Heraldic Dictionary of the Peerage and Baronetage together with Memoirs of the Privy Councillors and Knights.* Fortieth edition   1878

Burke, Sir Bernard: *A Genealogical and Heraldic Dictionary of the Peerage and Baronetage* . . . Forty-first edition   1879

Burke, Sir Bernard: *A Genealogical and Heraldic Dictionary of the Peerage and Baronetage* . . . Forty-second edition   1880

Burke, Sir Bernard and Ashworth P.: *A Genealogical and Heraldic History of the Peerage and Baronetage, The Privy Council, Knightage and Companionage*, Sixty-ninth edition   1907

Burke, Sir Bernard and Ashworth P.: *A Genealogical and Heraldic History of the Peerage and Baronetage* . . . Seventieth edition   1908

Burke, Sir Bernard and Ashworth P.: *A Genealogical and Heraldic History of the Peerage and Baronetage* . . . Seventy-first edition   1909

Burke, Sir Bernard and Ashworth P.: *A Genealogical and Heraldic History of the Peerage and Baronetage* . . . Seventy-second edition   1910

Burke, Sir Bernard and Ashworth P.: *A Genealogical and Heraldic History of the Peerage and Baronetage* . . . Seventy-third edition   1911

Burke, Sir Bernard and Ashworth P.: *A Genealogical and Heraldic History of the Peerage and Baronetage* . . . Seventy-fourth edition   1912

Burke, Sir Bernard and Ashworth P.: *A Genealogical and Heraldic History of the Peerage and Baronetage* . . . Seventy-fifth edition   1913

Burke, Sir Bernard and Ashworth P.: *A Genealogical and Heraldic History of the Peerage and Baronetage* . . . Seventy-sixth edition   1914

Burke, Sir Bernard and Ashworth P.: *A Genealogical and Heraldic History of the Peerage and Baronetage* . . . Seventy-seventh edition   1915

Burke, Sir Bernard and Ashworth P.: *A Genealogical and Heraldic History of the Peerage and Baronetage* . . . Seventy-eighth edition   1916

Burke, Sir Bernard and Ashworth P.: *A Genealogical and Heraldic History of the Peerage and Baronetage* . . . Seventy-ninth edition   1917

Thorpe, A. Winton: *A Genealogical and Heraldic History of the Peerage and Baronetage, The Privy Council, Knightage and Companionage, by Sir Bernard Burke, and Ashworth P. Burke, edited by A. Winton Thorpe.* Eightieth edition   1921

Butler, Alfred T.: *A Genealogical and Heraldic History of the Peerage and Baronetage, The Privy Council and Knightage, by Sir Bernard Burke and Ashworth P. Burke, edited by Alfred T. Butler.* Eighty-first edition   1923

Butler, Alfred T.: *A Genealogical and Heraldic History of the Peerage and Baronetage* . . . Eighty-second edition   1924

Butler, Alfred T.: *A Genealogical and Heraldic History of the Peerage and Baronetage* . . . Eighty-third edition   1925

Butler, Alfred T.: *A Genealogical and Heraldic History of the Peerage and Baronetage* . . . Eighty-fourth edition   1926

[Butler, A. T. and E. M. Swinhoe]: *A Genealogical and Heraldic History of the Peerage and Baronetage* . . . Eighty-fifth edition   1927

[Butler, A. T. and E. M. Swinhoe]: *A Genealogical and Heraldic History of the Peerage and Baronetage* . . . Eighty-sixth edition   1928

[Butler, A. T. and E. M. Swinhoe]: *A Genealogical and Heraldic History of the Peerage and Baronetage* . . . Eighty-seventh edition   1929

[Butler, A. T. and E. M. Swinhoe]: *A Genealogical and Heraldic History of the Peerage and Baronetage* . . . Eighty-eighth edition   1930

[Butler, A. T. and E. M. Swinhoe]: *A Genealogical and Heraldic History of the Peerage and Baronetage* . . . Eighty-ninth edition   1931

[Butler, A. T. and E. M. Swinhoe]: *A Genealogical and Heraldic History of the Peerage and Baronetage* . . . Ninetieth edition   1932

[Butler, A. T. and E. M. Swinhoe]: *A Genealogical and Heraldic History of the Peerage and Baronetage* . . . Ninety-first edition   1933

[Butler, A. T. and E. M. Swinhoe]: *A Genealogical and Heraldic History of the Peerage and Baronetage* . . . Ninety-second edition   1934

Swinhoe, E. M.: *A Genealogical and Heraldic History of the Peerage and Baronetage, The Privy Council and Knightage, by Sir Bernard Burke and Ashworth P. Burke, edited by E. M. Swinhoe.* Ninety-third edition   1935

Swinhoe, E. M.: *A Genealogical and Heraldic History of the Peerage and Baronetage*
... Ninety-fourth edition						1936
Swinhoe, E. M.: *A Genealogical and Heraldic History of the Peerage and Baronetage*
... Ninety-fifth edition						1937
[Smallshaw]: *Burke's Genealogical and Heraldic History of the Peerage, Baronetage
and Knightage, Privy Council, and Order of Precedence, by the late Sir Bernard
Burke.* Coronation Honours, Ninety-sixth edition			1938
[Smallshaw]: *Burke's Genealogical and Heraldic History of the Peerage, Baronetage*
... Ninety-seventh edition						1939
[Smallshaw]: *Burke's War Gazette and Corrigenda to the Peerage, Baronetage and
Knightage, The Privy Council, Lords Spiritual and the Ministry, by the late Sir
Bernard Burke.* Ninety-eighth edition				1940
Sometimes found bound with the Ninety-seventh edition, in which case the title page
reads: *Burke's Genealogical and Heraldic History of the Peerage, Baronetage and
Knightage with War Gazette and Corrigenda*
Pine, Leslie G.: *Burke's Genealogical and Heraldic History of the Peerage, Baronetage
and Knightage, Privy Council and Order of Precedence.* Ninety-ninth edition. With
separate Addendum						1949
Pine, Leslie G.: *Burke's Genealogical and Heraldic History of the Peerage, Baronetage*
... One-hundredth edition						1953
Pine, Leslie G.: *Burke's Genealogical and Heraldic History of the Peerage, Baronetage*
... One-hundred-and-first edition					1956
Pine, Leslie G.: *Burke's Genealogical and Heraldic History of the Peerage, Baronetage*
... One-hundred-and-second edition				1959
Townend, Peter: *Burke's Genealogical and Heraldic History of the Peerage, Baronetage*
... One-hundred-and-third edition					1963
Townend, Peter: *Burke's Genealogical and Heraldic History of the Peerage, Baronetage*
... One-hundred-and-fourth edition				1966
Townend, Peter: *Burke's Genealogical and Heraldic History of the Peerage, Baronetage*
... One-hundred-and-fifth edition					1970
Second impression under the title *Burke's Peerage and Baronetage*, omitting the
Royal Family and Knightage, with Supplement			1975

BURKE'S OFFICIAL KALENDAR

Burke, John: *The Official Kalendar for 1831*				**1831**

BURKE'S ROYAL REGISTER

Burke, Peter Joseph: *Royal Register, Genealogical and Historic for 1831*	**1831**

BURKE'S EXTINCT PEERAGES

Burke, John: *A General and Heraldic Dictionary of the Peerages of England, Ireland
and Scotland, Extinct, Dormant and in Abeyance* (England only was published) **1831**
Burke, John, and John Bernard: *A Genealogical and Heraldic Dictionary of the
Peerages of England, Ireland and Scotland, Extinct, Dormant and in Abeyance*,
Second edition							1840
Burke, John, and John Bernard: *The Extinct, Dormant and Abeyant Peerages of
England, Ireland and Scotland*, Third edition			1846
Burke, Sir Bernard: *A Genealogical History of the Dormant, Abeyant, Forfeited and
Extinct Peerages of the British Empire*, New edition		1866
Burke, Sir Bernard: *A Genealogical History of the Dormant, Abeyant, Forfeited and
Extinct Peerages of the British Empire*, New edition		1883
Reprint of 1883 edition						1962
Second Reprint							1969

BURKE'S PORTRAIT GALLERY

Burke, John: *The Portrait Gallery of Distinguished Females, including Beauties of the Courts of George IV and William IV.* With Memoirs, etc., two volumes   **1833**

BURKE'S LANDED GENTRY

Burke, John: *A Genealogical and Heraldic History of the Commoners of Great Britain and Ireland, enjoying Territorial Possessions or High Official Rank, but uninvested with Heritable Honours.* First published in three volumes   **1833-35**
Re-issued   1836-37
Additional volume IV   1837

Burke, John, and John Bernard: *A Genealogical and Heraldic Dictionary of the Landed Gentry of Great Britain and Ireland, a Companion to the Baronetage and Knightage.* With Supplement, Addenda, Corrigenda and Index. Published in Parts, usually bound in three volumes   1843-49

Burke, Sir Bernard: *A Genealogical and Heraldic Dictionary of the Landed Gentry of Great Britain and Ireland comprising particulars of upwards of 100,000 individuals.* With Supplement, Addenda, Corrigenda and Index. A re-issue of the 1843-49 edition with additional pages in the Addenda. It can be found variously dated and one copy dated 1847-53 had the joint editors of John and John Bernard Burke on the title page. Published in parts, usually bound in three volumes   1850-53

Burke, Sir Bernard: *A Genealogical and Heraldic Dictionary of the Landed Gentry of Great Britain and Ireland,* Third edition. With Supplement. Published in parts   1855-58

Can also be found in one volume dated 1858

Burke, Sir Bernard: *A Genealogical and Heraldic Dictionary of the Landed Gentry . . .* Fourth edition. Can be found in one volume with a single title page dated 1863 but was first issued as two parts with two title pages dated 1862 and 1863   1862-63

Burke, Sir Bernard: *A Genealogical and Heraldic Dictionary of the Landed Gentry . . .* Fourth edition revised and enlarged, with Supplement and Corrigenda   1868

Burke, Sir Bernard: *A Genealogical and Heraldic History of the Landed Gentry of Great Britain and Ireland,* Fifth edition with Supplement, two volumes   1871

Burke, Sir Bernard: *A Genealogical and Heraldic History of the Landed Gentry . . .* Fifth edition re-issued with two Supplements and Addenda, two volumes   1875

Burke, Sir Bernard: *A Genealogical and Heraldic History of the Landed Gentry . . .* Sixth edition with Supplement and Corrigenda, two volumes   1879

Burke, Sir Bernard: *A Genealogical and Heraldic History of the Landed Gentry . . .* Sixth edition re-issued with larger Supplement and Addenda, two volumes   1882

Burke, Sir Bernard: *A Genealogical and Heraldic History of the Landed Gentry . . .* Seventh edition, two volumes   1886

Burke, Ashworth P.: *A Genealogical and Heraldic History of the Landed Gentry . . .* Eighth edition, by Sir Bernard Burke, edited by his son, two volumes   1894

Burke, Ashworth P.: *A Genealogical and Heraldic History of the Landed Gentry . . .* Ninth edition, by Sir Bernard Burke, edited by his son, two volumes, including a separate section on Ireland (see *Landed Gentry of Ireland* for separate issue of this)   1898

Burke, Sir Bernard and Ashworth P.: *A Genealogical and Heraldic History of the Landed Gentry of Great Britain,* Tenth edition with Addenda   1900

Burke, Sir Bernard and Ashworth P.: *A Genealogical and Heraldic History of the Landed Gentry of Great Britain,* Eleventh edition   1906

Fox-Davies, A. C.: *A Genealogical and Heraldic History of the Landed Gentry of Great Britain,* Twelfth edition, by Sir Bernard Burke, revised by A. C. Fox-Davies   1914

Thorpe, A. Winton: *A Genealogical and Heraldic History of the Landed Gentry of Great Britain,* by Sir Bernard Burke, edited by A. Winton Thorpe, Thirteenth edition   1921

Butler, Alfred T.: *A Genealogical and Heraldic History of the Landed Gentry by the late Sir Bernard Burke*, Fourteenth edition. A re-issue of the 1921 edition, with Supplement   1925
Pirie-Gordon, H.: *Burke's Genealogical and Heraldic History of the Landed Gentry, Centenary Edition. Founded by the late Sir Bernard Burke, edited by H. Pirie-Gordon.* Includes an Irish Supplement   1937
[Pine, L. G. and others]: *Burke's Genealogical and Heraldic History of the Landed Gentry including American Families with British Ancestry*, Sixteenth edition   1939
Pine, L. G.: *Burke's Genealogical and Heraldic History of the Landed Gentry*, Seventeenth edition   1952
[Pine, L. G.]: *Supplement to Burke's Landed Gentry*   1954
Townend, Peter: *Burke's Genealogical and Heraldic History of the Landed Gentry*, Eighteenth edition, Volumes I and II   1965-69
Reprint of Volume I   1969
Montgomery-Massingberd, Hugh: Volume III of the Eighteenth edition, with Index to all three volumes   1972

BURKE'S EXTINCT BARONETCIES

Burke, John, and John Bernard: *A Genealogical and Heraldic History of the Extinct and Dormant Baronetcies of England*   **1838**
Burke, John, and John Bernard: *A Genealogical and Heraldic History of the Extinct and Dormant Baronetcies of England, Ireland and Scotland.* Second edition   1841
Reprint of the 1841 edition   1844
Reprint of the 1844 edition   1964

BURKE'S KNIGHTAGE

Burke, John, and John Bernard: *The Knightage of Great Britain and Ireland*   **1841**

BURKE'S GENERAL ARMORY

Burke, John, and John Bernard: *A General Armory of England, Scotland and Ireland*   **1842**
Burke, John, and John Bernard: *A General Armory of England, Scotland and Ireland.* Revised edition   1843
Burke, John, and John Bernard: *Encyclopaedia of Heraldry, or General Armory of England, Scotland and Ireland, comprising a registry of all armorial bearings from the earliest to the present time, including the late grants by the College of Arms.* Third edition with Supplement   1844
Reprint of 1844 edition with Supplement   1847
Second Reprint   1851
Burke, Sir Bernard: *The General Armory of England, Scotland, Ireland and Wales; comprising a Registry of Armorial Bearings from the Earliest to the Present Time.* (Enlarged edition)   1878
Burke, Sir Bernard: *The General Armory* . . . With a Supplement   1883
Burke, Sir Bernard: *The General Armory* . . . With a Supplement   1884
Reprint of the 1884 edition and Supplement   1961
Second Reprint   1962
Third Reprint   1966
Fourth Reprint   1969

THE CRIMINAL LAW

Burke, Peter: *The Criminal Law, and its Sentences, in Treasons, Felonies and Misdemeanours*   **1842**

A TREATISE ON THE LAW OF COPYRIGHT

Burke, Peter: *A Treatise on the Law of Copyright in literature, the drama, music, engraving and sculpture; and also in designs for ornamenting articles of manufacture: including recent Statutes on the subject*   **1842**

THE THREE STATUTES

Burke, Peter: *The Three Statutes forming the New Law for the Relief of Insolvent Debtors in the Court of Bankruptcy analysed, simplified and arranged; with the Acts themselves and an Index*   **1844**

THE WISDOM AND GENIUS OF EDMUND BURKE

Burke, Peter: *The Wisdom and Genius of the Right Hon. Edmund Burke; illustrated in a series of extracts from his writings and speeches; with a summary of his life* **1845**

BURKE'S HERALDIC ILLUSTRATIONS

Burke, John and John Bernard: *Heraldic Illustrations. With Explanatory Pedigrees.* Three volumes issued at various dates between 1843 and 1846. Usually found dated   **1845**

Burke, John Bernard: *Heraldic Illustrations; with Annotations* A re-issue of the 1845 edition   1853

Burke, John Bernard: *Illuminated Supplement to the Heraldic Illustrations, by John and John Bernard Burke, with Annotations by John Bernard Burke*   1851

Burke, Sir Bernard: *Illuminated Heraldic Illustrations, with Annotations*   1856

THE PATRICIAN

Burke, John, and J. Bernard: *The Patrician, A Periodical Publication.* May 1846-March 1848, edited by John Burke. April-October 1848 edited by J. Bernard Burke   **1846-1848**

BURKE'S HOUSE OF GWYSANEY

Burke, John Bernard: *A Genealogical History of the House of Gwysaney,* Privately printed   **1847**

BURKE'S ROYAL FAMILIES

Burke, John, and J. Bernard: *Royal Families of England, Scotland and Wales, with their Descendants, as well Subjects as Sovereigns,* two volumes. Each volume has an additional title page dated respectively 1848 and 1849   **1847 &**
1851

Burke, Sir Bernard: *Royal Families of England, Scotland and Wales, with pedigrees of Royal Descents in illustration.* An abridgement of the First edition   1876

BURKE'S ROLL OF BATTLE ABBEY

Burke, John Bernard: *The Roll of Battle Abbey, annotated*   **1848**
Reprint (Baltimore, USA)   1966

BURKE'S HISTORIC LANDS

Burke, John Bernard: *The Historic Lands of England,* two volumes   **1848/9**

BURKE'S ANECDOTES OF THE ARISTOCRACY

Burke, John Bernard: *Anecdotes of the Aristocracy, and Episodes in Ancestral Story*, two volumes   **1849**
Burke, John Bernard: *Anecdotes of the Aristocracy* ... Second edition, two volumes   **1849**
Burke, John Bernard: *Anecdotes of the Aristocracy* ... A new edition, two volumes   **1850**
Burke, John Bernard: *Romantic Records of Distinguished Families, Being the second series of the Anecdotes of the Aristocracy*, Second edition, two volumes   **1851**
Burke, Sir Bernard: *The Romance of the Aristocracy; or Anecdotes and records of distinguished families* (Selections from Anecdotes of the Aristocracy), new and revised edition, three volumes   **1855**

CELEBRATED TRIALS

Burke, Peter: *Celebrated Trials connected with the Aristocracy in the relations of private life*   **1849**
Burke, Peter: *Celebrated Trials connected with the Upper Classes of Society in the relations of private life*   **1851**

BURKE'S HERALDIC REGISTER

Burke, John Bernard: *The Heraldic Register 1849-50. With an Introductory Essay on Heraldry and an Annotated Obituary*, three volumes. Volumes II and III are entitled *The St. James's Magazine*, and *Heraldic and Historical Register*   **1850**

AN EXPLORATORY ANALYSIS

Burke, Peter: *An Exploratory Analysis of the Protection of Investors Act*   **1851**

SUPPLEMENT TO GODSON

Burke, Peter: *A Supplement to Godson's Practical Treatise on the Law of Patents for Inventors and of Copyright*   **1851**

THE LAW OF INTERNATIONAL COPYRIGHT

Burke, Peter: *The Law of International Copyright between England and France, in literature, the drama, music and the fine arts, analysed and explained*   **1852**

THE PATENT LAW

Burke, Peter: *The Patent Law Amendment Act, 15 and 16 Vict. c 83, and the Patent Law generally as affected by that Statute, analysed and explained*   **1852**

THE ROMANCE OF THE FORUM

Burke, Peter: *The Romance of the Forum, or Narratives, scenes and anecdotes from Courts of Justice*, two volumes   **1852**
Another edition   **1861**
Second Series, two volumes   **1854**

BURKE'S VISITATION OF SEATS AND ARMS

Burke, John Bernard: *A Visitation of Seats and Arms of the Noblemen and Gentlemen of Great Britain and Ireland*, two volumes   **1852/3**
Burke, John Bernard: *A Visitation of Seats and Arms* . . . Second series, two volumes   **1854/5**

THE PUBLIC AND DOMESTIC LIFE

Burke, Peter: *The Public and Domestic Life of the Right Hon. Edmund Burke*   **1853**

BURKE'S FAMILY ROMANCE

Burke, John Bernard: *Family Romance, or Episodes in the Domestic Annals of the Aristocracy*, two volumes   **1853**
Burke, Sir Bernard: *Family Romance* . . . Second edition, two volumes   1854
Burke, Sir Bernard: *Family Romance* . . . Third edition   1860

THE COPYRIGHT LAW

Burke, Peter: *The Copyright Law and the Press. An essay to show the necessity of an immediate amendment*   **1855**

BURKE'S ORDERS OF KNIGHTHOOD

Burke, Sir Bernard: *The Book of Orders of Knighthood and Decorations of Honours of all Nations. Comprising an historical account of each order, Military, Naval and Civil, from the Earliest to the Present Time. With lists of Knights and Companions of each British Order*   **1858**

PEDIGREE AND ARMS OF THE GLOVERS

Burke, Sir Bernard and Denis Fisher: *The Pedigree and Arms of the Glovers of Mount Glover*, etc.   **1858**

BURKE'S ROYAL DESCENTS

Burke, Sir Bernard: *Royal Descents and Pedigrees of Founders' Kin*. An additional title page bears the date 1855.   **1858**
Burke, Sir Bernard: *Royal Descents and Pedigrees of Founders' Kin*   1864

BURKE'S VICISSITUDES OF FAMILIES

Burke, Sir Bernard: *Vicissitudes of Families and other Essays*   **1859**
Burke, Sir Bernard: *Vicissitudes of Families and other Essays*, Second edition   1859
Burke, Sir Bernard: *Vicissitudes of Families and other Essays*, Third edition   1859
Burke, Sir Bernard: *Vicissitudes of Families and other Essays*, Fourth edition   1860
Burke, Sir Bernard: *Vicissitudes of Families*, Second Series, First edition   1860
Burke, Sir Bernard: *Vicissitudes of Families and other Essays*, Fifth edition   1861
Burke, Sir Bernard: *Vicissitudes of Families*, Second Series, Second edition   1861
Burke, Sir Bernard: *Vicissitudes of Families*, Third Series, First edition   1863
Burke, Sir Bernard: *Vicissitudes of Families*, Remodelled edition, two volumes   1869
Burke, Sir Bernard: *Vicissitudes of Families*, Third Series, Second edition   1873
Burke, Sir Bernard: *Vicissitudes of Families*, New edition, two volumes   1883

BURKE'S SELECTION OF ARMS

Burke, Sir Bernard: *A Selection of Arms authorized by the Laws of Heraldry. With Annotations*. (Originally published in Parts 1858-60. Title on Wrappers was *Authorized Arms of the Gentry of Great Britain and Ireland*)   **1860**
Burke, Sir Bernard: *A Selection of Arms authorized by the Laws of Heraldry. With Annotations*   1863
Burke, Sir Bernard: *Burke's Authorized Arms. An outstanding selection of over 300 Coats of Arms Authorized by the Laws of Heraldry*. Reprint of the 1860 edition, New York, USA   1971

NAVAL AND MILITARY TRIALS

Burke, Peter: *Celebrated Naval and Military Trials*   **1866**

BURKE'S RISE OF GREAT FAMILIES

Burke, Sir Bernard: *The Rise of Great Families, other Essays and Stories*   **1873**
Burke, Sir Bernard: *The Rise of Great Families* . . . Second edition   **1873**
Burke, Sir Bernard: *Reminiscences, Ancestral, Anecdotal and Historic.* A Remodelled
and Revised edition of *The Rise of Great Families* . . .   **1882**

BURKE'S SOVEREIGNS OF ENGLAND

Burke, Sir Bernard: *The Sovereigns of England from the Norman Conquest, in
rhyme*   **1876**

BURKE'S BOOK OF PRECEDENCE

Burke, Sir Bernard: *The Book of Precedence; the Peers, Baronets and Knights, and the
Companions of the Several Orders of Knighthood placed according to their Relative
Rank, together with A Scale of General or Social Precedence; A List of the Maids of
Honor to the Queen, with their Relative Precedence; Precedence of Diplomatic
Agents; Relative Rank of the Officers of the Navy and Army and Tables of Prece-
dence in the Colonies, Dominion of Canada and the Indian Empire*   **1881**

ROMAN CATHOLIC FAMILIES

Burke, Henry Farnham, and J. J. Howard: *Genealogical Collections illustrating the
History of Roman Catholic Families of England*   **1887**

DARWIN FAMILY

Burke, Henry Farnham: *Pedigree of the Family of Darwin*   **1888**

PEDIGREE OF DE TRAFFORD

Burke, Henry Farnham: *Pedigree and Quarterings of De Trafford compiled from the
Records of the Heralds' College, Record Offices, probate registries, etc.*   **1890**

PEDIGREE OF SMIJTH

Burke, Henry Farnham: *Pedigree of Smijth of Hill Hall, Essex*   **1891**

BURKE'S COLONIAL GENTRY

Burke, Sir Bernard: *A Genealogical and Heraldic History of the Colonial Gentry,* two
volumes. Volume II edited by Ashworth P. Burke   **1891 & 1895**
Reprint in one volume   **1970**

EXAMPLES OF IRISH BOOK-PLATES

Burke, Henry Farnham:*Example of Irish Book-Plates, From the collections of Sir
Bernard Burke, C.B., LL.D., Ulster King of Arms.* Privately issued by his son   **1894**

THEYDON MOUNT

Burke, Henry Farnham, and J. J. Howard: *Theydon Mount: Its Lords and Rectors* **1894**

BURKE'S FAMILY RECORDS

Burke, Ashworth P.: *Family Records*   **1897**
Reprint (New York, USA)   **1965**

BURKE'S LANDED GENTRY OF IRELAND/
IRISH FAMILY RECORDS

Burke, Ashworth P.: *A Genealogical and Heraldic History of the Landed Gentry of Ireland by Sir Bernard Burke, edited by his son Ashworth P. Burke.* (Re-issue of the Irish Supplement of the 1898 edition of the *Landed Gentry*, with a Supplement)   **1899**

Burke, Sir Bernard and Ashworth P.: *A Genealogical and Heraldic History of the Landed Gentry of Ireland.* Second edition but called New and Revised Tenth edition, referring to the numbering of the editions of the *Landed Gentry* of Great Britain   **1904**

Fox-Davies, A. C.: *A Genealogical and Heraldic History of the Landed Gentry of Ireland by Sir Bernard Burke, edited by A. C. Fox-Davies,* New edition (Third edition)   **1912**

Pine, L. G.: *Burke's Genealogical and Heraldic History of the Landed Gentry of Ireland,* Fourth edition   **1958**

Montgomery-Massingberd, Hugh: *Burke's Irish Family Records,* Fifth edition   **1976**
American edition   **1976**

HISTORICAL RECORD OF THE CORONATION, 1902

Burke, Henry Farnham: *The Historical Record of the Coronation of Their Most Excellent Majesties King Edward VII and Queen Alexandra, Solemized in the Abbey Church at Westminster on Saturday the Ninth day of August, In the Year of Our Lord 1902,* Privately printed. (With plates by Byam Shaw)   **1904**

BURKE'S PROMINENT FAMILIES OF THE USA

Burke, Arthur M.: *The Prominent Families of the United States of America.* Volume I (all published)   **1908**
Reprint (New York, USA)   **1975**

BURKE'S ANCIENT PARISH REGISTERS

Burke, Arthur M.: *Key to the Ancient Parish Registers of England and Wales*   **1908**
Burke, Arthur M.: *Key to the Ancient Parish Registers . . .* With Supplement   **1909**
Reprint of 1908 edition (Baltimore, USA)   **1962**
Second Reprint   **1971**

HISTORICAL RECORD OF THE CORONATION, 1911

Burke, Henry Farnham: *The Historical Record of the Coronation of Their Majesties King George V and Queen Mary, 1911*   **1911**

INDEXES TO ANCIENT TESTAMENTARY RECORDS

Burke, Arthur M.: *Indexes to the Ancient Testamentary Records of Westminster*   **1913**

MEMORIALS OF ST MARGARET'S, WESTMINSTER

Burke, Arthur Meredyth: *Memorials of St Margaret's Church, Westminster. The Parish Registers 1539-1660, edited with Introduction and Notes*   **1914**

BURKE'S HANDBOOK TO THE ORDER OF THE BRITISH EMPIRE

A. Winton Thorpe: *Burke's Handbook to the Most Excellent Order of the British Empire. Containing Biographies, A Full List of Persons appointed to the Order, showing their relative precedence, and coloured plates of the Insignia*   **1921**

BURKE'S DISTINGUISHED FAMILIES OF AMERICA

[Pine, L. G. and others]: *Burke's Distinguished Families of America. The Lineages of 1,600 Families of British Origin now resident in the United States of America.* A re-issue of pages 2529-3022 (the American section) of *Burke's Landed Gentry,* 1939 **1939**
Re-issue **1947**
Second Reprint (Baltimore, USA) **1975**

BURKE'S GUIDE TO THE ROYAL FAMILY

Montgomery-Massingberd, Hugh: *Burke's Guide to The Royal Family* **1973**

BURKE'S PRESIDENTIAL FAMILIES OF USA

Montgomery-Massingberd, Hugh: *Burke's Presidential Families of the United States of America* **1975**

BURKE'S INTRODUCTION TO IRISH ANCESTRY

Montgomery-Massingberd, Hugh: *Burke's Introduction to Irish Ancestry* **1976**

BURKE'S FAMILY INDEX

Montgomery-Massingberd, Hugh: *Burke's Family Index* **1976**

Guide to the Reader

THE *Family Index*, as mentioned in the PREFACE, provides a guide to the most complete and up-to-date version of a family's narrative pedigree in a *Burke's* publication since 1826. Every variation of surname has a separate entry and, in accordance with the usual *Burke's* rule, *compound surnames appear under the last* (*e.g.* "Loder-Old-Cobblers" would be found under "Cobblers"). It should be stressed that this is an Index of family names not of titles (nor of seats, for that matter, which will be covered in *Burke's Guide to Country Houses*) and the entry for a *Peerage* family whose name differs from its title will be found under the former. Cross-references have been inserted under the name of the title to aid the reader (*e.g.* "NEASDEN (*see* Snooks)"). A specimen entry for a *Peerage* family would begin with the family surname, followed by parentheses containing the title and rank, and then the reference to the book and edition (*e.g.* "SNOOKS (Neasden, B) **PB1970**"). Standard abbreviations for ranks have been used (*i.e.* "D" for Duke; "M" for Marquess; "E" for Earl; "V" for Viscount; "B" for Baron; and "Bt" for Baronet) and a list of the codes used for the books can be found at the foot of the next page. A *Peerage* (or *Baronetage*) family with a title of the same name merely has the surname followed by the rank (*e.g.* "BLOGGS, Bt **PB1970**"). The territorial designation of a Baronetcy is occasionally added for ease of identification (*e.g.* "SNODGRASS, Bt *of Longweed* **PB1917**").

An entry for a *Landed Gentry*, or other untitled, family has the heading of its article in the book referred to reproduced (*e.g.* "SHUFFLEBOTHAM *of Smallparc* **LG1925**"); and where there is no seat or territorial description, just the name and reference are given. A pedigree of one family is frequently included under another family name's article in *Burke's* books. These cases have been carefully indexed and cross-references have been inserted in the *Family Index* directing the reader to the family entry which accommodates another pedigree.

Where a family name has different (and often unconnected) articles in the same and separate books, the *Family Index* entry begins with the surname and then divides up into sub-entries, separated by semi-colons. These sub-entries are grouped in "sections" relating to books (*Peerage and Baronetage* references first; then *Dormant and Extinct Peerages*; *Extinct and Dormant Baronetcies*; *Landed Gentry*; and so on — the list of the codes hereunder is set out in the order followed by the sections of the sub-entries). The sequence of the

sub-entries within these sections is in reverse, *i.e.* the most recent
edition coming first, and then working backwards. A composite
specimen of a family name with various sub-entries would read as
follows:

"CODSWALLOP (Balderdash, V) **PB1970**; Bt **PB1970**; (Twaddle, M) **DEP**; (Codswallop
of Tripe, B) **DEP**; Bt *of Garbage* **EDB**; *of Old Rubbish Rectory* **LG1969**; *formerly of
Pigswill Park* **LG1952**; *of Piffle Priory* **LG1850/3**; *formerly of Nonsensetown*
LGI1958; *formerly of Eyewash* **DFUSA**; *of Banana Oil* **CG**; (*see also* Betty-Martin)"

As mentioned before, *every* variation of surname is treated
separately: for example, "MACAROON", "MacAROON" and
"McAROON" would all have separate entries; and even when the
surnames are the same but there is another name in the heading, this
still entails a separate entry, *e.g.* "BLISTER-BUNION (*now* CORNY)"
would have an entry to itself, not under plain "BLISTER-BUNION".
It cannot be reiterated too emphatically that the latter would come
under "BUNION", and there would only be a cross-reference under
"BLISTER" if there were a pedigree of "BLISTER" featured in the
"BLISTER-BUNION" article.

The *Family Index* refers the reader to particular editions of *Burke's*
works, which have been identified by the year of publication. This was
felt to be less ambigious than numbering the edition, though any
clarification needed can easily be obtained by consulting the
BIBLIOGRAPHY. If the reader can purchase or has access to the
relevant edition it should not be too difficult to locate the article he
seeks, bearing in mind that sometimes the article may be in an
"Addendum" or an incorporated "Supplement" at the front or back.
Most of the books have their own Indexes, though some are more
helpful than others, and it should be remembered that whereas in the
Peerage and Baronetage articles appear under titles, the articles in the
Dormant and Extinct Peerages appear under family names. As
announced in the PREFACE, the publishers can supply photocopies
from out-of-print editions.

Finally, here is a check-list of the codes used for *Burke's* books in
the text: **PB** *Peerage and Baronetage*; **DEP** *Dormant and Extinct
Peerages*; **EDB** *Extinct and Dormant Baronetcies*; **LG** *Landed Gentry*;
IFR *Irish Family Records*; **LGI** *Landed Gentry of Ireland*; **RL** "Royal
Lineage" in *Guide to The Royal Family*; **RF** *Royal Families*; **TNBE**
"Titled Nobility of the British Empire" in *Peerage and Baronetage*;
FT "Foreign Titles" in *Peerage and Baronetage*; **PresFUSA**
Presidential Families of USA; **DFUSA** *Distinguished Families of
USA*; **PromFUSA** *Prominent Families of USA*; **FR** *Family Records*;
CG *Colonial Gentry*; **AA** *Authorised Arms*; **HI** *Heraldic Illustrations*;
VF *Vicissitudes of Families*; **VSA** *Visitation of Seats and Arms*.

ABADAM *of Middleton Hall* **LG1875**; **VSA**

ABBEY *of Redlynch House formerly of Greyfriars* **LG1965**; *of Woldhurst Manor* **LG1925**

ABBOT (Colchester, B) **PB1917**; **DFUSA**

ABBOTT (Tenterden, B) **PB1939**; **CG**

WHITE ABBOTT *of Shire End formerly of Cowick Barton* **LG1972**

ABDY, Bt **PB1970**; Bt *of Felix Hall* **PB1868**; Bt *of Albans* **EDB**; Bt *of Moores* **EDB**

À BECKETT **CG**

ABEL, Bt **PB1902**; **DFUSA**

ABELL *of Foxcote Manor* **LG1937**; *formerly of Stapenhill and Hemington* **DFUSA**

ABERCONWAY (*see* McLaren)

ABERCORN (*see* Hamilton)

ABERCROMBIE, Bt **EDB**; **DFUSA**; *formerly of Falkirk* **DFUSA**; (*see also* Sandilands)

ABERCROMBY, Bt **PB1970**; B **PB1924**; (Dunfermline, Lord) **DEP**; (Glasford, Lord) **DEP**; **LG1833/7**

ABERDARE (*see* Bruce)

ABERDEEN (*see* Gordon)

ABERGAVENNY (*see* Nevill)

ABERTAY (*see* Barrie)

ABINGER (*see* Scarlett)

ABLETT *of Llanberr* **LG1850/3**

ABNEY *formerly of Measham Hall* **LG1972**; **PromFUSA**

ABOYNE (*see* Gordon)

ABRAHAM *formerly of Aughnacloy* **LG1937Supp**

ABRINCIS (Chester, E) **DEP**

ACHESON (Gosford, E) **PB1970**; **DFUSA**

ACHMUTY *of Brianstown* **LG1850/3**

ACKERS *of Huntley Manor* **LG1952**; *of Moreton Hall* **LG1900**

ACKROYD, Bt **PB1970**; *of Wheatleys* **LG1921**

ACLAND, Bt *of Columb John* **PB1970**; Bt *of Oxford* **PB1970**; Bt *of Fairfield* **PB1871**; *of Holnicote* **CG**; (*see also* Acland-Troyte)

FLOYER-ACLAND (*formerly* FLOYER) *of West Stafford* **LG1952**

ACTON, B **PB1970**; Bt **EDB**; *of Acton Scott* **LG1972**; *of Wolverton* **LG1972**; *of Gatacre Park* **LG1898**; **IFR1976**

BALL-ACTON *of Kilmacurrragh* (*see* Acton)

ADAIR, Bt **PB1970**; (Waveney, B) **PB1886**; *of Heatherton Park* **LG1894**;

of Rathdaire **LG1886**; *of Loughomore* **LG1858**; *of Belle Grove* **LG1858**; **DFUSA**

ADAM, Bt **PB1970**; Bt *of Blair Adam* **PB1922**; *of Blair Adam* **LG1972**; *of Denmore* **LG1972**

ADAMS, B **PB1959**; Bt **EDB**; *of Ansty Hall* **LG1965**; *of Greenfield* **LG1969**; *formerly of Woore Manor* **LG1969**; *of Clifton* **LG1952**; *formerly of Holyland* **LG1952**; *of Bowdon* **LG1886**; *of Ahavagurrah* **LG1858**; **IFR1976**; *of Drumelton House* **LG1958**; **PresFUSA**; *formerly of Charwelton* **DFUSA**; *formerly of Nottingham* **DFUSA**; plus 4 other entries in **DFUSA**; **CG**; *of Middleton Hall* **HI**; (*see also* Brodribb; and Clifton)

BOYS-ADAMS (*see* Carnegy-Arbuthnott)

COODE-ADAMS *of Sampford Grange* **LG1965**

GOOLD-ADAMS *formerly of Jamesbrook* **LG1958**

KILVERT-MINOR ADAMS *of Grinshill* **LG1952**

PHYTHIAN-ADAMS **LG1969**

STOPFORD ADAMS **LG1965**

WOOLCOMBE-ADAMS **LG1965**

ADAMSON *of Stracathro* **LG1972**; *of Linden Hall* **LG1952**; *late of Rushton Park* **LG1914**; *of Eglingham Hall* **LG1898**; *of Glenfarne Hall* **LG1912**

ADDAMS (*see* Altham)

ADDENBROOKE *formerly of The Lea* **LG1952**

ANDERLEY (Norton, B) **PB1970**

BROUGHTON-ANDERLEY *formerly of Tunstall Hall* **LG1972**

ADDINGTON (Sidmouth, V) **PB1970**; (*see also* Hubbard)

ADDIS *of Woodside* **LG1969**

ADDISON, V **PB1970**; *of Chilton* **LG1850/3**

ADDYES *of Great Barr* **LG1843/9**

ADEANE *of Babraham* **LG1965**

ADIE *of Brook House* **LG1952**

ADLAM *of Chew Magna* **LG1914**

ADLERCRON *of Londonthorpe Hall* **LG1952**

ADLINGTON (*see* Broke)

ADRIAN, B **PB1970**

AFFLECK, Bt **PB1939**

AGAR (Normanton, E) **PB1970**; (Callan, B) **DEP**

SHELTON-AGAR *of Melmerby Hall* **LG1965**

AGLIONBY *formerly of Nunnery*

LG1969; PromFUSA
AGNEW, Bt *of Clendry* **PB1970**; Bt *of Lochnaw* **PB1970**; Bt *of London* **PB1970**; *of Pythingdean Manor* **LG1952**; *(Tasmania)* **CG**
VANS AGNEW *(see* Vans *of Barnbarroch)*
AGUTTER *(see* Keeling)
AIKEN *of Dalmock* **LG1921**
CHETWOOD-AIKEN *formerly of Hillside* **LG1952**; *of Woodbrook* **LGI1958**
AIKENHEAD *formerly of Otterington Hall* **LG1952**
AIKINS *of Toronto and Winnipeg* **CG**
ROBERTSON-AIKMAN *of The Ross* **LG1965**
AILESBURY *(see* Brudenell-Bruce)
AILSA *(see* Kennedy)
AILWYN *(see* Fellowes)
AINSCOUGH *of Casterton Hall* **LG1969**
AINSLIE, Bt **PB1858**; *of Delgaty Castle* **LG1937**
AINSWORTH, Bt **PB1970**; *of Spotland* **LG1952**; *of Smithills Hall* **LG1921**; *of Harecroft and Ardanaiseig* **LG1914**; *of Backbarrow* **LG1914**; *VSA*
AIRD, Bt **PB1970**
STIRLING-AIRD *of Kippendavie* **LG1972**
AIREDALE *(see* Kitson)
AIREY, B **DEP**; **FR**; *(Australia)* **CG**
AIRLIE *(see* Ogilvy)
AIRMINE, Bt **EDB**
AITCHISON, Bt **PB1970**; *of Leamington Hall* **LG1937**
AITKEN, Bt (Beaverbrook, B) **PB1970**; *of Gleneske* **LG1952**
AIZLEWOOD *formerly of Whirlow Grange* **LG1952**
AKERMAN *(S Africa)* **CG**
AKROYD **LG1965**; *of Bank Field* **LG1886**; *of Bankfield, co York* **AA**
ALANBROOKE *(see* Brooke)
FORTESCUE-ALAND (Fortescue, B) **DEP**
ALBANY, D **PB1917**; *(see also* Stewart)
ALBEMARLE *(see* Fortibus; Keppel; and Monk)
ALBINI (Arundel, E) **DEP**
ALBU, Bt **PB1970**
ALCESTER *(see* Seymour)
ALCOCK **IFR1976**
ALDAM *(see* Pease *formerly of Chapel Allerton Hall)*
WARDE-ALDAM *of Hooton Pagnell, Healey and Frickley* **LG1965**
ALDBOROUGH *(see* Stratford)

ALDEBURGH, B **DEP**
ALDENHAM AND HUNSDON *(see* Gibbs)
ALDERSEY *of Aldersey* **LG1969**
ALDINGTON *(see* Low)
ALDOUS *formerly of Fressington* **LG1965**
ALDRIDGE *formerly of St Leonard's Forest* **LG1937**
ALDWORTH *of Frilford* **LG1969**; **IFR1976**
ALEN, Bt **EDB**; *of St Wolstans* **LG1833/7**
ALEXANDER (Alexander of Tunis, E) **PB1970**; (Caledon, E) **PB1970**; Bt *of Edgehill* **PB1970**; Bt *of Sundridge Park* **PB1970**; (Alexander of Hillsborough, E) **PB1963**; (Stirling, E) **DEP**; Bt **EDB**; *of Westerton* **LG1914**; *of Boydstone* **LG1875**; *(cos Antrim, Armagh, Carlow, Derry and Donegal)* **IFR1976**; *(cos Derry and Tyrone)* **IFR1976**; **DFUSA**; **PromFUSA**; *of Ahilly, co Donegal* **AA**; *(see also* Thomas *formerly of The Poolfold)*
ALEXANDER *(formerly* ALPIN) *of Woodlands* **LG1952**
CABLE-ALEXANDER, Bt **PB1970**
HAGART-ALEXANDER *of Ballochmyle,* Bt **PB1970**
ALFORD *formerly of Western Zoyland* **LG1952**
ALI MAHOMUD *of Bombay* **AA**
ALINGTON (Alington of Wymondley, B) **DEP**; *of Little Barford* **LG1972**; *of Swinhope* **LG1952**; *(see also* Sturt)
ALISON, Bt **PB1970**; *of Nyngan* **CG**
ALKIN *of Bonehill* **LG1937**
ALLAN *of Aros House* **LG1972**; *of Beacon Hill.* **LG1952**; *of Blackwell Grange* **LG1886**; **FR**; *of Blackwell Hall, co Durham* **AA**
HAVELOCK-ALLAN, Bt **PB1970**
ALLANBY *of Balbair* **LG1972**
BARCLAY-ALLARDICE **FR**; **CG**; *(see also* Barclay *of Mathers and Urie)*
ALLASON **LG1965**
ALLCROFT *of Stokesay Court* **LG1952**
MAGNUS-ALLCROFT, Bt **PB1970**
ALLDAY *of Halford* **LG1965**
ALLEN, B **PB1939**; Bt *of Marlow* **PB1939**; V **DEP**; Bt *of London* **EDB**; *formerly of Bathampton* **LG1965**; *formerly of Rickeston* **LG1969**; *of South Molton* **LG1972**; *of The Mote* **LG1972**; *of Bicton* **LG1952**; *of Davenham Hall* **LG1952**; *formerly of Evenley Hall*

LG1952; *of Wickeridge Woodland* LG1952; *late of Lyngford* LG1937; *of Upton Bishop* LG1937; *of Thornton House* LG1900; *of The Rhyd* LG1875; (1) & (2) **DFUSA**; *(S Africa)* **CG**
ALLEN (*now* HARDWICKE) *of Southfield Grange* LG1914
ALLEN (*now* SPENCER) *of Clifford Priory* LG1921
HARRISON-ALLEN (*see* Evans)
SANDEMAN-ALLEN LG1965
ALLENBY, V **PB1970**; (*see also* Allanby)
ALLENDALE (*see* Beaumont)
ALLERTON **PromFUSA**; (*see also* Jackson)
ALLEYN, Bt **EDB**
ALLEYNE, Bt **PB1970**; *of White Hall* LGI1958
ALLFREY *formerly of Wokefield Park* LG1965
ALLGOOD *of Nunwick* LG1965
ALLHUSEN *of Bradenham* LG1965
ALLIN, Bt *of Blundeston* **EDB**; Bt *of Somerleyton* **EDB**
ALLISON *formerly of Undercliffe and Tickford Abbey* LG1972; LG1969; *of Scaleby Hall* LG1937
ALLIX LG1965
ALLOTT *of Hague Hall* LG1914
ALLOWAY *of The Derries* LG1879; **HI**
ALLPORT *of Littleover* LG1894
ALLSEBROOK *formerly of Scropton* LG1972
ALLSOPP (Hindlip, B) **PB1970**; *of Hindlip Hall* LG1879
ALNESS (*see* Munro)
ALPORT **PB1970**
ALSTON, Bt *of Chelsea* **EDB**; Bt *of Odell* **EDB**; *formerly of The Tofte* LG1965; *of Hill House* LG1921; **DFUSA**; *of Elmdon Hall* **VSA**; (*see also* Lloyd-Jones; and Alston-Roberts-West)
MURRAY-ALSTON LGI1958
ALTHAM *formerly of Timbercombe* LG1972
ALTRINCHAM (*see* Grigg)
ALTRIE (*see* Keith)
ALVANLEY (*see* Arden)
ALVERSTONE (*see* Webster)
ALVINGHAM (*see* Yerburgh)
AMAN (Marley, B) **PB1970**
AMBLER *of Lawkland Hall* LG1952
AMCOTTS, Bt **PB1854**
CRACROFT-AMCOTTS *of Hackthorn* LG1965
AMERY *of Park House* LG1863
AMES *formerly of Longhorsley* LG1972;

formerly of Bruton **DFUSA**
AMES (*formerly* EAMES) **DFUSA**
AMESBURY (*see* Dundas)
AMHERST, E **PB1970**
AMHERST OF HACKNEY (*see* Cecil)
TYSSEN-AMHERST *of Didlington Hall* LG1886
AMMON, B **PB1959**
AMORIE (d'Amorie, B) **DEP**
HEATHCOAT-AMORY (Amory, V) **PB1970**
AMOS *of St Ibbs* LG1843/9
AMPHLETT *of Four Ashes Hall* LG1972; *of Wychbold* LG1972
AMPTHILL (*see* Russell)
AMULREE (*see* Mackenzie)
AMWELL (*see* Montague)
AMYLAND (*see* Cornewall)
ANCASTER (*see* Heathcote-Drummond-Willoughby)
ANCKETILL **IFR1976**
ANDERDON *of Henlade House* LG1937; (*see also* Salt, Bt *of Weeping Cross*)
ANDERSON (Waverley, V) **PB1970**; Bt *of Ardtaraig* **PB1940**; Bt *of Mullaghmore House* **PB1921**; Bt *of Broughton* **PB1891**; Bt *of Fermoy* **PB1861**; Bt *of Eyworth* **EDB**; Bt *of Mill Hill* **EDB**; Bt *of Penley* **EDB**; Bt *of St Ives* **EDB**; *of Northfield, formerly of St Germains and Bourhouse* LG1972; *of Standen Manor* LG1972; *of Little Harle Tower* LG1969; *of Notgrove* LG1965; *formerly of Tullichewan* LG1965; *of Glen Elvie* LG1952; *of Mill House* LG1952; *of Old Surrey Hall* LG1952, *of Moorcross House* LG1937; *of Walsworth House* LG1937; *of Jesmond House co Northumberland* LG1863; *of Havering Grange* LG1850/3; **IFR1976**, *of Ballyhossett* LGI1958; *of Ballyowan House* LGI1958; *formerly of Old Dunbell* LGI1958; **DFUSA**; **PromFUSA**
ANDERSON (*formerly* WOOD) *of Bilton Park* and *Efford Park* LG1952
DUNCOMBE-ANDERSON *of St John's* LG1937; (*see also* Feversham)
HARVIE ANDERSON *of Quarter* LG1972
ANDERTON Bt **EDB**; *of Euxton* LG1952; *of Spaynes Hall* LG1952; *of Vaila* LG1937
ANDRE, Bt **EDB**
ANDREW *of Ica* **CG**
ANDREWES *formerly of Maids Moreton Manor* LG1952; (*see also* Uthwatt)
ANDREWS, Bt *of Doddington* **EDB**; Bt *of*

Lathbury **EDB**; Bt *of Shaw Place* **EDB**; *of The Down House* **LG1952Supp**; *of Bantony* **LG1937**; *of St Briavel's House* **LG1937**; **IFR1976**; *of Rathenny* **LGI1912**; (*see also Crompton of Lever*)
ERVINE-ANDREWS *of Inish* **LGI1958**
FOX-ANDREWS (*see* Butler *cos Clare*)
ANDRUS *of Scadbury Manor* **LG1969**
ANGAS (*Australia*) **CG**
ANGELL *of Northey Island* **LG1952**
ANGERSTEIN (*see* Angerstein-Burton)
ANGLESEY (*see* Annesley; Paget; and Villiers)
ANGLE **DFUSA**
ANGUISH *of Somerleyton* **LG1850/3**
ANGUS (Moray, E) **DEP**; *of Ravenstone* **LG1972**; (*see also* Umfravill)
ANJOU (*House of*) **RL**
ANLEY *formerly of Ryecroft House* **LG1972**
ANNALY (*see* Grove; and White)
ANNAN, B **PB1970**
ANNAND *of Springwell House* **LG1952**
ANNANDALE (*see* Johnstone)
ANNE *formerly of Burghwallis* **LG1969**; (*see also* Charlton *of Hesleyside*)
ANNESLEY, E **PB1970**; (Valentia, V) **PB1970**; (Annesley, B) **PB1949**; (Anglesey, E) **DEP**; (*see also* Sowerby *of Lilley*)
GROVE ANNESLEY **IFR1976**; (*see also* Annesley)
ANSELL *of Cors-y-Gedol* **LG1921**
ANSLOW (*see* Mosley)
ANSON (Lichfield, E) **PB1970**; Bt **PB1970**; B **DEP**; (*see also* Neilson)
ANSTRUTHER, Bt **PB1970**
CARMICHAEL-ANSTRUTHER, Bt **PB1970**
ANTHONY *of Knight's Close* **LG1937 Supp**
ANTRIM (*see* McDonnell).
ANTROBUS, Bt **PB1970**
ANWYL *of Tywyn* **LG1972**; (*see also* Anwyl-Passingham)
AP-ADAM (de Ap-Adam, B) **DEP**; **LG1833/7**
APPERLY *formerly of Rodborough Court* **LG1952**
APPLETON, Bt **EDB**; *of Gaddon Uffculme* **LG1969**; *of Ipswich, Massachusetts* **DFUSA**
APPLEWHAITE *of Pickenham Hall* **LG1906**
APREECE, B **PB1845**
APSEY *formerly of Corfe Mullen* **LG1969**
APSLEY (*formerly* MEEKING) *formerly of Richings Park* **LG1952**

ARABIN *of Beech Hill* **LG1879**
ARBUTHNOT, Bt **PB1970**; Bt *of Kittybrewster* **PB1970**; (*see also* Prideaux)
ARBUTHNOTT, V **PB1970**; **AA**
CARNEGY-ARBUTHNOTT *of Balnamoon and Findowrie* **LG1972**
ARCEDEKNE *of Glevering Hall* **LG1875**
ARCHBOLD *of Davidstown* **LG1894**
ARCHDALE, Bt **PB1970**; **IFR1976**
ARCHDALL (*see* Archdale; and Montgomery (*cos Fermanagh and Tyrone*))
ARCHDEKNE, B **DEP**
ARCHER, B **DEP**; *of The Market Place* **LG1952**; *of Trelaske* **LG1952**; *of Salcombe Hill House* **LG1937**; *formerly of Londonderry* **DFUSA**; *of Brickendon* **CG**; *of Panshanger*; **CG**; (*Tasmania*) **CG**
ARCHIBALD, B **PB1970**; *of Rusland Hall* **LG1969**; *of Halifax and Truro* **CG**
ARDEN (Alvanley, B) **DEP**; *formerly of Longcroft* **LG1969**; *of Pontfaen* **LG1921**; (*Australia*) **CG**
BAILLIE-HAMILTON-ARDEN (*see* Haddington)
ARDGLASS (*see* Cromwell)
ARDILAUN (*see* Guinness)
ARGENTI **LG1965**
ARGENTINE (De Argentine, B) **DEP**
ARGLES *of Crudgington Manor* **LG1972**
ARGYLL (*see* Campbell)
ARKWRIGHT *formerly of Sanderstead Court* **LG1965**; *of Kinsham Court* **LG1965**; *formerly of Sutton Scarsdale* **LG1965**; *formerly of Willersley* **LG1965**; *of Overton* **CG**
ARLINGTON (*see* Bennet)
ARMAGHDALE (*see* Lonsdale)
ARMINE (Belasyse, B) **DEP**
ARMISTEAD, B **PB1915**; **DFUSA**
ARMITAGE *formerly of Farnley* **LG1965**; *of Longstone Grange* **LG1952**; *of Stoke Court* **LG1965**; *of Milnsbridge House* **LG1952**; **IFR1976**
ARMITSTEAD *of Stoke Court, formerly of Cranage Hall* **LG1965**
ARMS **DFUSA**
ARMSTEAD **DFUSA**
ARMSTRONG, Bt *of Gallen* **PB1970**; Bt **PB1940**; B **PB1900**; *of Gellidochlithe* **LG1952**; *of Nancealverne* **LG1952**; *of Hemsworth* **LG1875**; **IFR1976**; *of Garry Castle* **LGI1912**; (*see also* Kemmis)
HEATON-ARMSTRONG **IFR1976**
SAVAGE-ARMSTRONG *formerly of Corratinner* **LGI1958**

WATSON-ARMSTRONG (Armstrong, B) **PB1970**

ARMYTAGE, Bt **PB1970**; Bt **EDB**; *of Ingleby* **CG**

ARNOLD, B **PB1940**; *of Milton Hall* **LG1921**; *of Nethercott* **LG1921**; *of Little Missenden Abbey* **LG1886**; *formerly of Newry* **DFUSA**; **PromFUSA**; *of Hoppesford Hall* **VSA**

COAPE-ARNOLD *of Wolvey* **LG1952**

ARNOT, Bt **EDB**

ARNOTT, Bt **PB1970**

ARNOULD *of Broadbridge Mill* **LG1937**

ARRAGH, Bt **EDB**

ARRAN (*see* Boyd; Gore; and Stewart)

ARROWSMITH *formerly of Newbury* **DFUSA**

ARTHUR (Glenarthur, B) **PB1970**; Bt **PB1970**; *of Montgomerie Castle* **LG1937**; *formerly of Glanomera* **LGI1958**; **PresFUSA**

BOURNE-ARTON *of Tanfield Lodge* **LG1969**

ARUNDEL, B **DEP**; *of Lifton Park* **LG1850/3**; (*see also* Albini; and Fitz-Alan)

ARUNDELL (Arundell of Wardour, B) **PB1940**; (*see also* Talbot de Malahide)

HUNTER-ARUNDELL *of Barjarg* **LG1914**

MONCKTON-ARUNDELL (Galway, V) **PB1970**

ARWYN, B **PB1970**

ASGILL, Bt **EDB**

ASH *formerly of Packwood House* **LG1952**

BERESFORD-ASH **IFR1976**

ASHBOURNE (*see* Gibson)

ASHBRIDGE **DFUSA**

ASHBROOK (*see* Flower)

ASHBURN *formerly of Wyresdale* **DFUSA**

ASHBURNHAM, Bt **PB1970**; E **PB1924**

ASHBURTON (*see* Baring; and Dunning)

ASHBY, Bt **EDB**; *late of Naseby* **LG1914**; *of Quenby* **LG1894**; **PromFUSA**

ASHCOMBE (*see* Cubitt)

ASHCROFT (*formerly* SCOTT) *of Ancrum* **LG1952**

ASHE, Bt **EDB**; *of Langley* **LG1879**; **LGI1958**; *of Ashfield* **LG1863**

WINDHAM-ASHE (*see* Windham *formerly of Waghen*)

ASHFIELD, Bt **EDB**: (*see also* Stanley)

ASHHURST, Bt **EDB**; (*see also* Ruck Keene)

ASHLEY (Mount Temple, B) **PB1939**; Bt

EDB; (*see also* Shaftesbury)

ASHMAN, Bt **PB1916**

ASHMORE **DFUSA**; *of Clover Hill, co Antrim* **AA**

ASHPITEL **VSA**

ASHTON (Ashton of Hyde, B) **PB1970**; *formerly of Durwen* **LG1969**; *of Soulton Hall* **LG1952**: *of Welston Court* **LG1952**; *formerly of Woolton* **LG1952**; *of Scotsgrove House* **LG1937**; *of Lichford* **LG1921**; *of Polefield Hall* **LG1894**; (*see also* Bostock; and Williamson)

ASHTOWN (*see* Trench)

ASHWIN *of Bretforton Manor* **LG1972**

ASHWORTH *of Birtenshaw* **LG1952**; *formerly of Staghills* **LG1914**; *of Ashworth, Elland and Hall Carr* **LG1875**; (1) & (2) **FR**

ASKE, Bt **PB1970**

ASKEW *of Ladykirk, formerly of Pallinsburn* **LG1965**; (*see also* Askew-Robertson)

ASKWITH, B **PB1940**; *formerly of Ripon* **LG1969**

ASPINALL *of Standen Hall* **LG1952**

ASQUITH (Oxford and Asquith, E) **PB1970**; (Asquith of Bishopstone, B) **PB1953**; (*see also* Bonham Carter)

ASSHETON (Clitheroe, B) **PB1970**; Bt *of Lever* **EDB**; Bt *of Middleton* **EDB**

ASTBURY **FR**

ASTELL *of Woodbury and Everton* **LG1965**

ASTLEY (Hastings, B) **PB1970**; Bt **PB1970**; (Astley, B) **DEP**; (Astley, of Reading, B) **DEP**; Bt *of Melton Constable* **EDB**; Bt *of Patshull* **EDB**; *of Dukinfield Lodge* **LG1894**

LUDFORD-ASTLEY *of Ansley Park* **LG1921**

ASTON, B **DEP**; **EDB**

ASTOR, V **PB1970**; (Astor of Hever, B) **PB1970**

ATCHERLEY *formerly of Marton* **LG1952**

ATHERLEY *of Northbrook* **LG1914**

ATHERLEY (*now* Cator) *of Landguard Manor* **LG1921**

ATHERTON *formerly of Winstanley* **DFUSA**

ATHLONE (*see* Cambridge; and Ginkel)

ATHLUMNEY (*see* Somerville)

ATHOL (*see* Stewart; and Strathbogie)

ATHOLL (*see* Campbell; Douglas; Murray; and Stewart)

ATHOLSTAN (*see* Graham)

ATHORPE *of Thorpe Hall* **LG1952**

ATHY *of Renville* **LGI1912**
ATKIN, B **PB1940**; *of Leadington* **LG1863**
ATKINS, Bt **EDB**; *formerly of Stretton House* **LG1969**; *formerly of Waterpark* **LG1952**; *of Pouldrew* **LGI1958**
BURNABY-ATKINS *of Tolethorpe Hall, formerly of Halstead* **LG1965**
ATKINSON, B **PB1932**; *formerly of Morland* **LG1969**; *of Melbury* **LG1952**; *of Whitecroft, Wellington* **LG1952Supp**; *of Angerton* **LG1894**; *of Woolley Grange* **LG1894**; *of Lorbottle* **LG1886**; **IFR1976**; *of Cavangarden* **LGI1958**; *of Crowhill* **LGI1958**; **CG**; (*see also* Rawson)
ATLEE *formerly of Ford Hook House* **DFUSA**
ATON (Aton, B) **DEP**; (de Aton, B) **DEP**
ATTENBOROUGH *of Catesby* **LG1952**
ATTHILL *of Brandiston Hall* **LG1921**
ATTLEE, E **PB1970**
ATTREE **FR**
ATTWOOD **FR**
FREEMAN-ATTWOOD *formerly of Sion Hill* **LG1972**
ATTY *of Rugby* **LG1886**
ATTYE *late of Ingon Grange* **LG1921**
AUBERTIN *formerly of West Meon* **LG1972**
AUBREY, Bt **PB1856**; *of Dorton* **LG1900**
AUCHER, Bt **EDB**
AUCKLAND (*see* Eden)
AUCHINLECK (*see* Darling)
AUCHMUTY *of Brianstown* **LG1850/3**
STRACHAN-AUDAS *of Elloughton House* **LG1952**
AUDEN *formerly of Horninglow* **LG1965**
AUDLAND *of Ackenthwaite* **LG1969**
AUDLEY (Audley, B) **DEP**; (Audley of Walden, B) **DEP**; (Gloucester, E) **DEP**; (*see also* Tuchet-Jesson; and Touchet)
AUFRERE *of Burnside and Foulsham Old Hall* **LG1879**
AUNGIER, B **DEP**
AUSTEN, Bt *of Bexley* **EDB**; Bt *of Derhams* **EDB**; *of Capel Manor* **LG1921**; (*see also* Knight *of Chawton*)
GODWIN-AUSTEN *of Pirbright Manor* **LG1572**
AUSTIN, Bt **PB1970**; B **PB1940**; *of Roundwood* **LG1952**; *of Hollin Hall* **LG1921**; *of Brandeston Hall* **LG1900**
AVEBURY (*see* Lubbock)
AVELING *of Rochester* **LG1921**
AVERY, Bt **PB1917**
AVON (*see* Eden)

AVONDALE (*see* Stewart)
AVONMORE (*see* Yelverton)
AWDRY *of Notton* **LG1565**
AYKERODE (*see* Ecroyd)
AYKROYD, Bt *of Birstwith Hall* **PB1970**; Bt *of Lightcliffe* **PB1970**; of *Cliffe Hill* **LG1914**
AYLESBURY *of Packwood* **LG1914**
AYLESFORD (*see* Finch-Knightley)
AYLESTONE (*see* Bowden)
AYLESWORTH **DFUSA**
AYLMER, B **PB1970**; Bt **PB1970** *of Walworth Castle* **LG1937**; **IFR1976**
TOLER-AYLWARD **IFR1976**
AYLOFFE, Bt **EDB**
MURRAY-AYNSLEY *of Hall Court* **LG1921**; **CG**
AYRE *of The Limes* **LG1952**
SINCLAIR-AYTOUN *of Inchdairnie* **LG1900**
BABINGTON *formerly of Pinnacle Hill* **LG1972**; *of Cossington* **LG1952**; *of Creevagh* **LG11958**; **FR**
BACK **FR**
BACKHOUSE, Bt **PB1970**; Bt **EDB**; *late of Darlington* **LG1900**; *of Pilmore* **LG1894**; (*Australia*) **CG**
BACKWELL (*see* Tyringham)
BACON, Bt **PB1970**; (St Albans, V) **DEP**; Bt **EDB**; *of Eywood* **LG1898**; *formerly of Helmingham* **DFUSA**; (*see also* McCausland)
BADCOCK **LG1833/7**
BADD, Bt **EDB**
BADDELEY, Bt **PB1970**; *of Castle Hale* **LG1952**
BADELEY, B **PB1949**; *late of Guy Harlings* **LG1937**
BADEN (*Grand Ducal House of*) **RL**
BADENOCH *of Flamberts* **LG1952**
BADLESMERE, B **DEP**
BAGBY **DFUSA**
BAGGE, Bt **PB1970**; *formerly of Gaywood Hall* **LG1952**; *of Stradsett* **LG1863**; **FR**; **AA**
BAGENAL **IFR1976**
BAGNALL *of Newberries* **LG1886**
BAGNELL **IFR1976**
BAGOT, B **PB1970**; Bt *of Levens Hall* **PB1917**; *of Levens* **LG1906**; *of Churchdale House* **LG1879**; *of Elford House* **LG1875**; *of Pype Hall* **LG1858**; **IFR1976**; *of Ard and Ballymoe* **AA**
BAGWELL *of Accomack County, Virginia* **DFUSA**
BAGSHAWE *formerly of Ford Hall*

LG1965; *of Wormhill and Oakes-in-Norton* **LG1965**
GREAVES-BAGSHAWE (*see* Bagshawe)
BAGWELL **IFR1976**
BAIKIE *of Tankerness* **LG1952; AA**
BAILEY (Glanusk, B) **PB1970**; Bt **PB1970; LG1965**; *of Chaseley* **LG1937**; *of Ighthum* **LG1921**; *of Lofts Hall* **LG1914; HI**
BAILIE *of Manderston* **LG1952**; *of Rock House* **LGI1958**; *of Ringdufferin* **LGI1912**
BAILLIE (Burton, B) **PB1970**; Bt **PB1970**; Bt *of Berkeley Square* **PB1853**; Bt *of Lochend* **EDB**; *of Pyle Hill* **LG1952**; *of Dochfour* **LG1937**; *of Loch Loy* **LG1914**; *of Duntesborne Abbots* **LG1906**; *of Jerviswood* **LG1850/3**; *of Lamingtoun* **LG1833/7**; **FR; CG**; *of Hennington* **CG; HI**
COCHRANE-BAILLIE (Lamington, B) **BP1949**
BAILLIEU, B **PB1970**; *of Park Wood* **LG1952**
BAILWARD *of Horsington* **LG1972**
BAILY *of Hall Place* **LG1858**
BAIN *of Loadhall Grange* **LG1937**; **FR**
BAINBRIDGE *of Frankfield* **LGI1912**
DAINBRIGGE *formerly of Woodseat* **LG1969**
BAINES *formerly of Bawtry* **LG1969**; **FR**
BAIRD (Kintore, E) **PB1970**; (Stonehaven, V) **PB1970**; Bt *of Newbyth* **PB1970**; Bt *of Saughton* **PB1970**; *formerly of Elie* **LG1965**; *of Palmers Cross* **LG1952; IFR1976**; *of Gartsherrie Ironworks* **VF**
BAIRD (*formerly* ADAMSON) *of Auburn* **LGI1958**
MATURIN-BAIRD *of Langham Hall* **LG1952**
BAKER, Bt *of Ranston* **PB1956**; Bt *of Sissinghurst* **EDB**; *of Hasfield Court* **LG1969**; *of Sedbury Hall* **LG1965**; *formerly of Bayfordbury* **LG1952**; *of Elemore Hall* **LG1937**; *of Ramsden House* **LG1921**; *of West Hay* **LG1894**; *of Cottesmore* **LG1863; IFR1976**; (1) & (2) **DFUSA**; *of Adelaide* **CG**; *of Cottesmore, co Rutland* **AA**; *of Derby* **AA**; (*see also* Tower *formerly of Weald Hall*)
BELLYSE BAKER *of Highfields* **LG1972**
LLOYD-BAKER *of Hardwicke Court* **LG1972**
SHERSTON-BAKER, Bt **PB1970**
WINGFIELD-BAKER (*see* Wingfield-Digby)

BAKEWELL *of The Old Hall* **LG1900**
BALDERS *of West Barsham* **LG1879**
BALDOCK *of Hollycombe House* **LG1972**
BALDRIDGE **DFUSA**
BALDWIN *of Bewdley*, E **PB1970**; *of Ketton Hall* **LG1965**; *of Cressage Old Hall* **LG1952**; *of Dalton* **LG1937**; *of Levisham Hall* **LG1937**; *of Wilden House* **LG1906**; *of Clohina* **LG1863**; *formerly of Brookfield* **LGI1958**; *formerly of Aylesbury* **DFUSA**; *of Dunedin* **CG**
BALDWYN (*see* Childe *of Kinlet*)
BALE, Bt **EDB**
BALEAN *of The Green Hall* **LG1965**
BALERNO (*see* Buchanan-Smith)
BALFE **IFR1976**
BALFOUR, E **PB1970**; (Balfour of Burleigh, B) **PB1970**; (Balfour of Inchrye, B) **PB1970**; (Kinross, B) **PB1970**; (Riverdale, B) **PB1970**; (Balfour of Glenawley, B) **DEP**; Bt *of Langham Hall* **PB1915**; Bt *of Denmiln* **EDB**; *formerly of The Manor, Sidmouth* **LG1972**; *of Dawyck* **LG1965**; *of Balbirnie* **LG1965**; *of Balfour* **LG1952**; *of Balgonie and Newton Don* **LG1952**; *of Fernie Castle* **LG1937**; *of Kindrogan* **LG1937**; *of Townley Hall* **LGI1912**; (*Australia*) **CG**
BALGUY *formerly of Duffield* **LG1952**
BALIOL, B **DEP**
BALL, Bt **PB1970**; Bt *of Blofield* **PB1870**; *formerly of Veryan* **LG1969**; *formerly of Crouch End* **LG1952**; **IFR1976**; *formerly of Barkham* **DFUSA**; **FR**
ROLLO-BOWMAN-BALLANTINE *of Ashgrove and Castlehill* **LG1937**
BALLARD *of Maybole* **LG1937**
BALLIOL **RL**
BALLYANE (*see* Kavanagh)
BALMAIN *late of Alford House* **LG1937**
JONES-BALME *of High Close* **LG1952**
WHEATLEY-BALME (*see* Wheatley-Hubbard)
BALMERINOCH (*see* Elphinston)
BALOGH, B **PB1970**
BALTIMORE (*see* Calvert)
BALTINGLASS (*see* Eustace; and Roper)
BAMBURGH, Bt **EDB**
BAMFORD (*see* Bamford-Hesketh)
BAMPFYLDE (Poltimore, B) **PB1970**
BANBURY (Banbury of Southam, B) **PB1970**; (*see also* Knollys)
BANCKS *of Stockholm* **LG1833/7**
BANCROFT **IFR1976**; (1) & (2) **DFUSA**; *formerly of Salford* **DFUSA**

BAND *of Wookey House* **LG1886**
GLUSTINIANI-BANDINI (Newburgh, E) **PB1970**
BANDON (*see* Bernard)
BANFF (*see* Ogilvy)
BANGOR (*see* Ward)
BANKES, Bt **EDB**; *of Winstanley Hall* **LG1972**; *of Kingston Lacy and Corfe Castle* **LG1965**; *of Soughton Hall* **LG1965**; *of Weston* **LG1952**; **VSA**
BANKS, Bt *of London* **EDB**; Bt *of Revesby Abbey* **EDB**; *of The Park, Sutton Bridge* **LG1952**; *of Curlew Lodge* **LG1921**; *of Oxney* **LG1921**; *of Highmoor* **LG1921**; *of Golagh* **LGI1904**
BANKHEAD (*see* Jefferson)
BANNATYNE *of Haldon* **LG1921**
HARMOOD-BANNER, Bt **PB1970**
BANNERMAN (Bannerman of Kildonan, B) **PB1970**; Bt **PB1970**; *of Wyastone Leys* **LG1921**
BANNISTER *of Brantwood* **LG1952**
BANON *of Kilgreaney House* **LGI1958**
BANTRY (*see* Hedges-White)
BARBER, Bt **PB1970**; Bt *of Culham Court* **PB1927**; *of Englefield* **LG1937**
HILTON-BARBER **LG1972**
MITFORD-BARBERTON **LG1969**
BARBOUR, Bt **PB1949**; *of Bolesworth Castle* **LG1965**; *of Barlay* **LG1879**; **DFUSA**
BARCHARD *of Horsted* **LG1886**
BARCLAY, Bt **PB1970**; *of Higham* **LG1965**; *formerly of Mathers and Urie* **LG1965**; **DFUSA**; **PromFUSA**; *of Leyton, Essex* **AA**
BARCROFT **IFR1976**
BARD (Bellamont, V) **DEP**; Bt **EDB**
BARDOLF, B **DEP**
BARDSWELL *of The Chase, Chigwell* **LG1937**
BARDWELL *of Bolton Hall* **LG1937**
BARGENY (*see* Hamilton)
BARHAM *of Hole Park* **LG1972**; *of Trecwn* **LG1879**
BARING (Cromer, E) **PB1970**; (Ashburton, B) **PB1970**; (Howick of Glendale, B) **PB1970**; (Northbrook, B) **PB1970**; (Revelstoke, B) **PB1970**; Bt **PB1970**; (Northbrook, E) **PB1929**
BARKER, Bt *of Bishop's Stortford* **PB1914**; Bt *of Bocking Hall* **EDB**; Bt *of Bushbridge* **EDB**; Bt *of Grimston Hall* **EDB**; Bt *of Hambleton* **EDB**; *of Stanlake Park* **LG1965**; *of Dulas Court* **LG1952**; *of Lund Court* **LG1952**; *of Watchbury House* **LG1952**; *of Salt Hill*

LG1925; *of Brooklands* **LG1921**; *of St Germans* **LG1914**; *of Tong Lodge* **LG1914**; *of Albrighton Hall* **LG1900**; *of Needham House* **LG1894**; *of Hemsby Hall* **LG1894**; *of Croboy* **LG1886**; *formerly of Harwich* **DFUSA**; (*see also* May; Mill and Ponsonby)
PONSONBY-BARKER (*see* Ponsonby)
RAYMOND-BARKER *of Fairford Park* **LG1952**
SANKEY-BARKER *formerly of Horton* **LG1952**
BARKHAM, Bt *of South Acre* **EDB**; Bt *of Wainflete* **EDB**
BARLAS *of Craig Castle* **LG1972**
BARKLING, Bt **PB1940**
BARLOW, Bt *of Bradwell Hall* **PB1970**; Bt *of Fort William* **PB1970**; Bt *of London* **PB1970**; Bt *of Westminster* **PB1949**; Bt *of Slebetch* **EDB**; *of The Chace* **LG1952**; *of Pitt Manor* **LG1921**; *of Ashford* **LG1898**
OWEN-BARLOW, Bt **PB1851**
BARMSTON, Bt **PB1929**
BARNARD *of Furzebrook House* **LG1952**; *of Cave Castle* **LG1937**; *of Prestbury* **LG1894**; **DFUSA**; **PromFUSA**; (*see also* Vane)
BARNARDISTON, Bt *of Brightwell* **EDB**; Bt *of Kelton* **EDB**; *of The Ryes* **LG1952**
BARNBY (*see* Willey)
BARNE *of Sotterley* **LG1969**; *formerly of Broom Hall* **LG1952**
BARNEBY *of Llanerch-y-Coed formerly of Brockhampton* **LG1972**; *of Longworth* **LG1952**; *of Saltmarshe Castle* **LG1952**
LEWIS-BARNED **AA**
BARNES (Gorell, B) **PB1970**; *formerly of Ashgate* **LG1952**; *of Gateways* **LG1925**; *of Great Duryard* **LG1894**; *formerly of Soham* **DFUSA**
BARNETT *formerly of Glympton* **LG1965**; *of Stratton Park* **LG1898**
BARNEWALL (Trimlestown, V) **PB1970**; Bt **PB1970**; V **DEP**; *of Bloomsbury* **LG1894**; **AA**
BARNHAM, Bt **EDB**
BARNHILL **DFUSA**
BARNSTON *of Crewe Hill* **LG1921**
BARNWELL *formerly of Mileham* **LG1972**; **PromFUSA**
BARON, Bt **PB1934**
BARR, Bt **EDB**
BARRAN, Bt **PB1970**
BARRATT *of Blackwell Hall, formerly of*

Totteridge Park **LG1969**
BARRET (Barret of Newburgh, Lord) **DEP**
BARRETT, Bt **EDB**; *formerly of Court Lodge* **LG1969**; *of Bar House* **LG1965**; *of Milton House* **LG1952**; *of Wroughton Hall* **LG1937**; (1) & (2) **DFUSA**
MOULTON-BARRETT (*see* Altham *formerly of Timbercombe*)
BARRIE (Abertay, B) **PB1940**; Bt **PB1937**; *of Airlie Park* **LG1937**
BARRINGTON, V **PB1970**; Bt **PB1970**; Bt **EDB**; **IFR1976**
KENNETT-BARRINGTON *of The Manor House, Dorchester* **LG1900**
BARROGILL (*see* Sinclair)
BARRON, Bt **PB1900**; *of Belmont* **LG1886**; **IFR1976**; (*New Zealand*) **CG**
BARROW, Bt **PB1970**; *of Sydenham Hall* **LG1937**; *of The Red House* **LG1914**; *of Holmewood* **LG1900**; **IFR1976**; **FR**
BARROWS *formerly of Yarmouth* **DFUSA**
BARRY, Bt **PB1970**; (Barrymore, E) **DEP**; (Barry, B) **DEP**; Bt *of Dublin* **PB1891**; *of Hampton Gay Manor* **LG1937**; *of Firville* **LG1937Supp**; *of Rocklaveston* **LG1858**; *of St Leonard's Hill and Keiss Castle* **LG1898**; **IFR1976**; *of Castle Cor* **LGI1958**; *of Leamlara* **LGI1912**; *of Sandville* **LGI1912**; *of Summer Hill* **LGI1912**; *of Kilbolane Castle* **LGI1904**; **FR**
BURY-BARRY *formerly of Ballyclough* **LGI1958**; (*see also* Bury)
CREAGH BARRY (*see* Brasier-Creagh)
HAROLD-BARRY **IFR1976**
MILNER-BARRY *formerly of Kilgobbin and Hanover Hall* **LGI1958**
OTTER-BARRY *of Horkesley Hall* **LG1969**
SMITH-BARRY **IFR1976**
BARRYMORE (*see* Barry)
BARSTOW **FR**
JACKSON-BARSTOW *of Acomb* **LG1937**
BARTHOLOMEW *formerly of Burford* **DFUSA**
BARTHROPP *of Hacheston* **LG1925**
BARTLET *of Ludbrooke* **LG1921**
BARTLETT, Bt **PB1970**; *formerly of Holwell* **LG1952**; *of Burton House* **LG1937 Supp**; **FR**; *formerly of Emley and Stophem* **DFUSA**
BARTLEY *of East Clare, S Rhodesia* **LG1952 Supp**
BARTOL **DFUSA**

BARTON, Bt **PB1937**; *of Saxby Hall* **LG1972**; *formerly of Hadlow* **LG1952**; (*cos Donegal, Fermanagh, Kildare and Tipperary*) **IFR1976**; (*co Kilkenny*) **IFR1976**; (*co Wicklow*) **IFR1976**; **DFUSA**; (*Australia*) (1) & (2) **CG**; (*New Zealand*) **CG**
BARTTELOT, Bt **PB1970**
BARWICK, Bt **PB1970**; *of Inholmes* **LG1937**
BARWIS *of Langrigg Hall* **LG1886**
BASCOM **DFUSA**
BASING (*see* Sclater-Booth)
BASKERVILLE *of Clyro* **LG1952**; *of Crowsley Park* **LG1952**
BASKERVYLE (*see* Baskervyle-Glegg)
BASS (Burton, B) **PB1909**
BASSANO *of Hadenholme* **LG1937**
BASSET (Basset, of Drayton, B) **DEP**; (Basset of Sapcote, B) **DEP**; (Basset of Welden, B) **DEP**; (de Dunstanville, B) **DEP**; *formerly of Bonvilston* **LG1937**; *of Fledborough Hall* **LG1937**; *late of Tehidy* **LG1937**; *of Beaupré* **LG1914**
BASSET (*now* PENN-CURZON) *of Watermouth* **LG1937**
BASSETT, Bt **EDB**; **DFUSA**
BASTARD, Bt **EDB**; *of Kitley* **LG1969**; *of Charlton* **LG1898**
BATCHELOR *of Combe Florey* **LG1952**
BATE, Bt **EDB**; *of Marchwiel and Llanarmon-yn-läl* **LG1965**; (*see also* Charlton)
BATEMAN, V **DEP**; Bt **EDB**; *of Brightlingsea* **LG1937**; *of Hartington Hall* **LG1921**; *of Morley* **LG1914**; *of Middleton Hall* **LG1894**; *of Bartholey* **LG1894**, *of Bedford House* **LGI1912**; **FR**; (*see also* Bateman-Hanbury)
JONES-BATEMAN *of Inner Ting Tong* **LG1952**
LA TROBE-BATEMAN *of Moor Park* **LG1921**
BATES, Bt *of Bellefield, Gyrn Castle and Manydown* **PB1970**; *of Aydon* **LG1952**; *of Milbourne* **LG1886**; *of Manydown Park* **LG1879**; *of Denton* **LG1858**
BATESON, Bt **PB1870**
DE YARBURGH-BATESON (Deramore, B) **PB1970**
BATH, Bt **EDB**; *formerly of Alltyferin* **LG1972**; **FR**; (*see also* Bourchier; Granville; Nightingale; Pulteney; Shaunde; and Thynne)
BATHER *formerly of Meole Brace* **LG1969**
BATHO, Bt **PB1970**

BATHURST, E **PB1970** (Bledisloe, V) **PB1970**; Bt **EDB**; *of Marham House* **LG1921**
HERVEY-BATHURST, Bt **PB1970**
BATSON *of Horseheath* **LG1894**
BATT *of Gresham Hall* **LG1972**; *of Rathmullan* **LGI1912**
BATTEN *formerly of Aldon and Upcerne* **LG1972**; *of Stainforth* **LG1952 Supp**
CHISHOLM-BATTEN *of Thornfalcon* **LG1972**
BATTERSBY (*see* Maxwell)
HARFORD-BATTERSBY (*see* Harford *of Horton*)
BATTERSEA (*see* Flower)
BATTINE *formerly of Barrow Court* **LG1969**
BATTLE **DFUSA**
BATTLEY *of Belvedere Hall* **LGI1912**
BATTY *of Ballyhealy* **LG1879**
BATTYE *of Crosland Hill and Skelton Hall* **LG1914**
TREVOR-BATTYE *formerly of Little Hampton* **LG1972**
BAUMGARTNER **LG1937**
BAVARIA (*Royal House of*) **RL**
BAVENT, B **DEP**
BAVERSTOCK *of Alton and Windsor* **LG1833/7**
BAXENDALE *of Franfield Place* **LG1965**; *formerly of Hursley Park* **LG1952**; (*Fiji*) **CG**
BAXTER, Bt *of Invereighty* **PB1926**; Bt *of Kilmaron* **PB1872**; *formerly of Kincaldrum* **LG1965**; *of Sibdon Castle* **LG1921**
BAYARD (*Canada*) **CG**
BAYFORD (*see* Sanders)
BAYLDON *of Ingsdom and Oaklands* **LG1906**
BAYLES **CG**
BAYLEY *of Willasdon Hall* **LG1937**; **FR**
READETT-BAYLEY *formerly of Lenton Abbey* **LG1952**
BAYLIES (*now* HOOPER) *formerly of Alvechurch* **DFUSA**
BAYLY *formerly of Torr* **LG1969**; **IFR1976**; *of Ballyarthur* **LGI1912**; (*see also* Paget)
BAYNE **DFUSA**
BAYNES, Bt **PB1970**; **FR**
BAYNING (Bayning, V) **DEP**; Bt **EDB**; (*see also* Townshend)
BAYNTUN *of Bromham* **LG1833/7**
BAZLEY, Bt **PB1970**
BEACH *of Oakley Hall* **LG1921**
HICKS BEACH (St Aldwyn, E) **PB1970**

BEACONSFIELD (*see* Disraeli)
BEADLE **DFUSA**
BEADNELL *formerly of Gogarth* **LG1937**; *of Cynhinfa* **LG1879**
BEADON *of Gotton House* **LG1937**
BEALANDS **CG**
BEALE *of Drumlamford* **PB1922**; Bt *of Maidstone* **EDB**; *of Brettenham* **LG1914**; *of Heath House* **LG1894**
BEALS **DFUSA**
BEAM **DFUSA**
BEAMAN *formerly of Kingscote Grange* **LG1972**; **DFUSA**
BEAMISH **IFR1976**
BEARCE *formerly of Southampton* **DFUSA**
BEARCROFT *of Mere Hall* **LG1952**
BEARD *formerly of Grayshott Hall* **LG1952**
BEARDMORE (Invernairn, B) **PB1936**
BEARDSLEY *of New Quorn House* **LG1952**
BEARSTED (*see* Samuel)
BEATTY, E **PB1970**; (1) & (2) **DFUSA**
BEAUCHAMP, Bt *of Grosvenor Place* **PB1970**; Bt *of Woodborough* **PB1970**; (Warwick, E) **DEP**; (Beauchamp of Bletsho, B) **DEP**; (Beauchamp of Hache, B) **DEP**; (Beauchamp of Kydderminster, B) **DEP**; (Beauchamp of Powyke, B) **DEP**(St Amand, B) **DEP**; *of Trevince* **LG1952**; (*see also* Lygon)
PROCTOR-BEAUCHAMP, Bt **PB1970**
BEAUCLERK (St Albans, D) **PB1970**
BEAUFORD *of Troston Hall* **LG1952**
BEAUFORT (Dorset, M) **DEP**; (Exeter, D) **DEP**; (*see also* Somerset)
BEAULIEU (*see* Hussey)
BEAUMAN *of Hyde Park* **LG1886**
BEAUMONT (Allendale, V) **PB1970**; (Beaumont of Whitley, B) **PB1970**; Bt **PB1970**; V **DEP**; Bt *of Cole Orton* **EDB**; Bt *of Grace Dieu* **EDB**; Bt *of Whitley* **EDB**; *of Buckland Court* **LG1937**; *of Bretton* **LG1900**; *of Barrow-upon-Trent* **LG1894**; **DFUSA**; *of Canada* **AA**
BEAVAN *of Seldown House* **LG1921**
BEAVEN *of Holt* **LG1952**
BEAVER *formerly of Glyn Garth* **LG1952**
BEAVERBROOK (*see* Aitken)
BEAZLEY *formerly of Warborough* **LG1965**
BEC (Beke of Eresby, B) **DEP**
BECHE (La Beche, B) **DEP**
BECHER **IFR1976**
WRIXON-BECHER, Bt **PB1970**; *of*

Castle Hyde **LGI1912**
BECK, Bt **EDB**; *of Castle Point* **LG1952**
BECKETT (Grimthorpe, B) (Bt) **PB1970**; *formerly of Forty Hill* **LG1969**; *of Barnsley* **LG1850/3**; *formerly of Twemlow* **DFUSA**; **FR**
BECKFORD *of Fonthill and Basing Park* **LG1863**
BECKWITH, Bt **EDB**; *formerly of Trimdon* **LG1972**; (*see also* Lincoln)
MINTON BEDDOES *of Cheney Longville* **LG1969**
BEDELL, Bt **EDB**
BEDFORD *of Old Sleningford Hall* **LG1952**; **DFUSA**; (*see also* Couci; Plantagenet; Russell; and Tudor)
RILAND-BEDFORD *late of Sutton Coldfield* **LG1921**
BEDINGFELD *formerly of Bedinfield* **LG1952**
PASTON-BEDINGFELD, Bt **PB1970**
WYNTER BEE (*formerly* NUGENT) *of Cloncoskraine* **LGI1958**
BEEBEE *of Womaston* **LG1952**
BEECH *of Brandon Hall* **LG1952**
BEECHAM, Bt **PB1970**
BEECHING, B **PB1970**
BEECROFT *of Kirkstall* **LG1875**
BEEKMAN **PromFUSA**
TIDBURY-BEER *formerly of East Clandon* **LG1952**
BEETHAM *formerly of Betham and Little Strickland* **LG1972**; **CG**
BEEVOR, Bt **PB1970**
BEHRENS *of Swinton Grange* **LG1972**; **FR**
BEIT, Bt **PB1970**
BEITH *of Moniaive* **LG1952**
BEKE (*see* Bec)
BEKEN *of High Pauls* (*see* Lindley)
BELASYSE (Belasyse, of Worlaby, B) **DEP**; (Fauconberg, E) **DEP**; Bt **EDB**; (*see also* Armine)
BELCHER (*New Zealand*) **CG**
BELDAM *of Toft* **LG1921**
BELFIELD *of Primley Hill* **LG1937**
BELGRAVE *of North Kilworth* **LG1972**
BELHAVEN (*see* Douglas; and Hamilton)
HORE-BELISHA, B **PB1956**
BELK **DFUSA**
BELL, Bt *of Rounton Grange* **PB1970**; Bt *of Mynthurst* **PB1953** Bt *of Marlborough Terrace* **PB1940**; Bt *of Framewood* **PB1924**; *of Cottisford House* **LG1972**; *of Thirsk* **LG1972**; *formerly of Bourne Park* **LG1952**; *of Cleeve House* **LG1952**; *formerly of Pendell Court*

LG1952; *of Stubb House* **LG1952**; *of Woolsington, formerly of Northumberland* **LG1952**; *of Yewhurst* **LG1900**; *formerly of Felden* **LGI1958**; *formerly of Morpeth* **DFUSA**; (*see also* Smith-Barry)
BELL (*formerly* O'CALLAGHAN and PRESTON) *of Askham Bryan* **LG1965**
MORRISON-BELL, Bt **PB1970**
WILBERFORCE-BELL *of Portington Hall* **LG1937**
BELLAIRS *of Kirkby Bellairs* **VSA**; (*see also* Stevenson *of Uffington*)
BELLAMONT (*see* Bard and Coote)
BELLASIS **LG1952Supp**
OLIVER-BELLASIS (*see* Oliver)
BELLENDEN, Lord **DEP**
BELLEW, B **PB1970**; B **DEP**; **FR**
GRATTAN-BELLEW, Bt **PB1970**
TROLLOPE-BELLEW *of Carew, Casewick and Crowcombe* **LG1972**
BELLINGER **DFUSA**
BELLINGHAM, Bt **PB1970**; Bt **EDB**
BELLOMONT (Leicester, E) **DEP**; (*see also* Kirkoven)
BELLOT, Bt **EDB**
BELLVILLE *of Tedstone Court* **LG1952**
BELMORE (*see* Lowry Corry)
BELPER (*see* Strutt)
BELSTEAD (*see* Ganzoni)
BELVEDERE (*see* Rochfort)
BENCE (*see* Bence-Jones)
BENDISH, Bt **EDB**
BENDYSHE *formerly of Barrington Hall* **LG1952**
BENEDICT **DFUSA**
BENETT *of Pyt House* **LG1886**; (*see also* Benett-Stanford)
BENGOUGH *formerly of The Ridge* **LG1972**
BENHALE, B **DEP**
BENHAM *of Colchester* **LG1952**
BENJAMIN *of Holywell* **LGI1958**
BENN, Bt *of Old Knoll* **PB1970**; Bt *of Rollesby* **PB1970**; (Glenravel, B) **PB1937**
WEDGWOOD BENN (Stansgate, V) **PB1970**
BENNET (Tankerville, E) **PB1970**; (Arlington, E) **PB1936**; Bt **EDB**; Bt *of Babraham* **EDB**; Bt *of Bechampton* **EDB**; *formerly of Tresillian* **LG1952**; *of Rougham Hall* **LG1921**; *of Ballintaggart* **LGI1958**; **FR**
BENNETT, Bt **PB1970**; (Bennett of Edgbaston, B) **PB1956**; *of Cwmllecoediog* **LG1952**; *formerly of Fromehurst*

LG1952; *of Fryston* **LG1952**; *formerly of Llanvihangel Court* **LG1952**; *of Oxcombe* **LG1937**; *late of Sparkford Hall* **LG1921**; *of Faringdon House* **LG1894**; *of Castle Roe* **LGI1912**; *of Thomaston* **LGI1904**; *of Bennett's Court* **LG1886**; **DFUSA**
CURTIS-BENNETT **LG1972**
LEIGH-BENNETT *formerly of Thorpe Place* **LG1952**
BENNITT *of Stourton Hall, Stourbridge* **AA**
BENSLEY, Bt **EDB**
BENSON (Charnwood, B) **PB1953**; (Bingley, B) **DEP**; *of Newbrough Hall* **LG1972**; *formerly of Lutwyche* **LG1969**; *of Stanway House* **LG1969**; *formerly of The Fould* **LG1965**; *of Murley Grange* **LG1937**; *of Compton Bassett* **LG1937 Supp**; *of Old Mill House* **LG1937**; *of Utterby House* **LG1858**; **VSA**
BENT *of Wexham Lodge* **LG1863**; *of Basford House* **LG1833/7**; *formerly of Penton-Grafton* **DFUSA**
BENTHALL *of Benthall* **LG1972**
BENTINCK *of Bulstrode* **VF**
CAVENDISH-BENTINCK (Portland, D) **PB1970**
BENTLEY *of Pannal* **LG1952**; *of West House* **LG1886**; *of Birch House* **LG1858**; **FR**
BENUARRAT, B **TNBE1956**
BENYON, Bt **PB1959**; *of Englefield* **LG1952**; *of Carshalton* **LG1858**
BERE *of Timewell* **LG1900**; *of Morebath House* **LG1898**; *of Skilgate* **LG1875**
BERENS *of Bentworth Hall formerly of Kevington* **LG1969**
BERESFORD, B **PB1917**; V **DEP**; *of Learmount* **LGI1912**; *of Awbawn* **LGI1912**; *of Woodhouse* **LGI1912**; (*see also* Beresford-Ash; and Beresford-Peirse)
DE LA POER BERESFORD (Waterford, M) **PB1970**; (Decies, B) **PB1970**
MASSY-BERESFORD **LG1937 Supp**
PACK-BERESFORD **IFR1976**; **AA**
BERIDGE *of Algarkirk and Gosfield Place* **LG1921**
BERINGTON *of Little Malvern Court* **LG1969**; *of Bradwell and Sandbach* **LG1833/7**
BERKELEY, B **PB1970**; E **PB1940**; (Fitz-Hardinge, B) **PB1916**; M **DEP**; (Falmouth, E) **DEP**; (FitzHardinge, E) **DEP**; (Berkeley, of Stratton, B) **DEP**;

(Botecourt, B) **DEP**; Bt *of Bruton* **EDB**; Bt *of Wymondham* **EDB**; *of Spetchley* **LG1972**; *of Cotheridge* **LG1952**; *of Lisbuoy House* **LGI1958**
FOLEY-BERKELEY (*see* Foley)
BERKSHIRE (*see* Norreys)
BERMINGHAM (Louth, E) **DEP**; (Bermingham, B) **DEP**; (Carbery, B) **DEP**
BERNARD (Bandon, E) **PB1970**; Bt **PB1970**; Bt *of Nettleham* **PB1850**; Bt *of Huntingdon* **EDB**; *of High Hall* **LG1952**; *formerly of Snakemoor* **LG1952**; *of Dunsinnan and Buttergask* **LG1937**; (*see also* Paley)
BEAMISH-BERNARD (*see* Beamish)
MORROGH BERNARD **IFR1976**
BERNERS *of Marcham Park, formerly of Woolverstone Park* **LG1952**; *see also* Williams
BERNEY, Bt **PB1970**; *of Morton Hall* **LG1914**
BERRIDGE **IFR1976**
BERRY (Camrose, V) **PB1970**; (Kemsley, V) **PB1970**; (Hartwell, B) **PB1970**; (Buckland, B) **PB1928**; Bt **EDB**; *of Tayfield* **LG1952**; *of Farnham Chase* **LG1925**; *of Rowgardens Wood* **LG1921**; (1) & (2) **DFUSA**; *of Suva* **CG**
THORNTON-BETTY *of Swinithwaite Hall* **LG1952**
BERRYMAN **DFUSA**
BERTIE (Lindsey and Abingdon, E) **PB1970**; (Bertie of Thame, V) **PB1953**; (Lindsey, M) **DEP**; Bt **EDB**
BERTRAM, B **DEP**; *of Nisbert and Kersewell* **LG1952**
BERWICK (*see* Fitz-James; and Noel-Hill)
BESSBOROUGH (*see* Ponsonby)
BEST (Wynford, B) **PB1970**; **LG1972**; *of Donnington* **LG1914**; *of St Katherine's* **LG1894**; *of Eastbury House* **LG1879**
BEST (*formerly* ROBINSON) *late of Silksworth* **LG1937**
BEST (*now* BEST-DALISON) *of Park House* **LG1937**
DIGBY-BESTE *of Botleigh Grange* **LG1886**
MYERS-BESWICK *of Gristhorpe* **LG1921**
BETENSON, Bt **EDB**
BETHELL, B **PB1970**; (Westbury, B) **PB1970**; *of Rise* **LG1969**
BETHUNE *of Balfour* **LG1914**; *late of Blebo* **LG1914**
LINDESAY-BETHUNE (Lindsay, E) **PB1970**

PATTON-BETHUNE *formerly of Clayton Priory* **LG1921**
SHARP BETHUNE, Bt **PB1970**
BETTERTON (Rushcliffe, B) **PB1949**
BETTON *of Great Berwick* **LG1898**
BETTS *of Wortham* **LG1886**; *formerly of West Peckham* **DFUSA**; *(Australia)* **CG**
BEVAN *formerly of Trent Park* **LG1965**; *of Quatford Castle* **LG1952**; *late of Stone Park* **LG1921**; **IFR1976**; *(see also* Percy)
EVANS BEVAN, Bt **PB1970**
BEVERIDGE, B **PB1963**; *of Vallay* **LG1952**
BEVERLEY *of Beverley* **LG1875**; *formerly of Beverley* **DFUSA**
BEVINGTON **FR**
BEVIS **DFUSA**
BEWES *formerly of Beaumont* **LG1972**; *of Gnaton Hall* **LG1921**
BEWICKE *of Shawdon Hall and Urpeth Lodge* **LG1972**; *of Hallaton* **LG1900**
BEWLEY *of Binbrook* **LG1833/7**
BEXLEY *(see* Vansittart)
BEYNON, Bt **PB1940**
CROWTHER-BEYNON *late of Amwell House* **LG1921**
PROTHEROE-BEYNON *of Trewern* **LG1952**
O'CONNELL BIANCONI *(see* O'Connell)
BIBBY, Bt **PB1970**; *(see also* Thompson)
BICESTER *(see* Vivian Smith)
BICKERSTETH (Langdale, B) **DEP**; **FR**
BICKERTON, Bt **EDB**
BICKFORD *of Dunsland* **LG1833/7**
BICKLEY, Bt **EDB**
BIDDLE **PromFUSA**
BIDDULPH, B **PB1970**; Bt **PB1970**; *of Ledbury* **LG1900**; *of Burton* **LG1898**; **DFUSA**
MYDDLETON-BIDDULPH *(see* Myddelton)
BIDWILL *of Pihautea* **CG**
BIGELOW *formerly of Wrentham* **DFUSA**
BIGG, Bt **EDB**; **LG1833/7**
BIGGE (Stamfordham, B) **PB1931**; *late of Fowlden Hall* **LG1937**
SELBY-BIGGE, Bt **PB1970**
BIGGS **DFUSA**
YEATMAN-BIGGS *of Stockton* **LG1952**
BIGHAM (Mersey, V) **PB1970**; (Nairne, B) **PB1970**
BIGLAND *(see* Pain)
BIGNOLD *of Norwich* **LG1952**
BIGOD (Norfolk, E) **DEP**

BIGSBY *of Suffolk and Nottinghamshire* **LG1843/49**
BILL *of Farley Hall* **LG1952**; (1) & (2) **DFUSA**
BILLIAT *formerly of Aisthorpe* **LG1952**
BILLINGSLEY *formerly of Astley Abbotts* **DFUSA**
BILSLAND, B **PB1970**
BINDLOSSE, Bt **EDB**
BINDON *(see* Howard)
BINGHAM (Lucan, E) **PB1970**; (Clanmorris, B) **PB1970**; Bt *of Sheffield* **PB1940**; *formerly of Melcombe Bingham* **LG1969**; *of Bingham Castle* **LGI1912**; **DFUSA**; *formerly of Sheffield* **DFUSA**
SMITH BINGHAM *formerly of Mickleton Manor* **LG1965**
BINGLEY *(see* Benson; and Lane-Fox)
BINNEY *of Pampisford* **LG1972**
BINNING *(see* Monro *of Auchinbowie)*
BIRCH *of Beaumont Hall* **LG1952**; *formerly of Chartridge* **LG1952**; *formerly of Clare Park* **LG1952**; *of Watlington Hall* **LG1937**; *of Lympstone* **LG1921**; *late of Armitage* **LG1900**; *of Ardwick and Garnstone* **LG1833/7**; **DFUSA** *(see also* Birch Reynardson)
NEWELL-BIRCH *(see* Birch Reynardson)
WYRLEY-BIRCH *(see* Birch Reynardson)
BIRCHALL **FR**
BIRCHENOUGH, Bt **PB1937**
BIRCHENOUGH *(formerly* MESHAM) *formerly of Pontruffydd and of Dunwood Manor* **LG1952**
BIRD, Bt **PB1970**; *of Drybridge House* **LG1965**; *of Tudor Grange* **LG1921**
BIRDWOOD, B **PB1970**
BIRK, B **PB1970**
BIRKBECK, Bt **PB1908**; *formerly of Westacre* **LG1965**; *of Anley* **LG1952**; *of Norris Castle* **LG1952**
BIRKENHEAD *of Backford* **LG1833/7**; *(see also* Smith)
BIRKETT, B **PB1970**; *of Beldorney Castle* **LG1952**
BIRKIN, Bt **PB1970**; *of Ruddington Grange* **LG1900**
BIRKMYRE, Bt **PB1970**
BIRLEY *formerly of Kirkham* **LG1965**
BIRNEY *of Red Castle* **LG1952**
BIRRELL *of Uttershill* **LG1952**; *of Woodhouse* **LG1925 Supp**
BISCOE *formerly of Newton and Kingillie* **LG1952**
TYNDALE-BISCOE *formerly of Holton Park* **LG1952**

BISPHAM **DFUSA**
BISSE (*see* Challenor *of Portnall*)
BISSELL **DFUSA**
BISSETT *of Lessendrum* **LG1952**
BISSHOP, Bt **PB1870**
BLAAUW *late of Beechland* **LG1921**
BLACHFORD (*see* Rogers)
BLACK, B **PB1970**; Bt *of Midgham Park*
PB1970; Bt *of Louth Park* **PB1940**; *formerly of Ardmay* **LG1952**; *of Highfield
Park* **LG1952**; *of Prees Hall* **LG1952**; *of
Cailzie and Auchentoshan* **LG1937**; *of
Elton Manor* **LG1921**; *of Creagh Castle*
LGI1958; **FR**
BLACKADER, Bt **EDB**
BLACKALL **IFR1976**
BLACKBURN, B **PB1896**; *formerly of
Donhead Hall* **LG1952**; *of Oakville*
LG1952
BLACKBURNE *formerly of Hale and
Orford* **LG1969**; *of Gratwicks* **LG1952**;
(*see also* Townshend)
BLACKDEN *of The Jewell House* **LG1952**
BLACKER, Bt **EDB**; *of Coldhayes*
LG1952; *of Woodbrook* **LG1894**;
IFR1976; **FR**
BLACKET **LG1833/7**
BLACKETT, B **PB1970**; Bt **PB1970**; *of
Wylam* **LG1969**
BLACKFORD (*see* Mason)
BLACKHAM, Bt **EDB**
BLACKLEY **IFR1976**
BLACKMAN (*see* Harnage)
BLACKSTONE *of Castle Priory*
LG1850/3
BLACKWALL *of Blackwall* **LG1972**
BLACKWELL, Bt **EDB**; *of Brinkley Hall*
LG1952; *of The Cedars Harrow Weald*
LG1937
BLACKWOOD, Bt **PB1970**; *of Castle-
navin* **LGI1958**
HAMILTON-TEMPLE-BLACKWOOD
(Dufferin and Ava, M) **PB1970**
BLACQUE *of Castletown House*
LGI1958
BLADES (Ebbisham, B) **PB1970**
BLADON *of Kirk Ella* **LG1965**
BLAGDEN *formerly of Oxted* **LG1952**
BLAGG *of Car-Colston* **LG1969**
BLAGRAVE *formerly of Calcot Park*
LG1952
BLAGUE *of Hollinger* **LG1833/7**
BLAIR, Bt **PB1959**; *of Blair* **LG1952**; (1)
& (2) **DFUSA**; *formerly of Ballinteer*
DFUSA; (*see also* Blair-Imrie)
HUNTER-BLAIR, Bt **PB1970**
BLAKE, Bt *of Menlough* **PB1970**; Bt *of*

Langham **PB1970**; Bt *of Tillmouth*
PB1970; (Wallscourt, B) **PB1917**; Bt *of
Twizel Castle* **PB1860**; *of Barham
Court* **LG1972**; *of Mount Shannon*
LG1937Supp; *late of Danesbury*
LG1921; **IFR1976**; *of Tower Hill*
LGI1912; *of Heath House* **LGI1912**; (1)
& (2) **DFUSA**; **PromFUSA**; **CG**; (*see
also* Humfrey-Mason; White *Limerick*)
ALDRICH-BLAKE *of Weston Hall*
LG1965
JEX-BLAKE (*see* Humfrey-Mason)
BLAKEMOORE (*see* Booker)
BLAKEMORE *of The Leys* **LG1850/3**
BLAKENEY, B **DEP**; **IFR1976**
BLAKENHAM (*see* Hare)
BLAKER, Bt **PB1970**
BLAKISTON, Bt **PB1970**; Bt *of Blakis-
ton* **EDB**; Bt *of Gibside* **EDB**; *formerly
of Blakiston* **DFUSA**; (*New Zealand*)
CG
BLAMIRE *of Thackwood and The Oaks*
LG1858
BLANCHARD *of Grimsargh Hall*
LG1833/7; **DFUSA**
BLAND, Bt **EDB**; *of Copdock* **LG1965**;
of Debden Manor **LG1952**; (*co Kerry*)
IFR1976; (*co Leix*) **IFR1976**; **DFUSA**
DAVISON-BLAND *of Kippax Park*
LG1937
BLANDY *formerly of Inglewood and
Kingston Bagpuize* **LG1972**; (*see also*
Blandy-Jenkins)
BLANE, Bt **PB1916**; (*see also* De Hamel)
BLANESBURGH (*see* Younger)
BLANTON **DFUSA**
BLAQUIERE, Bt **PB1917**
BLATHWAYT *of Dyrham Park* **LG1952**
BLAXLAND *of Fordwich* **CG**
BLAXTER **DFUSA**
BLAYDES *formerly of High Paw and
Ranby* **LG1972**
BLAYNEY, B **DEP**; *of Evesham* **LG1858**
BLEDISLOE (*see* Bathurst)
BLENCOWE *of Marston St Lawrence*
LG1952; *of Thoby Priory* **LG1898**; **AA**;
(*see also* Tillard)
BLENKHORN *of Stirches* **LG1914**
BLENKINSOPP *of Sheriff Hutton*
LG1972; (*see also* Coulson)
LEATON-BLENKINSOPP *of Hoppyland
Park* **LG1914**
BLENNERHASSETT, Bt **PB1970**;
IFR1976
GARFORTH-BLES **LG1969**
BLESINGTON (*see* Boyle; and Stewart)
BLESSINGTON (*see* Gardiner)

BLEWITT *of Boxted* LG1952; *of Llantarnam* LG1850/3
BLIGH (Darnley, E) PB1970; (*see also* Barrington)
BLINN DFUSA
BLISS *of Brandon Park* LG1863; *formerly of Preston Parva* DFUSA; *formerly of Rochester* DFUSA
BLOCK LG1969
BLODGETT DFUSA
BLOFELD *of Hoveton House* LG1972
BLOIS, Bt PB1970
BLOMEFIELD, Bt PB1970
BLOOD IFR1976
BLOOMFIELD, B DER; *of Lisnafillon House* LG1937Supp; *of Castle Caldwell* LGI1904
BLOMMART *of Willett House* LG1886
LYNCH-BLOSSE, Bt PB1970
BLOUNT, Bt PB1970; (Devon, E) DEP, (Newport, F) DEP; B DEP; (Mountjoy, B) DEP; Bt EDB *late of Orleton* LG1914; *formerly of Bristol* DFUSA
DARELL-BLOUNT (*see* Riddell *of Felton and Swinburne*)
RIDDELL-BLOUNT (*see* Riddell *of Felton and Swinburne*)
BLOW *of Painswick* LG1952
BLUE *formerly of Kintyre* DFUSA
BLUETT *of Tor Mohun* LG1906
BLUNDEL, Bt EDB
BLUNDELL, V DEP; *of Crosby* LG1969
WELD-BLUNDELL (*see* Manchester; Weld; and Yarborough)
WHITLOCK BLUNDELL (*see* Blundell *of Crosby*)
BLUNDEN, Bt PB1970
BLUNT, Bt PB1970; *of Crabbet Park* LG1921
BLYTH, B PB1970; CG
BURN-BLYTH *of Woolhampton House* LG1900
CURRIE-BLYTH *of Sandown House* LG1906
BLYTHSWOOD (*see* Campbell)
BLYTON, B PB1970
BOARD *of Westerham* LG1921
BODDIE DFUSA
BODDINGTON *formerly of Pownall Hall* LG1965
BODEN *formerly of The Friary* LG1952
BODENHAM *of Rotherwas* LG1879; *of Biddenden and Ryal* LG1833/7
BODKIN *of Annagh* LGI1904
BODY *of Hindhead Court* LG1921
BOEHIN (*see* Boehm-Boteler; and Trafford *of Wroxham*)

CRAWLEY-BOEVEY, Bt PB1970
BOGER *formerly of Wolsdon* LG1952
BOGGIS *formerly of Edwardstone* LG1972
BOHUN (Northampton, E) DEP; (Bohun, B) DEP
BOILEAU, Bt PB1970
BOISSIER LG1965
BOLAM (*formerly* CALDECOTT) *of Holbrook Grange* LG1952
BOLCKOW *of Marton Hall* LG1937
BOLD *of Bold* LG1833/7
BOLDEN *of Hyning* LG1972
BOLDERO *formerly of Rattlesden* LG1952 Supp
BOLES, Bt PB1970
BOLEYNE (Ormonde, E) DEP; (Pembroke, M) DEP
BOLGER *of Ballinabarna* LG1858
BOLINGBROKE (*see* St John)
BOLITHO *of Trengwainton* LG1965
BOLLAND (*see* Dawson *of Langcliffe Hall*)
BOLLE, Bt EDB; *of Thorpe* LG1833/7
BOLLES, Bt EDB
BOLTON, B PB1970; *of Colwood Park* LG1952; *of Oakamoor* LG1952; *formerly of Brook Lodge* LG1937; *of Mount Bolton* LG1912; *of Castle Ring* LGI1912; *of Tullydonnell* LGI1904; *of Nenagh* LG1879; *of The Island* (*see* Hughes); DFUSA; (*see also* Paulet; and Orde-Powlett)
ROMFORD IFR1976
BONAPARTE PromFUSA
BONAR *formerly of Kilgraston and Kimmerghame* LG1952Supp; (*New Zealand*) CG
BOND, Bt *of Coolamber* EDB; Bt *of Peckham* EDB; *of Creech Grange* LG1969; *of Moigne Combe, formerly of Tyneham* LG1969; *of Ardglass* LG1850/3; *of Farragh* LGI1958; *formerly of Bury St Edmunds* DFUSA; *formerly of Laycock* DFUSA
MACGEOUGH BOND IFR1976
BONHAM, Bt PB1970; IFR1976
BONN *of Oaklands* LG1965
BONSALL *of Fronfraith* LG1952; *formerly of Morben* LG1952
BONSOR, Bt PB1970
BONTEIN *formerly of Ardoch and Barglas* LG1952; (*see also* Bontine Cunninghame Graham *of Ardoch*)
BONVILE, B DEP
BONYNGE LGI1912
BOOKER *of Velindra* LG1921

BOONE *formerly of Dipford* **DFUSA**
BOORD, Bt **PB1970**
BOORMAN *of St Augustine's Priory*
LG1952
BOOT (Trent, B) **PB1956**; *of Thornbridge
Hall* **LG1937**
BOOTH, Bt **PB1970**; Bt *of Portland
Place* **PB1896**; (Warrington, E) **DEP**;
Bt *of Dunham Massey* **EDB**; *of Glen-
don Hall and of Hawstead House*
LG1914; *of Darver Castle* **LGI1958**; *of
Rainsford Lodge* **LGI1958**
GORE-BOOTH, Bt **PB1970**
HAWORTH-BOOTH *formerly of Hull-
bank* **LG1972**
SCLATER-BOOTH (Basing, B) **PB1970**
BOOTHBY, B **PB1970**; Bt **PB1970**; Bt
EDB; (*see also* Cobham)
BORCHER **DFUSA**
BOREEL, Bt **PB1970**; Bt **EDB**
BORLASE, Bt **EDB**; *of Pendeen* **LG1937**
BOROUGH, Bt **PB1879**; *of Chetwynd
Park* **LG1952**
BORRER (*see* Orlebar)
BORROWES, Bt **PB1939**
BOURKE-BORROWES (*see* Bourke)
BORTHWICK, Bt **PB1970**; (Whitburgh,
B) **PB1967**; B **PB1910**; (Glenesk, B)
PB1908; *of Borthwick* **LG1969**
BORTON *formerly of Aynho* **DFUSA**
BORWICK, B **PB1970**
BOSANQUET *of Dingestow* **LG1965**; *for-
merly of Claysmore* **LG1965**; *of Rock
Hall* **LG1965**
SMITH-BOSANQUET *formerly of Brox-
bornebury* **LG1965**
BOSCAWEN (Falmouth, V) **PB1970**;
(Falmouth, E) **DEP**; (*see also* Jones *of
Godmond Hall*)
GRIFFITH BOSCAWEN *of Trevalyn* (*see*
Jones *of Godmond Hall*)
BOSSOM, Bt **PB1970**; B **PB1963**
BOSTOCK *formerly of Bostock* **LG1965**;
of Merefield House **LG1952**; *of Spar-
sholt Manor* **LG1952**; **LG1937 Supp**
BOSTON *formerly of Ettrick* **DFUSA**;
(*see also* Irby)
BOSVILE *formerly of Ravenfield Park*
LG1952
BOSVILLE *of Thorpe and Gunthwaite*
LG1906; **FR**
HOUSTOUN-BOSWALL, Bt **PB1970**
BOSWELL, Bt **PB1857**; *of Auchinleck*
LG1972; *formerly of Balmuto* **LG1952**;
DFUSA
BOTELER (Boteler, of Bramfield, B)
DEP; (Boteler, of Oversley and

Wemme, B) **DEP**; (Boteler, of Waring-
ton, B) **DEP**; Bt *of Branfield* **EDB**; Bt
of Hatfield Woodhall **EDB**; Bt *of
Teston* **EDB**; *formerly of Eastry*
LG1972
BOEHM-BOTELER, Bt **PB1928**
BOTETOURT, B **DEP**; (*see also* Berkeley)
BOTFIELD *of Norton Hall* **AA**; **VSA**
GARNETT-BOTFIELD *formerly of
Decker Hill* **LG1952**
BOTHWELL (Holyroodhouse, Lord)
DEP; (*see also* Hepburn; Ramsay; and
Stewart)
BOTREAUX (*see* Loudoun)
BOTSFORD **CG**
BOTT *of Benington* **LG1972**
BOTTOMLEY (*see* Cautley)
BOUCAUT *of Glenelg* **CG**
BOUCHER *of Trenean* **LG1952**; *of
Sharpcliffe Hall* **LG1921**
BOUCHERETT *of Willingham* **LG1900**
BOUGHEY, Bt **PB1970**; *of Brinkley
Grove* **LG1937**
ROUSE-BOUGHTON, Bt **PB1963**
BOULTBEE *late of Springfield* **LG1921**
BOULTON, Bt *of Braxted Park* **PB1970**;
Bt *of Copped Hall* **PB1970**; *of Tewpark*
LG1952; *of Moulton* **LG1858**
BOUMPHREY *formerly of The Nook*
LG1969
BOURCHIER (Bath, E) **DEP**; (Essex, E)
DEP; *formerly of Baggotstown*
LGI1958; *of Dromline and Ardinode*
LGI1912; **FR**
BOURK (*see* De Burgo)
BOURKE (Mayo, E) **PB1970**; (Conne-
mara, B) **PB1901**; (Bourke, of Mayo, V)
DEP; (Bourke, of Castleconnell, B)
DEP; *of Thornfields* **LGI1912**; *of
Curraghleagh* **LGI1899**; *of Heathfield*
LGI1899; (*see also* de Burgh)
LEGGE-BOURKE (*see* Dartmouth)
BOURN **PromFUSA**
BOURNE, B **PB1970**; Bt **PB1883**;
formerly of Garston Manor **LG1972**;
formerly of Symondsbury **LG1972**; *of
Burrough-on-the-Hill, formerly of
Epperstone Manor* **LG1952**; *of Fulston
Manor* **LG1952**; *of Hilderstone Hall*
LG1952; *of Fyfield Manor* **LG1937**; *of
Astley Court* **LG1921**; *of Dudley House*
LG1898; *of Wyersdale and Stalmine*
LG1858; **DFUSA**; **AA**; *of Hackinsall*
(*see* Bourne-May)
BOURRYAU (*see* Luard)
BOUSFIELD *formerly of Scarsykes*
LG1972

PLEYDELL-BOUVERIE (Radnor, E) PB1970
UTHWATT-BOUVERIE (see Andrewes)
BOVARD DFUSA
BOVEY, Bt EDB
HAIG-BOVEY LG1952 Supp
BOWATER, Bt of Friston PB1970; Bt of Hill Crest PB1970
BOWDEN (Aylestone, B) PB1970; B PB1970; Bt PB1970
CORNISH-BOWDEN of Black Hall LG1965
BOWDLER of Racketts LG1952; formerly of Marton LG1952 Supp
BOWDOIN (see Bence-Jones)
BOWDON of Pleasington Hall AA
BUTLER-BOWDON of Pleasington LG1952; (see also Grey)
BOWEN, Bt PB1970; B PB1894; formerly of Llwyngwair LG1969; formerly of Troedyraw LG1952; IFR1976; of Hollymount LGI1912; of Mantua and Burt House LGI1912; (New Zealand) CG
WEBB-BOWEN (see Penn of Camrose)
BOWER, Bt PB1940; formerly of Welham LG1965; of Fontmell Parva LG1952; of Claremont LG1937; of Cowlinge Hall LG1921; of Broxholme LG1900; of Iwerne LG1898; AA
BOWES, B DEP; formerly of Monkend LG1952; of Bradley LG1833/7
STONEY-BOWES (see Stoney)
BOWIE DFUSA
BOWKER CG
BOWLBY, Bt PB1970; of Culverthorpe Hall formerly of Gilston Park LG1965
SALVIN-BOWLBY of Coomhola Lodge LGI1958
BOWLES, B PB1970; Bt PB1943; of Abney Manor LG1921; late of Streatley LG1921; of North Aston LG1879; of Ahern LGI1912
BOWMAN, Bt of Holmbury St Mary PB1970; Bt of Killingworth PB1970
BOWRING, Bt PB1916; formerly of Larkbeare LG1972
BOWSER of Argaty and The King's Lundies LG1952 Supp
BOWYER (Denham, B) PB1970; Bt of Knipersley EDB; Bt of Leighthorne EDB
ATKINS-BOWYER of Steeple Aston LG1879
WINDHAM-BOWYER (see Windham formerly of Waghen)
BOXALT, Bt PB1945
BOXWELL IFR1976

MORSE-BOYCOTT (see Morse)
WIGHT-BOYCOTT formerly of Rudge Hall LG1952
BOYD (Kilmarnock, B) PB1970; Bt PB1970; (Arran, E) DEP; (Kilmarnock, E) DEP; Bt of Danson Hill PB1889; of Hollybush Hall LG1952; formerly of Westward Ho! LG1952; of Maxpoffle LG1937; of Moor House LG1921; of Hitcham Grange LG1914; of Rosslare LG1858; IFR1976; of Ballycastle LGI1958; formerly of Ballymacool LGI1958; formerly of Broadmeadows DFUSA; formerly of Newtown Hamilton DFUSA; (Canada) CG; of Glenfern CG
ROBERTS-HAY-BOYD of Townend of Symington LG1937
KEOWN-BOYD of Ballydugan LG1886
LENNOX-BOYD (Boyd of Merton, V) PB1970
BOYDELL of Burne House LGI1958
BOYLAN IFR1976
BOYLE (Cork and Orrery, E) PB1970; (Glasgow, E) PB1970; (Shannon, E) PB1970; Bt PB1970; (Ross, B) PB1890; (Burlington, E) DEP; (Guildford, E) DEP; (Blesington, V) DEP; (Shannon, V) DEP; (Carlton, B) DEP; IFR1976; of Limavady LGI1958
BOYNE (see Hamilton-Russell)
WICKHAM-BOYNTON of Burton Agnes LG1972
BOYS formerly of Betshanger LG1952
BOYSE of Bannow LGI1912 (see also Bruen)
BOYTON of Convoy House LGI1958
BRABANT of St John's CG
BRABAZON (Meath, E) PB1970; of Mornington House LG1894; of Brabazon Park LG1886
GIBSON-BRABAZON of Mount Dalton formerly of Stone Hall LGI1958
MOORE-BRABAZON (Brabazon of Tara, B) PB1970
BRABOURNE (see Knatchbull)
BRABY FR
BRACE formerly of Doveridge LG1921
COMPTON-BRACEBRIDGE of Atherstone Hall LG1952
BRACHER formerly of Wincanton DFUSA
BRACKEN, V PB1956
BRACKENBRIDGE of Ashfield Park LG1858
BRACKENBURY of Yerdley House formerly of Thorpe Hall LG1969

BRADBURY, B **PB1970**; *formerly of Altrincham* **DFUSA**

BRADDON *of Treglith* **CG**; *of Skisdon* **LG1937**

RICHMOND-GALE-BRADDYLL *formerly of Highhead and Conishead Priory* **LG1972**

BRADESTON, B **DEP**

BRADFORD, Bt **PB1970**; Bt *of Mawddwy* **PB1935**; **DFUSA**; (*see also* Bridgeman; and Newport)

BRADHURST (*see* Wood *of Wakes Hall*)

BRADISH *of Lonsdale* **LGI1958**

BRADLEY *of Ackton Hall* **LG1886**; *of Gore Court* **LG1850/3**; *of Slyne House* **LG1880/3**; (*see also* Shipman)

BRADNEY *formerly of Tal-y-Coed* **LG1969**; **FR**

BRADSHAIGH, Bt **EDP**; *of Kapnagorran* **AA**

BRADSHAW *formerly of Lifton* **LG1972**; *of Barton Blount* **LG1900**; *of Milecross* **LG1886**; **DFUSA**; (*see also* Bowles)

BRADSTOCK *of Yokehurst* **LG1969**

BRADY *of Myshall House* **LG1886**; (1) & (2) **DFUSA**

BRAILSFORD *of Barkwith House* **LG1850/3**

BRAIN, B **PB1970**

BRAINTREE (*see* Crittall)

BRAITHWAITE, Bt *of Burnham* **PB1956**; Bt *of Poston* **EDB**; **FR**; (*see also* Hotchkin)

BRAMHALL, Bt **EDB**

BRAMHAM **DFUSA**

BRAMPTON (*see* Hawkins)

BRAMSTON *late of Skreens* **LG1921**

BRAMWELL, B **PB1892**; Bt **PB1903**

BRANCH **DFUSA**; *formerly of Abingdon* **DFUSA**

BRAND (Hampden, V) **PB1970**; (Brand, B) **PB1963**

BRANDER (*see* Brander-Dunbar)

BRANDLING *of Gosforth* **LG1850/3**

BRANDON (Suffolk, D) **DEP**; **IFR1976**

BRANDRAM *formerly of Bickley* **LG1969**

BRANDRETH *of Houghton* **LG1886**

WATSON-GANDY-BRANDRETH *of Buckland Newton* **LG1972**

BRANFILL *formerly of Upminster Hall* **LG1972**

BRANSFORD (*see* Engalitcheff)

BRANSTON *of Branston* **LG1952**

BRAOSE, B **DEP**; (Braose, of Gower, B) **DEP**

BRASIER (*see* Brasier-Creagh)

BRASSEY (Brassey of Apethorpe, B) **PB1970**; E **PB1917**

BRATNEY **DFUSA**

BRAY *of Shere* **LG1952**; *of Langford Hill* **LG1850/3**; **DFUSA**; *of Adelaide* **CG**

BRAYBROOKE (*see* Neville)

BRAYE, B **DEP**; (*see also* Verney-Cave)

BRAYNE *formerly of Long Compton* **LG1952**

BRAYTON **DFUSA**

BREADALBANE (*see* Campbell)

BRECKINRIDGE **PromFUSA**

BRECON (*see* Lewis)

MAPLETON-BREE *of Allesley* **LG1952**

BREEN *of St Lucia* **AA**

BREESE *formerly of Abermynach* **DFUSA**

BREITMEYER **LG1969**

BRENAN **IFR1976**

BRENT **DFUSA**

BRENTFORD (*see* Joynson-Hicks)

BRENTON, Bt **PB1862**

BRERETON *of Winchester and Bedford* **LG1952Supp**; *of Brinton* **LG1875**; **IFR1976**; B **DEP**; Bt **EDB**

BRETHERTON *formerly of Runshaw* **LG1952**

STAPLETON-BRETHERTON *of Rainhill* **LG1952**

BRETT (Esher, V) **PB1970**; **DFUSA**; (*New Zealand*) **CG**

BREWIS *of Norton Grove* **LG1952**

BREWSTER *of Greenstead Hall and of Ashford Lodge* **LG1886**; *formerly of Scrooby, Notts* **DFUSA**

FRENCH-BREWSTER *of Cloonanartmore* **LGI1912**

FORTESCUE-BRICKDALE *formerly of Conway, Filton, West Monkton, Stoodleigh and Birchamp* **LG1972**

BRICKWOOD, Bt **PB1970**

BRIDGE *of Hurstpierpoint* **LG1952**; *of Fairfield* **CG**

WALLER-BRIDGE *formerly of Cuckfield* **LG1972**

BRIDGEMAN (Bradford, E) **PB1970**; V **PB1970**; Bt **EDB**

BRIDGER *of Buckingham House* **LG1921**; *of Halnaker* **LG1863**

BRIDGES, B **PB1970**; (FitzWalter, B) **PB1875**; *of Brickworth Park* **LG1952**; *of Fedderate formerly of Beddington* **LG1952**; **DFUSA**

BRIDGEWATER (*see* Daubeney; and Egerton)

BRIDGFORD *of Stansbach* **LG1952**

BRIDGMAN (*see* Sawbridge)
BRIDPORT (*see* Hood)
BRIDSON **FR**
BRIGG *of Brook House* **LG1972**
BRIGGES, Bt **EDB**
BRIGGS, Bt **PB1887**; *formerly of Hylton Castle* **LG1952**; *of Strathairly* **LG1921**; *formerly of Buckleshum* **DFUSA**
BRIGHAM **DFUSA**
BRIGHT, Bt **EDB**; **FR**; (*Australia*) **CG** *of Gawler and Willeston* **CG**; *of The Cedars, Harrow Weald* **AA**; (*see also* Lloyd)
BRIGSTOCKE *formerly of Blaenpant* **LG1972**; *of Ashley and Ryde* **LG1952**
BRINCKMAN, Bt **PB1970**
BRINE **FR**
BRINKLEY *of Fortland*; **LGI1912**
BRINSMADE **DFUSA**
BRINTON *formerly of Drayton House* **LG1972**; *formerly of Gornall* **DFUSA**; (*see also* Stocks)
BRISBANE, Bt **PB1860** *of Brisbane* **LG1921**
BRISCO, Bt **PB1970**; *of Coghurst* **LG1850/3**
BRISCOE, Bt **PB1970**; *of Coynton Manor and Hildon House* **LG1972**; *of Tinvane* **LG1886**; *of Fox Hills* **LG1875**; *of Riverdale and Screggan* **LGI1904**
DRAKE-BRISCOE *formerly of Penley Hall* **LG1952**
RUGGLES-BRISE, Bt **PB1970**
BRISTOL (*see* Digby; and Hervey)
BRISTOW *of Broxmore Park* **LG1850/3**; *of Crawley, Hants* **AA**
BRISTOWE *of Beesthorpe* **LG1937**
BRITTAIN *formerly of Shelley Hall* **LG1969**
BRITTON **FR**
CARLYON-BRITTON *of Hanham Court* **LG1921**
BRIXEY **DFUSA**
BROAD *of Nelson* **CG**
BROADBENT, Bt **PB1970**; **FR**
BROADBRIDGE, B **PB1970**
BROADE *of Fenton Vivian* **AA**
BROADHURST, Bt **PB1921**
HARRISON-BROADLEY *late of Welton* **LG1937**
BROADMEAD *of Enmore* **LG1952**
BROADRICK **FR**
BROADWOOD *of Lyne* **LG1952**
BROCK, B **PB1970**; *of Wyk House* **LG1952**
BROCKET *of Spains Hall* **LG1906**; (*see also* Nall-Cain)

FITZHERBERT - BROCKHOLES *of Claughton* **LG1969**
BROCKLEBANK, Bt **PB1970**; *formerly of Childwall Hall* **LG1965**
BROCKLEHURST, Bt **PB1970**; (Ranksborough, B) **PB1921**
DENT-BROCKLEHURST *of Sudeley Castle* **LG1972**
PHILLIPS-BROCKLEHURST *of Hare Hill* **LG1952**
DRAKE-BROCKMAN *formerly of Beachborough* **LG1972**
BROCKWAY, B **PB1970**
BRODERIP *formerly of Cossington Manor* **LG1952**
BRODIE, Bt **PB1970**; *of Brodie* **LG1972**; *of Lethen* **LG1972**; *of Bridge House* **LG1952**
JOHNSTONE-BRODIE (*formerly* Callender-Brodie) *of Idvies* **LG1952**; (*see also* Brodie-Innes)
BRODRIBB (*Australia*) **CG**
BRODRICK (Midleton, E) **PB1970**
BROKE *of Pilsgate House and Holme Hale* **LG1969**; **FR**; (*see also* Broke-Middleton)
BROME *of Salop, Herts and Kent* **LG1863**
BROMFIELD, Bt **EDB**
BROMFLETE (Vescy, B) **DEP**
BROMHEAD, Bt **PB1970**; *of Douglas House* **LG1952**
BROMILOW *of Bitteswell Hall* **LG1898**
BROMLEY, Bt **PB1970**; (Montfort, B) **DEP**
BRONSON **DFUSA**
BROOK (Normanbrook, B) **PB1967**; *of Upperwood House* **LG1952**
BROOKE (Alanbrooke, V) **PB1970**; (Brookeborough, V) **PB1970**; (Brooke of Cumnor, B) **PB1970**; Brooke of Ystradfellte, B) **PB1970**; Bt *of Almondbury* **PB1970**; Bt *of Norton Priory* **PB1970**; Bt *of Summerton* **PB1970**; Bt *of Armitage Bridge* **PB1908**; *of Sarawak* **LG1972**; *of Sibton Park* **LG1972**; *of Grimston Manor* **LG1952**; *of Haughton Hall* **LG1952** *of Trehill* **LG1952**; *of Ufford Place* **LG1952**; *formerly of Wrexham Park* **LG1952**; *late of Horton* **LG1937**; *of Mere* **LG1879**; *of Handford* **LG1879**; *of Dromavana* **LGI1912**; *of Ardeen* **LGI1912**; **DFUSA**; *formerly of Whitchurch* **DFUSA**; **PromFUSA**; (*NSW, Australia*) **CG**; (*see also* Cobham)

DE CAPELL BROOKE (Brooke of Oakley, B) **PB1940**
SERGISON-BROOKE (formerly SERGISON) of Cuckfield **LG1952**
BROOKES, Bt **EDB**; of Croft **LG1921**
BROOKFIELD **DFUSA**
BROOKHOUSE (see Scott of Logie-Montrose)
BROOKS (Crawshaw, B) **PB1970**; Bt **PB1900**; of Flitwick **LG1921**; of Woodcote Park **LG1914**; of Crawshaw Hall **LG1886**; of Barlow Hall **LG1879**; formerly of Limavady **DFUSA**
CLOSE-BROOKS **FR**
BROOKSBANK, Bt **PB1970**; of Lamplugh **LG1969**; of Healaugh **LG1914**
BROOMAN (see Brooman-White)
BROOM **IFR1976**
BROOME **FR**
BROTHERTON, B **PB1930**
RATCLIFFE-BROTHERTON of Kirkham Abbey **LG1952**
BROUGH (see Staunton)
BROUGHAM (Brougham and Vaux, B) **PB1970**
BROUGHSHANE (see Davidson)
BROUGHTON (Fairhaven, B) **PB1970**; **DFUSA**; (Australia) **CG**; (see also Broughton-Adderley; and Hobhouse)
DELVES BROUGHTON, Bt **PB1970**
BROUN Bt **PB1970**; of Johnstounburn **LG1900**; **DFUSA**; (see also Broun-Morison)
BROUNCKER V **DEP**; formerly of Boveridge **LG1952**
BROWELL of Merrow House **LG1952**
BROWN, B **PB1970**; Bt **PB1970**; (Ruffside, V) **PB1956**; Bt of Deptford **EDB**; of Edinburgh **EDB**; Bt of London **EDB**; Bt of Westminster **EDB**; Bt **EDB**; formerly of Coombe Lodge **LG1952**; formerly of Weens **LG1952**; of Arncliffe Hall **LG1921**; of Lockton **LG1921**; of Loftus Hill **LG1921**; of Brent Eleigh **LG1914**; of Newhall **LG1900**; of Ashley **LG1886**; of Rossington **LG1879**; of Tostock Place **LG1879**; of Beilby Grange **LG1850/3**; of Hare Hills Grove **LG1850/3**; of Woodthorpe Hall of Brandon **LG1833/7**; of Clonboy **LGI1912**; (1) (2) & (3) **DFUSA**; formerly of Ballymena **DFUSA**; formerly of Lavenham **DFUSA**; formerly of Londonderry **DFUSA**; of Burghwallis Hall (see Brown-Greaves); of Jarrow Hall (see Drewett); (see also Harvie

Anderson; Greenly; and Hamilton of Barns)
BROWN (formerly BROWNE) sometime of Betchworth **DFUSA**
CLERKE BROWN of Kingston Blount **LG1952**
DIXON-BROWN formerly of Unthank Hall **LG1952**
FOSTER BROWN (formerly FOSTER) of Clewer **LG1952Supp**
GARDNER-BROWN formerly of Petershill and Solitude **LGI1958**
GILPIN-BROWN of Sedbury Park **LG1882**
HARVIE-BROWN of Dunipace, Quarter and Shirgarton **LG1921**
McKERRELL-BROWN of Peasenhall Hall formerly of Fordell and Finmount **LG1952**
PIGOTT-BROWN, Bt **PB1970**
PIGGOTT-BROWN (formerly PIGOTT) of Doddershall Park **LG1952**
SCOTT-BROWN of Bourton **LG1952**
STEWART-BROWN of Bryn-y-Grog **LG1937**; (see also Brown, Bt)
TATTON BROWN of Westergate Wood **LG1969**
WEMYSS BROWN formerly of Cononsyth and of Lochton **LG1972**
WREFORD-BROWN formerly of Venn **LG1965**
BROWNE (Sligo, M) **PB1970**; (Craigton, B) **PB1970**; (Kilmaine, B) **PB1970**; (Oranmore and Browne, B) **PB1970**; (Kenmare, E) **PB1949**; (Montacute, V) **DEP**; Bt of Palmerston **PB1890**; Bt of Beechworth **EDB**; Bt of Caversham **EDB**; Bt of Kiddington **EDB**; Bt of Walcot **EDB**; of Buckland Filleigh and Torr House **LG1972**; of Callaly **LG1965**; of Leighton **LG1937Supp**; of Newgrove **LG1937Supp**; of Hall Court **LG1921**; of Venn **LG1921**; of Eastham Grange **LG1906**; of Doxford **LG1894**; of Elsing Hall **LG1894**; of Bronwylfa **LG1886**; of The Woodlands **LG1879**; of Higham Hall **LG1879**; of Mellington Hall **LG1879**; of Tallantire Hall **LG1879**; of Manulla **LG1863**; of Morley Hall **LG1863**; of Caughley **LG1863**; (cos Derry, Donegal and Tyrone) **IFR1976**; of Moyne Castle **LGI1958**; of The Hermitage **LGI1958**; of Leighton **LG1937Supp**; of Newgrove **LG1937 Supp**; of Brownestown **LGI1912**; of Rathain **LGI1912**; of Riverstown **LGI1912**; of Kilskeagh **LGI1904**; of

Woodstock **LGI1904**; (1) & (2) **DFUSA**; *formerly of High Wycombe* **DFUSA**; *formerly of Tolethorpe Manor and Stamford* **DFUSA**; *of Guilford Lodge* **CG**; *of Sweeny* (*see* Leighton *of Sweeny*); (*see also* Boyd *of Glenfern*; Goldson *of Blo' Norton Hall*; and Parker *of Terriers Green*)

BEALE-BROWNE (*see* Lombard-Hobson)

DU MOULIN-BROWNE **FR**

GORE-BROWNE *of Glaston House* **LGI965**

KENWORTHY-BROWNE *formerly of Wellbury* **LG1969**

KYNNERSLEY-BROWNE *of Leighton Hall* **LG1952**

SHAW BROWNE *of Cavendish Lodge* **LG1952**

STAPLES-BROWNE *of Brashfield* **LG1921**

WOGAN-BROWNE *of Castle Browne* **LGI1912**

BROWNELL *formerly of Rawmarsh* **DFUSA**

BROWNING *formerly of Legh, Melbury and Coaley* **LG1937**; **IFR1976**

BROWNLESS (*Australia*) **CG**

BROWNLOW (Lurgan, B) **PB1970**; (Tyrconnel, V) **DEP**; Bt *of Belton* **EDB**; Bt *of Humby* **EDB**; **IFR1976**; (*see also* Cust)

BROWNRIGG, Bt **PB1970**

BRUCE (Elgin and Kincardine, E) **PB1970**, (Aberdare, B) **PB1970**; Bt *of Downhill* **PB1970**; Dt *of Stenhouse* **PB1970**; (Bruce of Melbourne, V) **PB1967**; Bt *of Dublin* **PB1841**; (Ailesbury, E) **DEP**; B **DEP**; (Carrick, E) **DEP**; Bt *of Balcaskie* **EDB**; *of Blaen-y-Cym* **LG1969**; *of Sumburgh* **LG1952**; *of Inverquhomery and Longside* **LG1937**; *of Bruce Forest* **LG1937Supp**; *of Norton Hall* **LG1921**; *of Arnot* **LG1886**; *of Kennet* **LG1843/9**; *of Kinaird* **LG1875**; *formerly of Miltown Castle* **LGI1958**; *of Benburb* **LGI1912**; **RL**; **FR**; (*see also* Campbell *of Arduaine*)

BRUDENELL-BRUCE (Ailesbury, M) **PB1970**

HOVELL - THURLOW - CUMMING - BRUCE (Thurlow, B) **PB1970**

KNIGHT-BRUCE *of Roehampton Priory* **LG1914**

BRUDENELL (*see* Ailesbury)

BRUEN **IFR1976**; *formerly of Bruen Stapleford* **DFUSA**

BRUGES (Winchester, E) **DEP**

LUDLOW-BRUGES *of Seend* **LG1921**

PRIDEAUX-BRUNE *of Prideaux Place* **LG1965**

BRUNICARDI **LGI1958**

BRUNNER, Bt **PB1970**

BRUNSKILL **LGI1958**

BRUNSWICK **RL**

BRUNT *of Weston Green* **LG1965**

BRUNTISFIELD (*see* Warrender)

BRUNTON, Bt **PB1970**

BRUNWIN *of Park House* **LG1879**; **AA**

BRUSH **IFR1976**; *formerly of Tewkesbury* **DFUSA**

BRYAN, B **DEP**; *of Upton and Morris* **LGI1958**; *of Jenkinstown* **LGI1904**; **DFUSA**

BRYANS (*see* Playne)

BRYANT *of Stoke Park* **LG1921**; **DFUSA**; *formerly of Bampton* **DFUSA**

BRYCE, V **PB1922**

BRYDGES (Chandos, D) **DEP**; Bt **EDB**; (*see also* Lee-Warner)

BRYDSON *of Water Park, formerly of Byerswood* **LG1952**

BRYMER *of Islington* **LG1952**

BUCCLEUGH (*see* Montagu-Douglas-Scott)

BUCHAN (Tweedsmuir, B) **PB1970**; *of Auchmacoy* **LG1965**; (*Australia*) **CG**; (*see also* Cumyn; Erskine; and Stewart)

FORDYCE-BUCHAN *of Kelloe* **LG1900**

BUCHANAN, Bt **PB1970**; (Woolavington, B) **PB1935**; *of Powis* **LG1937**; *of Hales Hall* **LG1921**; *of Ardoch* **LG1879**; *formerly of Kilwaughter* **LGI1958**; **PresFUSA**; *sometime of Glenny* **DFUSA**; (*see also* Butler; and Hammond-Smith)

CARRICK-BUCHANAN *of Drumpellier and Corsewall* **LG1969**

FERGUSSON-BUCHANAN *of Auchentorlie* **LG1937**

GRAY-BUCHANAN *of Scotstown* **LG1952**

LEITH-BUCHANAN, Bt **PB1970**

MURRAY-BUCHANAN *of Leny* **LG1952**; (*see also* Murray)

BUCK, Bt **EDB**; *of Denholme and Glanarbeth* **LG1879**; *of Agecroft Hall* **LG1850**; *of Moreton and Hartland Abbey* **LG1850/3**; *of Sturry Court* **VSA**

BUCKINGHAM (1) & (2) **DFUSA**; (*see also* Giffard; Temple-Nugent-Brydges-Chandos-Grenville; Stafford; and Villiers)

BUCKINGHAMSHIRE (*see* Hobart-Hampden)
BUCKLAND (*see* Berry)
BUCKLE *formerly of Chaceley* **LG1952**; *formerly of Jordans* **LG1952**; *formerly of Norton House* **LG1952**; *of Burgh* **LG1914**
BUCKLEY (Wrenbury, B) **PB1970**; Bt **PB1917**; *of Castell Gorford* **LG1952**; *of New Hall* **LG1952**; *of Brynycaerau* **LG1925**
BUCKMASTER, V **PB1970**
LINDSEY-BUCKNALL *of Turin Castle* **LG1886**
BUCKSTON *formerly of Bradbourne Hall* **LG1965**
BUCKTON (*see* Storey)
BUCKWORTH *of Cockley Clay Hall* **LG1898**
BUCTON (*see* Foster *of Cold Hesledon*)
BUDAK, B **TNBE1956**
BUDDICOM *of Ticklerton Court* **LG1952**
BUDD *of Tattingstone Park* **LG1952**
BUDGEN (*see* Hewgill)
BUDGEN *of Ballindoney* **LGI1912**
BUDWORTH *of Greensted Hall* **LG1886**
BULEBEN, B **TNBE1956**
BULGARIA (*Royal House of*) **RL**
BULKELEY, V **DEP**; Bt **EDB**; **PromFUSA**
RIVERS BULKELEY *formerly of Whitchurch* **LG1952**
WILLIAMS-BULKELEY, Bt **PB1970**
BULL, Bt **PB1970**; **DFUSA**: *formerly of Stoke Ferry* **DFUSA**; **PromFUSA**
BULLEN **IFR1976**; (*see also* Garnons Williams)
SYMES-BULLEN *formerly of Catherston* **LG1972**
BULLER, Bt **EDB**; *of Downes* **LG1965**; *formerly of Erle Hall* **LG1952**; *of Morval* (*see* Tremayne)
MANNINGHAM-BULLER (Dilhorne, V) **PB1970**
YARDE-BULLER (Churston, B) **PB1970**
BULLEY *formerly of Lullingworth* **LG1952**
BULLIN (*see* Naylor-Leyland)
BULLIVANT (*Australia*) **CG**
BULLOCK, Bt **PB1963**; *of Middlefield* **LG1952**; *of St Leonard's* **LG1875**; *of Shipdham* **LG1850/3**; (*see also* Bullock-Webster; and Parker)
TROYTE-BULLOCK *of Zeals* **LG1952**
BULLOUGH, Bt **PB1939**
BULMER, B **DEP**

BULSTRODE **VF**
BULTEEL *of Leighon, formerly of Parnflete* **LG1952**
BULWER (Dalling and Bulwer, B) **PB1872**; (*see also* Long)
BUNBURY, Bt **PB1970**; *of Marlston House* **LG1886**; *formerly of Cranavonane* **LGI1958**
McCLINTOCK-BUNBURY (Rathdonnell, B) **PB1970**; (*see also* McClintock)
RICHARDSON-BUNBURY, Bt **PB1970**
BUND *of Wick House* **RFFK**
WILLIS-BUND (*see* Milward *formerly of Redditch*)
BUNDEY **CG**
BUNDY **DFUSA**
BUNKER **DFUSA**
BUNNY (*see* St John *of Slinfold*)
BUNTEN *of Dunalastair* **LG1906**
BUNTING *of Northbrook, West Hartlepool* **LG1965**; *formerly of Quainton* **DFUSA**
BURBIDGE, Bt **PB1970**
BURDEN, B **PB1970**; *formerly of Feddal* **DFUSA**
BURDETT, Bt **PB1970**; Bt *of Bramcote* **PB1949**; *of Shrubhurst* **LG1879**; **IFR1976**
BURDON *of Jervaulx Abbey* **LG1972**; *of Castle Eden* **LG1937**; (*see also* Burdon-Sanderson)
GRIFFITHS BURDON *of Newcourt* **LG1952**
BURGES, Bt **EDB**; **IFR1976**; **DFUSA**
BURGH (Kent, E) **DEP**; (St Albans, E) **DEP**; B **DEP**; (Downes, B) **DEP**; (*see also* de Burgh; and Leith)
BURGHCLERE (*see* Gardner)
BURGHERSH, B **DEP**
BURGOYNE, Bt **PB1871**
BURKE (Burke, V) **DEP**; (Galway, V) **DEP**; (Leitrim, B) **DEP**; *of Auberies* **LG1972**; *of Ballydugan* **LGI1912**; *of Springfield* **LGI1912**; *formerly of Ballinasloe* **DFUSA**; *of Elm Hall, co Tipperary* **AA**; (*see also* Burke Cole; Maxwell; and Teeling)
HAVILAND-BURKE *of Willistown* **LG1875**
BURKET **PromFUSA**
HUMBLE-BURKITT *of Stubbing Court* **LG1937**
BURLEIGH *of Carrickfergus* **LG1886**
BURLINGTON (*see* Boyle)
BURLTON *of Luntley Court formerly of Eaton Hill* **LG1969**
BURMAN *of Edgbaston* **LG1952**

BURN *of Orton Hall* **LG1886**; *of Coldoch* (*see* Burn-Murdoch)
CALLANDER-BURN (*see* Burn-Callander)
PELHAM BURN *formerly of Adstock* **LG1965**
BURNABY *formerly of Baggrove Hall* **LG1965**
BURNARD *of Northover* **LG1886**
BURNE *of Loynton Hall* **LG1965**
BURNELL, B **DEP**; (Burnell, of Holgate, B) **DEP**; (*see* Craven-Smith-Milnes)
BURNET *formerly of Elrick* **LG1952**
BURNETT, Bt *of Croydon* **PB1970**; Bt *of Leys* **PB1970**; *of Dunsa Manor* **LG1969**; *of Kemnay* **LG1952**; *of Monboddo* **LG1952**; *of Gadgirth* **LG1894**; *of Barns* **LG1843/9**; (1) & (2) **DFUSA**
PARRY-BURNETT *of Perfeddgoed* **LG1972**
BURNEY, Bt **PB1970**
DURNHAM **DFUSA**; (Canada) **CG**; (*see* also Lawson)
BURNS (Inverclyde, B) **PB1956**; *formerly of Kilmahew* **LG1952**; *of North Mymms Park* **LG1952**
BURNS (*formerly* BYRN) **DFUSA**
BURNTISLAND (*see* Wemys)
BURNSIDE *of Oulling* **LG1886**
BURR (1) & (2) **DFUSA**; *formerly of Redgrave* **DFUSA**; *of Aldermaston* (*see* Higford)
BURRA *of Rye* **LG1965**
BURRARD, Bt *of Walhampton* **PB1963**; Bt *of Lymington* **PB1870**
BURRELL, Bt **PB1970**; (Gwydyr, B) **PB1915**; *of Broome Park* **LG1952**; (1) & (?) **DFUSA**
BURROUGH **FR**
BURROUGHES *formerly of Burlingham* **LG1952**
BURROUGHS, Bt **EDB**; *of Ronsay* **LG1921**
BURROWES **IFR1976**
BURROWS, Bt **PB1917**; *of Long Crendon* **LG1965**; *formerly of Bonis Hall* **LG1952**
BURSLEY **DFUSA**
BURT (*Australia*) **CG**
BURTCHAELL *of Brandondale* **LGI1912**
BURTON (Burton of Coventry, B) **PB1970**; Bt *of Pollacton* **PB1902**; Bt *of Stockerston* **EDB**; *formerly of Longner Hall* **LG1972**; *formerly of Cherry Burton* **LG1965**; *formerly of Bakewell* **LG1965**; *of Orston Hall* **LG1952**; *formerly of Somersby* **LG1952**; *of St Leon-*

ards **LG1921**; *of Foggathorpe and Childrey* **LG1914**; *of Tunstall* **LG1863**; *of Sackett's Hill House* **LG1843/9**; *of Mount Anville and Eyre Court Castle* 1833/7; *of Carrigaholt Castle* **LGI1912**; **FR**; **VF**; *of Burton Hall* (*see* Mainwaring-Burton); *of Thurland* (*see* North *of Newton Hall*); (*see also* Baillie; and Bass)
ANGERSTEIN-BURTON *of West Lexham* **LG1952Supp**
MAINWARING-BURTON **IFR1976**
BURY (Charleville, E) **DEP**; *of St Leonard's House* **LG1952**; *of Bosmere Hall* **LG1937**; **IFR1976**
BURY (*formerly* PRYCE) *of Gunley* **LG1952**
HOWARD-BURY (*see* Suffolk and Berkshire)
BUSFEILD (*see* Ferrand *formerly of St Ives*)
BUSH *formerly of Eastington Park* **LG1972**; (*Australia*) **CG**
BUSH (*formerly* CROMWELL) *formerly of Cheshunt Park* **LG1952**
BUSHBY *of Wormley* **LG1952**; *of Bronwylfa Hall* **LG1937**
BUSHE *of Glencairn Abbey* **LGI1912**; **FR**
BUSK *formerly of Ford's Grove* **LG1972**
BUSWELL, Bt **EDB**
BUTCHER (Danesfort, B) **PB1935**
BUTE (*see* Crichton-Stuart)
BUTLER (Ormonde, M) **PB1970**; (Carrick, E) **PB1970**; (Lanesborough, F) **PB1970**; (Mountgarret, V) **PB1970**; (Butler of Saffron Walden, B) **PB1970**; (Dunboyne, B) **PB1970**; Bt *of Cloughgrenan* **PB1970**; Bt *of Old Park* **PB1970**; Bt *of Edgbaston* **PB1939**; B **PB1905**; (Ormonde, D) **DEP**; (Glengall, E) **DEP**; (Gowran, E) **DEP**; (Kilkenny, E) **DEP**; (Wiltshire, E) **DEP**; V **DEP**; (Galmoye, V) **DEP**; (Butler, of Weston, B) **DEP**; Bt *of Polestown* **EDB**; *formerly of Bourton* **LG1965**; *formerly of Ewart Park* **LG1969**; *of Shortgrove* **LG1969**; *of Warren Wood* **LG1937**; *of Standen Manor* **LG1921**; *of Cazenoves House* **LG1886**; *of Warminghurst* **LG1833/7**; *of Aston le Walls* **LG1833/7**; (*cos Clare and Tipperary*) **IFR1976**; (*co Tipperary*) **IFR1976**; *of Waterville* **LGI1958**; *of Ballycarron* **LGI1912**; *of Priestown* **LGI1912**; (1) (2) (3) & (4) **DFUSA**

BUTLER (*formerly* BUCHANAN) *sometime of Leny* **DFUSA**
BUTLER (*now* BUTLER-SLOSS) **IFR1976**
FOWLER-BUTLER *of Pendeford Hall* **LG1921**
WOOLSEY-BUTLER (*see* Barrow)
BUTLIN, Bt **PB1916**
BUTT, Bt **PB1970**
BUTTER *of Pitlochry* **LG1965**
BUTTERFIELD *of Cliffe Castle* **LG1937**
ANGUS-BUTTERWORTH *of Ashton New Hall* **LG1969**
BUTTON, Bt **EDB**
BUTTS *of The Salterns* **LG1921**
BUXTON, Bt **PB1970**; E **PB1934**; Bt *of Shadwell Lodge* **PB1888**
NOEL-BUXTON, B **PB1970**
BUZZARD, Bt **PB1970**
BYAM *of Antigua and Somersetshire* **LG1850/3**; **AA**
BYASS, Bt **PB1970**
BYE *sometime of Old Congress formerly of Horsleydown* **DFUSA**
BYERS, B **PB1970**; **IFR1976**; **DFUSA**
BYNG (Strafford, E) **PB1970**; (Torrington, V) **PB1970**; (Byng of Viny, V) **PB1935**; *of The Salutation* **LG1972**; (*see also* Lafone)
CRANMER-BYNG *formerly of Quendon Hall* **LG1952**
BYRD *formerly of Broxton* **DFUSA**
BYRDE *formerly of Goytrey House* **LG1952**
MOIR-BYRES *of Tonley* **LG1952**
TRAPPES-BYRNARD (*see* Trappes-Lomax)
BYRNE **IFR1976**; (*see also* Leicester)
BYROM (*see* Eden)
BYRON, B **PB1970**
BYTHESEA *of Freshford* **LG1921**
BOND-CABBELL *of Cromer* **LG1952**
CABELL *formerly of Warminster* **DFUSA**; **PromFUSA**
CABLE, B **PB1927**
CACCIA, B **PB1970**
CADBURY *of Northfield* **LG1972**
CARY-CADDELL *of Harbourstown* (*see* Stanley-Cary)
CADDY *formerly of Buckland Brewer* **LG1937**
CADELL *of Grange and Barnton and formerly of Cockenzie* **LG1969**
CADMAN, B **PB1970**; *of Walton Hall* **LG1937**; *of Westbourne House* **LG1921**
CADOGAN, E **PB1970**; E **DEP**; (*see also* Fenwick *of Brinkburn*)

CADWALADER *formerly of Ciltalgarth* **DFUSA**
CAFE **FR**
CAFFERY **DFUSA**
CAHILL **IFR1976**
CAHN, Bt **PB1970**
CAILLARD *formerly of Wingfield House* **LG1965**
CAILLI, B **DEP**
CAIN, Bt **PB1970**; *of Ballasalla* **LG1937**
NALL-CAIN (Brocket, B) **PB1970**
CAINE, Bt **PB1970**
CAIRD, Bt *of Glenfarquhar* **PB1953**; Bt *of Belmont Castle* **PB1916**
HENRYSON-CAIRD *of Cassencarie* **LG1952**
CAIRNES, Bt **EDB**; **IFR1976**
CAIRNS, E **PB1970**
CAITHNESS (*see* Campbell; Crichton; and Sinclair)
CALBURN *of Effingham Manor* **LG1972**
CALCOTT *of Caynham Court* **LG1858**
CALCRAFT *of Rempstone* **LG1900**
LUCAS-CALCRAFT *of Ancaster Hall* **LG1952**
ROPER-CALDBECK **IFR1976**
CALDECOTE (*see* Inskip)
CALDECOTT *of Holbrook Grange* (*see* Bolam); *of Holmer House* (*see* Hereford)
CALDER, Bt *of Muirtone* **PB1887**; Bt *of Southwick* **EDB**; *of Ardargie* **LG1952**
RITCHIE-CALDER, B **PB1970**
CALDWELL, Bt **PB1858**; *of The White House of Speen and of Caberfeidh* **LG1952**; *of Linley Wood* **LG1886**; *of Beech Lands* **LG1858**; *of New Grange* **LGI1912**; (1) & (2) **DFUSA**; **HI**
CALEDON (*see* Alexander)
CALENDAR (*see* Livingston)
CALL, Bt **PB1903**
CALLAN (*see* Agar)
CALLANDER, Bt **EDB**; *of Ardkinglas* **LG1921**
BURN-CALLANDER *of Preston Hall* **LG1972**
CALLEY *of Burderop* **LG1952**
CALHOUN *formerly of co Donegal* **DFUSA**
CALHOUN (*now* WATSON) **DFUSA**
CALLAWAY **DFUSA**
CALMADY *of Calmady* **LG1937**
CALROW *of Walton Lodge* **LG1879**
GOUGH CALTHORPE (Calthorpe, B) **PB1970**
ANSTRUTHER - GOUGH - CALTHORPE, Bt **PB1970**
CALTHROP, Bt **PB1917**; *of Stanhoe*

LG1937; *of Gosburton* LG1863
CALVERLEY, Bt EDB; *formerly of Oulton Hall* LG1952; VSA; (*see also* Muff; and Calverley-Rudston)
CALVERT (Baltimore, B) DEP; *of Ockley Court* LG1969; *of Foscombe* LG1952; *of Spexhall Manor* LG1952; *of Albury Hall* LG1833/7; *formerly of Danby Wiske* DFUSA; CG
CALVOCORESSI LG1965
CAMPBELL, Bt *of Clay Hall* EDB; Bt *of Woodford* EDB
CAMBORNE (*see* Paynter *formerly of Boskenna*)
CAMBRIDGE, M PB1970; (Athlone, E) PB1956; D PB1904; *of Bloxnorth* AA; (*see also* Guelph; and Stuart)
PICKARD-CAMBRIDGE (*see* Lane *of Poxwell*)
CAMDEN (*see* Pratt)
CAMELFORD (*see* Pitt)
CAMERON, Bt *of Fassifern* PB1863; *formerly of Inch* LG1969, *of Lochiel* LG1965; *of Garth* LG1952; *formerly in Worcester* LG1952; *of Murton House* LG1879; *of Fordon and Lowestoft* CG; (*see also* Cameron-Head)
CAMERON (*formerly* VAUGHAN-LEE) *of Dillington* LG1952
SOREL-CAMERON *of Glendruidh* LG1952
CAMMELL *formerly of Norton Hall* LG1937
CAMOYS (*see* Stonor)
CAMPBELL (Argyll, D) PB1970; (Breadalbane, E) PB1970; (Cawdor, E) PB1970; (Campbell of Eskan, B) PB1970; (Colgrain, B) PB1970; (Glenavy, B) PB1970; (Stratheden and Campbell, B) PB1970; Bt PB1970; Bt *of Aberuchill* PB1970; Bt *of Ardnamurchan* PB1970; Bt *of Auchinbreck* PB1970; Bt *of Barcaldine* PB1970; Bt *of Succoth* PB1970; (Blythswood, B) PB1940; (Breadalbane, M) PB1922; Bt *of Blythswood* PB1908; (Atholl, E) DEP; (Caithness, E) DEP; (Irvine, E) DEP; (Clyde, B) DEP; Bt EDB; Bt *of Inverneil* EDB; *of Arduaine* LG1972; *formerly of Auchendarroch and Inverawe* LG1972; *of Dunstaffnage* LG1972; *of Inverneill* LG1972; *of Jura* LG1972; *of Kilberry* LG1972; *of Skerrington* LG1972; *of Achelader* LG1969; *of Airds Bay* LG1969; *of Strachur* LG1969; *of Glendaniel* LG1965; *formerly of Achanduin and Barbreck*

LG1952; *formerly of Ardpatrick* LG1952; *of Dalhanna* LG1952; *formerly of Islay* LG1952; *of Kilmartin* LG1952; *formerly of South Hall* LG1952; *of Stonefield* LG1952; *formerly of Tullichewan* LG1952; *of Ord House* LG1952Supp; *of Auchmannoch* LG1937; *of Colgraine* LG1937; *of Lochnell* LG1937; *formerly of Skipness* LG1937; *late of Treesbank* LG1937; *of Woodseat* LG1937; *of Buscott Park* LG1886; *of Edenwood* LG1886; *of Blythswood* LG1879; *of Monzie* LG1879; *of Ballimore* LG1879; *of Sonachan* LG1875; *of Barquharrie* LG1863; *of Glenfalloch* LG1863; *of Gatcombe* LG1850/3; IFR1976; (1) (2) & (3) DFUSA; *of Kilbryde* CG; *of Yarralumla* CG; *of Barquharrie* AA; *of Colgrain* VSA; *of Altries* (*see* Adamson *of Strucathro*); *of Craigie* (*see* Wardlaw); *of Ormidale* (*see* Warrand); (*see also* Fender)
CAMPBELL (*formerly* BAX-IRONSIDE) *of Bleaton Hallet and Houghton-le-Spring* LG1952
CARTER-CAMPBELL *of Possil* LG1972
COCKBURN-CAMPBELL, Bt PB1970; CG
FLETCHER-CAMPBELL *late of Boqutian* LG1914
FRASER-CAMPBELL *of Dunmore* LG1972
GRAHAM-CAMPBELL *of Shirvan* LG1972
HAMILTON CAMPBELL *of Netherplace* LG1952
CLIFTON-HASTINGS-CAMPBELL (*see* Abney-Hastings)
HOMES - PURVES - HUME - CAMPBELL, Bt PB1970
MACIVER CAMPBELL *formerly of Ballochyle* LG1952
MACIVER-CAMPBELL *of Asknish* LG1921
LAMONT-CAMPBELL (*see* Carter-Campbell *of Possil*)
McORAN-CAMPBELL (*see* Adamson *of Stracathro*)
METHUEN-CAMPBELL (*see* Methuen)
RANKINE CAMPBELL (*see* Campbell *of Kilberry*)
WYNDHAM-CAMPBELL *of Dunoon* LG1894
CAMPERDOWN (*see* Haldane-Duncan)
CAMPION, B PB1956; *formerly of Danny* LG1952

CAMROSE (see Berry)
CAMVILLE, B **DEP**
CANDLER of Moreton Pinkney Manor LG1921; **PromFUSA**
CANE late of St Wolstans LG1937
CANN, Bt **EDB**
CANNING (Garvagh, B) **PB1970**; E **DEP**; (Stratford de Redcliffe, V **DEP**); of Restrop House LG1952; **FR**
DE BURGH-CANNING (Clanricarde, M) **PB1916**
GORDON-CANNING of Hartpury LG1952
CANTACUZENE (see Grant)
CANTERBURY (see Manners-Sutton)
CANTILUPE, B **DEP**
STEWART-CAPE of Bearnoch LG1952
CAPEL, B **DEP**; of Bulland Lodge LG1937Supp; **IFR1976**; formerly of Grove LG1925
CARNEGY-CAPEL (see Carnegy-Arbuthnott)
CAPELL (Essex, E) **PB1970**
CAPPER of Lyston Court LG1894
CAPRON of Southwick Hall LG1965
CAPSHAW **DFUSA**
CAPSTAFF **DFUSA**
CARACCIOLO (see Purcell-Fitzgerald)
CARADON (see Foot)
CARBERY (see Bermingham; Evans-Freke; and Vaughan)
CARDEN, Bt of Molesey **PB1970**; Bt of Templemore **PB1970**; **IFR1976**
CARDIFF of Easton Hall LG1972
CARDINALL of Holly Court and Tendring LG1906
CARDWELL, V **PB1886**
CAREW, Bt **PB1970**; B **DEP**; Bt of Anthony **EDB**; Bt of Beddington **EDB**; **IFR1976**; (see also Trollope-Bellew)
CONOLLY-CAREW (Carew, B) **PB1970**
POLE-CAREW (see Carew Pole)
CAREY (Dover, E) **DEP**; (Monmouth, E) **DEP**; formerly of La Ville-au-Roy LG1972
CARHAMPTON (see Luttrell)
CARINGTON (Carrington, B) **PB1970**; (see also Wynn-Carrington)
SMITH-CARINGTON of Ashby Folville LG1969
CARISBROOKE (see Mountbatten)
CARLETON (Dorchester, B) **PB1897**; V **DEP**; Bt **EDB**; formerly of Brightwell Park **DFUSA**; (see also Lowndes-Stone-Norton)
CARLETON (now CARLETON PAGET) **IFR1976**

LEIR-CARLETON of Ditcheat LG1921
L'ESTRANGE CARLETON (see L'Estrange)
CARLILE, Bt of Gayhurst **PB1949**; Bt of Ponsbourne Park **PB1940**
CARLING LG1952 **Supp**
CARLINGFORD (see Parkinson-Fortescue; Swift; and Taaffe)
CARLISLE of Wyken Hall LG1972; formerly of Oakley Hall LG1952; **PromFUSA**; (see also Harcla; Hay; and Howard)
CARLOS formerly of Broomhall LG1952
CARLTON (Dorchester, V) **DEP**; (see also Boyle)
CARLYLE, Lord **DEP**; (see also Douglas)
CARLYON of Tregrehen LG1965; **FR**; **CG**; (see also Carlyon-Britton)
CARMICHAEL (Hyndford, E) **DEP**; Bt **EDB**; of Carmichael LG1952; **DFUSA**; of Harton Mills **CG**; of Casspherne **VSA**
GIBSON-CARMICHAEL (Carmichael, B) **PB1926**
GIBSON - CRAIG - CARMICHAEL, Bt **PB1970**
THOMSON-CARMICHAEL of Eastend and Mansfield LG1914
RIVETT-CARNAC, Bt **PB1970**
CARNARVON (see Dormer; and Herbert)
STRADLING-CARNE (see Nicholl formerly of The Ham)
CARNEGIE (Fife, D) **PB1970**; (Northesk, E) **PB1970**; (Southesk, E) **PB1970**; of Stronvar LG1937
CARNEGIE (formerly FRANCE-HAYHURST) of Bostock House LG1972
LINDSAY-CARNEGIE of Spynie LG1937
CARNEGY of Lour LG1952
CARNEY **PromFUSA**
CARNOCHAN formerly of Gatehouse of Fleet **DFUSA**
CARNOCK (see Nicolson)
CARNWATH (see Dalzell)
CARON of Ottawa **CG**
CARPENTER (Tyrconnel, E) **DEP**; of Carreglwyd and Berw LG1952; of Haylands Manor LG1952; formerly of Dilwyn **DFUSA**; **FR**; (see also Carpenter-Garnier)
CARPENTIER, Bt **EDB**
CARR (Somerset, E) **DEP**; Bt **EDB**; of Ditchingham and Stackhouse LG1972; formerly of Holbrooke LG1965; of Newbiggin LG1972; of Farnsfield

LG1952; *formerly of Arnestown* LGI1912; *of Sydney Place, Cork* **HI**; (*see also* Carr-Ellison)
RIDDELL-CARRE *of Cavers* **LG1937**
CARRICK (*see* Bruce; Butler; Cunynghame; and Stewart)
CARRINGTON *of Great Missenden* LG1914; *formerly of Spaunton* **DFUSA**; (*see also* Carington; and Smith)
WYNN-CARRINGTON (Lincolnshire, M) **PB1928**
CARROLL *of Lissen Hall and Tulla House* **LGI1912**
CARROLL *formerly of Munduff, Ashford* **LG1937 Supp**; **IFR1976**; *formerly of Leap* **DFUSA**; **PromFUSA**
CARROLL (*now* VAN CLIEF) **DFUSA** *formerly of Old Court*
CARRON, B **PB1970**
CARRUTHERS *of Dormont* **LG1972**; (*Australia*) **CG**
CARSON, B **PB1935**; *of Spinfield* LG1875; *formerly of Annesville* LG1958; *formerly of Shanroe* **LGI1958**; *formerly of Dungannon* **DFUSA**
LLOYD-CARSON *of Hengwn* **LG1952**
CARTER *of Eccleshall Castle* **LG1972**; *of The Hermitage* **LG1952**; *of Wickhamford* LG1952; *late of Northwold* LG1937; *late of Paulton* LG1937; *formerly of Garston* **DFUSA**; **PromFUSA**; **FR**; *of Watlington Park* (*see* Shaen Carter); (*see also* Dawson *of Weston*)
BONHAM CARTER (Asquith of Yarnbury, B) **PB1967**; (*see also* Lubbock)
SHAEN CARTER **IFR1976**
CARTERET (Granville, E) **DEP**; Bt **EDB**
CARTHEW (*see* Carthew-Yorstoun)
CARTIER, Bt **PB1873**
CARTWRIGHT *of Aynhoe* **LG1952**; *formerly of Marnham and Wyberton* LG1952; *of Loughborough* **LG1900**; **CG**; (*see also* Rylands)
CARUS (*see* Carus-Wilson)
CARVELL (*Canada*) **CG**
CARVER (1) & (2) **DFUSA**; (*see also* Bagshawe *of Ford Hall*)
CARY (Falkland, V) **PB1970**; Bt **PB1970**; *of Torre Abbey* **LG1972**
STANLEY-CARY *of White Castle* **LG1875**
STANLEY-CARY *of Millicent* (*formerly* Cary-Caddell *of Harbourstown*) **LGI1958**
CARYSFORT (*see* Proby)
CASBORNE *of New House* **LG1879**
CASE *late of Beckford Hall* **LG1937**; *of*

Redhazels **LG1914**; **DFUSA**
CASEMENT **IFR1976**
CASEY, B **PB1970**; **CG**
CASS *of Little Grove* **LG1858**; **FR**
CASSAN *of Sheffield* **LGI1912**
CASSAR DE SAIN, M **TNBE1956**
CASSEL, Bt **PB1970**
CASSELS (*Canada*) **CG**
CASSIDI **IFR1976**
CASSIDY (1) & (2) **DFUSA**
CASSILHAS (*see* Thornton)
CASTEL CICCIANO (*see* Diar-LY Bniet and Bukana)
CASTELTHOMOND (*see* Ffrench)
CASTLE *of Burghcastle* **LG1952**; *of Hawford* **LG1886**; **DFUSA**
CASTLEHAVEN (*see* Touchet)
CASTLEMAINE (*see* Handcock; and Palmer)
CASTLEMAN *of Chettle* **LG1937**
CASTLE STEWART (*see* Stuart)
CASTLETON, Bt **EDB**; (*see also* Saunderson)
CASTLETOWN (*see* FitzPatrick)
CASWELL **DFUSA**
CATHCART, E **PB1970**; *of Pitcairlie* LG1937; *of Knockdolian* **LG1879**
CATHERLOUGH (*see* Fane; and Knight)
CATHERWOOD **IFR1976**
DEWLEY-CATHIE *of Barton-on-the-Heath* **LG1965**
CATLIN *formerly of Bedford* **DFUSA**
CATON *formerly of Binbrook* **LG1952**
CATOR *of Woodbustwick* **LG1965**
CATT *formerly of Owlesbury* **LG1965**
CATTO, B **PB1970**
CAULFEILD (Charlemont, V) **PB1970**; (Charlemont, B) **PB1892**
CAUNTER *of Hannafore* **LG1952**
CAUSTON (Southwark, B) **PB1929**
CAUTLEY, B **PB1940**; *late of Shelf Hall* **LG1914**
CAVAN (*see* Lambart)
CAVE, Bt **PB1970**; V **PB1928**; (Cave of Richmond, E) **PB1938**; *formerly of Ditcham Park and Stoner Hill* **LG1965**
CAVE-BROWNE-CAVE, Bt **PB1970**
VERNEY-CAVE (Braye, B) **PB1970**
CAVENDISH (Devonshire, D) **PB1970**; (Chesham, B) **PB1970**; (Waterpark, B) **PB1970**; (Newcastle, D) **DEP**; *of Chyknell* **LG1898**
CAWDOR (*see* Campbell)
CAWLEY, B **PB1970**
CAY *of Charlton Hall* **LG1833/7**
CAYLEY, Bt **PB1970**; *of Correen Castle* **LGI1958**; (*Canada*) **CG**

CAYZER (Rotherwick, B) **PB1970**; Bt *of Gartmore* **PB1970**; Bt *of Roffey Park* **PB1970**
CAZALET *of Fairlawne* **LG1969**; *of Alderton House* **LGI1958**
CAZENOVE *of Cottesbrooke* **LG1965**
CELY (*see* Cely Trevilian)
CECIL (Exeter, M) **PB1970** (Amherst of Hackney, B) **PB1970**; (Rockley, B) **PB1970** (Wimbledon, V) **DEP**; **DFUSA**
GASCOYNE-CECIL (Salisbury, M) **PB1970**; (Cecil of Chelwood, B) **PB1956**; (Quickswood, B) **PB1956**
CHAD, Bt **PB1855**
DUCKWORTH-CHAD *of Pynkney* **LG1972**
SCOTT-CHAD (*see* Duckworth-Chad)
CHADBOURNE **DFUSA**
CHADS *formerly of Donnington* **LG1972**
CHADWICK *of Chad Wyche* **LG1937**; *of High Bank* **LG1921**; *late of Healey and Mavesyn Ridware* **LG1906**; *of Daresbury Hall* **LG1894**; *of Ballinard* **LGI1912**; *formerly of Rochdale* **DFUSA**; (*Canada*) **CG**; **AA**; **VSA**
BURTON-CHADWICK, Bt **PB1970**
COOPER-CHADWICK (*see* Cooper)
CHAFY *formerly of Holnest Park and of Rous-Lench* **LG1952**
CHAINE *of Ballycraigy* **LGI1912**
CHALFONT (*see* Gwynne Jones)
CHALLEN *of Shermanbury Park* **LG1833/7**
CHALLENOR *of Portnall* **LG1875**
CHALLINOR *formerly of Pickwood* **LG1952**
CHALMER (*see* Stirling *late of Larbert*)
CHALMERS, B **PB1938**; *of Aldbar Castle* **LG1952**; *formerly of Almond Bank* **DFUSA**
CHALONER (Gisborough, B) **PB1970**; Bt **EDB**; *of King's Fort* **LGI1912**; (*see also* Enniskillen)
CHAMBERLAIN, Bt **PB1970**; *formerly of Highbury* **LG1965**
CHAMBERLAYNE, Bt **EDB**; *of Cranbury Park* **LG1972**; *of Stoney Thorpe* **LG1969**; *of Chamberlainstown* **LGI1958**; **HI**
INGLES-CHAMBERLAYNE *of Maugersbury* **LG1921**
CHAMBERLEN *of Alderton Hall* **LG1833/7**
CHAMBERLIN **DFUSA**
CHAMBERS *of Lochletter* **LG1952**; *of Clough House* **LG1937**; *of Fostertown* **LG1937Supp**; *of Hafod* **LG1875**; *of*

Fox Hall **LG1863**; *of Bredgar House* **LG1850/3**; (*S. Africa*) **CG**
CHAMBRÉ **IFR1976**
CHAMBRES *formerly of Plas Chambres* **LG1952**
CHAMNEY *of Schomberg* **LGI1912**
BATEMAN-CHAMPAIN *of Halton Park* **LG1886**
CHAMPERNOWNE *of Pound formerly of Dartington* **LG1937**
CHAMPION, B **PB1970**; *of Worthington Hall* **LG1921**; *of Riddlesworth Hall* (*see* Noel)
CHAMPNESS *formerly of Stansted Mountfitchet* **LG1952**
CHAMPNEYS *of Ostenhanger* **LG1850/3**
DALRYMPLE-CHAMPNEYS, Bt **PB1970**
CHANCE, Bt **PB1970**; *formerly of Great Alne* **LG1969**; *of Morton* **LG1969**; *formerly of Shepley* **DFUSA**; **FR**; *of Birmingham* **AA**
CHANCE (*formerly* CURWEN) *of Workington Hall* **LG1952**
CHANCELLOR *of Hunstrete House* **LG1965**; *of Shieldhill* **LG1952**
CHANDOS, B **DEP**; (*see also* Brydges; and Lyttelton)
CHANNING (Channing of Wellingborough, B) **PB1926**
CHANNON *of Kelvedon Hall* **LG1972**
CHAPLIN, V **PB1970**; Bt **EDB**
CHAPMAN, Bt **PB1970**; Bt *of Killua Castle* **PB1917**; Bt *of London* **EDB**; *formerly of Whitby* **LG1972**; *of Cleadon* **LG1952**; *formerly of Donhead House* **LG1952**; *formerly of Crooksbury* **LG1937**; *of Kilhendre* **LG1937**; *of Hill End* **LG1921**; *formerly of Hull* **DFUSA**; **FR**; (*New Zealand*) **CG**; *of Bowers* **VSA**; (*see also* Mungovan; and Thursby-Pelham)
CHAPELLE, Count **TNBE1956**
CHAPPELL *formerly of Goddon Leaze* **LG1965**
CHARDIN, Bt **EDB**
CHARLEMONT (*see* Caulfeild)
CHARLES, Bt **PB1970**; *formerly of Pelsall Hall* **LG1952**; **DFUSA**
CHARLESWORTH *of Abbot's Lodge* **LG1952**; *formerly of Bilton House* **LG1952**; *of Grinton Lodge* **LG1937**
CHARLETON, Bt **EDB**
NEWPORT-CHARLETT *of Hanley Court* **LG1833/7**
CHARLEVILLE (*see* Bury; and Moore)
CHARLEY **IFR1976**
CHARLTON, Bt **EDB**; *of Great Canfield*

Park **LG1969**; *of Hesleyside* **LG1969**; *of Chilwell* **LG1937**; *of Ludford* **LG1850/3**; *of Apley Castle* (*see* Tapps-Gervis-Meyrick); (*see also* Anne; and Staunton)

CHARLTON (*formerly* BATE) *of Kelsterton* **LG1952**

CHARNOCK *of Charnock und Astley* **LG1850/3**

CHARNWOOD (*see* Benson)

CHARRINGTON *of Bures Manor* **LG1965**; *of Cherry Orchard* **LG1965**; *of Field Place* **LG1965**; *of High Quarry* **LG1969**; *of Winchfield* **LG1965**

MONTGOMERIE-CHARRINGTON *of Hunsdon House* **LG1952Supp**

CHARTERIS (Wemyss and March, E) **PB1970**; *of Amisfield* **LG1972**; *of Cahir* **LGI1958**

CHARTRES **IFR1976**

CHASE *formerly of Chesham* **DFUSA**; **PromFUSA**

CHATFIELD, B **PB1970**

CHATHAM (*see* Pitt)

CHATTERIS *of Sandleford Priory* **LG1879**

CHATTERTON, Bt **PB1874**; *of Exeleigh* **LG1906**; **IFR1976**, **DFUSA**

CHAUNCEY **PromFUSA**

CHAUNCY *of Little Mundon* **LG1863**; *formerly of Skirpenbeck* **DFUSA**

CHAVASSE **IFR1976**

CHAVENT, B **DEP**

CHAWNER *formerly of Newton Manor* **LG1972**

CHAWORTH (Chaworth, N) **DEP**; (Chaworth, B) **DEP**

CHAYTOR, Bt **PB1970**; Bt **EDB**; *of Spennithorne* **LG1952**; *of Wilton Castle* **LG1898**

CHEALES *of Hagworthingham* **LG1952**; **FR** (*see also* Miles)

CHEAPE *of Strathtyrun and Lathockar* **LG1972**; *of Tiroran* **LG1952**

GRAY-CHEAPE *of Carse Gray* **LG1972**

ISMAY CHEAPE *of Fossoway* **LG1972**

CHEARNLEY *of Salterbridge* **LGI1912**

CHECKLAND *of Thurmaston Hall* **LG1921**

CHEDSEY *formerly of Chedzoy* **DFUSA**

CHEDWORTH (*see* Howe)

CHEERE, Bt **EDB**

CHEESE *of Huntington* **LG1863**

CHELMER (*see* Edwards)

CHELMSFORD (*see* Thesiger)

CHENEY, B **DEP**; *formerly of Puncknoll* **LG1969**; *of Gaddesby* **LG1898**; *of*

Monyash **LG1850/3**; **DFUSA**

CHERLTON (Cherlton of Powys, B) **DEP**

CHERNOCKE, Bt **EDB**; *of Chernocke Hall* **LG1833/7**

CHEROLS (*see* Stone)

CHERRY *of Buckland* **LG1863**; **FR**; (*see also* Cherry-Garrard)

CHERWELL (*see* Lindemann)

CHEESEBROUGH **DFUSA**

CHESHAM (*see* Cavendish)

CHESSHYRE (*formerly* ISACKE *of North Foreland Lodge*) **LG1972**

CHESTER, Bt **EDB**; *of Bush Hall* **LG1863**; *formerly of Chipping Barnet* **DFUSA**; *of Chicheley* (*see* Bagot); *of Poyle Park* (*see* Heron); (*see also* Abrincis; Georbodus; Meschines; and Scot)

CHESTERFIELD (*see* Stanhope; and Wotton)

CHESTON **DFUSA**

CHETHAM *of Mellor* **LG1833/7**

CHETWODE, B **PB1970**

WILMOT-CHETWODE *of Woodbrook* **LGI1912**

CHETWYND, V **PB1970**; B **PB1970**

CHEVALIER **DFUSA**

CHEVALLIER (*see* Guild)

CHEVERS (Mount Leinster, V) **DEP**; **IFR1976**; **AA**

CHEVERTON **DFUSA**

CHEW *of Vanor formerly of Chewton Mendip* **DFUSA**

CHEYLESMORE (*see* Eaton)

CHEYNE, Bt **PB1970**; (Newhaven, V) **DEP**

CHIBNALL *formerly of Sherington* **LG1937**

CHICHESTER (Donegall, M) **PB1970**; (Templemore, B) **PB1970**; Bt **PB1970**; (Ennishowen and Carrickfergus, B) **PB1883**; B **DEP**; Bt *of Arlington Court* **PB1881**; Bt *of Green Castle* **PB1847**; *formerly of Calverleigh* **LG1965**; *of Hall* **LG1965**; *of Grenofen* **LG1952**; **IFR1976**; (*see also* Chichester-Clark; Leigh; O'Neill; Pelham; and Wriothesley)

CHILD, Bt **PB1970**; (Tylney, E) **DEP**; Bt **EDB**; *of Bromley Palace* **LG1914**; *of Bigelly House* **LG1886**; *of Newfield* **LG1863**; **DFUSA**

CHILDE *of Kinlet* **LG1952**

BALDWYN-CHILDE *of Kyre* **LG1921**

CHILDERS **IFR1976**

CHILSTON (*see* Akers-Douglas)

CHILTON **DFUSA**

CHINNERY, Bt **PB1868**; *of Fringford* **LG1952**; (*see also* Chinnery-Haldane)
CHIRNSIDE (*formerly* CHARLTON) *of Croxall Hall* **LG1952**
CHISENHALL *of Arley* **LG1843/9**
CHISHOLM, Bt **PB1923**; *of Chisholm* **LG1952**; *formerly of Clachan* **DFUSA**; *formerly of Knockfin* **DFUSA**; (*Canada*) **CG**
CHITTENDEN *formerly of Marden* **DFUSA**
CHITTY, Bt **PB1970**; *formerly of Torrie Lodge* **LG1952**
CHITWOOD **DFUSA**
CHOLMELEY, Bt **PB1970**; *formerly of Riversdown* **LG1965**
FARIFAX-CHOLMELEY *formerly of Brandsby* **LG1952**
CHOLMLEY, Bt **EDB**; *of Place Newton* **LG1952**
CHOLMONDELEY, M **PB1970**; (Delamere, B) **PB1970**; (Leinster, E) **DEP**; Bt **EDB**; *formerly of Condover* **LG1952**
CHORLEY, B **PB1970**
CHOWNE *of Wheatleigh Lodge* **LG1863**
CHRISTIAN *formerly of Milntown and Ewanrigg* **LG1969**; (*S Africa*) **CG**
CHRISTIE *of Glyndebourne* **LG1969**; *of Durie* **LG1952**; *of Jervaulx Abbey* **LG1952**; *of Marston* **LG1952**; *of Melbourne Hall* **LG1886**; *of Stenton and Riddry* **LG1886**; *of Magherabuoy House* **LGI1958** (*see also* Christie-Miller)
CHRISTIN (*see* Christie *of Glyndebourne*)
CHRISTISON, Bt **PB1970**
CHRISTMAS *of Whitfield* **LG1863**
CHRISTOPHER *of Norton* **LG1952**; *of Bloxholm* **LG1850/3**
CHRISTY *of Watergate* **LG1937**; (*see also* Christie-Miller)
CHUBB (Hayter, B) **PB1970**; Bt **PB1956**
CHUDLEIGH, Bt **EDB**
CHURCH, Bt **PB1970**
CHURCHILL, B **DEP**; *of Muston formerly of Colliton* **LG1969**; **DFUSA**; (*see also* Spencer)
SPENCER-CHURCHILL (Marlborough, D) **PB1970**; B **PB1970**
CHURCHMAN (Woodbridge, B) **PB1949**; Bt **PB1940**
CHURSTON (*see* Yarde-Buller)
CHUTE, Bt *of The Vyne* **PB1956**; Bt *of Hinxhill Place* **EDB**; *of Chute Hall* **LGI1912**
CILCENNIN (*see* Thomas)
CITRINE, B **PB1970**

CLACK *formerly of Crowmarsh Gifford and Larkbeare* **LG1937**
CLAFLIN **DFUSA**
CLAGETT *formerly of Malling* **DFUSA**
CLAIBORNE *formerly of Cliburn* **DFUSA**; **PromFUSA**
CLANBRASSILL (*see* Hamilton; and Jocelyn)
CLANCARE (*see* M'Carty)
CLANCARTY (*see* Le Poer Trench; and MacCarthy)
CLANCHY *formerly of Charleville* **LGI1958**
CLANMALIER (*see* O'Dempsey)
CLANMORRIS (*see* Bingham)
CLANRICARDE (*see* De Burgh-Canning)
CLANWILLIAM (*see* Meade)
CLAPCOTT *of Keynstone* **LG1875**
CLAPHAM *of Ilmington* **LG1952**; *of Burley Grange* **LG1863**
CLAPP *formerly of Salcombe Regis* **DFUSA**
CLARE (Gloucester, E) **DEP**; (Pembroke, E) B **DEP**; (*see also* FitzGibbon; and Nugent)
CLARENCE (Clarence and Avondale, D) **PB1892**; (*see also* Guelph; and Plantagenet)
CLARENDON (*see* Villiers)
CLARGES, Bt **EDB**
CLARINA (*see* Massy)
CLARK, Bt *of Cavendish Square* **PB1970**; Bt *of Dunlambert* **PB1970**; Bt *of Edinburgh* **PB1970**; *formerly of Tal-y-Garn* **LG1972**; *of The Red Lodge* **LG1952**; *of The Croft* **LG1937**; *of Bellefield House* **LG1921**; *of Moorlands* **LG1921**; **IFR1976**; (1) & (2) **DFUSA**; *formerly of Cambridge* **DFUSA**; (*Tasmania*) **CG**
ATKINSON-CLARK *formerly of Belford Hall* **LG1952**
CHICHESTER-CLARK **IFR1976**
GILCHRIST-CLARK *of Speddoch* **LG1937**
GORDON CLARK *formerly of Mickleham Hall* **LG1965**
STEWART-CLARK, Bt **PB1970**
TOWERS-CLARK *of Wester Moffat* **LG1952**
CLARKE, Bt *of Dunham* **PB1970**; Bt *of Rupertswood* **PB1970**; (Sydenham of Combe, B) **PB1933**; Bt *of Salford Shirland* **PB1898**; Bt *of Snailwell* **EDB**; *of Borde Hill* **LG1965**; *of Achareidh* **LG1952**; *of Bridwell* **LG1952**; *of Gatcombe Court* **LG1952**; *of Tracy Park* **LG1952**; *of Welton Place* **LG1952**; *of*

LG1898; (see also Williams-Ellis; and Clough-Taylor)

CLOUSTON, Bt **PB1912**; of Clouston and Smoogro **LG1952**

CLOWES of Norbury formerly of Broughton **LG1969**; of Delaford **LG1863**; **DFUSA**

CLUDDE of Orleton (see Holt)

CLUTTERBUCK of Hornby Castle **LG1972**; of Rowington **LG1972**; of Micklefield Hall **LG1952**; of Newark Park **LG1937**; of Hardenhuish **LG1921**; of Warkworth **LG1900**

CLUTTON formerly of Chorlton **LG1972**

CLWYD (see Roberts)

CLYDE (see Campbell)

CLYDESMUIR (see Colville)

COALE **PromFUSA**

COALES of Newport Pagnell **LG1952**

COAPE (see Sherbrooke)

COATES, Bt **PB1970**; formerly of Combe House **LG1952**; of Eyton House **LG1952**; of Eastwood **LG1863**; of Rathmore **LGI1912**; **DFUSA**; formerly of Sproxton **DFUSA**

MILNES-COATES, Bt **PB1970**

COATS (Glentanar, B) **PB1970**; Bt **PB1970**

GLEN-COATS, Bt **PB1953**

COBB, Bt **EDB**

COBBE **IFR1976**

COBBOLD, B **PB1970**; of Glemham Hall formerly of Holywells **LG1965**

COBHAM, B **PB1970**; (Cobham of Kent, B) **DEP**; (Cobham, of Norfolk, B) **DEP**; (Cobham, of Rundell, B) **DEP**; (Cobham, of Sterborough, B) **DEP**; formerly of Shinfield Manor **LG1952**; (see also Lyttelton; and Oldcastle)

COCHRAN of Ashkirk **LG1952**; of Balfour **LG1952Supp**

COCHRANE (Dundonald, E) **PB1970**; (Cochrane of Cults, B) **PB1970**; Bt of Woodbrook **PB1970**; Bt of Woodbrook, Wicklow **PB1949**; formerly of The Heath **LG1937Supp**; **IFR1976**; of Red Castle **LGI1912**

COCK **FR**; (see also Trevor-Battye)

COCKBURN, Bt **PB1970**; Bt of Langton **PB1880**; formerly of Cockpen **LG1952**; formerly of Harmston and Redlynch **LG1952**; **CG**; (see also Chinnery-Haldane; and Rushout)

COCKERELL of The Brook House **LG1952**

COCKS, Bt **EDB**; **DFUSA**

SOMERS COCKS (Somers, B) **PB1970**; (Somers, E) **PB1883**

CODDINGTON, Bt **PB1917**; **IFR1976**; **DFUSA**

CODRINGTON, Bt of Dodington **PB1970**; Bt of Dodington Park **PB1970**; of Wroughton House **LG1972**

COE formerly of Gestingthorpe **DFUSA**

COFFEY **IFR1976**

COFFIN **DFUSA**; **CG**; (Canada) **CG**

PINE-COFFIN of Portledge **LG1972**

COGAN of Tinode **LGI1899**

COGGESHALL **DFUSA**

COGGILL **DFUSA**

COGHILL, Bt **PB1970**; **EDB**; formerly of Campster and Coghurst Hall **LG1972**; formerly of Knaresborough, Yorkshire **DFUSA**

COHAM of Dunsland, co Devon **AA**; (see also Coham-Fleming)

COHEN (Cohen of Birkenhead, B) **PB1970**; Bt **PB1970**; (Cohen of Brighton, B) **PB1967**; of Barwythe **LG1937**; (Australia) **CG**

WALEY-COHEN, Bt **PB1970**

COIT **DFUSA**

COKAYNE (Cullen of Ashbourne, B) **PB1970**; (Cullen, V) **DEP**

COKE (Leicester, E) **PB1970**; (Leicester, E) **DEP**; Bt **EDB**; of Brookhill **LG1965**; of Lemore **LG1900**; of Trusley (see Coke-Steel)

COKER of Bicester **LG1952**

COLBORNE, B **DEP**; (see also Colborne-Vivian)

COLBRAND, Bt **EDB**

COLBURN **DFUSA**

COLBY, Bt **EDB**; formerly of Beccles **DFUSA**; **FR**

SPENCE-COLBY of Donnington Hall **LG1952**

COLCHESTER (see Abbot)

COLCLOUGH, Bt **EDB**; **IFR1976**

COLDHAM formerly of Anmer Hall **LG1969**

COLE (Enniskillen, E) **PB1970**; B **PB1970**; (Ranelagh, B) **DEP**; Bt of Brancepeth **EDB**; Bt of Newland **EDB**; formerly of Twickenham **LG1969**; formerly of Llys Meirchion and Brandrum **LG1937**; of Hill House **LG 1886**; of Marazion **LG1863**; of Woodview **LGI1912**; (1) & (2) **DFUSA**; (1) & (2) **FR**; of Brancepeth **VF**; (see also Jarvis)

BURKE COLE **IFR1976**

COLEBROOKE, B **PB1939**

COLEGATE of Hill Grove **LG1952**

MANBY-COLEGRAVE *formerly of Cann Hall* **LG1952Supp**
COLEMAN *of Stoke Park* **LG1879**
COLEPEPER, B **DEP**; **LG1833/7**
COLERAINE (*see* Hanger; Hare; and Law)
COLERIDGE, B **PB1970**
COLES *of Ditcham* **LG1875**; *of Parrocks Lodge* **LG1875**; (1) & (2) **FR**
COLFOX, Bt **PB1970**
COLGATE *formerly of Sevenoaks* **DFUSA**
COLGRAIN (*see* Campbell)
COLHOUN *of Carrickbaldoey* **LGI1912**
COLLARD *of Entonhurst* **LG1952**; *of Stodmarsh Court* **LG1937**
COLLER **DFUSA**
COLLET, Bt **PB1940**
COLLETON, Bt **PB1938**
COLLETT, Bt **PB1970**
DAVIES-COLLEY *of Newbold* **LG1952**
COLLIE (*formerly* CLEGG) *of Backford* **LG1952**
COLLIER (Monkswell, V) **PB1970**; Bt **EDB**; *of Glassburn* **LG1969**; **DFUSA**; (1) & (2) **FR**
COLLING *formerly of Hurworth* **LG1972**
COLLINGS *of Guernsey* **LG1863**; *formerly of Clehonger* **DFUSA**
COLLINGWOOD, B **DEP** *of Cornhill House* **LG1972**; *of Lilburn Tower* **LG1965**; *of Dissington* **LG1952**
COLLINS (Stonham, B) **PB1970**; B **PB1911**; *formerly of Betterton* **LG1969**; *of Kelvindale* **LG1969**; *of Cundall Manor and Knaresborough* **LG1965**, *of Wythall Walford* **LG1952**, *of Peterborough, Ontario* **LG1952Supp**; *of Truthan* **LG1914**; *of Hatch Beauchamp* **LG1850/3**; *of Simmons Court* **LG1843/9**; (1) & (2) **DFUSA**; **PromFUSA**; (*New Zealand*) **CG**; (*see also* Aldworth; and Trelawny-Ross)
ABDY COLLINS *formerly of Deccan House* **LG1952**
EDWARD-COLLINS *of Trewardale* **LG1972**
PRIDE-COLLINS *of South Shore* **LG1952**
COLLINSON *of Beltoft* **LF1921**; *of The Chantry* **LG1833/7**
COLLIS *of Clotworthy House* **LGI1958**
COOKE-COLLIS **IFR1976**
COLLISON, Bt **PB1970**
COLLUM *of Bellevue* **LGI1912**
COLLYER *of Gimingham* **LG1937**; **DFUSA**

COLMAN, Bt **PB1970**; *of Crown Point* **LG1952**
CREGOE-COLMORE *of Moor End* **LG1898**
COLOMB *of Dromquinna and Dunkerron* **LGI1912**
COLOMBINE (*see* Humfrey-Mason)
COLQUHOUN, Bt **PB1970**; *of London* **LG1833/7**
CAMPBELL-COLQUHOUN *of Killermont* **LG1952**
COLSTON (Roundway, B) **PB1940**
COLT, Bt **PB1970**; *of Gartsherrie* **LG1937**
COLTHUP *of Hopebourne* **LG1952**
COLTHURST, Bt **PB1970**
BOWEN-COLHURST **IFR1976**
COLTMAN *of Daljarrock and Blair* **LG1952**; *of Naburn Hall* **LG1875**
POCKLINGTON COLTMAN *of Hagnaby Priory* **LG1898**; (*see also* Pocklington-Senhouse)
ROGERS-COLTMAN (*see* Coltman-Rogers)
COLTON (*Australia*) **CG**
CRONIN-COLTSMANN **IFR1976**
COLVILE, B **DEP**; *of Lullington* **LG1965**
COLVILL, Lord **DEP**; **IFR1976**
COLVILLE (Clydeomuir, B) **PB1970**; (Colville of Culross, V) **PB1970**; *of Penhealo* **LG1952**; *of Arncliffe* **LG1833/7**
WAKEMAN-COLVILLE *formerly of Bellaport* **LG1952**
COLVIN *formerly of Monkhams Hall* **LG1965**
COLWYN (*see* Smith)
COLYEAR (Portmore, E) **DEP**
COLYER *of Southfleet* **LG1886**
COLYTON (*see* Hopkinson)
COMBE *of Cobham Park* **LG1965**; *of Earnshill* **LG1972**; *formerly of Oaklands Park* **LG1965**; *of Strathconan* **LG1965**
COMBERMERE (*see* Stapleton-Cotton)
COMER *of Fitzhead* **LG1875**
COMMERELL *of Stroud* **LG1863**
COMPTON (Northampton, M) **PB1970**; (Wilminton, E) **DEP**; Bt **EDB**; *of Minstead Manor* **LG1952**; *of Carham Hall* **LG1833/7**; (*see also* Hall of Charnes Hall)
COMPTON (*formerly* VYNER) *of Newby* **LG1952**
COMYN (Northumberland, E) **DEP**. **IFR1976**; *of Woodstock and Kilcorney* **LGI1912**; *of Holywell* **LGI1912**
COMYNS *formerly of Wood* **LG1969**

CONANT, Bt **PB1970**; *of Willoughby Hall* **LG1898**
CONCANON **AA**
CONDER *of Terry Bank and Conigree Court* **LG1937**
CONESFORD (*see* Strauss)
CONEY *of Batcombe* **LG1952**
CONGLETON (*see* Parnell)
CONGREVE, Bt **PB1940**; *of Congreve* **LG1969**; **IFR**
CONINGSBY, E **DEP**
PHILLIPS-CANN *of Belturbet and Mount Ida* **LGI1912**
CONNAUGHT (*see* Windsor)
CONNELL (*see* O'Connell)
CONNELLAN *of Coolmore* **LGI1912**
CONNEMARA (*see* Bourke)
CONNER **IFR1976**
CONNOR (*Australia*) **CG**
CONOLLY *of Castletown House* **LGI1912**; *of Cottles, co Wilts* **AA**
CONRAN *of Backlands* **LG1952**; **FR**
CONROY, Bt **PB1900**
CONSETT *of Brawith Hall* **LG1969**; (*see also* Bell *of Thirsk*)
CONSIDINE **IFR1976**
CONSTABLE (Dunbar, V) **DEP**; Bt **EDB**
CHICHESTER-CONSTABLE *of Burton Constable* **LG1952**
GOULTON-CONSTABLE (*see* Marriott *of Cotesbach*)
STRICKLAND-CONSTABLE, Bt **PB1970**
CONSTANTINE, B **PB1970**; *of Laskill* **LG1972**
CONVERSE **PromFUSA**
CONWAY (Conway of Allington, B) **PB1937**; V **DEP**; Bt **EDB**; **PromFUSA** (*see also* Edge)
ROWLEY-CONWY (Langford, B) **PB1970**; *of Bodrhyddan* **LG1937**
CONYERS, B **PB1940**; Bt **EDB**; **IFR1976**; **VF**; (*see also* Pelham)
CONYNGHAM, M **PB1970**; E **DEP**; *formerly of Letterkenny* **DFUSA**
LENOX-CONYNGHAM **IFR1976**
COODE *formerly of Polapit Tamar* **LG1965**
COOK, Bt **PB1970**; *of Sennowe* **LG1969**; *formerly of Halesworth* **LG1965**; *of Roydon Hall* **LG1952**; *of Quatford Wood* **LG1937**; **DFUSA**; *formerly of Doncaster* **DFUSA**
COOKE, Bt **PB1970**; Bt **EDB**; *of Poland House* **LG1965**; *of Knockgraffon* **LG1894**; *of Cooksborough* **LG1863**; *of Retreat* **LG1858**; **IFR1976**; (*see also* Cooke-Collis)

DAVIES COOKE *of Owston and Gwysaney* **LG1937**
DENNY-COOKE *of Bergh Apton* **LG1952**
FALCON-COOKE *of Camerton* **LG1937**
KINLOCH-COOKE, Bt **PB1940**
COOKES, Bt **EDB**; *late of Bentley* **LG1900**
COOKMAN **IFR1976**
COOKSON *of Meldon Park* **LG1965**
FIFE-COOKSON *late of Whitehill* **LG1914**
SAWREY-COOKSON *formerly of Neasham Hall and Broughton Tower* **LG1965**
STIRLING-COOKSON *formerly of Renton* **LG1952**
COOKWORTHY (*see* Fox *of Penjerrick*)
COOLEY, **DFUSA**
COOLIDGE **PresFUSA**; *formerly of Cottenham* **DFUSA**; (*see also* Jefferson)
COOMBS *of Haddon House* **LG1965**
COOPER (Norwich, V) **PB1970**; Bt *of Gadebridge* **PB1970**; Bt *of Shenstone* **PB1970**; Bt *of Stockton Heath* **PB1970**; Bt *of Woollahra* **PB1970**; (Cooper *of Culross*, B) **PB1956**; Bt *of Hursley* **PB1959**; Bt *of Singleton* **PB1940**; Bt *of Berrydown Court* **PB1922**; Bt *of Gogar* **PB1842**; Bt *of Dublin* **EDB**; Bt *of Walcot* **EDB**; *of Hexton Manor* **LG1972**; *formerly of The Abbey, Abingdon* **LG1952**; *of Failford* **LG1937**; *of Toddington Manor* **LG1900**; *of Pain's Hill* **LG1875**; *of Finchley* **LG1863**; (*co Sligo*) **IFR1976**; (*co Tipperary*) **IFR1976**; *of Cooper's Hill* **LGI1912**; *sometime of Lower Edinton* **DFUSA**; *of Woollahra* **CG**; *of Failford* **AA**; *of New South Wales* **AA**; **VSA**; (*see also* Hone)
ASHLEY-COOPER (Shaftesbury, E) **PB1970**
COLLINSON-COOPER *formerly of Culland Hall* **LG1952**
DOUGLAS-COOPER *of The Hawfield, formerly of Killymoon Castle* **LG1952**
HERRING-COOPER *of Hanover House* **LG1886**
PASTON-COOPER (*see* Hervey-Bathurst)
COORE *of Scruton Hall* (*see* Gale)
COOTE, Bt **PB1970**; (Bellamont, E) **DEP**; (Mountrath, E) **DEP**; *of Haughton* **LG1952**; *of West Park* **LG1937**; *of Ballyclough Castle and Bearforest* **LGI1912**; *of Mount Coote* **LGI1912**; *of Carrowroe Park* **LGI1912**
COPE, Bt *of Hanwell* **PB1970**; Bt **EDB**;

formerly of Avebury **DFUSA**;
PromFUSA; *of Drummilly* **LG1937**
Supp; *of Osbaston Hall* **LG1914**; *of*
Loughgall Manor **LGI1912**
ARCHDALL-COPE (*see* Montgomery)
COPELAND *of Bishops Offley Manor*
and Kibblestone **LG1972**
COPEMAN *formerly of Sparham* **LG1972**
COPINGER *formerly of Buxhall* **LG1952**
COPLAND *of Colliston* **LG1921**
COPLESTON *of Ireson House* **LG1952**
COPLEY (Lyndhurst, B) **DEP**; Bt *of*
Sprotsborough **PB1883**; of *Sprot-*
borough **EDB**; **FR**
BEWICKE-COPLEY (Cromwell, B)
PB1970; *of Sprotborough and Coulby*
LG1914
WATSON-COPLEY (*see* Watson)
COPNER *of Laston* **LG1969**
COPPIN (*Australia*) **CG**
COPPINGER *of Rossmore* **LGI1912**; *of*
Midleton **LGI1912**; **PromFUSA**
COPSI (Northumberland, E) **DEP**
CORBALLIS **IFR1976**
CORBALLY *of Rathbeale* **LGI1912**
CORBET, Bt **PB1970**; V **DEP**; B **DEP**; Bt
of Leighton **EDB**; Bt *of Moreton Corbet*
EDB; Bt *of Sprouston* **EDB**; Bt *of*
Stoke **EDB**; Bt *of Stoke and Adderley*
EDB; *of Adderley Hall* **LG1937**; *of*
Sundorne **LG1937**; (*see also* Maurice)
BRICKDALE CORBET (*see* Fortescue-
Brickdale)
CORBETT (Rowallan, B) **PB1970**; *of*
Penlurth Ucha **LG1972**; *of Longnor*
LG1969; *of Shobdon Court* **LG1965**; *of*
Stableford **LG1937**; *of Ynysymaengwyn*
LG1937; *of Elsham* **LG1886**
FAWKNER-CORBETT *formerly of*
Brown Edge **LG1952**
HOLLAND CORBETT *of Admington*
Hall **LG1886**
CORBIN **DFUSA**
CORCOR *of Cor Castle* **LGI1912**
CORDEAUX *of Brackenborough Lawn*
LG1965
CORDELL, Bt **EDB**
CORDES *formerly of Silwood Park*
LG1965
CORDINER *formerly of Costes* **LG1952**
Supp
CORDNER *of Ardmay and Darleith*
LG1952
CORFIELD *of Chatwall Hall* **LG1972**
CORK AND ORRERY (*see* Boyle)
CORKER *formerly of Ringmahon*
LG1937Supp

CORKRAN *formerly of Fitzharry's Manor*
LG1952
CORNBROOKS **DFUSA**
CORNEWALL, Bt **PB1959**; *of Debury*
Hall **LG1900**
CORNEY *of Suva* **CG**
CORNISH, Bt **EDB**; *formerly of Thurle-*
stone **LG1972**; (*see also* Cornish-
Bowden)
CORNOCK *of Cromwellsfort* **LGI1912**
CORNWALL (Milbroke, B) **DEP**; (*see*
also Dunstanvill; Gaveston; Moreton;
and Plantagenet)
MARSHALL-CORNWALL *of Callander*
LG1952
CORNWALLIS, B **PB1970**; M **DEP**; (*see*
also Mann)
CORNWELL **DFUSA**
CORRANCE *of Parham Hall* **LG1914**
CORRIE *of Stansty Park* **LG1952**; **FR**
CORRIGAN, Bt **PB1883**
CORRY, Bt **PB1970**; *of Newry* **LG1886**
LESLIE-CORRY (*see* Leslie)
LOWRY-CORRY (Belmore, E) **PB1970**;
(Rowton, B) **PB1903**
CORSELLIS *of Wyvenhoe Hall* **LG1879**
CORSTORPHINE *of Pittowie* **LG1900**
CORWIN *formerly of Warwick* **DFUSA**;
PromFUSA
CORY, Bt **PB1970**; Bt *of Llantarnam*
Abbey **PB1940**; *formerly of Duffryn*
LG1952; *of Cranwells* **LG1898**
CORYTON, Bt **EDB**; *of Pentillie Castle*
LG1965
COSBURN **FR**
COSBY (Sydney, B) **DEP**; **IFR1976**
COSENS *of Samsons* **LG1952**
COSLETT *of Wyre Court* **LG1921**
COSPATRICK (Northumberland, E)
DEP
COSTELLO *of Edmundstown* **LG1886**;
AA
COSTIN *of St Mawes* **LG1952**
COSWAY (*see* Halliday *of Glenthorne*)
COTS *of Cots* **LG1937**
COTTENHAM (*see* Pepys)
COTTER, Bt **PB1970**; **DFUSA**
COTTERELL, Bt **PB1970**
COTTINGTON, B **DEP**; Bt **EDB**
COTTESLOE (*see* Fremantle)
COTTINGTON, B **DEP**; Bt **EDB**
COTTON, Bt *of Landwade* **PB1863**; Bt *of*
Thornton Hall **PB1848**; Bt *of Conning-*
ton **EDB**; *of Etwall* **LG1937**; *of Knol-*
ton Hall **LG1894**; *of Thomastown*
House **LGI1958**; *formerly of Cotton*

Hall **DFUSA**; *of Adelaide* **CG**; **AA**; (*see also* Gardner)
POWELL-COTTON *of Quex Park* **LG1937**; **FR**
STAPLETON-COTTON (Combermere, V) **PB1970**
COTTRELL *of Hadley* **LG1843/9**; (*see also* Cottrell-Dormer)
MITCHELL COTTS, Bt **PB1970**
COUCHMAN *of Solihull* **LG1952**
COUCI (Bedford, E) **DEP**
COULSON (*now* DU CANE) *formerly of Blenkinsopp* **LG1937**; (*see also* Wakeman-Colville)
COULSTON *of Hawksheads* **LG1952**
COULTHART *of Coulthart and Collyn* **LG1863**; **AA**
COULTHURST *of Gargrave* **LG1952**
COUNSELL *of Moreton Court* **LG1952**
COUPAR (*see* Elphinstone)
COUPER, Bt **PB1970**
COUPLAND *of Goscote* **LG1900**
COURAGE *of Edgcote* **LG1972**
COURT *formerly of Milton* **DFUSA**
COURT (*now* ROLT) *of Middlewich* **LG1937**
COURTAULD, Bt **PB1940**; *formerly of Gosfield* **LG1965**
COURTENAY (Devon, E) **PB1970**; (Exeter, M) **DEP**; (Devon, E) **DEP**; (*see also* Barry)
COURTHOPE, B **PB1953**; *of Whiligh* **LG1921**
COURTNEY (Courtney of Penwith, B) **PB1917**
COURTOWN (*see* Stopford)
COUTANCHE, B **PB1970**
BURDETT-COUTTS, B **PB1906**
MONEY-COUTTS (Latymer, B) **PB1970**
COUZENS *formerly of Edmonton* **DFUSA**
COVENTRY, E **PB1970**; B **DEP**
DARBY-COVENTRY *of Sunnyhill* **LG1894**
COVERNTON *formerly of Creeksea Hall* **LG1952**
COVERT, Bt **EDB**
COWAN, Bt *of The Baltic* **PB1956**; Bt *of Beeslack* **PB1900**; *of Rutherford* **LG1952Supp**; **FR**
COWDRAY (*see* Pearson)
COWDY *of Summer Island* **LGI1958**
COWEN *formerly of Stella Hall* **LG1952**
COWIE *of Glenrinnes* **LG1937**; *of Dufftown* **LG1925**; *formerly of Hamilton* **DFUSA**; (*New Zealand*) **CG**
SHADWELL-COWLAND *of Horfield,*

Natal **LG1952Supp**
COWLES (1) & (2) **DFUSA**
COWLEY (*see* Wellesley)
COWPER, E **PB1905**; *formerly of Carleton Hall* **LG1952**; *of High House, Hawkshead* **LG1952**; (*Australia*) **CG**; *of Carleton Hall, Cumberland* **AA**
COX, Bt *of Old Windsor* **PB1922**; Bt *of Castletown* **PB1873**; *of Blackhill* **LG1972**; *of Snaigow and Glenquaich* **LG1952**; *of Moat Mount* **LG1937**; *of Hillingdon* **LG1914**; *of Min-y-Garth* **LG1914**; *of Ballynoe* **LGI1899**; (1) & (2) **DFUSA**; **FR**; *of Fernside* **CG**; (*NSW, Australia*) **CG**; (*Tasmania*) **CG**; *of Winbourn* **CG**
HAMILTON-COX (*see* Boyne)
HIPPISLEY-COX *formerly of Gournay Court* **LG1972**
KENNEDY-COX *of Camerton Court* **LG1952**
ROXBEE COX (Kings Norton, B) **PB1970**
SNEAD-COX *of Broxwood* **LG1952**
TREVOR COX *of Roche Old Court* **LG1972**
HIPPISLEY COXE (*see* Buller; and Hippisley-Cox)
COXEN, Bt **PB1940**
COXON (*see* Cary *of Torre Abbey*)
COXWELL *of Ablington Manor* (*see* Coxwell-Rogers)
COYLE **DFUSA**
COYNEY *late of Weston Coyney* **LG1937**
CRABBE (*see* Sneyd *of Coldrenick*)
CRACKANTHORPE *formerly of Newbiggin* **LG1972**
CRACROFT (*see* Cracroft-Amcotts)
CRADDOCK *of Amberley Court* **LG1952**
CRADOCK (Howden, B) **DEP**; *of Hartforth* **LG1952**; *of Nighton* **LG1937**; *of Quorn Court* **LG1921**; *formerly of Trentham* **DFUSA**; **PromFUSA**; (*see also* Straker; and Newton *of Mickleover*)
CRAFTS **DFUSA**
CRAIG (Craigavon, V) **PB1970**; Bt **PB1933**; *of Carlton Hall* **LG1937**; *of Alsager* **LG1921**; *of Riccarton* **LG1833/7**; *of Drumcovit House* **LGI1958**; *of Preshute* **LGI1958**; (*see also* Craig-Laurie)
CRAIGIE *of Possingworth* **LG1952**
CRAIGMYLE (*see* Shaw)
CRAIGTON (*see* Browne)
CRAIK, Bt **PB1953**; (*see also* Barlas)
PENNY-CRAIK (*see* Barlas)
CRAIN **DFUSA**

CRAMER of Ballindinisk **LGI1912**; (see also Cramer-Roberts)

CRAMOND (see Richardson)

CRAMSIE (co Antrim) **IFR1976**; (cos Fermanagh and Tyrone) **IFR1976**

CRANAGE formerly of The Beum House **LG1952**

CRANBROOK (see Gathorne-Hardy)

CRANE, Bt of Chilton **EDB**; Bt of Woodrising **EDB**; of West Mersea **LG1952**; **DFUSA**; (see also Adams (Presidential); and Goodden)

CRANFIELD (Middlesex, E) **DEP**

CRANMER (see Cranmer-Byng)

CRANSTON **DFUSA**

CRANSTOUN, B **DEP**

EDMONSTOUNE-CRANSTOUN of Corehouse **LG1952**

TROTTER-CRANSTOUN of Dewar and Harviston **LG1914**

CRANWORTH (see Gurdon; and Rolfe)

CRASTER of Craster **LG1965**

CRATHORNE (see Dugdale)

CRAUFURD of Ardmillan (see Sterndale-McMikin of Grange)

CRAUFURD, Bt **PB1970**; formerly of Auchenames **LG1937**; **AA**

HOUISON-CRAUFURD of Craufurdland and Braehead **LG1952**

CRAVEN, E **PB1970**; E **DEP**; Bt **EDB**; of Cullingworth **LG1969**; of Kirklington Hall **LG1921**; of Brambridge **LG1863**; of Richardstown **LG1863**; of Chilton House **LG1833/7**

COLQUITT - CRAVEN formerly of Brockhampton Park **LG1972**

CRAWFORD (Hungarton, B) **PB1963**; formerly of Easter Setoune, Monorgan and Overton **LG1952**; of Wyld Court **LG1952**; of Derewyk Hall **LG1952Supp**; formerly of Cloreen **LGI1958**; late of Dunmucrum **LGI1958**; of Stonewold **LGI1912**; of Dunmucrum **LGI1912**; of Miramar **CG**; (see also Lindsay; and Pollock)

CRAWFORD (formerly CRAWFORD-LESLIE)'of Rothie **LG1952**

SHARMAN-CRAWFORD of Crawfordsburn **LGI1912**

CRAWFURD of Cartsburn **LG1937**; of Thornwood **LG1906**; of Saint Hill **LG1858**; (1) & (2) **FR**

CRAWFURD (formerly SMITH) formerly of Great Fenton **LG1952**

STIRLING CRAWFURD (see Stirling of Garden)

CRAWLEY formerly of Quarry Hill

LG1972; of Stockwood **LG1921**

CRAWSHAW (see Brooks)

CRAWSHAY formerly of Cyfarthfa Castle and Caversham Park **LG1965**; of Forest House **LG1921**

CREAGH formerly of Cahirbane **LGI1958**; of Dangan **LGI1912**; (see also Brasier-Creagh)

BRASIER-CREAGH **IFR1976**

BUTLER-CREAGH (see Butler)

CREAN of Ballenvilla **LG1858**

CREASY of Wiston **LG1952**

CREE of Ower Moigne **LG1952**

CREEL **DFUSA**

CREGOE (see Cregoe-Colmore of Moor End)

CREIGHTON of Crum Castle **LG1833/7**

CREMER **FR**

KETTON-CREMER of Felbrigg and Beeston Regis **LG1952**

CRESPIN of Modbury **LG1900**

CRESSWELL of Charingworth, formerly of Cresswell **LG1969**; of Crackenthorpe Hall **LG1937**; of Ocle Court **LG1937**

BAKER-CRESSWELL formerly of Cresswell **LG1965**

CRESWELL of Ravenstone **LG1921**

CRETING, B **DEP**

CREW, B **DEP**

CREWDSON of Helme Lodge **LG1952**

CREWE, Bt **PB1924**; (see also Crewe-Milnes)

CREYKE of Rawcliffe, late of Marton **LG1937**

CRICHTON (Erne, E) **PB1970**; (Caithness, E) **DEP**; (Frendraught, V) **DEP**, of Chadstone **LG1952**; of Broadward Hall **LG1894**; **IFR1976**

MAITLAND - MAKGILL - CRICHTON (see Lauderdale)

CRIGAN of Mount Pleasant **LG1843/9**

CRIPPS (Parmoor, B) **PB1970**; of Ampney Park **LG1952**; of Beechwood **LG1900**; of Novington **LG1886**; of Bath Lodge **LGI1958**

CRISP, Bt **PB1970**; of Little Wenham and Godalming **LG1937**

CRISPE, Bt **EDB**

CRISPEN late of Dodbrooke **LG1937**; **DFUSA**

CRITCHETT, Bt **PB1970**

CRITCHLEY formerly of Barrow Hills **LG1969**

CRITTALL (Braintree, B) **PB1959**

CROAD **LG1952Supp**

CROASDAILE **IFR1976**

CROCKER (see Bulteel)

CROFT, B **PB1970**; Bt *of Cowling Hall* **PB1970**; Bt *of Croft Castle* **PB1970**; *formerly of Aldborough Hall* **LG1952**; *of St Margaretsbury* **LG1952**; *of Fanhams Hall* **LG1937**; *of Greenham Lodge* **LG1879**; AA; (*see also* Huddleston)

CROFTON, B **PB1970**; Bt *of Longford House* **PB1970**; Bt *of Mohill* **PB1970**; *formerly of Trobridge* **LG1965**; *formerly of Lissadorn and Lakefield* **LGI1958**

CROFTS, B **DEP**; Bt **EDB**; *of Sompting Abbots* **LG1894**; **IFR1976**

CROKE *of Studley* **LG1900**

CROKER *of West Molesey* **LG1858**; **IFR1976**; *of The Grange* **LGI1912**; **DFUSA**

CROMARTIE (*see* Mackenzie)

CROMARTY (*see* Mackenzie)

CROMBIE *of Thornton Castle* **LG1894**

CROMER (*see* Baring)

CROMIE, Bt **EDB**; (*see also* Crumie)

DE LA CHEROIS-CROMMELIN (*see* Stone)

CROMPTON, Bt **PB1848**; *of Little Lever* **LG1952**; *of Flower Lilies* **LG1937**; *formerly of Holcombe* **DFUSA**; (*see also* Crompton-Stansfield)

CROMWELL (Essex, E) **DEP**; (Ardglass, B) **DEP**, B **DEP**; **VF**; (*see also* Bush; and Bewicke-Copley)

CRONIN (*see* Cronin-Coltsmann)

CRONK *formerly of New Barns* **LG1969**

CROOK, B **PB1970**; Bt **EDB**; **DFUSA**; *of Woodlands Hall* **LG1952**

CROOKE *formerly of Derreen* **LGI1958**

PARRY-CROOKE *of Friston House* **LG1972**

CROOKS *formerly of Eccleston Park* **LG1952**

CROOKSHANK, V **PB1959**; *formerly of Drumhalry and Johnstounburn* **LG1969**; *of Saint John, NB, Canada* **LG1952Supp**

CROOME *of Bagendon* **LG1952**

CROPLEY, Bt **EDB**

CROPPER *of Ellergreen* **LG1965**; **FR**

CROSBIE (Glandore, E) **DEP**; Bt **PB1936**; **IFR**

HERRIES-CROSBIE *of Flowerburn* **LG1937**

CROSBY **DFUSA**; *formerly of Holme-on-Spalding Moor* **DFUSA**

CROSFIELD, Bt **PB1938**; *of Embley Park* **LG1937**

CROSKEY **DFUSA**

CROSLEY **AA**

CROSS, V **PB1970**; Bt *of Marchbankwood* **PB1959**; *formerly of Wyke Hall* **LG1972**; *of Red Scar* **LG1937**; **DFUSA**; *formerly of Charlinch* **DFUSA**; *formerly of Uphill* **DFUSA**

COOKE-CROSS *of Dartan* **LGI1912**

INNES-CROSS *of Dromantine* **LGI1912**

SHEPHERD-CROSS *of Hamels Park* **LG1914**

CROSSE, Bt **EDB**; *of Shaw Hill* **LG1952**; *of Broomfield* **LG1863**

CROSSFIELD *late Stanningfield* **LG1937**

CROSSLEY (Somerleyton, B) **PB1970**; Bt **PB1970**; *formerly of Esthwaite Mount* **LG1965**

CROSSMAN *of Beara Court* **LG1972**; *of Cheswick and Holy Island* **LG1972**

CROWE, Bt **EDB**; *formerly of Dromore House* **LGI1958**

CROWFOOT **FR**

CROWLEY (*see* Myers)

CROWTHER, B **PB1970**

CROXALL *of Shustoke* **LG1937**

CROZIER *of West Hill* **LG1952**; *formerly of Enniskillen* **DFUSA**; **FR**

CRUDDAS *of Haughton Castle* **LG1952**

CRUIKSHANK *of Langley Park* **LG1952**; *of Herongate* **LG1886**

CRUM (*see* Hamilton *of Lowood and Castlehill*)

CRUMIE, Bt **PB1841**

CRUMP *of Chorlton* **LG1921**

CRUTCHLEY *of Mappercombe Manor* **LG1972**

CRUWYS *of Cruwys Morchard House* **LG1972**

CUBITT (Ashcombe, B) **PB1970**; *formerly of Bacton* **LG1969**; *formerly of Eden Hall, Edenbridge* **LG1965**; *of Honing Hall* **LG1952**; *formerly of Catfield Hall* **LG1921**

RICCARDI-CUBITT (*see* Ashcombe)

CUDDON *formerly of Dunwich and Shadingfield* **LG1952**

REID-CUDDON **FR**

CUDMORE (*Australia*) **CG**

CUFF (Tyrawley, B) **DEP**

CUFFE (Desart, E) **PB1934**

WHEELER-CUFFE, Bt **PB1934**

CULBERTSON *formerly of Kintyre* **DFUSA**

CULLEN, Bt **EDB**; **IFR1976**; *of Corry* **LGI1904**; *formerly of Ederny* **DFUSA**; (*see also* Cokayne)

CULLEY *late of Coupland Castle* **LG1937**

LEATHER-CULLEY *of Fowberry Tower* **LG1906**

CULLIMORE *of Morton* **LG1969**
CULLOM *formerly of Molland* **DFUSA**
CULLUM, Bt **PB1855**
MILNER-GIBSON-CULLUM *of Hardwick House* **LG1921**
CULPEPER, Bt *of Preston Hall* **EDB**; Bt *of Wakehurst* **EDB**
CULVERWELL *formerly of Snapes Manor* **LG1969**
CUMBERLAND (*see* Clifford; Denmark; Guelph; and Rupert)
CUMBY (*see* Spurrier)
CUMMIN **DFUSA**
GORDON CUMMING, Bt **PB1970**
CUMMINGS **DFUSA**
CUMMINS **IFR1976**
CUMYN (Buchan, E) **DEP**
CUNARD, Bt **PB1970**
CUNINGHAME *of Corsehill*, Bt **PB1970**; *of Caprington* **LG1969**; *of Balgownie* **LG1937**; *of Craigends* **LG1937**; *of Duchrae late of Lainshaw* **LG1937**; *of Monkredding* **LG1833/7**; *of Ashinyards* (*see* Rollo-Bowman-Ballantine), *of Cul dcl and Thorntoun* (*see* Wrey); (*see also* Stewart-Meiklejohn)
FAIRLIE-CUNINGHAME, Bt **PB1970**
GUN CUNINGHAME **IFR1976**
CUNLIFFE, B **PB1970**; Bt **PB1970**; *late of Petton* **LG1937**
PICKERSGILL-CUNLIFFE (*see* Duberly)
CUNNINGHAM, Bt **PB1970**; (Cunningham of Hyndhope, V) **PB1963**; Bt **EDB**; *of Mannings Heath* **LG1952**; *formerly of Birr* **LG1937Supp**; *formerly of Linlithgow* **DFUSA**
MILLER-CUNNINGHAM *of Leithenhopes* **LG1937**
CUNNINGHAME, Bt **EDB**
STEWART-DICK-CUNYNGHAM, Bt **PB1940**
CUNYNGHAME, Bt **PB1970**; (Carrick, E) **DEP**; (Glencairn, E) **DEP**
CUPPAGE **IFR1976**
CURDIE (*Australia*) **CG**
CAPEL CURE *of Blake Hall* **LG1965**
CURELL *of Knockmark* **LGI1958**
CURLING *formerly of Chilton* **LG1965**; *of Gosmore* **LG1925**
CURLL, Bt **EDB**
CURME *formerly of Cerne Abbas* **DFUSA**
CURRE, Bt **PB1930**; *of Ibton Court* **LG1921**
CURRER *of Kildwick* **LG1843/9**; *of Clifton House* (*see* Roundell)
RICHARDSON CURRER **RFFK**

CURREY *of Windmill House* **LG1965**
CURRIE, Bt **PB1970**; Bt **PB1906**; *of Dingley Hall and Dunbeath Castle* (*formerly of Minley Manor*) **LG1952**; *of Witley* **LG1952**; *of Christleton late of Boughton Hall* **LG1937**; *late of Seafield Park* **LG1921**; *of Rushton House* **LG1898**; *of Sandown House* **LG1898**; *of Linthill* **LG1898**; *of Beechwood House* **LGI1958**; (*Canada*) **CG**; *of St Kilda* **CG**; (*see also* Currie-Blyth)
CURRY *of Bishop-Oak* **LG1894**
CURSON, Bt **EDB**
CURTEIS *of Windmill Hill* **LG1952**
CURTINS, Bt **EDB**
CURTIS, Bt **PB1970**; *of Penbryn Hall* **LG1969**; *of Barcombe House* **LG1952**; *formerly of Denbury Manor* **LG1952**; *of Mayfield House* **LG1952**; **DFUSA**; *formerly of Stratford-on-Avon* **DFUSA**; **PromFUSA**
CURTLER *of Bevere Hill* **LG1937**
CURTOIS *of Branston* **LG1886**
CURWEN, Bt **FDB**; (*see also* Chance)
CURZON (Howe, E) **PB1970**; (Scarsdale, V) **PB1970**; (Curzon of Kedleston, M) **PB1925**; *of Lockington* **LG1972**; *of Breedon* **LG1914**
ROPER-CURZON (Teynham, B) **PB1970**
CUSACK **IFR1976**; **AA**
CUSHENDUN (*see* McNeill)
CUSHING *formerly of Hingham* **DFUSA**
CUSHMAN **DFUSA**
CUSSANS *formerly of Amity Hall, Jamaica* **LG1969**
O'HEA-CUSSEN *of Dundesmond* **LGI1958**
CUST (Brownlow, B) **PB1970**; (Brownlow, E) **PB1921**; Bt **PB1931**
CUSTANCE *of Elton Hall* **LG1972**
CUSTIS (*see* Washington)
CUTBILL *of Roskitt Lodge* **LG1937**
CUTCLIFFE *of Witheridge* **LG1921**
DRAKE CUTCLIFFE *of Lee Manor* **LG1921**
CUTHBERT *formerly of Berthier* **LG1969**; *of Beaufront Castle* **LG1952**
CUTHBERTSON **FR**
CUTLER, Bt **EDB**; *formerly of Yorkshire* **LG1858**; *of Upton* **LG1858**; *formerly of Sprowston* **DFUSA**
CUTTS, B **DEP**; Bt **EDB**
CUYLER, Bt **PB1940**
D'ABERNON (*see* Vincent)
D'ABO *of West Wratting Park* **LG1965**
D'ABREU **LG1972**
DACRE, B **DEP**; (*see also* Hampden)

D'AELT, Bt **EDB**
HUGHES-D'AETH *formerly of Knowlton* **LG1965**
DAGWORTH, B **DEP**
DAINTRY *of North Road* **LG1937**
DAKEYNE *of Derbyshire* **LG1843/9**; **FR**
DAKIN, **DFUSA**
DALBY *of Castle Donington* **LG1969**
DALE *of Glanville's Wootton* **LG1900**; *of Ashborne* **LG1850/3**; **DFUSA**; **HI**
DALGETY *of Lockerley Hall* **LG1972**; CG
DALGLEISH *formerly of Westgrange* **LG1952**
OGILVY-DALGLEISH, Bt **PB1913**; *of Springfield formerly of Boyne* **LG1969**
DALHOUSIE (*see* Ramsay)
DALISON, Bt **EDB**; *of Hamptons* **LG1952**
BEST-DALISON (*formerly* Best) *of Park House* **LG1952**
DALLAM **DFUSA**
DALLAS *formerly of Forres* **DFUSA**; *formerly of St Martins* **DFUSA**; **PromFUSA**; (*see also* Dallas-Yorke)
DALLING, Bt **PB1864**; (*see also* Bulwer)
DALMAHOY, Bt **EDB**
DALRYMPLE (Stair, E) **PB1970**; Bt *of Newhailes* **PB1970**; Bt *of High Merk* **PB1866**; Bt *of Hailes* **EDB**
ELPHINSTONE-DALRYMPLE, Bt **PB1970**
FORBES-DALRYMPLE (*see* Sempill)
HAMILTON DALRYMPLE, Bt **PB1970**
DALSTON, Bt **EDB**
DALTON, B **PB1959**; *of The Hutts* **LG1969**; *formerly of Stanmore* **LG1952Supp**; *of Thurnham* **LG1937**; (*Australia*) **CG**; *of Shanks House, Co Somerset*
GRANT-DALTON *of Brodsworth Hall* **LG1972**
PORTMAN-DALTON (*see* Wade-Dalton)
WADE-DALTON *of Hauxwell* **LG1952**
DALWAY *of Carrickfergus* **LG1899**
DALY (Dunsandle and Clanconal, B) **PB1911**; (*co Galway: Castle Daly*) **IFR1976**; (*co Galway: Dunsandle*) **IFR1976**; *of Tullamore* **LGI1912**; **DFUSA**; *formerly of Cahiraiveen* **DFUSA**; (*Australia*) **CG**; (*Canada*) **CG**; (*see also* Blake)
DALYELL *of The Binns*, Bt **PB1970**; *late of Lingo and Ticknevin* **LG1937**; **AA**
DALZELL (Carnwath, E) **PB1940**
DALZELL (*now* CRAIGIE-HALKETT)

late of Glenae **LG1937**
DALZIEL (Dalziel of Kirkcaldy, B) **PB1935**; (Dalziel of Wooler, B) **PB1928**
DAME **DFUSA**
DAMER (Dorchester, E) **DEP**; (Milton, B) **DEP**
DAWSON-DAMER (Portarlington, E) **PB1970**
LONGWORTH-DAMES *of Greenhill* **LGI1912**
DAMPIER *of Highfield* **LG1952**; *of Hilfield St Nicholas* **LG1952**
DANCE *of Idlicote House* **LG1952**
DANCER, Bt **PB1933**
DANE **IFR1976**
DANESFORT (*see* Butcher)
DANFORTH *formerly of Framlingham* **DFUSA**
DANGAR *formerly of Frensham House* **LG1965**; *of Sydney and Camden* **CG**
DANIEL *of Stockland* **LG1952**; *of Cwmgelly* **LG1921**; *of Lough Ree* **LGI1904**; **DFUSA**; **PromFUSA**; (*see also* Truman)
DANIELL *formerly of Daresbury* **LG1965**; *of Kenbury* **LG1900**; *of Trelissick* **LG1850/3**; **IFR1976**; (*see also* Willis)
DANSEY *formerly of Butterley* **LG1952**
DANVERS, B **DEP**
BUTLER-DANVERS *of Swithland* **LG1843/9**
D'ANVERS, Bt *of Culworth* **EDB**; Bt *of Swithland* **EDB**
DARBISHIRE **FR**
DARBY *of Adcote and Sunnyside* **LG1921**; *of Brymbo* **LG1921**; *of Coalbrookdale* **LG1898**; **IFR 1976**; **HI**
DARCY, (Darcy, of Chiche, B) **DEP**; Bt **EDB**; (*Australia*) **CG**
DARCY DE KNAYTH (*see* Ingrams)
D'ARCY (Holderness, E) **DEP**; (D'Arcy, B) **DEP**; (D'Arcy, of D'Arcy, B) **DEP**; (D'Arcy, of Navan, B) **DEP**; *of Dry Sandford* **LG1972**; *of Quatford Wood House* **LG1972**; *of Inch* **LG1894**; (*co Galway*) **IFR1976**; (*co Westmeath*) **IFR1976**; *of Corbetstown* **LGI1912**; (*see also* Conyers)
HALL-DARE **IFR1976**
DARELL, Bt **PB1970**; **EDB**; *formerly of Trewoman* **LG1952**; *of Calehill* **LG1894**; *of Littlecott* **LG1833/7**; (*see also* Sneyd *of Coldrenick*)
DARESBURY (*see* Greenall)
DARLEY *of Aldby Park* **LG1952**; (*Australia*) **CG**

DARLEY (*formerly* BUTLER) *of Cantley Hall* **LG1952**
BESWICK-DARLEY *of Muston* **LG1898**
DARLING, B **PB1970; IFR1976; DFUSA; FR;** (*see also* Bagshawe)
STORMONTH-DARLING *of Lednathie* **LG1965**
DARLINGTON *of Little Meon* **LG1952;** *of The Hill* **LG1914; DFUSA; PromFUSA**
DARNALL *formerly of Birds Place* **DFUSA**
DARNELL, Bt **EDB**
DARNLEY (*see* Bligh)
DARNTON (Von Schunck, B) **FT1939**
DARROCH *of Gourock* **LG1965**
DARTMOUTH (*see* Legge)
DARTON **LG1972**
DARTREY (*see* Dawson)
DARWEN (*see* Davies)
DARWIN *formerly of Downe* **LG1965;** *of Creskeld Hall* **LG1898; FR;** (*see also* Kindersley)
DARYNGTON (*see* Pease)
DASENT *late of Tower Hill* **LG1937**
DASHWOOD, Bt *of Kirtlington Park* **PB1970;** Bt *of West Wycombe* **PB1970;** (*see also* Peyton)
DAUBENEY (Bridgewater, E) **DEP;** *formerly of South Petherton* **LG1969**
DAUBENY *of The Beacon* **LG1900;** (*see also* Daubeney)
DAUGLISH **FR**
D'AUNEY, B **DEP**
DAUNT **IFR1976**
DAUNTESEY *late of Agecroft* **LG1937**
D'AUVERGNE **VF**
DAVENPORT *of Foxley* **LG1952;** *of Hinton Manor* **LG1952; PromFSUA; CG;** *of Davenport* (*see* Leicester-Warren); *of Clipsham Hall and of Bramhall Hall* (*see* Davenport-Handley)
BROMLEY-DAVENPORT *of Capesthorne* **LG1965**
DAVENTRY (*see* FitzRoy)
DAVERS, Bt **EDB**
DAVEY, B **PB1907;** *of Wraxall Court* **LG1952**
DAVEY (now LEE) *of Botchyn* **LG1921**
DAVID, Bt **PB1963;** *of Blackaldorn* **LG1952;** *of Fairwater* **LG1952**
DAVIDGE *of Little Haughton* **LG1969**
DAVIDSON, V **PB1970;** (Northchurch, B) **PB1970;** (Davidson of Lambeth, B) **PB1930;** Bt **EDB;** *formerly of Inchmarlo* **LG1965;** *formerly of Cantray* **LG1952;** *of Ockley Manor formerly of*

Muirhouse **LG1952; IFR1976;** (1) & (2) **DFUSA;** (*see also* Vickers)
DAVIE, Bt **PB1846;** *formerly of Inverness* **DFUSA**
FERGUSON DAVIE, Bt **PB1970**
DAVIES, B **PB1970;** (Darwen, B) **PB1970;** (Ystwyth, B) **PB1935;** Bt **EDB;** *of Elmley* **LG1969;** *of Brookland Hall* **LG1952;** *of Craig Wen* **LG1952;** *of Pentre* **LG1952;** *of Plas Llangoedmore* **LG1952;** *of Sandhampton* **LG1952;** *of Plas Darland* **LG1937;** *of Ryton* **LG1937;** *of Upland* **LG1937;** *of Castle Green* **LG1921;** *late of Moor Court* **LG1921;** *of Scoveston* **LG1921;** *of Sharcombe Park* **LG1921;** *of Tanybwlch* **LG1914;** *of Cardigan Castle* **LG1898;** *of Bronhewlog* **LG1850/3;** *of Gwasanau* **LG1833/7;** *of Llivior* **LG1833/7;** *formerly of Tregaron* **DFUSA; PromFUSA;** (*Australia*) **CG;** (*see also* Davies-Evans)
KEVILL-DAVIES (*see* Lacon)
LLEWELYN-DAVIES, B **PB1970;** (Llewelyn-Davies of Hastoe, B) **PB1970**
PRICE-DAVIES *of Marrington Hall* **LG1952**
ST AUBREY DAVIES *of Bredon* **LG1952**
TWISTON DAVIES *of The Mynde* **LG1572**
WOOTTON-DAVIES *of Bronwylfa Hull* **LG1952**
DAVIS, Bt **PB1970;** *of Well Close* **LG1969;** *of Beechwood House* **LG1952;** *of Chilham Castle* **LG1937;** *of Bryn-Derwen* **LG1921;** *of Whitmead* **LG1900;** *of Swerford* **LG1894;** *of Cranbrook Park* **LG1879; PresFUSA;** (1) & (2) **DFUSA;** *formerly of Marden* **DFUSA;** *formerly of Milford Haven* **DFUSA;** *formerly of Tewkesbury* **DFUSA;** *formerly of Tredegar* **DFUSA; PromFUSA;** *of Redcastle* **CG;** (*see also* Davies-Evans)
BOWEN-DAVIS *of Maes-y-Crygie* **LG1843/9**
HART-DAVIS *of Nether Stowey* **LG1952**
LLOYD-DAVIS *formerly of Lhittington* **LG1969**
DAVISON (Broughshane, B) **PB1970;** *formerly of Carlton* **LG1972;** *of Thorngrove* **LG1972;** *of Froxmere Court* **LG1952;** (*see also* Davison-Bland)
SPENCER-DAVISON *formerly of Brand Hall* **LG1937**
DAVY, Bt **EDB;** *of Owthorpe* **LG1952;**

formerly of Rose Ash **LG1952**; *of Kilverstone* **LG1898**
DAVYS (Mountcashel, V) **DEP**
CAMPBELL-DAVYS *of Newadd-Fawr* **LG1937**
DAWE *of Ditcheat Manor House* **LG1937**
DAWES *of Mount Ephraim* **LG1965**; *of Bolton* **HI**
DAWKINS *of Over Norton* **LG1952**; **DFUSA**
DAWNAY (Downe, V) **PB1970**
DAWSON, Bt *of Appleton Roebuck* **PB1970**; Bt *of Edgwarebury* **PB1970**; (Dawson of Penn, V) **PB1940**; (Dartrey, E) **PB1933**; *of Langcliffe Hall* **LG1972**; *of Weston Hall* **LG1972**; *of Leaden Hall* **LG1969**; *of The White House, Hadstock* **LG1969**; *of Launde Abbey* **LG1965**; *of Ball Hill formerly of Fawley Manor* **LG1952**; *of La Hague Manor formerly of Orchill* **LG1952**; *formerly of Sherne Hill* **LG1937**; *of The Nash* **LG1914**; *of Groton House* **LG1894**; (*see also* Chichester-Clark)
CROSBIE-DAWSON (*see* Dawson *of Langcliffe*)
FINCH DAWSON (*see* Dawson *of Launde Abbey*)
MASSY-DAWSON *of Ballynacourte* **LGI1912**
WESTROPP-DAWSON (*see* Westropp)
DAY *formerly of Woodland* **LG1952**; **LGI1958**; *formerly of Ipswich* **DFUSA**; **PromFUSA**
WENTWORTH DAY *of Wicken* **LG1952**
DAYMAN (*now* TURNER) *of Manbury* **LG1906**
DAYRELL *formerly of Lillingstone Dayrell* **LG1972**
DAYRELL (*formerly* ROLLESTON) *of Watnall* **LG1952**
DAYTON *formerly of Ashford* **DFUSA**
DE ALDITHELEY (*see* Audley)
DEACON *of Longcross House* **LG1843/9**; **IFR1976**
DEAKIN *of Werrington Park* **LG1879**; *of Llanarth* **CG**
DEALTRY *of Lofthouse Hall* **LG1843/9**
DEAN *of Haughton Hall* **LG1969**; *of Little Easton Manor* **LG1952**; *of Bonshaw* **LGI1958**
DEANE (Muskerry, B) **PB1970**; *formerly of Eastcote* **LG1952**; *of Littleton House* **LG1952**; *of The Boyce Court* **LG1914**; *of Glendaragh* **LGI1912**; **AA**
DE ANYERS (*see* Willis)
DEARDEN *of Holmstead* **LG1921**; *of*

Rochdale Manor and Walcot **LG1906**
DEASE (*see* Bland (*co Leix*))
O'REILLY-DEASE *of Charleville* **LG1886**
DEASY **IFR1976**
DE AUVERQUERQUE (*see* Nassau)
DE BARY *of Weston Hall* **LG1898**
DE BATHE, Bt **PB1940**
DEBENHAM, Bt **PB1970**
DE BERTODANO (Moral, M) **FT1939**
DE BLAQUIERE, B **PB1920**
DEBNAM **DFUSA**
DE BROTHERTON (*see* Plantagenet)
DE BUNSEN, Bt **PB1932**
DE BURGH (Ulster, E) **DEP**; *of West Drayton* **LG1937**; **IFR1976**; (*see also* Hussey de Burgh)
BLAKE DE BURGH (*see* Blake)
HUSSEY DE BURGH **IFR1976**
DE BURGHO, Bt **PB1873**
DE BURGO (*see* Moreton)
DE BURY, Count **FT1956**
DE BUSH, B **FT1939**
DE BUTTS *of Coolnakilly House* **LGI1958**; (*see also* Burdon)
DE CARTERET *of Bullswater Lodge* **LG1952**; **AA**
DE CASTELLA (*Australia*) **CG**
DE CAZENOVE (*see* Cazenove)
DE CHAIR **LG1965**
DECIE (*see* Deasy)
PRESCOTT-DECIE *of Bockleton Court* **LG1900**
DECIES (*see* de la Poer Beresford)
DECKER, Bt **EDB**
DE CLIFFORD (*see* Russell)
DE CONWAY **AA**
DE COSTOBADIE *of Gainsborough* **LG1952**
DE COURCY (Kingsale, B) **PB1970**; (Ulster, E) **DEP**
CHAMPION DE CRESPIGNY, Bt **PB1949**; **LG1969**
DE DREUX (Richmond, E) **DEP**
DE DUNSTANVILLE (*see* Basset)
DEEDES *formerly of Saltwood Castle* **LG1972**
DEELEY, Bt **PB1959**; *formerly of Halesowen* **LG1972**
DEERING (1) & (2) **DFUSA**
D'EIVILL, B **DEP**
DE FALBE *of Thundridge House* **LG1972**
DE FERRIERES **AA**
DE FERRY *of Kilymaenllwyd* **LG1898**
DE FOIX (Kendal, E) **DEP**
DE FONBLANQUE *formerly of Guildford* **LG1972**
DE FOREST, B **FT1917**; **DFUSA**

DE FREYNE (*see* French)
DE GREY (Walsingham, B) **PB1970**
DE HAMEL (*formerly Blane formerly of Foliejon Park*) **LG1952**
DE HAVILLAND *formerly of Havilland Hall* **LG1965**
DEHEUBARTH (*Kings and Princes of*) **RL**
DE HOGHTON, Bt **PB1970**
DE HOCHEPIED, B **FT1939**
DE HORNE *of Stanway Hall* **LG1843/9**
DE HORSEY **FR**
DE JERSEY (*see* de Jersey-Vavassour)
DE KENTON **LG1833/7**
DE KUSEL, B **FT1939**
DE LA BERE, Bt **PB1972**; *late of Porturet House* **LG1937**
BAGHOT-DE LA BERE *of The Hayes* **LG1937**
DE LABILLIÈRE **CG**
DE LA CHEROIS (*see* Stone)
DE LA COUR *of Clyda House* **LGI1958**
DELAFIELD *of Fieldston* **LG1843/9**; **PromFUSA**
DELAMER **IFR1976**
DELAMERE (*see* Cholmondeley)
DELAP *of Ray* **LGI1958**; *of Monellan* **LGI1912**
DE LA PASTURE *of Llandogo Priory* **LG1906**; M **FT1939**
DE LA POER **IFR1976**
DE LA POLE **VF**
DE LA RUE, Bt **PB1970**
DE LAS CASAS *of Washfield* **LG1952**
FAUNCE-DELAUNE *of Sharsted* **LG1937**
DE LAUTOUR (*see* Parker *of Houghton*)
DELAVAL, B **DEP**; Bt *of Ford* **EDB**; Bt *of Seaton* **EDB**
DE LA WARDE (*see* Warde)
DE LA WARR (*see* Sackville)
DE LISLE **LG1965**
DE L'ISLE (*see* L'Isle; and Sidney)
DELLA CATENA, Count **TNBE1956**; (*see also* Hornyold-Strickland)
DELLA GRUA, B **TNRE1956**
DELLA TAFLIA, M **TNBE1956**
DELMAINE (*see* Cooper)
DELME (*see* Delmé-Radcliffe)
DELMEGE **IFR1976**
DE LONGUEÜIL, B **TNBE1956**
DELORAINE (*see* Scott)
DE LOSADA, D **FT1939**
DELVES, Bt **EDB**
DE MANBEY *of Barrow Hill* **LG1952**
DE MAULEY (*see* Ponsonby)
DE MEDENE *of Witnesham Hall and*

Great Bealings **LG1863**
DEMETRIADI *of The Gote* **LG1937**
EVELEIGH DE MOLEYNS (Ventry, B) **PB1970**
DE MONTALT (*see* Maude)
DE MONTFORT **IFR1976**
DE MONTMORENCY, Bt **PB1970**; (Frankfort de Montmorency, B) **PB1917**; (Mountmorres, V) **PB1949**; **IFR1976**
DE MONTMORENCY (*formerly MICHEL*) *of Dewlish* **LG1952**
HALL-DEMPSTER *of Skibo Castle* **LG1875**; (*see also* Napier)
HAWKINS-DEMPSTER (*see* Hawkins)
DE MUSCHAMP *of Brotherlee* **LG1952**
DENBIGH AND DESMOND (*see* Feilding)
DENBY (*formerly DANBY*) *sometime of Farnley* **DFUSA**
DENDY *of Dorking* **HI**
DE NEUFVILLE, Bt **EDB**
D'ENGELBRONNER *of Redleaf* **LG1952**
DENHAM *of The Mill House* **LG1952**; *of Northbrook* **LG1937Supp**; (*see also* Bowyer)
STEUART-DENHAM (*see* Steuart)
DENIS, Bt **EDB**
DENISON (Londesborough, B) **PB1970**; (Londesborough, E) **PB1937**; (Ossington, V) **DEP**; *of Ossington* **LG1972**; **CG**
DENMAN, B **PB1970**; Bt **PB1970**
DENMARK, Prince of (Cumberland, D) **DEP**; (*Royal House of*) **RL**
DENNE (*see* Phythian-Adams)
DENNEHY *of Ballymanus* **LGI1958**; *of Brook Lodge* **LGI1912**
DENNEY **DFUSA**
DENNING, B **PB1970**
DENNIS (Tracton, B) **DEP**; **IFR1976**; **DFUSA**; **FR**; (*see also* Swifte)
DENNISTOUN *of Dennistoun* **LG1937**; *of Kelvin Grove* **LG1833/7**; **FR**; (*Canada*) **CG**
DENNY, Bt *of Castle Moyle* **PB1970**; Bt *of Dumbarton* **PB1970**; (Norwich, E) **DEP**; Bt **EDB**; *formerly of Combs* **LG1969**; *of Gurney's Manor* **LG1965**; *of Moorstown and Drumloane* **LGI1912**; **DFUSA**
DENNYS *of Heaslands* **LG1965**
DENT *of Flass* **LG1969**; *of Ribston Hall* **LG1969**; (*see also* Dent-Brocklehurst)
EDWARDS-DENT *of Hallaton Manor* **LG1937**
HEDLEY-DENT *of Shortflatt Tower* **LG1972**

DENTON, Bt **EDB**
DENYS, Bt **PB1959**
DE PARAVICINI **LG1952Supp**
DE PURTON *of Fort George* **LG1952**; *of Bertozerie* **LG1952**; *of Pierre Percée* **LG1952**
DE RAEDT, Bt **EDB**
DERAMORE (*see* de Yarburgh-Bateson)
DE RAMSEY (*see* Fellowes)
DERBY (*see* Ferrers; and Stanley)
DEREHAM, Bt **EDB**
DE REUTER, B **FT1956**
DERHAM *late of Henleaze Park* **LG1937**
DERING, Bt **PB1970**; (*see also* Blake *of Barham Court*)
DE RINZY *of Clobemon Hall* **LG1843/9**
DE RIVERS (*see* Ripariis)
DE ROBECK, Bt **PB1928**; **IFR1976**
DE ROEMAR *of Tilford* **LG1952**
DE ROS (*see* Maxwell)
DE RUTZEN, B **FT1939**
DERWENT (*see* Vanden-Bempde-Johnstone)
DERWENTWATER (*see* Radcliffe)
DE RYVERS *of Ongar Castle* **LG1833/7**
DE SALES LA TERRIÈRE *of Dunalastair* **LG1969**
DE SALIS **IFR1976**
DESART (*see* Cuffe)
DE SAUMAREZ (*see* Saumarez)
DE SAUSMAREZ, Bt **PB1940**
DESBOROUGH (*see* Grenfell)
DES CHAMPS *of Ealing* **LG1843/9**
DES GRAZ *of Castle Close* **LG1952**
DE SMIDT (*S Africa*) **CG**
DESMOND (*see* FitzGerald)
DESPARD *formerly of Larch Hill* **DFUSA**
DESPENCER (Gloucester, E) **DEP**; (Winchester, E) **DEP**
DE SPON *formerly of Landon House* **LG1969**
DE STACPOOLE **IFR1976**
DES VOEUX, Bt **PB1940**
DE TABLEY (*see* Leicester)
DE TEISSIER, B **FT1939**
DE TISSIER *of Woodcote Park* **LG1863**
DE TRAFFORD, Bt **PB1970**
DE VALERA **IFR1976**
DE VALLADO, M **FT1939**
DEVAS *of Hunton Court* **LG1972**
DEVENISH *formerly of Mount Pleasant* **LGI1958**
DEVER *of St John* **CG**
DE VERE, Bt **PB1904**; *of Curragh Chase* **LGI1912**; (*see also* Inchiquin; and St Albans)

DEVERELL *of Bossington* **LG1937**
DEVEREUX (Hereford, V) **PB1970**; (Essex, E) **DEP**; B **DEP**; *of Ballyrankin* **LGI1912**; *formerly of Kilrush* **DFUSA**; (*see also* Ferrers)
D'EVEREUX (Salisbury, E) **DEP**
DE VESCI (*see* Vesey)
DE VIC, Bt **EDB**
DE VILLIERS, B **PB1970**
DE VISME *of Devon and Gloucester* **LG1833/7**
DE VUMES, Count **FT1939**
DENIS DE VITRE (*see* Gaisford)
DEVITT, Bt **PB1970**; Bt *of Pangbourne* **PB1940**; *of Longspring Wood* **LG1937**
DEVLIN, B **PB1970**
DEVON (*see* Blount; Courtenay; and Stafford)
DEVONPORT (*see* Kearley)
DEVONSHIRE (*see* Cavendish)
DEWAR (Forteviot, B) **PB1970**; B **PB1930**; *formerly of Craigniven and King's Park* **LG1969**; *formerly of Doles* **LG1969**; *of Vogrie* **LG1921**; **FR**
BEAUCLERK-DEWAR (*see* Dewar *formerly of Craigniven and King's Park*)
DEWART *formerly of the Isle of Mull* **DFUSA**; *formerly of Stradone* **DFUSA**
D'EWES, Bt **EDB**; (*see also* Granville)
DEWEY, Bt **PB1970**; *formerly of Sandwich* **DFUSA**
DEWHURST *of Aireville* **LG1894**
DE WINDT (*see* Adams)
DE WINTON *formerly of Graftonbury* **LG1965**; *formerly of Hatherley* **LG1969**; *of Maesllwch Castle* **LG1965**; *of Maesderwen* **LG1965**
DE WOLF **PromFUSA**
DE WOLFE (*see* Harding)
DE WORMS (Pirbright, B) **PB1903**; B **FT1917**
DEWRANCE *of Wretham Hall* **LG1937**
D'EYNCOURT, B **DEP**
DEXTER (*see* Kemmis)
TENNYSON-D'EYNCOURT, Bt **PB1970**; *formerly of Bayons Manor* **LG1952**
DE ZULUETA **LG1965**
DIAR-IL-BNIET AND BUKANA, B **TNBE1956**
GERRARD-DICCONSON *of Wrightington* **LG1914**
DICEY *of Claybrook Hall* **LG1875**
DICK *formerly of Edinburgh* **DFUSA**; (*see also* Hume)
DICKENSON *late of Synston Court* **LG1921**

TROTMAN-DICKENSON *formerly of Bishops Court* **LG1952**
DICKERSON **DFUSA**
DICKEY *of Amherst* **CG**
DICKIE *formerly of Clonaleenan* **LG1958**
DICKIN *of Loppington* **LG1937**; **HI**
DICKINS *late of Cherington* **LG1937**
SCRASE-DICKINS *of Coolhurst* **LG1972**
DICKINSON, B **PB1970**; *of Arscott* **LG1952**; *of Glanhonddu* **LG1952**; *of Kingweston* **LG1952**; *of Stocksfield* **LG1952**; *of Roose* **LG1937**; *of Bambrough* **LG1921**; *of The Elms* **LG1900**; *of Farley Hill* **LG1858**; *formerly of Brampton* **DFUSA**; **FR**
RASTALL-DICKINSON **FR**
DICKSON, (Islington, B) **PB1936**; Bt **EDB**; *of Aldie* **LG1952**; *of Blackbeck* **LG1952**; *of Corstorphine formerly of Glassingall* **LG1952**; *of Monybuie* **LG1952**; *of Abbots Reading* **LG1937**; *of Stow* **LG1921**; *of Chatto* **LG1906**; *of Woodville* **LGI1912**; *formerly of Whitslaid* **DFUSA**; **FR**; *of Arnside* **CG**; (*see also* Maunsell)
WILSON-DICKSON *of Hartree* **LG1921**
DIGBY, B **PB1970**; E **PB1856**; (Bristol, E) **DEP**; (Offalcy, B) **DEP**; *of Landenstown* **LG1843/9**; *of Osbertstown* **LG1858**; *of Dry Stoke* **LG1833/7**; *of Luffenham and Red Hall* **LG1833/7**
WINGFIELD-DIGBY *of Sherborne Castle and Coleshill* **LG1965**
DIGGES *formerly of Chilham Castle* **DFUSA**; **PromFUSA**; (*see also* La Touche)
DIGGS, Bt **EDB**
DILHORNE (*see* Manningham-Buller)
DILKE, Bt **PB1970**; (*see also* Trafford of Wroxham)
FETHERSTON-DILKE *of Maxstoke Castle* **LG1952**
DILL **IFR1976**
DILLINGTON, Bt **EDB**
DILLON, V **PB1970**; Bt **PB1970**; (Clonbrock, B) **PB1926**; (Roscommon, E) **DEP**; *of The Hermitage* **LG1937**; **IFR1976**; *formerly of Listowel* **DFUSA**; (*see also* Dillon-Trenchard)
LEE-DILLON (*see* FitzGibbon)
DILLWYN *of Hendrefoilan* **LG1886**
DIMAN **DFUSA**
DIMOCK *formerly of Barnstaple* **DFUSA**
DIMSDALE, Bt **PB1970**; B **FT1956**
DINAN, B **DEP**
DINGWALL (*see* Keith)
DINORBEN (*see* Hughes)

DINSDALE *of Newsham Park* **LG1850/3**
DIPLOCK, B **PB1970**
DIRLETOWN (*see* Maxwell)
PASLEY-DIRON *of Mount Annan* **LG1921**
DISNEY *formerly of The Hyde* **LG1969**; **DFUSA**; (*see also* Cobham)
DISRAELI (Beaconsfield, E) **DEP**; *of Hughenden* **LG1952**
DISTLER **DFUSA**
DITMAS *of Countess Weir* **LG1965**
DIX **DFUSA**; (*see also* Dix Hamilton)
DIXIE, Bt **PB1970**
DIXON (Glentoran, B) **PB1970**; Bt *of Astle* **PB1970**; Bt *of Warford* **PB1920**; *of Kenwick Hall* **LG1952**; *of Rheda* **LG1937**; *of Cherkley Court* **LG1921**; *of Inveran House* **LG1898**; *of Gledhow* **LG1843/9**; *of Unthank* **1843/9**; *of The Knells* **LG1843/9**; *formerly of Camwhitton* **DFUSA**; **FR**; *of Eyrewell Park* **CG**; (*NSW, Australia*) **CG**
DIXON *of Holton-le-Moor* (*formerly* GIBBONS *of Boddington Manor*) **LG1952**
DIXWELL, Bt *of Brome* **EDB**; Bt *of Coton Hall* **EDB**; Bt *of Tirlingham* **EDB**
DOANE **DFUSA**
DOBBIN **IFR1976**
DOBBS **IFR1976**
DOBEDE *of Exning House* **LG1886**
DOBLE *of The Old Rectory, Ashbrittle* **LG1972**
DOBRÉE *of The Priory* **LG1972**
DOBSON *of Whitestock Hall* **LG1952**; *of Hobart and Melbourne* **CG**
DOBYNS *of Evesbatch* **1833/7**
DOCKER *late of The Gables* **LG1937**; **CG**
DOCKWRA, B **DEP**
DOD *of Cloverley* **VSA**; (*see also* Bellyse Baker)
WOLLEY DOD *of Edge* **LG1972**
DODD *of Godington* **LG1914**
DODDS, Bt **PB1970**; *of Sydney* **CG**
DODGE **PromFUSA**
DODINGTON (Melcombe, B) **DEP**; **VF**
MARRIOTT-DODINGTON *of Horsington* **LG1972**
DODSON (Monk Bretton, B) **PB1970**; *of Conyboro'* **LG1879**; **DFUSA**
SMITH-DODSWORTH, Bt **PB1970**
DODWELL *of Glenmore* **LG1875**; (*see also* Crichton)

DOHERTY *of Oaklands* **LGI1912**; **DFUSA**

DOLBEN, Bt **EDB**; *of Finedon Hall* **LG1875**

D'OLIER *of Wingfield* **LG1937Supp**

DOLLING *of Magheralin* **LGI1912**

DOLMAGE *(see* Delmege)

DOLPHIN *of Turoe* **LGI1912**

DOMVILE **IFR1976**

DOMVILLE, Bt **PB1970**; Bt *of Templeogue* **PB1935**; *of Thornhill, co Wicklow* **AA**

POË-DOMVILLE *(see* Poë)

DONALDSON (Donaldson of Kingsbridge, B) **PB1970**; *formerly of Hatton Hall* **LG1952**; **DFUSA**; *(Australia)* **CG**; *of Cheswick (see* Selby); *(see also* Donaldson-Hudson)

DONEGALL *(see* Chichester)

DONELAN *of Sylanmore* **LGI1912**; *of Killagh* **LGI1912**

DONERAILE *(see* St Leger)

DONGAN *(see* Dungan)

DONINGTON *(see* Abney-Hastings)

DONN **LG1969**

DONNELLY *of Auburn and Derrynoose* **LG1925**

DONNERE, Bt **PB1934**; *of Hurstbourne Park* **LG1952**

DONNITHORNE *of Colne Lodge* **LG1921**

DONOUGHMORE *(see* Hely-Hutchinson)

DONOVAN, B **PB1970**; *of Framfield Place* **LG1886**; *of Ballymore* **LGI1912**; *of Seafield* **LGI1912**; *formerly of Castle Donovan* **DFUSA**

DOOLITTLE *formerly of Bedford* **DFUSA**; *(see also* Adams *(Pres))*

DORCHESTER *(see* Carleton; Damer; and Sidley)

DORINGTON, Bt **PB1911**; *of Lypiatt Park* **LG1882**

DORMAN, Bt **PB1970**; **IFR1976**

DORMER, B **PB1970**; (Carnarvon, E) **DEP**; Bt **EDB**; *of Bowdown House* **LG1937**

COTTRELL-DORMER *of Rousham* **LG1972**

UPTON-COTTRELL-DORMER *(see* Upton *formerly of Ingmire Hall*; and Cottrell-Dormer)

DORSET *(see* Beaufort; Sackville; and Seez)

DOUBLEDAY **DFUSA**

DOUCE *of West Malling* **LG1858**

RONEY-DOUGAL *of Ratho* **LG1952**; **FR**

MAITLAND-DOUGALL *late of Scotscraig* **LG1921**

DOUGHTY **DFUSA**; *(see also* Doughty-Wylie)

DOUGLAS (Queensberry, M) **PB1970**; (Morton, E) **PB1970**; (Douglas of Barloch, B) **PB1970**; (Douglas of Kirtleside, B) **PB1970**; Bt *of Glenbervie* **PB1970**; Bt *of Springwood* **PB1970**; (Kelhead, B) **PB1894**; (Solway, B) **PB1837**; D **DEP**; (Dover, D) **DEP**; (Atholl, E) **DEP**; E **DEP**; (Dumbarton, E) **DEP**; (Forfar, E) **DEP**; (Ormond, E) **DEP**; (Belhaven, V) **DEP**; (Mordingtoun, V) **DEP**; (Carlyle, B) **DEP**; (Douglas, of Ambresbury, B) **DEP**; (Douglas, of Douglas Castle, B) **DEP**; (Glenervie, B) **DEP**; Bt **EDB**; Bt *of Glenbervie* **EDB**; *formerly of Salwarpe* **LG1972**; *of Hemingford Abbots* **LG1952**; *of Mains* **LG1952**; *of Tilquhillie* **LG1952**; *of Chardstock* **LG1937**; *of Bonjedward and Tinpindean* **LG1925**; *of Dervock* **LG1858**; *of Mountain Lodge* **LG1858**; *of Gyrn and Pendleton* **LG1833/7**; **DFUSA**

DOUGLAS *(now* PYE) *of Rosehall* **LG1833/7**

AKERS-DOUGLAS (Chilston, V) **PB1970**

MACMILLAN DOUGLAS *of Brigton* **LG1972**

PALMER-DOUGLAS *(formerly* MALCOLM) *of Burnfoot* **LG1952**

ROBINSON-DOUGLAS *of Orchardton* **LG1937**

DOUGLASS (Douglass of Cleveland, B) **PB1970**; **FR**

BLACKER-DOUGLASS *of Grace Hall* **LGI1912**

DOVER *(see* Carey; Douglas; and Agar-Ellis)

DOVERCOURT *(see* Holmes)

DOVERDALE *(see* Partington)

DOWDALL *of Ballyragget Grange* **LG1937** Supp; *of Ireland* **LG1858**; *formerly of Mounttown* **LGI1912**

DOWDESWELL *of Pull Court* **LG1937**

BERENS-DOWDESWELL *(see* Berens)

DOWDING, B **PB1970**

DOWELL *formerly of Bitteswell* **LG1952**; *of Ford* **LG1937**

GANDAR-DOWER *formerly of Clifton House* **LG1952**

DOWLING (*Australia*) **CG**; *of Luie* **CG**; *of Sydney* **CG**

DOWNE (*see* Dawnay; and Pope)

DOWNES *of Aspley Guise* **LG1937**; (*see also* Burgh)

DOWNHAM (*see* Fisher)

MACALPINE-DOWNIE *of Appin* **LG1972**; (*see also* Kavanagh)

DOWNING, Bt **EDB**

DOWNSHIRE (*see* HILL)

DOWNTON (*see* Duncombe)

DOXFORD *of Newby Wiske* **LG1952**

DOYLE, Bt **PB1970**; Bt **EDB**

CONAN DOYLE **LG1952Supp**

D'OYLEY, Bt **EDB**

D'OYLY, Bt **PB1970**; Bt **EDB**

DOYNE **IFR1976**

POLHILL-DRABBLE *formerly of Sundridge* **LG1952**

DRAFFEN **AA**; **VSA**

DRAKE, Bt *of Ashe* **EDB**; Bt *of Prospect* **EDB**; Bt *of Shardeloes* **EDB**; *of Inshriach* **LG1965**; *formerly of West Riddens* **LG1952**; *formerly of Ash* **LG1937**; *of Barnstaple* **LG1898**; *of Stokestown* **LGI1958**; **DFUSA**; **Prom FUSA**

TYRWHITT-DRAKE *formerly of Shardeloes* **LG1965**

DRAPER, Bt **EDB**; *formerly of Heptonstall* **DFUSA**; **PromFUSA**

PLUNKETT-ERNLE-ERLE-DRAX *of Charborough* **LG1952**

SAWBRIDGE-ERLE-DRAX *of Bilting House and formerly of Olantigh* **LG1972**

DRAYSON *formerly of Kilnsey* **LG1972**

DRAYTON *formerly of Atherstone* **DFUSA**

DREW *formerly of Bradninch* **LG1952**; *of Wadhurst Hall* **LG1906**; *of Drewscourt* **LGI1912**; *of Mocollop* **LGI1912**; *of Strand House, Youghal* **AA**; (*see also* Daly)

DREWE *of Castle Drogo* **LG1969**; *of Grange* **LG1886**

DREWETT (*now* CHAYTON) *of Jarrow Hall and Iridge* **LG1921**

DREYER **LG1969**

DRING *of Little Massingham* **LG1937**; **IFR1976**

DRINKER *formerly of Pevensey* **DFUSA**

DRINKWATER *of Kirby* **LG1952**

DROGHEDA (*see* Moore)

DROUGHT *formerly of Whigsborough* **LGI1958**; *of Glencarrig* **LGJ1912**: *of Lettybrook* **LGI1912**

DRUGHORN, Bt **PB1940**

DRUMALBYN (*see* Macpherson)

DRUMMOND (Perth, E) **PB1970**; (Strange, B) **PB1970**; (Melfort, E) **PB1902**; (Melfort, D) **DEP**; (Perth, B) **DEP**; Bt *of Lasswade* **PB1924**; *of Megginch Castle* **LG1952**; *of Cadland* **LG1937**; *of Sissinghurst Place* **LG1937**; (*see also* Evans *of Lovegrove*)

DEANE-DRUMMOND *formerly of The Boyce Court and Dymock Grange* **LG1952**

HOME DRUMMOND (*see* Stirling Home Drummond Moray)

WILLIAMS-DRUMMOND, Bt **PB1970**

DRURY, Bt *of Overstone* **EDB**; Bt *of Riddlesworth* **EDB**; *formerly of North Huish* **LG1969**; (*Canada*) **CG**

DRU DRURY **LG1952**

DRYDEN, Bt **PB1970**; Bt **EDB**

DRYSDALE *of Pitlethie House* **LG1937**

DOCKAR-DRYSDALE *of Wick Hall* **LG1952**

DUBERLY *of Gaynes Hall and Staughton Manor* **LG1972**

DU BOULAY (*see* Houssemayne du Boulay)

DU BUISSON *of Saints Hill House* **LG1952**; *of Glynhir* **LG1906**

DU CANE *of East Hoe Manor, formerly of Braxted* **LG1965**

DUCIE, Bt **EDB**; (*see also* Moreton)

DUCK, Bt **EDB**

DUCKETT, Bt **PB1902**; **LG1952Supp**

EUSTACE-DUCKETT **IFR1976**

DUCKINFIELD, Bt **PB1858**

DUCKWORTH, Bt **PB1970**; *of Dalingridge Place and Pityoulish* **LG1972**; *of Orchardleigh* **LG1972**

DU CROS, Bt **PB1970**

DUDGEON *of Cargen* **LG1952**; *of Burton Hall* **LGI1958**

DUDLEY (Dudley, D) **DEP**; (Northumberland, D) **DEP**; (Leicester, E) **DEP**; (Warwick, E) **DEP**; Bt *of Clapton* **EDB**; Bt *of Kilscoran House* **EDB**; *of Stradishall Manor* **LG1952**; **DFUSA**; (*see also* Smith; Somerie; Sutton; and Ward)

DUER **DFUSA**

DUFF, Bt **PB1970** (Fife, B) **DEP**; Bt *of Hatton* **PB1949**; *of Meldrum and Hatton* **LG1969**; *of Combe, Bradford Abbas* **LG1937**; *of Woodcott House* **LG1843/49**; (*see also* Carnegie; and Darwin)

GORDON-DUFF *of Park and Drummuir*
LG1965
GRANT DUFF *formerly of Eden* **LG1952**
SCOTT-DUFF *(formerly* DUFF) *formerly*
of Fetteresso **LG1952**
WHARTON-DUFF *of Orton* **LG1952**
DUFFERIN AND AVA *(see* Hamilton-
Temple-Blackwood)
DUFFIELD *formerly of Marcham Park*
LG1952; *of Coverdale, co York* **AA**;
(see also Crutchley)
DAWSON-DUFFIELD **AA**
DUFFUS *of Dalclaverhouse* **LG1972**;
(see also Sutherland)
DUFFY *(Australia)* **CG**
GAVAN DUFFY **IFR1976**
DUGAN (Dugan of Victoria, B) **PB1949**;
formerly of Coleraine **DFUSA**
DUGDALE (Crathorne, B) **PB1970**; Bt
of Merevale **PB1970**; *of Wroxall Abbey*
LG1965; *of Crowthorne Hall* **LG1937**;
of Dutton Manor **LG1937**; *of Gilmonby*
Hall **LG1937**; *of Merevale* **LG1937**; **FR**
DUGGAN *(see* Cronin-Coltsmann)
DUKE (Merrivale, B) **PR1970**; Bt *of*
London **PB1935**; Bt *of Benhall* **EDB**;
of Lake House **LG1921**; *of Newpark*
LGI1912
DUKES (Dukeston, B) **PB1947**
DUKESTON *(see* Dukes)
DULANY **DFUSA**
DULVERTON *(see* Wills)
DUMARESQ *of Mount Ireh* **CG**
DUMBARTON *(see* Douglas)
DUMBLETON **FR**
DUNALLEY *(see* Prittie)
DUNBAR, Bt *of Durn* **PB1970**; Bt *of*
Hempriggs **PB1970**; Bt *of Mochrum*
PB1970; Bt *of Northfield* **PB1970**; Bt
of Boath **PB1937**; (Dunbar and March,
E) **DEP**; Bt **EDB**; *(see also* Constable;
Hume; and Pack-Beresford)
BRANDER-DUNBAR *of Pitgaveny*
LG1952
HOPE-DUNBAR, Bt **PB1970**
NUGENT-DUNBAR *of Machermore*
LG1937
DUNBOYNE *(see* Butler)
DUNCAN, Bt **PB1970**; Bt *of Horsforth*
Hall **PB1963**; Bt *of Maryle Bone* **EDB**;
late of Knossington Grange **LG1921**;
of Darnside **LG1875**; **DFUSA**;
PromFUSA; **CG**
DUNCAN *(formerly* TOWNSHEND) *of*
Wincham **LG1952**
GOMME-DUNCAN *of Dunbarney*
LG1952

HALDANE-DUNCAN (Camperdown, E)
PB1933; *(see also* Chinnery-Haldane)
DUNCOMBE (Feversham, B) **PB1970**;
(Feversham, E) **PB1963**; Bt *of Wood*
Hall **PB1933**; (Downton, B) **DEP**; *of*
Great Brickhill **LG1850/3**
PAUNCEFORT DUNCOMBE, Bt
PB1970
PIERCE-DUNCOMBE *of Winthorpe*
Hall **LG1914**
DUNCUMB, Bt **EDB**
DUNDAS (Zetland, M) **PB1970**; (Mel-
ville, V) **PB1970**; Bt *of Arniston*
PB1970; Bt *of Beechwood* **PB1970**; Bt
of Richmond **PB1868**; (Amesbury, B)
DEP; *of Dundas* **LG1972**; *of Arniston*
LG1898; *of Fingask and Carron Hall*
LG1886; *of Barton Court* **LG1879**; *of*
Duddingstoun **LG1858**; *of Blair*
Castle **LG1858**; *of Clobemon Hall*
LGI1912; **FR**
DUNDEE *(see* Graham; Scrimgeour;
and Scrymgeour-Wedderburn)
DUNDONALD *(see* Cochrane)
DUNEDIN *(see* Murray)
DUNFERMLINE *(see* Abercromby)
DUNGAN (Limerick, E) **DEP**
DUNGANNON *(see* Trevor)
DUNHAM **DFUSA**
DUNKELD *(see* Galloway)
DUNLAP **DFUSA**; *formerly of Campbell-*
town **DFUSA**
DUNLEATH *(see* Mulholland)
DUNLOP, Bt **PB1970**; Bt *of Dunlop*
PB1853; *formerly of Arthurlee* **LG1952**;
of Doonside **LG1952**; *formerly of*
Lockerbie House **LG1952**; *(see also*
Delap; and Hildyard)
BUCHANAN DUNLOP *of Drumhead*
LG1969
MURRAY-DUNLOP *of Corsock* **LG1937**
DUNMORE *(see* Murray)
DUNN, Bt *Bathurst* **PB1970**; Bt *of*
Clitheroe **PB1970**; Bt **PB1912**; *formerly*
of Titcomb Manor and Wallingtons
LG1969; *of Ashford* **LG1952**; *of*
Mariners **LG1952**; *of Tudor Hall*
LGI1958; **DFUSA**; *(Australia)* **CG**;
(see also Bower)
DUNNE *of Gatley Park* **LG1965**;
formerly of Kilcavan **LGI1958**;
of Brittas **LGI1912**; *late of Kilcoony*
LGI1912
DUNNING, Bt **PB1970**; (Ashburton, B)
DEP
DUNRAVEN AND MOUNTEARL
(see Wyndham-Quin)

DUNROSSIL (see Morrison)
DUNSANDLE (see Daly)
DUNSANY (see Plunkett)
DUNSCOMBE of Mount Desert LGI1912
DUNSTAN of East Burnham End LG1952
DUNSTANVILL (Cornwall, E) DEP
DUNSTERVILLE formerly of Halse LG1952
DUNTZE, Bt PB1970
DUNVILLE of Redburn LGI1912
DU PARCQ, B PB1949
DUPPA de UPHAUGH of Hollingbourne LG1952
DU PRE of Wilton Park LG1952
DUPREE, Bt PB1970
DURAND, Bt PB1970
DURANT of Pelham Place LG1952; (see also Kirk; and Parke)
DURAS (Feversham, E) DEP
DURDIN (see Durdin-Robertson)
DURHAM (Lambton, E) PB1970
CUNINGHAME DURHAM of Cromer Grange LG1952
DURRANT, Bt PB1970
DURTNELL of Sevenoaks LG1969
DURY formerly of Ronsall Hall LG1952
DU SAUTOY formerly of Warren Hill LG1952
DUTRY, Bt EDB
DUTTON (Sherborne, B) PB1970; Bt EDB; of Tushingham LG1972; of Hinton Ampner House LG1937; CG; AA; (see also Naper; and Egerton-Warburton)
DUVALL DFUSA
DWIGHT formerly of Dedham DFUSA
DUVEEN, B PB1939
DWIGHT of The Pheasantries LG1952
DYCER, Bt EDB
DYER, Bt PB1970; Bt EDB; of Westhope LG1937; DFUSA
DYER (formerly BYTHERSEA) formerly of Freshford LG1952
DYKE, Bt PB1970
BALLANTINE DYKES formerly of Dovenby LG1952
DYMOCK of Penley Hall and Ellesmere LG1833/7
DYMOKE, Bt PB1866; of Scrivelsby LG1965
DYMOND of Burntwood Hall and Brierley LG1952
DYNE of Gore Court LG1863; of Westfield LG1833/7
DYNEVOR (see Rhys)
DYOTT of Freeford LG1972

BURNABY-DYOTT (see Burnaby)
DYSART (see Greaves)
DYSON formerly of Belmore LG1952
EADE of Walworth Castle LG1972
EADON LG1969
EADY (Swinfen, B) PB1970
EAGAR formerly of Ballymalis Castle LGI1958; AA
EAGER (see Shelton-Agar)
EAGLETON DFUSA
EALES FR
EARDLEY, B DEP; Bt PB1875
EARLE, Bt PB1970; Bt EDB; of Enham Place LG1921; PromFUSA; (see also Willis)
EARLY DFUSA
EARNSHAW formerly of Sheffield DFUSA
EAST, Bt of Hall Place PB1932; of Calcutta Bt PB1878; Bt of Hall Place EDB; (see also Thomas)
EASTCOTT of Endsleigh LG1937
EASTLEY of Loventor Manor LG1952
EASTMAN formerly of Langford DFUSA
EASTWOOD formerly of Gosden House LG1965; of West Stoke LG1965; of Castletown LG1863
EATON, Bt EDG; formerly of Eaton Hall LG1972; formerly of Messing Park LG1952; of Tolethorpe LG1937; of Stetchworth Park LG1875; (see also Hall-Dare)
EBBISHAM (see Blades)
EBDEN (see Penn)
EBRAHIM, Bt PB1970
EBURY (see Grosvenor)
ECCLES V PB1970; of Halston Place LG1937; of Clonroe LG1858; (see also McClintock)
ECHLIN, Bt PB1970; of Ardquin LGI1912
ECKERSALL (see Boynton-Wood)
ECKERSLEY of Carlton LG1921
ECKFORD of Templeknowe LG1937 Supp
ECKLEY of Creden Hill LG1843/9
ECKSTEIN, Bt PB1940
ECROYD of Low House, formerly of Homeshaye LG1969
EDDINGTON formerly of Glencreggan LG1921; of Ballangeich CG
EDDY (Australia) CG
CHUTER-EDE, B PB1967
EDEN (Avon, E) PB1970; (Auckland, B) PB1970; (Henley, B) PB1970; Bt PB1970; (Auckland, E) DEP; of Beamish Park LG1879

EDEN (*formerly* BYROM) *of Culver* LG1969

EDGAR, Bt PB1934; *of Hambleden* LG1972; *of Red House Park* LG1921; *formerly of Keithock* DFUSA; AA

EDGCOMB DFUSA

EDGCUMBE (Mount Edgcumbe, E) PB1970; *of Edgcumbe House* LG1898

PEARCE-EDGCUMBE *formerly of Reperry Manor* LG1952

EDGE, Bt PB1970; *of Strelley* LG1972; *of Clonbrook* LGI1912

EDGELL *of Standerwick Court* LG1914; AA

WYATT-EDGELL *of Cowley Place* LG1952

EDGEWORTH *formerly of Kilshrewly* LGI1958; *of Edgeworthstown* LGI1912; (*see* Forrest)

EDINBURGH (*see* Guelph)

EDLESTON *of Buckden Palace* LG1952

EDMANDS *of Sutton* LG1879; AA

EDMEADES *of Nurstead Court* LG1972

EDMONDSON (Sandford, B) PB1970

EDMONSTON *of Buness* LG1969; DFUSA

EDMONSTONE, Bt PB1970; *formerly of Cambus Wallace* LG1937Supp

EDMUNDS *of Cholderton* LG1972

MARTIN-EDMUNDS *of Worsbro' Hall* LG1937

EDRINGTON, B DEP

EDWARD *of Fernhill* LG1952

EDWARDES (Kensington, B) PB1970; Bt PB1900; *late of Treffgarne* LG1937; *of Sealy Ham* LG1900; *of Rhyd-y-Gôrs* LG1898; *of Gileston Manor* LG1879; HI

HOPE-EDWARDES *of Netley* LG1937

EDWARDS (Chelmer, B) PB1970; Bt *of Pye Nest* PB1970; Bt *of Treforis* PB1970; Bt *of Knighton* PB1927; Bt *of Garth* PB1850; Bt *of York* EDB; *of Empshott* LG1972; *of Hardingham* LG1969; *formerly of Longparish and Worting, and of Ivybridge* LG1969; *of Elsich Manor* LG1952; *of Finchampstead* LG1952; *of Trevor Tower* LG1937; *of Trematon Hall* LG1921; *of Dolserau* LG1914; *of Ness Strange* LG1906; *of Arlesbury* LG1875; *of Old Court* LG1875; *of The Hayes* LG1850/3; *of Henlow Grange* LG1850/3; *formerly of Diss* DFUSA; AA

EDWARDS (*now* GOUGH) *of Nanhoran* LG1937

HOPE-EDWARDS (*see* More)

KING-EDWARDS *of Dartans House* LGI1912

PALMOUR-EDWARDS *of Saint Florence* LG1952

POWELL-EDWARDS *of Novington* LG1972

WYNNE-EDWARDS *of Plas Nantglyn* LG1952

EELES *of Sandyden House* LG1969

EFFINGHAM (*see* Howard)

EGERTON (Sutherland, D) PB1970; (Wilton, E) PB1970; (Egerton of Tatton, B) PB1956; (Salford, V) PB1909; (Bridgewater, D) DEP; (Grey de Wilton, B) DEP; *of Mountfield Court formerly of Tatton* LG1969

GREY EGERTON, Bt PB1970

EGGLETON (*see* Kemp)

EGLINTON AND WINTON (*see* Montgomerie)

EGMONT (*see* Perceval)

EGREMONT *of Reedness* LG1921; (*see also* Percy; and Wyndham)

EHLEN DFUSA

EISENHOWER PresFUSA

ELBORNE *of Water Newton* LG1972

ELCOCKE LG1833/7

ELD *of Seighford Hall* LG1965

ELDERTON *of Amersham* LG1952

ELDER (*Australia*) CG

ELDON (*see* Scott)

ELDRED, Bt EDB

ELEY, Bt PB1949; *of East Bergholt* LG1965

ELFORD, Bt EDB

ELGAR, Bt PB1934

ELGIN AND KINCARDINE (*see* Bruce)

ELGOOD *of Brewery House* LG1952

ELIAS (Southwood, V) PB1940

ELIBANK (*see* Murray; and Erskine-Murray)

ELIOT (St Germans, E) PB1970; *formerly of East Coker* DFUSA

ELIOTT, Bt *of Stobs* PB1970; (Heathfield, B) DEP

ELKINGTON *of Adbury Holt* LG1952; *of Clunes* LG1921

BRADISH-ELLAMES *formerly of Little Marlow* LG1972

ELLEGOOD DFUSA

ELLENBOROUGH (*see* Law)

ELLERMAN, Bt PB1970

ELLETSON *of Parrox Hall* LG1969

ELLICE *of Invergarry* LG1952

ELLICOTT *formerly of Collumpton* DFUSA

ELLIOT (Elliot of Harwood, B) **PB1970**; Bt **PB1911**; *of Clifton Park formerly of Harwood* **LG1952**; *late of Wolfelee* **LG1921**

FOGG-ELLIOT *formerly of Bedburn* **LG1972**

SCOTT-ELLIOT *of Arkleton* **LG1972**; *of Kirkconnel Lea* **LG1972**

ELLIOTT, Bt **PB1970**; Bt **EDB**; *formerly of Nethermilne* **LG1965**; **DFUSA**

ELLIS, Bt **PB1912**; *formerly of Osselt* **LG1972**; *of Ponsbourne Park* **LG1863**; *of Abheyfeale* **LGI1912**; **DFUSA**; *formerly of Dedham* **DFUSA**

AGAR-ELLIS (Dover, B) **PB1899**

HEATON-ELLIS *formerly of Wyddiall Hall* **LG1965**

LESLIE-ELLIS *of Seaview House* **LGI1958**

SCOTT-ELLIS (Howard de Walden, B) **PB1970**

WILLIAMS-ELLIS *of Glasfryn* **LG1965**

ELLISON *of Butts Hall formerly of Footherley Hall* **LG1952**; *of Boultham* **LG1921**; *of Sudbrooke Holme* **LG1863**

CARR-ELLISON *of Hedgeley Hall* **LG1965**

ELLYS, Bt **EDB**

ELPHINSTON (Balmerinoch, Lord) **DEP**

ELMES *of Culm Davy House* **LG1952**

ELMHIRST *of Dartington Hall and Elmhirst* **LG1972**; *of West Ashby* **LG1937**

ELPHINSTONE, B **PB1970**; Bt *of Logie* **PB1970**; Bt *of Sowerby* **PB1970**; (Keith, V) **PB1867**, (Coupar, Lord) **DEP**; Bt **EDB**; **DFUSA**

ELSLEY *of Patrick Brompton* **LG1886**

ELTISLEY (*see* Newton)

ELTON, B **PB1970**; Bt **PB1970**; *of Trerice manor* **LG1965**; *of Ledbury* **LG1921**; **HI**

MARWOOD-ELTON *of Widworthy* **LG1952**

ELVIN *of East Dereham and Swaffham* **AA**

ELWES, Bt **EDB**; *of Colesbourne* **LG1965**; *of Congham* **LG1965**; *of Roxby* **LG1965**; *of Ennistown* **LGI1958**; *of Great Billing* **AA**

ELWILL, Bt **EDB**

ELWIN *formerly of Stalisfield Lodge* **LG1952**

ELWON *of Saltburn* **LG1900**

ELWOOD *of Strand Hill* **LG1863**; *of Clayton Priory* **LG1863**

ELY (*see* Tottenham)

ELY O'CARROLL (*see* O'Carroll)

EMBURY *formerly of Ballygaran* **DFUSA**

EMERIS *of Louth* **LG1906**

EMERSON *of Easby Hall* **LG1952**; *of Ulverscroft Abbey* **LG1863**; *formerly of Foxton* **DFUSA**; *of Lincolnshire* **HI**

EMERY *of The Grange Banwell* **LG1863**; *formerly of Stroud* **DFUSA**

RUSCOMBE-EMERY **LG1969**

EMERTON *of Banwell Castle* **LG1900**

EMLY (*see* Monsell)

EMMET (Emmet of Amberley, B) **PB1970**; *of Amberley Castle* **LG1965**; **IFR1976**

EMMOTT, B **PB1926**

GREEN-EMMOTT *of Emmott Hall* **LG1969**

EMORY **DFUSA**

EMPSON *of Yokefleet Hall* **LG1972**

LISTER-EMPSON *of Ousefleet* **LG1900**

ENERGLYN (*see* Evans)

ENGAINE, B **DEP**

ENGALITCHEFF (*formerly* BRANSFORD) **DFUSA**

ENGLEFIELD, Bt **EDB**

ENGLEHEART *of Stoke Priory* **LG1965**

ENGLAND *of Ferrises* **LG1969**

ENGLISH *of The Rookery* **LG1906**

ENNISDALE (*see* Lyons)

ENNISHOWEN (*see* Chichester)

ENNISKILLEN (*see* Cole)

ENO **PromFUSA**

ENSOR *of Rollesby Hall* **LG1891**

ENTWISLE *of Beachfield formerly of Entwisle* **LG1952**; *of Foxholes* **LG1952**

FNYON, Bt **EDB**

ENYS *of Enys* **LG1952**

EPPES (*see* Jefferson)

ERDMANN (*see* Wright)

ERICHSEN, Bt **PB1896**

ERLE (*see* Plunkett-Ernle-Erle-Drax)

ERNE (*see* Crichton)

ERNLE, Bt **EDB**; (*see also* Money-Kyrle; and Prothero)

ERNST (*see* Sword)

ERRINGTON, Bt **PB1970**; Bt *of Lackham Manor* **PB1917**; Bt *of Hooton* **PB1893**; *of Beeslack* **LG1969**; *of Chadwell Hall* **LG1969**; *of High Warden* **LG1921**

GLADWIN-ERRINGTON *formerly of Hinchley Wood* **LG1952**

ERROLL (Erroll of Hale, B) **PB1970**; (*see also* Hay)

ERSKINE (Mar and Kellie, E) **PB1970**; (Erskine of Rerrich, B) **PB1970**; Bt *of*

Cambo **PB1970**; *formerly of Cardross*
LG1937; **FR**
BIBER-ERSKINE *late of Dryburgh*
LG1921
KENNEDY-ERSKINE *of Dun* **LG1937**;
(*see also* Ailsa)
ST CLAIR-ERSKINE (Rosslyn, E)
PB1970
WEST-ERSKINE *of Hindmarsh Island*
CG
ERVINE *of Honey Ditches* **LG1952**
SWEET-ESCOTT *formerly of Hartrow*
LG1965
ESDAILE *of Cothelestone* **LG1952**; *of*
Hazelwood **LG1906**
ESHER (*see* Brett)
ESMONDE, Bt **PB1970**; B **DEP**
ESPEUT (*Jamaica*) **CG**
ESPLEN, Bt **PB1970**
ESSENDON (*see* Lewis)
ESSENHIGH *of Kenwood Bank* **LG1952**
ESSEX, Bt **EDB**; (*see also* Bourchier;
Capell; Cromwell; and Mandeville)
COWPER-ESSEX *of High House* (*alias*
Yewfield Castle) **LG1914**
ESSINGTON **DFUSA**
ESTCOURT, B **PB1915**; Bt **EDB**; (*see*
also Oswald)
SOTHERON-ESTCOURT *of Estcourt*
and Darrington Hall **LG1937**
ESTRIDGE (*St Kitts*) **CG**
ETHELSTON *formerly of Hinton Hall*
LG1972
ETHERINGTON, Bt **EDB**
ETHERTON *of Greentree Hall* **LG1972**
ETHERIDGE **DFUSA**
ETTRICK (*now* MAUGHAN-ETTRICK)
of Little Ilford, late of High Barnes
LG1937
EURE, B **DEP**
EUSTACE (Baltinglass, V) **DEP**; Bt **EDB**;
formerly of Stoodwell **LG1972**; (*co*
Kildare) **IFR1976**; (*co Meath*) **IFR1976**;
(*see also* Eustace-Duckett)
EUSTIS (*formerly* EUSTACE) *sometime*
of Bledlow **DFUSA**
EVANS (Energlyn, B) **PB1970**; (Evans of
Hungershall, B) **PB1970**; (Mountevans,
B) **PB1970**; Bt *of Roltingdean* **PB1970**;
Bt *of Tubbendens* **PB1970**; Bt *of*
Wightwick **PB1970**; B **PB1959**; Bt *of*
Allestree Hall **PB1892**; Bt *of Kilcreene*
EDB; *formerly of Broom Hall* **LG1972**;
of Eyton **LG1972**; *of Whitbourne Hall*
LG1972; *of Yew House, Bramshott*
LG1972; *of Lovesgrove* **LG1969**; *of*
Ffrwdgrech **LG1965**; *of Caterham*

LG1952; *formerly of Hatley Park*
LG1952; *of Nantymoch* **LG1952**;
of Ridlington **LG1952**; *of Walton*
LG1952; *of Worsall Hall* **LG1952**;
of Brynbella **LG1937**; *of Glas-*
coed **LG1937**; *late of Llwynartchan*
LG1937; *of Darley Abbey* **LG1937**; *of*
Henblas **LG1921**; *Nash Mills* **LG1914**;
of Llantrissant **LG1906**; *of Forde Abbey*
LG1900; *of North Tuddenham* **LG1900**;
of Moreton Court **LG1900**; *of Haydock*
LG1894; *of Ash Hill and Miltown Castle*
LG1863; *of Knockaderry* **LG1894**; *of*
Portrane **LG1833/7**; *of Carker*
LGI1912; *of Churchlands* **LGI1912**; *of*
Gortmerr House **LGI1912**; *of*
Rockfield **LGI1912**; **PromFUSA**; *of*
Henblas, co Anglesey **AA**; *of Sufton*
Court, co Hereford **AA**; (*see also* Carr;
Pugh; and Twemlow)
EVANS (*formerly* HARRISON-ALLEN)
of Cresselly **LG1969**
DAVIES-EVANS *of Highmead formerly*
of Penylan **LG1972**
EMRYS-EVANS (*formerly* TWEMLOW)
of Peatswood **LG1952**
GWYNNE-EVANS, Bt **PB1970**
RICE-EVANS *of Eaglebush* **LG1937**
SEYMOUR-EVANS (*see* Davies-Evans)
TYRRELL-EVANS *of Capel End* **LG1972**
WORTHINGTON-EVANS, Bt **PB1970**
EVATT *of Mount Louise* **LGI1912**
TRUSTRAM EVE (Silsoe, B) **PB1970**
EVELEGH *formerly of West Evelegh*
LG1965
EVELYN, Bt *of Wotton* **PB1848**; Bt *of*
Godstone **EDB**; Bt *of Long Ditton*
EDB; *of Wotton* **LG1965**
EVERARD, Bt **PB1970**; Bt *of Ballybay*
EDB; Bt *of Much Waltham* **EDB**;
formerly of Bardon **LG1972**; *of Rat-*
cliffe Hall **LG1972**; *of Miltons* **LG1965**;
of Fulney House **LG1879**; *of Middleton*
LG1863; *of Randlestown* **LGI1904**; *of*
Middleton, co Norfolk **AA**
EVERED (*see* Everard *of Miltons*)
EVERINGHAM, B **DEP**
EVERSFIELD *of Denne Park* **LG1937**
EVERSHED, B **PB1963**; *formerly of*
Albury House **LG1972**
EVERSLEY (*see* Shaw-Lefevre)
EVERY, Bt **PB1970**
EVETTS *formerly of Tackley Park*
LG1952; *of Base Court* **LG1937Supp**
EVRE (*see* Eure)
EWART, Bt **PB1970**; Bt *of White House*
PB1928; *of Sailfoot formerly of Bodes-*

beck and *Allershaw* **LG1952**; **DFUSA**; (*see also* Monro)

EWBANK *formerly of Snotterton Hall* **LG1972**

EWELL *formerly of Sandwich* **DFUSA**

EWING *late of Burton Grange* **LG1921**; **DFUSA**

CRUM EWING (*see* Hamilton *of Lowood and Castlehill*)

ORR EWING, Bt **PB1970**

ORR-EWING, Bt *of Hendon* **PB1970**

EXETER (*see* Beaufort; Cecil; Courtenay; and Holland)

EXMOUTH (*see* Pellew)

EXSHAW **IFR1976**

EYERMAN **PromFUSA**

EYKYN *of Gaynton* **LG1952**

EYLES, Bt **EDB**

EYRE, B **DEP**; *of Lytes Cary Manor* **LG1972**; *formerly of St John's Wood* **LG1965**; *formerly of Brickworth and Landford* **LG1937**; *late of Welbury* **LG1937**; *of Lindley Hall* **LG1921**; *late of Rampton* **LG1921**; **IFR1976**; *of Uppercourt* **LGI1912**; **DFUSA**; (*see also* Archer-Houblon; Eyre Matcham; and Speir)

CROSTHWAITE-EYRE (*formerly* EYRE*) of Warrens* **LG1965**

MAUNSELL-EYRE (*see* Maunsell)

EYRES *of Nuts Court* **LG1965**; *of Cut Heath* **LG1937**; (*see also* Eyres-Monsell)

EYSTON *of East Hendred* **LG1965**

EYTON *of Plas-yn-Cwm* **LG1952**; (*see also* Morris-Eyton)

MORRIS-EYTON *of Eyton* **LG1972**

FAIRBAIRN-WYNNE-EYTON (*formerly* EYTON) *of Leeswood* **LG1952**

FABER (Wittenham, B) **PB1931**; B **PB1917**; *of Ampfield House* **LG1972**

FAGAN **IFR1976**; *of Feltrim House, Philadelphia* **DFUSA**

FAGGE, Bt **PB1970**

FAIR (*see* Ruttledge)

FAIRBAIRN, Bt **PB1970**; (*Australia*) **CG**

WAILES-FAIRBAIRN *of Berrington House* **LG1972**

FAIRBANKS *formerly of Sowerby* **DFUSA**

FAIRFAX (Fairfax of Cameron, B) **PB1970**; (Fairfax, V) **DEP**; *of Manor West* **LG1972**; **DFUSA**; (*see also* Smith)

FAIRFIELD (*see* Greer)

FAIRHAVEN (*see* Broughton)

FAIRHOLME *of Lugate* **LG1972**

FAIRLES (*see* Fairles-Humphreys)

FAIRLIE *of Myres* **LG1969**; (*see also* Morris)

FALCON (*formerly* COOK) *of Camerton* **LG1914**

FALCONAR (*see* Falconar-Stewart)

FALCONER, Bt *of Bath* **LG1921**; *formerly of Inveravon* **DFUSA**

KEITH-FALCONER (Falconer of Halkerton, B) **PB1963**; (Kintore, B) **PB1963**

FALDER (*see* Roddam)

FALKINER, Bt **PB1970**; Bt **EDB**; *of Holly Park* **LGI1958**; *of Mount Falcon* **LGI1912**

FALKLAND (Hunsdon of Scutterskelfe, B) **PB1884**; (*see also* Cary)

FALKNER *formerly of Claverley* **LG1972**; *of North Newnton* **LG1952**

FALLE (Portsea, B) **PB1940**

FALLON *of Netterville Lodge* **LGI1912**

FALMOUTH (*see* Berkeley; and Boscawen)

FALVESLEY, B **DEP**

FANE (Westmorland, E) **PB1970**; V **DEP**; (Catherlough, B) **DEP**; *of Boynton Manor* **LG1937**

FANE DE SALIS *of Bourne House* **LG1965**; (*Australia*) **CG**

CLIVE-PONSONBY-FANE (*see* Clive *of Perrystone*)

FANNING *formerly of Bozedown and Hardwick* **LG1972**

FANSHAWE, V **DEP**; Bt **EDB**; *formerly of Dengie* **LG1965**; *formerly of Donnington Hall* **LG1965**; *formerly of Parsloes* **LG1965**

FARDELL *of Little Warley* **LG1952Supp**

FAREWELL *of Hillfield House* **LG1952**

FARGUS *of Woodlands* **LG1952**

FARIE *of Farme* **LG1952**

FARINGDON (*see* Henderson)

FARINGTON, Bt **EDB**

FARLEY *of Wornditch Hall* **LG1952**; **DFUSA**

KING-FARLOW *formerly of Wood Lees* **LG1969**

FARMAR *of Millwood* **LG1972**

FARMBROUGH *of Denbigh Hall, co Bucks* **AA**

FARMER, Bt **PB1913**; *formerly of Nonsuch* **LG1969**; *of Ifield Wood* **LG1952**; *of Ascot Place* **LG1914**

FARMER (*formerly* SMITH) *formerly of Aston Munslow* **LG1952**

FARMILOE (*see* Congleton)

FARNABY, Bt **PB1859**

FARNALL *of Manor House* **LG1879**

FARNBOROUGH (see Long; and May)
FARNHAM of Quorn House LG1965;
(see also Maxwell)
FARQUHAR, Bt PB1970; B PB1923;
formerly of Acheron and Drum-na-Gesk
LG1965; of Gilminscroft LG1900
FARQUHARSON of Invercauld LG1972;
of Langton House LG1972; of Finzean
LG1952; of Haughton LG1921; of
Whitehouse LG1914; of Baldovie
LG1850/3; of Haughton, co Aberdeen
AA; HI; (see also Leslie formerly of
Kininvie)
FARR of Shortwood House LG1965; of
Newnham Hall LG1952; of Staunton
LG1937; (Australia) CG
FARRAN of Clifton LG1952
FARRANT of Roskrow LG1952; of Balla-
moar LG1914
FARRELL of Dalyston LG1858; of
Moynalty LGI1912; (see also Skeffing-
ton)
FARRER, B PB1963; of Ingleborough
LG1972; of Brayfield LG1952; of Whit-
barrow LG1952; of Eastwoodside and
Botcherby LG1952Supp; (see also
Knox)
FARRINGTON, Bt PB1970
FARROW of Surlingham LG1952
FARSYDE of Fylingdales LG1879
FASSON formerly of Lanton Tower
LG1972
FAUCOMBERGE (see Fauconberge)
FAUCONBERG (see Pelham)
FAUCONBERG (see Belasyse; and Nevill)
FAUCONBERGE, B PB1940
FAULCONER (now JEFFERYS) DFUSA
FAULKNER formerly of Castletown
LGI1958
FAUNCE DFUSA; of Sharsted HI; (see
also Faunce-Delaune)
GODFREY-FAUSSETT formerly of
Heppington LG1965
FAWCETT of Somerford Keynes LG1972;
of Thornhill House and Gardenhill
LGI1958; CG
HORTON-FAWKES of Farnley LG1965
FAXON DFUSA
FAY of Faybrook LGI1912
FAYRER, Bt PB1970
FAZAKERELY of Burwood LG1875
FEACHEM formerly of Chillandham
LG1952
FEARNLEY of Hetton LG1894; (see also
Fearnley-Whittingstall)
FEATHERSTON (New Zealand) CG

FEATHERSTONE of Yoxall Lodge
LG1952
FEATHERSTONHAUGH of Hopton AA
FEETHAM late of Whinfield LG1937
FEHR of Monk Sherborne LG1952; of
Hatton House and Slodden LG1937
Supp
FEILDEN, Bt PB1970; of Cokethorpe
formerly of Witton Park LG1965; of
Dulas Court LG1921; of Mollington
LG1843/9
FEILDING (Denbigh and Desmond, E)
PB1970
FELL formerly of Daltongate LG1972;
of Lismore LG1969; of Peinmore
LG1952
FELLOWES (Ailwyn, B) PB1970; (de
Ramsey, B) PB1970; of Shotesham
Park LG1965; of Court Hall formerly of
Woodfield LG1952; (see also Benyon;
and Fellowes-Gordon)
FELLOWS formerly of Beeston LG1952;
(Canada) CG
FELTON, B DEP; Bt EDB; of Sandgate
LG1921; DFUSA
FENDER (formerly CAMPBELL) formerly
of Brickendon Grange LG1952
FENNELL of Burtown House LGI1958
FENTON, Bt EDB; LG1969; of Dutton
Manor LG1921; of Underbank Hall HI
DE WEND-FENTON of Ebberston Hall
LG1972
FENWICK, Bt EDB; formerly of Thirle-
staine House LG1965; of Brinkburn
LG1952; of Longframlington LG1952;
of Burrow Hall LG1937; formerly of
Stockerston Hall LG1921; (see also
Dugdale)
FENWICKE (see Fenwicke-Clennell)
FERGUSON, Bt PB1860; of Dummer
LG1972; of Kinmundy LG1952; for-
merly of Pitfour LG1965; of Polebrooke
Hall LG1937; of Carlisle LG1898; of
Ballyvally House LGI1958; (see also
Mar)
JOHNSON-FERGUSON, Bt PB1970
MUNRO-FERGUSON (Novar, V)
PB1934; of Raith and Novar LG1969
FERGUSSON, Bt of Kilkerran PB1970;
of Baledmund LG1972; of Ebbes-
bourne Wake LG1952; formerly of
Dalmally DFUSA) (see also Cuning-
hame of Caprington)
COLYER-FERGUSSON, Bt PB1970
GILLON-FERGUSSON of Isle LG1921
FERMOR (Pomfret, E) DEP; Bt EDB;
(see also Hesketh)

FERMOY (see Roche)
FERNALD formerly of Bristol **DFUSA**
FERNANDES formerly of Haddon Lodge and Crofton Grange **LG1972**
CARMICHAEL-FERRALL of Augher Castle **LGI1912**
FERRAND formerly of St Ives **LG1965**; **HI**
THOMAS-FERRAND of Edgarley Hall **LG1937**
FERRARD (see Massereene and Ferrard; and Tichborne)
FERRERS (Ferrers of Chantley, B **PB1855**); (Derby, E) **DEP**; (Ferrers of Chartley, B) **DEP**; (Ferrers, of Groby, B) **DEP**; (Ferrers, of Wemme, B) **DEP**; Bt **EDB**; of Baddesley Clinton **LG1952**; (see also Shirley)
FERRIER of Hemsby **LG1969**; formerly of Belsyde **LG1952**; (see also Noel-Paton)
FERRIS of Hawkhurst **LG1880/3**; **DFUSA**
GRANT-FERRIS of Hazleton **LG1952**
FESTING of Birks **LG1972**
FETHERSTON, Bt **EDB**; of Packwood **LG1879**
FETHERSTONAUGH, Bt **PB1846**
FETHERSTONHAUGH of Kirkoswald **LG1965**; formerly of Hopton Court **LG1952**; of Kinmel **LG1952**; of Staffield Hall **LG1886**; **IFR1976**
FETTIPLACE, Bt **EDB**
GORGES-FETTIPLACE (see Gorges)
FEVERSHAM (see Duncombe; Duras; and Sondes)
FFARINGTON of Worden **LG1886**
FFEILDEN of Witton **HI**
FFOLKES, Bt **PB1970**
FFOLLIOTT of Hollybrook House **LGI1912**; of Tierernane **LGI1912**
FFOOKS of Sherborne **LG1965**
FFORDE of Raughlin **LGI1912**
FFOULKE **PromFUSA**
FFOULKES of Eriviat Hall **LG1937**
FFRENCH, B **PB1970**; **IFR1976**
FFYTCHE of Thorpe Hall **LG1886**; of Pyrgo Park **LG1886**
FICKLIN of Tasburgh **LG1937**
FIDDIEN, M **TNBE1956**
FIELD, B **PB1907**; of Rest Harrow **LG1952**; of Laceby **LG1937**; of The Grove **LG1906**; of Yorkshire **LG1843/9**; of Heaton Hall **LG1833/7**; **PromFUSA**
MORRIS-FIELD of Ashurst Park **LG1921**
FIELDEN of Witton Park **AA**

FIELDEN of Grimston Park **LG1965**; (see also Villiers-Stuart)
FIELDING (see Denbigh)
TWISLETON - WYKEHAM - FIENNES (Save and Sele, B) **PB1970**; Bt **PB1970**
FIFE (see Carnegie; and Duff)
FIFE (formerly FIFE-COOKSON) of Langton Hall **LG1952**
FIFE (formerly RUTSON) of Nunnington Hall **LG1952**
FILGATE **IFR1976**
FILLEY **DFUSA**
FILLINGHAM of Syerston Hall **LG1952**
FILLMORE **PresFUSA**
FILMER, Bt **PB1916**; formerly of East Luton **DFUSA**; (see also Wilson)
WYNNE FINCH of Voelas **LG1952**; (see also Aylesford)
FINCH, B **DEP**; of Ayston formerly of Burley-on-the-Hill **LG1952**; of Chedworth **LG1952**; formerly of Willesden **LG1952**; of Redheath **LG1921**; (1) & (2) **DFUSA**; **FR**; (see also Dring)
FINDLATER **IFR1976**; of Fernside **LGI1912**; (see also Ogilvy)
FINDLAY, Bt **PB1970**, of Boturich **LG1965**; of Stansted Hall **LG1952**
FINGALL (see Plunkett)
FINLAY, Bt **PB1970**; B **PB1940**; formerly of Castle Toward **LG1952**; of Corkagh **LGI1912**
FINLAYSON **CG**
GORDON-FINLAYSON of Wickerstreet House **LG1952**
FINLEY formerly of Dublin **DFUSA**
FINNIE of Newfield **LG1900**
FINNY of Leixlip and Ellesmere Port **LG1973Supp**
FINUCANE of Stamer Park **LG1850/3**
FINZEL of Frankfort Hall **LG1882**; **AA**
FIRBANK of St Julian's **LG1921**
FIREBRACE, Bt **EDB**; formerly of Elmstone Court **LG1965**
FIRMAN late of Gateforth **LG1937**
FIRTH, Bt **PB1936**; formerly of Coates Manor **LG1969**; of Heckmondwike **LG1875**; of Hartford Lodge **LG1870/3**
FISH, Bt **EDB**; **DFUSA**
FISHER, B **PB1970**; (Fisher of Lambeth, B) **PB1970**; (Downham, B) **PB1917**; Bt of Packington Magna **EDB**; Bt of St Giles **EDB**; of Framfield **LG1952**; of Helme Hall **LG1952**; of Nunfield in Cumwhitton **LG1952**; of Winton House **LG1952**; late of Distington Hall **LG1937**; of Higham-on-the-Hill **LG1900**; of Thornecombe **LG1894**; of

Tretwind **LG1858**; *of Cossington and Fields Place* **LG1875**; *formerly of Syleham* **DFUSA**; (*see also* Fisher-Rowe)
WILLIAMS-FISHER (*formerly* FISHER) *formerly of Eastcote* **LG1952**
FISKE, B **PB1970**; *formerly of Laxfield* **DFUSA**
FISON, Bt **PB1970**
FITCH *of Olivers formerly of Hadleigh House* **LG1952**; *formerly of Bocking* **DFUSA**
FITTON, B **DEP**; Bt **EDB**; *of White Hall* **LG1952** .
FITZALAN (*see* Fitzalan-Howard)
FITZ-ALAN (Arundel, E) **DEP**
FITZ-CHARLES (Plymouth, E) **DEP**
FITZCLARENCE (Munster, E) **PB1970**
FITZGERALD, (Leinster, D) **PB1970**; Bt (*Knight of Kerry*) **PB1970**; Bt *of Cork* **PB1970**; (FitzGerald of Kilmarnock, B) **PB1889**; (Desmond, E) **DEP**; (Fitz-Gerald and Vesey, B) **DEP**; (Lecale, B) **DEP**; *of Holbrook* **LG1894**; (Knight of Glin) **IFR1976**; (*co Mayo*) **IFR1976**; *formerly of Ballynard* **LGI1958**; *formerly of Coolanowle* **LGI1958**; *of Mondellihy* **LGI1958**; *of Moyvane* **LGI1912**; *of Moyrhea* **LGI1912**; *of Carrigoran* **LGI1912**; *of Rathgar and Laccagh* **LG1904**; **PromFUSA**; (*see also* Butler; Nugent; and Purefoy)
FOSTER - VESEY - FITZGERALD **IFR1976**
JUDKIN-FITZGERALD, Bt **PB1921**; (*see also* Uniacke)
PENROSE-FITZGERALD (*see* Uniacke)
UNIACKE - PENROSE - FITZGERALD, Bt **PB1919**; (*see also* Uniacke)
PURCELL-FITZGERALD **IFR1976**
WILSON-FITZGERALD *of Chalcombe and Inchoveagh* **LGI1912**;. (*see also* Wilson *of Cliffe Hall*)
FITZGIBBON (Clare, E) **DEP**; (*co Kilkenny*) **IFR1976**; (*co Limerick*) **IFR1976**; (*see also* Dillon; and Foster-Vesey-FitzGerald)
FITZHARDINGE (*see* Berkeley)
FITZHARRIS, Bt **EDB**
FITZHERBERT (Stafford, B) **PB1970**; Bt **PB1970**; (St Helens, B) **DEP**; *of Synwnerton* **LG1906**; **IFR1976**
FITZ-HERBERT, B **DEP**
FITZHUGH *of Plas Power* **LG1969**; **PromFUSA**
FITZ-HUGH, B **DEP**; *formerly of Bedford* **DFUSA**
FITZ-JAMES (Berwick, D) **DEP**

FITZJOHN (*see* FitzGerald, Knight of Glin)
FITZ-JOHN, B **DEP**
FITZMAURICE **IFR1976**
FITZ-MAURICE (Orkney, E) **PB1970**
PETTY-FITZMAURICE (Lansdowne, M) **PB1970**; B **PB1935**
FITZPATRICK (Castletown, B) **PB1937**
FITZ-PATRICK (Upper Ossory, E) **DEP**
LINDSEY-FITZPATRICK *of Hollymount* **LGI1912**
FITZ-PAYNE, B **DEP**
FITZRANDOLPH **DFUSA**
FITZROY (Grafton D) **PB1970**; (Daventry, V) **PB1970**; (Southampton, B) **PB1970**
FITZ-ROY (Cleveland, and Southampton, D) **DEP**; (Northumberland, D) **DEP**; (Richmond and Somerset, D) **DEP**
FITZ-SIMON *of Glencullen House* **LGI1958**
FITZWALTER (*see* Plumptre)
FITZ-WALTER, B **DEP**; (*see also* Bridges; and Mildmay)
FITZ-WARINE, B **DEP**
WENTWORTH-FITZWILLIAM (Fitzwilliam, E) **PB1970**
FITZ-WILLIAM (Southampton, E) **DEP**; (Tyrconnel, E) **DEP**; B **DEP**
FITZWILLIAMS *of Gilgwyn* **LG1965**
FITZWYGRAM (*see* Wigram)
FLAGG **PromFUSA**
WOULFE FLANAGAN *formerly of Rathfudagh and Rathtermon* **LGI1958**
FLANNERY, Bt **PB1959**
FLAVEL **FR**
FLAVELLE, Bt **PB1970**
FLECK, B **PB1967**
FLEET *of Darenth* **LG1952**
FLEETWOOD, Bt **EDB**
FLEMING (Wigton, E) **DEP**; (Longford, V) **DEP**; Bt **EDB**; Bt *of Brompton Park* **EDB**; *of Nettlebed* **LG1965**; *of Spring Grove* **LG1952**; *of Rayrigg and Belfield* **LG1900**; *formerly of New Court* **LGI1958**; *Barraghcore House* **LG1904**; **DFUSA**; **FR**
BARBER-FLEMING (*see* Hamilton Fleming)
COHAM-FLEMING *of Coham* **LG1952**
HAMILTON FLEMING *of Court Hall* **LG1972**
WILLIS FLEMING *formerly of Stoneham* **LG1965**
FLETCHER (Winster, B) **PB1959**; Bt *of Carrow* **PB1876**; Bt *of Hutton Le Forrest* **EDB**; *formerly of Allerton*

LG1972; *of Saltoun* LG1972; *of Dunans* LG1969; *of The Lodge, Little Tew* LG1969; *of Atherton Hall* LG1952; *formerly of Dale Park* LG1952; *of Southridge* LG1952; *of Wyrley and Strete End formerly of Lawneswood* LG1952; *of Aldwick Manor* LG1937; *Rosehaugh* LG1937; *late of Kenward* LG1914; *of Brigham Hill* LG1906; *of Kevanila* LG1858; *of Corsock* LG1858; *of Water Eyton* LG1850/3; DFUSA; *formerly of Cockermouth* DFUSA
AUBREY-FLETCHER, Bt PB1970
HAMILTON-FLETCHER LG1969
FLINT *of Hembury Castle* LG1972; PromFUSA; CG; (*see also* Corbett *of Longnor*)
FLOOD, Bt EDB
SOLLY-FLOOD *of Ballynaslaney House* LGI1912
FLOREY, B PB1967
FLOREY FR
FLOWER (Ashbrook, V) PB1970; (Battersea, B) PB1907; Bt PB1876; *formerly of Furze Down Park* LG1972; *of The Hill* LG1965; *of Pennyghael* LG1952; *of Aston Clinton* LG1886; FR
FLOWERS DFUSA
FLOWERS (*formerly* SMITH) DFUSA
FLOYD, Bt PB1970, PromFUSA
FLOYER *of Martin Hall* LG1882; *of Hints* LG1858; (*see also* Floyer-Acland)
FLUDYER, Bt PB1922
FOCK (*see* de Robeck)
FOGG (*see* Fogg-Elliot)
FOGO *of Row* LG1921
FOLEY, B PB1970; Bt EDB; (*see also* Berkeley)
FOLIOT, B DEP
FOLJAMBE (Liverpool, E) PB1970; Bt EDB; *of Osberton* LG1972
FOLLETT (*see* Noel)
FOLLIOT, B DEP
FOLLIOTT *of Stapeley House* LG1858
FONNEREAU *of Dale Hall formerly of The Moat* LG1952
FOOKS *formerly of Langton House* LG1969; *of Sudbrooke House* LG1952; (*see also* Ffooks)
FOOT (Caradon, B) B PB1970; B PB1970; *Pencrebar* LG1952; *formerly of Holly Park* LG1952; *formerly of The Rower* LGI1912
FOOTT *of Carngacunna Castle* LGI1912
FORBES (Granard, E) PB1970; B PB1970; Bt *of Craigievar* PB1970; Bt *of Newe* PB1970; B DEP; *of Callendar*

LG1965; *of Rothiemay* LG1965; *of Culloden* LG1952; *formerly of Winkfield Place* LG1952; *of Inverernan* LG1921; *of Medwin* LG1921; *of Skellater and Kingarelock* LG1854; *of Echt House* LG1858; (1) & (2) DFUSA; *formerly of Newe* DFUSA; *of Casterton* CG; *of Sydney* CG; (*see also* Forbes-Mitchell)
OGILVIE-FORBES *of Boyndlie and formerly of Aucheries* LG1972
STUART-FORBES, Bt PB1970
FORD, Bt PB1970; *formerly of Enfield Old Park* LG1952; *of Abbeyfield* LG1858; PresFUSA; (1) & (2) DFUSA; *formerly of Clonakilty* DFUSA
ST CLAIR-FORD, Bt PB1970
FORDE IFR1976
FORDHAM *of Melbourn Bury* LG1969; *of Odsey* LG1969
DINGWALL-FORDYCE *of Brucklay* LG1952
WELD-FORESTER (Forester, B) PB1970
FORFAR (*see* Douglas)
FORMBY *of Formby* LG1952
FORRES (*see* Williamson)
FORREST, Bt PB1928
FORREST (*Canada*) CG; *of Perth* CG
FORRESTER LG1972
FORSTER (Forster *of Harraby*, B) PB1970; B PB1936; Bt *of Lysways Hall* PB1930; Bt *of The Grange* PB1930; Bt *of Coolderry* PB1904; Bt *of Aldermaston* EDB; Bt *of Bamborough*, EDB; Bt *of East Greenwich* EDB; Bt *of Stokarly* EDB; *of Wellisford Manor* LG1952; *of Great Carlton* LG1921; *of Malverlies* LG1906; *of Lysways* LG1858; *of Swords* LGI1912; *of Walthamstow* HI; (*see also* Foster *of Cold Hesledon*)
ARNOLD-FORSTER (*formerly* STORY-MASKELYNE) *of Basset Down* LG1952
SADLEIR-FORSTER (*see* Trench)
FORSYTH *late of Quinish* LG1937; (*Canada*) CG; (*see also* Forsyth-Grant)
FORT *of Hare Hatch House, formerly of Read Hall* LG1952
FORTE (*Barbados*) CG
FORTEATH *formerly of Newton* LG1952
FORTESCUE, E PB1970; (Clermont, E) DEP; (Clinton, E) DEP; Bt *of Fallapit* EDB; Bt *of Fowellscombe* EDB; Bt *of Salden* EDB; Bt *of Wood* EDB; *of Fallapit* LG1921; *formerly of Barnstaple* DFUSA; (*see also* Fortescue-Brickdale; and Hamilton (*co Louth*))

INGLETT-FORTESCUE (see Fortescue-Brickdale)
IRVINE-FORTESCUE of Kingcausie LG1969
PARKINSON-FORTESCUE (Carlingford, B) PB1898
FORTEVIOT (see Dewar)
FORTH (see Ruthven)
FORTIBUS (Albemarle, E) DEP
FORTNUM of The Hill House LG1898
FORTUNE of Bengairn LG1972
FORWOOD, Bt PB1970
FOSBERY formerly of Clorane LGI1958
FOSBROOKE of Ravenstone LG1952
FOSTER, Bt PB1970; (Ilkeston, B) PB1949; Bt of Norwich PB1959; of Cold Hesledon and Hawthorne LG1965; formerly of Hornby Castle LG1965; of Ashe Grange LG1952; formerly of Kempston LG1952; of Old Mill House LG1952; of Pontlands LG1952; of Apley LG1937; of Fontridge LG1937; of Killhow LG1921; of Lanwithan LG1914; of Warmwell LG1906; of Horton-in-Ribblesdale LG1882; of Wadsworth Banks LG1882; of Castlering LG1858; (1) & (2) DFUSA; formerly of Bradford DFUSA; of Thurnby CG; of Brickhill House, co Bedford AA; (see also Foster Brown; Foster-Vesey-FitzGerald; and Foster-Melliar)
HYLTON-FOSTER, B PB1970
FOTHERBY (see Blake of Barham Court)
FOTHERGILL of Lowbridge LG1969; formerly of Carr End LG1952 Supp
SCRYMSOURE STEUART FOTHRINGHAM of Murthly LG1972
FOULIS, Bt of Ingleby PB1877; Bt EDB
LISTON FOULIS, Bt PB1970
FOULQUES VF
FOUNTAINE of Narford LG1972
FOUNTAYNE (see Montagu of Upton)
FOURNIER, Count TNBE1956
FOWELL, Bt EDB; of Devonshire LG1880/3
FOWKE, Bt PB1970; of Hale Hill LG1937; of Saling LG1914
FOWLE DFUSA
FOWLER (Wolverhampton, V) PB1940; Bt of Braemore PB1933; Bt of Gastard House PB1902; Bt of Harnage Grange EDB; Bt of Islington EDB; of Ashby Manor LG1952; of Woodthorp LG1921; of Gunton Hall LG1886; of Walliscote House LG1882; IFR1976; (1) & (2)

DFUSA; of Georgia DFUSA; (see Fowler-Butler)
FOWNES, Bt EDB
FOX (Holland, B) DEP; Bt PB1959; of Penjerrick (and of Falmouth) LG1972; formerly of The Cleve LG1952; formerly of Girsby LG1952; of Wellington LG1952; of Chacombe Priory LG1833/7; of Fox Hall LGI1912; formerly of The Cleve LG1952; formerly of Coton LG1952; formerly of Girsby LG1952; of Wellington LG1952; of Chacombe Priory LG1833/7; of Fox Hall LGI1912; formerly of Exeter DFUSA; PromFUSA
(THE) FOX IFR1976
LANE-FOX (Bingley, B) PB1940; (Bingley, B) DEP; of Bramham Park LG1965; (see also Conyers; and Fauconberge)
FOXCROFT (see Robertson-Glasgow)
FOY DFUSA
FOYLE of Beeleigh Abbey LG1972
FETHERSTONHAUGH-FRAMPTON of Moreton LG1969
FRANCE (see France-Hayhurst)
FRANCIS of Llwyn Helyg LG1965; of Quy Hall LG1952
FRANCIS (formerly BOWEN) of Tyddyn LG1952
FRANCIS (formerly LOVELL) formerly of Cole Park LG1952
FRANCKEN of Halstock and Maldon LG1921
FRANCKLIN of Gonalston LG1969
FRANCKLYN, Bt EDB; of Chart Sutton, Maidstone and Wye LG1937
FRANCO (see Lopes)
FRANK, Bt PB1970; of Campsall LG1937
FRANKFORT (see de Montmorency)
FRANKLAND (Zouche, B) PB1970
FRANKLYN formerly of Burton Grange LG1952; late of Furze Hall and formerly of Jamaica and Antigua LG1937; of Longcroft Hall LG1937
FRANKS, B PB1970; IFR1976
FRASER (Fraser of Allander, B) PB1970; (Fraser of Lonsdale, B) PB1970; (Fraser of North Cape, B) PB1970; (Lovat, B) PB1970; (Saltoun, B) PB1970; (Strathalmond, B) PB1970; Bt of Cromarty PB1970; Bt of Ledeclune PB1970; Bt of Tain PB1970; B DEP; Bt EDB; formerly of Brook House LG1972; of Reelig LG1969; of Tornaveen LG1969; formerly of Ardachy LG1952; formerly of Mongewell Park LG1952; formerly of Seend Head House LG1952; of

Wardlaw **LG1952**; *of Buckham Hill House* **LG1937**; *of Findrack* **LG1921**; *of Lochavich* **LG1921**; *of Hospitalfield* **LG1894**; *of Skipness Castle* **LG1875**; *of Moniack* **LG1850/3**; *formerly of Gortfoyle* **LGI1958**; **DFUSA**; (*see also* Hewgill; and Fraser-Mackintosh)
CROFT-FRASER *of Inverallochy* **LG1952**
FRAZER **DFUSA**
FREAKE, Bt **PB1949**
FREDERICK, Bt **PB1970**
FREELAND *of Oaklands* **LG1886**; *of Cornbrook Park, Manchester* **AA**
FREELING, Bt **PB1940**
FREEMAN, Bt **PB1970**; *of Pylewell* **LG1863**; (1) & (2) **DFUSA**
FREEMAN (*formerly* CHILDE-FREEMAN) *formerly of Gaines* **LG1952**
WILLIAMS-FREEMAN *formerly of Clapton* **LG1969**
FREER, Bt **EDB**; *of Ditchford Hill* **LG1952**; *of Pedmore* **LG1894**
FREKE, Bt **EDB**
EVANS-FREKE (Carbery, B) **PB1970**
HUSSEY-FREKE *of Hannington* **LG1969**
FREMANTLE (Cottesloe, B) **PB1970**
FREMLIN *formerly of Kemsing and Maidstone* **LG1952**
FRENCH (Ypres, E) **PB1970**; (de Freyne, B) **PB1970**; (de Freyne of Artagh, D) **PB1856**; **LG1969**; *of Cudworth Manor* **LG1952**; (*Dublin*) **IFR1976**; (*cos Galway and Roscommon*) **IFR1976**; (*co Wexford*) **IFR1976**; *of Cuskinny* **LG1937Supp**; **LGI1912**, *sometime of Ardsallagh* **LGI1912**; *formerly of Knoddishall* **DFUSA**; **PromFUSA**; *of Prescott and Toronto* **CG**
STUART-FRENCH *of Marino* **LGI1958**
FREND **IFR1976**
FRENDRAUGHT (*see* Crichton)
FRERE, Bt **PB1933**; *formerly of Roydon Hall* **LG1969**
FRESCHEVILLE, B **DEP**
FRESHFIELD *of Wych Cross Place* **LG1921**
FREUND *of Wilcote and of Pitsford* **LG1952**
FREVILLE, B **DEP**
FREW **DFUSA**
FREWEN *of Northiam* **LG1965**
FREYBERG, B **PB1970**
FRIAR *formerly of Duddo* **LG1937**
FRIEND *of Eastnorthdown and Winnington Grange* **LG1965**
FRISBY *formerly of The Holt* **LG1965**
FROST *formerly of West Wratting*

LG1952; *of Dolcorsllwyn* **LG1937**; *formerly of Binsted* **DFUSA**; *formerly of Pulham* **DFUSA**
FRY, Bt **PB1976**; **IFR1976**; **DFUSA**
FRYE **DFUSA**
FRYER, Bt **EDB**; *formerly of Chatteris* **LG1952**; *of The Wergs* **LG1875**
FULFORD *of Fulford* **LG1965**
BROWN-FULLARTON *of Kilmichael* **LG1952**
FULLER, Bt **PB1970**; Bt **EDB**; *of Glashnacree* **LG1937Supp**; *of Neston Park* **LG1906**; *of The Rookery* **LG1898**; *of Hyde House and Germans* **LG1894**; *of Rose Hill* **LG1858**; **DFUSA**; **PromFUSA**; (*Canada*) **CG**; (*see also* Meyrick)
FULLERTON *of Norwood Grange* **LG1972**; *of Hambleden Place formerly of Ware* **LG1952**; *of Thribergh* **LG1937**; *formerly of Ballintoy* **LGI1958**; **DFUSA**
FULTON, B **PB1970**; *of Braidujle* **LGI1912**; **DFUSA**; *of Napier* **CG**; (*New Zealand*) **CG**
FURNELL **IFR1976**
FURNESE, Bt **EDB**
FURNESS, V **PB1970**; Bt *of Tunstall Grange* **PB1970**
FURNIVAL, B **DEP**; (*see also* Talbot)
FURNIVALL, B **PB1970**
FURSDON *of Fursdon* **LG1969**
FURSE *of Halsdon* **LG1965**
COLDHAM-FUSSELL (*Australia*) **CG**
FUST, Bt **EDB**
JENNER-FUST *of Hill Court* **LG1972**
FYFFE *of Smithfield* **LG1875**; (*see also* Phyfe)
MAXWELL FYFE (Kilmuir, V) **PB1967**
FYLER *of Woodlands and Hethfelton* **LG1921**
FYTCHE, Bt **EDB**
GABBETT **IFR1976**
GABRIEL, Bt **PB1891**
GADESDEN *of Holwell Manor* **LG1925 Supp**
GADSDEN *formerly of Little Gaddesden* **DFUSA**
GAEL *of Charlton Kings* **LG1858**
GAGE, V **PB1970**; B **DEP**; Bt **PB1872**; *formerly of Willbrook House* **LG1972**; *of Widdington* **LG1952**; **IFR1976**; (*see also* McCausland)
McCAUSLAND-GAGE (*see* McCausland)
GAINFORD (*see* Pease)
GAINSBOROUGH (*see* Noel)
GAINSFORD *of Skendleby* **LG1921**

GAIRDNER *formerly of Lisbeg House* **LGI1958**; **DFUSA**
GAISFORD *of Gresgarth Hall* **LG1972**; (*see also* Gaisford-St Lawrence)
GAITHER **DFUSA**
GAITSKELL, B **PB1970**
GALBRAITH (Strathclyde, B) **PB1970**; Bt **EDB**; *of Barskimming* **LG1952**; *of Clanabrogan* **LGI1912**
GALBRAITH (*formerly* MURRAY) *of Murraythwaite* **LG1952**
GALE *of Bardsea Hall* **LG1921**; *of Scruton Hall* **LG1900**; **FR**
MORANT-GALE (*see* Morant)
GALLOWAY (Dunkeld, Lord) **DEP**; *of Auchendrane* **LG1952**; *of Blervie* **LG1952**; *formerly of Holmsted Manor* **LG1952Supp**; **IFR1976**; **DFUSA**; (*see also* Stewart)
GALLWEY **IFR1976**
FRANKLAND-PAYNE-GALLWEY, Bt **PB1970**
GALMOYE (*see* Butler)
GALT *of Ballysally* **LGI1912**
GALTON *late of Hadzor House* **LG1937**; **AA**; **HI**
GALVIN **DFUSA**
GALWAY (*see* Monckton-Arundell; Burke; and Massue)
GALWEY, Bt **EDB**; **IFR1976**
GAMAGE **PromFUSA**
GAMBIER, B **DEP**
GAMBLE, Bt **PB1970**; *of Windlehurst* **LG1894**; *of Killoly Hall* **LGI1912**; *of Ballynacourty House* **LGI1958**; **DFUSA**
GAMBRILL **DFUSA**
GAMMAGE **DFUSA**
GAMMANS, Bt **PB1956**
GAMMELL *of Alrick* **LG1972**
GAMMIE *of Shotover House* **LG1863**
GANDELL *formerly of Slinfold Manor* **LG1972**
GANDOLFI, D **FT1939**; (*see also* Hornyold)
GANDY *of Skirsgill* **LG1921**
WATSON-GANDY (*see* Watson-Gandy-Brandreth)
GANE *of Warren Farm House* **LG1952**
PHILIPPS-GANGE *of Faversham* **LG1969**
GANNON *of Lara* **LG1875**
GANS, Bt **EDB**
GANT (Lincoln, E) **DEP**; B **DEP**
GANTT (*see* McDougall)
GANZONI (Belstead, B) **PB1970**
GAPE *of St Michael's Manor* **LG1952**
GARDE *of Ballinacurra* **LG1854**

GARDEN *of Troup* **LG1972**
GARDINER, B **PB1970**; (Blessington, E) **DEP**; Bt *of Roche Court* **PB1868**; Bt *of Roche Court* **EDB**; *of Goring* **LG1921**; *of Narragansett* **DFUSA** *formerly of Collynbyn Hall*
GARDNER, B **PB1970**; (Burghclere, B) **PB1921**; *formerly of Conington* **LG1952**; *of Culdees Castle* **LG1952**; **IFR1976**; (1) (2) (3) & (4) **DFUSA**; *of Coombe Lodge* **HI**
BRUCE-GARDNER, Bt **PB1970**
DUNN-GARDNER *of Chatteris House* **LG1921**
BRUCE-GARDYNE *of Middleton* **LG1972**
GREENHILL-GARDYNE *of Finavon* **LG1952**
GARFIELD **PresFUSA**
GARFIT *formerly of Kenwick Hall* **LG1972**; *formerly of Hopedene* **LG1969**
GARGRAVE *of Nostel* **VF**
GARLAND *late of Michaelstow Hall* **LG1937**
GARNER, B **PB1970**
GARNETT *of Quernmore Park* **LG1969**; *formerly of Wyreside* **LG1952**; *of Williamston* **LGI1912**; *of Summerseat* **LGI1912**; **PromFUSA**
CARPENTER-GARNIER *of Rookesbury Park* **LG1965**
GARNSWORTHY, B **PB1970**
GARRARD, Bt *of Lamer* **EDB**; Bt *of Langford* **EDB**
CHERRY-GARRARD *formerly of Lamer* **LG1952**
GARRATT *of Bishop's Court* **LG1972**
GARRETT *formerly of Cromac, Court* **LG1969**; *of Gower House* **LG1921**; *of Kilgaran* **LGI1912**; **DFUSA**
GARSIDE **DFUSA**
GARSTIN *of Braganstown* **LGI1912**
GARTH *of Morden Hall* **LG1886**
GARTHWAITE, Bt **PB1970**
GARTON *of Fyfield Manor* **LG1965**
GARTSHORE *of Gartshore* **LG1858**
GARVAGH (*see* Canning)
GARVEY *of Murrisk Abbey* **LG1937 Supp**; *of Porthill* **LG1937Supp**
GASCOIGNE *of Sanders* **LG1965**; *of Parlington, Lotherton and Craignish* **LG1952**; *late of Fishleigh* **LG1937**; *of Henley Hall* **LG1937**
GASCOINE, Bt **EDB**
GASKELL *of Kiddington Hall* **LG1952**;

of Ingersley Hall **LG1921**; *of Church-down* **LG1906**;

MILNES-GASKELL *formerly of Thomas House* **LG1965**

PENN-GASKELL *of Shanagarry* **LG1886**

GASON **IFR1976**

GASSIOT *of Carshalton* **LG1898**

GASTON *formerly of Clough Water* **DFUSA**; **PromFUSA**

GATACRE *of Gatacre* **LG1972**

GATAKER *formerly of Mildenhall* **LG1972**

GATE *of St Michael's Manor* **LG1882**

GATES *of Old Buckenham Hall* **LG1925**

GATTY *formerly of Ossemsley Manor* **LG1972**

GAULD *of Kinnaird Castle* **LG1952**

GAULT *of Hatch Court and Mont St Hilaire* **LG1952**

GAUSSEN *formerly of Brookmans* **LG1969**; *of Shanemullagh* **LGI1912**

GAVESTON (Cornwall, E) **DEP**

GAVIN *formerly of Braikie* **LG1972**

GAW **DFUSA**

GAWDY, Bt *of Crow's Hill* **EDB**; Bt *of West Herling* **EDB**

GAWTRY *formerly of Elvington* **DFUSA**

GAY *of Thurring Hall* **LG1914**; *of Falmouth* **AA**; (*see also* Lilly)

RIVERS-GAY (*see* Rivers)

GAYER *formerly of Liskeard* **LG1972**

GAYRE **LG1952Supp**

GAZZAM **DFUSA**

GEARY, Bt **PB1940**

GEDDES, B **PB1970**; (Geddes of Epsom, B) **PB1970**

GEE **DFUSA**

GELDART *of Kirk Deighton* **LG1921**

GELL *of Hopton Hall* **LG1972**

GELL, Bt **EDB**

CHANDOS-POLE-GELL (*see* Chandos-Pole)

GEMMELL *of Peatling Hall* **LG1921**

GENEVILL, B **DEP**

HENN-GENNYS *formerly of Whitleigh Hall* **LG1952**

GENT *of Moyns* **LG1882**

GENTLEMAN *of Ballyhorgan* **LGI1912**

GEOGHEGAN (*see* O'Neill)

GEORBODUS (Chester, E) **DEP**

GEORGE, Bt **PB1856**; *formerly of Haughs* **LG1972**; *of Thorington House* **LG1952**; *of Sessiagh Lodge* **LGI1958**; **FR**

LLOYD GEORGE (Lloyd George of

Dwyfor, E) **PB1970**; (Tenby, V) **PB1970**

GERARD, B **PB1970**; (Macclesfield, E) **DEP**; B **DEP**; Bt *of Fiskerton* **EDB**; Bt *of Harrow-on-the-Hill* **EDB**; *of Wrightington* **LG1952**; *of Rochsoles* **LG1921**; *of Ince* **LG1833/7**

GERARD (*now* RIDDELL) *of Kinwarton* **LG1921**

GERMAINE, Bt **EDB**

GERNON *of Athcarne Castle* **LGI1912**

GERRARD *formerly of Greenoge* **LGI1958**; *late of Gibbstown* **LG1937 Supp**

GERVASE *of Cecil* **LGI1912**

TAPPS-GERVIS (*see* Tapps-Gervis-Meyrick)

WADE-GERY *of Bushmead* **LG1969**

GETHIN, Bt **PB1970**

GHAIN KAJET, M **TNBE1956**

GHAIN TOFFIEHA, Count **TNBE1956**

GHISNES, B **DEP**

GIBB, Bt **EDB**; *of Easter Caribber* **LG1965**; *of Pyrgo Park* **LG1921**

GIBB (*formerly* JUDGE) *sometime of Gaichborough* **DFUSA**

STILEMAN-GIBBARD *of Sharnbrook* **LG1952**

GIBBES **PromFUSA**;

OSBORNE-GIBBES, Bt **PB1940**

GIBBINGS *of Gibbings Grove* **LGI1912**

GIBBON *of Little Stretton* **LG1952**; *of Getacre* **LG1875**; **IFR1976**

GIBBONS, Bt **PB1970**; Bt *of Sitting-bourne* **PB1876**; *of Roddington Manor* **LG1937**

GIBBS (Aldenham and Hunsdon, B) **PB1970**; (Wraxall, B) **PB1970**; *of Kingswood* **LG1952**; *of Derry* **LG1882**; *of The Yews, Sheffield* **AA**

GIBSON (Ashbourne, B) **PB1970**; Bt *of Linconia* **PB1970**; Bt *of Great Warley* **PB1970**; Bt *of Regent Terrace* **PB1912**; Bt **EDB**; *of Burnside, formerly of Whelprigg* **LG1969**; *of Glenarn* **LG1952**; *of Sandgate Lodge* **LG1886**; *of Shalford and Sullington* **LG1863**; *of Quernmore Park* **LG1833/7**; *of Rockforest* **LGI1912**; *formerly of Goldingstones* **DFUSA**

MILNER-GIBSON *of Theberton* **LG1921**

GIBSONE *formerly of Pentland* **LG1952**

GIDEON, Bt **EDB**

GIFFARD (Halsbury, E) **PB1970**; (Buckingham, E) **DEP**; B **DEP**; *formerly of Rushall* **LG1972**; *of*

Chillington **LG1969**; *of Brightley* **LG1858**
GIFFORD, B **PB1970**; Bt *of Burstall* **EDB**; Bt *of Castle Jordan* **EDB**; *late of Westbrook* **LGI1912**
GILBERT *of Chedgrave* **LG1972**; *of Lancarffe formerly of Treore* **LG1969**; *of Compton* **LG1965**; *of The Priory* **LG1921**; *of Trelissick* **LG1921**; **DFUSA**; *formerly of Bridgwater* **DFUSA**
DAVIES-GILBERT *formerly of Eastbourne* **LG1969**
GILBEY, Bt **PB1970**; (Vaux of Harrowden, B) **PB1970**
GILCHRIST *of Oppisdale* **LG1900**; *(Australia)* **CG**; *(New Zealand)* **CG**
GILCHRIST *(now STRONG)* **DFUSA**
GILDEA *of Clooncormack* **LGI1912**
GILFILLAN **DFUSA**
GILFOYLE *of Carrowcullen* **LGI1912**
GILKEY *formerly of Londonderry* **DFUSA**
GILL *of Bwlch-y-Cibau* **LG1952**; *of Mountquhanie* **LG1900**; *of Springhill* **LG1900**; *of Bickham* **LG1894**; *of Wyrardisbury* **LG1850/3**; **AA**
MITCHELL-GILL *of Auchinroath formerly of Savock* **LG1952**
MACKENZIE-GILLANDERS *formerly of Highfield* **LG1952**
GILLBANKS *of Whitefield House* **LG1875**
GILLESPIE *of Kirkton* **LG1906**; (1) & (2) **DFUSA**; *(see also* Gillespie-Stainton)
GILLETT, Bt **PB1970**; *formerly of Woodgreen* **LG1972**; *formerly of Chorley Wood Cedars* **LG1965**; *of Halvergate* **LG1921**; **DFUSA**; *(see also* Lort-Phillips)
GILLETTE **DFUSA**
GILLILAND *of Brookhall* **LGI1958**
GILLMAN, Bt **EDB**; **IFR1976**
GILLON *of Abbey St Bathans and formerly of Wallhouse* **LG1952**
GILLOW *of Leighton Hall* **LG1952**
GILMOUR, Bt *of Liberton* **PB1970**; Bt *of Lundin* **PB1970**; Bt **EDB**; *of Eaglesham* **LG1921**
GORDON-GILMOUR *of Liberton and Craigmillar* **LG1921**
GILPIN *of Hockliffe Grange* **LG1858**; *formerly of Kentmere Hall,* **DFUSA**
GILSTRAP, Bt **PB1896**
MACRAE-GILSTRAP *of Ileane Donan and Ballimore* **LG1937**

GINKEL (Athlone, E) **DEP**
GIRARDOT *of Car-Colston Hall* **LG1875**
GISBORNE *of Yoxall Lodge* **LG1875**; *(New Zealand)* **CG**
GISBOROUGH *(see* Chaloner)
GIST *of Wormington Grange* **LG1900**
GLADSTONE, Bt **PB1970**; (Gladstone of Hawarden, V) **PB1935**; V **PB1930**; *of Capenoch* **LG1972**
GLADWIN *(see* Gladwyn-Errington)
GLADWYN *(see* Jebb)
GLANDORE *(see* Crosbie)
GLANELY *(see* Tatem)
GLANTAWE *(see* Jenkins)
GLANUSK *(see* Bailey)
GLANVILLE *late of Catchfrench* **LG1937**
GLASCOTT *of Alderton* **LGI1912**
GLASFORD *(see* Abercromby)
GLASGOW *of Old Court* **LG1858**; *(see also* Boyle)
ROBERTSON-GLASGOW *formerly of Montgreenan* **LG1969**
GLASIER *(Canada)* **CG**
GLASSE **LG1850/3**
GLASTONBURY *(see* Grenville)
GLEAN-O'MALLUN *(see* O'Mallun)
GLEANE, Bt **EDB**
GLEDSTANES *of Fardross* **LGI1958**
GLEED *of Park House, Donington* **LG1952**
GLEGG *(now* COLLIE) *of Backford* **LG1937**
BASKERVYLE-GLEGG *of Withington* **LG1937**
GLEN *of Stratton Audley Park* **LG1886**
GLENARTHUR *(see* Arthur)
GLENAVY *(see* Campbell)
GLENCAIRN *(see* Cunynghame)
GLENCONNER *(see* Tennant)
GLENCROSS *formerly of Luxstowe* **LG1969**
GLENDEVON *(see* Hope)
GLENDONWYN *of Parton* **LG1858**
GLENDYNE *(see* Nivison)
GLENELG *(see* Grant)
GLENERVIE *(see* Douglas)
GLENESK *(see* Borthwick)
GLENGALL *(see* Butler)
GLENLYON *(see* Murray)
GLENN **DFUSA**
GLENRAVEL *(see* Benn)
GLENTANAR *(see* Coats)
GLENTORAN *(see* Dixon)
GLIDDEN **DFUSA**
GLIN, KNIGHT OF *(see* FitzGerald)
GLOSSOP *formerly of Silver Hall*

LG1965; *of Bramwith Hall* **LG1937**
GLOUCESTER (*see* Audley; Clare; Despencer; Guelph; Monthermer; Plantagenet; and Stuart)
GLOVER, Bt **PB1934**; *of Pytchley House* **LG1952**; (1) & (2) **DFUSA**
GLYN (Wolverton, B) **PB1970**; Bt *of Berbice* **PB1970**; Bt *of Ewell and Gaunts* **PB1970**; Bt **PB1959**
GLYNN *formerly of Glynn* **LG1972**; *of Harlesford House* **LG1972**; *of South Cerney House* **LG1952**; (*see also* Oglander)
GLYNNE, B **PB1874**
GNIEN-IS-SULTAN, M **TNBE1956**
GODBER, B **PB1970**
GODBEY **DFUSA**
GODDARD, B **PB1970**; *formerly of Blacknest* **LG1952**; *of Swindon* **LG1921**, *of Hartham* **LG1833/7**; *of Purton* **LG1833/7**; *of Clyffe Pypard* (*see* Wilson); *formerly of Eaglesham* **DFUSA**
GODFREY, Bt **PB1970**; *of Brooke Street House* **LG1969**; *of Kennett Hall* **LG1900**; **FR**
GODLEE, Bt **PB1925**
GODLEY (Kilbracken, B) **PB1970**
GODMAN *formerly of Park Hatch* **LG1965**
GODOLPHIN, E **DEP**; Bt **EDB**
GODSAL *of Iscoyd Park* **LG1965**
GODSON *of The Court, Tenbury* **LG1952**
GODWIN *formerly of Crowland* **DFUSA**
GOFF, Bt **PB1939**; *formerly of Standerwick Court and Hale Park*; **LG1969** *of Oakport* **LG1894**; *of Carrowroe Park* **LGI1912**; **DFUSA**
GOGARTY **IFR1976**
GOING *formerly of Traverston* **LGI1912**; *formerly of Ballyphilip* **LGI1912**; (*see also* Mansergh)
GOLD *formerly of Hedsor* **LG1965**
GOLDFINCH *late of Rotherhurst* **LG1937**
GOLDIE (*see* Goldie-Scot; and Fry-Goldie-Taubman)
GOLDING, Bt **EDB**; *of Maiden Erlegh* **LG1882**
GOLDINGHAM *of Horsendon* **LG1952**
GOLDISBROUGH *of Goldisbrough* **LG1833/7**
GOLDNEY, Bt **PB1970**
GOLDSBOROUGH *formerly of Goldsborough* **DFUSA**
GOLDSMID, Bt **PB1896**

D'AVIGDOR-GOLDSMID, Bt **PB1970**
GOLDSON *of Blo' Norton Hall* **LG1972**
GOLDSWORTHY *of Charton* **LG1952**
GOLLOP *of Strode* **LG1894**
GOMERINO, B **TNBE1956**
CARR-GOMM *formerly of Ockley Lodge* **LG1972**
GOOCH, Bt *of Benacre* **PB1970**; Bt *of Clewer Park* **PB1970**; *of Wivenhoe Park* **LG1972**
GOODACRE *of Ullesthorpe* **LG1952**
GOODALE *formerly of Dennington* **DFUSA**
GOODALL *of Dinton Hall* **LG1914** (*see also* Coryton)
GOODBAUDY (*see* Goodbody)
GOODBODY **IFR1976**
GOODCHILD *of Rotherby Manor* **LG1900**
GOODDEN *of Compton* **LG1965**
GOODE *formerly of Whitstone* **DFUSA**
GOODENOUGH, Bt **PB1970**; *formerly of Shaftesbury* **DFUSA**
GOODERE, Bt **EDB**
GOODFORD *of Shilton Cantelo* **LG1972**
GOODHART, Bt **PB1970**; *of Langley Park* **LG1850/3**
SIMONDS-GOODING *of Buncar House* **LGI1958**
GOODLAD *of Hill Place* **LG1886**
GOODLAKE *of Wadley House* **LG1898**
GOODLIFFE *of Richmond Park* **LGI1958**
GOODMAN *of Eccles House* **LG1952**; **FR**
GOODPASTURE **DFUSA**
GOODRICH *formerly of Bury St. Edmunds* **DFUSA**; **PromFUSA**
GOODRICKE, Bt **EDB**
GOODSON, Bt **PB1970**
GOODWIN *of Orton Hall* **LG1937**
GOOLD, Bt **PB1970**; (*see also* Goold-Adams)
GOODSELL *formerly of Staplegrove* **DFUSA**
GOODWIN *formerly of Bocking* **DFUSA**
GORDON (Aberdeen, M) **PB1970**; (Huntly, M) **PB1970**; Bt *of Earlston* **PB1970**; Bt *of Embo* **PB1956**; (Gordon of Drumearn, B) **PB1879**; Bt *of Northcourt* **PB1876**; Bt *of Dalpholly* **PB1850**; D **DEP**; (Norwich, E) **DEP**; (Aboyne, V) **DEP**; (Kenmure, V) **DEP**; (Melgum, V) **DEP**; Bt **EDB**; Bt *of Cluny* **EDB**; Bt *of Newark-upon-Trent* **EDB**; *of Letterfourie* **LG1972**; *of Abergeldie* **LG1969**; *of Ballindoun House* **LG1965**; *formerly of Kinharvie* **LG1965**; *of Cairnfield*

LG1952; *of Drimnin* LG1952; *of Lane Head* LG1952; *formerly of Newtimber* LG1952; *of Pitlurg* LG1952; *of Threave* LG1952; *of Wincombe Park* LG1952; *of Auchendolly* LG1937; *of Cairness* LG1937; *formerly of Ellon* LG1937; *of Wardhouse* LG1937; *of Culvennan* LG1882; *of Balmagie* LG1875; *of Cairnbulge* LG1875; *of Haffield* LG1833/7; *formerly of Kirkcudbright* **DFUSA**; **PromFUSA**; *of Nanaimo and Comax* **CG**; *of Culvenan* **HI**; *of Manar* (*see* Risley)

GORDON (*now* GORDON-PUGH) **IFR1976**

GORDON (formerly STEUART) *of Tanachie formerly of Auchlunkart* **LG1952**

CONWAY-GORDON *formerly of Lynwode* **LG1952**

DUFF GORDON, Bt **PB1970**

FELLOWES-GORDON *of Knockespoch* **LG1965**

FORBES-GORDON *of Rayne* **LG1937**

HAMILTON-GORDON (Stanmore, B) **PB1956**

HAY-GORDON *of Avochie* **LG1900**

MAITLAND-GORDON *late of Kenmuir* **LG1937**

PIRIE-GORDON *of Buthlaw* **LG1965**

SMITH-GORDON, Bt **PB1970**

WOLRIGE-GORDON *of Hallhead and Esslemont* **LG1965**

GORE (Arran, E) **PB1970**; Bt **PB1970**; (Ross, E) **DEP**; (Annaly, B) **DEP**; *of Hawkington* **LGI858**; *of Derrymore* **LGI1912**; *of Fedney* **LGI1912**; **DFUSA**

HUME-GORE *formerly of Derryluskan* **LG1952**

KNOX-GORE (*see* Knox)

PERY-KNOX-GORE (*see* Limerick)

SAUNDERS-KNOX-GORE (*see* Knox)

ORMSBY-GORE (Harlech, B) **PB1970**

GORELL (*see* Barnes)

BARNES-GORELL (*see* Barnes)

GORGES, B **DEP**; (Gorges of Dundalk, B) **DEP**; Bt **EDB**; *of Wraxall* **LG1965**

GORING, Bt **PB1970**; (Norwich, E) **DEP**; Bt **EDB**; *of Wiston* **LG1937**

GORMANSTON (*see* Preston)

GORST *of Catts Place* **LG1952**

GORT (*see* Vereker)

GORTON **FR**

GOSCHEN, V **PB1970**; Bt *of Beacon Lodge* **PB1970**; Bt *of Durrington House* **PB1940**

GOSFORD (*see* Acheson)

GOSLING *of Thrimley House, formerly of Hassobury* **LG1965**

GOSSELIN *of Blakesware* **LG1914**

GOSSET *formerly of Town Court* **LG1952**

GOSSETT **DFUSA**

GOSSIP **FR**; (*see also* Hatfeild)

GOSTWICK, Bt **EDB**

GOTT *formerly of Armley* **LG1969**

GOUGH, V **PB1970**; *of Corsley House* **LG1972**; *of Glenthorn* **LG1937**; *of Yniscedwyn* **LG1937**; *of Perry Hall* **LG1833/7**

GOULBURN *of Betchworth, Apley and Woodcote* **LG1972**

GOULD, Bt **EDB**; *of Upwey* **LG1952**; **DFUSA**; *formerly of Milton* **DFUSA**; (*see also* Muirhead)

BARING-GOULD *of Lew Trenchard* **LG1972**

GOULDING, Bt **PB1970**; (Wargrave, B) **PB1936**

GOULTON (*see* Goulton-Constable)

MURRAY-GOURLAY *of Kincraig* **LG1952**

GOUVERNEUR (*see* Monroe)

GOW *of Howwood* **LG1952**

BUTT-GOW *of Little Fowlers* **LG1937**

GOWEN **DFUSA**

GOWER *formerly of Glandovan* **LG1972**; *of Sandown Court* **LG1952**

LEVESON-GOWER (Granville, B) **PB1970**; (*see also* Sutherland)

GOWRAN (*see* Butler)

GOWRIE (*see* Ruthven)

GOYDER (*Australia*) **CG**

GRAAFF, Bt **PB1970**

GRACE, Bt **PB1970**; *of Knowle House* **LG1850/3**; *of Mantua, co Roscommon* **AA**; (*see also* Bowen)

GRACEY *of Northcote Manor* **LG1952**

GRADWELL *formerly of Dowth Hall* **LGI1958**; *of Platten Hall* **LGI1912**

GRAEME *formerly of Garvock* **LG1969**; *of Aberuthven and formerly of Inchbrakie* **LG1952**; (*Canada*) **CG**

HAMOND-GRAEME, Bt **PB1970**

SUTHERLAND GRAEME *of Graemeshall* **LG1952**

GRAFTON (*see* FitzRoy)

GRAESSER *of Argoed Hall* **LG1952**

GRAEVENITZ *of The Wolds* **LG1952**

GRAHAM (Montrose, D) **PB1970**; Bt *of Dromore* **PB1970**; Bt *of Esk* **PB1970**; Bt *of Larbert* **PB1970**; Bt *of Netherby* **PB1970**; Bt *of Norton Conyers* **PB1970**; (Atholstan, B) **PB1938**; Bt *of Kirkstall* **PB1895**; (Dundee, V) **DEP**; (Lynedoch,

B) **DEP**; (Preston, V) **DEP**; (Strathern, E) **DEP**; Bt *of Braco* **EDB**; Bt *of Gartmore* **EDB**; *of Mossknowe* **LG1972**; *formerly of Auchenloich and Tamrawer* **LG1965**; *of Old Mill House* **LG1965**; *of Pulham St Mary* **LG1952**; *of Rednock formerly of Duchray* **LG1952**; *of Summerhill formerly of Drumgoon* **LG1952 Supp**; *of Breckness* (*see* Scarth); *of Airth* **LG1937**; *of Edmond Castle* **LG1937**; *formerly of Fintry* **LG1937**; *of Carefin and Stonebyers* **LG1921**; *of Leitchtown* **LG1921**; *of Balgowan* **LG1858**; *of Meiklewood* **LG1858**; **IFR1976**; *of Larchfield* **LGI1958**; *of Summerhill* **LGI1958**; (1) & (2) **FR**; *of Largs* **AA**; *of Breckness* (*see* Scarth); *of Duntrune* (*see* Graham-Wigan); (*see also* Sheppard)
BARNS-GRAHAM *of Lymekilns* **LG1972**
BONTINE CUNNINGHAME GRAHAM *of Ardoch* **LG1952**
MAXTONE GRAHAM *of Cultoquhey* **LG1972**
MURRAY-GRAHAM (*see* Maxtone Graham)
GRAHAME *of Lingo formerly of Drumquhassil and Ballagan* **LG1952**; *of Overglenny* **LG1937**
BARCLAY GRAHAME *of Morphie* **LG1952**
LIDDELL-GRAINGER *of Ayton Castle* **LG1965**
GRANGER *of Littleton Hall* **LG1952**
GRANARD (*see* Forbes)
GRANDISON (Grandison, B) **DEP**; (*see also* Villiers)
GRANLEY (*see* Grey)
GRANT (Strathspey, B) **PB1970**; Bt *of Dalvey* **PB1970**; Bt *of Monymusk and Cullen* **PB1970**; Bt *of Forres* **PB1940**; Bt *of Househill* **PB1932**; (Glenelg, B) **DEP**; *of Cotes* **LG1965**; *of Rothiemurchus* **LG1965**; *of Beil and Dirleton formerly of Kilgraston* **LG1952**; *of Carron formerly of Elchies* **LG1952**; *formerly of Corrimony* **LG1952**; *of Druminnor* **LG1952**; *of Glenmoriston* **LG1937**; *of Porth-y-Felin House* **LG1937**; *of Kincorth* **LG1882**; *of Kilmurray* **LGI1912**; **PresFUSA**; (1) (2) & (3) **DFUSA**; *formerly of Auchernach* **DFUSA**; (Glenmoriston) **DFUSA**; *of Windsor, Conn.* **DFUSA**; **FR**; (*S Africa*) **CG**; *of Tullochgorum* **CG**; *of Arndilly* (*see* Stewart-Menzies); *of Hillersdon* (*see*

Grant-Sturgis); *of Lichborough* (*see* Grant-Rennick)
FORSYTH-GRANT *of Ecclesgreig* **LG1952**
MACPHERSON-GRANT, Bt **PB1970**
OGILVIE GRANT (Strathspey, B) **PB1884**; (*see also* Seafield)
GRANTCHESTER (*see* Suenson-Taylor)
GRANTHAM *of Chailey* **LG1952**; **FR**; (*see also* Grantham-Hill; and Nassau)
GRANTLEY (*see* Norton)
GRANVILLE (Granville of Eye, B) **PB1970**; (Bath, E) **DEP**; (Lansdowne, B) **DEP**; *of Wellesbourne* **LG1969**; (*see also* Carteret; and Leveson-Gower)
GRATTAN **IFR1976**
ARCHDALL-GRATWICKE (*see* Montgomery)
GRAVES, B **PB1970**; *of Cloghan Castle* **LGI1912**; *of Mickleton* **LG1863**; **DFUSA**; *formerly of Beeley* **DFUSA**
GRAY, Bt **PB1970**; Bt **EDB**; *of Stewkey Old Hall late of Farley Hill Place* **LG1937**; *of Nunraw* **LG1921**; *of East Bolton* **LG1882**; *of Darcy Lever Hall* **LG1875**; *of Gilmilnscroft* **LG1833/37**; *of Carntyne* **LG1833/37**; **IFR1976**; *of Graymount* **LGI1958**; *of Enagh* **LGI1912**; *formerly of Currie* **DFUSA**; *formerly of Newtown Stewart* **DFUSA**; (*Australia*) **CG**; *of Carntyne, co Lanark* **AA**; *of Charleville House, Rathmines, co Dublin* **AA**; (*see also* Gray-Cheape)
GRAY (*formerly* SMYTH) *of Heath and Ripple* **LG1952**
ANSTRUTHER-GRAY (Kilmany, B) **PB1970**
CAMPBELL-GRAY (Gray, B) **PB1970**
GRAYRIGGE *of Wood Broughton* **LG1952**
GRAYSON, Bt **PB1970**
GRAZEBROOK *of Blakeshall* **LG1965**; *of Stourton Castle* **LG1965**
GREATHED (*see* Oldfield)
GREAVES (Dysart, E) **PB1970**; *of Broneifion and Glangwna* **LG1937**; *of Weston House* **LG1937**; *of The Cliff* **LG1882**; *of Staffordshire* **LG1875**; *of Irlam Hall* **LG1833/37**; *of Mayfield Hall* **LG1833/37**; *of Avonside* **LG1863**; (*see also* Bagshawe *of Ford Hall*)
GREAVES (*formerly* BRADSHAW) *formerly of Culcheth Hall* **LG1952**
BROWN-GREAVES *of Woodthorpe Hall* **LG1921**
GREECE (*Royal House of*) **RL**

GREEN, Bt **PB1970**; Bt *of Belsize Park*
PB1959; Bt *of Marras* **EDB**; Bt *of
Milnrow* **EDB**; Bt *of Mitcham* **EDB**; Bt
of Sampford **EDB**; *formerly of Ring-
stead* **LG1972**; *formerly of Hainault
Lodge* **LG1952**; *of The Whittern*
LG1952; *formerly of Court Henry*
LG1952Supp; *formerly of Felmersham
Grange* **LG1937**; *of King's Ford*
LG1921; *of Wyvehoe Hall* **LG1898**; *of
Wilby* **LG1886**; *of Dunsbye* **LG1882**;
DFUSA; (1) & (2) **FR**; (*see also* Red-
mond; and Young-Thompson)
LANCELYN-GREEN *of Poulton-
Lancelyn* **LG1972**
GREENALL (Daresbury, B) **PB1970**
GREENAWAY, Bt **PB1970**; *of Barring-
ton Grove* **LG1863**
GREENE, B **PB1949**; *formerly of Harston
House* **LG1965**; *of Midgham* **LG1900**;
of Rolleston **LG1858**; **IFR1976**;
PromFUSA; **CG**; (*see also* Marshall)
GREENE (*now* BROOKE *and* PHILIPS)
formerly of Slyne and Whittington
LG1937
CONYNGHAM GREENE **IFR1976**
CROFTS-GREENE (*see* Crofts)
GREENFIELD **FR**
GREENHAM *formerly of Norton sub
Hamdon* **LG1972**; *of Wentworth*
LG1937
GREENHILL, B **PB1970**; *of Knowle Hall*
LG1952
GREENLY *of Titley Court* **LG1972**
GREENSHIELDS *of Houghton-le-Spring*
LG1952
GREENWAY, B **PB1970**
GREENWELL, Bt **PB1970**; *of Greenwell
Ford* **LG1972**; *late of Broomshields*
LG1937
GREENWICH (*see* Townshend)
GREENWOOD, V **PB1970**; *of Swarcliffe
Hall* **LG1972**; *of Stone Hall* **LG1972**;
formerly of Wallingford **LG1965**; late
of Broadhanger **LG1914**
GREER (Fairfield, B) **PB1940**; **IFR1976**;
DFUSA
GREEVES **IFR1976**
GREG *formerly of Norcliffe Hall* **LG1972**;
late of Escowbeck **LG1937**
GREGG **LGI1958**; *of Ballyknockane
House* **LGI1958**; **FR**
GREGOR *of Trewarthenick* **LG1886**
GREGORY, Bt **PB1949**; *of Tayfletts*
LG1969; *of Ireland House* **LG1952**; *of
Adcote* **LG1937**; *of Ashfordby and
West Court* **LG1925**; *of Bramcote*

LG1882; **IFR1976**; **CG**; (*see also* Hood)
GREGSON *of Murton and Burdon*
LG1952
GREHAN *of Clonmeen* **LGI1958**
GREIG *of Binsness* **LG1972**; *of Eccles*
LG1969; *formerly of Glen Park*
LG1937; *of Glencarse* **LG1914**
GRENDON, B **DEP**
GRENFELL, B **PB1970**; (St Just, B)
PB1970; (Desborough, B) **PB1940**
GRENVILLE (Glastonbury, B) **DEP**;
(Grenville, B) **DEP**
TEMPLE - NUGENT - BRYDGES -
CHANDOS - GRENVILLE (Bucking-
ham and Chandos, D) **PB1889**
FREEMAN-GRENVILLE (Kinloss, B)
PB1970
MORGAN-GRENVILLE (*see* Kinloss)
GRESHAM, Bt **EDB**
GRESLEY, Bt **PB1970**; B **DEP**; (*see also*
Ball)
GRESSON (*New Zealand*) **CG**
GRESWOLDE (*see* Greswolde-Williams)
GRETTON, Bt **PB1970**
GREVILLE (Warwick, E) **PB1970**; B
PB1970
GREVIS (*see* Grevis-James)
GREY, E **PB1970**; (Stamford, E) **PB1970**;
(Grey de Ruthyn, B) **PB1970**; (Grey of
Naunton, B) **PB1970**; Bt *of Fallodon*
PB1970; (Grey of Falloden, V) **PB1933**;
(Grey de Radclyffe, B) **PB1885**; (Kent,
D) **DEP**; (Suffolk, D) **DEP**; (Tanker-
ville, E) **DEP**; (Warrington, E) **DEP**;
(Graney, V) **DEP**; (L'Isle, V) **DEP**;
(Grey, of Codnor, B) **DEP**; (Grey,
of Rotherfield, B) **DEP**; (Grey of
Wilton, B) **DEP**; Bt **EDB**; *formerly of
The Manor House, Shipman* **LG1952**;
of Milfield **LG1952**; *of Norton* **LG1875**;
of Morwick **LG1833/37**; (*New Zealand*)
CG; (*see also* Best)
GREY (*formerly* HOARE) *of Hocker
Edge* **LG1937**
GREY DE WILTON (*see* Egerton)
BACON-GREY *of Styford* **LG1921**
GREYSTOCK, B **DEP**
GRIDLEY, B **PB1970**
GRIERSON, Bt **PB1970**
MACFARLANE-GRIEVE *of Penchrise
and Edenhall* **LG1937**
MACKENZIE-GRIEVE *of Eastwater
House* **LG1937**
GRIFFIN, B **DEP**; *of Bourn Hall* **LG1952**;
of Colehurst **LG1937**; *of Towersey*
LG1921; *of Violet Hill* **LG1882**; *of The
Hurn* **LG1894**; (1) & (2) **DFUSA**

GRIFFITH, Bt **EDB**; *formerly of Garn* **LG1972**; *of Plasnewydd* **LG1952**; *of Braich y Celyn* **LG1937**; *Castle Neynoe* **LG1894**; *of Trevalyn* **LG1882**; *of Brisbane* **CG**; (*see also* Heaton; and Richmond)
DARBY-GRIFFITH *of Padworth* **LG1937**
ELLIS-GRIFFITH, Bt **PB1934**
WALDIE-GRIFFITH, Bt **PB1933**
GRIFFITHS **FR**; (*see also* Williams)
COPLAND-GRIFFITHS *of Potterne, formerly* Griffiths *of Erryd* **LG1952**
NORTON-GRIFFITHS, Bt **PB1970**
GRIGG (Altrincham, B) **PB1970**
GRIGGS *of Wigwell Grange* **LG1952**
GRIGSON *of Saham Toney* **LG1875**
GRIMSHAW *of Hutton Lodge* **LG1921**; *formerly of Priorsland* **LGI1958**
GRIMSTON (Verulam, E) **PB1970**; (Grimston of Westbury, B) **PB1970**; Bt **EDB**; *formerly of Grimston Garth* **LG1972**
GRIMTHORPE (*see* Beckett)
GRISEWOOD *formerly of Daylesford* **LG1965**
GRISSELL *formerly of Redisham Hall* **LG1952**
GRISWOLD **DFUSA**; **PromFUSA**
GROGAN, Bt **PB1927**; *formerly of Plattenstown* **LGI1958**; *of Slaney Park* **LGI1958**
GRONOW *of Ash Hall* **LG1894**
GROOM (*Fiji*) **CG**
GROSVENOR (Westminster, D) **PB1970**; (Ebury, B) **PB1970**; (Stalbridge, B) **PB1949**; *of Blakodown formerly of Broome* **LG1952**; **IFR1976**
GROSVENOR (*formerly* GRAVENOR) **DFUSA** *sometime of Bridgnorth*
GROTRIAN, Bt **PB1970**; *of North Stainley Hall* **LG1937**
GROVE, Bt **PB1970**; *of Pollards Park* **LG1921**; *of Coldbrook* **CG** (*see also* Grove Annesley; Troyte-Bullock; and Grove-White)
CAMPBELL-GROVE **IFR1976**
CHAFFYN-GROVE (*see* Troyte-Bullock)
GROVES *formerly of Holehird* **LG1969**
GRUBB **IFR1976**
HUNT-GRUBBE *of Eastwell* **LG1952**
GRUEBER (*of Ormley*) **CG**
GRUNDY *of Park House* **LG1952**
GRYLLS *of Winterbourne Zelston* **LG1969**; *late of St Neot* **LG1937**
GUADER (*see* Wayer)
GUBBINS *of Dunkath* **LG1937Supp**

GUELPH (Cumberland and Teviotdale, D) **PB1917**; (Edinburgh, D) **PB1900**; (Cambridge, D) **DEP**; (Clarence, D) **DEP**; (Cumberland, D) **DEP**; (Cumberland and Strathern, D) **DEP**; (Edinburgh, D) **DEP**; (Gloucester and Edinburgh, D) **DEP**; (Kent and Strathern, D) **DEP**; (Sussex, D) **DEP**; (York and Albany, D) **DEP**
GUEST (Wimborne) **PB1970**; B **PB1970**; **DFUSA**
HADEN-GUEST, B **PB1970**
GUILD *formerly of Balquharn* **LG1972**
GUILD (*formerly* CHEVALLIER) *of Aspall Hall* **LG1972**
GUILDFORD (*see* Boyle)
GUILFORD (*see* North)
GUILLAMORE (*see* O'Grady)
GUINNESS (Iveagh, E) **PB1970**; (Moyne, B) **PB1970**; Bt **PB1970**; (Ardilaun, B) **PB1915**; (*co Dublin*) **IFR1976**; (*co Kildare*) **IFR1976**; **AA**
LEE-GRATTAN-GUINNESS **AA**
GUIRY **IFR1976**
GUISE, Bt **PB1970**; Bt **EDB**
GULDEFORD, Bt **EDB**
GULL, Bt **PB1970**
GULLION **DFUSA**
GULLIVER **DFUSA**
GULLY (Selby, V) **PB1970**; *of Trevennen* **LG1882**
STEPNEY-GULSTON *of Derwydd* **LG1969**
MAXWELL-GUMBLETON *of Twyning* **LG1952**
GUN *of Rattoo* **LGI1912**, (*see also* Gun Cuninghame)
GUNDRY *of The Hyde* **LG1965**
GUNNING, Bt **PB1970**; *of Torney's Court and Langridge* **LG1863**; *of Woolley* **LG1863**; *of Swainswick* **LG1863**
GUNSTON, Bt **PB1970**
GUNTER, Bt **PB1970**
GUNTHER **LG1921**
GURDON (Cranworth, B) **PB1970**; *of Burgh House* **LG1952**; *late of Assington* **LG1921**
GURNEY, Bt **EDB**; *of Keswick and Bawdeswell* **LG1965**; *formerly of North Runcton* **LG1965**; *of Walsingham Abbey and Earlham* **LG1965**; *of Hare Street* **LG1952**
GUROWSKI *formerly of Woolhampton Park* **LG1972**
GURWOOD **HI**
GUTHE *of Kepwick Hall* **LG1952**

GUTHRIE, Bt ?**B1970**; *of Craigie* **LG1972**; *of Guthrie* **LG1972**; *of Haukerton* **LG1850/53**; **CG**
LINGARD GUTHRIE *of Carnoustie* **LG1952**
GUYON **FR**
GWATKIN (1) & (2) **FR**
GWYDYR (*see* Burrell)
GWYN *formerly of Stanfield Hall* **LG1965**
MOORE-GWYN *formerly of Dyffryn* **LG1969**
GWYNEDD (*Kings and Princes of*) **RL**
GWYNN **IFR1976**
GWYNNE *of Folkington Manor* **LG1952**; *formerly of Glangrwyney* **LG1952**; *formerly of Monachty* **LG1952**; *of Cynghordy, co Carmarthen* **AA**
GYLL *of Remenham* **LG1900**; *of Wyddial Hall* **HI**
HABIN *of Newton House* **RFFK**
HACCHE, B **DEP**
HACKER *of East Bridgford* **LG1882**
HACKETT *late of Moor Hall* **LG1937**; **IFR1976**; B **FT1917**
HACKING, B **PB1970**
HACKNEY **DFUSA**
HADDEN *of Stonehouse* **LG1952**
HADDINGTON (*see* Baillie-Hamilton)
HADDOCK **DFUSA**
HADFIELD, Bt **PB1940**
HADLEY (1) & (2) **DFUSA**; *formerly of Ballynakill* **DFUSA**
HADOW *formerly of Kemsing* **LG1969**; *of Coates House* **LG1952**
HADWEN **LG1952Supp**
HAFFENDEN *of Homewood* **LG1858**
HAGART *of Eastbury Manor* **LG1894**
HAGGARD *formerly of Bradenham* **LG1965**; *of Hemsby* **LG1900**
HAGGART *of Aberfeldy* **LG1937**
HAGGAS *formerly of Walmsgate Hall* **LG1937**
HAGGERSTON, Bt **PB1970**
HAGGITT (*see* Wegg-Prosser)
HAIG, E **PB1970**; *formerly of Bemersyde* **LG1969**; *formerly of Blairhill* **LG1969**; *of Dollarfield* **LG1969**; *formerly of Pen-Ithon* **LG1969**; *formerly of Ramornie* **LG1969**; *of Grainsby* **LG1952**; **FR**
HAGUE *of Norman Hill* **LG1952**
HAIGH *of Grainsby Hall* **LG1937**
HAILEY, B **PB1967**
HAINES *of Bagendon* **LG1921**; *of Hasketon* **LG1921**
HAILES (*see* Buchan-Hepburn)
HAILSHAM (*see* Hogg)
HAIRE (Haire of Whiteabbey, B)

PB1963; *of Armagh Manor* **LG1937 Supp**
HALD (*see* Hildyard)
HALDANE, V **PB1928**
HALDANE (*now* STUMP) **DFUSA**
CHINNERY-HALDANE *of Gleneagles* **LG1972**
HALDON (*see* Pack)
HALE *of Plumpton* **LG1969**; *of King's Walden* **LG1921**; *of Somerston Hall* **LG1882**; *formerly of King's Walden* **DFUSA**
HALE (*formerly* SEYMOUR) *of Ballymore Castle* **LGI1958**
SHERWOOD-HALE *of Alderley* **LG1972**
HALES, Bt *of Beaksbourne* **EDB**; Bt *of Coventry* **EDB**; Bt *of Woodchurch* **EDB**; *of Copdock and Washbrook* **LG1921**
HALFORD, Bt **EDB**; *of East Bergholt* **LG1921**; (*see also* Vaughan)
HALIBURTON, B **PB1907**
HALIDAY *of Squires Hill* **LG1863**
HALIFAX (*see* Montagu; Savile; and Wood)
HALKETT, Bt **PB1904**
CRAIGIE-HALKETT *of Cramond* **LG1914**
HALL, V **PB1970**; (Roberthall, B) **PB1970**; Bt *of Burton Park* **PB1970**; Bt *of Dunglass* **PB1970**; Bt *of Grafham* **PB1970**; (Llanover, B) **DEP**; *formerly of Hall Park* **LG1972**; *of Charnes Hall* **LG1965**; *formerly of Jamaica* **LG1965**; *formerly of Barton Abbey* **LG1952**; *of Glebe House* **LG1952**; *of Hales Hall* **LG1952**; *formerly of Holly Bush* **LG1952**; *of Melyniog* **LG1952**; *formerly of Foxcote* **LG1937**; *of Pentreheylen Hall* **LG1937**; *of Sutton* **LG1937**; *formerly of Weeting Hall* **LG1937**; *late of Whatton Manor* **LG1937**; *of Park Hall* **LG1921**; *formerly of Six Mile Bottom* **LG1921**; *of Burton Park* **LG1914**; *of Farnham Chase* **LG1900**; *of Walton on the Hill* **LG1886**; *of Scorbro'* **LG1882**; *of Hallstead* **LG1882**; *of Blacklands Park* **LG1875**; *of Abercarne* **LG1833/37**; (*co Cork*) **IFR1976**; (*co Down*) **IFR1976**; *of Barmeen* **LGI1958**; *of Rowantree House* **LGI1958**; *formerly of Henbury* **DFUSA**; *of Hororata* **CG**; **AA**; *of Blacklands Park, Wilts* **AA**; (*see also* FitzWilliams; and Knight)
HALL (*formerly* McARTHUR and MARSHALL) *of Treworgey Manor* **LG1972**
KING-HALL, B **PB1967**

MACALISTER HALL *of Torrisdale* **LG1972**
HUGHES-HALLETT *formerly of Higham* **LG1965**
HALLEWELL *of Stratford Park* **LG1886**
HALLIDAY *of Glenthorne* **LG1972**; *formerly of Chicklade* **LG1969**; *of Chapel Cleeve* **LG1906**; *of Rodborough* **LG1833/37**; *of Scotland* **LG1833/37**; *of Wilts and Somerset* **LG1833/37**
HALLIFAX *of Chadacre Hall* **LG1882**
HALLINAN **IFR1976**
HALLOWES *formerly of Glapwell Hall* **LG1921**
HALLOWELL *formerly of Sutton* **DFUSA**
HALPIN *of Ford Lodge* **LGI1958**
HALSALL (*see* Clifton)
HALSBURY (*see* Giffard)
HALSEY, Bt **PB1970**; *of Gaddesden Place* **LG1914**; *formerly of Great Gaddesden* **DFUSA**
EVERY-HALSTED *formerly of Rowley* **LG1937Supp**
HALSWELL *of Wylmington Hayes* **LG1952**
HALTON, Bt **EDB**; *formerly of Greenthwaite Hall* **LG1972**
HALYBURTON, Lord **DEP**; Bt **EDB**
HAM (*Australia*) **CG**
HAMBLEDEN (*see* Smith)
HAMBLING, Bt **PB1970**
HAMBLY *of Treharrock Manor* **LG1969**
HAMBRO *of The Hyde* **LG1965**
HAMBROUGH *of Pipewell Hall* **LG1914**; *of Steephill Castle* **AA**
HAMER *formerly of Glan-yr-Afon* **LG1972**
DUCAT HAMERSLEY *of Pyrton Manor* **LG1965**
HAMERTON (*now* BOWER) *of Hellifield* **LG1937**
HAYTER-HAMES *of Chagford* **LG1952**
HAMILTON (Abercorn, D) **PB1970**; (Belhaven and Stenton, B) **PB1970**; (Hamilton of Dalzell, B) **PB1970**; (Holm Patrick, B) **PB1970**; Bt *of Ilford* **PB1970**; Bt *of Silverton Hill* **PB1970**; Bt *of Trebinshun* **PB1970**; (Sumner, B) **PB1940**; Bt *of Cadogan Square* **PB1928**; Bt *of Woodbrook* **PB1876**; (Hamilton of Wishaw, B) **PB1868**; (Melrose, B) **PB1858**; (Clanbrassill, E) **DEP**; (Ruglen, E) **DEP**; (Bargeny, Lord) **DEP**; (Hamilton, of Glenawly, B) **DEP**; Bt **EDB**; Bt *of Broomhill* **EDB**; Bt *of London* **EDB**; Bt of *Monella* **EDB**; Bt *of Rosehall* **EDB**; *formerly of*

Barns and Cochno **LG1972**; *of Lowood and Castlehill* **LG1972**; *of Rozelle* **LG1969**; *of Craighlaw* **LG1952**; *of Fyne Court* **LG1952**; *of Carrwood House* **LG1937**; *formerly of The Retreat* **LG1937**; *of Brownhall* **LG1937Supp**; *late of Hillston* **LG1921**; *of Kiftsgate Court* **LG1921**; *of Pinmore* **LG1921**; *of Cairn Hill and Westport* **LG1900**; *of Wilton* **LG1882**; *of Orbiston and Dalzell* **LG1875**; *of Newton* **LG1833/7**; *of Westburn* **LG1833/7**; (*co Leix*) **IFR1976**; (*co Louth*) **IFR1976**; (*co Meath*) **IFR1976**; *formerly of Ballymacoll* **LGI1958**; *of Cornacassa* **LGI1912**; *of Mossville* **LGI1912**; *of Castle Hamilton* **LGI1912**; **DFUSA**; **FR**; (*Canada*) **CG**; *of Hobart* **CG**; *of Elderslie* **CG**; *of Fyne Court, co Somerset* **AA**; *of Glasgow* **AA**; *of Hamwood, co Meath* **AA**; (*see also* Douglas)
HAMILTON (*now* AMES) *of Sundrum* **LG1921**
HAMILTON (*now* COLTMAN) *of Daljarrock* **LG1937**
HAMILTON (*formerly* RICARDO) *of Bramley Park* **LG1952**
BAILLIE-HAMILTON (Haddington, E) **PB1970**
BUCHANAN-BAILLIE-HAMILTON *of Arnprior* **LG1937**
BARRETT-HAMILTON *of Kilmanock House* **LGI1912**
DIX HAMILTON *formerly of Wickmere Hall* **LG1969**
DOUGLAS-HAMILTON (Hamilton and Brandon, D) **PB1970** (Selkirk, E) **PB1970**
FINDLAY-HAMILTON *of Westport and Carnell* **LG1952**
MACNEILL-HAMILTON *of Raploch* **LG1937**
ROWAN-HAMILTON **IFR1976**
STEVENSON HAMILTON *of Fairholm* **LG1969**
STIRLING-HAMILTON, Bt **PB1970**
WALDRON-HAMILTON *of Ashfort House* **LGI1958**
HAMLIN (*see* Blacker)
HAMLYN *of Buckfastleigh* **LG1972**; *of Widecombe-in-the-Moor* **LG1972**; *of Clovelly* **LG1937**
CALMADY-HAMLYN *of Leawood* **LG1972**
HAMMETT (*see* Kirkwood; and Williams)
HAMMICK, Bt **PB1970**

HAMMOND (Hammond of Kirkella, B)
PB1890; *formerly of Cressners* LG1972;
formerly of Newmarket LG1937; *of St
Alban's Court* LG1937; DFUSA; *formerly of Lavenham* DFUSA
HAMON, Bt **EDB**
HAMOND *formerly of Westacre* LG1965;
late of Pampisford Hall LG1921
HARBORD-HAMOND (Suffield, B)
PB1970
HAMPDEN (*see* Trevor-Battye; Brand;
and Trevor)
HOBART-HAMPDEN (Buckinghamshire, E) PB1970
HAMPSON, Bt PB1970
HAMPTON (*see* Pakington)
VIVIAN-HAMPTON (*see* Vivian)
HANBURY *of Drumstinchall, formerly of
Poles* LG1965; *formerly of Kingston
Maurward* LG1965; *of Hitcham House*
LG1937; *of Bishopstowe* LG1921; (*see
also* Hanbury-Williams; and Hill *of
Holfield Grange*)
BATEMAN-HANBURY (Bateman, B)
PB1931
BOWRING-HANBURY *of Islam and
Norton* LG1921
HANCE **DFUSA**
HANCOCK (*see* Ligon)
HANCOCKS *of Wolverley Court* LG1921
HANDCOCK (Castlemaine, B) PB1970;
(Castlemaine, V) PB1839; *of Cole Hill
House* LG1882; *of Carantrila* LG1912
HANDFIELD *of Melbourne* **CG**
HANDFORD *of Guyers* LG1952
HANDFORD (-FLOOD) *of Flood Hall*
LGI1912
HANDLEY *formerly of Muskham Grange*
LG1937
DEVONPORT-HANDLEY *of Clipsham
Hall* LG1898
HANDYSIDE (*New Zealand*) **CG**
HANDLO, B **DEP**
HANEY **DFUSA**
HANGER (Coleraine, B) **DEP**
HANHAM, Bt PB1970
HANKEY, B PB1970
ALERS-HANKEY *of Stanton* LG1972
BARNARD-HANKEY *formerly of
Fetcham Park* LG1965
HANLEY **DFUSA**
HANMER, Bt PB1970; (Hanmer, of
Hamner and Flint, B) PB1881; Bt **EDB**
HANNA **DFUSA**
HANNAY, Bt PB1842; *formerly of Sorbie*
LG1952; *of Spring Hill House* LG1952;
of Kingsmuir LG1937; **FR**

RAINSFORD-HANNAY *of Kirkdale*
LG1972
HANNEN, B PB1894
HANOVER (*House of*) **RL**
HANSEN, Bt PB1956
HANSON, Bt *of Bryanston Square*
PB1970; Bt *of Fowey* PB1970
HANWORTH (*see* Pollock)
HARBEN *of Newland Park* LG1921
HARBERTON (*see* Pomeroy)
HARBIN *of Newton House* **HI**
BATES-HARBIN (*see* Rawlins *of Newton
Surmaville*)
HARBORD *formerly of Stutton* LG1965;
(*see also* Suffield)
HARBOROUGH (*see* Sherard)
HARBY, Bt **EDB**
HARCOURT, V PB1970; *of Ankerwycke*
LG1921; *of Nuneham and Stanton
Harcourt* LG1914; (*see also* Vernon)
HARCLA (Carlisle, E) **DEP**
HARCOURT, E **DEP**
HARDCASTLE *of Asthall Manor*
LG1972; *of New Lodge, Hawkhurst*
LG1906; *of Blidworth Dale* LG1875; *of
Nether Hall* LG1875
HARDEN *formerly of Harrybrook*
LGI1958
HARDING (Harding of Petherton, B)
PB1970; *formerly of Madingley*
LG1972; *of Old Springs* LG1969; *of
Ballathie* LG1952; *of Birling Manor*
LG1952; *of Baraset* LG1921; *of Upcott*
LG1900; *of Tamworth* LG1858:
PresFUSA; (*Australia*) **CG**; (*see also*
Harding-Newman)
HARDINGE, V PB1970; B PB1970;
(Hardinge of Penhurst, B) PB1970
HARDRES, Bt **EDB**
HARDMAN *formerly of Clough Hall*
LG1952
HARDWICK *of Brentford* LG1921
HARDWICKE *of Friarmayne* LG1952; *of
Tytherington Manor* LG1952; (*see also*
Yorke)
HARDY, Bt PB1970; Bt *of The Navy*
PB1839; *of Boughton Court formerly of
Chilham Castle* LG1952; *of Poole Hall*
LG1937; *of Sandling Park* LG1937; *of
Isenhurst Park* LG1921; DFUSA
COZENS-HARDY, B PB1970; (*see also*
Knott)
GATHORNE-HARDY (Cranbrook, E)
PB1970
MEREDITH-HARDY *formerly of
Poughley Priory* LG1965
HARE (Listowel, E) PB1970; (Blakenham,

V) **PB1970**; Bt **PB1970**; Bt *of Stow Hall* **PB1940**; (Coleraine, B) **DEP**; Bt *of Stow Bardolph* **EDB**; *of Blairlogie* **LG1952**; *of Docking Hall* **LG1952**
MORDAUNT-HARE *formerly of Hurstmonceaux* **LG1972**
HAREWOOD (*see* Lascelles)
HARFORD, Bt **PB1970**; *of Horton* **LG1965**; *formerly of Down Place* **LG1952**; *of Blaise Castle and Falcondale* **LG1921**; *of Holme* **LG1921**; *of Petty France* **LG1921**
HARGRAVE (*see* Hargrave-Pawson)
HARGREAVES *of Drinkstone Park formerly of Arborfield* **LG1952**; *of Knightley Grange* **LG1952**; *of Longwood formerly of Cuffnells* **LG1952**; *of Ormerod House* **LG1833/7**; *of Broad Oak* **HI**
HARINGTON, Bt **PB1970**; B **DEP**; (Harington, of Exton, B) **DEP**
HARKNESS *of Garryfine* **LGI1912**
HARELAND, Bt *of Brompton* **PB1895**; Bt *of Sproughton* **PB1848**; Bt *of Sutton Hall* **EDB**; *of Sutton Hall* **LG1863**
HARLECH (*see* Ormsby-Gore)
HARLEY (Oxford, E) **DEP**; *of Brampton Bryan* **LG1969**
HARMAN *formerly of Frinton Hall* **LG1972**; *formerly of Halesworth* **LG1952**; *of Crossdrum* **LGI1958**; *late of Palace* **LGI1912**
KING-HARMAN *of Newcastle* **LG1937 Supp**; (*see also* Kingston)
STAFFORD - KING - HARMAN, Bt **PB1970**
HARMSWORTH (Rothermere, V) **PB1970**; B **PB1970**; Bt *of Freshwater Grove* **PB1970**; Bt *of Moray Lodge* **PB1970**; (Northcliffe, V) **PB1922**
HARNAGE, Bt **PB1888**
HARPER *formerly of Lamberts* **LG1972**; (1) & (2) **DFUSA**
HARPUR *of Burton Latimer* **LG1952**; (*see also* Crewe)
HARRIES, Bt **EDB**; *of Rickestone and Trevacoon* **LG1937**; *of Llanunwas* **LG1921**; *of Tregwynt* **LG1921**; *of Heathfield* **LG1894**; *of Cruckton* **LG1882**; *of Cwydwig* **LG1882**
HARRINGTON **DFUSA**; (*see also* Stanhope)
HARRIS (Malmesbury, E) **PB1970**; B **PB1970**; Bt *of Bethnal Green* **PB1970**; Bt *of Chepping Wycombe* **PB1970**; Bt *of Boreatton* **EDB**; Bt *of Hayne* **EDB**; *formerly of Westcotes* **LG1969**; *of*

Brackenburgh Tower and Greysouthen **LG1952**; *formerly of The Hayes* **LG1952**; *of Donnington* **LG1952Supp**; *of Bowden* **LG1921**; *of Halwill* **LG1921**; *of Sheldons* **LG1900**; *of Tylney Hall* **LG1898**; *of Rosewarne, Rosteage, and Trelil* **LG1850/3**; *formerly of Curglasson* **LGI1958**; (1) & (2) **DFUSA**; *formerly of Antrim* **DFUSA**; *of Leicester* **AA**; *of Thornton Hall* (*see* Young)
HARRIS (*now* HOWRY) **DFUSA**
LEWIN-HARRIS **LG1965**
MOHUN-HARRIS *of Cross House* **LG1914**
HARRISON, Bt *of Bugbrooke* **PB1970**; Bt *of Eaglescliffe* **PB1970**; Bt *of Le Court* **PB1934**; *of Harthover formerly of Ashton* **LG1969**; *of Copford Hall* **LG1952**; *of Fron Llwyd* **LG1952**; *of King's Walden* **LG1952**; *of Maer* **LG1952**; *of Tremeer formerly of Brandesburton* **LG1952**; *of Wychnor Park* **LG1952**; *of Kerrhowel* **LG1937**; *of Coombe* **LG1937**; *of Teaninich* **LG1925**; *late of Seascale* **LG1921**; *of Snelston Hall* **LG1900**; *of Winscales and Stainburn* **LG1882**; *of Greenbank* **LG1863**; **IFR1976**; *of Holywood* **LGI1899**, **PresFUSA**; *formerly of Langton* **DFUSA**; *formerly of Thurstonfield* **DFUSA**; *of Linethwaite, Cumberland* **AA**; (*see also* Boynton-Wood)
CHOLMELEY HARRISON **IFR1976**
SLATOR HARRISON *of Shelswell* **LG1937**
HARRISSON *of Mathon Court* **LG1937**; *of Tollthorpe Hall* **LG1863**
HULTON-HARROP *of Gatton, formerly of Bardsley* **LG1965**
HARROWINE *of Low Stakesby* **LG1937**
HARROWBY (*see* Ryder)
HART, Bt **PB1970**; *of Kilderry* **LG1937 Supp**; *of Netherbury* **LG1900**; *of Esperanza* **LG1894**; (*see also* Hart-Synnot)
HART (*formerly* SHAKESPEARE) *formerly of New Place* **LG1952**
HARTCUP *formerly of Upland Hall* **LG1952**
HARTER *formerly of Cranfield Court* **LG1972**; *of Salperton Park* **LG1952**
HARTIGAN *of Lavendon Grange* **LG1952**
HARTLAND *of Oaklands* **LG1886**; (*see also* Mahon)
DIXON-HARTLAND, Bt **PB1909**
HARTLEY *of Fletton Tower* **LG1952**; *of*

Silchester House **LG1952**; *formerly of Wheaton-Aston Hall* **LG1952**; *of Gill-foot* **LG1858**; *of Marton* **LG1833/7**; *formerly of Beech Park* **LGI1958**
HORTON-SMYTHE-HARTLEY *of Hartley* **LG1952**
HARTOPP, Bt **EDB**
BURNS HARTOPP *of Dalby* **LG1952**
CRADOCK-HARTOPP, Bt **PB1970**
HARTSTONGE, Bt **EDB**
HARTWELL; Bt **PB1970**; (*see also* Berry)
HARTY, Bt **PB1939**
HARVEST **FR**
HARVEY, B **PB1970**; Bt *of Threadneedle Street* **PB1970**; Bt *of Langley Park* **PB1931**; *formerly of Dundridge* **LG1972**; *formerly of Ringstead Bury* **LG1969**; *of Little Chishall Manor* **LG1937**; *late of Thorpe* **LG1937**; *of Langley Park* **LG1863**; *of Blurton House* **LG1863**; *of Rolls Park* **LG1833/7**; **IFR1976**; *of Malin Hall* **LGI1912**; *late of Mintiaghs* **LGI1912**; (1) & (2) **DFUSA**; (*see also* Bateson)
HARVEY (*now* STEWART) *late of Carnousie* **LG1937**
BARCLAY-HARVEY *of Dinnet* **LG1965**
CRAIG-HARVEY *of Lainston* **LG1969**
SHAND-HARVEY *of Castle Semple* **LG1921**
HARVIE (*see* Harvie-Brown)
ROBERTSON-SHERSBY-HARVIE *of Brownlee* **LG1952**
HARWOOD *of Woodhouse* **LG1972**; *of Hagbourne and Streatley* **LG1850/3**
HASELL *of Dalemain* **LG1952**; **DFUSA**
HASELTON **DFUSA**
HASKARD *of Tragariff House* **LGI1958**
HASLER *formerly of Aldingbourne* **LG1965**
HASLEWOOD (*see* Blake *of Barham Court*)
HASSARD *of Edington* **LG1921**; *of Waterford* **LG1886**; *of Skea* **LG1873**; **FR**
HASSELL **LG1833/7**; (*see also* Hassell-Maw)
HASTANG, B **DEP**
HASTIE *formerly of The Place Land* **LG1952**
HASTINGS (Huntingdon, E) **PB1970**; Bt *of Willesley Hall* **PB1858**; (Pembroke, E) **DEP**; (Hastings, of Gressing Hall, B) **DEP**; (Hastings of Loughborough, B) **DEP**; *of Martley* **LG1937**; *of Tipperary* **LG1833/7**; (*see also* Astley; and Rawdon)

ABNEY-HASTINGS (Loudoun, E) **PB1970**; (Donington, B) **PB1927**
WOODMAN-HASTINGS *of Stubb Hill* **LG1952**
HASZARD (*formerly* LEVETT) *of Milford Hall* **LG1952**
HATCH, Bt **PB1927**; *of Ardee Castle* **LG1863**; *of The Manor of Sutton* **LG1850/3**; **DFUSA**
PERRIN-HATCHELL *of Fortfield House* **LGI1912**
HATCHER **DFUSA**; *formerly of Careby* **DFUSA**
HATCHETT **LG1880/3**
HATFEILD *formerly of Hartsdown* **LG1952**; *of Thorp Arch* **LG1952**
HATHERELL *of Chacombe* **LG1965**; **FR**
HATHERLEY (*see* Wood)
HATHERTON (*see* Littleton)
HATHORN *of Castle Wigg* **LG1921**
HATTON, V **DEP**; Bt *of Long Stanton* **EDB**; *of Clonard* **LGI1912**; *of Prospect* **LGI1912**
FINCH HATTON (Winchilsea and Nottingham, E) **PB1970**
HAUGHTON **IFR1976**
HAUSTED, B **DEP**
HAVELOCK (*see* Havelock-Allan)
HAVERS *of White Hill* **LG1882**
HAVERSHAM (*see* Hayter; and Thompson)
HAVILAND *of Delrow House* **LG1937**; *of Ditton Hall* **LG1900**; **HI**; (*see also* Haviland-Burke)
HAWARDEN (*see* Maude)
HAWDON *of Westerfield* **CG**
HAWKE, B **PB1970**
HAWKER *of Longparish House* **LG1921**; (*Australia*) **CG**
HAWKES *formerly of Carhue* **LGI1958**; **DFUSA**; (*Australia*) **CG**
HAWKESWORTH, Bt **EDB**; *formerly of Forest* **LGI1958**
HAWKEY, Bt **PB1970**
HAWKINS, Bt **PB1970**; (Brampton, B) **PB1907**; Bt **EDB**; *of Everdon Hall* **LG1952**; *of Grafton Underwood formerly of St Fenton's* **LG1952**; *formerly of Horringer Court* **LG1952**; *of Trewithen* **LG1898**; *of Tredunnoc* **LG1875**; *of Middlesex* **LG1863**; *of Alresford Hall* **LG1863**; *of Bignor Park* **LG1850/3**; **LG1833/7**; **IFR1976**; (1) & (2) **DFUSA**
HAWKSLEY *of Bronllys Castle* **LG1952**
HAWKSWORTH (*see* Horton-Fawkes)

HAWLEY, Bt **PB1970**; B **DEP**; Bt **EDB**; *of West Green House* **LG1875**
HAWORTH, Bt **PB1970**; (*see also* Haworth-Booth)
HAWTHORNE **PromFUSA**
HAY (Tweeddale, M) **PB1970**; (Erroll, E) **PB1970**; (Kinnoull, E) **PB1970**; Bt *of Alderston* **PB1970**; Bt *of Hay Park* **PB1970**; (Carlisle, E) **DEP**; Bt *of Alderston* **EDB**; Bt *of Linplum* **EDB**; *of Hopes* **LG1875**; *of Pitfour* **LG1850/3**; *formerly of Dundee* **DFUSA**; *of Rose Bay* **CG**
HAY *of Rannes* (*see* HAY-GORDON)
PATERSON-BALFOUR-HAY *of Carpow* **LG1906**
DALRYMPLE-HAY, Bt **PB1970**
DRUMMOND-HAY *of Seggieden* **LG1965**; (*see also* Kinnoull)
LEITH-HAY *of Leith Hall* **LG1952**
RICHARDSON-HAY (*see* Drummond Hay)
HAYCOX *formerly of Ludlow* **DFUSA**
HAYDOCK *formerly of Charlemont* **DFUSA**
HAYES, Bt **PB1896**; **IFR1976**; **PresFUSA**
FRANCE-HAYHURST (*see* Carnegie)
HAYMAN *of Springfield House* **LG1952**
HAYMES *formerly of Great Glen* **LG1952**
HAYNE **PromFUSA**
SEALE-HAYNE *of Pitt House, Fuge House and Kingswear Castle* **LG1900**
HAYNES *of Courtlands* **LG1937**; *of Thimbleby Lodge* **LG1894**
HAYS *formerly of Londonderry* **DFUSA**
MANSFIELD-HAYSOM **LG1925**
HAYTER (Haversham, B) **PB1917**; *of Winterbourne* **CG**; (*see also* Chubb)
HAYWARD *of Shilton Manor* **LG1972**; (*see also* Rose)
HAYWOOD (*now* FRANCKLIN) *of Sillins* **LG1921**; *of Brownhills* **LG1863**
HAZLERIGG, B **PB1970**
HEAD, V **PB1970**; Bt *of Rochester* **PB1970**; Bt *of Hermitage* **PB1868**; *of Hartburen Hall* **LG1921**; *formerly of Derrylahan Park* **LGI1958**
CAMERON-HEAD *of Inverailort* **LG1952**
HEADFORT (*see* Taylour)
HEADLAM Bt **PB1963**; *formerly of Gilmonby Hall* **LG1972**; *of Egleston* **CG**
HEADLEY (*see* Winn)
BALLS-HEADLEY *of Melbourne* **CG**

HEAL *of Knotty Green* **LG1952**
HEALD *late of Parrswood* **LG1921**
HEALE *of Woolston Grange formerly of FitzRoy House* **LG1952**; *of Highfield House* **LG1863**
CHADWYCK-HEALEY, Bt **PB1970**
HEALY **IFR1976**
FORTREY-HEAP *formerly of North Cove Hall* **LG1952**
HEAPE *of Trow Hall* **LG1937**
HEAPS **DFUSA**
HEARD **LG1969**; *of Kinsale* **LGI1899**
HEARN **CG**
HEATH, Bt **PB1940**; *formerly of Biddulph Grange* **LG1952**; *of Kitlands* **LG1952**; (*Australia*) **CG**; *formerly of Nazeing* **DFUSA**
HEATHCOTE, Bt **PB1970**; *of Conington Castle* **LG1937**; (*see also* Ancaster)
EDWARDS-HEATHCOTE *formerly of Longton Hall* **LG1952**
HEATHFIELD (*see* Eliott)
HEATLIE *of Glen Heatlie* **CG**
HEATON *of Rhual and Plas Heaton* **LG1972**; *of Helsington* **LG1952**; *formerly of Round Down* **LG1952**
HEATON (*formerly* PHILIPS) *of Rhual* **LG1952**
HENNIKER HEATON, Bt **PB1970**
HEAVEN *formerly of Kingsgate Court, The Forest of Dirse and Lundy* **LG1972**
HUDSON-HEAVEN (*see* Heaven)
HEBDEN *of Eday* **LG1937**
HEBER *of Hodnet* **LG1882**; (*see also* Heber-Percy)
HEBERDEN **FR**
HEDDLE *of Melsetter* **LG1937**
HEIGHAM *of Hunston* **LG1937**
HEIGHINGTON *of Donard House* **LGI1912**
HELE, Bt **EDB**
SHAW-HELLIER *of The Wombourne Wodehouse* **LG1952**
RUDYERD-HELPMAN *of Quarr Hill* **LG1937**
HELSBY, B **PB1970**
HELSHAM *of St Mary's Hall* **LG1900**
HELY *of Foulkscourt* **LGI1904**
HELYAR *of Poundisford* **LG1937**; *of Coker Court* **LG1875**
HEMINGFORD, (*see* Herbert)
HEMMING *formerly of Castle House* **LG1972**
HEMMING (*now* CHEAPE) *of Bentley Manor* **LG1894**
HEMPHILL *of Rathkenny* **LGI1904**

MARTYN-HEMPHILL (Hemphill, B) **PB1970**
HEMSWORTH *formerly of Shropham* **LG1952**; *of Monk Fryston* **LG1937**
O'CONNOR-HENCHY *of Stonebrook* **LGI1912**
HENDERSON, B **PB1970**; (Faringdon, B) **PB1970**; (Rowley, B) **PB1967**; *formerly of Fordel* **LG1972**; *formerly of Sedgwick Park* **LG1965**; *of Stemster* **LG1937**; **LGI1958**; **DFUSA**; **FR**
CLAYHILLS-HENDERSON *formerly of Invergowrie* **LG1952**
GORE-BROWNE-HENDERSON (*see* Gore-Browne)
MERCER-HENDERSON (*see* Buckinghamshire)
HENDRY *of Gagie* **LG1952**
HENDLEY (*see* Kirkwood)
HENE, Bt **EDB**
HENEAGE, B **PB1967**; *formerly of Coker Court* **LG1972**; *of Hainton* **LG1972**
CATHCART-WALKER-HENEAGE (*see* Heneage *formerly of Coker Court*)
WALKER-HENEAGE (*see* Heneage *formerly of Coker Court*)
HENLEY (Northington, E) **DEP**; Bt **EDB**; *formerly of Waterperry* **LG1965**; *of Ippleden Priory* **LG1937**; (*see also* Eden)
HENN **IFR1976**
HENNELL *of Undershaw* **LG1952**
HENNESSY (Windlesham, B) **PB1970**; **IFR1970**; *of Ballindeasig* **LGI1912**
HENNIKER Bt **PB1970**; (*see also* Henniker-Major)
HENNING **FR**
HENRY Bt *of Cahore* **PB1970**; Bt *of Campden House Court* **PB1931**; Bt *of Parkwood* **PB1917**; *of Fort Henry* **LGI1912**; *of Lodge Park* **LGI1912**; **DFUSA**; **PromFUSA**; *of Kylemore Lodge, co Galway* **AA**; (*see also* Buchanan; and Warburton-Lee)
HENSHAW (*see* Innes-Smith)
HENSLEY *formerly of Hensleigh House* **LG1952**
HENSON *of Bickleigh Castle* **LG1937**
HENTY **CG**
HEPBURN (Bothwell, E) **DEP**; *of Waughton* **LG1952**; *of Monkridge* **LG1937**; *of The Hooke* **LG1882Supp**; **DFUSA**
BUCHAN-HEPBURN (Hailes, B) **PB1970**; Bt **PB1970**
DOPPING-HEPENSTAL *formerly of Derrycassan* **LGI1958**

HEPWORTH **FR**
HERAPATH **LG1965**
HERBERT (Carnarvon, E) **PB1970**; (Pembroke and Montgomery, E) **PB1970**; (Powis, E) **PB1970**; (Hemingford, B) **PB1970**; (Tangley, B) **PB1970**; Bt *of Wilton* **PB1940**; Bt *of Boyton* **PB1939**; (Treowen, B) **PB1933**; (Powis, M) **DEP**: (Pembroke, E) **DEP**; (Torrington, E) **DEP**; (Herbert, of Chirbury, B) **DEP**; Bt *of Blomfield* **EDB**; Bt *of Durrow* **EDB**; Bt *of Red Castle* **EDB**; *of Upper Helmsley and Old Leigh Place* **LG1972**; *of Clytha* **LG1952**; *of Orleton* **LG1937**; *of Llanarth* **LG1900**; *of Glantlafren* **LG1894**; **IFR1976**
KENNEY-HERBERT *late of Castle Island* **LGI1912**
OGILVIE-GRANT STUDLEY HERBERT (Seafield, E) **PB1970**
HERCY *of Winkfield* **LG1937**
HERDMAN **IFR1976**
HEREFORD *of Sufton* **LG1952**; (*see also* Devereux)
MAITLAND-HERIOT (*formerly* WILSON-WOOD) *formerly of Timsbury Manor* **LG1952**
HERMON *of Necairne* **LG1937Supp**
BURCHELL-HERN *of Bushey Grange* **LG1921**
HERON, B **DEP**; Bt *of Newark* **PB1854**; **IFR1976**
MAXWELL-HERON *of Heron* **LG1898**; (*see also* Heron-Maxwell)
HERRICK *of Beaumanor* **LG1937**; *formerly of Beaumanor* **DFUSA**
CURZON-HOWE-HERRICK (*see* Howe)
TABUTEAU-HERRICK *of Shippool* **LGI1912**
HERRIES *of St Julians and formerly of Halldykes* **LG1937**; (*see also* Constable-Maxwell; and Norfolk)
YOUNG-HERRIES *of Spottes* **LG1952**
HERSCHEL, Bt **PB1949**
HERSCHELL, B **PB1970**
HERSEY *formerly of Hingham* **DFUSA**
HERTFORD (*see* Seymour)
HERVEY (Bristol, M) **PB1970**; (Hervey, of Kidbroke, B) **DEP**; (Hervey, of Ross, B) **DEP**; Bt **EDB**; *of Little Bealings* **LG1952**; *of Killiane* **LGI1912**
HESELTINE *formerly of Bambridge Park* **LG1952**
BAMFORD-HESKETH *of Gwrych Castle* **LG1898**

FERMOR-HESKETH (Hesketh, B) **PB1970**
FLEETWOOD-HESKETH *of North Meols* **LG1952**; (*see also* Bibby)
HESSE **RL**
HETT *of Littleworth and Eildon Hall* **LG1952**
HEUGILL *of Hornby Grange* **LG1858**
HEWART, B **PB1963**
HEWET, Bt **EDB**
HEWETT, Bt **PB1970**; Bt *of Chesterfield Street* **PB1891**; B **DEP**; Bt *of Headley Hall* **EDB**; *of Tyr Mab Ellis* **LG1886**
HEWGILL (*Canada*) **CG**
HEWITT (Lifford, V) **PB1970**; Bt **PB1970**; *of Bodfarei* **LG1937**; **DFUSA**; (*see also* Oliphant-Sheffield)
BRADFORD HOWLAND HEWITT (*see* Alington)
LUDLOW-HEWITT *formerly of Clan coole* **LGI1958**
WOOLSEY HEWITT (*see* Alington)
HEWLETT **DFUSA**
HEWSON *late of Ovington Park* **LG1921**; (*cos Kerry and Limerick*) **IFR1976**; (*co Limerick: Castle Hewson*) **IFR1976**
HEXT *of Trenarren* **LG1972**; *formerly of Tredethy* **LG1952**
HEYCOCK, B **PB1970**; *of East Norton* **LG1952**
HEYGATE, Bt **PB1970**
HEYLAND *of Glendarugh and Tamlaght* **LG1882Supp**
HEYMAN, Bt **EDB**, *formerly of Shanganagh Castle* **LGI1958**
HEYTESBURY (*see* Holmes à Court)
CURTIS-HEYWARD *formerly of Quedgeley* **LG1952**
HEYWOOD, Bt **PB1970**; *of Haresfield Court* **LG1972**; *of Pentney House* **LG1952**; *of Caradoc Court* **LG1937**; *formerly of Hatley St George* **LG1937**
HEYWORTH, B **PB1970**; *of Yewtree, co Lancaster* **AA**
HIBBERT, Bt **PB1927**; *formerly of Ashby St Ledgers* **LG1965**; *formerly of Birtles and Chalfont* **LG1965**; *of Crofton Grange* **LG1898**; *of Birtles Hall* **LG1875**; *of Marple* **LG1833/7**; *of Woodpark* **LGI1912**
HOLLAND-HIBBERT (Knutsford, V) **PB1970**
HICKEY *of Haddenham* **LG1921**; **IFR1976**
TYNTE-HICKEY (*see* Tynte-Irvine)
HICKIE **IFR1976**; (*see also* Hickey)

HICKING, Bt **PB1940**; (*see also* North)
HICKMAN, Bt **PB1970**; Bt **EDB**; *of Fenlowe* **LGI1952** *of Charlton House* **LG1921**; *of Wightwick* **LG1900**
GORE-HICKMAN *formerly of Tyredagh* **LGI1958**
HICKOK **DFUSA**
HICKS, Bt **EDB**; *of Wilbraham Temple* **LG1952**; **DFUSA**; *formerly of Whitehaven* **DFUSA: FR**
JOYNSON-HICKS (Brentford, V) **PB1970**
HICKSON *of Fermoyle* **LGI1912**; *of Ballintaggart* **LGI1912**
HIDE, Bt **EDB**
HIERN **FR**
HIGFORD *of Hartsfield* **LG1906**; *of Aldermaston* **LG1898**
HIGGIN *of Puddington Hall* **LG1952**
HIGGINS *of Turvey House* **LG1952**; *of Bosbury House* **LG1875**; *of Skellow Grange* **LG1863**; (*see also* O'Higgins)
LONGUET-HIGGINS *formerly of Turvey Abbey* **LGI1912**
PLATT HIGGINS **FR**
HIGGINSON; **IFR1976**; **FromFUSA**; *of Lisburn, co Antrim* **AA**; (*see also* Barneby)
HIGGON *of Scolton* **LG1972**
DE PREMOREL-HIGGONS **LG1965**
HIGGS *of Cold Ash* **LG1952**; *of Winthorpe* **LG1952**
HIGHETT (*of Toorak and Mitiamo Park*) **CG**
HIGHSMITH **DFUSA**
HIGSON *of Burton Lazars Hall* **LG1937**
HILDER *of Huskards* **LG1952**
HILDYARD, Bt **EDB**; *of Flintham Hall* **LG1969**; *of Middleton Hall formerly of Horsley Hall* **LG1969**; *of Winestead* **LG1969**
HILL (Downshire, M) **PB1970**; (Hill of Luton, B) **PB1970**; (Hill of Wivenhoe, B) **PB1970**; (Sandys, B **PB1970**); Bt *of Bradford* **PB1970**; Bt *of Brooke Hall* **PB1970**; Bt *of Green Place* **PB1940**; B **DEP**; *of Waughton* **EDB**; *of Brynderi* **LG1965**; *of Good-a-Meavy* **LG1952**; *Crux Easton* **LG1952Supp**; *of Oakhurst* **LG1937**; *of Thornton Hall* **LG1937**; *of St Catherine's Hill* **LG1900**; *of Gressenhall Hill* **LG1894**; *of Rockhurst* **LG1894** *of Graig* **LG1886**; (1) & (2) **DFUSA**; *formerly of Hodnet* **DFUSA**; *formerly of Houndston and Spaxton, Somerset, and Hills Court, Exeter*

DFUSA; *formerly of Shrewsbury*
DFUSA; **PromFUSA; FR**; (*Fiji*); **CG;**
of Castle Bank (*see* Holmes)
HILL (*formerly* HANBURY) *of Holfield
Grange* **LG1965**
CLEGG-HILL (Hill, V) **PB1970**
ERSKINE-HILL, Bt **PB1970**
GRANTHAM-HILL (*Australia*) **CG**
NOEL-HILL (Berwick, B) **PB1953**
STAVELEY-HILL *formerly of Oxley
Manor* **LG1965**
HILLARY, Bt **PB1855**
HILLAS *of Doonecoy* **LGI1912**
NEWLAND HILLAS *of Etton Hall*
LG1952
HILLES *formerly of Banbridge* **DFUSA**
HILLINGDON, (*see* Mills)
HILLS, Bt **PB1953**; *of Redleaf* **LG1821**;
of Colne Park **LG1886**
HILLYER **DFUSA**
HILTON (Hilton of Upton, B) **PB1970**;
B **DEP**; (Hilton, of Hilton, B) **DEP**; *of
Glynhiriaeth* **LG1952**; *of Bramling*
LG1886; *of Preston House* **LG1858**;
(1) & (2) **DFUSA**
HINCHCLIFFE *of Mucklestone* **LG1972**;
of Woodside **LG1937**
HINCKES *of Tetton Hall* **LG1900**
HINCKS *formerly of Breckenbrough*
LG1952
ARCHER-HIND *of Olington Lodge*
LG1921
HINDE *of Shrewton House* **LG1965**
HINDLEY (Hyndley, B) **PB1963**
HINDLIP, (*see* Allsopp)
HINGLEY, Bt **PB1917**
HINGSTON *of Horsehead* **LGI1958**
HINSDALE *formerly of Dedham* **DFUSA**
HINSHAW **DFUSA**
HINTON (Hinton of Bankside, B)
PB1970; DFUSA
HINXMAN *of Little Durnford* **LG1898**
HIPPESLEY, Bt **PB1867**
HIPPISLEY *of Ston Easton* **LG1972**;
of Sparsholt **LG1952**
HIRSCH (*see* Hirst)
HIRSHFIELD, B **PB1970**
HIRST, B **PB1940**; *formerly of Great
Ropers* **LG1965**
HITCHCOCK *of Bay Lodge* **LG1952**
HITCHINS *of Ashcroft Tower* **LG1952**
HIVES, B **PB1970**
HOARE, Bt *of Annabella* **PB1970**;
Bt *of Fleet Street* **PB1970**; Bt *of
Luscombe* **PB1970**; (Templewood, V)
PB1959; *of Gateley Hall* **LG1972**;
of Stourton **LG1965**; *of Luscombe*

Castle **LG1937**; *of Chelsworth* **LG1937**;
of Ellisfield **LG1937**; *of Limerick*
LG1833/7
HAMILTON HOARE (*see* Hoare *of
Stourton*)
HOBART, Bt **PB1970**
HOBBS *of Barnaby* **LGI1912**; **DFUSA**
HOBHOUSE, Bt **PB1970**; B **PB1904**;
(Broughton, B) **PB1869**; *of Hadspen
House* **LG1965**
HOBKIRK *formerly of Cleddon* **LG1952**
HOBLYN **FR**
PETER-HOBLYN *of Colquite* **LG1952**
HOBSON, B **PB1967**; *formerly of
Misterton Hall* **LG1965**
LOMBARD-HOBSON *of Middleham*
LG1972
HOBY, Bt **EDB**
HOCKIN (*Canada*) **CG**
HODDER **IFR1976; FR**
HODGE, Bt **PB1970**
HERMON-HODGE (Wyfold, B) **PB1970**
HODGES, Bt **EDB**; *formerly of
Dorchester* **LG1952**; *of Hagley*
LG1858
HODGKINSON (*Australia*) **CG**
HODGSON *of Geerings* **LG1969**;
formerly of Ashgrove **LG1952**; *formerly
of Houghton House* **LG1952**; *formerly
of Merlin Park* **LG1952**; *of Scarah Hill
formerly of Nocton Hall* **LG1952**;
of Westons Place **LG1952**; *of Clopton
House* **LG1921**; *of Highthorne*
LG1886; *of Newby Grange* **LG1875**;
CG; (*see also* Pemberton *of Trumping-
ton*; Archer-Hind *of Ovington;* Wells *of
Mere House and Marlands*)
HODSOLL *formerly of Loose Court*
LG1952
HODSON, B **PB1970**; Bt **PB1970**; **FR**
HODSON (*formerly* PAGET) *formerly of
Stuffynwood Hall* **LG1952**
HODY *of Chedington* **LG1894**
HOES **DFUSA**
HOESE, B **DEP**; (Hoese of Beechworth,
B) **DEP**
HOG *of Newliston* **LG1952**; (*see also*
Charteris)
HOGARTH *of Firhill* **LG1969**
HOGG (Hailsham, V) **PB1970**; Bt
PB1970; *of Norton* **LG1952**
LINDSAY-HOGG, Bt **PB1970**
McGAREL-HOGG (Magheramorne, B)
PB1956
HOHLER *of Long Crendon* **LG1965**
HOLAND, B **DEP**
HOLBECH *of Farnborough* **LG1965**

HOLBECHE *of Hillybroom* **LG1952**
HOLBROOKE *formerly of Broadway* **DFUSA**
HOLBURNE, Bt **PB1874**
HOLCOMB **DFUSA**
HOLCROFT, Bt **PB1970**; Bt *of The Shrubbery* **PB1917**
HOLDEN, Bt *of the First* **PB1970**; Bt *of Oakworth House* **PB1970**; B **PB1949**; *of Hawton and Sibdon* **LG1969**; *formerly of Aston* **LG1969**; *of Bromson* **LG1952**; *of Holden* **LG1921**; *of Wednesbury* **LG1900**; *of Palace House* **LG1858**; *formerly of Lindsey* **DFUSA**; *of Palace House, co Lancaster* **AA**; (*see also* Rose *of Wolston Grange*)
HOLDER, Bt **PB1970**
HOLDERNESS, Bt **PB1970**; (*see also* D'Arcy; and Ramsay)
HOLDICH *OF Wadenhoe* **LG1972**
HOLDSWORTH *of Scargill* **LG1952**; *formerly of Widdicumbe* **LG1952**; *formerly of Sandal Hall* **LG1921**
HOLE *of Caunton* **LG1952**; *of Parke* **LG1952**
HOLFORD, B **PB1970**; *of Duntish Court* **LG1972**; *of Westonbirt* **LG1898**; *of Castle Hill* **LG1898**
KING-HOLFORD (*see* Holford)
GWYNNE-HOLFORD *late of Cilgwyn and of Buckland* **LG1937**
HOLLADAY (*now* PHILBIN) **DFUSA**
HOLLAND, Bt **PB1970**; (Rotherham, B) **PB1949**; (Exeter, D) **DEP**; (Surrey, D) **DEP**; Bt *of Quiddenham* **EDB**; Bt *of Wittersham* **EDB**; *formerly of Romiley and Stalybridge* **LG1952**; *of Lulings* **LG1937**; *of Cropthorne* **LG1898**; *of Mount Ephraim* **LG1898**; *of Caerleon* **LG1886**; (*see also* Fox; Rich; and Wilde)
HEYCOCK-HOLLAND *of Benhall Lodge* **LG1952**
HOLLENDEN, (*see* Hope-Morley)
HOLLES (Newcastle, D) **DEP**; (Holles of Ifield, B) **DEP**; Bt **EDB**
HOLLEY *late of Oaklands* **LG1937**
HOLLIDAY *of Mount St John* **LG1972**; *of Copgrove Hall* **LG1952**; *of Kirkburton* **LG1937**
HOLLINGS *of The Watchetts* **LG1921**
HOLLINGTON *formerly of Redditch* **DFUSA**
HOLLINGWORTH **LG1969**; *of Colyford* **LG1937**
HOLLINS, Bt **PB1963**; (*see also* Gibson)

HOLLISTER **DFUSA**
HOLLOND *of Benhall Lodge* **LG1937**
HOLLYDAY **DFUSA**
HOLLYNGWORTH *of Hollyngworth* **LG1858**
HOLMAN, Bt **EDB**; *formerly of Dunley Manor* **LG1972**; *of Martinhoe* **LG1952**; *of Hyes* **LG1937**
HOLMAN (*formerly* DIXON) *of Rheda* **LG1952**
HOLMDEN *formerly of Marlpit House* **LG1952**
HOLME *of Paull-Holme* **LG1921**
HOLMES (Dovercourt, B) **PB1959**; B **DEP**; (*formerly* HILL) *of Castle Bank* **LG1952**; *of Strumpshaw Hall* **LG1952**; *of Udimore* **LG1952**; *of Gawdy Hall* **LG1937**; *of Brook Hall* **LG1921**; *of Scole House* **LG1886**; *formerly of Moycashel* **LGI1958**; *of St David's* **LG1912**; (*of Hawkestone House*) **CG**; (*New Zealand*) **CG**
HOLMES À COURT (Heytesbury, B) **PB1970**
HOLM PATRICK (*see* Hamilton)
HOLROYD **CG**
HOLT, Bt **PB1940**; *of Orleton Hall*; *formerly of Mount Muscal* **LG1969**; *of Riffhams* **LG1952**; *of Farnborough Grange* **LG1921**; *of Stubbylee* **LG1906**; *of Sefton Park* **LG1894**; **FR**; *of Parramatta and Rockhampton* **CG**; (*see also* Holt-Wilson)
HILLIER-HOLT *of Hope Court* **LG1952**
HOLTE, Bt **EDB**
HOLYNGWORTHE *of Holyngworthe Hall* **AA**
HOLYROODHOUSE (*see* Bothwell)
HOMAN, Bt **PB1852**
HOME, Bt **PB1970**; Bt **EDB**; *of Bassendean* **LG1886**; (*see also* Hume)
BINNING-HOME *of Argaty and Softlaw* **LG1882**
DOUGLAS-HOME (Home, E) **PB1970**
LOGAN-HOME *of Edrom formerly of Broomhouse* **LG1952**
MILNE-HOME (*see* Robertson)
HOMER *formerly of Sedgley* **LG1952**
HOMFRAY *formerly of Otterbourne Court* **LG1969**; *of Penllyn Court* **LG1969**; *of Stradissall* **LG1875**
HONE **IFR1976**
HONEYBALL (*formerly* MARTYN) *formerly of Tonacombe* **LG1952**
HONYWOOD, Bt **PB1970**
HOO, B **DEP**
HOOD, V **PB1970**; (Bridport, V) **PB1970**;

Bt **PB1970**; (Hood of Avalon, B) **PB1901**; (Bridport, V) **DEP**; *of Nettleham Hall* **LG1921**; *of Bardon Park* **LG1875**; *(Australia)* (1) & (2) **CG**
COCKBURN-HOOD *late of Stainrigg* **LG1921**
FULLER-ACLAND-HOOD (St Audries, B) **PB1970**
GREGORY HOOD *(formerly GREGORY) of Loxley Hall and Styvechale* **LG1952**; *(see also* Bridport)
HOOK, Bt **EDB**
HOOKE *of Crookes Park* **LG1969**
HOOKER *formerly of Blaston* **DFUSA**
HOOKER *(formerly* McMICHAEL*)* **DFUSA** *sometime of Muirkirk*
HOOKEY *(see* Gaskell *of Churchdown)*
HOOPER, Bt **PB1970**; **DFUSA**; **FR**; *(see also* Baylies)
HOOVER **PresFUSA**
HOPCRAFT *of Brackley* **LG1921**
HOPE (Glendevon, B) **PB1970**; (Linlithgow, M) **PB1970**; (Rankeillour, B) **PB1970**; Bt *of Craighall* **PB1970**; Bt *of Kinnettles* **PB1970**; Bt *of Kerse* **EDB**; Bt *of Kirklistun* **EDB**; *of West Park* **LG1969**; *of Preston House* **LG1952**; *of Amsterdam* **LG1937**; *formerly of Havering Grange* **LG1937**; *of Loughness* **LG1937**; *of Gartlandstown* **LG1937Supp** *of Carriden* **LG1882**; *of Timaru* **CG DFUSA**;
BERESFORD-HOPE *of Bedgebury Park* **LG1914**
PELHAM-CLINTON-HOPE (Newcastle-under-Lyme, D) **PB1970**
HOPER *of Thornhill* **LG1858**
HOPES *of Brampton Crofts* **LG1875**
HOPKINS, Bt *of St Pancras* **PB1940**; Bt *of Athboy* **PB1860**; *formerly of Tidmarsh Manor* **LG1952**; (1) & (2) **DFUSA**; **FR**
HOPKINSON (Colyton, B) **PB1970**; *of Llanvihangel Court formerly of Wotton Court and Edgeworth Manor* **LG1952**; *of Netherton Hall* **LG1952**
HOPPER *formerly of Wolsingham* **DFUSA**; *of Shincliffe* (*see* Williamson); *(see also* Shipperdson *of Hermitage)*
HOPTON, B **DEP**; *of Canon-ffrome* **LG1937**; *(see also* Adams *of Ansty Hall)*
HOPWOOD (Southborough, B) **PB1970**; *of Blackburn* **AA**
HOPWOOD *(formerly* GREGGE-HOPWOOD) *formerly of Hopwood* **LG1952**

HOPWOOD (Southborough, B) **PB1970**
HORD **DFUSA**
HORDER, B **PB1970**
HORDERN *formerly of Alverstoke* **LG1965**; *of Throwley House* **LG1952**; *of Oxley House* **LG1863**
HORE *of Pole Hore* **LG1882**; *of Harperston* **LG1863**
HORLICK, Bt **PB1970**
HORN *of Woodcote Park* **LG1952**; *of Holmwood* **CG**
HORNBY Bt **PB1970**; *of Pusey House, formerly of Chantmarle* **LG1965**; *of St Michael's-on-Wyre* **LG1969**; *of Ribby* **LG1914**; **DFUSA**
HORNBY *(now* HOOD) *of The Hooke and Upham House* **LG1937**
PENRHYN-HORNBY *(formerly* Hornby) *of Dalton Hall* **LG1952**
PHIPPS HORNBY *of Ord, formerly of Lordington Park* **LG1969**
HORNDON *formerly of Pencrebar* **LG1937**
HORNE, Bt **PB1970**; (Horne of Slammenan, V) **PB1940**; B **PB1929**; *formerly of Shelley Hall* **LG1952**
HORNER *of Mells Park* **LG1937**; *of Strathmore* **LGI1904**
HORNIDGE **IFR1976**; *of Calverston* **LGI1958**
HORNSBY *late of Laxton Park* **LG1937**
HORNUNG *of Ivorys* **LG1965**
HORNYOLD *formerly of Blackmore Park and Hanley Castle* **LG1969**
HORRIDGE *of Elton Lodge* **LG1952**
HORROCKS *(Australia)* **CG**
HORROCKS *(now* MORGAN) *of Mascalls* **LG1921**
HORSBRUGH, B **PB1970**; *of Horsbrugh* **LG1900**
HORSFALL, Bt **PB1970**; *of Bellamour* **LG1937**; *(Australia)* **CG**
CAMPBELL-HORSFALL *(see* Campbell *of Glendaruel)*
HORSFORD *of Bosvathick* **LG1952**
HORSMAN *of Castle Hywel and Terra Coed Vawr* **LG1882**
HORT, Bt **PB1970**
HORTON Bt **EDB**; *of Guilsborough Hall* **LG1952**; *late of The Holt* **LG1937**; *of Howroyde* **LG1937**; **FR**; *of Southwark* **AA**
ANSON-HORTON *(see* Neilson *of Catton Hall)*
WILMOT-HORTON, Bt **PB1931**
HOSKEN *of Ellenglaze* **LG1886**
HOSKINS *of Higham* **LG1900**

HOSKYNS, Bt **PB1970**; *of North Perrott Manor* LG1952
HOSMER **PromFUSA**
HOSTE *of Barwick House* LG1863
HOTBLACK *of Deakes Manor* LG1937
HOTCHKIN *of Woodhall Spa* LG1972
HOTCHKIS *formerly of Hoxwood* LG1965
HOTCHKISS **DFUSA**
HOTHAM, B **PB1970**
HOTHFIELD (*see* Tufton)
ARCHER-HOUBLON *of Welford and formerly of Hallingbury Place* LG1952; **IFR1976**
HOUGHTON *formerly of Westwood* LG1952; **DFUSA**
HOULDSWORTH, Bt *of Heckmondwike* **PB1970**; Bt *of Reddish* **PB1970**; *of Coltness* LG1969
HOULT *of Norton Place* LG1937
HOULTON *of Farley Castle* LG1898
HOUSSEMAYNE DU BOULAY *formerly of Donhead Hall* LG1965
HOUSTON, Bt *of West Toxteth* **PB1926**
BLAKISTON-HOUSTON **IFR1976**
DAVIDSON-HOUSTON LG1969
DAVIDSON - HOUSTON (*formerly WOODGATE*) *of Pembury* LG1952
HOUSTOUN, Bt **EDB**; *of Johnstone* LG1937; *of Mayshiel* LG1937
HOVELL *formerly of Wyverstone* LG1972, (*New Zealand*) **CG**
HOVENDEN *of Gurteen* LGI1912
HOW *of Hill House* LG1969; *of Balnacarron House* LG1937
HOWARD (Carlisle, E) **PB1970**; (Effingham, E) **PB1970**; (Suffolk and Berkshire, E) **PB1970**; (Wicklow, E) **PB1970** (Howard of Penrith, B) **PB1970** (Strathcona and Mount Royal, B) **PB1970**; Bt **PB1970**; Bt *of Bushey Park* **PB1873**; (Norfolk, D) **DEP**; (Bindon, E) **DEP**; (Northampton, E) **DEP**; (Norwich, E) **DEP**; (Stafford, E) **DEP**; V **DEP**; B **DEP**; (Howard, of Escrick, B) **DEP**; *of Ashmore* LG1969; *of Tintinhull Court* LG1969; *of Broughton Hall* LG1952; *of The Moat* LG1952; *of Wigfair* LG1952; *of Clapham Park* LG1937; *of Corby* LG1937; *of Stone House* LG1937; *of Strawberry Hill* **LG1925Supp**; (1) & (2) **DFUSA**; **PromFUSA**; *of Toronto, Canada* **AA**; (*see also* Frere; Furnivall; Gorges; and Howard-Vyse)

HOWARD DE WALDEN (*see* Scott-Ellis)
FITZALAN-HOWARD (Norfolk, D) **PB1970**; (Beaumont, B) **PB1970**; (Howard of Glossop, B) **PB1970**; (FitzAlan of Derwent, B) **PB1959**
FORWARD-HOWARD (*see* Wicklow)
HOWARTH *formerly of Crimbourne* LG1969
KIRKPATRICK-HOWAT *formerly of Mabie* **DFUSA**
HOWDEN (*see* Cradock)
HOWE, E **DEP**; V **DEP**; (Chedworth, B) **DEP**; Bt *of Cold Barwick* **EDB**; Bt *of Compton* **EDB**; *of Chart Place* LG1937; (1) & (2) **DFUSA**; *formerly of Hatfield* **DFUSA**; (*see also* Curzon)
HOWELL *of Prinknash* LG1858; *formerly of Westbury Manor* **DFUSA**
HOWES *formerly of King's Cliffe* LG1952; *of Morningthorpe* LG1886
HOWICK OF GLENDALE (*see* Baring)
HOWITT *formerly of Hoping Hall* LG1972; *of Farndon formerly of Farnsfield and Heanor* LG1952
HIPWELL-HOWITT (*see* Howitt)
HOWLAND **DFUSA**
HOWLETT *of Briningham House* LG1952
HOWLIN *of Ballycronigan* LGI1904
HOWRY (*see* Harris)
HOWTH (*see* St Lawrence)
HOYLE, Bt **PB1939**; *Gnaton Hall* LG1937; *of Soyland and Denton* LG1886; *of Hooton Levet Hall* LG1886
HOYSTED *formerly of Walterstown* LG1937
HOYT **DFUSA**; **PromFUSA**
HOZIER (Newlands, B) **PB1929**
HUBAND, Bt **EDB**; *formerly of Ipsley Lodge* LG1952
HUBBARD (Addington, B) **PB1970**; *of Somerby House* LG1972; *late of Tingrith Manor* LG1937; **DFUSA**
WHEATLEY-HUBBARD *of Berkswell Hall* LG1969
CANTRELL-HUBBERSTY *of Ragdale Hall* LG1952
HUBERT *formerly of Showborough House* LG1952
HUDDLESTON *of Upwell* LG1914
EYRE-HUDDLESTON *of Sawston and Lindley* LG1952
HUDLESTON *of Hutton John* LG1969
HUDSON, V **PB1963**; Bt *of North Hackney* **PB1956**; *of Westwards* LG1952; *of Henden Manor* LG1937;

of Low Hall **LG1937**; *of Wick House* **LG1937**; *of Colley Manor* **LG1906**; *formerly of Manchester* **DFUSA**
DONALDSON-HUDSON *of Cheswardine* **LG1952**
HUFTY **DFUSA**
HUGER **PromFUSA**
KNATCHBULL-HUGESSEN (*see* Brabourne)
HUGGINS (Malvern, V) **PB1970**; *of Berkswell Grange* **LG1965**
HENNIKER-HUGHAN (*see* Henniker)
HOUGHTON-HUGHAN *of Airds* **LG1900**
HUGHES, Bt **PB1970**; Bt *of Denford* **PB1956**; (Dinorben, B) **DEP**; *of Coedhelen* **LG1952**; *of Furneaux Pelham Hall* **LG1952**; *of Allt Llwyd* **LG1937**; *of Middleton Hall* **LG1937**; *of Sherdley Hall* **LG1937**; *of Ystrad* **LG1906**; *of Plâs-yn-Llangoed* **LG1894**; *of Donnington Priory* **LG1875**; *The Grove* **LG1875**; *of Newbery* **LG1833/7**; *of Penymaes* **LG1833/7** **IFR1976**; *of Spring Gardens* **LG1937 Supp**; *of Ballycross* **LGI1912**; *of Dalchoin* **LGI1912**; **FR**; *of Betshanger* (*see* Hughes-D'Àeth; and Hughes-Hallett); *of Kinmel Park* (*see* Fetherstonaugh)
GWYNNE-HUGHES *of Tregib* **LG1937**
HUGHES-HUGHES *formerly of Lees Priory* **LG1952**
VAUGHAN-HUGHES *of The Wyelands* **LG1952**
HUGONIN *of Stainton House* **LG1952**
HUIDEKOPER **PromFUSA**
HUISH *of Smalley Hall* **LG1886**
HULBERT *of Finmere* **LG1965**; *of Fir Hill* **LG1952**; (*see also* Hulbert-Powell)
HULL *formerly of Carnbane* **LG1952**
HULSE, Bt **PB1970**
HULTON, Bt **PB1970**; Bt *of Downside* **PB1925**; *of Hulton* **LG1900**
HUMBLE, Bt *of Kensington* **EDB**; *of London* **EDB**
HUME (Dunbar, E) **DEP**; (Marchmont, E) **DEP**; (Hume, of Berwick, B) **DEP**; Bt **EDB**; *of Auchendolly* **LG1937**; *of Humewood* **LGI1912**; (*see also* Brodribb; and Macartney)
HUME (*now* DICK) *of co Wicklow* **LGI1912**
ROSS-HUME *of Ninewells* **LG1952**
HUMFFREYS *of Llwyn* **LG1858**
HUMFREY *of Cavanacor* **LGI1912**

BLAKE-HUMFREY (*see* Humfrey-Mason)
HUMISTON *formerly of Walkern* **DFUSA**
HUMPHERY *of Senton House* **LG1937**
HUMPHREY *of Blewbury Down* **LG1952**; **DFUSA**
HUMPHREY (*or* HUMPHREYS) *formerly of Lyme Regis* **DFUSA**
HUMPHREYS, Bt **EDB**; *formerly of Broomfield House* **LGI1958**; (*see also* Richards *of Caerynwch*)
FAIRLES-HUMPHREYS *of Bank House* **LG1921**
DAVENPORT-HANDLEY-HUMPHREYS *of Clipsham Hall* **LG1952**
HUMPHRIES *formerly of Bristol* **DFUSA**
PERCIVAL-HUMPHRIES *of Drayton House* **LG1952**
HUMPHRY *of Horham Hall* **LG1952**
HUMPHRYS *of Ballyhaise* **LGI1912**
HUNGARTON (*see* Crawford)
HUNGATE, Bt **EDB**
HUNGERFORD (Hungerford, B) **DEP**; (Hungerford, of Heytesbury, B) **DEP**; **IFR1976**; (*Australia*) **CG**; *of co Cork* **AA**; (*see also* Loudoun; and Strange of Knokin)
HOLDICH-HUNGERFORD (*see* Holdich)
HUNLOKE, Bt **PB1856**
HUNSDON (*see* Falkland; and Gibbs)
HUNT, B **PB1970**; Bt *of Kensington* **PB1904**; *of Boreatton* **LG1969**; *formerly of Dartmouth* **LG1969**; *of Pittencrief and Logie* **LG1969**; *of Wadenhoe* **LG1952**; *of Ketton* **LG1863**; *of Shermanbury Park* **LG1863**; *of Danesfort* **LGI1912**; *of Cummer More* **LGI1912**; (1) & (2) **DFUSA**; *formerly of Halifax* **DFUSA**; *formerly of Lee* **DFUSA**; *formerly of Longner* **DFUSA**; *formerly of Lyndon* **DFUSA**; (*see also* Wolley-Dod)
DE VERE HUNT, Bt **PB1904**
HUSEY-HUNT *late of Compton Castle* **LG1925**
PHILLIPS-HUNT *of Ballysinode* **LGI1912**
VERE-HUNT *of Ardmayle House* **LGI1958**
HUNTER *formerly of Crichton Dean* **LG1972**; *of Hunterston* **LG1972**; *formerly of Westmorland* **LG1965**; *of Beech House* **LG1937**; *formerly of Medonsley* **LG1937**; *of Stoke Hall*

LG1937; *of Thirston* LG1937; *of The Elms, Leamington Spa* LG1921; *of Tynemount* LG1921; *of Mount Severn* LG1900; *of Stradarran* LG1894; *of Blackness* LG1882; *of Burnside* LG1882Supp; *of Seaside and Glencarse* LG1858; *of Stradarran* LG1904; DFUSA; FR; (*see also* Hunter-Arundell)

CHAMBERS-HUNTER *of Tillery* LG1952

HUGHES-HUNTER *of Plâs Côch* LG1906

SWINTON-HUNTER (*see* Swinton *of that Ilk*)

HUNTERCOMBE, B DEP

HUNTINGDON (*see* Clinton; Hastings; and St Liz)

HUNTINGFIELD, B DEP; (*see also* Vanneck)

HUNTINGTON, Bt PB1928; *of Bonawe House* LG1972; *formerly of Woodhall Manor* DFUSA; (*see also* Parker)

HUNTLEY *of Boxwell* LG1937; FR

HUNTLY (*see* Gordon)

HUNTSMAN *of West Retford* LG1952

HURCOMD, B PB1970

HURD, B PB1967

COOKE-HURLE *formerly of Kilve Court* LG1972; FR

HURLY *of Glendalough* LGI1958; *of Glenduffe* LG1894

HURST *formerly of Horsham Park* LG1972; *formerly of Battersea* DFUSA; (*see also* Wright *of West Bank and Hurstfield*)

HURT *formerly of Alderwasley* LG1965

HUSEE (*see* Hoese)

HUSKINSON *of Langar Hall* LG1972

HUSKISSON *of Eastham, co Sussex* AA; (*see also* Milbanke)

HUSSEY (Beaulieu, E) DEP; (Hussey, B) DEP; Bt *of Caythorpe* EDB; Bt *of Honington* EDB; *of Scotney Castle* LG1952; *of Rathkerry* LGI1912; *of Westown* LGI1912; *of Edenburn* LGI1912; (*see also* Wallace (*formerly* Macpherson) *of Little Wyrley Hall*)

HUSTLER *formerly of Acklam Hall* LG1969

HUSTED DFUSA

HUSTON DFUSA; *formerly of Ballymoney* DFUSA

HUTCHINS *formerly of Ardnagashel* LGI1958

HUTCHINSON (Ilford, B) PB1970;

(Hutchinson of Montrose, B) PB1949; B DEP; *of Howden* LG1898

FOX-HUTCHINSON *formerly of Kyo and Riding Hills* LG1952

HELY-HUTCHINSON (Donoughmore, E) PB1970

PARKER-HUTCHINSON *of Timoney* LGI1912

HUTCHISON, Bt *of Hardiston* PB1970; Bt *of Rossie* PB1970; Bt *of Thurle* PB1970; *of Balmaghie formerly of Rockend* LG1952; DFUSA

HUTH (*now* BOORD) *of Wan's Dycke End* LG1972

HUTTON *formerly of Gate Burton* LG1972; *of Harescombe Grange* LG1972; *of Marske* LG1952; *late of Sowber Grange* LG1937; *of Beetham House* LG1921; *of Houghton Hall* LG1921; *formerly of Spridlington* LG1921; *of Overthwaite* LG1863; FR; (*New Zealand*) CG

HUXLEY LG1965

HUYSHE *of Sand and Clyst Hydon* LG1952

HYDE (Rochester, E) DEP; Bt *of Birmingham* PB1940; *of Longworth* LG1937, IFR1976; DFUSA

HYDE (*now* SEALY) IFR1976

HYETT *of Painswick House* LG1952

HYLTON (*see* Jolliffe; and Musgrave)

HYNDFORD (*see* Carmichael)

HYNDLEY (*see* Hindley)

HYNE *of Kettlewell* LG1937

HYNES *of Beara Court* LG1937

HYSLOP *formerly of Lotus* LG1965; DFUSA

SELWYN-IBBETSON (Rookwood, B) PB1902

IDDESLEIGH (*see* Northcote)

IEVERS IFR1976

ILBERT *of Bowringsleigh* LG1952

ILCHESTER (*see* Fox-Strangways)

ILDERTON *of Ilderton* LG1900

ILFORD (*see* Hutchinson)

ILIFFE, B PB1970

ILKESTON (*see* Foster)

ILLINGWORTH, B PB1940; LG1969

IMAGE *of Herringswell House* LG1906

IMBRIE DFUSA

BLAIR-IMRIE *of Lunan* LG1969

INCHBALD *of Holdfast and Wraxall* LG1965

INCHCAPE (*see* Mackay)

INCHIQUIN (*see* O'Brien)

INCHYRA (*see* Hoyer Millar)

INCLEDON *of Buckland* (*see* Incledon-Webber)

IND *formerly of Whitehall* **LG1972**

INGE *of Brightwell Manor* **LG1965**; *of Thorpe Constantine* **LG1952**

INGHAM, B **DEP**; *formerly of Blake Hall* **LG1965**; *of Augill Castle* **LG1937**; *of Sugwas Court* **LG1937**; *of Marton* **HI**

INGILBY Bt **PB1970**; *late of Lawkland Hall* **LG1937**

AMCOTTS-INGILBY (*see* Cracroft-Amcotts)

INGLEBY, Bt *of Ripley* **PB1854**; Bt *of Ripley* **EDB**; *of Sedgeford Hall* **LG1937**; *of Valentines* **LG1898**; (*see also* Peake)

INGLEFIELD **LG1965**

CROMPTON-INGLEFIELD (*see* Inglefield)

INGLETT (*see* Fortescue-Brickdale) **LG1972**

INGLEWOOD (*see* Vane)

INGLIS, Bt *of Glencorse* **PB1970**; Bt *of Milton Bryan* **PB1855**; Bt *of Cramond* **EDB**; *formerly of Redhall* **LG1952**; *of Riokhinghall* **LG1914**; (*see also* McCulloch *of Auchindinny*)

INGOLDSBY, Bt **EDB**

INGRAM, Bt **PB1970**; (Irvine, V) **DEP**; *formerly of Ades* **LG1965**; *of Swinshead Abbey* **LG1886**

MEYNELL INGRAM *of Hoar Cross* **LG1900**

INGRAMS (Darcy de Knayth, B); **PB1970**

INMAN, B **PB1970**; *of Upton Manor* **LG1921**

INNES, Bt *of Balvenie* **PB1970**; Bt *of Coxtown* **PB1882**; Bt *of Lochalsh* **EDB**; *of New Seat of Scurdargue* **LG1972**; *of Fordoun* **LG1952**; *of Inverisla* **LG1952**; *of Learney* **LG1952**; *of Roffey Park* **LG1952**; *of Cowie* **LG1937**; *of Crommey* **LG1937**; *formerly of Islips Manor* **LG1937**; *late of Muiryfold* **LG1937**; *late of Raemoir* **LG1937**; *of Ayton* **LG1894**; *formerly of Dromantine* **LG1958**; (*Australia*) **CG**; (*see also* Farquharson *of Invercauld*; and Innes-Cross)

BRODIE-INNES *of Milton Brodie* **LG1921**

MITCHELL-INNES *of Whitehall* **LG1972**

ROSE-INNES *formerly of Netherdale* **LG1952**

INSKIP (Caldecote, V) **PB1970**

INVERCHAPEL (*see* Clark Kerr)

INVERCLYDE (*see* Burns)

INVERFORTH (*see* Weir)

INVERNAIRN (*see* Beardmore)

INVERNESS (*see* Underwood)

IONIDES *of Buxted Park* **LG1952**

IPRE (Kent, E) **DEP**

IRBY (Boston, B) **PB1970**; *of Tenterfield* **CG**; (*see also* Boteler *formerly of Eastry*)

IREDELL *formerly of Belton* **LG1972**

IRELAND *of Oldfield Lodge* **LG1952**; *of Altringham* **LG1937**; **DFUSA**; (*see also* Vere)

CLAYFIELD-IRELAND *of Brislington Hall and Dourich* **LG1921**

DE COURCY-IRELAND *of Abington Pigotts* **LG1972**

IREMONGER *formerly of Wherwell Priory* **LG1972**

IRONSIDE, B **PB1970**; *formerly of New Deer* **DFUSA**

BAX-IRONSIDE (*see* Campbell)

TURNER-IRTON *of Swanwick Glen* **LG1921**

IRVIN *formerly of The Elms* **LG1952** **Supp**

IRVINE, Bt **EDB**; *of Brynllwyn* **LG1965**; *formerly of Under-the-Hill House* **LG1969**; *of Castle Irvine* **LGI1912**; *of Killadeas* **LGI1912**; (*see also* Campbell; and Ingram)

DOUGLAS-IRVINE (*see* Queensberry)

FORBES-IRVINE *of Drum* **LG1965**

TYNTE-IRVINE **IFR1976**

IRVING, Bt **PB1866**; *of Dumfries* **LG1969**; *of Well Place* **LG1952**; *of Bonshall* **LG1894**; *of Barwhinnock* **LG1886**; *formerly of Shapinsay* **DFUSA**; **AA**

BELL-IRVING *of White Hill* **LG1965**

WINTER-IRVING **CG**

IRWIN *of Justicetown* **LG1952**; *of Lynehowe and Solport* **LG1898**; *of Richmount* **LG1898**; **IFR1976**; *of Mount Irwin* **LGI1958**

ISAACS (Swanborough, B) **PB1970**; (*see also* Courthope-Munroe)

RUFUS ISAACS (Reading, M) **PB1970**

ISACKE (*see* Chesshyre)

ISHAM, Bt **PB1970**

ISHERWOOD, Bt **PB1940**

BRADSHAW-ISHERWOOD *of Marple* **LG1952**

ISLINGTON (*see* Dickson)

ISMAY, B **PB1963**; *formerly of Dawpool* **LG1952**

ISTED *of Ecton* **LG1882**

IVEAGH (*see* Guinness)

IVERS (see Ievers)
GORDON-IVES of Bentworth **LG1937**
GRANT-IVES of Bradden **LG1972**
IVORY of Brewlands **LG1969**
IZARD **PromFUSA**
IZOD of Chapel Izod **LGI1912**
JACKSON (Allerton, B) **PB1970**; (Jackson
  of Burnley, B) **PB1970**; Bt of Arlsey
  PB1970; Bt of Stansted **PB1970**; Bt of
  Wimbledon **PB1970**; B **PB1953**; Bt of
  Wandsworth **PB1937**; Bt of Fork Hill
  PB1851; Bt of Hickleton **EDB**; of
  Barston **LG1952**; of Duddington
  LG1952; formerly of Fairburn **LG1952**;
  of Kirkbuddo **LG1952**; of Rignell
  House **LG1952**; of Clay Cross Hall
  LG1937; of Felix Hall **LG1937**; of
  Leighton Court **LG1937**; of Springfield
  House **LG1937**; of Swordale **LG1921**;
  of Ahanesk **LG1894**; of Manor House
  LG1863; of Fanningtown Castle
  LG1863; of Carrowmore **LGI1912**;
  PresFUSA; (1) & (2) **DFUSA**; (Aus-
  tralia) **CG**; of Jackson Dale and Telan
  CG; of Sandford House **CG**; of Car-
  ramore **HI**; (see also Barstow; Calvert;
  Duckett; and Lane-Fox)
MATHER-JACKSON Bt **PB1970**
ROTHWELL-JACKSON of Moorfield
  LG1921
WARD-JACKSON of Normanby Hall
  LG1937
JACOB, Bt **EDB**; of Ard na Greine
  LGI1958; of Silverfort House **LGI1958**;
  AA
JACOBS of Wooland Court **LG1937**;
  DFUSA
JACOMB **RFFK**
JACQUES, B **PB1970**; Bt **PB1970**
JACSON of Tedsmore **LG1952**; of Barton
  LG1898; of Barton, co Lancaster **AA**
JAFFRAY, Bt **PB1970**
JAFFREY, Bt **PB1953**
JAGO (see Sneyd of Coldrenick)
JALLAND late of Holderness House
  LG1937
JAMES (James of Rusholme, B) **PB1970**;
  (Northbourne, B) **PB1970**; Bt **PB1970**;
  (James of Hereford, B) **PB1911**; Bt of
  Creshall **EDB**; Bt of Elthan **EDB**; of
  West Dean **LG1972**; of Wynd House
  LG1972; of Chevington **LG1952**; late of
  Otterburn **LG1937**; of Water House
  LG1937; late of Pantsaison **LG1937**;
  PromFUSA; **FR**; (Australia) **CG**; (see
  also Powell of Barrock)

GREVIS-JAMES of Ightham Court
  LG1906; **FR**
JAMESON, Bt **PB1917**; **IFR1976**; (see
  also McCulloch of Ardwall)
JANSON (Sutherland, E) **PB1970**
JANSSEN, Bt **EDB**
JAQUES of Easby Abbey **LG1952**
JARDINE, Bt of Applegirth **PB1970**; Bt
  of Godalming **PB1970**; Bt of Notting-
  ham **PB1963**; of Chesterknowes for-
  merly of Hallside **LG1952**; **DFUSA**
BUCHANAN-JARDINE, Bt **PB1970**
JARRETT of Glasfryn **LG1972**
JARRETT (now COLCLOUGH) of
  Camerton Court **LG1921**
JARVIS, Bt **PB1963**; of Doddington
  LG1972; late of Middleton **LG1937**
JARY of Burlingham House **LG1914**
JASON, Bt **EDB**
JAUNCEY of Tullichettle **LG1972**
JAY **PromFUSA**
JEAFFRESON of Dullingham **LG1863**
JEANS of Fisherton de la Mere **LG1952**
JEBB (Gladwyn, B) **PB1970**; Bt **EDB**; of
  The Lyth **LG1952**
JEFFCOCK of Worlingham Grove
  LG1965
JEFFERSON of Springfield **LG1952**;
  PresFUSA
DUNNINGTON - JEFFERSON, Bt
  PB1970
JEFFERYS formerly of Nevis, B.W.I.
  DFUSA; (see also Faulconer)
ALLEN-JEFFERYS (see Allen of Lyng-
  ford)
JEFFREY **DFUSA**
JEFFREYS, B **PB1970**; B **DEP**; Bt **EDB**;
  of Doddington Place **LG1972**; formerly
  of Canterton Manor **LG1969**; of Burk-
  ham **LG1952**; formerly of Llywell
  LG1937
CRAIG JEFFREYS formerly of Aber-
  cynrig **LG1972**
JEHANGIR, Bt **PB1970**
JEJEEBHOY, Bt **PB1970**
JEKYLL **FR**
JELLICOE, E **PB1970**
JENINGS of Ironpool **LGI1912**
KEMEYS-JENKIN of Glan Mor **LG1952**
PRYCE-JENKIN of Clanna **LG1952**
JENKINS, B **PB1967**; (Glantawe, B)
  PB1915; of Hampnett Manor **LG1969**;
  of Broseley Hall and Charlton Hill
  LG1937; of Westhide **LG1937**; of
  Bicton Hall **LG1882**; **DFUSA**; (see also
  Stewart-Killick)

BLANDY-JENKINS *of Llanharan* LG1952
VAUGHAN-JENKINS *of Combe Grove* LG1952
JENKINSON, Bt PB1970; (Liverpool, E) DEP; Bt EDB; *of Knapp Hill Manor* LG1937
JENKS, Bt, PB1970
JENNER *of Wenvoe* LG1952; (*see also* Jenner-Fust)
JENNEY *of Calke Abbey* LG1952; *of Drayton Beauchamp* LG1952
JENNINGS *of Gelli-Dêg* LG1955; (*Australia*) CG
JENOUR *of Crossways* LG1952
JENOURE, Bt EDB
JENYNS *of Bottisham Hall* LG1969
JEPHCOTT, Bt PB1970
JEPHSON IFR1976
JEPSON DFUSA
JERMY (*see* Back; and Gwyn)
JERMYN (St Albans, E) DEP; B DEP
JERNEGAN, Bt PB1935
JERNINGHAM *of Longridge Towers* LG1914; (*see also* FitzHerbert; and Jernegan)
JERSEY (*see* Child-Villiers)
JERVEY DFUSA
JERVIS (St Vincent, V) PB1970; (St Vincent, E) DEP; *formerly of Chatcull and Darlaston* LG1972
JERVIS-WHITE-JERVIS, Bt PB1940
JERVOIS IFR1976
JERVOISE, Bt PB1933; *of Herriard* LG1965
JESSE *of Llanbedr Hall* LG1894
JESSEL, B PB1970; Bt *of Ladham* PB1970
JESSON *formerly of Oakwood* LG1937 Supp; *of Oakwood, co Stafford* AA
TUCHET-JESSON (Audley, B) PB1970
JESSOP *formerly of Overton Hall* LG1937; *of Doory Hall* LGI1912
JESSOPP *formerly of Lexham Hall* LG1952Supp
JESSUP DFUSA
JESUP PromFUSA
JENNE (St Helier, B) PB1906
SYMONS-JEUNE *formerly of Watlington Park* LG1952
JEWELL *formerly of Romsey* LG1952
JEWETT DFUSA; *formerly of Bradford* DFUSA
JILLARD (*see* Martineau *of Clapton Court*)
JOCELYN (Roden, E) PB1970; (Clanbrassill, B) PB1897

JODRELL, Bt PB1929
COTTON-JODRELL (*now* RAMSDEN-JODRELL) *of Yeardsley* LG1937
JOEL *formerly of Wyphurst* LG1965
JOHNSON, Bt *of Bath* PB1970; Bt *of New York* PB1970; Bt *of Dublin* PB1917; *of Strathaird* LG1972; *of Castlesteads* LG1965; *of Seacroft* LG1952; *formerly of Winkleigh Court* LG1952; *of Heronbrook House* LG1937; *of Marsh Court* LG1937; *of Goscobe Hall* LG1921; *late of Withan-on-the-Hill* LG1906; *of Ayscough Fee Hall* LG1900; *of Temple Belwood* LG1900; *of Ulverscroft* LG1894; *of Deanery* LG1863; *of Burleigh Field* LG1863; *of Monksfields* LG1863; *of Tildesley* LG1833/7; *of Rockenham and Skahanagh* LGI1912; PresFUSA; (1) (2) & (3) DFUSA; *formerly of Canterbury* DFUSA; *formerly of Liverpool* DFUSA; *of Wairakaia* CG; *of Wellington* CG; *of Burleigh Field, co Leicester* AA; *of Rockeenham, co Cork* AA; *of Runcorn, co Chester* AA; *of Ayscough Fee Hall* HI; (*see also* Adams)
CROOM-JOHNSON *of Hillbrook House* LG1952
DIXON-JOHNSON *formerly of Aykleyheads* LG1969
HILTON-JOHNSON *of Sarre Court* LG1921
WEBB-JOHNSON, B PB1956
JOHNSTON, Bt *of Caskieben* PB1970; Bt *of City of London* PB1933; Bt *of Elphinston* EDB; *formerly of Lesmurdie* LG1972; *of Brent Knoll formerly of Hilton* LG1969; *of Bryn-y-Groes* LG1952; *of Coubister and Orphir House* LG1952; *formerly of Cashel Johnston* LG1952Supp; *of Cowhill* LG1900; *of Kincardine* LG1900; IFR1976; *formerly of Aughawood* LGI1958; *of Lisgoole Abbey* LGI1958; *of Wild Forest* LGI1958; *of Ballykilbeg* LGI1912; *of Fort Johnston* LGI1912; *of Magheramenc* LGI1912; *of Kinlough House* LGI1912; DFUSA; (*New Zealand*) CG; (*see also* Barton; and Broom)
CAMPBELL JOHNSTON *formerly of Carnsalloch* LG1972
LAWSON JOHNSTON (Luke, B) PB1970
JOHNSTONE, Bt PB1970; (Annandale, M) DEP; Bt EDB; *of Galabank* LG1952; *late of Alva* LG1937; *of Trewithen* LG1937; *of Bignor Park*

LG1906; *of Snow Hill* **LGI1912**; *of Bawnboy House* **LGI1912**; (1) & (2) **DFUSA**
HOPE-JOHNSTONE *of Annandale* **LG1952**; (*see also* Linlithgow)
VANDEN-BEMPDE-JOHNSTONE (Derwent, B) **PB1970**
JOICEY, B **PB1970**; *of Blenkinsopp Hall* **LG1969**; *of Poulton Priory* **LG1925 Supp**
JOLIFFE *of Ammerdown Park* **AA**
JOLLIE *of Waireka* **CG**
JOLLIFFE (Hylton, B) **PB1970**
JOLY DE LOTBINIERE *of Brandon Hall* **LG1969**
JONES (Maelor, B) **PB1970**; Bt **PB1970**; Bt *of Pentower* **PB1949**; (Ranelagh, V) **PB1885**; Bt *of Albemarlis* **EDB**; Bt *of Ramsbury Manor* **EDB**; *of Godmond Hall formerly of Llay* **LG1969**; *formerly of Bron Crw* **LG1952**; *of Foxoote* **LG1952**; *of Gwynfryn* **LG1952**; *formerly of Neath Abbey* **LG1952**; *of Sandersteud* **LG1952**; *of Fronheulog* **LG1937**; *of Gungrog Hall* **LG1937**; *of Hartsheath* **LG1937**; *of Llanmiloe* **LG1937**; *of Penyrallt* **LG1937**; *of Underdean formerly of Nass* **LG1937**; *of Vynter's Manor* **LG1937**; *late of Headfort* **LG1937Supp**; *of Derry Ormond* **LG1921**; *of Fonmon Castle* **LG1921**; *of Kilsall Hall and Shakerley Hall* **LG1921**; *of Llanerchrugog Hall and Eglwyseg Manor House* **LG1894**; *of Glandenys and Balenôs* **LG1894**; *of Larkhill* **LG1886**; *of Trewithen* **LG1863**; *of Wepre Hall* **LG1863**; *of Ystrad* **LG1863**; *of Moneyglass* **LG1863**; *of Clytha* **LG1863**; *of Esgair Evan* **LG1863**; *of Caton* **LG1833/7**; *of Llanarth* **LG1833/7**; *formerly of Roscrea* **LGI1958**; *of Mount Charles* **LGI1958**; *of Mullinaboro'* **LGI1912**; *of Ardnaree* **LGI1912**; *late of Jonesboro'* **LGI1912**; (1) (2) (3) (4) (5) & (6) **DFUSA**; (1) & (2) **FR**; (*Canada*) **CG**; *of Langford Court* (*see* Somers *of Mendip Lodge*); *of Pantglas* (*see* Spence-Colby); *of Ynysfor* (*see* Roche); (*see also* Robertson-Glasgow; Longueville; and Godfrey)
ARMSTRONG-JONES (Snowdon, E) **PB1970**
BENCE-JONES **IFR1976**
BOOTH-JONES *of Hale Park* **LG1952**
BOWEN-JONES, Bt **PB1925**
BURNE-JONES **PB1926**
CATON-JONES *of Earlsdale* **LG1937**

CHOLMELEY-JONES *formerly of Nass* **DFUSA**
GRESFORD JONES (*see Jones* of Godmond)
GWYNNE JONES (Chalfont, B) **PB1970**
HAMILTON-JONES *of Moneyglass* **LGI1912**
HEYWOOD-JONES *of Badsworth Hall* **LG1921**
INGLIS-JONES *formerly of Derry Ormond* **LG1952**
INIGO-JONES (*see* Neeld)
LAWRENCE-JONES, Bt **PB1970**
LEIF-JONES (Rhayader, B) **PB1939**
LLOYD-JONES (*formerly* ALSTON) *of Harrold Hall formerly of Odell Castle* **LG1952**; *formerly of Llandyssul* **DFUSA**
MAKEIG-JONES *formerly of Southerton House* **LG1972**
MORGAN-JONES (*formerly* JONES) *formerly of Llanmiloe* **LG1969**
PEYTON-JONES **LG1952**
PRICHARD-JONES, Bt **PB1970**
PROBYN-JONES, Bt **PB1949**
PRYCE-JONES, Bt **PB1963**; **FR**
QUAYLE JONES *of Barton Mere* **LG1937**
SALISBURY-JONES *of Mill Down* **LG1952**
SPENCE-JONES *of Pantglâs* **LG1921**
STEWART-JONES (*see Jones of God-mond*)
TALBOT JONES *formerly of Rich Hill* **DFUSA**; (*see also* Post)
WHITMORE-JONES *of Chasleton* **LG1937**
WILLDING-JONES *of Hampton Hall* **LG1952**
WYNNE-JONES *of Penmaenucha* **LG1952**
JORDAN *of Rosslevin Castle* **LG1886**; *of Pigeonsford* **LG1882**; (*Australia*) **CG**
JOSEPH, Bt **PB1970**; Bt *of Stoke-on-Trent* **PB1949**; *of Alsager* **LG1937**
JOSSELYN *formerly of Little Horksley* **LG1965**
JOWETT *of Manningham and Coverdale* **LG1937**
JOWITT, E **PB1956**
JOY *of Grimston amd Marelands* **LG1952**
JOYCE *formerly of Blackfordby* **LG1952**; *formerly of Mervue* **LGI1958**; *of Corgary* **LG1894**
JOYES *formerly of Belmont* **DFUSA**

JUDD *formerly of Maces Place* **LG1965**; *of Stewkley Grange* **LG1965**; **DFUSA**
JUDGE (*see* Gibb)
JULIUS (*New Zealand*) **CG**
JUXON, Bt **EDB**
KABERRY, Bt **PB1970**
KAHN, B **PB1970**
KAINS **DFUSA**
KANE *of Drumreask* **LGI1912**; *of Saunderscourt* **LG1894**
SETON-KARR *formerly of Kippilaw* **LG1937**
KARSLAKE *of Nymet St George* **LG1972**
KATER **CG**
KAULBACK *of Ardnagashel House* **LGI1958**
KAVANAGH (Ballyane, B) **DEP**: **IFR1976**
KAY, Bt **PB1917**; *of Poppleton Hall* **LG1952**; *of Davenham Hall* **LG1906**; *of Farfield* **LG1886**; (*see also* Shuttleworth)
KAYE, Bt **PB1970**; Bt **EDB**; *of Old House, Coolham* **LG1937**
LISTER-KAYE, Bt **PB1970**
KEANE, Bt **PB1970**; B **PB1901**; *of Mardon* **LG1937**; **IFR1976**
KEARLEY (Devonport, V) **PB1970**
KEARNEY *of The Ford* **LG1882Supp**
BUTLER-KEARNEY *of Drom* **LGI1912**
CUTHBERT-KEARNEY *of Garrettstown* **LG1863**
KEARSLEY *formerly of Fullwood Park* **LG1937**
KEATE, Bt **EDB**
KEATES *of Bishop's Nympton* **LG1921**
KEATING (*see* Singer)
MORRIS-KEATING (*see* Morris *formerly of Allerton Priory*; and Singer)
KEATINGE **IFR1976**; *formerly of Kilcowan* **LGI1958**
KEAY (*see* Warburton-Lee)
KEBLE *of Keble House* **LG1969**
POWIS-KECK *of Stoughton Grange* **LG1937**
POWYS-KECK (*see* Lilford)
KEELING *formerly of Walton Grange* **LG1952**; **DFUSA**; **FR**
KEENE *formerly of Worplesdon* **DFUSA**
RUCK KEENE *of Waterstock, formerly of Swyncombe House* **LG1969**
KEEVIL **LG1969**
KEIGWIN *of Mousehole* **LG1880/3**; **HI**
KEIR *of Kindrogan* **LG1898**
KEITH (Keith of Avonholme, B) **PB1963**; (Marischal, E) **DEP**; (Altrie, Lord) **DEP**; (Dingwall, Lord) **DEP**; Bt *of*

Ludquhairn **EDB**; Bt *of Powburn* **EDB**; *of West Barsham Hall* **LG1965**; (*see also* Elphinstone)
KEKEWICH, Bt **PB1932**; *formerly of Peamore* **LG1969**
KELHAM *of Bleasby Hall* **LG1921**
KELHEAD (*see* Douglas)
KELLETT, Bt **PB1970**
KELLOGG *formerly of Bocking* **DFUSA**
KELLY *of Kelly* **LG1972**; *of Leesthorpe Hall* **LG1972**; *of Dundermot* **LGI1958**; *of Tara House* **LGI1958**; *of Mucklon* **LGI1912**; *of St Helens* **LGI1912**; *of Newtown* **LGI1904**; *formerly of Ballinasloe* **DFUSA**
ALIAGA-KELLY (*see* O'Kelly) **LGI1958**
HARVEY-KELLY **IFR1976**
ROCHE-KELLY **IFR1976**
KELSEY *formerly of Braintree* **DFUSA**
KELSO *of Kelsoland and Sauchrie* **LG1937**; **DFUSA**
KELVIN (*see* Thomson)
KEMBLE *of Laggan* **LG1965**; *formerly of Runwell Hall* **LG1972**
KEMEYS, Bt **EDB**; *of Kevanmably* **LG1833/7**; (*see also* Kemmis *of Hanger*)
KEMMIS *of Hanger* **LG1969**; **IFR1976**
WALSH-KEMMIS **IFR1976**; (*see also* Kemmis *of Hanger*)
KEMP (Rochdale, V) **PB1970**; Bt **PB1936**
KEMPE, Bt **EDB**; *of Roseteage* **LG1833/7**
KEMPSON *of Densy Lodge* **LG1937**
KEMSLEY (*see* Berry)
KENDAL (*see* de Foix; and Stuart)
KENDALL *of Pelyn* **LG1972**; *of Great Nineveh* **LG1952**; (1) & (2) **DFUSA**
KENILWORTH (*see* Siddeley)
KENMARE (*see* Browne)
KENMURE (*see* Gordon)
KENNAN **IFR1976**
KENNARD, Bt **PB1970**; *late of Cawley Court and of The Haining* **LG1937**; (*see also* Oglander)
KENNAWAY, Bt **PB1970**
KENNEDY (Ailsa, M) **PB1970**; Bt **PB1970**; Bt *of Clowburn* **EDB**; Bt *of Garvinmains* **EDB**; *of Underwood* **LG1972**; *of Knockgray* **LG1969**; *formerly of Stone Cross* **LG1969**; *of Doonholm* **LG1965**; *of Dunure* **LG1937**; *late of Bennane and Finnarts* **LG1937**; *of Knocknalling and Knockrioch* **LGI1921**; *of Romanoe* **LG1900**; *of Hayesleigh* **LG1886**; *of Cultrea* **LGI1958**; **PresFUSA**; (1) & (2) **DFUSA**; *of Ellerslie* **CG**; *of Knockgray* **HI**; (*see*

also Brodribb; MacFarlan; Kennedy-Skipton; and Skipton)
SHAW-KENNEDY *of Kirkmichael* **LG1937**
KENNET (*see* Young)
KENNETT (*see* Kennett-Barrington)
KENNEY *of Kilclogher, co Galway* **AA**
FITZGERALD-KENNEY *of Kilclogher* **LGI1912**
KENNY **IFR1976**
KELLY-KENNY *of Treanmore and Managh* **LGI1912**
KENRICK, Bt **EDB**; *of Caer Rhun Hall formerly of Maenan Abbey* **LG1952**
KENRY (*see* Wyndham-Quin)
KENSINGTON (*see* Edwardes)
KENSWOOD (*see* Whitfield)
KENT, Bt **PB1848**; *late of Anmer* **LG1925**; **DFUSA**; *formerly of St Blazey Gate* **DFUSA**, (*see also* Burgh; Grey; Guelph; Ipre; Odo; and Plantagenet)
KENWORTHY (Strabolgi, B) **PB1970**
KENYON *of St George's Lodge* **LG1952**; *of Gillingham Hall* **LG1937**; *of Pradoe* **LG1937**
TYRELL-KENYON, (Kenyon, B) **PB1970**
KEOGH *of Kilbride* **LG1886**; **FR**
KEPPEL (Albemarle, E) **PB1970**; V **DEP**
KER, E **DEP**; *formerly of Leintwardine* **LG1965**; **IFR1976**
INNES-KER (Roxburghe, D) **PB1970**
KERDESTON, B **DEP**
KERN **DFUSA**
KERR (Lothian, M) **PB1970**; (Teviot, B) **PB1970**; Bt **PB1970**; Bt **EDB**; *formerly of Maer Craig* **LG1972**; *of Newnham formerly of The Haie* **LG1952**; **IFR1976**; **DFUSA**; (*see also* Lamar)
CLARK KERR (Inverchapel, B) **PB1949**
KIDSTON-KERR (*see* Kidston)
MURRAY-KERR *of New Bliss House* **LGI1912**
SCOTT-KERR *of Chatto and Sunlaws* **LG1937**
KERRICH *of Geldestone* **LG1921**
KERRISON, Bt **PB1886**; *of Burgh Hall* **LG1969**
KERSHAW *of Endon Hall* **LG1969**
KESTEVEN (*see* Trollope)
KETTLE *of Merridale and Glan-y-don* **LG1894**; (*New Zealand*) **CG**
KETTLEWELL *of Harptree Court* **LG1937**
KETTON *of Felbrigge Park* **LG1886**
KEY, Bt **PB1932**; *of Fulford Hall* **LG1952**
COOPER-KEY *of Burnt Wood* **LG1965**

KEYES, B **PB1970**; **DFUSA**
O'MALLEY-KEYES (*see* O'Malley)
KEYNES, B **PB1940**
KEYT, Bt **EDB**
KIDNER *of Old Hall, Colton* **LG1952**
KIDSTON *of Redenham Park* **LG1965**
KROYER-KIELBERG *of Sefton Lodge* **LG1952**
KILBRACKEN (*see* Godley)
KILGOUR *of Tulloch* **LGI1937**
KILKENNY (*see* Butler)
KILLANIN (*see* Morris)
KILLEARN (*see* Lampson)
KILLEGREW, Bt **EDB**
KILLICK (*see* Stewart-Killick)
STEWART-KILLICK *formerly of Whitehall* **LG1969**
KILMAINE (*see* Browne)
KILMANY (*see* Anstruther-Gray)
KILMARNOCK (*see* Boyd)
KILMOREY (*see* Needham)
KILMUIR (*see* Maxwell Fyfe)
KILPATRICK **DFUSA**
KILSYTH (*see* Livingston)
KILWARDEN (*see* Wolfe)
KILVERT (*see* Kilvert-Milnor Adams)
KIMBALL *of Alderholt Park* **LG1965**; *formerly of Rattlesden* **DFUSA**
KIMBER, Bt **PB1970**
KIMBERLEY (*see* Wodehouse)
KIME **DFUSA**
KIMMINS *formerly of Marks Barn and Rodwell House* **LG1972**
KIMPTON *of Sarunds House* **LG1972**
KINAHAN **IFR1976**
HUDSON-KINAHAN, Bt **PB1949**
KINASTON (*see* Mainwaring *of Oteley*)
KINCAID *formerly of Alloa* **DFUSA**
KINCHANT *late of Park Hall* **LG1914**
KINDER *of Harrytown* **LG1937**
KINDERSLEY, B **PB1970**; *formerly of Elston Hall* **LG1972**; *of Clyffe* **LG1921**
KING (Lovelace, E) **PB1970**; Bt *of Campsie* **PB1970**; Bt *of Charlestown* **PB1970**; Bt *of Cornwall Gardens* **PB1933**; (Kingston of Mitchelstown, B) **PB1869**; (Kingston, B) **DEP**; *formerly of Chadshunt* **LG1969**; *of Brinkley Hall* **LG1952**; *of The Old House* **LG1952**; *of Tertowie* **LG1937**; *of Ford House* **LG1925Supp**; *of Preston Candover* **LG1875**; *of Umberslade* **LG1858**; *formerly of Ballylin* **LGI1958**; *formerly of Roebuck Hall* **LGI1958**; **DFUSA**; **FR**; (*Australia*) **CG**; *of Double Bay* **CG**; *of Nambrok* **CG**; (*see also* Ford *Pres*; and Kingston)

DUCKWORTH-KING, Bt **PB1970**
KING-KING *formerly of Staunton-on-Arrow* **LG1972**
LESLIE-KING **IFR1976**
MEADE-KING *formerly of Walford* **LG1965**
REEVE-KING (*see* Reeve *of Leadenham*)
SEALY-KING *formerly of Richmount* **LGI1958**
KINGAN **IFR1976**
KINGDON *of Launcells* **LG1863**
KINGHAN (*see* Kingan)
KINGSALE (*see* de Courcy)
KINGSBURY *formerly of Hagbourne and Chewton Mendip* **LG1965**; *formerly of Boxford* **DFUSA**; **PromFUSA**
KINGSCOTE *of Kingscote* **LG1969**
KINGSDOWN (*see* Pemberton-Leigh)
KINGSMILL, Bt **EDB**; *of Sydmonton* **LG1952**; *of Hermitage Park* **LGI1912**
KINGS NORTON (*see* Roxbee Cox)
KINGSTON (*see* King; and King-Tenison)
KINGSTON-UPON-HULL (*see* Pierrepont)
KINGSTOUN (*see* Seton)
KINKEAD **DFUSA**
KINLOCH, Bt *of Gilmerton* **PB1970**; Bt *of Kinloch* **PB1970**; Bt **EDB**
KINLOSS (*see* Freeman-Grenville)
KINNAIRD, B **PB1970**; (Rossie, B) **PB1878**
KINNEAR, B **PB1917**; **CG**
BALFOUR-KINNEAR *formerly of the Laws and Cross* **LG1969**
BOYD-KINNEAR *of Kinnear and Kinloch* **LG1921**
KINNERSLY *of Binfield Manor, Berks* **AA**
KINNOULL (*see* Hay)
KINROSS (*see* Balfour)
KINSOPP (*see* Leadbitter)
KINTORE (*see* Baird; and Keith-Falconer)
KIPPEN **FR**
KIRBY *of Brandsby* **LG1952**; **DFUSA**
KIRK *formerly of Wavertree, Sevenoaks* **LG1952**; *of Sharpham* **LG1937**
LLOYD-KIRK *of North Hill Park* **LG1952**
KIRKCALDY, Bt **EDB**
KIRKCUDBRIGHT (*see* Maclellan)
KIRKBRIDE *formerly of Kirkbride* **DFUSA**
KIRBY (*see* Bagnall-Wild)
KIRKE *of Markham House* **LG1965**;

late of The Eaves **LG1921**; *of Mirfield Hall* **LG1898**
KIRKETON, B **DEP**
KIRKHOVEN (Bellomont, E) **DEP**
KIRKLEY (*see* Noble)
KIRKPATRICK, Bt **PB1970**; **IFR1976**; *of Donacomper* **LGI1958**; *of Closeburn* **CG**
KIRKWOOD, B **PB1970**; *formerly of Gore Court* **LG1969**; *late of Yeo* **LG1937**; *formerly of Woodbrooke and Cloongoonagh* **LGI1958**
KIRSOPP *of The Spital* **LG1921**
KIRWAN *of Gregg* **LGI1912**; *of Blindwell* **LG1886**; (*see also* Paley)
MAITLAND-KIRWAN *of Gelston Castle* **LG1937**
KITCHENER (Kitchener of Khartoum, E) **PB1970**; (Kitchener of Khartoum, B) **PB1916**; **CG**
KITCHING *of Ayton Firs* **LG1952**
KITSON (Airedale, B) **PB1970**; *formerly of Shiphay Manor* **LG1952**
KITTOE *of Leafland* **LG1952**
KLEINWORT, Bt **PB1970**
KNAPP *formerly of Little Linford Hall and Shenley* **LG1972**; (1) & (2) **DFUSA**
KNAPTON *of Boldre* **LG1921**
KNARESBOROUGH (*see* Meysey-Thompson)
KNATCHBULL (Brabourne, B) **PB1970**
KNELLER, Bt **EDB**
KNESHAW *of Penmaemawr* **LG1921**
KNIGHT (Catherlough, E) **DEP**; *of Lockinge Manor* **LG1972**; *of Tythegston Court* **LG1972**; *of Chawton* **LG1969**; *formerly of Court House* **LG1952**; *of The Oaks, Queniborough* **LG1952**; *of Wolverley* **LG1937**; *of Firbeck* **LG1833/7**; (1) (2) & (3) **DFUSA**; (*see also* Webb *of The Berrow*)
ROUSE - BOUGHTON - KNIGHT *of Downton Castle* **LG1937**
KNIGHTLEY (Knightley of Fawsley, B) **PB1895**; Bt **EDB**
FINCH-KNIGHTLEY (Aylesford, E) **PB1970**
KNILL, Bt **PB1970**
KNIVETON, Bt **EDB**
KNOLLES *of Oatlands* **LG1894**
KNOLLYS, V **PB1970**; (Banbury, E) **DEP**; Bt *of Grove Place* **EDB**; Bt *of Thame* **EDB**
(DE) KNOOP *of Tingewick House* **LG1925**
KNOTT, Bt **PB1949**
KNOTT (*formerly* COZENS HARDY) *of Cley-Next-The-Sea* **LG1952**

FORTESCUE-KNOTTESFORD   (see Fortescue-Brickdale)
KNOVILL, B **DEP**
KNOWLES, Bt **PB1970**; Bt of Westwood **PB1928**; formerly of Swinton Old Hall **LG1952**; of Colston Bassett Hall **LG1921**
KNOX (Ranfurly, E) **PB1970**; of Place **LG1952**; **IFR1976**; of Creagh **LGI1912**; of Netley Park, co Mayo **AA**; (see also Carnegy-Arbuthnott)
KNUTSFORD (see Holland-Hibbert)
GRAVES-KNYFTON of Uphill **LG1952**
KNYVETT, B **DEP**; Bt **EDB**; **FR**
KOCH DE GOOREYND **LG1965**
KONIG formerly of Tyringham **LG1965**
KYAN of Ballymurtag **LG1858**
KYD of Pitcastle **LG1952**
KYFFIN of Whitehall **LG1972**
KYLE of Laurel Hill **LGI1912**
KYLSANT (see Philipps)
KYME, B **DEP**
KYNASTON, Bt **PB1866**; of Hardwick **LG1952**; (see also Williams of Trwylun; and Mainwaring of Oteley)
KYNNERSLEY (see Kynnersley-Browne)
SNEYD-KYNNERSLEY of Loxley **LG1952**
ELLIOT - MURRAY - KYNYNMOUND (Minto, E) **PB1970**
KYRKE formerly of Nantyffrith **LG1937**
VENABLES KYRKE (formerly Hoyle) of Gnaton Hall **LG1952**
KYRLE, Bt **EDB**
MONEY-KYRLE, Bt **PB1843**; of Whetham **LG1965**
LA BECHE (see Beche)
LABERTOUCHE of Melbourne **CG**
LABOUCHERE (Taunton, B) **DEP**; of Broome Hall **LG1863**
LACON, Bt **PB1970**; of Wigmore and Ormesby Hall **LG1972**
LACY, Bt **PB1970**; (Lincoln, E) **DEP**
LADD **DFUSA**
LADE, Bt **EDB**; of Nash Court **LG1875**
MILLES-LADE (Sondes, E) **PB1970**
LAFFAN, Bt **PB1848**
LAFONE formerly of Hanworth Park **LG1972**
LA FONTAINE, Bt **PB1867**
LAIDLAW of Somerton **LGI1958**
LAIDLAY formerly of Seacliff **LG1969**
LAIDLEY **CG**
LAING of Thornhill and Etal Manor **LG1906**
LAKE, Bt **PB1970**; V **DEP**; Bt **EDB**
LAKIN, Bt **PB1970**
LAKING, Bt **PB1930**

LALOR of Gregg **LGI1899**
POWER-LALOR of Long Orchard **LGI1912**; (see also de la Poer)
LAMAR (formerly KERR) **DFUSA**
LA MARE (see Mare)
L'AMAY of Dunkenny **LG1952**
LAMB (Rochester, B) **PB1970**; (Melbourne, V) **DEP**; of Warkton **LG1969**; of Knighton Manor **LG1965**; of Ryton **LG1965**; of Temon and Scotby **LG1952**; of West Denton, Northumberland **AA**
LAMBARD of Beechmont **LG1937**
LAMBART (Cavan, E) **PB1970**; Bt **PB1970**; of Beau Parc **LGI1899**
LAMBERT, V **PB1970**; Bt **PB1970**; of Blechingley, formerly of Banstead **LG1969**; formerly of Telham Court **LG1952**; formerly of West Bridgford **LG1952**; co Galway **IFR1976**; of Dysertmore **LGI1958**; of Carnagh **LGI1912**; **FR**; of Carnugh, co Wexford **AA**; (see also Ruttledge)
CAMPBELL LAMBERT of Burlton Hall **LG1969**; **FR**
LAMBOURNE (see Lockwood)
LAMBTON (Durham, E) **PB1970**
LAMBURY (see Lord)
LAMING of Alresford Place **LG1937**
LAMINGTON (see Cochrane-Baillie)
LAMONT, Bt **PB1949**; of Gribton **LG1937**; of Lamont **LG1921**; of Knockdow **LG1906**
LAMPLUGH (see Brooksbank of Lamplugh)
LAMPSON (Killearn, B) **PB1970**; Bt **PB1970**
LANCASHIRE **DFUSA**
LANCASTER, B **DEP**; of Kelmarsh Hall **LG1952**; (see also Plantagenet)
LANCE of Wentfield **LG1937**
LAND **DFUSA**
LANDALE of Dalswinton **LG1972**
LANDON formerly of Monnington Straddle and Credenhill **LG1972**; of Uxmore **LG1952**; **DFUSA**
LANDOR of Llanthony Abbey formerly of Ipsley Court **LG1952**
LANE, Bt **PB1970**; (Laneborough, V) **DEP**; Bt **EDB**; formerly of King's Bromley **LG1965**; of College Barn **LG1952**; of Glenden **LG1937**; of Pemberton House **LG1937**; of Moundsley Hall **LG1921**; of Grattans **LG1906**; of Badgmore **LG1886**; of Ryelands **LG1886**; **DFUSA**
LANE (now BOTHAMLEY) of Middleton **LG1921**

LANE (*formerly* PICKARD-CAM-BRIDGE) *of Poxwell* **LG1969**
LANEBOROUGH (*see* Lane)
LANESBOROUGH (*see* Butler)
LANEY **DFUSA**
LANG *formerly of Paisley* **LG1969**; **DFUSA**
LANG OF LAMBETH (*see* Lang *formerly of Paisley*)
LANGDON **DFUSA**
LANGDALE, B **DEP**; *of Compton* **LG1952**; *of Haughton* **LG1937**; (*see also* Bickersteth; Kelham; and Mowbray, Segrave and Stourton)
LANGFORD, Bt **EDB**; **IFR1976**; (*see also* Rowley-Conwy)
LANGLEY, *of Clayton Holt* **LG1921**; **IFR1976**; **FR**
LANGHAM, Bt **PB1970**
LANGHORNE, Bt **EDB**
LANGLEY, Bt **EDB**
LANGMAN, Bt **PB1970**
LANGRISHE, Bt **PB1970**
LANGSTON *of Sarsden House* **LG1858**; **FR**
LANGTON *of Langton* **LG1972**; *of Little Hadham Place* **LG1937**; *of Danganmore* **LG1886**; (*Australia*) **CG**
GORE-LANGTON *of Newton Park* **LG1875**
TEMPLE-GORE-LANGTON (Temple of Stowe, E) **PB1970**
LANNIGAN **LG1833/7**; (*see also* Bancroft)
LANSDOWNE (*see* Granville; and Petty-Fitzmaurice)
LARCOM, Bt **PB1970**
SOMERVILLE-LARGE *of Vallombrosa* **LGI1958**
LARNACH *of Adderbury* **LG1921**; (*Australia*) **CG**
LAROCHE, Bt **EDB**
LARPENT, Bt **PB1899**
LASCELLES (Harewood, E) **PB1970**; (Harewood, E) **DEP**
LASCELS, B **DEP**
LASLETT *of Abberton Hall* **LG1886**
LATHAM, B **PB1970**; Bt **PB1970**; *of Oak Knoll* **LG1952**; *of Theydon Towers* **LG1952**; *of Bradwall* **LG1886**
LATHOM (*see* Bootle-Wilbraham)
LATHROP **PromFUSA**
LATIMER (Latimer, of Braybrooke, B) **DEP**; (Latimer, of Danby, B) **DEP**; (*see also* Nevill)
FREWEN-LATON (*see* Frewen)
LA TOUCHE **IFR1976**

LATTA, Bt **PB1940**
LATTER *of Cropredy and Weald Place* **LG1937**
LATTIN (*see* Mansfield)
LATYMER (*see* Money-Coutts)
DICK-LAUDER, Bt **PB1970**
LAUDERDALE (*see* Maitland)
LAUGHTON *of Eastfield, Yorks* **LG1921**; **FR**
LAURIE, Bt *of Bedford Square* **PB1970**; Bt *of Maxwelton* **PB1848**; *of South Weald* **LG1972**
CRAIG-LAURIE (*see* Birney)
DYSON-LAURIE (*see* Vere-Laurie)
NORTHALL-LAURIE (*see* Vere-Laurie)
VERE-LAURIE *of Carlton* **LG1972**
LAUTOUR (*see* Parker *of Houghton*)
LAVINGTON (*see* Payne)
LAW (Coleraine, B) **PB1970**; Ellenborough, B) **PB1970**; (Ellenborough, E) **PB1871**; **IFR1976**; *of Marble Hill* **LG1937Supp**; *of Killaloe* **LGI1912**; **DFUSA**; *of Lauriston* **VF**
LAWDAY, Bt **EDB**
LAWDER *of Lawderdale* **LGI1912**
LAWES Bt **PB1970**; *formerly of Old Park* **LG1952**
LAWLESS (Cloncurry, B) **PB1929**
LAWLEY (Wenlock, B) **PB1932**
LAWLOR *of Grenagh House* **LG1858**
LAWRANCE *of Golden House, Minstead* **LG1952**; *of Dunsby Hall* **LG1921**
LAWRANCE (*formerly* LAWRENCE) *sometime of St Albans* **DFUSA**
LAWRENCE, B **PB1970**; (Trevethin and Oaksey, B) **PB1970**; Bt *of Chelsea* **PB1970**; Bt *of Ealing Park* **PB1970**; Bt *of Lucknow* **PB1970**; (Lawrence of Kingsgate, B) **PB1927**; Bt *of Westbourne Terrace* **PB1897**; Bt *of Iver* **EDB**; Bt *of St Ives* **EDB**; *of Pilgrims' Hill* **LG1969**; *of Cowesfield House* **LG1937**; *of Ellerton Hall* **LG1937**; *of Sandywell Park* **LG1914**; *of Lisreaghan* **LG1912**; (1) & (2) **DFUSA**
DURNING-LAWRENCE, Bt **PB1914**
PETHICK-LAWRENCE, B **PB1959**
LAWSON, (Burnham, B) **PB1970**; Bt *of Brough Hall* **PB1970**; Bt *of Knavesmire* **PB1970**; Bt *of Westwood Grange* **PB1970**; (Lawson, B) **PB1963**; Bt *of Brayton* **PB1959**; (Burnham, V) **PB1933**; Bt *of Brough Hall* **EDB**; Bt *of Isell* **EDB**; *formerly of Longhirst* **LG1937**; *of Hall Barn* **LG1886**; (*see also* Lawson-Tancred)

LAWTON *of Lawton* **LG1952**; *of Copmanthorpe Manor* **LG1937**; *of Wyvenhoe* **LG1886**
LAYARD *formerly of Corton Denham* **LG1972**
LAYCOCK *of Wiseton* **LG1969**
LAYMAN (*Australia*) **CG**
LAYTON, B **PB1970**; *of Chettisham Hall* **LG1863**
LEA, Bt **PB1970**; *formerly of Astley Hall* **LG1972**; *formerly of Orchardlea* **LG1952**; *of The Larches* **LG1886**
LEACH *of Corstock* **LG1937**
LEACOCK (*Canada*) **CG**
LEADBETTER *formerly of Stobieside* **LG1952**
LEADBITTER *formerly of Warden* **LG1972**
LEADER **IFR1976**
LEAF *formerly of Park Hill, Streatham, and Bishop Monckton* **LG1969**
LEAHY *of Southill* **LGI1912**; *formerly of Whitechurch* **DFUSA**; *of Shunakiel, co Cork* **AA**
CARROLL-LEAHY *of Eglantine* **LGI1958**
LEAKE **DFUSA**, *formerly of Norton* **DFUSA**; (*Tasmania*) **CG**
BYRES-LEAKE *late of Rockside* **LG1921**
MARTIN-LEAKE *of Marshalls formerly of Thorpe Hall* **LG1952**
LEAPER (*see* Curzon)
LEAR, Bt **EDB**
LEARMONTH *of Eumoralla West* **CG**; *of Prestonholme* **CG**
LIVINGSTONE-LEARMONTH *formerly of Parkhall* **LG1965**
LEATHAM *formerly of Hemsworth Hall* **LG1965**
LEATHER *of Middleton Hall* **LG1937**; *of Leventhorpe Hall* **AA**; (*see also* Leather-Culley)
LEATHERLAND, B **PB1970**
LEATHERS, V **PB1970**
LEATHES *formerly of Herringfleet* **LG1972**
LE BRETON *formerly of Loders Court* **LG1972**
LECALE (*see* FitzGerald)
LECHE *of Carden* **LG1972**
LECHMERE, Bt **PB1970**; B **DEP**; *of Fownhope Court* **LG1952**
LECKY **IFR1976**; *of Ballykealey* **LG1937** **Supp**
BROWNE-LECKY (*see* Browne)
LECKY-BROWNE-LECKY (*see* Browne)

LEDGARD *formerly of Roundhay* **LG1952**
LEDSAM *of Chad Hills* **LG1875**
LEE (Lee of Fareham, V) **PB1940**; (Lichfield, E) **DEP**; Bt *of Hartwell* **EDB**; Bt *of Langley* **EDB**; Bt *of Quarendon* **EDB**; *of Dinas Powis* **LG1972**; *of How Caple Court* **LG1972**; *of Coton* **LG1921**; *of Yarner* **LG1921**; *of Grove Hall* **LG1914**; *of Hartwell* **LG1906**; *of Kingsgate House* **LG1886**; *of Holborough* **LG1882**; *of Balsdon* **LG1863**; *of Lauriston Hall* **LG1850/3**; *of The Mount* **LG1850/3**; *formerly of Barno* **LGI1958**; **DFUSA**; *of Maryland and Virginia* **DFUSA**; **FR**; (*Canada*) **CG**; (*see also* Eyre; Shand-Harvey; Lee-Warner; and Washington)
VAUGHAN-LEE (*see* Cameron *of Dillington*)
WARBURTON-LEE *of Broad Oak* **LG1972**
LEECH *of Cloonconra* **LGI1912**; *late of Kippure* **LGI1912**
LEEDS, Bt **PB1970**; (1) & (2) **DFUSA**; (*see also* Osborne)
LEEKE *of Longford and Aston Hall* **LG1937**
LEEFE (*Tonga*) **CG**
LEES, Bt *of Black Rock* **PB1970**; Bt *of Longendale* **PB1970**; Bt *of Lytchet Manor* **PB1970**; *formerly of Thurland Castle* **LG1972**; *of Whittlebury Lodge* **LG1952**; *of Etherow* **LG1937**; (*see also* Phythian-Adams; and Lees-Milne)
DUMVILLE LEES (*see* Luxmoore *of Okehampton*)
LEESE, Bt **PB1970**
LEESON (Milltown, E) **PB1970**
LE FANU **IFR1976**
SHAW LEFEVRE (Eversley, B) **PB1928**; (Eversley of Heckfield, V) **PB1888**
LEFFINGWELL **PromFUSA**
LE FLEMING, Bt **PB1970**; *of Rydal* **LG1952**
LEFROY **IFR1976**; (*Canada*) **CG**
LEGARD, Bt **PB1970**
LEGGATT **AA**
LEGGE (Dartmouth, E) **PB1970**; (Stawel, B) **DEP**; *of Malone House* **LG1882**; *of Cullenswood House* **CG**
LEGH (Newton, B) **PB1970**; *of Radipole* **LG1972**; *of High Legh* **LG1965**; *of Adlington* **LG1952**; **LG1972**; *of Lyme* **LG1886**
LE GRICE *of Trereife* **LG1952**

LEGUEN DE LACROIX *of Chediston* **LG1952**

BAINBRIGGE-LE HUNT (*see* Bainbrigge *formerly of Woodsteat*)

LE HUNTE *of Artramont* **LGI1912**

LEICESTER, Bt **PB1967**; (De Tabley, B) **PB1895**; Bt **EDB**; (*see also* Coke; Dudley; Montfort; and Sydney)

LEIGH, B **PB1970**; Bt **PB1970**; Bt *of South Carolina* **PB1870**; Bt *of Whitley* **PB1844**; (Chichester, E) **DEP**; (Leigh of Stoneleigh, B) **DEP**; Bt **EDB**; Bt *of Newnham* **EDB**; Bt *of Stoneleigh* **EDB**; *of Thorpe Satchville Hall, formerly of Luton Hoo* **LG1965**; *of Belmont* **LG1952**; *of Brocastle* **LG1952**; *formerly of West Hall, High Legh* **LG1952**; *late of Bardon* **LG1937**; *late of Bouldnand* **LG1921**; *of Hindley Hall* **LG1921**; *of Woodchester Park* **LG1921**; *of Mayfield* **LG1906**; *of Stoneleigh* **LG1833/7**; *of Leather Lake House* **LG1833/7**; *of Northcourt* **LG1833/7**; **IFR1976**; **DFUSA**; (*see also* Hare)

AUSTEN-LEIGH (*see* Knight *of Chawton*)

GERARD LEIGH (*see* Leigh *of Thorpe Satchville Hall*)

HANBURY-LEIGH *of Ponty Pool Park* **AA**

PEMBERTON-LEIGH (Kingsdown, B) **DEP**

WARD-BOUGHTON-LEIGH *of Brownsover Hall* **LG1972**

LEIGHTON, Bt **PB1970**; B **PB1896**; *formerly of Medomsley* **LG1952**; *of Sweeney Hall* **LG1952**; (*see also* Seager)

LEINSTER (*see* FitzGerald; and Cholmondeley)

LEIR (*see* Leir-Carleton) *of Ditcheat*

LEITH (Burgh, B) **PB1976**; Bt *of Newcastle* **PB1956**; *of Freefield and of Glenkindie* **LG1914**

FORBES-LEITH, Bt *of Fyvie* **PB1970**; (Leith of Fyvie, B) **PB1925**; *of Whitehaugh* **LG1914**; *of Fyvie* **LG1900**

LEITRIM (*see* Burke; and Clements)

LEKE (Scarsdale, E) **DEP**; Bt *of Newark-upon-Trent* **EDB**; Bt *of Sutton* **EDB**

LELAND **DFUSA**

LELY *of Carlton Scroop* **LG1937**

LEMAN, Bt **EDB**; *of Brampton Hall* **LG1900**

LE MARCHANT, Bt **PB1970**

LEMON, Bt **PB1868**

LEMPRIERE *of Roselle Manor* **LG1937**

LENDRUM (*see* Cramsie)

LENIGAN *of Castle Fogerty* **HI**

RYAN-LENIGAN *of Castle ffogerty* **LGI1912**; (*see also* Ryan)

LENNARD, Bt **PB1970**; (Sussex, E) **DEP**; Bt **EDB**; (*see also* Cator)

BARRETT-LENNARD, Bt **PB1970**

LENNIG **DFUSA**

LENNOX (*see* Stewart)

GORDON-LENNOX (Richmond and Gordon) **PB1970**

PEARETH KINCAID LENNOX *of Downton Castle* **LG1952**

LENTAIGNE **IFR1976**; *of Tallaght, co Dublin* **AA**

LENTHALL *of Bessels Leigh* **LG1952**

MACALPINE-LENY (*see* Macalpine-Downie)

LEON, Bt **PB1970**

LEONARD *of Queensfort* **LGI1912**; **DFUSA**

LEPPER *of Elsinore* **LG1937Supp**

LEPPINGTON **AA**

LERMITTE (*now* BROOME) *formerly of Woodhouse* **LG1952**

LESCHER *formerly of Boyles Court* **LG1952**; **FR**

LESLIE, (Rothes, E) **PB1970**; Bt *of Glaslough* **PB1970**; Bt *of Wardis* **PB1970**; Bt *of Juniper Hill* **PB1849**; (Lindores, B) **DEP**; (Newark, Lord) **DEP**; Bt *of Tarbert* **EDB**; *of Brancaster* **LG1965**; *formerly of Kininvie* **LG1952**; *of Balquhain* **LG1937**; *formerly of Courtmacsherry* **LG1937**; (*co Antrim*) **IFR1976**; (*co Kerry*) **IFR1976**; *of Ballyward* **LGI1912**; (1) & (2) **FR**; *of Warthill, co Aberdeen* **AA**

ARBUTHNOT-LESLIE (*see* Stainton)

CRAWFORD-LESLIE (*see* Crawford)

L'ESTRANGE; Bt **EDB**; **IFR1976**

LE STRANGE *of Hunstanton* **LG1972**

LETHBRIDGE, Bt **PB1970**; *of Tregeare* **LG1952**; *of Exbourne Manor* **LG1921**; *of Homebush* **CG**

KINGSFORD-LETHBRIDGE *of Wood* **LG1952**

LETT, Bt **PB1963**; *formerly of Waters Edge* **LG1972**

LEVELIS (*see* Vosper)

LEVEN AND MELVILLE (*see* Leslie Melville)

LEVENTHORPE, Bt **EDB**

LEVER (Leverhulme, V) **PB1970**; Bt **PB1970**; Bt *of Allerton* **PB1940**; (*see also* Goldie-Scot)
LEVERHULME (*see* Lever)
LEVETT *formerly of Wychnor Park* **LG1952**; *of Milford Hall* **LG1937**
LEVEY **DFUSA**
LEVIEN (*Australia*) **CG**
LEVINGE, Bt **PB1970**
LEVY, Bt **PB1970**
LEWES *of Llysnewydd* **LG1937**
LEWIN *formerly of Cloghans* **LGI1958**; *of The Hollies* **LG1898**; *of The Hollies* **LG1858**; *of Lancaster* **CG**; *of The Hollies, Bexley, Kent* **AA**; (*see also* Roberts)
ROSS-LEWIN *of Ross Hill* **LGI1912**
LEWIS (Brecon, B) **PB1970**; (Essendon, B) **PB1970**; (Merthyr, B) **PB1970**; Bt *of Portland Place* **PB1940**; Bt *of Brighton* **PB1893**; Bt **EDB**; *of Parwich and Evancoyd* **LG1972**; *of Henllan* **LG1952**; *formerly of Seafort House* **LG1952**; *of Dormie House* **LG1952 Supp**; *of Llwyncelyn* **LG1937**; *of Stradey* **LG1937**; *of St Pierre* **LG1906**; *of Plâs-Draw* **LG1900**; *of Greenmeadow* **LG1882**; *of Harpton Court* **LG1850/3**; *of Llanthewy Court* **LG1850/3**; *of Penlline* **LG1880/3**; *of Dallinagar* **LGI1912**; *of Inniskeen and Seatown* **LGI1912**; **DFUSA**; *formerly of Eglwysilan* **DFUSA**; *formerly of The Van* **DFUSA**; (*see also* Washington)
HAMPTON-LEWIS (*now* DWYER-HAMPTON) *of Henllys and Dodior* **LG1937**
LE ROY-LEWIS *of Westbury* **LG1921**
ORR-LEWIS, Bt **PB1970**
LEWTHWAITE, Bt **PB1970**
LEWYS, Bt **EDB**
LEXINGTON (*see* Sutton)
LEY, Bt **PB1970**; (Marlborough, E) **DEP**; Bt **EDB**
LEY (*now* JENKINSON) *of Trehill* **LG1937**
LEYCESTER *of Hilton* **LG1952**; *of White Place* **LG1894**; (*see also* Penrhyn; and Leycester-Roxby)
LEYLAND *formerly of Haggerston* **LG1952**
NAYLOR-LEYLAND, Bt **PB1970**
LEYBURN, B **DEP**
STEWART-LIBERTY *of The-Lee* **LG1972**
LIBBY (*see* Wyman)
LICHFIELD (*see* Anson; and Lee)

LIDDELL (Ravensworth, B) **PB1970**; (Ravensworth, B) **PB1904**; (Ravensworth, B) **DEP**; *of Warwick-on-Eden* **LG1969**; *of Shirenewton* **LG1952**
LIDDELL (*now* ELWES) *of Warwick Hall* **LG1952**
LIDWILL **IFR1976**
LIFFORD (*see* Hewitt)
LIGHTON, Bt **PB1970**
LIGON *formerly of Madresfield* **DFUSA**
LIGONIER, V **DEP**
LILBURN *of Coull* **LG1969**
LILFORD (*see* Powys)
LILLEY **CG**
LILLIE **DFUSA**
INGE-INNES-LILLINGSTON *of Thorpe Constantine* **LG1965**
LILLY (*formerly* GAY) *of Aldborough Hall* **LG1969**
LIMERICK (*see* Dungan; and Pery)
LINCOLN **Pres FUSA**; *formerly of Hingham* **DFUSA**; (*see also* Grant; Lacy; Pole; and Romare)
LINCOLNSHIRE (*see* Wynn-Carrington)
LIND *of Hyde* **LG1858**
LINDEMANN (Cherwell, V) **PB1956**
LINDESAY *formerly of Loughry* **LGI1958**
LINDGREN, B **PB1970**
LINDLEY, B **PB1921**; (1) & (2) **DFUSA**
LINDLEY (*formerly* BEKEN) *of High Pauls* **LG1952**
LINDORES (*see* Leslie)
LINDOW *of Ingwell, co Cumberland* **AA**
BURNS-LINDOW *of Ingwell and Ehen Hall* **LG1937**
LINDSAY (Crawford, E) **PB1970**; (Lindsay of Birker, B) **PB1970**; Bt *of Dowhill* **PB1970**; Bt *of West Ville* **PB1931**; (Montrose, D) **DEP**; (Spynie, Lord) **DEP**; Bt *of Evelick* **EDB**; *of Houston House* **LG1952**; (*see also* Lindesay-Bethune)
BROUN-LINDSAY *of Colstoun and formerly of Wellwood* **LG1952**
LOYD-LINDSAY (Wantage, B) **PB1901**
LINDSEY *formerly of Fenstanton* **DFUSA**; (*see also* Bertie)
LINDSEY AND ABINGDON (*see* Bertie)
LINDSELL *formerly of Fairfield* **LG1952**
LINGARD *of Fellside* **LG1952**
LINGEN, B **PB1905**; *of Penlanolen*

LG1900; (*see also* Burton *of Longner Hall*)
LINLITHGOW (*see* Livingston; and Hope)
LINTON *of Stirtloe* **LG1952**
STUART-LINTON *formerly of Cabarston House* **LG1952**; **DFUSA**
LIPPE **RL**
LIPPINCOTT, Bt **EDB**
LIPSCOMBE *late of Claverton Lodge* **LG1937**
LIPTON, Bt **PB1931**
LISBURNE (*see* Loftus; and Vaughan)
LISGAR (*see* Young)
LISLE **DFUSA**; (*see also* Lysaght)
L'ISLE (de L'Isle, B) **DEP**; (de L'Isle, *of Rougemont*, B) **DEP**; (*see also* Grey; Plantagenet; and Talbot)
LISMORE (*see* O'Callaghan)
LISTER (Riddell, B) **PB1934**; B **PB1912**; *formerly of Armitage Park and Westby Hall* **LG1972**; *of Shibden* **LG1906**; *of Finningley Park* **LG1900**; *of Cefn Ila* **LG1894**; *of Ousefleet Grange* **LG1863**
CUNLIFFE-LISTER (Swinton, E) **PB1970**; (Masham of Ilton, B) **PB1970**; (Masham, B) **PB1924**
LISTOWEL (*see* Hare)
LITCHFIELD *of Snowfield* **LG1972**
LITHGOW, Bt **PB1970**
LITTLE *of Newbold Pacey* **LG1952**; *of Pitchcombe* **LG1937**; *late of Llanvair Grange* **LG1921**; *of Stewartstown* **LGI1912**
BROOKE-LITTLE *of Heyford Horvoe* **LG1972**
CARUTHERS-LITTLE *of Pitchcombe* **LG1952**
LITTLEBOY *of Howe* **LG1969**
LITTLEDALE *of Bunbury* **LG1937**; **FR**
LITTLEHALES (*see* Baker)
LITTLEJOHN *of Invercharron* **LG1921**
LITTLER *of Cheshire* **LG1850/3**
LITTLETON (Hatherton, B) **PB1970**; Bt *of Pillaton Hall* **EDB**; Bt *of Stoke Milburgh* **EDB**
LITTLEWOOD *late of The Hyde* **LG1921**
LITTON *formerly of Woolmer Lodge* **LG1952**; *of Ardavilling* **LGI1912**; (*Australia*) **CG**
LIVERMORE *formerly of Little Thurlow* **DFUSA**; (*see also* Martin)
LIVERPOOL (*see* Foljambe; and Jenkinson)

LIVESEY, Bt **EDB**; *of Stourton Hall* **LG1886**
LIVINGSTON, Bt **PB1862**; (Calendar, E) **DEP**; (Linlithgow, E) **DEP**; (Kilsyth, V) **DEP**; (Teviot, V) **DEP**; Bt *of Newbiggin* **EDB**; *of Clermont* **DFUSA**; **PromFUSA**
LIVINGSTONE, Bt **EDB**; Bt *of Dunipace* **EDB**; (*see also* Newburgh)
FENTON-LIVINGSTONE *late of Westquarter* **LG1921**
LLANDAFF (*see* Mathew)
LLANGATTOCK (*see* Rollo)
LLANOVER (*see* Hall)
LLEWELLIN, B **PB1956**; *of Upton House* **LG1937**; *of Tregwynt* **LG1863**
PURCELL-LLEWELLIN *of Eynant* **LG1882**
LLEWELLYN, Bt *of Baglan* **PB1970**; Bt *of Bwllfa* **PB1970**; *of Court Colman and Baglan Hall* **LG1952**
DILLWYN-VENABLES-LLEWELYN, Bt **PB1970**; *of Llysdinam Hall* **LG1952**
LLOYD, B **PB1970**; (Lloyd of Hampstead, B) **PB1970**; Bt *of Rhu* **PB1970**; Bt *of Bromwydd* **PB1933**; Bt *of Lancing* **PB1844**; Bt *of Garth*; Bt *of Mitfield* **EDB**; Bt *of Peterwell* **EDB**; Bt *of Woking* **EDB**; Bt *of Yale* **EDB**; *of Abercynrig, formerly of Dinas* **LG1972**; *formerly of Blaenglyn* **LG1972**; *of Coedmore* **LG1969**; *of Dolobran* **LG1969**; *of Aston* **LG1952**; *formerly of Castell Forwyn* **LG1952**; *formerly of Cowesby* **LG1952**; *of Cynghordy* **LG1952**; *of Fosseway House formerly of Leaton Knolls* **LG1952**; *of Penty Park* **LG1952**; *of Plâs Tregayan* **LG1952**; *of Stockton Hall* **LG1952**; *formerly of White Hall* **LG1952**; *of Brunant* **LG1937**; *of Bryndyfrydog* **LG1937**; *of Dan-yr-Allt* **LG1937**; *of Dolobranisaf* **LG1937**; *of Rhagatt* **LG1937**; *of Shelton Hall* **LG1921**; *of Trallwyn* **LG1921**; *of Glansevin* **LG1900**; *of Sutton Coldfield* **LG1886**; *of Welcombe* **LG1833/7**; *of Gwyrch* **LG1833/7**; *of Ferney Hall* **LG1833/7**; *of Bronwydd* **LG1863**; *of Plymog, Gwerclas, and Bashall* **LG1863**; *of Laques* **LG1863**; *of Pale* **LG1863**; (*co Limerick*), **IFR1976**; (*Offaly*) **IFR1976**; (*co Tipperary*) **IFR1976**; *formerly of Lossett* **LGI1958**; *formerly of Rockville* **LGI1958**; *of Croghan* **LGI1912**; *of Strancally Castle* **LGI1912**; **DFUSA**;

(Australia) **CG**; *of Cum Bychan (see* Lloyd-Roberts); *of Hafodunos (see* Howard *of Wigfair); of Trawscoed (see* Trevor); *(see also* Iremonger; and Mostyn)

LLOYD *(formerly* BRIGHT) *of Colwall* **LG1965**

LLOYD *(formerly* HASTINGS) *of Martley* **LG1952**

CARR-LLOYD *of Lancing* **LG1914**

JONES-LLOYD *formerly of Moely-garnedd and Plasyndre* **LG1972**

LLUELLYN *of Strethall* **LG1900**

LOAKE *formerly of Hampden House and of Desborough* **LG1952**

LOANE **IFR1976**

LOCH, B **PB1970**; *of Drylaw* **LG1882**; *of Tittensor* **LG1863**

LOCHEE *(see* Robertson)

LOCK *of York House* **LG1952**

LOCKE *formerly of Cleeve House* **LG1952**; *late of Grange* **LG1914**; **DFUSA; FR**

LOCKETT *of Clonterbrook* **LG1965; FR**

LOCKHART *formerly of Milton Lockhart* **LG1972**

ELIOTT LOCKHART *of Cleghorn* **LG1972**

SINCLAIR-LOCKHART, Bt **PB1970**

LANGTON-LOCKTON *of Teeton Hall* **LG1952**

LOCKWOOD (Lambourne, B) **PB1928; PromFUSA**

LOCKYER *of Plymouth* **LG1898**

LOCOCK, Bt **PB1963**

LODER (Wakehurst, B) **PB1970**; Bt **PB1970**

LOFFT *(now* BEVAN) *of Troston Hall* **LG1921**

LOFTUS, Bt **PB1864**; (Lisburne, V) **DEP**; (Loftus, V) **DEP**; *of Oaklands* **LG1898**; *of Breconash Lodge* **LG1886**; **IFR1976**; *(see also* Ely)

LOGAN *of The Pool House* **LG1952**

LOMAS *of Cornborough* **LG1952**

LOMAX *formerly of Cockayne Hatley* **LG1952**; *formerly of Grove Park* **LG1952; DFUSA**

TRAPPES-LOMAX *of Great Hockham* **LG1965**

FITZGERALD-LOMBARD *formerly of South Hill* **LGI1958**

LOMBE *(see* Jodrell)

EVANS-LOMBE *of Marlingford formerly of Bylaugh* **LG1969**

LONDESBOROUGH *(see* Denison)

LONDON *of Coldharbour* **LG1952**

LONDONDERRY *(see* Pitt; Ridgeway; and Vane-Tempest-Stewart)

LONG, V **PB1970**; (Farnborough, B) **DEP**; Bt *of Westminster* **EDB**; Bt *of Whaddon* **EDB**; *of Sydenham, formerly of Hurts Hall* **LG1969**; *of Clifton House* **LG1952**; *of Dunstan* **LG1952**; *of Preshaw* **LG1921**; *of Rood Ashton* **LG1914**; *of Hampton Lodge* **LG1863**; *of Bainton and Wootton Basset* **LG1833/7**; *of Beckington and Stratton* **LG1833/7**; *of Semington and Trowbridge* **LG1833/7**; **DFUSA**; *of West Hackney, co Middlesex* **AA**; *of Preshaw* **HI**

LONG *(formerly* BULWER) *of Heydon* **LG1952**

LONGCROFT *formerly of Llanina* **LG1952**

LONGE *formerly of Spixworth* **LG1969**

LONGFELLOW **PromFUSA**

LONGFIELD (Longueville, V) **DEP; IFR1976**

LONGFORD *(see* Fleming; and Pakenham)

LONGLEY *formerly of Angley Park* **LG1952**

LONGMAN, Bt **PB1940**; *late of Shendish* **LG1937**

LONGMORE *formerly of Bengeo Wick and Porthill House* **LG1972**; *of Pipits Hill* **LG1952**

LONGRIGG **LG1969**

LONGSDON *of Little Longstone* **LG1972**

LONGSTAFF *formerly of Nearfield House* **LG1958**

LONGUEVILLE, Bt **EDB**; *formerly of Penylan* **LG1965**; *(see also* Longfield)

LONGVILLIERS, B **DEP**

DAMES-LONGWORTH *of Glynwood* **LGI1912**

LONGYEAR **DFUSA**

LONSDALE (Armaghdale, B) **PB1924**; *(see also* Lowther)

HEYWOOD-LONSDALE *of Shavington* **LG1965**

LOPDELL *formerly of Raheen* **LGI1958**

LOPES (Roborough, B) **PB1970**; (Ludlow, B) **PB1922**

LORAINE, Bt **PB1959**

LORD (Lambury, B) **PB1967**; *of Newbus Grange* **LG1952; DFUSA**

LOREBURN *(see* Reid)

LORIMER *of Gibliston* **LG1969**; *of Strone* **LG1952**

LORING **DFUSA**

GUTHRIE-LORNIE *of Burnham* LG1921

LORT, Bt **EDB**

L'ORTI, B **DEP**

LOTHIAN (*see* Kerr)

LOUDON *of Olantigh* LG1972

LOUDOUN (*see* Abney-Hastings)

LOUGHBOROUGH (*see* Wedderburn)

LOUSADA *of Peak House* LG1875

LOUTH (*see* Bermingham; and Plunkett)

LOVAT (*see* Fraser)

LOVE **DFUSA**

LOVEDAY *of Arlescote and formerly of Williamscote* LG1972; *of Williamscote, co Oxford* **HI**

LOVEJOY **DFUSA**

LOVEL, V **DEP**; (Lovel of Kary, B) **DEP**

LOVELACE, B **DEP**; (*see also* Hewgill; and King)

LOVELAND **AA**

LOVELL *of Cole Park* LG1937; *late of Chilcote Manor and Dinder* LG1898

LOVETT, Bt **EDB**: *of Henlle Hall* LG1952; *formerly of Liscombe* LG1952; *of The Grange* LG1900; *of Belmont* LG1894; *of Bath* **HI**

LOVIEBOND *of Hatfield Peverell* LG1863

LOW (Aldington, B) **PB1970**; *of Blebo* LG1937; *of Kilshane* LGI1912; *of Sunvale* LGI1912; *formerly of Boxford* **DFUSA**; **PromFUSA**

MORRISON LOW, Bt **PB1970**

LOWE, Bt **PB1970**; (Sherbrooke, V) **PB1892**; *formerly of Highfield* LG1952; *of Gosfield* LG1937; *of Whitehall* LG1921; (*see also* Lowndes-Stone-Norton; and Sherbrooke)

DRURY-LOWE *of Locko Park* LG1965

PACKE-DRURY-LOWE *of Prestwold Hall* LG1965

HILL-LOWE *formerly of Court of Hill.* LG1952

LOWES *formerly of Ballyclare* **DFUSA**

LOWIS *formerly of Merchiston Castle and Plean* LG1972

LOWNDES *of Hassall* LG1972; *late of Barrington* LG1914; *of Arthurlie* LG1886; **PromFUSA**; *of Chesham, Bucks* **AA**; (*see also* Maurice; and Lowndes-Stone-Norton)

LOWNDES (*now* LYSLEY) *of Castle Combe* LG1937

FRITH-LOWNDES *of Beel House* LG1952

SELBY-LOWNDES *formerly of Whaddon* LG1965

LOWRY **IFR1976**

LOWSLEY *of Hampstead Norris* LG1952; *formerly of Hagbourne* **DFUSA**

LOWSON, Bt **PB1970**; *of Quarnwood* LG1952

LOWTEN *of Manley* LG1863

LOWTH *of Bollitree Lawns* LG1952

LOWTHER (Lonsdale, E) **PB1970**; (Ullswater, V) **PB1970**; Bt **PB1970**; Bt *of Belgrave Square* **PB1916**; (Lonsdale, B) **DEP**; Bt *of Marske* **EDB**; Bt *of Swillington* **EDB**; Bt *of Whitehaven* **EDB**

BRABAZON-LOWTHER *of Shrigley* LG1965

LOXDALE *of Castle Hill* LG1937

LOYD (Overstone, B) **PB1883**; *of Lockinge* LG1972; *formerly of Monks' Orchard* LG1972

LUARD *formerly of Blyborough* LG1965

SELBY-LUARD (*see* Selby *formerly of Shotton and Pawston*; and Luard *formerly of Blyborough*)

LUBBOCK (Avebury, B) **PB1970**; *of Adhurst St Mary* LG1965

LUCAN (*see* Bingham; and Sarsfield)

LUCAS, B **PB1970**; Bt **PB1970**; B **DEP**; Bt *of Fenton* **EDB**; *formerly of Northwood* LG1965; *formerly of Oakash* LG1952; *of Warnham* LG1952; *of Great Colverden* LG1921; *of Stout Hall* LG1863; **IFR1976**; **FR**; (*see also* Hotchkin; and Wood)

LANCASTER-LUCAS *of Wateringbury Place* LG1882

LUCKOCK *of Hormead Hall* LG1965

LUCY, B **DEP**; Bt **EDB**

CAMERON-RAMSAY-FAIRFAX-LUCY, Bt **PB1970**

LUDLOW, E **DEP**; *of Heywood* LG1863; (*see also* Lopes)

LUDINGTON **DFUSA**

LUGARD, B **PB1940**

LUKE *formerly of Crook of Devon* **DFUSA**; (*see also* Lawson Johnston)

LUM, Bt **EDB**

LUMB *of Northcroft House* LG1937; *of Brigham Hall, co Cumberland* **AA**

LUMLEY (Scarbrough, E) **PB1970**; B **DEP**; Bt **EDB**; *formerly of Harleston* LG1952

SANDYS-LUMSDAINE *of Lumsdaine* LG1937

LUMSDEN, Bt **EDB**; *of Arden* LG1952

BURGES-LUMSDEN *of Pitcaple* **LG1969**; (*see also* Burges)
LUND *of Ellerton Hall* **LG1952**; **FR**
COMPTON-LUNDIE *of Spital* **LG1921**
LUNDIN *of Auchtermairnie* **LG1863**; *of Auchtermairnie, co Fife* **AA**
LUPTON **LG1969**
LURGAN (*see* Brownlow)
LUSHINGTON, Bt **PB1970**; (*see also* Saville)
WILDMAN-LUSHINGTON *formerly of Norton Court* **LG1952**
LUTEREL, B **DEP**
LUTLEY *of Brockhampton* (*see* Barneby); **FR**
LUTTRELL (Carhampton, V) **DEP**; *of Dunster* **LG1965**
LOWTHORPE-LUTWIDGE *of Holm Rook Hall* **LG1921**
LUTWYCHE *formerly of Kynerston* **LG1921**
LUXEMBOURG (*Grand Ducal House of*) **RL**
ROBERTSON-LUXFORD *of Higham* **LG1937**
LUXMOORE *of Crackanthorpe, formerly of Ardochy* **LG1972**; *formerly of Okehampton* **LG1972**; *of Kerslake, Devon* **AA**
LYALL *of Headley* **LG1952**
POWYS-LYBBE *late of Hardwick House* **LG1937**
LYCETT **DFUSA**
LYDALL *formerly of Uxmore* **LG1965**
LYDE, Bt **EDB**; (*see also* Ames; and Brodribb)
LYDEKKER *of Harpenden Lodge* **LG1969**
LYELL, B **PB1970**; Bt *of Kinnordy* **PB1875**; *of Gardyne* **LG1952**; *of Kinnordy and Pitmuis* **LG1894**; **FR**
LYGON (Beauchamp, E) **PB1970**
LYLE (Lyle of Westbourne, B) **PB1970**; Bt *of Glendelvine* **PB1970**; Bt *of Greenock* **PB1923**; Lord **DEP**; *of Knocktarna* **LGI1912**; *of Cairnagariff* **LGI1912**; *of The Oaks* **LGI1912**; *of Portstewart House* **LGI1912**; **DFUSA**
LYMAN *formerly of High Ongar* **DFUSA**
LYNCH *of Barna* **LGI1912**; *of Clonmaine House* **LGI1912**; **DFUSA**
BLOSSE LYNCH **IFR1976**
WILSON LYNCH *of Belvoir formerly of Duras and Renmore* **LGI1958**
LYNDHURST (*see* Copley)
LYNE *of Gala and Sydney* **CG**; (*see also* Harford)

LYNEDOCH (*see* Graham)
LYNES *of Ashley Moor formerly of Cyfronydd Hall* **LG1952**; **FR**
LYON *formerly of Appleton Hall* **LG1972**; *late of Goring* **LG1937**; *of Kirkmichael* **LG1937**; *of Tutbury* **LG1921**; *of Cossins* **LG1863**; *of Auldbar* **LG1833/6**; **DFUSA**; *formerly of Enniskillen* **DFUSA**; *formerly of Glen Lyon* **DFUSA**; *formerly of Heston* **DFUSA**
BOWES-LYON (Strathmore and Kinghorne) **PB1970**
LYONS (Ennisdale, B) **PB1963**; (Lyons, V) **PB1887**; *formerly of Oldpark* **LGI1958**; *formerly of Rathcoursey* **LGI1958**; *of Croome* **LGI1912**; *of Ledestown* **LGI1912**; *of Old Park, co Antrim* **AA**
PENRICE-LYONS *of Glazebrook* **LG1952**
LYSAGHT (Lisle, B) **PB1970**; (*co Cork; Kilmacoom*) **IFR1976**; (*cos Cork and Clare*) **IFR1976**
LYSLEY *of Pewsham* **LG1937**
LYSONS *of Hempsted* **LG1898**
LYSTER *of Lysterfield* **LG1898**; *of Rowton* **LG1863**; *of Rocksavage* **LGI1912**; *of Grange* **LGI1912**
LYTTELTON (Chandos, V) **PB1970**; (Cobham, V) **PB1970**; *of Studley Castle* **LG1833/7**; *of Teddesley* **LG1833/7**
LYTTLETON (Lyttleton of Frankley, B) **DEP**; (Lyttleton, of Mounslow, B) **DEP**
LYTTON, E **PB1970**
LYVEDEN (*see* Vernon)
LYWOOD *of Woodlands* **LG1952**
MABANE, B **PB1967**
M'ADAM *of Greenhill* **LG1921**
MACADAM *of Blackwater* **LGI1912**
MacADAM *of Waterhead, Kirkcudbright* **AA**
McADAM *of Craigengillan* **LG1937**
McALESTER *of Loup and Kennox* **LG1937**; **AA**
MACALISTER *of Glenbarr* **LG1952**
MacALISTER, Bt **PB1934**
M'CALL **FR**
McALLISTER **DFUSA**
McALPIN **DFUSA**
MACALPINE (*see* Macalpine-Leny)
McALPINE, Bt **PB1970**
MACAN *of Drumcashel* **LGI1912**
MACANDREW, B **PB1970**; *late of Westwood House* **LG1921**
MacANDREW *of Newfield* **LG1952**; *of Pallinghurst* **LG1952**

McANDREW *of Headley Park* **LG1952**
MACANSH *of Canning Downs* **CG**
MACARA, Bt **PB1970**
McARTHUR *of Ardstraw* **LG1898**;
(*Australia*) **CG**; *of Wyandra* **CG**; (*see
also* Hall)
MACARTNEY, Bt **PB1970**; E **DEP**;
of Lissamore **LGI1912**
ELLISON-MACARTNEY *of Mountjoy
Grange* **LGI1912**; **AA**
M'CARTY (Clancare, E) **DEP**
MACAULAY, B **DEP**; *of Red Hall*
LGI1912
MACAULEY **DFUSA**
McAULIFFE **DFUSA**
MacBAIN *of Scotsburn* **CG**
MacBRAIRE *of Tweedhill and Broad-
meadows* **LG1882**
MACBRAYNE *formerly of Glenbranter*
LG1952
McBRYDE *formerly of Stranraer* **DFUSA**
McCAHAN (1) & (2) **DFUSA**
McCAHILL **DFUSA**
POLLOK-McCALL *of Daldowie* **LG1972**
MacCALLUM (*see* Malcolm)
McCALMONT **IFR1976**
McCANN **DFUSA**
MacCARTHY (Clancarty, E) **DEP**; *of
Dunmanway* **VF**; (*see also* MacCarthy-
Morrogh)
MacCARTHY (GLASS) **AA**
McCARTHY *of Srugrena Abbey* **LGI1912**
MacCARTIE *of Carrignavar* **LGI1912**
McCAUSLAND *of Woodbank* **LG1937
Supp**; **IFR1976**; (*see also* Gorges)
McCAUSTLAND **DFUSA**
McCAW *formerly of Newton Stewart*
DFUSA
McCAWLEY **PromFUSA**
McCLELAN *of Hopewell* **CG**
McCLELLAND **DFUSA**
McCLENNEN **DFUSA**
MACCLESFIELD (*see* Gerard; and
Parker)
McCLINTIC **DFUSA**
McCLINTOCK (*cos Derry and Tyrone*)
IFR1976; (*cos Antrim, Armagh,
Carlow, Donegal, Louth, Tyrone, and
Tipperary*) **IFR1976**
McCLINTOCK (*now* CLOPPER)
DFUSA
McCLUNG **DFUSA**
McCLURE, Bt **PB1893**
McCOMB **DFUSA**
McCONNELL, Bt **PB1970**
McCORKELL *of Ballyarnett* **LGI1958**;
of Glengallaugh **LGI1912**

MacCORMAC, Bt **PB1901**
McCORMICK **DFUSA**
McCORNIE (*see* MacThomas)
McCORQUODALE OF NEWTON,
B **PB1970**; *formerly of Cound Hall*
LG1952
McCOWAN, Bt **PB1970**
MORE-MOLYNEUX-McCOWEN
(*now* LONGBOURNE) *of Lowseley
Park* **LG1921**
MacCRACKEN **DFUSA**
McCRAITH *of Normanton Grange*
LG1952
MacCUBBIN *formerly of Knockdolian*
DFUSA
McCULLAGH, Bt **PB1970**
McCULLOCH *of Ardwall* **LG1972**;
of Auchindinny **LG1972**; **DFUSA**
MacCURDY **DFUSA**
MacDERMOT, PRINCE OF
COOLAVIN **IFR1976**
MacDERMOTT, B **PB1970**; *formerly of
Ramore* **LGI1958**; *of Alderford*
LGI1912
MACDONALD, B **PB1970**; (Macdonald
of Gwaenysgor, B) **PB1970**; (Mac-
donald of Earnscliffe, B) **PB1920**;
of Clanranald **LG1972**; *of Tote*
LG1969; *of Balranald* **LG1952**; *of
Hyde Hall* **LG1952**; *of Rammerscales*
LG1937; *of St Martin's* **LG1937**;
of Glenaladale **LG1921**; *'of Dalchosnie*
LG1906; *of Sandside* **LG1886**; *of
Gribune and Inchkenneth* **LG1863**;
of Vallay co Inverness **LG1880/3**;
(*Canada*) **CG**; *of Charlottetown* **CG**
BOSVILLE MACDONALD *of Sleat*, Bt
PB1970
MAXWELL-MACDONALD (*see* Ducie)
MAXWELL MACDONALD (*formerly*
MORETON-MACDONALD) *of
Largie* **LG1952**
ROBERTSON-MACDONALD *of
Kinlochmoidart* **LG1879**
MACDONNEL, Bt **EDB**; *of Glengarry*
LG1972; *of Keppoch* **LG1937**; (*see
also* Maxwell Macdonald)
McDONELL (*Toronto, Canada*) **CG**;
(*Canada*) (1) & (2) **CG**
MACDONNELL, B **PB1925**; Bt **PB1875**;
DEP
MACDONNELL *of New Hall and Kilkee*
LGI1912; *of Dunfierth* **LGI1912**;
of New Hall, co Clare **AA**
McDONNELL (Antrim, E) **PB1970**;
IFR1976; (1) & (2) **DFUSA**
McDONNELL (*now* SILVERTOP) *of*

Brackney and Kilmore, in Glens of Antrim **LGI1912**

ARMSTRONG-MacDONNELL   (*see* Heaton-Armstrong)

McDONOUGH *of Wilmont House* **LGI1912**

McDOUALL *of Logan* **LG1937**

MACDOUGALL *of Macdougall and Dunollie* **LG1972**; *of Mackerston* **LG1833/7**

LINDSAY-MacDOUGALL *of Lunga* **LG1952**

PATTEN-MACDOUGALL *of Gallanach* **LG1937**

McDOUGALL *of Ottawa* **CG**; *of Rosalie Plains* **CG**

McDOUGALL (*formerly* GANTT) **DFUSA**

MACDOWALL *of Garthland* **LG1972**

McDOWALL (*Australia*) **CG**

McDOWEL *of Gillespie* **LG1921**

McDOWELL **DFUSA**

McDOWELL (*formerly* PLATT) *formerly of Highfield Hall* **LG1969**

MACDUFF *of Bonhard* **LG1937**

MACELROY **DFUSA**

McENTEE, B **PB1953**

McEVOY **DFUSA**; (*see also* de Stacpoole)

McEWAN **DFUSA**

McEWEN, Bt **PB1970**; *of Marchmont and of Bardrochat* **LG1952**; **DFUSA**

McFADZEAN, B **PB1970**

MACFARLAN (*formerly* KENNEDY) *of Dunure* **LG1952**

McFARLAN *formerly of Nether Auchandrane and of Bullancleroch* **LG1952**; *of Ballencleroche* **AA**

McFARLAND, Bt **PB1970**

MACFARLANE *of Carlung* **LG1952**; *late of Hunstown House* **LGI1912**; **DFUSA**; *formerly of Paisley* **DFUSA**; (*New Zealand*) **CG**; (*Tasmania*) **CG**

McFERRAN *of Rickerscote House* **LG1921**; *of Camus* **LGI1958**

MACFIE *formerly of Langhouse and Beach* **LG1958**

McGAW *of St Leonard's Forest* **LG1952**

M'GEACHY *of Shenley Hill* **LG1886**

MACGEORGE *of Hames Hall* **LG1886**; *of Nether Larg* **LG1886**; *formerly of Dumfries* **DFUSA**

McGEOUGH (*see* MacGeough Bond)

McGILDOWNY *of Clare Park* **LGI1958**

MACGILL (Oxfurd, V) **DEP**

MACGILLIVRAY *of High Hesket* **LG1952**

McGILLYCUDDY OF THE REEKS **IFR1976**

McGOODWIN **DFUSA**

McGOWAN, B **PB1970**

MACGREGOR, Bt **PB1970**; *of Bole Hall Manor* **LG1937**; *of Glengyle* **LG1863**; *of Craigroston and Inversnaid* **LG1880/3**; *of Leragan Rannoch, co Perth* **LG1880/3**

MACGREGOR *of MacGregor*, Bt **PB1970**

McGRIGOR, Bt **PB1970**; *of Cairnoch* **LG1952**

MACGUFFIE *of Crossmichael* **LG1863**

McGUFFIE *of Woolton Hall* **LG1937**

MACGUIRE (McGUIRE) *of Clonea House* **LGI1904**

McHARDY **FR**

McHATTON **DFUSA**

MACHELL *formerly of Crackenthorpe* **LG1952**; *of Pennybridge* **LG1900**

MACHEN *of Bicknor* **LG1952**

MACHIN *of Gateford* **LG1972**

MACILVAINE **DFUSA**

MAC INNES *of Rickerby* **LG1914**

McINNES (*Canada*) **CG**

McINTYRE *of Sorn* **LG1952**

MAC IVER (*see* Mac Iver-Campbell)

McIVER, Bt **PB1920**; *formerly of Stornoway* **DFUSA**

MACK *formerly of Paston Hall* **LG1952**; (*Australia*) **CG**

MACKANESS *of Boughton Hall* **LG1969**

MACKAY (Inchcape, E) **PB1970**; (Reay, B) **PB1970**; (Reay, B) **PB1921**; *of Bighouse and Sandwood* **LG1952**; *of Strathkyle and Glengloy* **LG1894**

McKAY *of Rothay Manor* **LG1937**

MACKAYE *formerly of Norham-on-Tweed* **DFUSA**

MACKEAN *of Loughanmore* **LGI1958**

McKEAN **DFUSA**

McKEITH **DFUSA**

MACKELLAR (*of Dunara*) **CG**; *of Strathkeller* **CG**

McKELVY **DFUSA**

McKENDREE **DFUSA**

McKENNA *of Ardogena* **LGI1912**

MACKENZIE (Cromartie, E) **PB1970**; (Amulree, B) **PB1970**; Bt *of Coul* **PB1970**; Bt *of Glen Muick* **PB1970**; Bt *of Scatwell* **PB1970**) (Cromarty, E) **DEP**; (Seaforth, E) **DEP**; *of Farr* **LG1965**; *of Mornish* **LG1965**; *of Black-Stone Grange* **LG1952**; *of Kincraig* **LG1952**; *formerly of Ord* **LG1952**; *formerly of Tarlogie* **LG1952**; *of Edinbarnet* **LG1937**; *late of Portmore*

LG1937; *of Dailuaine* LG1921; *of Glack*
LG1921; *of Findon* LG1882; *of Kintail*
LG1882; *of Muirton House* LG1850/3;
of Applecross co Ross LG1850/3; *of*
Flowerburn (*see* Crosbie); *of Gairloch*
(*see* Stirling *of Fairburn*); (*see also*
Baillie; Martineau *of Clapton Court*;
and Stevenson *of Bolton Old Hall*)
MACKENZIE (*formerly* LLOYD-
WILLIAMS) *of Gwernant* LG1952
McKENZIE *formerly of Kelso* DFUSA;
(*Tasmania*) CG
BLUNT-MACKENZIE (*see* Cromartie)
BURTON-MACKENZIE (*see* North *of*
Newton Hall)
FRASER-MACKENZIE *of Bunchrew*,
formerly of Allangrange LG1972
HODSON-MACKENZIE *of Polstead*
formerly of Rockalls Hall LG1952
LEARMONTH-MACKENZIE (*see*
Livingstone-Learmonth)
MUIR MACKENZIE, Bt PB1970; B
PB1930
SHAW-MACKENZIE (*see* Shaw *of Tor-*
darroch)
STEWART-MACKENZIE (Seaforth, B)
PB1923; *of Seaforth* LG1937; (*see also*
Midleton)
MONTAGU - STUART - WORTLEY -
MACKENZIE (Wharncliffe, E) PB1970
McKERGOW *of Twineham Grange*
LG1937
McKERRELL *of Hillhouse* LG1969
MACKESON, Bt PB1970
MACKESY *of Aughmacart and Dunkitt*
LG1875
McKIBBEN DFUSA
MACKIE, Bt PB1924
McKIE *of Bargaly, of Auchencairn, of*
Ernespie and of Glencaird LG1952; *of*
Corraith and Glen Reasdell LG1914; *of*
Kirkthorpe LG1898
McKINLEY PresFUSA
McKINNELL *formerly of Wigtown*
DFUSA
MACKINNON, Bt PB1893; *of Dunakin*
LG1969; *of Mackinnon* LG1972; *of*
Dalness CG; *of Mountford* CG
MACKINTOSH (Mackintosh of Halifax,
B) PB1970; Bt EDB; *of Daviot-Kinrara*
LG1969; *of Mackintosh*; *of Balvraid*
LG1952; *of Clan Chattan* LG1952; *of*
Kyllachy LG1937; *of Dalmunzie*
LG1921; *of Rothiemurchus* (*see* Shaw
of Tordarroch)
FRASER-MACKINTOSH *of Drummond*
LG1921

M'KIRDY *of Birk Wood* LG1858
SCOTT-MACKIRDY *of Abbey House*
formerly of Birkwood LG1952
McKITTRICK DFUSA
MACKRILL *of Lanwath Hall* LG1952
MACKWORTH, Bt PB1970; Bt EDB;
of Normanton VF; (*see also* Mackworth-
Praed)
MACKY *of Belmont* LGI1912
MACLACHLAN *of Maclachlan* LG1952
McLACHLAN *of Rendcomb Manor*
LG1952
McLAGAN *of Pumpherston* LG1900
MACLAINE *of Lochbuie* LG1972; *of*
Kyneton LG1906; AA
McLANE *formerly of the Island of Coll*
DFUSA
MACLAREN *of Craigs* LG1937
McLAREN (Aberconway, B) PB1970
MACLAUGHLIN *of Ballinamona for-*
merly of Ramelton LGI1958
McLAUGHLIN *formerly of The Lydiates*
LG1952; DFUSA
MACLAVERTY *of Wessington Court*
LG1952
MACLAY (Muirshiel, V) PB1970; B
PB1970
MACLEAN *of Duart*, Bt PB1970; Bt *of*
Strachur PB1970
MACLEAN *of Ardgour* LG1972; *Ardgour*
(*Mac-mhic-Eoghainn*) LG1972; *of King-*
airloch LG1972; *of Westfield* LG1972;
formerly of Kingairloch LG1965; *of*
Balnaboth LG1952; *of Dochgarroch*
LG1952; *formerly of Lazonby Hall*
LG1952; *formerly of Pennycross*
LG1952; *of Haremere Hall* LG1886
O'HARA MACLEAN (*see* Maclean
formerly of Kingairloch)
McLEAN (1) & (2) DFUSA
HOWARD-McLEAN *of Aston Hall*
LG1937
McLEAVY, B PB1970
MACLEAY DFUSA
MACLEISH DFUSA
MACLELLAN (Kirkcudbright, Lord)
DEP; VF
MACLEOD *of Raasay* LG1969; *of*
Suardal LG1969; *of Glendale* LG1965;
of Macleod LG1965; *of Cadboll*
LG1952; *of Dalvey* LG1952; *of Talisker*
LG1937
MacLEOD OF FUINARY, B PB1970
ROBERTSON-MACLEOD *of Gres-*
hornish and Orborst LG1937
McLEOD, Bt PB1970
VON HAUPT-McLEOD LG1925Supp

McLINTOCK, Bt **PB1970**
MACLIVER *of Kilchoman* **LG1894**
MacLOSKEY *of Rothwell, co Northampton* **AA**
McLOUGHLIN (*Maelseachlainn*) **LG1958**
MACLURE, Bt **PB1970**; *of Whalley Range* **LG1894**
M'CLURE *of Belmont* **LG1875**
McLURE **DFUSA**
MACMAHON, Bt **EDB**; *of Woodville* **LGI1958**
McMAHON, Bt **PB1970**; Bt **PB1926**; *of Hollymount* **LGI1912**
MACMANNUS **LG1880/3**
MACMASTER, Bt **PB1922**
McMASTER *of Waikaura* **CG**
McMICHAEL (*see* Hooker)
MACMICKING (*Australia*) **CG**
McMICKING *of Miltonise* **LG1952**
STERNDALE-McMIKIN *of Grange* **LG1937**
MACMILLAN, B **PB1949**; *formerly of Lochaber* **DFUSA**
MacMILLAN *of Holm of Dalquhulrn and Glencrosh* **LG1952**; *of Botton Hall* **LG1937**
McMILLAN *of Sydney* **CG**
(THE) MACMORROUGH (*see* Kavanagh)
MACNAB *of Macnab* **LG1969**; (*Canada*) **CG**; (*see also* Cassels)
MACNABB *of Kinnell House* **LG1952**
MACNAGHTEN, Bt **PB1970**; B **PB1913**
McNAIR; B **PB1970**; **DFUSA**; *formerly of Donaghmore* **DFUSA**
MACNAMARA *of Caddington Bury* **LG1914**; **IFR1976**
MAC NEALE *of Portraine* **LGI1912**
MACNEIL *of Barra* **LG1972**
McNEILE *of Nonsuch* **LG1972**; *of Parkmount* **LGI1904**
MacNEILL *of Wolfelee* **LG1900**; **FR**; **IFR1976**; **LGI1899**; (*see also* MacNeill-Hamilton)
McNEILL (Cushendun, B) **PB1934**; *formerly of Colonsay* **LG1952**; *of Gardenvale* **LG1937Supp**; *of Craigdunn* **LGI1912**; (*see also* McNeill-Moss)
McNEIR **DFUSA**
MACONCHY *of Rathmore* **LGI1912**
MACONOCHIE *of Avontoun* **LG1952**; (*see also* Maconochie-Welwood)
MACPHERSON (Drumalbyn, B) **PB1970**; (Macpherson of Drumochter, B) **PB1970**; (Strathcarron, B) **PB1970**; Bt **EDB**; *of Pitmain* **LG1969**; *of Banchor* **LG1952**; *of Blairgowrie* **LG1952**; *of Cluny Macpherson* **LG1952**; *of Glen-*

truim **LG1952**; *formerly of Radbrook Hall* **LG1952**; *of Countesswells* **LG1937**; *of Wyrley Grove* **LG1921**; **CG**; (*see also* Wallace)
CHEYNE-MACPHERSON *of Dalchully* **LG1952**
McPHERSON (*Australia*) **CG**
MACQUAKER *of Auchendrane* **LG1952**
MACQUARIE *of Ormaig* **LG1863**
MACQUEEN *of Corryborough* **LG1886**
McQUEEN *of Braxfield* **LG1886**
McQUITTY **LGI1958**
MACRAE *of Ballimore* **LG1972**; *of Clunes formerly of Inverinate* **LG1952**; *of Feoirlinn* **LG1952**
MACREADY, Bt **PB1970**
MURE-MACREDIE *of Perceton* **LG1898**
MACROBERT, Bt **PB1940**
MACTAGGART, Bt **PB1970**
McTAGGART, Bt **PB1867**
MACTERNAN *of Mount Allen* **LGI1925**
MACTHOMAS *of Finegand* **LG1972**
MACULLOCK, Bt **EDB**
McVEAGH *of Galtrim Lodge formerly of Drewston* **LGI1958**
MACY *formerly of Chilmark* **DFUSA**
MADDEN, Bt **PB1970**; **IFR1976**; *of Tinode* **LGI1912**; (*Australia*) **CG**
MADDISON *formerly of Partney Hall* **LG1952**; (*see also* Combe *of Earnshill*)
ASHBY-MADDOCK *of Naseby* **VSA**
MADDOX, Bt **EDB**
MADEN *of Rockcliffe House* **LG1937**
MADGE, Bt **PB1959**
MADISON **PresFUSA**
MADOCKS *of Glanywdrn* **LG1863**
MAELOR (*see* Jones)
MAENAN (*see* Taylor)
MAFFEY (Rugby, B) **PB1970**
MAGAN **IFR1976**
MAGAWLY CERATI DE CALRY, Count **FT1939**
MAGENNIS, V **DEP**; *of Finroy Lodge* **LGI1912**
MAGHERAMORNE (*see* McGarel-Hogg)
MAGILL, Bt **EDB**; **IFR1976**; *of Littleton* **LGI1912** (*see also* Hawkins)
HAWKINS-MAGILL (*see* Hawkins)
M'GILL, Bt **EDB**
MAGNAY, Bt **PB1959**
MAGOR *of Lamellen* **LG1952**
MAGRATH, Bt **EDB**
MAGRUDER **DFUSA**
MAGUIRE, B **DEP**; *of Gortoral House* **LG1886**; *of Gortoral House* **AA**; *of Tempo* **VF**

MAGUIRE (*now* SCHUMACHER) **DFUSA**
MAHAFFY **IFR1976**
MAHER **IFR1976**
MAHON, Bt **PB1970**; (Hartland, B) **DEP**; *of Corbally* **LGI1912**; *of Ballydonelan and Killareny* **LGI1912**
HALES PAKENHAM MAHON **IFR1976**
MAHONY **IFR1976**; **DFUSA**
MAINWARING, Bt *of Over Peover* **PB1934**; Bt *of Over Peover* **EDB**; *of Oteley* **LG1969**; *of Bwlchybendy* **LG1952**; **DFUSA**
CAVENAGH-MAINWARING *of Whitmore and Biddulph* **LG1969**
MILMAN-MAINWARING *of Monks* **LG1937**
MAIR (*New Zealand*) **CG**
MAIS, B **PB1970**; *of Hobcroft House* **LG1952**
MAISTER *of Beverley* **LG1863**; *of Beverley* **AA**
MAITLAND (Lauderdale, E) **PB1970**; Bt **PB1970**; (Lauderdale, D) **DEP**; Bt **EDB**; *of Cumstoun and Dundrennan* **LG1972**; *of Harrington Hall, formerly of Loughton* **LG1965**; *of Southerndown* **LG1937**; *of Eccles* **LG1882**
RAMSAY-STEEL-MAITLAND, Bt **PB1963**
MAJENDIE *of Hedingham Castle* **LG1972**
MAJOR *formerly of Frome* **DFUSA**
HENNIKER-MAJOR (Henniker, B) **PB1970**
MAKGILL, Bt **PB1970**
MAKINS (Sherfield, B) **PB1970**; Bt **PB1970**; *of Rotherfield* **LG1900**
MALCOLM, Bt **PB1970**; (Malcolm of Poltalloch, B) **PB1902**; *of Poltalloch* **LG1965**; *of Freeland Lodge* **LG1882 Supp**; **DFUSA**; (*see also* Douglas)
MALCOLMSON *of Icomb Place, formerly of Aston Bury* **LG1972**
MALET, Bt **PB1970**
MALET DE CARTERET *of St Ouen's* **LG1952**
MALIM *formerly of Myddlyton House* **LG1972**
MALISE (Strathern, E) **DEP**
MALKIN *of Corrybrough* **LG1952**; *of Rock Cliffe* **LG1952**
MALLALIEU *of Tan-y-Marian* **LG1937**
MALLET *of Curry Mallet* **LG1972**; *of Wittersham House* **LG1972**; *formerly of Ash* **LG1952**; *of Ash, Devon* **AA**; *of Jersey* **AA**
MALLET DE CARTERET **AA**

MALLINSON, Bt **PB1970**
MALLOCK *formerly of Cockington* **LG1972**
MALLORY **PromFUSA**
LEIGH-MALLORY *formerly of Mobberley* **LG1952**
MALMESBURY (*see* Harris)
MALONE (Sunderlin, B) **DEP**; *of Rosemorran formerly of Trevayler* **LG1952**; *of Baronston* **LGI1912**; **DFUSA**
L'ESTRANGE MALONE (*see* L'Estrange)
MALTBY *of Greenacre* **LG1952**; **DFUSA**; *formerly of Kexby* **DFUSA**
MALTRAVERS, B **DEP**
MALVERN (*see* Huggins)
MAMHEAD (*see* Newman)
MANBEY (*Canada*) **CG**
MANBY (*see* Manby-Colegrave)
MILLIGAN-MANBY *of Thorganby Hall* **LG1952**
MANCHESTER (*see* Montagu)
MANCILL **DFUSA**
MANCLE *formerly of Burley* **LG1972**
MANCROFT, B **PB1970**
MANDER, Bt **PB1970**
MANDEVILLE (Essex, E) **DEP**; **IFR1976**
HACKETT-MANDEVILLE (*see* Hackett)
MANIFOLD (*Australia*) **CG**
MANLEY *of Bacton* **LG1952**; *of Manley Hall and Shenstone Park* **LG1952**; *formerly of Spofforth Hall* **LG1952**; *of Whitehouse* **LGI1912**
MANN, Bt **PB1970**; Bt *of Brome* **PB1852**; Bt *of Linton Hall* **EDB**; *of Thelveton Hall* **LG1900**; *of Dunmoyle and Corvey Lodge* **LG1894**; *of Linton* (*see* Cornwallis)
MANNERS (Rutland, D) **PB1970**; B **PB1970**; *of Netherseale* **LG1937**
MANNING *of Coldbrook Park and Diss* **LG1882**; *of Eversfield* **LG1882**; *of Wallaroy* **CG**; (*see also* Marriott-Dodington)
WATTS-MANNING *of Harpole* **LG1894**
MANNIX, Bt **EDB**
MANNOCK, Bt **EDB**; *of Gifford's Hall* **LG1886**
MANNY, B **DEP**
MANSEL, Bt **PB1970**; B **DEP**; Bt *of Margam* **EDB**; Bt *of Trimsaren* **EDB**; *of Cosgrove Hall* **LG1882**
COLVILE-MANSEL (*see* Colvile *of Lullington*)
MANSERGH **IFR1976**
MANSFIELD (Sandhurst, B) **PB1970**; (Sandhurst, V) **PB1921**; **IFR1976**; *of*

Castle Wray LGI1912; (*see also* Maunsell)
MANSFIELD AND MANSFIELD (*see* Murray)
MANT FR
MANTELL CG
MANTON (*see* Watson)
MANVERS (*see* Pierrepont)
MAPLE, Bt PB1903
MAPLES, Bt EDB; *of Grassgarth* LG1952
MAPOTHER *of Kilteevan* LGI1912
MAPPIN, Bt PB1970
MARCON *late of Swaffham* LG1921
MAR, E PB1970; (*see also* Stewart)
MAR AND KELLIE (*see* Erskine)
MARCH (*see* Mortimer)
MARCHAMLEY (*see* Whiteley)
MARCHMONT (*see* Hume)
MARCHWOOD (*see* Penny)
MARDON *of Cameley House, formerly of Halsway Manor* LG1972; *of New Court* LG1937
MARE (La Mare, B) DEP
MARESCAUX DE SABRUIT IFR1976
MARETT *of Haule* LG1952
MARGADALE (*see* Morrison)
MARGARY AA
MARGESSON, V PB1970; *formerly of Findon Place* LG1952
MARGETTS (*Australia*) CG
MARINDIN *formerly of Fordel* LG1972
MARISCHAL (*see* Keith)
MARJORIBANKS (Tweedmouth, B) PB1935; Bt *of Lees* PB1888; *formerly of Marjoribanks* LG1952; *of Lees* LG1925
MARKER *of Combe* LG1952
MARKHAM, Bt PB1970; Bt EDB; *of Morland* LG1972
MARKLAND (*see* Entwisle)
MARKLOVE *of Lullingworth House* LG1875
MARKS (Marks of Broughton, B) PB1970; B PB1938
MARLAY *of Belvedere* LGI1912
MARLBOROUGH (*see* Spencer-Churchill; and Ley)
MARLEY (*see* Aman)
MARLING, Bt PB1970; *of Stanley Park* LG1882
MARMION (*see* Dymoke; and Marmyon)
CARPENTER MARMON (*see* Tchkotoua)
MARMYON (Marmion, B) DEP; (Marmion of Wetrington, B) DEP; (Marmyon, B) DEP
MARNEY, B DEP

MAROCHETTI, B FT1939
MAROW, Bt EDB
MARPLES *of Thornbridge Hall* LG1921
MARQUIS (Woolton, E) PB1970
MARR, Bt PB1970
FREIRE MARRECO *of St Mawes* LG1952
MARRIOTT *of Cotesbach* LG1972; *of Athelington House* LG1952; *of Harcourt House* LG1937; *of Avonbank* LG1906; FR; *of Horsmonden, Kent* AA
SMITH-MARRIOTT, Bt PB1970; *of Horsmonden* LG1863
MARRIS *of Burton Corner* LG1952; *of Clinton House* LG1952
WINSTON - DAVIS - DE - MARRIS *of Pattyndenne Manor* LG1952
MARROW LG1969; FR
ARMFIELD-MARROW (*see* Marrow)
MARRYAT (*Australia*) CG
MARSACK *formerly of Caversham Park* LG1937
MARSDEN, Bt PB1970; *of Chelmorton* LG1969; FR
MARSH, Bt PB1868; *of Woodsetts Grange* LG1921; *of Winterbourne Park* LG1894; *of Snave Manor and Ivy Church* LG1886; *of Ramridge* LG1882; *of Jerpoint* LGI1958
CHISENHALE-MARSH *of Gaynes Park* LG1965
MARSHAL (Pembroke, E) DEP; B DEP
MARSHALL (Marshall of Chipstead, B) PB1936; *of Rachan and Glenhove* LG1972, *formerly of Heathfield* LG1952; *of Lanwithan House* LG1952; *formerly of Patterdale Hall* LG1952; *of Sarnesfield Court* LG1937; *of Hardres Court* LG1921; *of Broadwater* LG1900; *of Penworthan Hall* LG1886; *of Barron Court* LGI1912; DFUSA; *formerly of Aberdeen* FR; (*New Zealand*) (1) & (2) CG; *of Roskille and Fairlight* CG; *of Belmont, co Somerset* AA; *of Broadwater, Surrey* AA; *of Treworgey* (*see* Hall)
MARSHALL (*now* GREENE) *formerly of Pembroke* DFUSA
LEESON-MARSHALL *of Callinafercy House* LGI1912
MARSHAM (Romney, E) PB1970; *formerly of Rippon Hall* LG1952; *of Headfort* LGI1912
FIELD-MARSHAM *of Ashurst Park* LG1952
MARSLAND *of Henbury* LG1882

MARSTON *formerly of Afcot* **LG1952**; *of Hampton* **DFUSA**; (*see also* Ryder)

MARTEL *of Bulford Lodge* **LG1952**

MARTEN *formerly of Marshals Wick* **LG1972**

MARTIN, B **DEP**; Bt *of Overbury Court* **PB1916**; Bt *of Cappagh* **PB1901**; Bt *of Long Melford* **PB1854**; *of Norton* **LG1972**; *of The Brand* **LG1972**; *of Bwlch* **LG1952**; *of Colleton Manor* **LG1952**; *of Hemingstone* **LG1952**; *of Nether Hall* **LG1952**; *late of Ledbury* **LG1937**; *of Bideford* **LG1914**; *of Ensham* **LG1833/7**; **IFR1976**; *of Wiche* **LGI1912**; *formerly of Drumavalla* **DFUSA**; (1) & (2) **FR**; (*Canada*) (1) & (2) **CG**; (*see also* Martin-Edmunds *of Worsbro' Hall*)

MARTIN (*formerly* LIVERMORE) **DFUSA**

MARTIN (*formerly* STOTT) *of Craigdun* **LGI1958**

BROMLEY-MARTIN *formerly of Ham Court* **LG1965**

HOLLAND-MARTIN *of Overbury* **LG1965**

STAPLETON MARTIN (*see* Martin *of Norton*)

WOOD-MARTIN *of Cleveragh* **LGI1912**

WYKEHAM-MARTIN *formerly of Leeds Castle* **LG1952**; (*see also* Cornwallis)

MARTINDALE *formerly of Hurworth* **LG1937**

MARTINEAU *of Clapton Court* **LG1972**; *of Walsham-le-Willows* **LG1972**

MARTLEY *late of Ballyfallon* **LGI1912**

MARTON *of Capernwray* **LG1937**

MARTONMERE (*see* Robinson)

MARTYN *of Tulira* **LGI1912** (*see also* Honeyball)

MARVIN **DFUSA**

MARWOOD, Bt **EDB**; *of Busby Hall* **LG1972**

MARX *of Atle-Bury* **LG1886**

MARYBOROUGH (*see* Wellesley)

MASEFIELD *formerly of Rosehill* **LG1952**; *late of Ellerton Hall* **LG1921**

MASHAM, B **DEP**; Bt **EDB**; (*see also* Cunliffe-Lister)

MASHAM OF ILTON (*see* Cunliffe-Lister)

STORY-MASKELYNE (*see* Forster)

MASON (Blackford, B) **PB1970**; *of Eden Place* **LG1952**; *of Morton Hall* **LG1952**; *of Eversley Cross House* **LG1937**; *of Aldenham Lodge* **LG1882**; **DFUSA**

HUMFREY-MASON & BLAKE *formerly*

of Necton and Scottow **LG1972**

MASSEREENE AND FERRARD (*see* Skeffington)

MASSEY *of Pool Hall* **LG1921**; *also* **LG1863**; **DFUSA**

MASSIE *formerly of Coddington* **LG1952**

MASSINGBERD, Bt **EDB**; (*see also* Langton; and Massingberd-Mundy)

MONTGOMERY-MASSINGBERD *of Gunby* **LG1972**; (*see also* Montgomery (*cos Fermanagh and Tyrone*))

MASSUE (Galway, E) **DEP**

MASSY, B **PB1970**; (Clarina, B) **PB1949**; Bt **PB1870**; (*co Limerick*) **IFR1976**; (*cos Louth, Limerick and Tipperary*) **IFR1976**

MASTER *of Barrow Green Court* **LG1952**

CHESTER-MASTER *of The Abbey, formerly of Knole Park* **LG1965**

MASTERS *of Stanton Fitwarren* **LG1952**

SMITH-MASTERS *of Camer* **LG1937**

MASTERSON **DFUSA**

EYRE MATCHAM *of Newhouse* **LG1952**

MATHER *formerly of Lowton* **DFUSA**; **PromFUSA**

MATHERS, B **PB1963**

MATHESON, Bt **PB1970**; Bt *of The Lews* **PB1878**; *of Brahan* **LG1972**; *formerly of Little Scatwell* **LG1952**; *of Ardross* **LG1863**; *of Shinness* **LG1850/3**; *of Achany* **LG1850/3**

MATHEW (Llandaff, E) **DEP**; *of Pentlowe Hall* **LG1886**; *of Tresunger, Pennitenny and The Leeward Islands* **LG1882**; **IFR1976**

MATHEWS, Bt **PB1920**; *of Mount Hanover* **LG1937Supp**

ATTWOOD-MATHEWS *of Pontrilas Court* **LG1900**

MATHIAS, Bt **PB1970**; *of Hyde* **LG1952**; *of Lamphey Court* **LG1952**

MATON *formerly of Maddington* **LG1952**

MATTERSON *of Langford Manor* **LG1952**

MATTHEWS (Llandaff, B) **PB1913**; Bt **EDB**; *of Aston Hall* **LG1937**; *of Madley* **LG1894**; *of Hereford* **LG1863**

MATTINGLY **DFUSA**

MAUD *formerly in Yorkshire* **LG1952**

REDCLIFFE-MAUD, B **PB1970**

MAUDE (Hawarden, V) **PB1970**; (de Montalt of Dundrum, E) **PB1905**; *formerly of Burley* **LG1972**; *of Leylands* **LG1937**; (*see also* Leycester-Roxby)

MAUDSLAY *of North Coker House* **LG1952**

MAUDUIT, B **DEP**

MAUGHAM, V **PB1970**
MAULE (Panmure, B) **DEP**; (Panmure, E) **DEP**
MAULEVERER *of Arncliffe* **LG1886**
MAULEY, B **DEP**
MAULIVERER, Bt **EDB**
MAUNSELL **IFR1976** *of Auckland* **CG**
MAURICE *formerly of Lloran* **LG1972**
MAURICE *(formerly* LOWNDES) *of Castle Combe* **LG1952**
BONNOR-MAURICE *of Bodynfoel* **LG1921**
HASSELL-MAW *formerly of Thornton Dale* **LG1937**
MAWBEY, Bt **EDB**
MAXSE (*see* Berkeley)
MAXTONE *of Cultoquhy* **LG1863**
MAXWELL (De Ros, B) **PB1970**; (Farnham, B) **PB1970**; Bt *of Monreith* **PB1970**; Bt *of Cardoness* **PB1924**; (Dirletoun, E) **DEP**; (Nithsdale, E; **DEP**; Bt *of Pollock* **EDB**; *of Brynhir, formerly of Dargavel* **LG1972**; *formerly of Glenlee* **LG1952**; *of Munches* **LG1952**; *of Westfield House* **LG1937**; *of Terraughty* **LG1886**; *of Kirkconnell* **LG1894**; *of Williamwood* **LG1880/3**; **IFR1976**; *of Ballyrolly* **LGI1912**; **DFUSA**; *of Merksworth* **AA**; (*see also* Smith *formerly of Craigend and Jordanhill*)
CLARK-MAXWELL *of Carruchan and Mackworth* **LG1972**; *of Speddoch* **LG1952**
CONSTABLE-MAXWELL (Herries, B) **PB1908**, (*see also* Norfolk)
HALL-MAXWELL (*see* Maxwell *of Brynhir*)
HERON-MAXWELL, Bt **PB1970**
PERCEVAL-MAXWELL (*co Down*) **IFR1976**; (*co Waterford*) **IFR1976**
STIRLING-MAXWELL *of Pollok* Bt **PB1970**; (*see also* Stirling *of Garden*)
WEDDERBURN-MAXWELL *of Middlebie* **LG1952**
MAY, B **PB1970**; (Farnborough, B) **PB1886**; Bt *of Mayfield* **PB1834**; Bt **EDB**; (*formerly* BARKER) *of Clare Priory* **LG1952**; *of Greenstead Green* **LG1952**; *of Rockbeare Court and Johnstone Castle* **LG 1952**; *formerly of Hale House* **LG1937**; (1) & (2) **DFUSA**; (*see also* **LG1952Supp**)
BOURNE-MAY *formerly of Hackinsall* **LG1972**
MAYALL *formerly of Mossley* **LG1969**
MAYCOCK *of Foxton Lodge* **LG1875**

MAYHEW *formerly of Newton* **LG1965**; *of Clayton Priory* **LG1921**
MAYNARD, **DEP**; Bt **EDB**; *of Skinningrove* **LG1969**
MAYNE (Newhaven, B) **DEP**; Bt **EDB**; *formerly of Gidleigh Park* **LG1952**; *formerly of Powis* **LG1952**; *of Glynch House* **LG1875**
MAYNEY, Bt **EDB**
MAYO *formerly of Cheshunt* **LG1952**; *formerly of Eccles* **DFUSA**; *formerly of Poulshot, Wilts* **DFUSA**; *formerly of West Malling* **DFUSA**; (*see also* Bourke)
WYNELL-MAYOW *of Brave and Hangorth* **LG1952**
MAZE *of Bristol* **HI**
BLACKBURNE-MAZE (*see* Blackburne *formerly of Hale and Orford*)
MAZYCK **PromFUSA**
MEABY *of Burgage Court* **LG1952**
MEADE (Clanwilliam, E) **PB1970**; *formerly of Farley Court and Tissaxon* **LG1972**; *of Earsham Hall* **LG1937**; *formerly of Ballymartle and Ballintober* **LGI1958; AA**
MEADOWS *of Witnesham Court* **LG1952**; *of Burgersh House* **LG1833/7**; *of Wexford and Thornville, co Wexford* **LGI1912**
MEALY *of Perfeddgoed* **LG1863**
MEARES *of Meares Court* **LG1937**; (*Australia*) **CG**
MEARNS *of Disblair* **LG1937**
MEATH (*see* Brabazon)
MECKLENBURG (*House of*) **RL**
MEDCALF *of Capel House* **LG1937**
MEDHURST *of Kippax Hall* **LG1879**
MEDLEN *of Lowlands* **LGI1912**
MEDLICOTT *of Medlicott* **LG1952** **IFR1976**
MEDLYCOTT, Bt **PB1970**; (*see also* Medlicott)
MEDOWS (*see* Pierrepont)
MEEK *of Brantridge Park* **LG1886**; **DFUSA**
MEEKING (*see* Apsley)
MEEKINS *of Glasthule House* **LG1863**
MEETKIRKE (*see* Metcalfe)
MEGGOTT (*see* Elwes *of Roxby*)
MEIGH *of Ash Hall* **LG1921**
MEIKLE *of Lochlibo* **LG1937**
STEWART-MEIKLEJOHN *of Eradynate* **LG1965**
MEIN **CG**
MEINELL, B **DEP**
MEINERTZHAGEN **LG1969**

MELBOURNE (*see* Lamb)
MELCHETT (*see* Mond)
MELCOMBE (*see* Dodington)
MELDON LG1886
MELDRUM (and SETON) LG1833/7
MELFORT (*see* Drummond)
MELGUM (*see* Gordon)
MELLER *of The Limes* LG1937
MELLES *formerly of Gruline* LG1952; FR
FOSTER-MELLIAR *of North Aston Hall* LG1914
MELLOR, Bt PB1970; *of Box House* LG1952; *of Knipoch* LG1952; *formerly of Idridgehay* DFUSA
MELROSE (*see* Hamilton)
MELVILLE DFUSA; (*see also* Dundas)
BALFOUR-MELVILLE *of Mount Melville* LG1906
LESLIE MELVILLE (Leven and Melville, E) PB1970
WHYTE-MELVILLE *of Bennochy and Strathkiness* LG1879
MENTELT, E DEP
STUART-MENTETH, Bt PB1970
MENZIES *of Hallyburton* LG1937; (*see also* Clayhills; and Wombwell)
STEWART-MENZIES *of Culdares* LG1952; *of Chesthill and Foss* LG1914
MERCER *formerly of Huntingtower* LG1972; *of East Farleigh* LG1937; *of Norton Court* LG1937
TOD-MERCER *of Hope Park formerly of Scotsbank* LG1952
MERCES, Bt EDB
MEREDITH, Bt *of Montreal* PB1929; Bt *of Carlanstown* PB1923; Bt EDB; *formerly of Broadward Hall* LG1952; *Pentre Bychan* LG1921; *of Dicksgrove* LGI1912; *of Cloonamahon* LG1875; CG: (*Tasmania*) CG
WARTER-MEREDITH (*see* Meredith *of Pentre Bychan*)
MEREDYTH, Bt *of Greenhills* PB1909; Bt *of Henbury* EDB; Bt *of St Catherine's Grove* EDB
MEREWETHER *of Bowden Hill* LG1875
MERRIMAN, B PB1959; *formerly Mildenhall* LG1952
MERRITT DFUSA
MERRIVALE (*see* Duke)
MERRY *of Highlands* LG1875
MERSEY (*see* Bigham)
MERTHYR (*see* Lewis)
MERTON *of Stubbings House* LG1965; *of Winforton House* LG1937
MERYON (*see* Brocket)

MESCHINES (Chester, E) DEP
MESHAM *of Ewloe Hall* LG1914; (*see also* Birchenough)
MESSEL *of Nymans* LG1965
MESSER *of Springwood* CG
MESSERVY *formerly of La Ville-Es-Gaudins* LG1972
MESSITER *of Barwick House* LG1921
MESTON, B PB1970
METAXÀ, Count FT1939
METCALF *formerly of Norwich* DFUSA
METCALFE, Bt PB1970; *formerly of Inglethorpe Hall* LG1937; *of Hawstead House* LG1886; DFUSA; *of Northallerton* (*see also* Marwood)
METGE *of Athlumney* LGI1912
METHUEN, B PB1970; Bt PB1924; *formerly of Stratton Lodge* LG1952
METHVEN (*see* Stewart)
MEUX, Bt *of Theobalds Park* PB1900; Bt *of Kingston* EDB; (*see also* Durham; and Montgomery-Massingberd)
MEWBURN (*see* Mewburn-Watson)
MEXBOROUGH (*see* Savile)
MEYER, Bt PB1970
MEYERS, Bt EDB
MEYLER AA
MEYNELL *of Meynell Langley* LG1965; *of Kilvington* LG1952; *of Hoar Cross* LG1937; (*see also* Halifax)
MEYRICK, Bt PB1970; *of Ramsbury* LG1972; *of Apley Castle* LG1937; *of Bush* LG1879; *of Bodorgan* LG1875; *of Goodrich Court* LG1875
TAPPS-GERVIS-MEYRICK, Bt PB1970
MEYSEY LG1833/7
MICHEL (*see* de Montmorency)
MICHELHAM (*see* Stern)
MICHELL *formerly of Forcett* LG1972; *of Holwell* LG1898; (*see also* Hambly)
MICKLEM *formerly of Rose Hill* LG1965
MICKLETHWAIT, V DEP; *of Ardsley* LG1965; *of Taverham Hall and Iridge Place* LG1900
MIDDELTON, *of Hackney* EDB; Bt *of Ruthyn* EDB; *of Stockeld* LG1921
MIDDLEBROOK, Bt PB1970
MIDDLEMORE, Bt PB1970; *of Hawkeslowe* LG1937
MIDDLESEX (*see* Cranfield)
MIDDLETON, Bt PB1970; Bt *of Crowfield* PB1860; E DEP; Bt *of Chirke* EDB; Bt *of Leighton Hall* EDB; LG1969; *of Bradford Peverell* LG1952; *of Rose Farm* LG1952; *of The Grove* LG1875; *of Leam* LG1863; *formerly of Crowfield Hall* DFUSA; PromFUSA; *of Norwich*

AA; (see also Broke; Norfolk; and Willoughby)
BROKE-MIDDLETON, Bt **PB1887**
MIDLETON (see Brodrick)
MIERS formerly of Ynyspenllwch **LG1969**
MIGNON of Mignonville **HI**
MILBANK, Bt **PB1970**; of Thorp Perrow **LG1879**
MILBANKE, Bt **PB1949**
MILBROKE (see Cornwall)
MILBURN, Bt **PB1970**; of Wardrew **LG1900**; of Clogham House **LGI1958**
MILDMAY (Mildmay of Flete, B) **PB1949**; (Fitz-Walter, E) **DEP**; of Moulsham Bt **EDB**
ST JOHN-MILDMAY, Bt **PB1970**
MILES, Bt **PB1970**; formerly of Kings Weston **LG1972**; of Tilstock **LG1952**; of Keyham **LG1937**
MILES (now CHEALES) of Nether Hall **LG1952**
MILFORD (see Philipps)
MILFORD HAVEN (see Mountbatten)
MILL, Bt of Mottisfont **PB1860**; Bt of Camois Court **EDB**
MILLAIS, Bt **PB1970**
HOYER MILLAR (Inchyra, B) **PB1970**
MACDONALD-MILLAR formerly of Wick **DFUSA**
MILLEAR **CG**
MILLER Bt of Chichester **PB1970**; Bt of Glenlee **PB1970**; Bt of Oxenhoath **EDB**; of Myres **LG1972**; formerly of Dummer Grange **LG1952**; formerly of Great Billing Hall **LG1952**; formerly of Cricklade Manor House **LG1937**; of Milford **LGI1912**; of Brentry **LG1894**; of Monk Castle **LG1875**; of Collier's Wood **LG1863**; **DFUSA**; formerly of Bishops Stortford **DFUSA**; of Auchat **CG**; of Crag Miller **CG**; (New Zealand) **CG**; of Glaskenny (see Williams of Warpool Court)
MILLER (now MILLS) of Radway **LG1921**
CHRISTIE-MILLER of Clarendon Park, formerly of Britwell **LG1969**
NORIE-MILLER, Bt **PB1970**
PITT MILLER of Foxboro' Hall **LG1972**
RULON-MILLER **PromFUSA**
MILLIGAN of Caldwell Hall **LG1952**
MILLINGTON (see Synge)
MILLS, V **PB1970**; (Hillingdon, B) **PB1970**; Bt **PB1970**; of Bisterne **LG1969**; of Little Barrington **LG1969**; of Hilborough Hall and Bodney Hall formerly of Stockgrove and Langton

Hall **LG1952**; of Sudgrove **LG1952**; of Saxham Hall **LG1898**; of Clermont **LG1894**; of Tolmers **LG1879**; of Lexden Park co Essex **LG1850/3**; **DFUSA**; (see also Miller)
MILLTOWN (see Leeson)
MILMAN, Bt **PB1970**
MILN of Ivy House **LG1972**
MILNE, B **PB1970**; Bt of Inveresk **PB1938**; of Logie **LG1952**; formerly of Melgum and Ardmiddle **LG1952Supp** (Australia) **CG**
GRINNELL-MILNE **LG1965**
LEES-MILNE formerly of Wickhamford Manor **LG1965**
MILNER (Milner of Leeds, B) **PB1970**; Bt **PB1970**; V **PB1925**; formerly of Totley Hall **LG1952**
MILNES, Bt **PB1841**; of Stubbin Edge **LG1875**; of Fryston **LG1863**; of Beckingham Hall **LG1858**; of Alton Manor (see also Walthall)
CRAVEN-SMITH-MILNES of Hockerton Manor and Dunston, and formerly of Winkburn **LG1969**
CREWE-MILNES (Crewe, M) **PB1940**
PEGGE - BURNELL - SMITH - MILNES (see Craven-Smith-Milnes)
MILSOM of Bath **LG1952**
MILTON **DFUSA**; (see also Damer)
MILVAIN of Eglingham Hall **LG1952**
MILVERTON (see Richards)
MILWARD formerly of Redditch **LG1972**; formerly of Thurgarton and Hexgreave **LG1972**; formerly of East Bridgford **LG1952**; formerly of Lechlade **LG1937**; of Tullogher **LGI1912**
CORBET-MILWARD (see Milward formerly of Redditch)
SAYER-MILWARD of Fairlight Place **LG1921**
MINCHIN **IFR1976**; of Woodburn **CG**
MINET **FR**
MINNITT of Annaghbeg **LGI1912**; (see also Groom)
MINOPRIO of Haulfryn **LG1969**
MINOR formerly of Chew Magna **DFUSA**
MINOT formerly of Saffron Walden **DFUSA**; **PromFUSA**
MINTO (see Elliot-Murray-Kynynmound)
MINTOFT of Alne **LG1952**
MIREHOUSE of Hambrook **LG1937**; late of St George's Hill **LG1937**
ALLEN-MIREHOUSE of Angle **LG1972**
MIRRLEES (see Grinnell-Milne)
MITCHEL (see de Montmorency)

MITCHELL, Bt **PB1970**; Bt **EDB**; *formerly of Seaborough Court* **LG1969**; *of Glenfall House* **LG1952**; *of Carwood* **LG1937**; *of Pyrgo Park* **LG1937**; *of Walcot* **LG1937Supp**; *late of Polmood* **LG1921**; *of Llanfrechfa Grange* **LG1900**; *of Castlestrange* **LG1875**; *of Drumreaske* **LG1863**; **DFUSA**; (*see also* Brasier-Creagh)

MITCHELL (*formerly* MUIR *of Postlip Hall*) **LG1952**

MITCHELL (*now* MAJENDIE *of Holbrook Hall*) **LG1921**

FORBES-MITCHELL *of Thainstone* **LG1921**; (*see also* Sempill)

MITCHELSON, Bt **PB1940**

MITCHISON, B **PB1970**

MITFORD *of Mitford* **LG1969**; *of Pitshill* **LG1952**

FREEMAN-MITFORD (Redesdale, B) **PB1970**; (Redesdale, E) **PB1886**

OSBALDESTON-MITFORD (*see* Mitford)

MITTON *of Craven, Yorks* **LG1952**; (*see also* Eadon)

JONES MITTON *of Mitton Manor* **LG1937**

MOAT *of Johnson* **LG1952**

MOBBS *formerly of Stoke Park House* **LG1965**

MOBERLY **LG1972**; **DFUSA**

MODYFORD, Bt **EDB**

MOELS, B **DEP**

MOENS *formerly of Tweed* **LG1972**

MOFFAT **DFUSA**

MOFFATT **CG**; *of Goodrich Court* (*see* Trafford)

REES-MOGG *of Cholwell* **LG1969**

MOHUN, B **DEP**; (Mohun of Okehampton, B) **DEP**; Bt **EDB**

MOILLIET *of Abbotsleigh* **LG1898**

MOIR, Bt **PB1970**; Bt **EDB**; *of Leckie* **LG1921**; (*see also* Moir-Byers)

MOLESWORTH, V **PB1970**; **CG**

MOLINES, B **DEP**

MOLINEUX *of Isfield* **LG1937**

LE CHAMPION-MOLLER *of Butterston* **LG1863**

MOLLOY *of Clonbela* **LGI1912**

MOLONY, Bt **PB1970**; **IFR1976**

MOLSON, B **PB1970**

MOLTANO *of Glen Lyon House and Chesthill formerly of Parklands* **LG1952**

MOLYNEUX (Sefton E) **PB1970**; Bt *of Castle Dillon* **PB1940**; Bt *of Teversall* **EDB**; **FR**

MORE-MOLYNEUX *of Loseley Park* **LG1972**

MONCK, V **PB1970**; (Rathdowne, E) **DEP**; *of Coley Park* **LG1952**

MONCKTON (Monckton of Brenchley, V) **PB1970**; (Ruthven of Freeland, B) **PB1970**; *of Hilton* **LG1921**; (*see also* Monckton-Arundell)

MONCREIFF, B **PB1970**

MONCREIFFE *of that Ilk*, Bt **PB1970**

MONCRIEFF, *of Kinmonth* **LG1969**; *formerly of Barnhill, Bandiran and Culfargie* **LG1952**

SCOTT-MONCRIEFF *formerly of Fossaway* **LG1969**

SCOTT-MONCRIEFF (*formerly* SNEYD) *of Basford Hall* **LG1952**

MOND (Melchett, B) **PB1970**

MONEY (*see* Money-Kyrle)

MONINS *of Ringwold* **LG1952**; *of Waldershare, Kent* **AA**

MONK (Albemarle, D) **DEP**

LINGARD-MONK (*see* Lingard)

MONK BRETTON (*see* Dodson)

MONKS *formerly of Old Castle* **DFUSA**

MONKSWELL (*see* Collier)

MONMOUTH (*see* Carey; and Scott)

MONNOUX, Bt **EDB**

MONRO, Bt **PB1929**; *of Auchinbowie* **LG1952**; *of Edmondsham* **LG1952**; *of Allan* **LG1921**; *of Islington* **LG1906**; *of Ingsdon* **LG1894**

MONRO (*formerly* EWART) *of Crigleuch* **LG1952**

MONROE **PresFUSA**; *sometime of Katewell* **DFUSA**

MONSELL, V **PB1970** (Emly, B) **PB1932**

DE LA POER MONSELL **IFR1976**

EYRES-MONSELL (*formerly* EYRES) *of Dumbleton Hall* **LG1952**

MONSLOW, B **PB1963**

MONSON, B **PB1970**; (Oxenbridge, V) **PB1898**; V **DEP**

MONTACUTE (Salisbury, E) **DEP**; B **DEP**; (*see also* Browne)

MONTAGU (Manchester, D) **PB1970**; (Sandwich, E) **PB1970**; (Montagu of Beaulieu, B) **PB1970**; (Swaythling, B) **PB1970**; D **DEP**; (Halifax, E) **DEP**; (Montagu of Boughton, B) **DEP**; *of Upton formerly of Shortgrove formerly of Ingmanthorpe* **LG1952**; (*S Africa*) **CG**; (*see also* Nevill; and Pole)

MONTAGUE (Amwell, B) **PB1970**

MONTALT, B **DEP**

MONTALTO, Count **TNBE1956**

MONTEAGLE (*see* Stanley)
MONTEAGLE OF BRANDON (*see* Spring Rice)
MONTEATH *of Duchally* LG1952; *of Cranley* LG1900
MONTEFIORE, Bt *of Worth Park* PB1935; Bt *of Isle of Thanet* PB1885; AA
GOLDSMID-MONTEFIORE (*see* Sebag-Montefiore)
SEBAG-MONTEFIORE LG1965
MONTFORT (Leicester, E) DEP; B DEP; (*see also* Bromley; and de Montfort)
MONTGOMERIE (Eglinton and Winton, E) PB1970; *of Stocks* LG1965; *of Hunsdon House* LG1952; *of Southallan House formerly of Garnsgate and Auchans* LG1937; *of Lainshaw and Brigend, co Ayr* AA; (*see also* Allanby; and Kidston)
KIDSTON-MONTGOMERIE (*see* Kidston)
MOLINEUX-MONTGOMERIE (*now* HOWARD) *formerly of Garboldisham* LG1952
MONTGOMERY (Montgomery of Alamein, V) PB1970; Bt PB1970; (Mount Alexander, E) DEP; B DEP; Bt *of Magbie Hill* EDB; Bt *of Skelmorlie* EDB; *of Marche Manor* LG1952; *of Crilly House* LG1894; *of Milton* LG1858; (*co Antrim*) IFR1976; (*co Down*) IFR1976; (*cos Fermanagh and Tyrone*) IFR1976; *of Kilmer* LGI1904; *of Convoy House* LGI1899; (*see also* Waddington)
LESLIE-MONTGOMERY (*see* Leslie)
LYONS-MONTGOMERY IFR1976
MONTHERMER (Gloucester and Hertford, E) DEP
MONTRESOR *late of Denne Hill* LG1894
MONTROSE (*see* Graham; and Lindsay)
MONYPENNY, Lord DEP; *of Pitmilly* LG1969
MOOD *of Chapel* LG1898
MOODIE *of Henley Park* LG1937
MOODY, Bt EDB; *of Aspley Guise* LG1875; *of Kingsdon* LG1863
MOON, Bt *of Copsewood Grange* PB1970; Bt *of Portman Square* PB1970
ENRAGHT-MOONY IFR1976
MOOR, Bt EDB
MOORE (Drogheda, E) PB1970; Bt *of Colchester* PB1970; Bt *of Hancox* PB1970; Bt *of Kylesburn* PB1970; Bt *of Moore Lodge* PB1970; (Mount Cashell,

E) PB1915; Bt *of Ross Carbery* PB1926; (Drogheda, M) PB1892; (Charleville, E) DEP; Bt EDB; Bt *of Fawley* EDB; Bt *of Jamaica* EDB; *of Broadway and Little Buckland, formerly of Keresley Manor* LG1969; *of Kinderton House* LG1952; *formerly of Mayes Park* LG1952; *of Grimeshill* LG1937; *of Mowbray House* LG1937; *of Willbrook House* LG1937Supp; *of Appleby Hall* LG1906; *of Stockwell* LG1875; IFR1976; *of Moore Lodge* LGI1912; *ofMolenan* LGI1912; *of Manor Kilbride* LGI1912; *of Cremorgan* LGI1912; *of Rowallane* LGI1912; (1) & (2) DFUSA; *of Glenmark* CG; *of Springwood* CG; (*Western Australia*) CG; *of Wierton* CG; (*see also* Perceval-Maxwell)
BRAMLEY-MOORE *of Langley Lodge* LG1875
CARRICK-MOORE *of Corswall* LG1898
MONTGOMERY-MOORE *late of Garvey* LGI1912
PARKIN-MOORE *formerly of Whitehall* LG1952
STEWART MOORE IFR1976
STREATFEILD-MOORE *formerly of Oakhanger Park and of Woodcock Hill* LG1952
THOMSON-MOORE IFR1976
TUNNARD-MOORE *formerly of Frampton Hall* LG1952
MOORHEAD LG1969; *of Derryleckagh House* LGI1958
MORAL (*see* de Bertodano)
MORAN *of Dullinamore, co Leitrim* AA; (*see also* Wilson)
MORANT *of Roydon, formerly of Brokenhurst* LG1972
STIRLING HOME DRUMMOND MORAY *of Abercairny* LG1969
MORAY (*see* Angus; Randolph; and Stuart)
MORDAUNT, Bt PB1970; (Peterborough, E) DEP
MORDEN, Bt EDB
MORDINGTOUN (*see* Douglas)
MORE, Bt *of Loseley* EDB; Bt *of More Hall* EDB; *of Linley and Netley* LG1952: *of Barnborough* LG1833/7
MORETON (Ducie, E) PB1970; (Cornwall, E) DEP; *of Pickenham Hall* LG1952; (*Australia*) CG
PALMER-MOREWOOD *of Alfreton* LG1952
MORGAN (Tredegar, B) PB1959; Bt *of Whitehall Court* PB1916; Bt *of Green*

Street **PB1897**; Bt *of Llangattock* **EDB**; Bt *of Llantarnam* **EDB**; *of Llanwenog* **LG1952**; *of Nantcaerio* **LG1937**; *of Plâs Coed Mor* **LG1937**; *of Woolcombe* **LG1937**; *ofDefynog* **LG1898**; *ofBiddlesdon Park* **LG1894**; *of Golden Grove* **LG1894**; *of Hendrescythan* **LG1894**; *of Hengwrtucha* **LG1886**; *of Cottelstown* **LG1850/3**; *of St Clere and Tredegar* **LG1880/3**; *formerly of Ealing* **DFUSA**; *of Wall Hall* **DFUSA**; **PromFUSA**; (*see also* de Winton *formerly of Graftonbury*; and Morgan-Stratford)

DEANE-MORGAN (*see* Muskerry)

DELMAR-MORGAN *formerly of Effingham House* **LG1952**

GROGAN-MORGAN *ofJohnstown Castle* **LG1863**

HUGHES-MORGAN, Bt **PB1970**; (*see also* Jones-Parry)

PATERSON-MORGAN *of Sandiway Lodge* **LG1952**

VAUGHAN-MORGAN, Bt **PB1970**

MORICE, Bt **EDB**; *of Springfield* **LGI1904**

MORIN *of Allanton* **LG1898**

BONNOR-MORIS *of Bryn-y-Gwalia* **LG1937**

MORISON *of Bognie* **LG1937**

BROUN-MORISON *of Finderlie and Murie* **LG1921**

WALKER-MORISON *of Falfield* **LG1937**

MORKILL *of Newfield Hall* **LG1921**

MORLAND, Bt **EDB**; *of Lamberhurst Court Lodge* **LG1952**; *of Sheepstead* **LG1937**

MORLEY (Morley of Blackburn, V) **PB1923**; B **DEP**; *formerly of Dishforth* **LG1952**; *of Hall Place* **LG1906**; *of Marrick Park* **LG1898**; *of Islanmore and Rockstown* **LGI1958**; *of Marrick Park, co York* **AA**; (*see also* Parker; Roche-Kelly; and Saunders *formerly of Wennington*)

HOPE-MORLEY (Hollenden, B) **PB1970**

MORONY *of Odell Ville* **LG1937SUPP**

MORRALL *of Plâs-Yolyn* **LG1952**

MORRELL *of Headington Hill Hall* **LG1952**; *of Dorchester Manor* **LG1921**; *of Milton* **LG1898**

MORRES, Bt **EDB**; (*see also* de Montmorency)

MORRICE *of Brampton Hall* **LG1921**; *of Catthorpe* **LG1879**; *of Betshanger* **LG1850/3**

MORRIS (Killanin, B) **PB1970**; B **PB1970**; (Morris of Borth-y-Gest, B) **PB1970**;

(Morris of Grasmere, B) **PB1970**; (Morris of Kenwood, B) **PB1970**; Bt **PB1970**; (Nuffield, B) **PB1963**; B **PB1901**; Bt *of Cavendish Square* **PB1926**; *formerly of Allerton Priory* **LG1969**; *formerly of Bolton Lodge* **LG1952**; *of Bryn Myrddin* **LG1952**; *of Llansannan and Llanfair Talhaiarn* **LG1952**; *formerly of Netherby* **LG1937**; *Dol-Llys Hall* **LG1921**; *of Wretham Hall* **LG1906**; *of The Hurst* **LG1898**; *of Wood Eaton* **LG1898**; *of Cwm* **LG1898**; *of Dunkathel* **LG1879**; *of Fishleigh* **LG1858**; **IFR1976**; *of Newrath and Clonmore* **LGI1958**; **DFUSA**; *formerly of Milton* **US**; *formerly of Morrisania and sometime of Tintern Parva* **DFUSA**; *of Philadelphia* **DFUSA**; *formerly of Piercefield* **DFUSA**; *formerly of Waltham Cross* **DFUSA**; *of Nunburnholme, co York* **AA**; *of Peckham, Surrey* **AA**

ARCHDALE MORRIS **IFR1976**

O'CONNOR-MORRIS *of Gortnamona or Mount Pleasant* **LGI1912**

POLLOK-MORRIS (*see* Pollok-McCall)

WALL MORRIS *formerly of Rockenham* **LGI1958**

MORRISON (Dunrossil, V) **PB1970**; (Margadale, B) **PB1970**; B **PB1970**; (Morrison of Lambeth, B) **PB1963**; *of The Hemploe* **LG1952**; *formerly of The White House* **LG1937Supp**; *of Coolegegan* **LGI1912**; **DFUSA**; *formerly of Greenock* **DFUSA**

MORRITT *of Rokeby* **LG1952**

MORROGH **IFR1976**; (*see also* Morrogh Bernard)

MacCARTHY-MORROGH **IFR1976**

MORROUGH (*see* Morrogh Bernard)

MORSE *formerly of Lound* **LG1965**; **DFUSA**; *of Sprowston, co Norfolk* **AA**

MORSHEAD, Bt **PB1905**; *of Lamerton* **LG1965**; *of Wyde Court* **LG1875**

MORTIMER (March, E) **DEP**; (Mortimer of Chirke, B) **DEP**; (Mortimer, of Richard's Castle, B) **DEP**; *of Milbourne Hall* **LG1952**; *formerly of Wigmore* **LG1952**; *of Redisham Hall* **LG1937**

JONES-MORTIMER *of Hartsheath and Plas Newydd* **LG1972**

MORTLOCK *of Abington* **LG1937**

MORTON (Morton of Henryton, B) **PB1970**; Bt **EDB**; *formerly of Crosshouse* **LG1952**; *ofLittle Island* **LGI1912**; *formerly of Bawtry* **DFUSA**; **PromFUSA**; (*see also* Douglas)

MOSELEY *formerly of Darland Hall* **LG1969**; *formerly of Buildwas* **LG1952**; *of Leaton Hall* **LG1914**; *of Owsden* **LG1850/3**; **PromFUSA**
MOSER **LG1969**
MOSLEY (Ravensdale, B) **PB1970**; Bt **PB1970**; (Anslow, B) **PB1933**; Bt **EDB**
MOSMAN *late of Auchtyfardle* **LG1937**
EDWARDS-MOSS, Bt **PB1970**; *of Roby Hall* **LG1863**
McNEILL-MOSS **IFR1976**
MOSSE *formerly of Loriners* **LG1965**; *of Knockfinne* **LG1850/3**
MOSTYN, Bt **PB1970**; Bt **EDB**; *of Llewesog* **LG1875**; *of Bryngwyn* **LG1850/3**; *of Kiddington* **LG1833/7**; **IFR1976**; (*see also* Vaux of Harrowden)
LLOYD-MOSTYN (Mostyn, B) **PB1970**
MOTION *formerly Stisted Hall* **LG1952**
MOTT Bt **PB1970**; *of The Bell House formerly of Wall* **LG1952**; *of Barningham Hall* **LG1921**; (1) & (2) **DFUSA**; (*see also* Mott-Radclyffe)
MOTTET, Bt **EDB**
MOTTISTONE (*see* Seely)
MOUAT, Bt **EDB**
MOUBRAY *of Broonlands formerly of Naemoor* **LG1952**; *of Cockairnie and Otterston* **LG1937**
BLACKWALL-MOULSDALE (*see* Blackwall *of Blackwall*)
MOULTON, B **PB1921**; **DFUSA**; *formerly of Ormsby* **DFUSA**
MOULTRIE *of Aston Hall* **LG1875**
MOUNSELL (*see* De La Poer Monsell)
MOUNSEY *of Castletown* **LG1875**
MOUNT, Bt **PB1970**; *of Wasing Place* **LG1900**
MOUNTAIN, Bt **PB1970**; *of The Heath* **LG1863**
MOUNT ALEXANDER (*see* Montgomery)
MOUNTBATTEN (Milford Haven, M) **PB1970**; (Mountbatten of Burma, E) **PB1975**; (Carisbrooke, M) **PB1959**
MOUNT CASHEL (*see* Davys)
MOUNT CASHELL (*see* Moore)
MOUNTCASTLE **DFUSA**
MOUNT EDGCUMBE (*see* Edgcumbe)
MOUNT EVANS (*see* Evans)
MOUNTGARRET (*see* Butler)
MOUNTJOY (*see* Blount)
MOUNT LEINSTER (*see* Chevers)
MOUNTMORRES (*see* De Montmorency)
MOUNTRATH (*see* Coote)
MOUNT SANDFORD (*see* Sandford)
MOUNT STEPHEN (*see* Stephen)

MOUNT TEMPLE (*see* Ashley)
MOUTRAY *of Favour Royal*; *of Fort Singleton and Auburn* **LGI1912**
MOWAT **CG**
MOWBRAY, Bt **PB1970**; (Norfolk, D) **DEP** *formerly of Surburton House* **LG1952**; *of Mortimer and Bishopwearmouth* **LG1879**; **AA**
MOWBRAY, SEGRAVE AND STOURTON (*see* Stourton)
MOYER, Bt **EDB**
MOYLE, B **PB1970**; (*see also* Copley)
MOYNE (*see* Guinness)
MOYNIHAN, B **PB1970**
MOYSEY *of Highfield formerly of Bathelton Court* **LG1952**
MUDD **DFUSA**
MUDGE *of Sydney* **LG1952**
MUDIE *of Pitnuies* **LG1875**
MUFF (Calverley, B) **PB1970**
MUIR, Bt **PB1970**; *of Billingbear House* **LG1969**; *of Farmingwoods* **LG1914**; *formerly of Kirkcudbright* **DFUSA**; (*see also* Mitchell)
MUIRHEAD *of Craigieburn House* **LG1952**; *of Haseley Court* **LG1937**; (*see also* Gould)
MUIRSHIEL (*see* Maclay)
MULCAHY *of Abbey View* **LGI1912**
MULCASTER *of Benwell Park* **LG1914**; *of Laversdale* **LG1900**
MULDOON (*see* Meldon)
MULES *of Devon and Somerset* **LG1850/3**; **HI**
MULGRAVE (*see* Phipps)
MULHOLLAND (Dunleath, B) **PB1970**; Bt **PB1970**; *of Eglantine* **LG1879**; *of Springvale, co Down* **AA**
MULLAN *of Cairn Hill* **LGI1958**
MULLENS *of Walland Manor* **LG1937**
MULLER (*see* Stewart-Killick)
MULLINER *of Clifton Court* **LG1952**
MULLINGS *of East Court* **LG1875**
MULLINS *of Ballyeigan* **LG1875**; (*see also* Ventry)
MULLOWNEY **DFUSA**
MULLOY *of Hughestown* **LGI1912**; *of Oakport* **LG1880/3**
MULOCK *of Kilnagarna* **LGI1912**
HOMAN-MULOCK *of Bellair*; *of Ballycumber* **LGI1912**
MULTON (Multon, of Egremont, B) **DEP**; (Multon, of Gillesland, B) **DEP**
MUNCASTER (*see* Pennington)
MUNCHENSI, B **DEP**
MUNDY *formerly of Caldrees Manor* **LG1969**; *late of Shipley Hall* **LG1937**;

of *Markeaton* **LG1921**; of *Burton*
LG1833/7; (*see* Clark-Maxwell)
MASSINGBERD-MUNDY of *Ormsby*
LG1972
MUNFORD **PromFUSA**
MUNGOVAN (*formerly* CHAPMAN)
formerly of Tainfield **LG1952**
MUNN *of Heath Hill* **LG1937**
MUNRO, Bt *of Foulis-Obsdale* **PB1970**;
Bt *of Lindertis* **PB1970**; (Alness, B)
PB1953; *of Foulis* **LG1952**; *of Novar*
LG1863; (*Australia*) **CG**; *of Teaninich*
(*see* Munro-Spencer)
COURTHOPE-MUNROE *of Woodbridge*
LG1952
MUNSON **DFUSA**; *formerly of South
Carlton* **DFUSA**
MUNSTER (*see* FitzClarence; and
Schulenberg)
MUNTZ, Bt **PB1940**; *of Umberslade*
LG1972
MURCH *of Cranwells* **LG1894**
MURCHISON, Bt **PB1871**
MURDOCH *of Buckhurst* **LG1921**
BURN-MURDOCH *formerly of Gartin-
caber* **LG1972**
MURE, Bt **EDB**; *formerly of Caldwell*
LG1969; *of Perceston* **LG1921**; *of
Perringswell House* **LG1875**
LOCKHART-MURE of *Livingston*
LG1952
MURPHY, Bt *of Wyckham* **PB1963**;
Bt *of Altadore* **PB1922**; (co Cork)
IFR1976; (*co Tipperary)* **IFR1976**; *of
The Grange* **LGI1912**; *of Kilbrew*
LGI1912; *formerly of Giant's Cause-
way* **DFUSA**; *formerly of the Isle of
Arran* **DFUSA**; (*see also* Loftus)
MACMURROGH-MURPHY (*see* O'
Morchoe) **LGI1912**
MURRAY (Atholl, D) **PB1970**; (Dun-
more, E) **PB1970**; (Mansfield and
Mansfield, E) **PB1970**; (Murray of New-
haven, B) **PB1970**; Bt *of Blackbarony*
PB1970; Bt *of Dunerne* **PB1970**; Bt
of Ochtertyre **PB1970**; (Dunedin, V)
PB1940; (Glenlyon, B) **PB1956**; (Murray
of Elibank, B) **PB1920**; Bt *of Melgund*
PB1882; Bt *of Stanhope* **PB1878**;
(Annandale, E) **DEP**; (Tullibardine, E)
DEP; (Bayning, V) **DEP**; Bt **EDB**; *of
Folla* **LG1969**; *of Coles Park* **LG1952**;
of Dinmore Manor **LG1952**; *of Dollerie*
LG1952; *of Geanies* **LG1952**; *formerly
of Ossemsley Manor* **LG1952**; *of
Cringletie* **LG1937**; *formerly of New-
stead in Wimbledon* **LG1937**; *of Touch-*

adam and Polmaise **LG1937**; *of Twyford
House* **LG1937**; *of North Inveramsay*
LG1921; *late of Philiphaugh* **LG1921**;
of Wootton Court **LG1921**; *of Danes-
field* **LG1894**; *of Lintrose* **LG1879**; *of
Broughton* **LG1879**; *of Eriswell Lodge*
LG1853; *of Casterton* **CG**; *of Mitta-
gong* **CG**; *of Murraythwaite* (*see
Galbraith*); (*see also* Maxtone Graham)
MURRAY (*formerly* WILLIAMS) *of Pen-
pont* **LG1952**
DRUMMOND-MURRAY *formerly of
Mastrick* **LG1965**
ERSKINE-MURRAY (Elibank, B) **PB1970**
GORDON MURRAY *of Craigie* **LG1952**
GREY-MURRAY (*see* Murray *of Folla*)
SCOTT MURRAY *late of Hambledon*
LG1937
MURROUGH *of Watersfield Towers*
LG1921
MUSGRAVE, Bt *of Hartley Castle*
PB1970; Bt *of Tourin* **PB1970**; Bt *of
Drumglass* **PB1904**; Bt *of Hayton
Castle* **PB1875**; B **DEP**; *of Ashleigh*
LG1921; *of Shillington Manor and
Borden* **LG1894**; (*New Guinea*) **CG**
SAGAR-MUSGRAVE *formerly of Bram-
ley* **LG1952**
WYKEHAM-MUSGRAVE of *Swalcliffe*
LG1952
MUSKER *of Shadwell Park* **LG1965**
MUSKERRY (*see* Deane)
MUSKETT *of Clippesby* **LG1898**
MUSPRATT, Bt **PB1934**; *formerly of
Cornist* **LG1952**
(de) MUSSENDEN (*see* Leathes)
MUST (*Australia*) **CG**
CHAWORTH-MUSTERS **LG1969**
MYDDELTON *of Chirk Castle* **LG1972**;
of Gwaynynog **LG1972**; *of Woodhall
Spa* **LG1952**
MYERS *late of Swanmore* **LG1937**;
DFUSA
MYERS (*formerly* CROWLEY) **DFUSA**
MYLNE *of Mylnefield* **LG1863**
MYLTON (*see* Thorneycroft)
MYNORS, Bt **PB1970**; *of Weatheroak*
LG1921
MYRTON, Bt **EDB**
MYTTON *of Garth and Penylan* **LG1937**;
of Cleobury North **LG1879**; *of Shipton*
LG1875; *of Halston* (*see* Thornycroft)
NAESMYTH, Bt **PB1928**; **LG1969**
NAGLE, Bt **PB1850**; *of Clogher* **LGI1912**;
of Calverleigh (*see* Chichester)
NAIRN, Bt **PB1970**; Bt **EDB**
SPENCER-NAIRN, Bt **PB1970**

NAIRNE, Bt **PB1940**; *of Dunsinnan* **LG1898**; (*see also* Bigham)
HOARE NAIRNE (*see* Hoare *of Stourton*)
NAISH *of Ballycullen* **LG1875**
NALL, Bt **PB1970**
NANGLE **IFR1976**; *of Kildalkey* **AA**
NANNEY, Bt **PB1917**; *of Maes-y-Neuadd* **LG1875**; *of Cefndeuddwr* **LG1875**; *of Belmont* **LG1833/7**
ELLIS-NANNIE *of Gwynfryn* **LG1894**
NANSLADRON, B **DEP**
NAPER **IFR1976**
NAPIER (Napier and Ettrick, B) **PB1970**; (Napier of Magda, B) **PB1970**; Bt *of Merchistoun* **PB1970**; Bt *of Merrion Square* **PB1970**; Bt *of Luton Hall* **EDB**; Bt *of Middle Marsh Hall* **EDB**; Bt *of Puncknoll* **EDB**; *of Pennard House* **LG1965**; **DFUSA**
NAPIER (*formerly* HALL-DEMPSTER) *formerly of Dunnichen* **LG1952**
NARBOROUGH, Bt **EDB**
NARBROUGH (*see* Hughes-D'Aeth)
NASH *of Sutton Waldron* **LG1952**; *of Martley* **LG1886**; *of Worcestershire* **LG1875**; **IFR1976**
NASON (*see* Crofts)
NASSAU (Grantham, E) **DEP**; (Rochford, E) **DEP**; (*House of*) **RL**
NATHAN, B **PB1970**; (*New Zealand*) **CG**
NAYLOR *formerly of Leighton Hall* **LG1969**; *of Hooton Hall* **LG1886**; *of Leighton Hall, co Montgomery* **AA**; (*see also* Leyland)
NEAL, Bt **PB1940**; **DFUSA**
VIVIAN-NEAL **LG1972**
NEALE *of Yate and Corsham* **LG1921**; *of Allesley Park* **LG1875**; *of Newington* **LGI1912**; **DFUSA**; **FR**; (*see also* Otter-Barry)
NEALE (*formerly* PHILLIPPS) *of Berwick House* **LG1952**
BURRARD-NEALE (*see* Burrard)
VANSITTART-NEALE *of Bisham Abbey* **LG1952**
NEAME *of Kent* **LG1952**
NEAVE, Bt **PB1970**; *of Mill Green Park* **LG1937**
NEDHAM *of Glen Doon* **LG1937**; *of Jamaica* **LG1850/3**
NEED *of Winthorpe Hall* **LG1937**; *of Woodhouse Castle* **LG1900**
NEEDHAM (Kilmorey, E) **PB1970**; *of Lenton* **LG1863**
HOLT-NEEDHAM **LG1965**
NEELD (*formerly* INIGO-JONES) *of*

Kelston Park and Grittleton **LG1952**
NEGRETTI **LG1969**
NEGUS **LG1972**
NEILL *of Midfield* **LG1898**; *of Sydney and Kiama* **CG**
SMITH-NEILL *late of Barnweil* **LG1937**
NEILSON *of Catton Hall* **LG1972**; (*see also* Graham-Wigan)
NELIGAN (*late* PUTLAND) *of Bray Head* **LGI1912**
NELSON, E **PB1970**; (Nelson of Stafford, B) **PB1970**; Bt **PB1970**; *of Gledstone* **LG1969**; *of Holme* **LG1969**; *of Muckairn* **LG1969**; *of Gelt Garth* **LG1952**; *of Hanger Hill House* **LG1898**; **PromFUSA**
NELTHORPE, Bt **PB1865**
SUTTON-NELTHORPE *of Scawby Hall* **LG1937**
NEPEAN, Bt **PB1970**
NEREFORD, B **DEP**
NESBITT (*see* Burrowes *of Lismore*)
BEAUMONT-NESBITT *formerly of Penton Lodge* **LGI1958**
NETHERCOTE *of Moulton Grange* **LG1886**
NETHERLANDS (*Kings and Queens of*) **RL**
NETHERTHORPE (*see* Turner)
NETTERVILLE, V **DEP**; (*see also* de Stacpoole; and Synnott)
NETTLEFOLD *of Nether Lypiatt* **LG1965**
NETTLES *of Nettleville* **LGI1912**
NEVILE, Bt **EDB**; *formerly of Skelbrooke and Chevet* **LG1965**; *formerly of Thorney* **LG1965**; *of Wellinggore and Aubourn* **LG1965**
NEVILE *of Skelbrook Park, co York* **AA**
NEVILL (Abergavenny, M) **PB1970**; (Montagu, M) **DEP**; (Salisbury, E) **DEP**; (Westmoreland, E) **DEP**; (Fauconberg, B) **DEP**; (Latimer, B) **DEP**; B **DEP**; (Nevill of Essex, B) **DEP**; *of Kewland Hall formerly of Nevill Holt* **LG1969**; *of Tasburgh Hall* **LG1937**; *late of Westfa* **LG1898**; *of Lanlliedi* **LG1850/3**; (*see also* Neville)
LARNACH-NEVILL *of Uckfield House formerly of Brambletye* **LG1937**
NEVILLE (Braybrooke, B) **PB1970**; Bt **PB1970**; *of Shenstone House* **LG1921**; *of Belmont Lodge* **LG1850/3**; *of Moyfin* **LGI1899**; **IFR1976**; (*see also* Furnivall)
NEWALL, B **PB1970**; *formerly of Forest Hall* **LG1952**; *of Stelling Hall* **LG1952**; *of Shepherds Dene* **LG1937**; *of Hare Hill* **LG1921**

NEWARK (see Leslie)
NEWBOLD formerly of Hackenthorpe
DFUSA
NEWBOROUGH (see Wynn)
NEWBURGH (see Giustiniani-Bandini)
PB1970; (Warwick, E) DEP
NEWCASTLE (see Cavendish; and
Holles)
NEWCASTLE-UNDER-LYME (see
Pelham-Clinton-Hope)
NEWCOMB (1) & (2) DFUSA
NEWCOME formerly of Hale Place
LG1972
NEWCOMEN, V DEP; Bt EDB; Bt of
Kenagh EDB; of Kirkleatham LG1937
FITZROY NEWDEGATE of Arbury and
Harefield LG1952
NEWDIGATE, Bt EDB; (see also Fitz-
Roy Newdegate)
NEWELL DFUSA; formerly of Notting-
ham DFUSA
BARRON-NEWELL (see Barron)
NEWENHAM IFR1976
NEWHAVEN (see Mayne)
NEWINGTON formerly of Lewes DFUSA
NEWLANDS (see Hozier)
NEWMAN, Bt of Mamhead PB1970; Bt
of Newmarket PB1970; (Mamhead, B)
PB1940; Bt EDB; of Great Brake
LG1952; of Panfield Hall LG1952; of
Brands House LG1921; of Thornbury
Park LG1921; of Barwick House
LG1850/3; of Dromore LG1899; of
Thornbury Park AA
BRAMSTON-NEWMAN of Castlefield,
formerly of Newberry Manor LGI1958
HARDING-NEWMAN formerly of
Nelmes Place LG1969
NEWMARCH, B DEP
NEWNES, Bt PB1953
NEWPORT, Bt PB1862; (Bradford, E)
DEP; (Torrington, B) DEP; (see also
Blount)
NEWSON, Bt PB1949
NEWSUM formerly of Eastwood House
LG1969
NEWTON, Bt of Beckenham PB1970;
Bt of The Wood PB1970; (Eltisley, B)
PB1940; Bt of Barrs Court EDB; Bt
of Charlton EDB; Bt of London EDB;
formerly of Barton Grange LG1952;
of The Downs Croxton LG1952; of Hill-
mount LG1875; of Cheadle Heath
LG1858; of Killymeal LGI1912; of Bally-
beg LGI1912; DFUSA; of Carrickfergus
AA; of Mickleover (see Curzon of Lock-

ington); (see also Bagenal; and Legh
HAY-NEWTON of Newton LG1900
LEAPER-NEWTON (see Curzon of Lock-
ington)
NIALL IFR1976
NIBLET of Haresfield Court HI
NIBLETT late of Haresfield LG1898
GRUBB-NICHOL (see Grubb)
NICHOLAS of Ashton Keynes LG1863;
of Bothwell CG
NICHOLL of Merthyr Mawr LG1965;
formerly of The Ham LG1965; of
Tredunnock LG1858; of Theydon
Gernon, Essex AA; (see also Hawkins
of Tredunnoc)
NICHOLLS, Bt PB1970
NICHOLS of Lawford Hall LG1965;
formerly of Ampthill DFUSA
NICHOLSON, Bt of Kensington PB1970;
Bt of Luddenham PB1970; Bt of Winter-
bourne PB1970; B PB1917; Bt of Lass-
wade PB1959; of Arisaig LG1952;
of Coles Farm formerly of Basing Park
LG1952; formerly of Highfield Hall
LG1952; of Parehayne Farm formerly
of Eastmore LG1952; late of Newton
Green Hall LG1937; of Ashfield LG1900;
of Waverley Abbey LG1875;
of Roundhay Park LG1863; IFR1976;
of Listoke LG1958; of Ballow LG1912;
of Crannagael LGI1912; formerly of
Orston DFUSA; of Sydney and Ludden-
ham CG; of Ballow, co Down AA; (see
also MacMicking)
NICKISON of Hinton Manor LG1937
NICKOLS formerly of Bramley Hill Top
LG1972
CHAINE-NICKSON formerly of Munny
LGI1958
NICOL of Ballogie LG1972; formerly of
Falkirk DFUSA
NICOLAS of East Looe LG1850/3; of
London LG1880/3
NICOLL PromFUSA
VERE NICOLL LG1969
NICOLLS, Bt EDB; of Garisker LG1879
NICOLS (see Trafford)
NICOLSON (Carnock, B) PB1970; of
Lyndhurst CG
BANENACH-NICOLSON of Glenbervie
LG1958
NIGHTINGALE, Bt PB1970; of Worms-
hill LG1965; of Lea Hurst LG1937
NIHELL (see Niall)
NISBET of Southbroome House LG1875;
of Dirleton LG1858; formerly of Kirk-
cudbright DFUSA

NISBETT *of Cairnhill* **LG1900**
MORE NISBETT **LG1972**
NITHSDALE (*see* Maxwell)
NIVEN *of Carswell* **LG1894**
NIVISON (Glendyne, B) **PB1970**
NIX **LG1965**
NIXON, Bt **PB1970**; *of Fermanagh and Cavan* **LG1875**; *of Belcoo* **LGI1958**; *of Cragbeg* **LGI1912**; **PresFUSA**; **FR**
NOBLE, Bt *of Ardkinglas* **PB1970**; Bt *of Ardmore* **PB1970**; (Kirkley, B) **PB1935**; *of Ash Lodge* **LG1952**; *of Glassdrummond* **LGI1912**
NOEL (Gainsborough, E) **PB1970**; (Gainsborough, E) **DEP**; Bt *of Brook* **EDB**; Bt *of Kirkby Mallory* **EDB**; *of Bell Hall* **LG1914**
NOEL (*formerly* CHAMPION and FOLLETT) *of Edale, Riddlesworth and Rockbeare* **LG1972**
NOLAN *of Ballinderry* **LGI1912**
NORBURY *of Sherridge* **LG1952**; **HI**; (*see also* Graham-Toler)
WARDE-NORBURY (*see* Warde-Aldam)
NORCLIFFE (*see* Howard-Vyse)
RADFORD-NORCOP *of Bettom Hall* **LG1952**
NORFOLK (*see* Bigod; Howard; Fitzalan-Howard; Mowbray; Plantagenet; and Wayer)
NORMAN, Bt **PB1970**; B **PB1949**; *of Bromley Common* **LG1965**; *of St Clere and Moor Place* **LG1965**; *of Iwood Manor and Brundon Hall* **LG1952**; *formerly of Mistley Place* **LG1952**; *of Doncombe* **LG1886**; *of Claverham* **LG1875**; *of Goadby Marwood* **LG1875**; *of Beech Park* **LGI1958**; *of Glengollen* **LGI1912**; **DFUSA**; **FR**; (*Australia*) **CG**
LEE-NORMAN *formerly of Corbollis* **LGI1958**
NORMANBROOK (*see* Brook)
NORMANBY (*see* Phipps; and Sheffield)
NORMAND, B **PB1959**
NORMANDY (*Dukes of*) **RL**
NORMANTON (*see* Agar)
NORQUAY *of Parkdale Farm* **CG**
NORREYS (Berkshire, E) **DEP**; Bt **EDB**; *of Davyhulme Hall* **LG1879**; (*see also* Jephson)
JEPHSON-NORREYS (*see* Jephson)
NORRIE, B **PB1970**
NORRIS *formerly of Barons Down* **LG1952**; *of Hackney* **LG1952**; *of Wood Norton Hall* **LG1937**; *of Sudbury House*

and Hurst Dene **LG1894**; *of Swalcliffe* **LG1886**
NORTH (Guilford, E) **PB1970**; B **PB1970**; Bt **PB1970**; (Grey, B) **DEP**; Bt *of Mildenhall* **EDB**; *of Colleton Hall and Ardura* **LG1972**; *formerly of Keythorpe Hall* **LG1972**; *of Newton Hall* **LG1965**; *formerly of Comeragh Court* **LG1952**; *of Netherbury* **LG1952**; *of Vale Mascal formerly of Elton* **LG1952**
NORTHAMPTON (*see* Bohun; Compton; Howard; and Parr)
NORTHBARING (*see* Baring)
NORTHBOURNE (*see* James)
NORTHBROOK (*see* Baring)
NORTHCHURCH (*see* Davidson)
NORTHCLIFFE (*see* Harmsworth)
NORTHCOTE (Iddesleigh, E) **PB1970**; B **PB1911**; *of Somerset Court* **LG1952**
NORTHEN *of Lea House* **LG1858**
NORTHESK (*see* Carnegie)
NORTHEY *of Epsom* **LG1965**
WILBRAHAM-NORTHEY *formerly of Cheney Court* **LG1969**
NORTHINGTON (*see* Henley)
NORTHMORE *formerly of Cleve* **LG1969**
WELBY-NORTHMORE (*see* Northmore)
NORTHUMBERLAND (*see* Comyn; Copsi; Cospatrick; Dudley; Fitz-Roy; Percy; and Walcher)
NORTHWICK (*see* Rushout)
NORTHWODE, B **DEP**
NORTON (Grantley, B) **PB1970**; (Rathcreedan, B) **PB1970**; Bt **EDB**; Bt *of Coventry* **EDB**; Bt *of Rotherfield* **EDB**; *of Ragden Hall* **LG1952**; *formerly of Northwood Park and The Dell* **LG1952**; *of Downs House* **LG1937**; *formerly of Ockley* **DFUSA**; *of Ecclesbourne and Euchora* **CG**; (*see also* Adderley)
BORTHWICK-NORTON (*formerly Thistlethwayte*) *formerly of Southwick Park* **LG1952**
LOWNDES-STONE-NORTON *of Brightwell Baldwin* **LG1952**
NORWAY (*Royal House of*) **RL**
NORWICH, B **DEP**; Bt **EDB**; *of Brampton* **VF**; (*see also* Cooper; Denny; Gordon; Goring; and Howard)
NORWOOD *of Ashford* **LG1875**; **AA**
NOTLEY *of Diptford* **LG1921**; *of Combe Sydenham* **LG1898**
NOTT **LG1972**; **HI**
PYKE-NOTT *of Bydown* **LG1952**
NOURSE *of New House Ross* **LG1850/3**
NOVAR (*see* Munro-Ferguson)
NOWELL *of Linton House* **LG1952**

NOYES *of East Mascalls* **LG1863**; *formerly of Cholderton* **DFUSA**
NUFFIELD (*see* Morris)
NUGENT (Westmeath, E) **PB1970**; B **PB1970**; (Nugent of Guildford, B) **PB1970**; Bt *of Donore* **PB1970**; Bt *of Waddesdon* **PB1970**; Bt *of Portaferry* **PB1959**; Bt *of Donore* **PB1929**; (Westmeath, M) **PB1871**; (Clare V) **DEP**; B **DEP**; Bt **EDB**; *of Clonlost* **LG1921**; *of Farren Connell* **LGI1912**; (*see also* Johnson; and Douglas-Nugent)
DOUGLAS-NUGENT **IFR1976**
NUNN **IFR1976**
NUNNELEY **LG1965**
NUSSEY, Bt **PB1970**
NUTTALL, Bt **PB1970**; *of Kempsey House* **LG1858**; *of Tittour* **LGI1958**
NUTTING, Bt **PB1970**
NYE **DFUSA**
OAKDEN *of Ladham House* **LG1875**
OAKELEY, Bt **PB1970**
OAKES, Bt **PB1970**; Bt *of Hereford* **PB1927**; Bt *of The Army* **EDB**; *of Nowton Court* **LG1969**; *of Skipness and Riddings* **LG1965**
OAKLEY *of Lawrence End* **LG1972**; *of Appleby* **LG1969**; *of Oakeley* **LG1898**; *of Plas Tan-y-Bwlch* **LG1833/7**
OAKSHOTT, B **PB1970**
OATES *of Besthorpe* **LG1969**; *formerly of Gestingthorpe Hall* **LG1969**; *formerly of Kilnahone* **DFUSA**
OBBARD **LG1969**
O'BEIRNE *of Jamestown* **LGI1912**
OBRE *of Clantilew* **LG1894**
O'BRIEN (Inchiquin, B) **PB1970**; Bt **PB1970**; (Shandon, B) **PB1930**; B **PB1914**; (Thomond, M) **DEP**; (O'Brien, V) **DEP**; *of Ballynalacken* **LGI1912**; *of Cahirmoyle* **LGI1912**; *formerly of Bird Hill* **DFUSA**; *formerly of Nenagh* **DFUSA**; (*see also* Wyndham)
STAFFORD-O'BRIEN *of Blatherwycke Park* **LG1952**
WYNDHAM-O'BRIEN (Thomond, E) **DEP**
O'BYRNE *late of Allardstown and Corville* **LGI1912**
O'CALLAGHAN (Lismore, B) **PB1898**; *of co Cork* **LG1879**; **IFR1976**; *formerly of Cahirduggan* **LGI1958**; (*see also* Bell *of Askham Bryan*)
O'CARROLL (Ely O'Carroll, Lord of) **DEP**; *formerly of Athgoe Park* **LGI1958**
OCHILTREE (*see* Stewart)

OCHTERLONY, Bt *of Ochterlony* **PB1963**; Bt **EDB**
O'CONNELL, Bt **PB1970**; **IFR1976**; *of Ballynabloun* **LGI1912**
O'CONNOR **IFR1976**; *of Charleville* **LGI1912**; *of Toronto* **CG**; (*see also* Conner)
O'CONOR *of Mount Druid* **LGI1912**; *formerly of Thomastown, co Kilkenny* **DFUSA**; (*see also* O'Conor Don)
O'CONOR DON **IFR1976**
O'DÁLAIGH **IFR1976**
ODDIE (*Australia*) **CG**
ODELL *of Kilcleagh Park* **LGI1958**; (Canada) **CG**
O'DEMPSEY (Clanmalier, V) **DEP**
ODO (Kent, E) **DEP**
O'DONEVEN *formerly of Clerahan* **LGI1958**
O'DONNELL (Tyrconnell, E) **DEP**; Bt **PB1889**; *formerly of Trough* **LGI1958**
O'DONOGHUE *of The Glens* **IFR1976**
O'DONOVAN **IFR1976**; (*Australia*) **CG**
O'FARRELL *of Dalystown* **LGI1912**; **AA**
MORE O'FERRAL (*co Kildare: Balyna*) **IFR1976**; (*co Kildare: Kildangan*) **IFR1976**
OFFALEY (*see* Digby)
OFFICER (*Australia*) **CG**
O'FFLAHERTIE *of Lemonfield* **LG1886**
OFFLEY (*see* Crewe-Milnes; and Crewe-Read)
OGDEN **DFUSA**
OGILBY *of Ardnargle and Pellipar House* **LG1937Supp**; *of Altnachree Castle* **LGI1899**; **DFUSA**
OGILVIE, Bt *of Barras* **PB1861**; Bt *of Carnoustie* **PB1861**; *of Sizewell Hall* **LG1969**; *of Chesters* **LG1937**; (*Australia*) **CG**; (*Canada*) **CG**
OGILVY (Airlie, E) **PB1970**; Bt **PB1970**; (Banff, Lord) **DEP**; (Findlater, E) **DEP**; *of Inshwean* **LG1965**; *of Pityoulish* **LG1937**; **FR**; (*Canada*) **CG**; (*Tasmania*) **CG**
NISBET-HAMILTON-OGILVY *of Belhaven Dirleton and Pencaitland* **LG1914**
OGLANDER, Bt **PB1874**; *of Nunwell* **LG1972**; **VF**
ASPINALL-OGLANDER (*see* Oglander)
OGLE, V **DEP**; B **DEP**; Bt **PB1940**; *formerly Kirkley Hall* **LG1952**; *of Eglingham* **LG1879**; **IFR1976**
OGMORE (*see* Rees-Williams)

O'GORMAN *of Bellevue* **LGI1912**; Count **FT1917**

O'GOWAN **IFR1976**

O'GRADY (Guillamore, V) **PB1953**; *of Aghamarta* **LGI1912**; *of Landscape* **LGI1912**; *of Carlton and Queenscliff* **CG**

OGSTON *of Ardoe* **LG1937**

O'HAGAN (*see* Strachey)

O'HALLORAN **CG**

O'HARA (Tyrawly, B) **DEP**; *of Crebilly* **LG1863**; **IFR1976**; *of Mornington* **LGI1958**; *of O'Hara Brook* **LGI1912**; *of Lenaboy* **LGI1912**; *formerly of Lenaboy* **DFUSA**

O'HEA *formerly of Aghamilla Castle* **LGI1958**

O'HEHIR (*otherwise* HARE) *formerly of Deerpark* **LGI1958**

O'HIGGINS **IFR1976**

OHLSON, Bt **PB1970**

PARRY OKEDEN *formerly of Moor Critchell* **LG1965**

LANIGAN O'KEEFFE *of Ryemore* **LGI1958**

O'KELLY *of Screen* **LG1863**; *co Galway*; *Gallagh* **IFR1976**; *co Galway: Gurtray* **IFR1976**; *of Ballygoran Park* **LGI1958**, (*see also* Deasy)

O'KELLY DE CONEJERA *formerly of Kellysmeadow* **LGI1958**

DE PENTHENY O'KELLY **LGI1958**

WALKER-OKEOVER, Bt **PB1970**

OLCOTT **DFUSA**

OLDCASTLE (Cobham, D) **DEP**

OLDENBURG (House of) **RL**

OLDER **DFUSA**

OLDFIELD, Bt **EDB**; *of Doddington Place* **LG1965**; *formerly of Finkley House* **LG1952**; *of Moor House* **LG1952**; *of Cantray House* **LG1937**; *of Oldfield* **LG1863**; *of Oldfield Lawn* **LG1863**; **FR**

OLDFIELD (*formerly* GREATHEAD) *of Uddens* **LG1952**

OLDHAM *of Leatom Grange* **LG1952**

OLDNALL *of Chaddesley Corbett* **LG1972**

RUSSELL-OLDNALL (*see* Oldnall)

OLDS *formerly of Shirborne* **DFUSA**

MacCARTHY-O'LEARY (*see* MacCarthy-Morrogh)

OLIPHANT, Lord **DEP**; *formerly of Condie* **LG1965**; *of Rossie* **LG1921**

KINGTON-BLAIR-OLIPHANT *of Ardblair* **LG1965**

OLIVE *of The Ton* **LG1863**

OLIVER **IFR1976**; *of Uplands Hall* **LG1898**; **DFUSA**; **CG**

OLIVERSON *of Coney Weston Hall* **LG1914**; **FR**

OLIVIER B **PB1940**; *of Notley Abbey* **LG1952**

TESTAFERRATA-OLIVIER, M **TNBE1956**

OLMINS (Waltham, B) **DEP**

O'LOGHLEN, Bt **PB1970**; **CG**

OLPHERT *of Ballyconnell* **LGI1912**

OLPHERTS *of Dartrey* **LG1875Supp**

O'MAHONY (*see* Mahony)

O'MALLEY, Bt **PB1892**; *late of Denton House* **LG1937**; **IFR1976**; **LGI1958**; *of Kilmilkin* **LGI1958**

O'MALLUN (Glean-O'Mallun, B) **DEP**

OMAN *formerly of Kirbister and Onstay* **LG1937**

OMMANEY **LG1972**

O'MOONY (*see* Enraght-Moony)

O'MORCHOE **IFR1976**

O'MORE (*see* More O'Ferrall)

O MULLOY *of Hughestown* **LG1833/7**

O'NEILL, B **PB1970**; (O'Neill of The Maine, B) **PB1970**; (Rathcavan, B) **PB1970**; Bt **EDB**; **IFR1976**; *of Clanaboy* **AA**; *of Sandford Park, co Dublin* **AA**

ONGLEY, B **DEP**

SAVILL-ONLEY *of Ash Priors* **LG1937**

ONSLOW (Onslow, E) **PB1970**; Bt **PB1970**; *of Stoughton House* **LG1875**; (*Australia*) **CG**

OPPENHEIMER, Bt **PB1970**

ORANMORE AND BROWNE (*see* Browne)

ORBY, Bt **EDB**

ORCUTT **DFUSA**

BLACKETT-ORD *of Whitfield* **LG1965**

HASTINGS-ORD *of Packam House* **LG1937**

ORDE *of Nunnykirk* **LG1965**; *formerly of Weetwood* **LG1952**; (*see also* Walter *of Hopton*)

CAMPBELL-ORDE, Bt **PB1970**

O'REILLY *of Yorkshire* **LG1863**; (*cos Dublin, Kildare, Longford and Wexford*) **IFR1976**; (*co Louth*) **IFR1976**; *of Clondrisse formerly of Colamber* **LGI1958**; *of Baltrasha* **LGI1912**; *of Scarborough, Yorkshire* **AA**

ORFORD (*see* Russell; and Walpole)

ORGILL (*see* Leman)

ORKNEY (*see* Fitz-Maurice; Sinclair; and Stewart)

ORLEBAR *of Hinwick* **LG1965**

ORLEBAR *(formerly* BORRER) *of Pakyns Manor* **LG1952**
ORMATHWAITE *(see* Walsh)
ORME *of Owenmore* **LGI1912**
GARNETT-ORME *formerly of Hill Lodge and Greenfield* **LG1969**
ORMEROD *of Tyldesley* **LG1965**
ORMISTON *of Trood House* **LG1972**
ORMOND *(see* Douglas)
ORMONDE *(see* Butler)
ORMSBY, Bt **EDB; IFR1976**
O'RORKE *of Ballyboltan* **LG1875**
ORPEN **IFR1976; CG**
ORR **DFUSA; CG**
ORR *(formerly* GODFREY-FAUSSETT-OSBORNE) *of Hartlip Place* **LG1952**
BOYD-ORR, B **PB1970**
ORREBY, B **DEP**
ORRED *of Tranmere* **LG1898**
ORTON *formerly of Reresby Manor* **LG1952; DFUSA**
OSBALDESTON, Bt **EDB;** *(see also* Firman)
OSBORN, Bt **PB1970; DFUSA**
OSBORNE, Bt **PB1970;** (Leeds, D) **PB1963;** *of Balmadies* **LG1972; DFUSA;** *(Australia)* **CG;** *(see also* Orr)
SMYTH-OSBOURNE *formerly of Ash* **LG1969**
OSGOOD *formerly of Marlborough* **DFUSA;** *formerly of Wherwell* **DFUSA**
O'SHEE **IFR1976**
OSLER, Bt **PB1917**
OSMAND *of Stawell* **CG**
OSMASTON *of Lowfold* **LG1952**
OSSINGTON *(see* Denison)
OSTLER *of Arnold Field* **LG1886**
O'SULLIVAN *(see* Sullivan)
OSWALD *of Newmore* **LG1972;** *of Little Orchard* **LG1965;** *of Cavens and formerly of Auchincruive* **LG1952;** *of Dunniker* **LG1937**
OSWALD *(formerly* ESTCOURT) *formerly of Pinkney* **LG1952**
LLOYD-OSWELL **LG1965**
O'TOOLE *(see* Hall)
OTTER *of Royston Manor* **LG1965**
OTTLEY *formerly of Alces Place* **LG1952;** *of The West Indies* **LG1863; AA**
OTWAY *(see* Otway-Ruthven)
OUGHTON, Bt **EDB**
OULTON *of Stoneleigh* **LG1937;** *of Muxna Lodge* **LGI1958**
OURSLER **DFUSA**
OUTERBRIDGE **DFUSA**
OUTRAM, Bt **PB1970**

OVENS *of Aughnagaddy House* **LG1937 Supp**
OVERBEEK (S Africa) **CG**
OVERSTONE *(see* Loyd)
OVERTOUN *(see* White)
OVEY *of Hernes* **LG1969**
OVINGTON **DFUSA**
OWEN, Bt **PB1970;** *of Candlesby Hall* **LG1972;** *of Ash Hall* **LG1937;** *of Bettws* **LG1937;** *late of Huntspill, now of Sampford Brett* **LG1937;** *of Ymwlch* **LG1898;** *of Withybush* **LG1898;** *of Hemgwrtucha* **LG1898;** *of Cwmgloyne* **LG1886;** *of Condover* **LG1875;** *of Broadway Hall* **LG1875;** *of Garthynghared* **LG1863;** *formerly of Dolgelly* **DFUSA;** *formerly of Mathavan* **DFUSA;** *(see also* Owen-Barlow; Bowen; and Evans *of Lovesgrove)*
BULKELEY-OWEN *(see* Jacson)
CUNLIFFE-OWEN, Bt **PB1970**
HUMPHREYS-OWEN *of Glansevern* **LG1937**
MOSTYN-OWEN *of Woodhouse* **LG1969**
OWENS *of Holestone* **LGI1912**
OWSLEY *of Skeffington* **LG1833/7**
OWTRAM *of Newland Hall* **LG1952**
OXENBRIDGE *(see* Monson)
DIXWELL-OXENDEN, Bt **PB1924**
OXFORD *(see* Harley)
OXFORD AND ASQUITH *(see* Asquith)
OXFURD *(see* Macgill)
OXLEY *of Queen Camel* **LG1969;** *of Ripon Hall* **LG1952**
OZANNE *of Guernsey* **AA**
PACK (Haldon, B) **PB1939;** *(see also* Pack-Beresford)
REYNELL-PACK *of Netherton* **LG1937**
PACKARD *of Bramford* **LG1921**
PACKE *(see* PACKE-DRURY-LOWE)
PACKMAN *of Monks Ditch* **LG1937**
PADDOCK *of Hartwell Hall* **LG1969**
PADDON *of Thralesend* **LG1863**
PADWICK *of Horsham* **LG1937**
PAGE, Bt **EDB;** *formerly of Holebrook* **LG1969;** *of Ivythorne Manor* **LG1952;** *of Newton House* **LG1952; PromFUSA; FR;** *of Holebrook* **HI**
PAGET (Anglesey, M) **PB1970;** Bt *of Cranmore* **PB1970;** Bt *of Harewood Place* **PB1970;** (Queenborough, B **PB1949);** Bt *of Sutton Bonington* **PB1936;** (Uxbridge, E) **DEP;** *of Ibstock* **LG1972;** *of Chipping Norton* **LG1894;** *of Cranmore Hall* **LG1879;** *(see also* Paget-Tomlinson)
PAGET *(now* HODSON) *of Stuffynwood*

Hall **LG1921**
CARLETON PAGET (*see* Carleton)
PAIN (*see* Bigland *of Bigland*)
PAKENHAM (Longford, E) **PB1970**
PAKINGTON (Hampton, B) **PB1970**;
Bt **EDB**
PALEY *formerly of Ampton and Langcliffe* **LG1969; IFR1976**
PALGRAVE, Bt **EDB**; *of Henstead Hall* **LG1921**
PALK, Bt **PB1940**
PALLES *of Mount Palles, Cavan* **LG1879**
PALLISER, Bt **PB1868**; (*see also* Galloway)
PALMER (Lucas, B) **PB1970**; (Palmer, B) **PB1970**; (Rusholme, B) **PB1970**; Selborne, E) **PB1970**; Bt *of Carlton* **PB1970**; Bt *of Grinkle Park* **PB1970**; Bt *of Wanlip Hall* **PB1970**; Bt *of Reading* **PB1910**; Bt *of Wingham* **EDB**; (Castlemaine, E) **DEP**; *of Bow Lodge* **LG1952**; *of Dorney Court* **LG1952**; *of Withcote Hall* **LG1898**; *of Nazing* **LG1879**; *of Summer Hill* **LG1875**; *of Clifton Lodge* **LG1863**; *of Wood Court* **LG1850/3**; *of Boyne House* **LG1850/3**; *formerly of Derreen*) **LGI1958**; *of Rahan* **LG1912**; **CG**; (*see also* Michell *formerly of Forcett*)
FENWICK PALMER (*see* Fenwick *formerly of Thirlestaine House*)
LLEWELLEN-PALMER *of Great Somerford* **LG1972**
ORPEN-PALMER *formerly of Killowen* **LGI1958**
PRIOR-PALMER *formerly of Rathdoury and Cuffsborough* **LGI1958**
WADE-PALMER *late of Holme Park* **LG1937**
PALMERSTON (*see* Temple)
PALMES *of Naburn* **LG1965**; *of Lindley* **LG1833/7**
PALMOUR (*see* Palmour-Edwards)
PANCOAST **DFUSA**
PANMURE (*see* Maule)
PANNILL **DFUSA**
PANTON (*Australia*) **CG**
PAPILLON *formerly of Acryse and Crowhurst* **LG1972**
PARDOE *formerly of Leyton Manor* **LG1969**; *late of Nash Court* **LG1937**
PARES **LG1965**
PARFITT *of Bruton, co Somerset* **AA**
PARGITER, B **PB1970**
PARISH *formerly of Bamburgh Old Hall* **LG1969**
PARKE (Wensleydale, B) **DEP**; *of Henbury House* **LG1952**; *of Dunally* **LGI1912**

PARKER (Macclesfield, E) **PB1970**; (Morley, E) **PB1970**; (Parker of Waddington, B) **PB1970**; Bt *of Melford Hall* **PB1970**; Bt *of Shenstone* **PB1970**; Bt *of Carlton House Terrace* **PB1932**; Bt *of Harburn* **PB1903**; (Morley, B) **DEP**; Bt *of Arwarton* **EDB**; Bt *of Langley* **EDB**; Bt *of Ratton* **EDB**; *of Browsholme* **LG1972**; *formerly of Hanthorpe House* **LG1969**; *formerly of Clopton Hall* **LG1952**; *formerly of Fairlie* **LG1952**; *of Faulkbourne* **LG1952**; *of Feathercombe* **LG1952**; *of Parknook* **LG1952**; *of Terriers Green* **LG1952**; *formerly of Upton House* **LG1952**; *formerly of Warwick Hall* **LG1952**; *of Grindon Ridge Hall* **LG1937**; *late of Rothley Temple* **LG1921**; *of Sharpham* **LG1921**; *of Swannington Hall* **LG1906**; *of Woodham Mortimer* **LG1898**; *of Castle Lough* **LG1894**; *of Whiteway* **LG1879**; *of Petteril Green Cumberland* **LG1858**; *of Bally Valley* **LGI1912**; *of Passage West* **LGI1912**; (1) (2) & (3) **DFUSA**; *formerly of Huntington* **DFUSA; PromFUSA**; *of Perth* **CG**; (*see also* Wolley-Dod)
PARKER (*formerly* WELLS) *of Houghton Lodge* **LG1972**
PARKER (*formerly* BULLOCK) *of Radwinter formerly of Faulkbourne* **LG1952**
DODDS-PARKER *formerly of Little Norton* **LG1972**
OXLEY PARKER *of Faulkbourne* **LG1972**
TOWNELEY-PARKER (*see* Tatton)
WALKER-PARKER (*see* Dodds-Parker)
PARKHOUSE *of Eastfield Lodge* **LG1863**
PARKHURST **FR**
PARKIN *of Sharrow Bay* **LG1952**
PARKINSON *late of Ludford* **LG1921**; *late of Easthill* **LG1914**; *of Winkleigh Court* **LG1898**; **DFUSA**; *of Ravensdale Hall* (*see* Robertson); (*see also* Milward *formerly of Thurgarton and Hexgreave*)
PARKYNS, Bt **PB1970**; (Rancliffe, B) **DEP; VF**
PARLANE *of Derrie formerly of Appleby and Craigdhu* **LG1952**
PARLBY *of Manadon* **LG1952**
PARLOUR *of Monkend, Bedburn, Newbiggin and Hunstanworth* **LG1952**
PARMINTER *formerly of Dawes Hall and Bevingdon House* **LG1952**
PARMOOR (*see* Cripps)
PARNELL (Congleton, B) **PB1970**; *of Avondale* **LG1899**

PARR (Northampton, M) **DEP;** (Parr of Horton, B) **DEP;** *of Mill House* **LG1972;** *Grappenhall Hayes* **LG1900;** *of Paytoe Hall* **LG1898;** *of Killiechronan* **LG1886;** *of Parr* **LG1863;** *of Ashchurch* **LG1863;** *of Stonelands* **LG1863;** *of Shropshire* **LG1858;** *of Taunton* **LG1858;** *of Tonbridge, Kent* **AA**
PARRINGTON *of Blackwood Hall* **LG1937**
PARRY, Bt **PB1917;** *of Twysog* **LG1875;** *of Noyadd Trefawr* **LG1875;** **FR**
GAMBIER-PARRY *of Highnam Court* **LG1952**
JONES-PARRY (*now* HUGHES-MORGAN) *of Llwyn Onn* **LG1969**
PARSONS (Rosse, E) **PB1970;** Bt *of Winton Lodge* **PB1940;** (Rosse, E) **DEP;** Bt *of Langley* **EDB;** *of Digges Court* **LG1952;** *of Carskiey* **LG1937;** **PromFUSA;** (*see also* Warburton-Lee)
PART *of Houghton Hall* **LG1952**
PARTINGTON (Doverdale, B) **PB1949;** *of Merklands House* **LG1875**
PARTRIDGE *of Hockham Hall* **LG1952;** *of Bacton Manor* **LG1921;** *late of Bishop's Wood* **LG1921;** *of Horsenden Hall* **LG1875;** *of Bishop's Wood* **AA;** *of Horsendon House, Bucks* **AA;** *of Cornwell Manor* (*see* Penyston)
PASLEY, Bt **PB1970**
PASSFIELD (*see* Webb)
ANWYL-PASSINGHAM (*see* Anwyl *of Tywyn*)
PASSMORE *of Withyshaw* **LG1937**
PASTON (Yarmouth, E) **DEP;** Bt **EDB**
PATE, Bt **EDB;** *formerly of Eye Kettleby* **DFUSA**
PATERSON, Bt **EDB;** *of Balgray* **LG1952;** *formerly of Castle Huntley* **LG1952;** *formerly of Holmewood* **LG1952;** *late of Montgomerie* **LG1921;** *of Carpow* **LG1894;** **FR**
PATESHALL *of Allensmore* **LG1937**
PATESHULL, B **DEP**
PATON *formerly of Crailing* **LG1972;** *of Grandhome* **LG1898;** **FR**
HADDEN-PATON *of Rossway* **LG1952**
NOEL-PATON (Ferrier, B) **PB1970**
PATRICK *of Roughwood and Hessilhead formerly styled of Trearne* **LG1937;** *of Dunminning* **LG1894;** **IFR1976**
KENNEDY-COCHRAN-PATRICK *of Ladyland* **LG1969**
PATRICKSON *of Kirklinton Park* **LG1863**
WILSON PATTEN (Winmarleigh, B) **PB1892;** *of Bank Hall* **LG1875**
TYLDEN-PATTENSON *of Dashmonden*

and formerly of Ibornden **LG1952**
PATTESON *of Great Hautbois House* **LG1952**
PATTINSON *of Gossel Ridding* **LG1952**
PATTISON **DFUSA**
PATTON *of Clayton Priory* **LG1886;** *of Bishop's Hall* **LG1875;** **DFUSA;** (*see also* Patton-Bethune)
PAUL, Bt **PB1970;** Bt *of Paulville* **PB1959;** Bt *of Rodborough* **EDB;** *formerly of Cakemuir Castle* **LG1965;** *of Freston* **LG1969;** *of High Grove* **LG1875;** *formerly of Ilminster* **DFUSA**
PAULET (Winchester, M) **PB1970;** (Bolton, D) **DEP**
PAUNCEFOTE, B **PB1902;** *of Preston Court, co Gloucester* **LG1875;** **AA**
PAUNCEFORT (*see* Pauncefort Duncombe)
RUSSELL-PAVIER *of Newlands* **LG1898;** **FR**
HARGRAVE-PAWSON *of Shawdon* **LG1952**
PAXTON, Bt **PB1930;** *of Cholderton* **LG1875;** (*see also* Norman *of Claverham*)
PAYLER Bt **EDB**
PAYNE (Lavington, B) **DEP;** *of Badgeworth End* **LG1921;** *of Sulby Hall* **LG1863;** **DFUSA, PromFUSA;** **CG**
PAYNEL (Paynell, B) **DEP**
PAYNELL (*see* Paynel)
PAYNTER *formerly of Boskenna* **LG1972;** *of Gate House* **LG1900;** **FR**
PENDARVES PAYNTER (*see* Paynter)
PAYSON (*see* Smith)
PEABODY *formerly of St Albans* **DFUSA**
PEACH *of Tockington* **LG1875**
KEIGHLEY-PEACH *of Idlicote House* **LG1898;** **AA**
PEACHEY (Selsey, B) **DEP**
PEACOCK *of South Runcton* **LG1952;** *of Springfield Place* **LG1952;** (*see also* Willson)
PEACOCKE, Bt **PB1875;** *of Efford Park* **LG1906;** *of Reeves Hall* **LG1863;** *of Skebanish* **LGI1912**
PEAKE (Ingleby, V) **PB1970;** *formerly of Burrough-on-the-Hill* **LG1965;** *of Cottrells* **LG1952;** *of Lleweny* **LG1875**
PEARCE, B **PB1970;** Bt **PB1907;** *of Ffrwdgrech* **LG1875;** **RFFK;** **PromFUSA**
PEARD *of Coole Abbey* **LG1863**
PEARETH *of Thorpe Mandeville* **LG1914;** *of Usworth House* **AA**
PEARSALL *of Willsbridge* **LG1863**
PEARSE *of Hurlington* **LG1875;** **CG**

PEARSON (Cowdray, V) **PB1970; B PB1970**; Bt *of Dunstan's* **PB1970**; Bt *of Gressingham* **PB1970**; *of Bulcote* **LG1972**; *of Bramcote* **LG1952**; *of Johnston* **LG1952**; *of Wroxton Abbey* **LG1952**; *of South Wingfield* **LG1937**; *of Greenwich* **LG1850/3**; *formerly of Pownall* **DFUSA**; **FR**; **CG**; *of Kilmony Park and Craigellachie* **CG**

PEART *formerly of Glenwood* **LGI1958**

PEASE (Daryngton, B) **PB1970**; (Gainford, B) **PB1970**; (Wardington, B) **PB1970**; Bt *of Hummersknott* **PB1970**; Bt *of Hutton Lowcross and Pinchinthorpe* **PB1970**; *formerly of Chapel Allerton Hall* **LG1972**; *formerly of Hesslewood* **LG1952**; *of Middleton Tyas* **LG1952**; *of Binkburn* **LG1914**; *of Pendower* **LG1898**; *of Mowden* **LG1898**; **DFUSA**; *(see also* Warde-Aldam)

PEATLING *of Leverington Hall* **LG1937**

PECHE (Peche, of Brunne, B) **DEP**; (Peche, of Wormleighton, D) **DEP**

PECHELL, Bt **PB1970**

PECK *formerly of Penmore House* **LG1952**; *of Cornish Hall and Temple Coombe* **LG1875**; **DFUSA**; *formerly of Knoston* **DFUSA**; **PromFUSA**

PECKHAM *formerly of Nyton* **LG1952**

PECKOVER, B **PB1917**; *of Wisbech* **LG1906**

PEDDER *formerly of Ashton Park* **LG1952**; *of Finsthwaite* **LG1952**; *of Brandeston Hall* **LG1900**; *of Ashton Park* **AA**

PEDDIE, B **PB1970**

PEDLER *of Hoo Mavey* **LG1833/7**

PEEK, Bt **PB1970**

PEEL, E **PB1970**; Bt *of Eyworth* **PB1938**; Bt of *Tyersall Hall* **PB1911**; *of Trenant Park, formerly of Peele Fold* **LG1969**; *of Brynypys* **LG1952**; *of Knowlmere* **LG1952**; *of Taliaris* **LG1952**; *of Singleton Brook, co Lancaster* **AA**; *of Stone Hall, co Pembroke* **AA**; *(see also* Ethelston; and Thursby-Pelham *(formerly* PEEL) *formerly of Danyrallt)*

PEEL *(formerly* MACONCHY) *of Rathmore* **LGI1958**

PEELE *late of Shrewsbury* **LG1937**

PEGGE *(see* Craven-Smith-Milnes)

GARRETT-PEGGE *of Chesham Bois* **LG1952**

PEILE *of Ogle Castle* **LG1952**

PEIRCE *formerly of Winscombe* **DFUSA**

PEIRSE *of Bedale* **LG1863**

BERESFORD-PEIRSE, Bt **PB1970**

PELHAM (Chichester, E) **PB1970**; (Yarborough, E) **PB1970**

ANDERSON-PELHAM *(see* Conyers; and Fauconberge)

THURSBY-PELHAM *(now* CHAPMAN) *of Upton Cressett* **LG1965**

THURSBY-PELHAM *(formerly* PEEL) *formerly of Danyrallt* **LG1965**;

PELL *of Wilburton* **LG1937**; *of Hazelbeach* **LG1900**; *formerly of Water Willoughby* **DFUSA**; **PromFUSA**

PELLEW (Exworth, V) **PB1970**

PELLEY **DFUSA**

PELLY, Bt **PB1970**; *formerly of Heronsbrook* **LGI1958**

PELSANT, Bt **EDB**

PELTON **DFUSA**

PEMBERTON *of Trumpington* **LG1972**; *of Bainbridge Holme, Ramside formerly of Hawthorn Tower* **LG1952**; *of Newton* **LG1894**; *formerly of Wigan* **DFUSA**: *(see also* Cholmondeley)

CHILDE PEMBERTON *(see* Childe *of Kyre)*

LEIGH PEMBERTON **LG1965**

PEMBROKE *(see* Clare; Hastings; Herbert; Marshal; and Valence)

PEMBROKE AND MONTGOMERY *(see* Herbert)

BENCE-PEMBROKE *(see* Bence-Jones)

PENDARVES *of Pendarves* **LG1952**

PENDER, Bt **PB1921**; *of Middleton Hall and Footscray Place* **LG1894**; **DFUSA**

DENISON-PENDER (Pender, B) **PB1970**

PENDLETON **PromFUSA**

PENDOCK *(see* Otter-Barry)

PENEYSTONE, Bt **EDB**

PENFOLD *(Australia)* **CG**

PENHALLOW *formerly of Penhalow* **DFUSA**; **PromFUSA**

PENN *of Camrose House* **LG1952**; *(formerly* EBDEN) *formerly of Newton House* **LG1952**; *of Stoke Park* **LG1863**

PENNANT (Penrhyn, B) **DEP**; *of Bodfari* **LG1952**; *of Penrhyn* **LG1863**; *of Bagillt* **LG1833/7**

DOUGLAS-PENNANT (Penrhyn, B) **PB1970**

PENNEFATHER, Bt **PB1933** *of Marlow* **LGI1958**

FREESE-PENNEFATHER *of Rathsallagh* **LGI1958**

PENNEY, B **PB1970**

PENNIMAN **DFUSA**

PENNINGTON (Muncaster, B) **PB1917**;

of Broome Hall **LG1894;** *of Thickthorn*
LG1875; (*see also* Pennington-Ramsden)
PENNOYER **DFUSA**
PENNY (Marchwood, V) **PB1970**
PENNYMAN, Bt *of Ormsby* **PB1852;** Bt
of Marske **EDB;** *of Ormesby Hall*
LG1952
PENNYSTON *of Cornwell Manor* **LG1921**
PENOYRE (*formerly* BAKER STAL-
LARD-PENOYRE) *of The Moor*
LG1972
PENRHYN *of East Sheen* **LG1914;** (*see
also* Pennant; and Douglas-Pennant)
PENRICE *of Kilbrough* **LG1900;** (*see
also* Penrice-Lyons)
PENROSE *of Pentney House* **LG1972;** *of
Shandangan* **LG1875;** *formerly of
Woodhill* **LGI1958; PromFUSA; FR**
PENRUDDOCKE *formerly of Compton
Chamberlayne* **LG1952; AA**
PENRY *of Newport* **LG1921**
PENTLAND (*see* Sinclair)
PENTON *of Pentonville* **LG1898**
PENZANCE (*see* Wilde)
PEPLOE *formerly of Garnstone* **LG1952**
PEPPARD *of Cappagh House* **LG1875;**
(*see also* Blundell)
PEPPER *late of Redlynch Park* **LG1937;**
of Baliygarth **LGI1912;** (*see also*
Staveley; and *Pepper-Staveley*)
PEPPERELL, Bt *of Boston* **EDB;** Bt *of
Massachusetts* **EDB**
PEPYS (Cottenham, E) **PB1970;** (*see also*
Leslie)
PERCEVAL (Egmont, E) **PB1970;** *of
Bishops Lydeard* **LG1952; IFR1976;** *of
Barntown* **LGI1912;** (*New Zealand*)
CG; (*see also* Perceval-Maxwell)
PERCIVAL *formerly of The Hermitage*
LG1969; *of Kimsbury House* **LG1952**
PERCY (Northumberland, D) **PB1970;**
(Percy of Newcastle, B) **PB1956;** (North-
umberland, E) **DEP;** (Worcester, E)
DEP; (Egremont, B) **DEP;** (Prudhoe,
B) **DEP**
HEBER-PERCY *of Hodnet* **LG1952;** (*see
also* Northumberland)
PEREIRA **LG1965**
PERINE **DFUSA**
PERKINS *of Bure House, formerly of
Chipstead Place* **LG1965;** *of Orton Hall*
LG1906; *formerly of Hillmorton*
DFUSA
PERKS, Bt **PB1970**
PERNET **DFUSA**
PERRIER *of Cork* **LG1875**
PERRING, Bt **PB1970**

PERRINS *formerly of Davenham*
LG1969
PERROTT, Bt *of Plumstead* **PB1922;**
formerly of Wackland **LG1952;** (*see
also* Noel)
PERRY B **PB1956;** *of Donnington
Manor* **LG1952;** *of Bitham Hall*
LG1937; *of Moor Hall and Jervis Hall,
co Essex* **LG1850/3; IFR1976;** *formerly
of Bideford* **DFUSA;** (*New Zealand*)
CG; *of Bitham House, co Warwick,*
AA
PERSSE **IFR1976**
PERTH (*see* Drummond)
PERY (Limerick, E) **PB1970;** V **DEP**
PESHALL, Bt **EDB**
WELLS-PESTELL, B **PB1970**
PETER *of Chyverton* **LG1921; DFUSA;**
(*New Zealand*) **CG**
PETERBOROUGH (*see* Mordaunt)
PETERS *of Harefield* **LG1937;** (*see also*
Turton; and Washington)
PARSONS-PETERS *of South Petherton*
LG1952
PETERSON **PromFUSA**
PETERSWALD **CG**
PETHERICK **LG1965**
PETHICK *formerly of Lanoy* **LG1921**
PETIT, Bt **PB1970**
PETLEY *of Riverhead* **LG1937**
PETO, Bt *of Barnstaple* **PB1970;** Bt *of
Somerleyton* **PB1970**
PETRE, B **PB1970;** (*see also* Furnivall)
PETRIE; Bt **PB1970**
PETTENGILL *formerly of Shottesham*
DFUSA
PETTIT *of Castle Weir* **LG1937; DFUSA**
PETTIWARD *formerly of Finborough
Hall* **LG1937**
PETTUS, Bt **EDB**
PETTY (Shelburne, E) **DEP**
PEW **HI**
DE PEYER *of Newent Court* **LG1921**
PEYTON, Bt *of Doddington* **PB1959;**
Bt **EDB;** Bt *of Doddington* **EDB;** Bt *of
Isleham* **EDB;** Bt *of Knowlton* **EDB;** *of
Laheen* **LGI1912**
PHAIRE *of Killoughrum Forest* **LG1858**
PHAYRE *formerly of Grange* **LG1969**
PHELIPS, Bt **EDB;** *formerly of Monta-
cute* **LG1972**
PHELPS **IFR1976;** *formerly of Tewkes-
bury* **DFUSA;** (*see also* Clifford of
Chestal)
PHIBBS *of Lisheen* **LGI1912;** *of Doobeg*
LGI1912
PHILBIN (*see* HOLLADAY)

PHILIPPS (St Davids, V) **PB1970;** (Milford, B) **PB1970;** (Strange of Knokin, B) **PB1970;** (Kylsant, B) **PB1937;** (Milford, B) **DEP;** *of Cwmgwilie* **LG1972;** *of Picton* **LG1886**
FOLEY-PHILIPPS, Bt **PB1959**
LLOYD-PHILIPPS *of Dale Castle* **LG1952**
PHILIPS *formerly of Abbey Cwmhir* **LG1969;** *of The Heath House; formerly of Heybridge* **LG1965;** *of Welcombe* **LG1886;** *of Bank Hall* **LG1886;** (*see also* Heaton)
FAUDEL-PHILIPS, Bt **PB1940**
PHILIPSE (*see* Heaton)
MURRAY-PHILIPSON *formerly of Stobo Castle* **LG1952**
PHILLIMORE, B **PB1970**
PHILLIPPS, Bt **PB1872;** *formerly of Lower Eaton* **LG1952;** *of Bryngwyn* **LG1875,** *of Longworth, co Hereford* **LG1850/3;** (*see also* Neale)
MARCH PHILLIPPS (*see* de Lisle)
PHILLIPS, D **PD1970,** Dt **PB1970;** *formerly of Haverfordwest* **LG1969;** *formerly of Sunningdale and Royston* **LG1965;** *of Burnworthy Manor* **LG1952;** *of Cilyblaidd* **LG1952;** *of Well End* **LG1952;** *of Culham House* **LG1921;** *of Gaile* **LGI1912;** *of Glenview* **LGI1899;** *of Witston House, co Monmouth* **LG1875;** *of Dry River Station* **CG;** *of Garendon Park, co Leicester* **AA**
LORT PHILLIPS *formerly of Down Grange* **LG1965;** *of Lawrenny* **LG1965**
PAGE-PHILLIPS *of Brough* **LG1952**
SPENCER-PHILLIPS *formerly of Riffhams* **LG1952**
PHILLPOTTS *of Porthgwidden* **LG1886**
PHIPPS (Normanby, M) **PB1970;** (Mulgrave, B) **DEP;** *of Chalcot* **LG1965;** *of Dilton Court* **LG1875; IFR1976**
PHYFE (*formerly* FYFFE) **DFUSA**
PICKARD (*see* Lane (*formerly* Pickard-Cambridge) *of Poxwell*)
PICKERING Bt *of Tidmarsh* **EDB;** *of Whaddon* **EDB; DFUSA;** *of Hindmarsh* **CG**
PICKERSGILL (*see* Duberly)
PICKFORD (Sterndale, B) **PB1923;** *of King Sterndale* **LG1937**
PICKTHORN, Bt **PB1970**
PIDCOCK *of Bury Hill House* **LG1952;** *of The Platts* **LG1863**
PIERCE *of Frettons* **LG1921; PresFUSA; DFUSA;** *formerly of Norwich*

DFUSA; *formerly of Stepney* **DFUSA;** *of Liverpool* **AA**
PIERCY, Bt **PB1970;** *late of Marchwiel Hall* **LG1937**
PIERREPONT (Manvers, E) **PB1953;** (Kingston-upon-Hull, D) **DEP;** (Pierrepont, of Hanslope, B) **DEP;** *of St Austins* **LG1914**
PIERS, Bt **PB1970;** Bt **EDB;** (*S Africa*) **CG**
PIGGOTT *formerly of Fitzhall* **LG1952**
PIGOT, Bt **PB1970; DEP**
PIGOTT, Bt **PB1970;** *formerly of Widmoore* **LG1937;** *of Doddershall Park* **LG1900;** *of Sundorne* **LG1894;** *of Edgmond* **LG1875;** *of Eagle Hill* **LG1875;** *of Archer Lodge* **LG1863;** *of Capard* **LGI1912;** *of Slevoy* **LGI1912;** FR; (*Australia*) **CG;** (*see also* Pigott-Brown)
GRAHAM-FOSTER-PIGOTT (*see* De Courcy-Ireland)
CARLETON-PIGOTT **LG1879**
SMYTH-PIGOTT **LG1969**
PIKE *formerly of Besborough and Kilnock* **LGI1958**
PILCHER *of Laggan House* **LG1952;** *of Englefield Green* **LG1937**
PILDITCH, Bt **PB1970**
PILE, Bt **PB1970;** Bt **EDB**
PILKINGTON, B **PB1970;** *of Reay* **LG1965;** *formerly of Sutton* **LG1965;** *of Windle Hall* **LG1965;** *of Halliwell Hill* **LG1894;** *of Park Lane Hall* **LG1863;** *formerly of Tore* **LGI1958;** *of Park Lane Hall* **AA**
MILBORNE-SWINNERTON-PILKINGTON, Bt **PB1970**
PILLANS *of Myres* **CG**
PIM *formerly of Newpark* **LGI1958**
PINCARD *of Combe Court* **LG1894**
PINCKNEY *of Monkton Farleigh* **LG1952;** *of Milford Hill* **LG1914**
PINDAR, Bt **EDB**
PINE (*see* Pyne; and Pine-Coffin)
PINFOLD *of Walton Hall* **LG1875; AA**
PINK *formerly of Shrover Hall* **LG1952**
PINKNEY, B **DEP**
PRETOR-PINNEY *of Somerton Erleigh* **LG1965**
PINSENT, Bt **PB1970**
PIPARD, B **DEP**
PIPER (*see* Cox)
PIPON *formerly of Noirmont* **LG1952**
PIRBRIGHT (*see* de Worms)
PIRIE, Bt **PB1851;** (*see also* Pirie-Gordon)

PIRRIE, B **PB1924**
PITCAIRN *of Pircairns* **LG1858**
PITMAN *of Eastcourt House* **LG1972**; *of Dunchideock House* **LG1863**
PITT (Chatham, E) **DEP**; (Londonderry, E) **DEP**; (Camelford, B) **DEP**; *formerly of Cricket Court* **LG1937**; (*see also* Pitt-Rivers)
PITTENWEEM (*see* Stewart)
PITTS (1) & (2) **DFUSA**
PIXLEY *formerly of Wooburn House* **LG1952**; **FR**
PLANTAGENET (Bedford, D) **DEP**; (Clarence, D) **DEP**; (Cornwall, D) **DEP**; (Gloucester, D) **DEP**; (Kent, E) **DEP**; (Lancaster, D) **DEP**; (York, D) **DEP**; (Cornwall, E) **DEP**; (Kent, E) **DEP**; (Norfolk, E) **DEP**; (Salisbury, E) **DEP**; (L'Isle V) **DEP**
PLATT, B **PB1970**; Bt **PB1970**; *of Highfield Hall* **LG1952**; *of Gorddinog* **LG1937**; **DFUSA**; (*see also* McDowell)
PLAYER *of Whatton Manor* **LG1952**; *of Wernfadog* **LG1937**; (*see also* Brigstocke)
PLAYFAIR, B **PB1939**
PLAYFORD **CG**
PLAYNE *of Aswarby and Minchinhampton* **LG1972**; *of Longfords* **LG1900**
PLAYTERS, Bt **EDB**
PLAYZ, B **DEP**
PLENDER, B **PB1940**
PLESSETIS (*see* Plessets)
PLESSETS (Warwick, E) **DEP**
PLEYDELL, Bt **EDB**
MANSEL-PLEYDELL *of Whatcombe* **LG1952**; (*see also* Mansel)
PLIMPTON **DFUSA**
PLOMER, Bt **EDB**
PLOWDEN, B **PB1970**; **LG1972**; *of Ewhurst Park, Hants* **AA**
CHICHELE PLOWDEN (*see* Plowden)
CHICHELEY-PLOWDEN (*see* Plowden)
PLUGENET, B **DEP**
PLUMB **DFUSA**; **PromFUSA**
PLUMER, B **PB1940**; *formerly of Newbury* **DFUSA**; **FR**
PLUMMER, B **PB1970**; *of Mount Plummer, co Limerick* **LGI1912**
SCOTT-PLUMMER *of Sunderland Hall* **LG1972**
PLUMPTRE (FitzWalter, B) **PB1970**; **LG1972**
PLUNKET, B **PB1970**; (Rathmore, B) **PB1917**

PLUNKETT (Fingall, E) **PB1970**; (Dunsany, B) **PB1970**; (Louth, B) **PB1970**; *of Portmarnock* **LGI1912**
PLYMLEY (*see* Corbett *of Longnor*)
PLYMOUTH (*see* Fitz-Charles; Windsor-Clive; and Windsor)
PLYMPTON **PromFUSA**
POCOCK, Bt **PB1921**
POCHIN *of Barkby Hall* **LG1952**
POCKLINGTON (*now* CHENEVIX-TRENCH) *of Chelsworth* **LG1921**
POCKLINGTON *of Hagnaby Priory* **LG1886**; (*see also* Pocklington-Senhouse)
PODE *of Bonvilston* **LG1952**
POË **IFR1976**
POINTZ, B **DEP**
POLAND *of Bramshott* **LG1952**
POLE, Bt **PB1970**; (Suffolk, D) **DEP**; (Lincoln, E) **DEP**; (Montagu, B) **DEP**; Bt **EDB**
CAREW POLE, Bt **PB1970**
CHANDOS-POLE *of Newham Hall* **LG1965**; *of Radbourne* **LG1965**
POLEY *of Boxted Hall* **HI**
WELLER-POLEY *of Boxted Hall* **LG1972**
POLHILL *of Howbury* **LG1972**; (*see also* Polhill-Drabble)
POLK **PresFUSA**
POLLARD, Bt **EDB**; **LG1969**; *of King's Nympton* **LG1952**; *of Scarr Hall* **LG1921**; *of Haynford Hall* **LG1906**; *of Hundhill* **LG1875**; (*see also* Pollard-Urquhart)
POLLEN, Bt **PB1970**
WILLOCK-POLLEN *of Little Bookham* **LG1937**
POLLEXFEN (*see* Calmady)
POLLOCK (Hanworth, V) **PB1970**; Bt **PB1970**; Bt *of Kilbirney* **PB1885**; Bt *of Pollock* **EDB**; *of Erchfont Manor late of Avening* **LG1937**; *of Mountainstown* **LG1937Supp**
MONTAGU-POLLOCK, Bt **PB1970**
POLLOK *formerly of Lismany* **LGI1958** (*see also* Pollok-McCall)
POLTIMORE (*see* Bampfylde)
POLWARTH (*see* Hepburne-Scott)
POLWHELE *of Polwhele* **LG1952**; **AA**
POMEROY (Harberton, V) **PB1970**; *formerly of Beaminster* **DFUSA**; **PromFUSA**
POMFRET *of Mystole* **LG1952**; (*see also* Fermor)
PONSONBY (Bessborough, E) **PB1970**; (de Mauley) B) **PB1970**; (Ponsonby of Shulbrede, B) **PB1970**; (Sysonby, B)

POWYS WENWYNWYN (*Princes of*) RL
DICKSON-POYNDER (*see* Dickson)
POYNINGS, B **DEP**; (St John, of Basing, B **DEP**)
POYNTZ *of Tylston Lodge* **LG1965**
POYSER **FR**
PRAED (*see* Tyringham)
MACKWORTH-PRAED, Bt **PB1920**; *formerly of Mickleham* **LG1969**
PRAIN *of Mugdrum* **LG1965**
PRATT (Camden, M) **PB1970**; Bt **EDB**; *of Ryston* **LG1972; LG1937Supp; DFUSA;** *formerly of Stevenage* **DFUSA; FR;** (*see also* de Montmorency)
WESTBROOK-PRATT *of Woolston* **LG1952**
PRENDERGAST, Bt **EDB**; *late of Ardfinnan Castle* **LG1937Supp**; (*Australia*) **CG**
PRENTIS **DFUSA**
PRESCOTT, Bt **PB1970**; Bt *of Theobalds Park* **PB1959;** *of Bockleton Court* **LG1952;** *of Wilmslow* **LG1937;** *of Dalton Grange* **LG1921; FR**
PRESCOTT (*now* BRANDLE) *formerly of Arborfield Court* **LG1952**
DECIE-PRESCOTT (*see* Deasy)
PRESSWELL **LG1972**
PRESTIGE *formerly of Bourne Park* **LG1969**
PRESTON (Gormanston, V) **PB1970**; Bt **PB1970**; Bt *of Valleyfield* **PB1873**; (Tara, V) **DEP**; (Tara, V) **DEP**; Bt **EDB**; Bt *of Airdrie* **EDB**; *of Flasby Hall* **LG1952;** *of Moreby Hall* **LG1952;** *of Landford Manor* **LG1937;** *of Helgholme Hall* **LG1914;** *of Dalby Park* **LG1914;** *of Bellinter* **LG1875;** *of Cockerham* **LG1850/3;** *of Westderby Lower House* **LG1833/7; IFR1976;** (1) and (2) **DFUSA**; (*see also* Bell *of Askham Bryan*; Graham; and O'Callaghan)
PRESTON (*now* WILD) *of Warcop Hall* **LG1937**
CAMPBELL-PRESTON *of Ardchattan* **LG1952**
SHAW PRESTON (*formerly* SHAW) *of Bourton* **LG1952**
PRESTWICK, Bt **EDB**
PRETOR (*see* Pretor-Pinney)
PRETYMAN, Bt **EDB;** *of Orwell Park* **LG1965**
PREVOST, Bt **PB1970; PB1913;** *of Elfords* **LG1921**
MALLET-PREVOST **PromFUSA**
PREZIOSI, Count **TNBE1956**

PRICE, Bt **PB1970**; Bt *of Ardingly* **PB1963**; Bt *of Foxley* **PB1857**; Bt *of Newton* **EDB**; *of Abbots Morton Manor* **LG1952**; *of Tanglee* **LG1952**; *of Rhiwlas* **LG1952**; *of Tibberton Court* **LG1952**; *late of Culverwood* **LG1937**; *of Glynllech* **LG1937**; *of Greenstead Hall formerly of Glynllech* **LG1937**; *of Marks Hall* **LG1937**; *late of Tregate Castle* **LG1921**; *of Plâs Cadnant* **LG1914**; *of Waterhead House* **LG1906**; *of Broomfield Hall* **LG1898**; *of Triley Court* **LG1898**; *of Norton* **LG1875**; *of Glangwilly* **LG1875**; *of Castle Madock* **LG1858**; *of Birkenhead Priory* **LG1858**; **DFUSA**; *formerly of Shrewsbury* **DFUSA;** (*see also* Fountaine; and Price-Davies)
GREEN-PRICE, Bt **PB1970**
PERCEVAL-PRICE **IFR1976**
RUGGE-PRICE, Bt **PB1970**
PRICHARD *of Pwellywrach* **LG1972**
PRICHETT *formerly of Tunnymore* **DFUSA**
PRICKARD *of Dderw* **LG1952**
PRICKETT *formerly of Browston Hall* **LG1952**; *of Octon Lodge* **LG1833/7**; *of Bridlington* **AA**
PRIDE (*see* PRIDE-COLLINS)
PRIDEAUX, Bt **PB1875**; **LG1972**; (*see also* Prideaux-Brune)
PRIESTLEY *of Terrier's House* **LG1937**
PRIESTMAN, Bt **PB1940**; *of Slaley Hall formerly of Shotley Park* **LG1952**
PRIME *of Combrook House* **LG1894**; **DFUSA**
PRIMROSE (Rosebery, E) **PB1970**; Bt **PB1970**
PRINGLE, **PB1970**; Bt **EDB**; *of Whytbank* **LG1972**; *of Torwoodlee* **LG1952**; *of Farmhill and Elmhall* **LGI1899**; *of Thorncliffe* **LG1886**; *of Haining, Selkirk* **LG1863**
PRINSEP *of Glenbrook St Francis* **LG1952**
LEVETT-PRINSEP *late of Croxall Hall* **LG1937**
PRIOLEAU **DFUSA**
PRIOR *of Adstock Manor* **LG1952**; *formerly of Netherfield* **LG1952**; *of Rathdowney* **LG1863**
MURRAY-PRIOR **CG**
PRITCHARD *of Dolwcheorhyd* **LG1952**; *of Broseley* **LG1894**; *of Trescawen* **LG1894**
PRITT *of Rampsbeck* **LG1898**
PRITTIE (Dunalley, B) **PB1970**

PRIVETT *formerly of Crookley Park* **LG1952**
PROBERT *of Bevills* **LG1965**
PROBY, Bt **PB1970**; (Carysfort, B) **PB1909**; Bt **EDB**
PROBYN *late of Huntly Manor* **LG1937**
PROCTER *of Cowden Park, Allon* **LG1952**; *of Brockton* **LG1921**
PROCTOR *of Tullydoey* **LGI1958**
PRODGERS *of Garthmeilio, formerly of Ayot Bury* **LG1937**
PROFUMO *formerly of Avon Carrow* **LG1952**; B **FT1939**
PROGER *of Llanmaes* **LG1937**
WEGG-PROSSER *(now* CHICHESTER) *of Belmont* **LG1952**
PROTHERO (Ernle, B) **PB1937**; (*see also* Wiseman-Clarke)
PROUT **DFUSA**
PROWER *of Purton House* **LG1863**
PROWETT *of Oxfordshire* **LG1850/3**
PRUDHOE (*see* Percy)
PRUSSIA (*Royal House of*) **RL**
PRYCE, Bt **EDB**; *of Cyfronydd* **LG1937**; (*see also* Bury)
BRUCE-PRYCE (*see* Bruce *of Blaen-y-Cym*)
PRYKE, Bt **PB1970**
DE LA PRYME **FR**
PRYOR *formerly of Bentworth Hall* **LG1965**; *of Weston* **LG1965**; **DFUSA**
PRYSE, Bt *of Gogerddan* **PB1959**; Bt *of Gogarthen* **EDB**
WEBLEY-PARRY-PRYSE *of Noyadd Trefawr and formerly of Paro-y-gors* **LG1937**
PRYTHERCH *of Abergole* **LG1863**
PUCKERING, Bt **EDB**
PUDSEY (*see* Littledale)
THORN-PUDSEY (*formerly* ASTON-PUDSEY) *of Seisdon Hall* **LG1952**
PUGH *of Hatching Green House formerly of Abermad* **LG1965**; *formerly of Llanedy* **LG1965**; *of Manoravon* **LG1879**; *of Llanerchydol* (*see* Lovell)
GORDON-PUGH (*see* Gordon)
STORIE-PUGH (*see* Pugh *formerly of Llanedy*)
PUGSLEY **DFUSA; CG**
PULLEINE (*now* CURZON-HOWE) *of Crakehall and Clifton Castle* **LG1937**
GILES-PULLER *formerly of Youngsbury* **LG1952**
PULLEY, Bt **PB1901**
PULLING *formerly of Whitestone House* **LG1972**

PULTENEY (Bath, E) **DEP**; (*see also* Fawcett)
PUMPHREY *formerly of Hindley Hall* **LG1969**
PUNCH **IFR1976**
PURBRECK (*see* Villiers)
PURCELL *of Albert House* **LG1937Supp**; *of Ashton* **LG1937Supp**; **IFR1976**; **DFUSA**; *of Burton Park* (*see* Ryan-Purcell)
RYAN-PURCELL **IFR1976**
CHAPMAN-PURCHAS **LG1969**
PURDON **IFR1976**
PUREFOY, Bt **EDB**; *of Shalstone* **LG1952**
BAGWELL-PUREFOY *formerly of Greenfields* **LGI1958**
PURNELL *of Staverton* **LG1894**; *of Kingshill* **LG1863**; (*see also* Brodribb)
PURNELL (*now* PURNELL-EDWARDS) *of Stancombe Park* **LG1921**
PURTON *late of Faintree Hall* **LG1937**
PURVES (*see* Campbell)
PURVIS *of Kinaldy* **LG1952**; *of Earlshall* **LG1937**; *of Darsham* **LG1863**
BOUVERIE-PUSEY (*see* Fletcher *of Saltoun*)
PUTLAND (*see* Neligan) **LGI1912**
PUTNAM *formerly of Aston Abbots* **DFUSA**
PUTT, Bt **EDB**
PUXLEY *of Llethr Lestri and Welford Park* **LG1972**; (*see also* Wroughton)
PYBUS, Bt **PB1935**
PYDDOKE *formerly of the Austins* **LG1937**
PYE, Bt *of Hone* **EDB**; Bt *of Lekhampstead* **EDB**; **LG1969**; *formerly of Blythe* **LG1952**; *late of Clifton Hall* **LG1921**; *formerly of Quernmore* **DFUSA**; (*see also* Alington)
PYEMONT *formerly of The Grove* **LG1921**
PYKE *of Elswick Manor formerly of Thistleton Lodge* **LG1952**; (*see also* Pyke-Nott)
PYM, Bt **EDB**; *of Hazell Hall* **LG1965**
PYMAN *of Netherclay House* **LG1952**
PYNE *of East Downe Manor* **LG1952**; *of Northbrook* **LG1921**; *sometime of East Down* **DFUSA**
PYNSENT, Bt **EDB**
PYRKE *of Deane Hall* **LG1898**
PYTCHES *of The Little Grange* **LG1937**
PYTTS (*see* Childe *of Kinley*; and Baldwyn-Childe)
QUAIN, Bt **PB1898**

QUANTOCK *of Norton House* **LG1863; HI**
QUARLES **DFUSA;** *(see also* Back)
QUAYLE *of Clogga* **LG1937**
QUEENSBERRY *(see* Douglas)
QUEENSBOROUGH *(see* Paget)
QLEJJGHA, B **TNBE1956**
QUEROUAILLE (Portsmouth, D) **DEP**
QUIBELL, B **PB1959**
QUICKE *of Newton St Cyres* **LG1965**
QUICKSWOOD *(see* Gasgoyne-Cecil)
QUILTER, Bt **PB1970;** *of Belstead House* **LG1937**
QUIN *of Ballinacourty* **LG1937Supp**
WYNDHAM-QUIN (Dunraven and Mountearl, E) **PB1970;** (Kenry, B) **PB1926**
QUINCHANT *(see* Kinchant)
QUINCY (Winchester, E) **DEP**
QUINNELL *formerly of Edenburn* **LGI1958**
RABETT *late of Bramfield Hall* **LG1937; AA**
RABY *(see* Reibey)
RADCLIFFE, V **PB1970;** Bt **PB1970;** (Derwentwater, E) **DEP;** *formerly of Tuesley Court* **LG1969;** *of Warleigh* **LG1969;** *formerly of Bag Park* **LG1965;** *of Beverley House* **LG1952;** *formerly of Hurleston* **LG1937;** *of Tinnakilly* **LG1879;** *(see also* Thomas *of The Poolfold)*
DELMÉ-RADCLIFFE *of Hitchin Priory* **LG1952**
FARNABY-RADCLIFFE *(see* Farnaby)
RADCLYFFE, Bt **EDB;** *of Lew* **LG1972;** *of Little Park* **LG1921**
MOTT-RADCLYFFE *of Barningham Hall* **LG1972**
RADFORD *formerly of Rockbeare* **DFUSA;** *(see also* Radford-Norcop)
RADNOR *(see* Pleydell-Bouverie; and Roberts)
RADSTOCK *(see* Waldegrave)
RAE, Bt **PB1840**
RAEBURN, Bt **PB1970**
RAFF *(Australia)* **CG**
RAFFLES *formerly of High Wood* **LG1952;** *of Liverpool* **HI**
RAGLAN *(see* Somerset)
RAGLAND *(see* Judd)
RAIKES *of Llwynegryn* **LG1952;** *of Treberfydd* **LG1952;** *of Bennington* **LG1925**
RAINCOCK *(see* Fleming)
RAINES *of Wyton* **LG1863**

RAINSFORD *formerly of Tew Magna* **DFUSA; PromFUSA**
RAIT *(now* LINDSAY-CARNEGIE) *of Anniston* **LG1921**
RALLI, Bt **PB1970**
RALSTON *(Australia)* **CG;** *of Hampden* **CG**
RAM **IFR1976**
RAMACCA (Newburgh, E) **PB1970**
RAMAGE **DFUSA**
RAMBAUT *of Etton* **LG1965**
RAMSAY (Dalhousie, E) **PB1970;** Bt *of Balmain* **PB1970;** Bt *of Bamff* **PB1970;** (Holderness, E) **DEP;** (Bothwell, Lord of) **DEP;** Bt *of Abbotshall* **EDB;** Bt *of Whitehill* **EDB;** *late of Croughton Park* **LG1937;** *of Howletts* **LG1937;** *of Kildalton* **LG1921;** *of Hill Lodge* **LG1863;** *of Barnton* **LG1863;** *formerly of Chester-le-Street* **DFUSA;** *of Barra (see* Forbes Irvine); *(see also* Dix Hamilton)
WARDLAW-RAMSAY *formerly of Whitehill* **LG1952**
RAMSBOTHAM (Soulbury, V) **PB1970;** *of Crowborough Warren* **LG1937**
RAMSDEN, B **PB1953;** *of Old Sleningford Hall* **LG1965;** *of the Jumples* **LG1952;** *late of Siddinghurst* **LG1937;** *of Chadwick Manor* **LG1900;** *(see also* Horton-Fawkes)
PENNINGTON-RAMSDEN, Bt **PB1970**
RAMSEY **DFUSA**
RANCHHODLAL, Bt **PB1970**
RANCLIFFE *(see* Parkyns)
RAND (1) & (2) **DFUSA**
RANDALL *of Blacklands* **LG1952;** *of Haldon Grange* **LG1952**
RANDOLPH (Moray, E) **DEP;** *formerly of Biddenden* **LG1972;** *formerly of Kimpton Lodge* **LG1952;** *formerly of Sheen House* **LG1952;** *of Eastcourt* **LG1937; DFUSA;** *(see also* Jefferson)
RANELAGH *(see* Jones)
RANFURLY *(see* Knox)
RANK, B **PB1970**
RANKEILLOUR *(see* Hope)
RANKIN, Bt **PB1970;** Bt *of Broughton Tower* **PB1959;** *of Auchengray* **LG1937;** *of Broughton Tower* **LG1937; DFUSA**
RANKINE *(see* Campbell *of Kilberry)*
RANKSBOROUGH *(see* Brocklehurst)
RANNIE *of Conheath* **LG1898**
RANSOM *(now* WITHERSPOON) **DFUSA**
RANTOUL **DFUSA**
RAPER *(see* Brooksbank *of Lamplugh)*

LAMPLUGH-RAPER (*see* Brooksbank *of Lamplugh*)
RAPHAEL, Bt **PB1924**
RASBOTHAM *of Ebnal Grange* **LG1937**
RASCH, Bt **PB1970**; *of Woodhill* **LG1898**
RASHLEIGH, Bt **PB1970**; *of Menabilly* **LG1965**
RATCLIFF *of Black Notley Hall* **LG1952**; *of Wyddrington* **AA**
RATCLIFFE (Sussex, E) **DEP**
RATHBONE *formerly of Greenbank* **LG1952**; (*see also Rathborne*)
RATHBORNE **IFR1976**
RATHCAVAN (*see* O'Neill)
RATHCREEDAN (*see* Norton)
RATHDONNELL (*see* McClintock-Bunbury)
RATHDOWNE (*see* Monck)
RATHMORE (*see* Plunket)
RATTRAY *of Rattray* **LG1972**; *of Barford House* **LG1863**
RAVENEL **PromFUSA**
RAVENSDALE (*see* Mosley)
RAVENSHAW *of Fulham* **LG1937**
RAVENSWORTH (*see* Liddell)
RAWDON (Hastings, M) **DEP**
GREEN-EMMOTT-RAWDON (*see* Green-Emmott)
RAWLINGS *formerly of Padstow* **LG1952**; *formerly of Southwark* **DFUSA**
RAWLINS *formerly of Stoke Courcy* **LG1969**
RAWLINS (*formerly* BATES HARBIN) *of Newton Surmaville* **LG1969**
RAWLINSON, Bt **PB1970**; B **PB1925**; *of Duddon Hall* **LG1898**; *of Graythwaite* **LG1863**; *of New Place, Alresford* **LG1850/3**; *of Graythwaite co Lancaster* **AA**
RAWNSLEY *of Well Vale* **LG1972**
RAWORTH *of St John's Manor* **LG1937**
RAWSON (Clontarfe, V) **DEP**; *of Sowerby* **LG1972**; *of the Haugh End and Mill House* **LG1952**; *of Gravenhurst* **LG1921**; **IFR1976**; *formerly of Langley Marish* **DFUSA**; **FR**; **CG**
TRAFFORD-RAWSON *of Nidd Hall* (*see* Trafford *of Hill Court*)
RAWSTORNE *formerly of Balderstone Grange* **LG1965**; *of Penwortham* **LG1937**
RAYER *formerly of Holcombe Court* **LG1952**
RAYLEIGH (*see* Strutt)
RAYMOND, B **DEP**; *of Belchamp Hall* **LG1972**; *of Symondsbury* **LG1863**; *of Kilmurry* **LG1863**; (*see also* Penoyre)

RAYNER *of Chievely Manor* **LG1937**; *late of Worthenbury Manor* **LG1937**
PRITCHARD-RAYNER *of Trescawen* **LG1937**
RAYNEY, Bt **EDB**
RAYNSFORD *of Milton Malsor* **LG1972**
REA, B **PB1970**; *of Berrington House* **LG1952**; *formerly of Drumskee* **LGI1958**
READ *of Barton Bendish* **LG1921**; *of Honynghamthorpe* **LG1894**; *of Hayton* **LG1863**; **DFUSA**
CREWE-READ **LG1965**
RUDSTON-READ (*see* Calverley-Rudston)
READE, Bt **PB1970**; Bt **EDB**; *of Ipsden* **LG1972**; *of Crowe Hall* **LG1952**; *of Carncairn Lodge* **LGI1958**; (*see also* Hibbert of Woodpark)
READHEAD, Bt **PB1970**
READING, Bt **EDB**; (*see also* Rufus Isaacs)
READSHEW (*see* Morley)
REAVELY *of Kinnersley Castle* **LG1937**
REAY *of Gill House, co Cumberland* **LG1850/3**; (*see also* Mackay)
GURDON-REBOW *of Wyvenhoe* **LG1921**
RECKITT, Bt **PB1940**; *of The Elms, Roose* **LG1952**
REDDAWAY *of Winmarleigh Hall* **LG1937**
REDE *of Ashmuns* **LG1863**
REDESDALE (*see* Freeman-Mitford)
MILNE-REDHEAD *formerly of Springfield and Holden Clough* **LG1952**
REDINGTON *of Kilcornan* **LG1899**
REDMAYNE, B **PB1970**
REDMOND (*now* GREEN) **IFR1976**; *of Popefield* (*see also* **LG1937Supp**)
REDWOOD, Bt **PB1970**; *of Boverton* **LG1858**; *of Boverton, co Glamorgan* **AA**
REED *of The Cragg* **LG1969**; *of Sidbury Hall* **LG1965**; *of Heathpool and Hoppen* **LG1863**
REES, Bt **PB1970**; *of Killymaenllwyd* **LG1879**; *formerly of Llanelly* **DFUSA**; (*see also* de Ferry)
REEVE, Bt **EDB**; *of Leadenham* **LG1972**; *of Colne Park* **LG1894**
REEVES *of Besborough* **LGI1912**; *of Danemore Park* **LG1914**; *formerly of Blandford* **DFUSA**; **DFUSA**
REGISTER **DFUSA**
REIBEY **CG**
REICHEL *of A la Ronde* **LG1937**

REID, B **PB1970**; Bt *of Ellon* **PB1970**; Bt *of Springburn* **PB1970**; Bt *of Rademon* **PB1939**; (Loreburn, E) **PB1923**; Bt *of Barra* **PB1885**; *of Robertland* **LG1969**; *of Thorpe Mandeville* **LG1952**; *of Ardmeallie* **LG1898**; **LGI1912**; *of Elderslie* **CG**; *of Hokitika* **CG**; *of Ratho* **CG**; (*see also* Fenwick *of Burrow Hall*; and Durdin-Robertson)

PELHAM-REID (*see* Keane)

ROBERTSTON-REID *of Gatlowflat* **LG1898**

REILLY *of Scarvagh* **LGI1912** (*see also* More O'Ferrall)

REITH, B **PB1970**

REITMEYER (*see* Calburn)

REMINGTON *formerly of Melling* **LG1952**; **DFUSA**

REMNANT, B **PB1970**

RENALS, Bt **PB1970**

RENDALL *formerly of Tidcombe* **LG1952**; (*see also* Clarke)

RENDEL, B **PB1913**

RENDLESHAM (*see* Thellusson)

RENNELL (*see* Rodd)

GRANT-RENNICK **LG1972**

RENNIE *of Osmington House* **LG1952**; *of Frensham Vale* **LG1898**

RENNY *of Panbride House* **LG1952**

RENSHAW, Bt **PB1970**

RENTON *of Thaxted* **LG1952**

CAMPBELL-RENTON *of Mordington* **LG1952**

RENWICK, B **PB1970**; Bt **PB1970**; *of Holystone Grange* **LG1937**; (Australia) **CG**

REPINGTON *of Amington* **LG1833/7**

RERESBY, Bt **EDB**; *of Thrybergh* **VF**

REUSS (Princes) **RL**

JELF-REVELEY *of Bryn-y-gwyn* **LG1952**

REVELSTOKE (*see* Baring)

SMITH-REWSE **CG**

REYNARD *of Sunderlandwick* **LG1952**

BIRCH REYNARDSON *of Adwell House* **LG1972**

ACLAND-HOOD-REYNARDSON (*see* Birch Reynardson)

REYNELL, Bt **EDB**; *of Newton Abbot* **LG1850/3**; *of London* **LG1850/3**; *of Malston* **LG1850/3**; *of Laleham and Shepperton* **LG1850/3**; *of Ogwell* **LG1833/7**; *of Killymon* **LGI1912**: *of Montecillo* **CG**

REYNOLDS, Bt **PB1970**; **PB1896**; *of Ardachy Horoe* **LG1972**; *of Haslemere* **LG1952**; *of Lurley* **LG1952**; *of The*

Mullens **LG1937Supp**; *of Norfolk and Devon* **LG1863**

RHAYADER (*see* Leif-Jones)

RHINELANDER **PromFUSA**

RHOADES *of Lower Close* **LG1937**

RHOADS *formerly of Winegreaves* **DFUSA**

RHODES, B **PB1970**; Bt **PB1970**; *late of Brockhampton Park* **LG1937**; *of Hennerton* **LG1937**; *of Bellair and Chapwick* **LG1863**; *formerly of Great Houghton* **DFUSA**; (*see also* Kindersley (*formerly* Darwin))

PARKER-RHODES *of Finningley Park* **LG1937**

RHONDDA (*see* Thomas)

RHYS (Dynevor, B) **PB1970**

RIALL *of Ballyorney House* **LGI1958**

RIBBLESDALE (*see* Lister)

RIBTON, Bt **PB1901**

RICARDO *formerly of Gatcombe House* **LG1972**

RICE *of Dane Court* **LG1952**; *of Bushmount* **LGI1912**; *of Loughor* **LG1863**; **DFUSA**; *formerly of Berkhampstead* **DFUSA**

PRICE-RICE *of Llwyn-y-brain* **LG1952**

SPRING RICE (Monteagle of Brandon, B) **PB1970**

TALBOT RICE (*see* Dynevor)

VAUGHAN-PRICE-RICE (*see* Price-Rice)

RICH, Bt **PB1970**; Bt *of Sunning* **PB1869**; (Holland, E) **DEP**; (Warwick, E) **DEP**; Bt *of London* **EDB**; Bt *of Sunning* **EDB**; **DFUSA**; (*see also* Bostock)

RICHARDES (*now* NAPIER) *of Bryneithin* **LG1937**

RICHARDS (Milverton, B) **PB1970**; Bt **EDB**; *of Gawsworth* **LG1972**; *of Caerynwch* **LG1969**; *of Macclesfield* **LG1952**; *of Solsborough* **LGI1912**; *of Monksgrange* **LGI1912**; *of Ardamine* **LGI1912**; *of Macmine Castle* **LGI1912**; (1) & (2) **DFUSA**; **FR**; *of Croft House, co Pembroke* **AA**

RICHARDSON, Bt *of Eccleshall* **PB1970**; Bt *of Weybridge* **PB1970**; Bt *of Yellow Woods* **PB1970**; (Cramond, Lord) **DEP**; *formerly of Glanbrydan Park* **LG1969**; *formerly of Hitchin* **LG1952**; *formerly of Kirkleavington Grange* **LG1952**; *of Park Hall, Aislaby* **LG1952**; *formerly of Potto Hall* **LG1952**; *of Longbridge Manor* **LG1937**; *of Capenhurst Hall* **LG1921**; *of Shotley* **LG1921**; *of Sneaton Castle* **LG1921**; *of Aber-*

hirnant **LG1858**; *of Findon Place* **LG1858**; *of Riccall Hall* **LG1858**; **IFR1976**; *formerly of Poplar Vale* **LG1958**; *of Lisburn* **LGI1912**; **PromFUSA**; **FR** (*Victoria, Australia*) **CG**
STEWART-RICHARDSON, Bt **PB1970**; **DFUSA**
RICHEY **CG**
RICHMOND, Bt **PB1970**; *of Kincairney* **LG1965**; (*see also* de Dreux; Fitz-Roy; Stewart; and Tudor)
RICHMOND AND GORDON (*see* Gordon-Lennox)
RICKABY *of Ulrome, co York* **LG1850/3**
RICKARD *formerly of Hand Park* **DFUSA**
RICKARDS *formerly of Woodside* **LG1965**; *of South Hill* **LG1952**
RICKETTS, Bt **PB1970**; *formerly of Twyford, Hants* **LG1965**; *of Coombe* **LG1850/3**; (*see also* Tempest)
RICKMAN *of South Hill Park* **LG1937**
RICKS **DFUSA**
RIDDELL, Bt *of Riddell* **PB1970**; Bt *of Walton Heath* **PB1934**; Bt *of Ardnamurchan* **PB1907**; *of Felton and Swinburne* **LG1972**; *formerly of Bullymeuth* **DFUSA**; (*see also* Lister)
THORNE-RIDER **DFUSA**
RIDGELY (1) & (2) **DFUSA**
RIDGEWAY (Londonderry, E) **DEP**; Bt **EDB**
RIDGWAY *formerly of Blenheim and Riverview House* **LGI1958**; *of Hittisleigh* **LG1952**; *of Wallsuches* **LG1886**
RIDLEY, V **PB1970**; *of Park End* **LG1952**; *of The Elms* **LG1937**
RIDOUT (*Canada*) (1) & (2) **CG**
RIGBY, Bt **PB1970**; *of The Rookery* **LG1965**
RIGG *formerly of Burnley* **DFUSA**
RIGGALL *of The Great Meadow* **LG1965**
RIGGE *of Wood Broughton* (*see* Grayrigge)
RIGGS **DFUS**
RILAND (*see* Riland-Bedford *of Sutton Coldfield*)
RILEY *of La Trinité* **LG1969**; *formerly of Hamstall Ridware* **LG1952**; *of Brearley House and Putley Court* **LG1921**; *of Forest Hill, Berks* **LG1875**
RIMINGTON (*see* Rimington-Wilson)
RINGROSE (*see* Ringrose-Voase)
RIPARIIS, B **DEP**
RIPLEY, Bt **PB1970**
RIPON (*see* Robinson)
RIPPON *of Waterville* **LG1863**; **FR**

RISLEY (*fomerly* GORDON) *formerly of Manar* **LG1952**
RITCHIE (Ritchie of Dundee, B) **PB1970**; Bt **PB1970**; Bt *of Highlands* **PB1912**; *formerly of West Burton* **LG1969**
MacIVER RITCHIE *of Ardlarach* **LG1937**
RIVERDALE (*see* Balfour)
RIVERS, Bt *of Chafford* **PB1870**; (*see also* Savage; and Widvile)
PITT-RIVERS (Rivers, B) **DEP**
FOX-PITT-RIVERS *of Hinton St Mary and Tollard Royal* **LG1972**
RIVERSDALE (*see* Tonson)
ALCOCK-STAWELL-RIVERSDALE (*see* Stawell)
RIVIERE **LG1965**
RIVINGTON *of Appleby* **LG1921**
RIVIS *of Newstead House* **LG1921**
ROBARTES Bt **EBD**; *of Lanhydrock* **LG1863**; (*see also* Roberts)
AGAR-ROBARTES (Clifden, V) **PB1970**
ROBARTS *of Lillingstone Lovell* **LG1969**
ROBB **IFR1976**; (*see also* Johnson)
ROBBINS, B **PB1970**; *of Castle Malwood* **LG1863**; **DFUSA**
ROBENS, B **PB1970**
ROBERT **DFUSA**
ROBERTHALL (*see* Hall)
ROBERTS (Clwyd, B) **PB1970**; Bt *of Eccleshall* **PB1970**; Bt *of Glassenbury and Brightfieldstown* **PB1970**; Bt *of Milner Field* **PB1970**; E **PB1953**; Bt *of Martholme* **PB1949**; Bt *of Bow* **EDB**; Bt *of Glassenbury* **EDB**; Bt *of Willesdon* **EDB**; *formerly of Caer Penrhos* **LG1969**; *formerly of Coeddû* **LG1952**; *of Dorsington Manor* **LG1952**; *of Hollingside* **LG1952**; *of Upland Hall* **LG1952**; *of Trethill* **LG1937**; *of Plâs-yn-rhiw* **LG1894**; *of Milford Haven* **LG1863**; **IFR1976**; *formerly of Mount Rivers* **LGI1958**; *of Dormstown Castle* **LGI1912**; *of Kilmoney* **LGI1912**; (1) (2) & (3) **DFUSA**; **FR**; (*NSW, Australia*) (1) & (2) **CG**; *of Woodrising* **CG**
ATKIN-ROBERTS (*see* Nettelbladt-Roberts)
BEOR-ROBERTS *of Glyn Celyn* **LG1952**
CRAMER-ROBERTS *formerly of Sallymount* **LGI1958**
CROMPTON-ROBERTS *of Drybridge* **LG1906**
LLOYD-ROBERTS *of Plâs Glanafon formerly of Brynysguboriau and Amnodd Wên* **LG1969**

NETTELBLADT-ROBERTS *of Glassenbury Park* **LG1952**
ROBERSTON (Robertson of Oakridge, B) **PB1970**; (Lochee, B) **PB1911**; B **PB1909**; Bt **EDB**; *of Crogen* **LG1972**; *of Struan* **LG1972**; *of Bragleenmore* **LG1969**; *of Colton* **LG1952**; *of Newmore* **LG1952**; *of Orchardton* **LG1952**; *of Glenview* **LG1952Supp**; *of Palé and Llantysilio* **LG1937**; *of Kindeace* **LG1921**; *of Widmerpool* **LG1921**; *of Tulliebelton and Ballathie* **LG1879**; *of Chilcote* **LG1879**; *of Lushes* **LG1875**; *of Hazel Hill* **LG1875**; (1) (2) & (3) **DFUSA**; *formerly of Dunoon* **DFUSA**; *formerly of Edinburgh* **DFUSA**; *formerly of Huntly* **DFUSA**; **PromFUSA**; (*Victoria, Australia*) **CG**; *of Huntington Castle* (*see* Durdin-Robertson); *of Muirton and Gledney* (*see* Williamson *of Lawers*); *of Prenderguest* (*see* Glasgow); (*see also* Robertson-MacDonald)
ASKEW - ROBERTSON *of Pallinsburn* **LG1921**
DESPENCER-ROBERTSON *of Wilbury Park* **LG1937**
DUNDAS ROBERTSON *formerly of Auchleeks* **LG1972**
DURDIN-ROBERTSON **IFR1976**
FORBES-ROBERTSON *of Chardwar* **LG1952**
HASTIE-ROBERTSON *of Gossaburgh* **LG1937**
HOME-ROBERTSON (*formerly* MILNE-HOME) *of Wedderburn and Paxton* **LG1952**
STEWART-ROBERTSON (*see* Stewart-Meiklejohn)
LEMPRIERE-ROBIN *of Rosel* **LG1972**
ROBINS, B **PB1959**; **DFUSA**; *formerly of Upton and Long Buckby* **DFUSA**
ROBINSON (Martonmere, B) **PB1970**; Bt *of Hawthornden* **PB1970**; Bt *of London* **PB1970**; Bt *of Toronto* **PB1970**; B **PB1949**; Bt *of Batts House* **PB1940**; (Rosmead, B) **PB1933**; (Ripon, M) **PB1923**; (Rokeby, B) **PB1883**; (Rokeby, B) **DEP**; Bt *of Kentwall Hall* **EDB**; Bt *of Newby* **EDB**; *formerly of Poston* **LG1972**; *of Hinxton* **LG1969**; *of Chatburn* **LG1952**; *of Knapton* **LG1952**; *of Moorwood* **LG1952**; (*formerly* PARKINSON) *of Ravendale Hall* **LG1952**; *of Mill House* **LG1937**; *late of Reedley Hall* **LG1937**; *of Roos Hall* **LG1937**; *of Rothley Grange* **LG1937**; *formerly of Worksop Manor* **LG1937**; *of Lynhales*

LG1921; *of Silksworth* **LG1921**; *of Poston Court* **LG1900**; *of Denston Hall* **LG1894**; *of Sudley, co Lancaster* **LG1850/3**; *of Guersfelt* **LG1833/37**; *of Hull* **LG1833/7**; *formerly of Boston* **DFUSA**; **PromFUSA**; **FR**; (*Australia*) **CG**; (*New Zealand*) **CG**; (*see also* Best *late of Silksworth*; Burton *of Cherry Burton*; Robinson-Douglas; Evans *of Lovesgrove*; and Garnett-Orme)
ROBINSON (*formerly* PARKINSON) *of Ravendale Hall* **LG1952**
ELLIS-ROBINSON *formerly of Begbroke, Kidlington and Yarnton* **LG1972**
GAVIN ROBINSON (*see* Robinson *formerly of Poston*)
LYNCH-ROBINSON, Bt **PB1970**
RAINEY-ROBINSON **LGI1912**
STEWART-ROBINSON (*see* Stewart-Meiklejohn)
ROBOROUGH (*see* Lopes)
ROBSART, B **DEP**
ROBSON, B **PB1917**; *of Addyheugh Lodge* **LG1952**; *of Holtby* **LG1875**
ROCH *of Woodbine Hill* **LGI1958**; *of Maesgwyn* **LG1937**; *of Butter Hill* **LG1858**; **FR**
ROCHDALE (*see* Kemp)
ROCHE (Fermoy, B) **PB1970**; Bt **PB1970**; B **PB1956**; V **DEP**; Bt **EDB**; (*now* WARNER) *formerly of Ardeer* **LG1952**; (*formerly* JONES) *of Ynysfor* **LG1952**; *of Granagh Castle and Rye Hill* **LGI1912**
ROCHESTER (*see* Hyde; Lamb; and Wilmot)
ROCHFORD (*see* Nassau)
ROCHFORT (Belvedere, E) **DEP**; *of Rochfort Bridge* **LGI1912**; *of Cloughgrenane* **LGI1912**
BOYD-ROCHFORT **IFR1976**
ROCHEAD, Bt **EDB**
ROCKE *of Clungunford House* **LG1952**
ROCKINGHAM (*see* Watson; and Wentworth)
ROCKLEY (*see* Cecil)
RODD (Rennell, B) **PB1970**; *of Crapstone House* **LG1952**; *formerly of Treburtha* **LG1952**; *of Turnworth House* **LG1937**
RODDAM *of Roddam* **LG1969**
RODEN (*see* Jocelyn)
RODES, Bt **EDB**; *of Barlborough* **LG1886**
RODGER *of Hadlow Castle* **LG1898**
RODGERS, Bt **PB1970**; **DFUSA**
RODICK **DFUSA**; *of Gateacre* **HI**
RODNEY, B **PB1970**

RODOCANACHI **LG1969**
RODON *of Vere in the Island of Jamaica* **LG1879**
HUNTER-RODWELL *of Woodlands* **LG1969**
ROE, B **PB1923**; Bt **PB1866**; *of Ballyconnell House* **LGI1912**; *of Loran Park* **LGI1912**; *of Gnaton Hall* **LG1875**
ROGERS (Blackford, B) **PB1889**; *of Ellary, formerly of Coltishall Hall* **LG1972**; *of Penrose* **LG1969**; *of the Bramblings, Rustington* **LG1952**; *of Nanslow* **LG1937**; *of Rainscombe Park* **LG1937**; *of River Hill* **LG1937**; *of Lota* **LG1863**; (1) (2) & (3) **DFUSA**; *of Society Hill* **DFUSA**
BURCHAM ROGERS (*see* Rogers *of Ellary*)
COLTMAN-ROGERS *of Stanage Park* **LG1969**
COXWELL-ROGERS *of Rossley Manor* **LG1969**
WRIGHT-ROGERS *of Yarlington* **LG1937**
ROGERSON *of Gillesbie* **LG1914**
ROHDE *of Ranfold Grange* **LG1952**
ROKEBY, Bt **EDB**; *late of Arthingworth* **LG1937**; (*see also* Robinson)
ROLFE (Cranworth, B) **DEP**; *of Heacham* **HI**
BOGGIS-ROLFE **FR**; (*see also* Boggis)
NEVILLE-ROLFE *formerly of Heacham* **LG1972**
ROLL, Bt **PB1970**
ROLLASON *formerly of Hampton Manor* **LG1952**
ROLLE, B **DEP**
ROLLESTON, Bt **PB1940**; *of Watnall* **LG1937**; *of Saltford House* **LG1921**; **IFR1976**; (*New Zealand*) **CG**
ROLLO, B **PB1970**
ROLLS (Llangattock, B) **PB1916**; *of Banstead House* **LG1921**; *of The Hendre* **LG1886**
ROLT *of Ozleworth Park and Misenden Park* **LG1875**; **FR**
BAYNTUNN-ROLT, Bt **EDB**
ROMANIS *of Hurtmore* **LG1952**
ROMARE (Lincoln, E) **DEP**
ROMER, B **PB1940**
ROMILLY, B **PB1970**; *of Huntington Park* **LG1965**
ROMNEY (*see* Marsham; and Sydney)
RONALD (*Australia*) **CG**
ROOKE *of Bigsweir House* **LG1952**; *of The Ivy* **LG1921**; **LGI1958**
ROOKWOOD (*see* Selwyn-Ibbetson)

ROOME *late of Lota* **LG1898**
ROOPER *formerly of Abbot's Ripton* **LG1972**
ROOS (*see* Ros)
ROOSEVELT **PresFUSA**
ROOTES, B **PB1970**
ROPER (Baltinglass, V) **DEP**; *of Forde Abbey* **LG1952**; *of The Grove* **LG1914**; *formerly of Hazlebrook* **LGI1958**; *of Rathgar and Lackagh* **LGI1912**
TREVOR-ROPER (*see* Roper-Curzon)
ROPNER, Bt *of Preston Hall* **PB1970**; Bt *of Thorp Perrow* **PB1970**
ROS (Ros, B) **DEP**; (Ros, of Werke, B) **DEP**
ROSBOROUGH (*see* Crozier)
ROSCOE (*formerly* Townsend) *of Clifton Manor* **LG1952**
ROSCOMMON (*see* Dillon)
ROSE, Bt *of Hardwick House* **PB1970**; Bt *of Leith* **PB1970**; Bt *of Montreal* **PB1970**; Bt *of Rayners* **PB1970**; (Strathnairn, B) **PB1885**; *of Holme* **LG1969**; *of Leweston* **LG1969**; *of Worth Court* **LG1952**; *of Auchernach* **LG1937**; *of Wolston Grange* **LG1921**; *of The Ferns* **LG1898**; *of Cransley Hall* **LG1886**; *of Leiston Old Abbey* **LG1863**; *of Glastullick* **LG1863**; *of Ahabey and Foxhall* **LGI1912**; **FR**; (*see also* Rose-Innes; Ross; Thomas; and Trippe)
ROSE (*formerly* HAYWARD) **DFUSA**
LANG-ROSE (*see* Rose *of Holme*)
ROSEBERY (*see* Primrose)
ROSKELL *of Gatacre* **LG1850/3**
ROSMEAD (*see* Robinson)
ROSS, Bt **PB1970**; Bt *of Dunmoyle* **PB1958**; Bt *of Carstairs* **PB1940**; Lord **DEP**; *of Cromarty* **LG1972**; *of Pitcalnie* **LG1898**; *late of Netherley* **LG1894**; *of Dalton* **LG1863**; *of Dunmoyle* **LGI1912**; (*Australia*) **CG**; *of Westfield House* **CG**; (*see also* Boyle; de Ros; Gore; Ross-Hume; and Stewart)
ROSS-OF-BLADENSBURG *of Rostrevor* **LGI1912**
GROVE-ROSS *of Invercharron* **LG1886**
LEITH-ROSS *of Arnage* **LG1952**
ROBERTSON-ROSS *of Glenmoidart* **LG1894**
TRELAWNY-ROSS *of Fulford Grange formerly of Ham* **LG1952**
ROSSE (*see* Parsons)
ROSSIE (*see* Kinnaird)
ROSSITER **DFUSA**

ROSSLYN (*see* St Clair-Erskine) **PB1970**
ROSSMORE (*see* Westenra)
ROTHBAND, Bt **PB1940**
ROTHE *late of Mount Rothe* **LGI1912**
ROTHERHAM *formerly of Crossdrum* **LGI1958**; (*see also* Holland)
ROTHERMERE (*see* Harmsworth)
ROTHERWICK (*see* Cayzer)
ROTHERY *of Littlethorpe* **LG1879**
ROTHES (*see* Leslie)
ROTHSCHILD, B **PB1970**
ROTHWELL, Bt **EDB**; *of Morebath Manor* **LG1952**; *of Rockfield* **LGI1912**; *formerly of Newchurch* **DFUSA**; *of Sharples Hall* **AA**
ROUGHSEDGE *of Foxghyll* **LG1863**
ROUGHT-ROUGHT *of Viking Lodge* **LG1952**
ROUMANIA (*Royal House of*) **RL**
ROUND *of Birch Hall* **LG1965**; *of Tipton* **LG1898**
TURNER-ROUND (*see* Round)
ROUNDELL *of Dorfold Hall formerly of. Gledstone* **LG1965**; **AA**
ROUNDWAY (*see* Colston)
ROUPELL *formerly of Charlton* **LG1952**; *of Loddon* **LG1875**
ROUS (Stradbroke, E) **PB1970**; *of Courtyrala* **LG1879**
ROUSE, Bt **EDB**; *formerly of Halton* **LG1952**; *of Woodbridge* **LG1952**
ROWALLAN (*see* Corbett)
ROWAN *of Mount Davys* **LGI1912**; **DFUSA**; (*Australia*) **CG**
CONAL ROWAN *of Meiklewood* **LG1952**
HAMILTON ROWAN (*see* Rowan-Hamilton)
ROWCLIFFE *of Pinkney Park* **LG1972**
ROWCROFT *of Ash Vale* **LG1952**
ROWE *of Ballycross* **LG1858**
FISHER-ROWE *formerly of Thorncombe* **LG1969**
ROWLAND, Bt **PB1970**
ROWLEY, Bt *of Hill House* **PB1970**; Bt *of Tendring* **PB1970**; Bt **PB1842**; *of Priory Hill* **LG1972**; *of Glassonby* **LG1898**; *of De Beauvoir* **LG1894**; *of Morcott* **LG1875**; *of Maperath* **LG1863**; *of Mount Campbell* **LGI1912**; *of Maperath, co Meath* **AA**; (*see also* Rowley-Conwy; and Henderson)
ROWTON (*see* Lowry-Corry)
ROXBURGHE (*see* Innes-Ker)
ROXBY *of Blackwood* **LG1863**

LEYCESTER-ROXBY *of Toft* **LG1969**
ROY *of Nenthorn* **LG1898**
ROYCE, Bt **PB1933**
ROYDEN, Bt **PB1970**; B **PB1949**
ROYDS *of Falinge* **LG1965**; *formerly of Brizes Park* **LG1972**
ROYLE, B **PB1970**; **LG1952**
ROYSE *of Nantenan House* **LG1850/3**
RUDD, Bt **EDB**; (*see also* Rudd-Clarke *of Knedlington Manor*)
RUDGE *of Evesham* **LG1952**; *of Folkingham* **LG1921**
RUDKIN *formerly of Corries* **LG1937Supp**
RUDSTON, Bt **EDB**
CALVERLEY-RUDSTON *of Hayton* **LG1921**
RUEGG *formerly of Highfields Hall* **LG1972**
RUFFIN (*see* Jefferson)
RUFFSIDE (*see* Brown)
RUGBY (*see* Maffey)
RUGGLES *formerly of Sudbury* **DFUSA**
RUGLEN (*see* Hamilton)
RUMBOLD, Bt **PB1970**
RUMSEY *formerly of Trellick* **LG1969**
RUNCIMAN (Runciman of Duxford, V) **PB1970**
RUNCORN (*see* Vosper)
RUNK **DFUSA**
RUPERT (Cumberland, D) **DEP**
RUSH *of Farthinghoe* **LG1900**; **DFUSA**; **PromFUSA**
RUSHBROOKE *formerly of Rushbrooke* **LG1952**
RUSHCLIFFE (*see* Betterton)
RUSHOLME, B **PB1970**
RUSHOUT, Bt *of Sezincote* **PB1931**; (Northwick, B) **PB1887**
RUSHTON (*now* SHEPHERD-CROSS) *of Barnacre Lodge* **LG1952**; *of Phepson Manor* **LG1952**
RUSKELL *of Coolmaine Castle* **LGI1958**
RUSSEL *of Blackbraes* **LG1921**
RUSSELL (Bedford, D) **PB1970**; E **PB1970**; (Ampthill, B) **PB1970**; (de Clifford, B) **PB1970**; Bt *of Littleworth Corner* **PB1970**; Bt *of Swallowfield* **PB1970**; (Russell of Killowen, B) **PB1940**; Bt *of Olney* **PB1921**; (Russell of Killowen, B) **PB1900**; (Orford, E) **DEP**; Bt *of Chequers Court* **EDB**; Bt *of Chippenham* **EDB**; Bt *of Langherne* **EDB**; Bt *of Strensham* **EDB**; *formerly of Aden* **LG1952**; *of Bucklebury* **LG1952**; *of Crooksbury Hurst* **LG1952**; *of Scarbank House* **LG1937**; *of Cleveden* **LG1921**; *of Maulside* **LG1921**; *of*

Stone Comberton **LG1894**; *of Killough* **LG1863**; *of Ashiesteel* **LG1863**; *of Kings Heath, co Worcester* **LG1850/3**; **IFR1976**; *of Glanmire* **LGI1958**; *of Seafield formerly of Glanmire House* **LGI1958**; Count **FT1917**; (1) & (2) **DFUSA**; *of Golfhill* **CG**; (*Victoria, Australia*) **CG**; *of Jamaica* **AA**; (*see also* Bramfill; and Bush (*formerly* Cromwell) *late of Cheshunt Park*; and Russel-Pavier)

HAMILTON - RUSSELL (Boyne, V) **PB1970**

OLDNALL-RUSSELL *of Stone and Comberton* **LG1863**

WATTS-RUSSELL *formerly of Ilam Hall* **LG1969**

RUSSIA (*Imperial House of*) **RL**

RUST *of Alconbury House* **LG1921**

RUSTON *late of Monks Manor and Aisthorpe Hall* **LG1937**

RUTH (*formerly* LEESON-MARSHALL) *of Callinafercy* **LGI1958**

RUTHERFOORD *formerly of Glasgow* **DFUSA**

RUTHERFORD, Bt *of Liverpool* **PB1940**; (Rutherford of Nelson, B) **PB1937**; Bt *of Beardwood* **PB1932**; (Teviot, E) **DEP**

RUTHERFURD *of Edgerston* **LG1921**; *of Fairnington* **LG1921**; *formerly of Edgerson* **DFUSA**

RUTHVEN (Gowrie, E) **PB1970**; (Forth, E) **DEP**; (Gowrie, E) **DEP**

RUTHVEN OF FREELAND (*see* Monckton)

HORE RUTHVEN (*see* Monckton)

OTWAY-RUTHVEN **IFR1976**

RUTLAND (*see* Manners)

RUTLEDGE (*of Wetronggurt*) *and Farnham Park* **CG**

RUTSON *of Newby Wiske and Nunnington Hall* **LG1900**

RUTTLEDGE **IFR1976**; **LGI1912**; (*see also* Lambert)

RUXTON *of Broad Oak* **LG1921**; *formerly of Cairnhill* **DFUSA**; **Prom FUSA**; (*see also* Fitz Herbert)

RYALL *of The Fosse House* **LG1952**

RYAN, Bt **PB1970**; (*co Limerick*) **IFR1976**; (*co Tipperary*) **IFR1976**; *of Ballymackeogh* **LGI1912**; *of Kilkefernan* **LGI1912**; **DFUSA**; *of Derriweit Heights* **CG**

RYCROFT, Bt **PB1970**

RYDER (Harrowby, E) **PB1970**

RYDER (*formerly* MARSTON) *of Rempstone* **LG1952**

RYDON *of Pyrland House* **AA**

TONSON-RYE **IFR1976**

RYLAND (*formerly* CARTWRIGHT) *of Preston Bagot* **LG1952**; **FR**

SMITH-RYLAND *of Sherbourne Park* **LG1965**

RYLANDS, Bt **PB1940**; *of The Mount* **LG1952**; *of Massey Hall* **LG1937**; **FR**

RYLE *formerly of Barkhale* **LG1965**

RYND *of Ryndville* **LGI1912**

RYRIE (*Australia*) **CG**

DE RYTHER *of Riverstown House* **LG1863**

RYTHRE, B **DEP**

RYVERS *of Ongar Castle* **LG1833/7**

RYVES (*see* Eley)

SABINE, Bt **EDB**

SACH (*see* Dickinson)

SACKVILLE (De La Warr, E) **PB1970**; (Dorset, D) **DEP**; (*see also* Sackville-West)

SADLER *of Keynsham Bury* **LG1863**; **DFUSA**

SADLEIR, Bt **EDB**; (*see also* Trench)

SAINSBURY, B **PB1970**

ST ALBANS (*see* Bacon; Beauclerk; Burgh; and Jermyn)

ST ALDWYN (*see* Hicks Beach)

ST AMAND (St Amand, B) **DEP**; (*see also* Beauchamp)

ST AUBYN (St Levan, B) **PB1970**; Bt **EDB**

MOLESWORTH-ST AUBYN, Bt **PB1970**

ST AUDRIES (*see* Fuller-Acland-Hood)

ST BARBE, Bt **EDB**; *of Lymington* **LG1858**

ST CLAIR (Sinclair, B) **PB1970**; *formerly of Staverton Court* **LG1921**; *of Roslin* **LG1863**

ST COLME (*see* Stewart)

ST DAVIDS (*see* Philipps)

ST GEORGE, Bt **PB1970**; B **DEP**; Bt **EDB**; **IFR1976**; *of Tyrone* **LGI1912**; M **TNBE1956**; (*see also* Usslier)

MANSERGH ST GEORGE (*see* Mansergh)

ST GERMANS (*see* Eliot)

ST HELENS (*see* FitzHerbert; and Hughes-Young)

ST HELIER (*see* Jeune)

SAINTHILL **LG1969**

ST JOHN (Bolingbroke, V) **PB1970**; (St John of Bletso, B) **PB1970**; (Bolingbroke, E) **DEP**; (St John, of Basing, B) **DEP**; (St John, of Lagenham, B) **DEP**;

(St John, of Stanton St John, B) **DEP**; (Tregoze, B) **DEP**; Bt **EDB**; *of Slinfold* **LG1952**; (*see also* Poynings)
HARRIS-ST JOHN *formerly of West Court* **LG1969**
ST JUST (*see* Grenfell)
ST LAWRENCE (Howth, E) **PB1909**
GAISFORD-ST LAWRENCE **IFR1976**
ST LEGER (Doneraile, V) **PB1970**; *late of Park Hill* **LG1937**; *of Heywards Hill* **LG1883/7**; (*see also* Aldworth)
ST LEONARDS (*see* Sugden)
ST LEVAN (*see* St Aubyn)
ST LIZ (Huntingdon, E) **DEP**; **LG1833/7**
ST MAUR, E **PB1885**; B **DEP**
ST OSWALD (*see* Winn)
ST PAULE, Bt **EDB**
ST PHILIBERT, B **DEP**
ST QUINTIN, B **DEP**; Bt **EDB**; *formerly of Hatley Park* **LG1937**
ST QUINTIN (*now* L'ESTRANGE MALONE) *of Scampston* **LG1952**
ST VINCENT (*see* Jervis)
SALE *of Aston Rowant* **LG1952**; *formerly of Twyford Hall* **LG1952**
SALFORD (*see* Egerton)
(DE)SALIS **IFR1976**
SALISBURY (*see* Cecil; d'Evereux; Greenham; Montacute; Nevill; and Plantagenet)
SALKELD *formerly of Holme Hill* **LG1952**
SALMON *of Tockington* **LG1937**; *of Penllyne Court* **LG1885**
SALMOND *formerly of Waterfoot* **LG1952**
CRITCHLEY-SALMONSON **LG1952 Supp**
GOLDSMID-STERN-SALOMONS, Bt **PB1925**
SALT, Bt *of Saltaire* **PB1970**; Bt *of Weeping Cross* **PB1970**; *of Saltaire* **AA**; *of Crow Nest, co York* **AA**
SALTER, B **PB1970**; *formerly of Salter's Hall* **LG1972**
SALTMARSHE *of Saltmarshe* **LG1952**
SALTONSTALL *formerly of Rookes Hall* **DFUSA**; **PromFUSA**
SALTOUN (*see* Fraser)
SALUSBURY, Bt **EDB;** *of Firgrove* **LG1952**
SALVESEN *formerly of Polmont* **LG1965**
SALVIN *of Croxdale* **LG1952**; *of Sutton Place* **LG1898**
SALWEY *of The Lodge, Overton* **LG1952**
SAMBORNE *of Timsbury* **LG1952**
SAMMAN, Bt **PB1959**

SAMMOND **DFUSA**
SAMPSON *of Buxhalls* **LG1921**; *of Henbury* **LG1894**
SAMUDA *of Bruern Abbey* **LG1921**
SAMUEL (Bearsted, V) **PB1970**; V **PB1970**; Bt **PB1970**; Bt *of Chelwood Vetchery* **PB1926**; **CG**; (*see also* Edgar)
SAMUELSON, Bt **PB1970**; *of Breckenbrough* **LG1937**
SAMWELL, Bt **EDB**
SANBORN **DFUSA**
SANDARS *of Gate Burton Hall* **LG1952**; *of Chesterford Park, co Essex* **AA**
SANDBACH *of Hafodunos* **AA**
MACKESON-SANDBACH *of Hafodunos* **LG1952;** (*see also* Mackeson)
SANDEMAN *formerly of Morden House* **LG1972**; **FR**
STEWART-SANDEMAN, Bt **PB1940**
SANDERS (Bayford, B) **PB1940**; *of Street Court* **LG1921**; **IFR1976**; **DFUSA**; (*see also* Sandars)
SANDERSON (Sanderson of Ayot, B) **PB1970**; Bt **PB1970**; B **PB1939**; B **PB1923**; Bt *of Combe* **EDB**; Bt *of London* **EDB**; *of Jenkin Place* **LG1921**; *of Clover Hill* **LG1912**; **FR, CG**
BURDON-SANDERSON, Bt **PB1905**; *of West Jesmond* **LG1921**
SANDES *late of Greenville* **LG1937Supp**; *of Sallow Glen* **LGI1912**
COLLIS-SANDES *of Oak Park* **LGI1912**
SANDFORD, B **PB1893**; (Mount Sandford, B) **DEP**; Bt **EDB**; *of The Isle of Rossall* **LG1972**; *of Sandford* **LG1900**; (*see also* Edmondson)
WILLS-SANDFORD *formerly of Willsgrove* **LGI1958**
SANDHURST (*see* Mansfield)
SANDILANDS (Torpichen, B) **PB1970**; (Abercrombie, Lord) **DEP**; *of Lagganmore* **LG1972**
SANDWICH (*see* Montagu)
SANDYS (Sandys, of Ombersley, B) **DEP**; (Sandys, of The Vine, B) **DEP**; Bt *of Northborne* **EDB**; Bt *of Wilberton* **EDB**; *of Graythwaite* **LG1969**; *of St Minver* **LG1858**; (*see also* Hill; and Sandys-Lumsdaine)
BAYNTUN-SANDYS, Bt **PB1848**
SANFORD *of Hamilton and Wesanford* **CG**
AYSHFORD-SANFORD *of Chipley Park* **LG1972**
SAN GIOVANNI, B **TNBE1956**
SANKEY, V **PB1940**; *of Coolmore* **LGI1912**; *of Fort Frederic* **LGI1912**

SAN MARCIANO, B **TNBE1956**
SANT-CASSIA, Count **TNBE1956**
SAN VINCENZO FERRERI, M **TNBE1956**
SANXAY **PromFUSA**
SARELL *of Braeside* **LG1937**
SARGEAUNT **LG1965**
SARGENT *formerly of Exeter* **DFUSA**; **PromFUSA**
SARGINT *late of Cahir Lodge* **LG1937 Supp**
SARGOOD **CG**
SARSFIELD (Lucan, E) **DEP**; (Sarsfield, V) **DEP**; Bt **EDB**; *of Fairy Hill* **LGI1958**
SARTORIS *late of Rushton* **LG1937**
SARZANO, M **FT1917**
SASSOON, Bt *of Bombay* **PB1959**; Bt *of Kensington Gore* **PB1939**; *formerly of Ashley Park* **LG1972**
SAS-VAN-BOSCH, Bt **EDB**
SATTERTHWAITE **DFUSA**
SAUMAREZ (de Saumarez, B) **PB1970**
SAUNDERS *formerly of Wennington* **LG1972**; *of Alton Pancras* **LG1952**; *formerly of Dolphinton House* **LG1952**; *of Downs House* **LG1921**; *of Largay* **LG1886**; *of Saunders Grove* **LGI1912**; *of Kilavalla* **LGI1912**; *of Tullig* **LGI1912; DFUSA**
WAKEFIELD-SAUNDERS (*see* Saunders)
SAUNDERSON (Castleton, E) **DEP**; Bt **EDB; IFR1976**
SAURIN *late of Orielton* **LG1937**
SAVAGE (Rivers, E) **DEP**; Bt **EDB**; *of St Leonard's* **LG1863**; *of Ballymadun* **LG1863**; *of Norelands* **LG1858**, **DFUSA**; *formerly of Savage's Neck* **DFUSA; FR**; (*see also* Nugent)
BYRCHE-SAVAGE (*see* Birch Reynardson)
HEYWORTH SAVAGE (*now* HEYWORTH) *of Bradwell Grove* **LG1952**
SAVERY *of Benn* **LG1863**
SAVILE (Mexborough, E) **PB1970**; (Halifax, M) **DEP**; (Sussex, E) **DEP**; Bt *of Copley* **EDB**; Bt *of Methley* **EDB**; Bt *of Thornhill* **EDB**; *formerly of Oaklands* **LG1972**
LUMLEY-SAVILE (Savile, B) **PB1970**
STEWART-SAVILE (*see* Savile)
SAVILLE (*formerly* LUSHINGTON) *of Aldington Court formerly of Park House* **LG1952**
SAVORY, Bt *of The Woodlands* **PB1959**; Bt *of Buckhurst Park* **PB1921**
SAWBRIDGE *of Coney Weston and East*

Haddon **LG1972**; *of Olantigh* **LG1850/3**
COBBOLD- SAWLE (*see* Cobbold *of Glemkan Hall, formerly of Holywells*)
GRAVES-SAWLE, Bt **PB1932**
SAWREY *of Broughton Tower* **LG1863**
SAWYER *formerly of Haseley* **LG1952**; *of Heywood* **LG1937**; (1) & (2) **DFUSA**
SAXTON, Bt **PB1857**
SAY *of Oakley Court* **LG1898**; *of Tilney* **LG1863**
SAYCE *of Dineterwood* **LG1952**
SAYE, B **DEP**
SAYE AND SELE (*see* Twisleton-Wykeham-Fiennes)
SAYER *of Sparham Hall* **LG1969**; *of Pett Place* **LG1952**
SAYRE (*see* Wilson)
SAYRES **DFUSA**
SAYWELL (*see* Eustace-Duckett)
SCALES, B **DEP**
SCANDRETT **DFUSA**
SCANLON *formerly of Lispole* **DFUSA**
SCARAMANGA **LG1952**
SCARBROUGH (*see* Lumley)
SCARISBRICK, Bt **PB1953**
SCARLETT (Abinger, B) **PB1970**; *of Rudhall House* **LG1969**; (*see also* Scarlett-Streatfeild)
SCARSDALE (*see* Curzon; and Leke)
SCARTH *of Breckness* **LG1972**
SCAWEN (*see* Blunt)
SCEALES *of Thornhill House* **LG1937**
SCHANK *of Castlerig* **LG1914**; *of Barton House* **LG1863**
SCHAUMBURB-LIPPE **RL**
SCHIEFFELIN **PromFUSA**
SCHILIZZI *of Chacombe House* **LG1972**
SCHLESWIG-HOLSTEIN **RL**
SCHOFIELD *of Low Burton Hall* **LG1952**; *of Langston House* **LG1937**
SCHOLEFIELD *of Sandhall* **LG1952**
SCHOLEY *of Eyhurst* **LG1965**
SCHOMBERG, D **DEP**; *of Glycing House* **LG1952**
SCHOMBURGK (*Australia*) **CG**
SCHOOLING *formerly of Park Place, Milton* **LG1969**
SCHOTT (*see* Scott *of The Yews*)
SCHREIBER *of Marlesford* **LG1965**; *of Henhurst, co Kent* **HI**
SCHRODER, Bt **PB1910**
SCHULENBERG (Munster, D) **DEP**; (Walsingham, C) **DEP**
SCHUMACHER (*see* Maguire)
SCHUSTER, Bt **PB1970**; B **PB1956**
SCHWAB *of Kingfield* **LG1937**

SCLATER, Bt **EDB**; *formerly of Newick Park* **LG1972**; *of Hoddington House* **LG1863**; (*see also* Basing)

SCOBELL *of Kingwell* **LG1952**; *of Nancealverne, co Cornwall* **HI**

SCONCE **DFUSA**

SCOON *formerly of Hawick* **DFUSA**

SCOT (Chester, E) **DEP**; (*see also* Scott-Watson)

GOLDIE-SCOT *of Craigmuie* **LG1921**

SCOTLAND (*Kings and Queens of*) **RL**

SCOTT (Eldon, E) **PB1970**; Bt *of Beauclerc* **PB1970**; Bt *of Great Barr* **PB1970**; Bt *of Rotherfield* **PB1970**; Bt *of Witley* **PB1970**; Bt *of Yews* **PB1970**; Bt *of Lytchet Minster* **PB1959**; Bt *of Dunninald* **PB1940**; (Clonmell, E) **PB1935**; Bt *of Connaught Place* **PB1912**; Bt *of Ancrum* **PB1902**; Bt *of Abbotsford* **PB1847**; (Monmouth, D) **DEP**; (Deloraine, E) **DEP**; (Tarras, E) **DEP**; (Stowell, B) **DEP**; *of Glenaros* **LG1972**; *of Lasborough, formerly of Betton* **LG1972**; *of Logie-Montrose and Usan* **LG1969**; *of Dittisham Court* **LG1952**; *of Gala* **LG1952**; *of Orchard* **LG1952**; *of Raeburn* **LG1952**; *of Rotherfield Park* **LG1952**; *formerly of Malleny* **LG1937**; *of Matson Ground* **LG1937**; *of Bretherton* **LG1921**; *of Great Barr and of Ratlinghope and Norbury* **LG1921**; *late of Melby* **LG1921**; *of Thorpe* **LG1921**; *of The Yews* **LG1906**; (*co Cork*) **IFR1976**; (*co Fermanagh*) **IFR1976**; (*co Tyrone*) **IFR1976**; *of Willsboro'* **LGI1912**; *of Annegrove Abbey* **LGI1912**; **DFUSA**; **PromFUSA**; (*S Australia*) **CG**; (*see also* Ashcroft *of Ancrum*; Corbett *of Peniarth Ucha*; Scott-Elliot; Johnston Stewart (*formerly* Corse-Scott) *of* Synton; and Watson *of Burnhead*)

CORSE-SCOTT *of Synton* **LG1937**

ERSKINE-SCOTT (*see* Scott *of Lasborough*)

FOLLIOTT SCOTT (*see* Scott *of Lasborough*)

GRAHAM SCOTT (*see* Scott *of Logie Montrose*)

LINDSAY - ORROCK - GRAHAM - SCOTT (*see* Scott *of Logie Montrose*)

HEPBURNE-SCOTT (Polwarth, B) **PB1970**

JOHNSTONE-SCOTT *of Wood Hall* **LG1937**

LOCKHART SCOTT (*see* Lockhart *of Milton Lockhart*)

McMILLAN SCOTT *of Howcleuch* **LG1937**

McNAIR SCOTT *of Huish House* **LG1972**

CONSTABLE-MAXWELL-SCOTT (*see* Norfolk)

MONTAGU-DOUGLAS-SCOTT (Buccleuch, D) **PB1970**

SHAW SCOTT *of Ashtead* **LG1952**

STODDART-SCOTT *of Creskeld Hall.* **LG1952**

SCOTTER, Bt **PB1911**

DAVIES-SCOURFIELD *of The Mote* **LG1952**

SCRASE (*see* Scrase-Dickins)

SCRATCHLEY **LG1965**

SCRATTON *of Prittewell and Ogwell* **LG1937**

SCRIMGEOUR (Dundee, E) **DEP**

SCRIVEN *of The Priory* **LG1863**

LEVETT-SCRIVENER *of Sibton Abbey* **LG1952**

SCROPE (Sunderland, E) **DEP**; (Wiltes, E) **DEP**; (Scrope of Masham, B) **DEP**; Bt **EDB**; *of Danby* **LG1965**

SCUDAMORE, V **DEP**; Bt *of Ballingham* **EDB**; Bt *of Holme Lacy* **EDB**

LUCAS-SCUDAMORE *of Kentchurch* **LG1972**

SCUDDER **PromFUSA**

SCULLY *of Mantle Hill* **LGI1912**

SCURFIELD *of Ford and formerly Hurworth* **LG1937**

SEABURY **PromFUSA**

SEAFIELD (*see* Ogilvie-Grant Studley Herbert)

SEAFORTH (*see* Mackenzie; and Stewart-Mackenzie)

SEAGER (Leighton of Saint Mellons, B) **PB1970**; *of Ty Gwyn Court* **LG1952**

SEAGRAVE **DFUSA**

SEAGRIM **LG1952Supp**

SEALE, Bt **PB1970**

SEALY *of Richmount* **LGI1912**; *of Gortnahorn* **LGI1912**; (*see also* Hyde)

SEAMAN, Bt **PB1936**

PIERCE-SEAMAN *of Rotherby Hall* **LG1863**

SEARLE **DFUSA**

SEARS *formerly of Colchester* **DFUSA**

SEATON (*see* Colborne-Vivian)

SEAVER *formerly of Heath Hall* **LGI1958**

SEAY *of Richmond, Virginia* **DFUSA**

SEBAG (*see* Sebag-Montefiore)

SEBRIGHT, Bt **PB1970**

SECKER *formerly of Callast* **LG1952**; *of Standford Grange* **LG1952**

SECKHAM *of Whittington* **LG1937**

SECRETAN *of Swaynes* **LG1952**
SEDGWICK *formerly of Woburn* **DFUSA**
SEEBOHM *formerly of Poynder's End* **LG1972**
SEED *of Melbourne Hall* **LG1952**
MOLYNEUX-SEEL *of Huyton Hey* **LG1898**
SEELY (Mottistone, B) **PB1970**; (Sherwood, B) **PB1970**
SEEZ (Dorset, E) **DEP**
SEFTON (*see* Molyneux)
SEGAL, B **PB1970**
SEGESSER **FT1917**
SEGRAVE, B **DEP**; *of Isfield Place* **LG1972**
SEIGNE *formerly of Grennane House* **LGI1958**
SELBORNE (*see* Palmer)
SELBY, Bt **EDB**; *formerly of Shotton and Pawston* **LG1969**; *formerly of Ightham Mote* **LG1969**; *of Biddleston* **LG1921**; *of Yearl* **LG1898**; *of Twizell House* **LG1863**; *of Cheswick House* **LG1863**; *of Whitley Hall* **AA**; (*see also* Gully)
SELDEN *formerly of Wadhurst* **DFUSA**
SELKIRK (*see* Douglas-Hamilton)
SELLAR **LG1952Supp**
SELSDON (*see* Mitchell-Thomson)
SELSEY (*see* Peachey)
SELWYN *of The Orchards* **LG1969**; *of Pagoda House* **LG1875**
FORBES-SEMPILL (Sempill, B) **PB1970**
SEMPLE **DFUSA**
POCKLINGTON SENHOUSE *of Netherhall* **LG1972**
SERGISON (*now* SERGISON-BROOKE) *of Cuckfield* **LG1937**
SERJEANSTON **LG1969**
SEROCOLD (*see* Skeels *of Chatteris*)
PEARCE-SEROCOLD *of Ashe House* **LG1972**
SEROTA, B **PB1970**
SETON, Bt *of Abercorn* **PB1970**; Bt *of Pitmedden* **PB1970**; (Wintoun, E) **DEP**; (Kingstoun, V) **DEP**; Bt *of Garletoun* **EDB**; Bt *of Windygoul* **EDB**; *of Mounie* **LG1952**; *late of Cariston and Treskerby* **LG1952**; *of Mounie, co Aberdeen* **AA**; (*see also* Meldrum)
CHEESMENT-SEVERN *of Penybont Hall* **LG1863**
SEVERNE *of Shakenhurst* **LG1965**
SEVIER *of Hulland Hall* **LG1969**
SEWELL *of Tysoe Manor* **LG1952**
SEYMER *of Hanford* **LG1952**
SEYMOUR (Somerset, D) **PB1970**; (Hertford, M) **PB1970**; (Alcester, B) **PB1895**; (Somerset, D.) **DEP**; (Seymour, of Sudeley, B) **DEP**; Bt **EDB**; *of Knoyle* **LG1914**; *of Castletown* **LG1863**; *formerly of Somerset House* **LGI1958**; *of Ballymore Castle* **LGI1912**; *of Killagally* **LGI1912**; *of Limerick* **LGI1912**
CULME-SEYMOUR, Bt **PB1970**
SEYS *formerly of Wirewoods Green* **LG1969**
SHACKELFORD (*see* Jefferson)
SHACKFORD **DFUSA**
SHACKLE *of Seymour Court* **LG1937**
SHACKLETON, B **PB1970**
SHADWELL (*see* Shadwell-Cowland)
LUCAS-SHADWELL *of Fairlight* **LG1921**
SHAEN, Bt **EDB**
SHAFTESBURY (*see* Ashley-Cooper)
SHAFTO *of Whitworth* **LG1952**
SHAIRP *of Honstoun* **LG1937**
SHAKERLEY, Bt **PB1970**
SHAKESPEARE, Bt **PB1970**; (*see also* Hart)
SHAND, B **PB1904**; *of The Laines* **LG1952**; (*see also* Shand-Harvey)
SHANDON (*see* O'Brien)
SHANK *of Castlerig* **LG1863**; **HI**
SHANN **FR**
SHANNON (*see* Boyle)
SHARD *of Warfield Hall* **LG1937**
SHARLAND (*see* Cruwys)
SHARP, B **PB1970**; Bt *of Heckmondwike* **PB1970**; Bt *of Maidstone* **PB1970**; Bt **EDB**; *of Clyth Lodge and Bank House* **LG1952**; *of Balmuir* **LG1937**; *of Maryfield* **LG1921**; *of Linden Hall* **LG1886**; **DFUSA**
SHARPE **FR**
SHARPLES (*or* SHARPLESS) **DFUSA**; *formerly of Wybunbury*
SHAUGHNESSY, B **PB1970**
SHAUNDE (Bath, E) **DEP**
SHAW (Craigmyle, B) **PB1970**; Bt **PB1970**; Bt *of Wolverhampton* **PB1940**; Bt *of Kilmarnock* **PB1868**; *of Welburn Hall* **LG1972**; *of Tordarroch* **LG1972**; *formerly of Arrowe Park* **LG1952**; *of Cobbe Place* **LG1952**; *formerly of Calmington Manor* **LG1952**; *of Preston and Kirk Bride formerly of Shaw Place, Heath Charnock and High Bulhalgh* **LG1952**; *of Bourton Hall* **LG1937**; (*Tasmania*) **CG**; (*see also* Dyott; Shaw-Kennedy; and Shaw-Mackenzie)
BEST-SHAW, Bt **PB1970**
SHAWCROSS, B **PB1970**

SHAWE *formerly of Weddington Hall* **LG1952**
SHEAFFE, Bt **PB1851**
SHEARER **DFUSA**
SHEARS *formerly of Cork* **DFUSA**
SHEDDEN *of Hardmead* **LG1952**; *of Morris Hill* **LG1863**
SHEE, Bt **PB1869**; (*see also* Gordon *of Letterfourie*; and O'Shee)
ARCHER-SHEE *formerly of Ashurst Lodge* **LG1972**
SHEEHAN **DFUSA**
SHEEHY (*co Cork*) **IFR1976**; (*Dublin*) **IFR1976**
SHEEPSHANKS *of Arthington Hall* **LG1952**; *of Broom House* **LG1952**
SHEFFIELD, Bt **PB1970**; E **PB1909**; (Normanby, D) **DEP**; (*see also* Stanley)
OLIPHANT-SHEFFIELD *of Broadfield House* **LG1937**
WENTWORTH-SHEILDS *formerly of Wainstown* **LG1937Supp**
SHEKELL *of Pebworth* **LG1858**
SHELBURNE (*see* Petty)
SHELDON *of Brailes House* **LG1898**
SHELLEY, Bt **PB1970**
SHELLY *of Avington House* **LG1879**
SHELTON *of Springfort* **LGI1958**
MACGEOUGH BOND SHELTON (*see* MacGeough Bond)
SHENNAN (*New Zealand*) **CG**
SHENSTONE *of Sutton Hall* **LG1914**
SHEPHERD, B **PB1970**; *of Higham Bury* **LG1937**; *of Shaw End* **LG1937**
SHEPLEY *of Woodthorpe Hall* **LG1969**
SHEPPARD *of Cabra Castle* **LGI1958**; *formerly of Fromefield* **LG1952**; *formerly of Kilcunahanbeg* **LG1952**; *of Clifton* **LG1894**; *of Rednock* **LG1900**; *of High House* **LG1863**; *formerly of Tipperary* **DFUSA**; (*see also* Cotton)
SHEPPERSON, Bt **PB1949**; *of Keyworth House* **LG1937**
SHERARD, B **PB1931**; (Harborough, E) **DEP**; Bt **EDB**
SHERBORN *of Bedfont* **LG1969**
SHERBORNE (*see* Dutton)
SHERBROOKE *of Oxton* **LG1965**; (*see also* Lowe)
SHERBURNE, Bt **EDB**
SHERFIELD (*see* Makins)
SHERIDAN *late of Frampton Court* **LG1937**
SHERLOCK *of Rahan* **LGI1912**
SHERMAN **PromFUSA**
SHERRERD **DFUSA**
SHERSTON *formerly of Evercreech* **LG1965**
SHERWIN *of Bramcote Hills* **LG1858**
SHERWOOD *of Prested Hall* **LG1952**; *of Rysome Garth* **LG1879**; **DFUSA**; (*see also* Seely)
SHIELDS *formerly of Wainstown* **LG1875Supp**
SHIERS, Bt **EDB**
SHIFFNER, Bt **PB1970**
SHIPBROOK (*see* Vernon)
SHIPLEY *of Twyford Moors* **LG1937**; **DFUSA**; (*see also* Rowley-Conwy *of Bodrhyddan*)
SHIPMAN (*formerly* BRADLEY) **DFUSA**
SHIPPEN **PromFUSA**
SHIPPERDSON *of Hermitage* **LG1879**
SHIPPEY **DFUSA**
SHIRLEY (Ferrers, E) **PB1970**; Bt *of Oat Hill* **EDB**; Bt *of Preston* **EDB**; *of Ettington and Lough Fea* **LG1952**; (1) & (2) **DFUSA**
SHOBER **DFUSA**
SHOBINGTON *of Bulstrode* **VF**
SHOLL (*Australia*) **CG**
SHORE (Teignmouth, B) **PB1970**; *late of Norton Hall* **LG1914**; *of Embley* **LG1875**; **FR**
SHORT (*now* FRADGLEY) *of Bickham* **LG1952**; *of Heslerton Hall* **LG1898**
HASSARD-SHORT *formerly of Edlington* **LG1952**
SHORTT **AA**
SHOWERS (*see* Stirling *of Garden*)
SHREVE *late of Poplar Hill and sometime of Rugby* **DFUSA**
SHREWSBURY (*see* Talbot)
SHREWSBURY AND WATERFORD (*see* Chetwynd-Talbot)
SHRIVER **DFUSA**
SHRUBB *formerly of Boldre* **LG1937**
SHUCKBURGH, Bt **PB1970**; *late of Bourton Hall* **LG1914**; *of Downton House* **LG1833/7**
SHULDHAM, B **DEP**; *of Marlesford Hall* **LG1863**; *of Ballymulveg* **LGI1912**; *of Dunmanway, co Cork* **AA**
QUANTOCK-SHULDHAM *of East Stoke House and Norton* **LG1972**
SHUTE *of Bramshaw Hill* **LG1875**
SHUTTLEWORTH *of Hathersage* **LG1969**; *of Old Warden* **LG1952**; *of Hodsack Park* **LG1863**
KAY-SHUTTLEWORTH (Shuttleworth, B) **PB1970**
SIBBALD, Bt *of Rankelour* **PB1846**; Bt **EDB**; *of Westcott* **LG1863**; (*see also* Scott)

SIBLEY *formerly of St Albans* **DFUSA**
SIBTHORP *formerly of Canwick Hall* **LG1952**
SICKLEMORE *of Nether Court* **LG1886**; *of Wetheringsett* **LG1863**
SIDDELEY (Kenilworth, B) **PB1970**
SIDEBOTTOM *of Etherow House* **LG1921**
SIDLEY (Dorchester, E) **DEP**; Bt *of Ailesford* **EDB**; Bt *of Great Chart* **EDB**; *of Southfleet* **EDB**
SIDMOUTH (*see* Addington)
SIDNEY (De L'Isle, V) **PB1970**; *of Cowper Hall* **LG1937**
SIEFF, B **PB1970**
SIER *of Ravensden, Beds* **AA**
SIKES *of The Chauntry House* **LG1858**
SILKIN, B **PB1970**
SILLIFANT *of Coomb* **LG1921**
SILLITOE *formerly of Fordhall* **LG1969**
SILLS **DFUSA**
SILSOE (*see* Trustram Eve)
SILVA *of Testcombe* **LG1921**
SILVERTOP *of Minsteracres* **LG1952**
SILVESTER, Bt **EDB**
SIMCOE *of Wolford* **LG1921**
VOWLER-SIMCOE *late of Penhele* **LG1921**
SIMCOX *of Harborne House* **LG1898**
SIMEON, Bt **PB1970**; Bt **EDB**
SIMEY, B **PB1967**
SIMMONS *of Churchill* **CG**
SIMMS **IFR1976**; *of Trowell Hall* **LG1952**
SIMON, V **PB1970**; (Simon of Wythenshawe, B) **PB1970**
SIMONDS, V **PB1970**; *of Abbott's Barton* **LG1952**; *formerly of Winchester* **DFUSA**
BLACKALL-SIMONDS *of Bradfield House* **LG1921**
SIMPSON, Bt **PB1970**; Bt *of Strathavon* **PB1924**; *of Bowerswood* **LG1952**; *of The Ryelands, Taynton* **LG1952**; *of Spitchwick Manor* **LG1952**; *of Walton Hall* **LG1952**; *of Waye formerly of Maypool* **LG1952**; **LG1952Supp**; *of Mellor Lodge* **LG1875**; *of Cloncorick Castle* **LG1875**; *of Castle Lodge, Knaresborough* **LG1875**; *of Babworth Hall* **LG1875**; *of Merklands House* **LG1863**; *of Cloncorick Castle* **LG1863**; *of Whitburn, Westhouse* **LG1858**; (1) & (2) **DFUSA**
SIMS (*formerly* SYMES) *sometime of Chard* **DFUSA**
SIMSON *of Brunton and Pitcorthie* **LG1898**

SINCLAIR (Caithness, E) **PB1970**; (Thurso, V) **PB1970**; (Pentland, B) **PB1970**; (Sinclair of Cleeve, B) **PB1970**; Bt *of Dunbeath* **PB1970**; (Barrymore, B) **PB1925**; (Orkney, E) **DEP**; *of Cleeve Court* **LG1952**; *of Misarden Park* **LG1952**; *of Mey* **LG1921**; *of Forss* **LG1886**; *of Holyhill and Bonnyglen* **LGI1912**; *of Hopefield House* **LGI1912**; (*see also* Buchan)
ALEXANDER-SINCLAIR *formerly of Freswick* **LG1952**
SING (*see* Synge)
SINGER **LG1972**; (*see also* Longsdon)
SINGLETON *of Aclare* **LG1937Supp**; *of Fort Singleton* **LG1879**; *of Mell* **LGI1912**; *of Quinville Abbey* **LGI1912**
SINGTON *of Dunham House* **LG1937**
SINHA, B **PB1970**
SINNOTT *of Tuffley Grange* **LG1937**
SIRR **LGI1958**
SISMEY *of Offord Cluny* **LG1952**
SISSON **DFUSA**
SITWELL, Bt **PB1970**; *of Burmoor Castle* **LG1972**; *late of Ferney Hall* **LG1937**
SITWELL (*formerly* WARING) *of Lennel* **LG1952**
WILMOT-SITWELL *formerly of Stainsby* **LG1965**
SIVRIGHT *of South House and Meggatland* **LG1921**
SKEELS *of Chatteris* **LG1952**
SKEET *of Stortford Park* **LG1937**
SKEFFINGTON (Massereene and Ferrard, V) **PB1970**; Bt *of Skeffington* **PB1851**; (Massereene, E) **DEP**; Bt *of Fisherwick* **EDB**
SKELMERSDALE (*see* Bootle-Wilbraham)
SKELTON *of Papcastle* **LG1863**
SKENE, Bt **EDB**; *of Hallyards* **LG1952**; *of Rubislaw* **LG1879**; *of Marnoo* **CG**; *of St Kilda* **CG**
GORDON-CUMING-SKENE *of Pitlurg* **LG1921**
SKERRETT *of Finavara* **LGI1912**; *of Athgoe Park* **LG1886**
SKEVINGTON *formerly of Sherwood* **DFUSA**
SKEY *of Spring Grove, co Worcester* **LG1850/3**
SKILTON *formerly of Coventry* **DFUSA**
SKINNER, Bt **PB1970**; *of The Chantry* **LG1972**
CRAWLEY ROSS SKINNER *of Warmwell* **LG1972**
SKIPTON *of the Casino, co Derry* **AA**

KENNEDY-SKIPTON **IFR1976**
SKIPWITH, Bt **PB1970**; Bt *of Metheringham* **EDB**; Bt *of Newbold Hall* **EDB**; **PromFUSA**
SKIPWORTH *of Moortown House* **LG1863**
SKIRROW (*see* Woodroffe)
SKIRVING (*formerly* WISE) *formerly of Leamington* **LG1952**
SKRINE *of Warleigh* **LG1972**
SLACK *of Derwent Hill* **LG1921**
SLACKE *late of Ashleigh* **LGI1912**
SLADE, Bt **PB1970**; (1) & (2) **DFUSA**
SLADEN *formerly of Hartsbourne Manor* **LG1965**; *formerly of Ripple Court* **LG1965**; *of Rhydoldog* **LG1952**; *formerly of Rochdale* **DFUSA**; *of Hartbourne Manor, Herts* **AA**
KENYON-SLANEY (*see* Kenyon)
SLANNING, Bt **EDB**
SLATER *of Woolhanger* **LG1937**; *of Chesterfield* **LG1863**; *of Newick Park* **LG1863**
WILSON-SLATOR *of White Hill* **LGI1912**
SLAUGHTER *formerly of Slaughter* **LG1937**
SLEDGE **DFUSA**
SLEECH *of Sussex* **LG1833/7**
SLEEMAN *formerly of Pool Park, St Tudy* **LG1965**
SLEIGHT, Bt **PB1970**
SLESSER *of Cornerways* **LG1937**
SLIGO (*see* Browne)
SLIM, V **PB1970**
SLINGSBY, Bt *of Scriven* **PB1869**; Bt *of Newcells* **EDB**; Bt *of Scriven* **EDB**; *formerly of Scriven* **LG1952**
SLIPPER *of Braydestone* **LG1921**
SLOAN *formerly of Ballymoney* **DFUSA**; *formerly of Lisburn* **DFUSA**
SLOANE, Bt **EDB**; **DFUSA**; (*Australia*) **CG**
BUTLER-SLOSS (*see* Butler)
SMAIL *of Bodorgan* **LG1952**
SMAILES *of Fairhaven* **LG1937**
SMALL (*Canada*) **CG**; (*see also* Kerr)
SMALWOOD (*see* Fetherston)
SMALLWOOD (*see* Fetherstonhaugh)
SMART *formerly of Bere Mill* **LG1952**; *of Trewhit* **LG1863**
SMEATON *of Coul* **LG1863**
MARSDEN-SMEDLEY *of Lea Green* **LG1965**
SMETHURST *of Chorley* **LG1898**
SMILEY, Bt **PB1970**

SMIRTHWAITE *of Normanton Rise* **LG1921**
SMITH (Birkenhead, E) **PB1970**; (Hambleden, V) **PB1970**; (Colwyn, B) **PB1970**; (Dudley, B) **PB1970**; Bt *of Crowmallie* **PB1970**; Bt *of Eardiston* **PB1970**; Bt *of Keighley* **PB1970**; Bt *of Stratford Place* **PB1970**; Bt *of Kidderminster* **PB1959**; (Strathcona and Mount Royal, B) **PB1914**; Bt *of Long Ashton* **PB1849**; (Carrington, V) **DEP**; Bt *of Crantock* **EDB**; Bt *of Edmonthorpe* **EDB**; Bt *of Hatherton* **EDB**; Bt *of Isleworth* **EDB**; Bt *of Long Ashton* **EDB**; Bt *of Pickering* **EDB**; *formerly of Craigend and Jordanhill* **LG1972**; *formerly of Woodmancote* **LG1969**; *formerly of Barnes Hall* **LG1965**; *formerly of Hertingfordbury Park and of Duffield* **LG1965**; *of Longhills* **LG1965**; *formerly of Midhurst* **LG1965**; *of Shottesbrooke Park and Ashford* **LG1965**; *formerly of Wilford House* **LG1965**; *of Woodhall Park* **LG1965**; *formerly of Woodhill and Goldings* **LG1965**; *formerly of Edwalton and Foelalt* **LG1952**; *of Pollard Hall* **LG1952**; *of Wickham Hall* **LG1952**; *of Balerno* **LG1937**; *of Bramcote* **LG1937**; *of Cromallie House* **LG1937**; *late of Walcote House* **LG1937**; *of Tusmore Park and Mount Clare* **LG1937**; *of Grovehurst* **LG1937**; *of Horbling* **LG1921**; *of The Limes* **LG1921**; *of Halesowen Grange* **LG1914**; *of Consall Hall* **LG1898**; *of Shortgrove* **LG1898**; *of Hammerwood* **LG1898**; *of Camer* **LG1894**; *of Beabeg* **LG1875**; *of Blackwood House* **LG1875**; **IFR1976**; *of Duneira* **LGI1958**; *of Rathcoursey* **LGI1958**; *of Annesbrook* **LGI1912**; (1) (2) & (3) **DFUSA**; *formerly of Bristol* **DFUSA**; *formerly of Ilkley* **DFUSA**; **PromFUSA**; (1) & (2) **FR**; *of Adelaide* **CG**; *of Bathurst and Gamboola* **CG**; *of Gordon Brook* **CG**; *of Kyogle* **CG**; *of Marryatville* **CG**; (*Sydney, NSW*) (1) & (2) **CG**; (*Tasmania*) **CG**; *of Aston* (*see* Farmer); *of Ryhope* (*see* Scurfield); (*see also* Acton *of Acton Scott*; Downs *of Aspley Guise*; Eardley; Flowers; Lee; Neale; Ogilvy; O'Gowan; and Pauncefote)
SMITH (*now* CRAWFORD) *of Great Fenton* **LG1921**
SMITH (*formerly* FAIRFAX) **DFUSA**
SMITH (*now* PAYSON) **DFUSA**

ABEL SMITH (see Smith of Longhills; Smith formerly of Wilford House; Smith of Woodhall Park; Smith formerly of Woodhill and Goldings)

ALEC-SMITH of Winestead **LG1969**

AUDLEY SMITH (see Smith formerly of Midhurst)

BABINGTON SMITH (see Smith formerly of Cruigend and Jordanhill)

BECKWITH-SMITH formerly of Stratton Audley and Aberarder **LG1969**

BICKFORD-SMITH of Younghouse **LG1952**

BOSWORTH-SMITH (see Smith-Marriott)

BOWDEN-SMITH formerly of Carey's **LG1952**

BUCHANAN-SMITH (Balerno, B) **PB1970**; (see also Smith formerly of Craigend and Jordanhill)

CLOSE-SMITH of Boycott Manor **LG1972**

COCHRAN-SMITH (see Alec Smith)

CUSACK-SMITH, Bt **PB1970**

DELACOURT-SMITH, B **PB1970**

DENROCHE SMITH (see Smith formerly of Craigend and Jordanhill)

DORMAN-SMITH (see O'Gowan)

DYER SMITH **LG1952Supp**

FULLERTON-SMITH (see Acton of Acton Scott)

GUTHRIE SMITH (see Smith formerly of Craigend and Jordanhill)

HAMMOND-SMITH **IFR1976**

HEATHCOTE-SMITH (see Smith-Marriott)

HERIZ SMITH formerly of Slade Park **LG1952**

INNES-SMITH **LG1972**

LAVERS-SMITH (see Wontner-Smith)

LAWRENCE SMITH (see Smith formerly of Woodmancote)

LAWSON-SMITH formerly of Colton **LG1952**

LEADBITTER-SMITH (see Leadbitter formerly of Warden)

LEIGH SMITH of Scalands **LG1952**

LOCKHART SMITH of Ellingham Hall **LG1972**

MARTIN SMITH (see Smith formerly of Midhurst)

NEWSON-SMITH, Bt **PB1970**

PARKER-SMITH (see Smith formerly of Craigend and Jordanhill)

PRINCE-SMITH, Bt **PB1970**

REARDON- SMITH, Bt **PB1970**

RUTHVEN-SMITH (see Smith of Woodhall Park)

SETH-SMITH **LG1972**

SMITH-DORRIEN-SMITH of Tresco Abbey **LG1969**

HAMILTON - SPENCER - SMITH, Bt **PB1970**

STANLEY SMITH formerly Treliske **LG1952**

STRAKER-SMITH of Carham Hall **LG1965**

TAYLOR-SMITH (now BELLORD) of Colepike Hall **LG1952**

VASSAR-SMITH, Bt **PB1970**

VIVIAN SMITH (Bicester, B) **PB1970**

WALKER-SMITH, Bt **PB1970**

WILSON-SMITH of Curnledge **LG1965**

WONTNER-SMITH of Amberley Place **LG1952Supp**

WYLDBORE-SMITH (see Smith-Marriott)

SMITHSON late of Inverernie **LG1937**

SMITHWICK (co Kilkenny) **IFR1976;** (co Tipperary) **IFR1976**

TELFER-SMOLLETT of Bonhill **LG1969**

SMYLY of Stratton Audley Hall, formerly of Camus **LG1952**

SMYTH, Bt **PB1970**; Bt of Eske Hall **PB1940**; Bt of Isfield **PB1940**; Bt of Redcliffe **EDB**; of Little Houghton **LG1952**; of Ashton Court **LG1937**; formerly of Barrowmore Hall **LG1937**; of Elkington **LG1937**; of Fladbury Manor House **LG1937**; of Rathcoursey **LG1937Supp**; of Heath Hall **LG1898**; **IFR1976;** of Aston Court VF; (see also Davidge; Nevill; Smith; and Upton of Ingurire Hall)

BARTELOTT-SMYTH of Stopham **LG1833/37**

BLOOD-SMYTH (see Blood)

BOWYER-SMYTH, Bt **PB1970**

HOLROYD-SMYTH **IFR1976**

MOORE-SMYTH (see Perceval-Maxwell (co Waterford))

MORE-SMYTH (see Perceval-Maxwell (co Waterford))

SMYTHE (Strangford, V) **DEP;** of Methven **LG1937**; of Hilton (see Monckton); (see also Cholmondeleigh late of Condover; and **IFR** Smyth)

SNADDON (see Vere-Laurie)

AIKIN-SNEATH of Tibberton Court **LG1921**

SNELL, B **PB1940**; of Mengeham House **LG1952**; of Hertfordshire **LG1863**

SNEYD *formerly of Keele Hall* **LG1969;** *of Ashcombe* **LG1863**

SNEYD (*now* SCOTT-MONCRIEFF) *of Basford Hall* **LG1969**

SNEYD (*formerly* TRELAWNY) *of Coldrenick* **LG1969**

SNOW, B **PB1970;** *formerly of Cleve* **LG1972**

SNOWDEN, V **PB1937;** (*see also* Ehlen)

SNOWDON (*see* Armstrong-Jones)

SNOWE, Bt **EDB**

SOAME, Bt **EDB**

BUCKWORTH - HERNE - SOAME, Bt **PB1970**

SOAMES *of Hamsell Manor formerly of Sheffield Park* **LG1965**

MURPHY-SOLARI (*see* Murphy (*co* Tipperary))

SOLTAU *of Little Efford* **LG1879**

SOLWAY (*see* Douglas)

SOMERIE (Dudley, B) **DEP**

SOMERLEYTON (*see* Crossley)

SOMERS, B **DEP;** *of Bell Hall* **LG1952;** *late of Mendip Lodge* **LG1937;** (*see also* Somers-Cocks)

SOMERSET (Beaufort, D) **PB1970;** (Raglan, B) **PB1970;** V **DEP;** (*see also* Carr; Seymour; and Tudor)

SOMERVELL *of High Borrans* **LG1937;** *of Sorn* **LG1921**

SOMERVILLE, Bt **PB1970;** (Athlumney, B) **PB1929;** B **DEP; IFR1976**

SONDES (Feversham, E) **DEP;** (*see also* Milles-Lade)

SONDS, Bt **EDB**

SOPER, B **PB1970**

SORENSEN, B **PB1970**

SOSKICE (Stow Hill, B) **PB1970**

SOULBURY (*see* Ramsbotham)

SOUTER *of Gosforth* **LG1952**

SOUTHAM *of Shrewsbury* **LG1906**

SOUTHAMPTON (*see* FitzRoy; and Fitz-William)

SOUTHBOROUGH (*see* Hopwood)

SOUTHBY, Bt **PB1970;** *of Carswell* **LG1894**

SOUTHCOMBE *of Honiton House* **LG1886**

SOUTHCOTT, Bt **EDB**

SOUTHEBY *of Eckton* **LG1952**

SOUTHESK (*see* Carnegie)

SOUTHWARK (*see* Causton)

SOUTHWELL, V **PB1970;** (*see also* Trafford *of Wroxham*)

SOUTHWOOD (*see* Elias)

SOUTHWORTH **DFUSA**

SOWERBY *of Lilley Manor* **LG1972;** *of*

Putteridge Park **LG1900**

SPAFFORD *formerly of Silkstone* **DFUSA**

SPAIGHT *formerly of Ardnatagle* **LG1969**

GARTSIDE-SPAIGHT *of Derry Castle* **LGI1912**

SPAIN (*Royal House of*) **RL**

SPALDING **DFUSA**

SPALDING (*now* UPTON) *of Holme* **LG1937**

SPAN (*see* Forrest)

SPARKE *of Gunthorpe Hall* **LG1952;** *of Tanyard House* **LG1952;** *of Pennyworlodd* **LG1875**

SPARKS *of West Lodge* **LG1863**

SPARLING (*see* Cunliffe *of Petton*)

SPARROW *of Albrighton* **LG1952;** *of Colne Engaine* **LG1952;** *of Stansgate Abbey* **LG1952;** *of Penn, co Stafford* **AA;** *of Worlingham Hall* (*see* Bence)

BODYCHAN-SPARROW *of Bodychan* **LG1921**

HANBURY-SPARROW *formerly of Rushbury and Eaton-under-Heywood* **LG1952**

SPEAIGHT *formerly of Bishop's Hatfield* **LG1952**

SPEAKMAN *of Culcheth* **LG1952**

SPEARMAN, Bt **PB1970;** *of Thornley and Eachwick* **LG1894**

SPEARS, Bt **PB1970**

SPEDDEN **DFUSA**

SPEDDING *of Windebrowe and Mirehouse* **LG1969;** *of Wotton-under-Edge* **LG1969;** *of Summergrove* **LG1900**

SPEELMAN, Bt **PB1970;** Bt **EDB**

SPEER *formerly of Desertoghill* **DFUSA**

LITCHFIELD-SPEER (*see* Litchfield *of Snowfield*)

SPEID *of Ardovie* **LG1886**

SPEIR *of Linkside* **LG1972;** *formerly* Eyre *of Middleton Tyas* **LG1952;** *of Burnbrae and Culdees* **LG1900**

SPEIRS **FR**

HAGART SPEIRS *of Elderslie* **LG1952**

SPEKE, Bt **EDB; LG1972**

NEVEN-SPENCE *of Uyea* **LG1952**

TORRENS-SPENCE *of Drumcullen* **LGI1958**

SPENCER, E **PB1970;** (Churchill, V) **PB1970;** (Teviot, V) **DEP;** Bt *of Offley* **EDB;** Bt *of Yarnton* **EDB;** *of Coles Hall* **LG1972;** *of Summerfield Court* **LG1921;** *of Bramley Grange* **LG1858;** *formerly of Edworth* **DFUSA;** *formerly of Northampton* **DFUSA**

MUNRO-SPENCER *of Teaninich* **LG1921**
SPENS, B **PB1970**; *of Lathallan* **LG1969**; *(now* DUNNING) *of Craigsanquhar* **LG1900**
SPENSLEY *of Westoning Manor* **LG1937**
SPERLINE *of Teviot Bank* **LG1972**
SPEYER, Bt **PB1932**
SPICER, Bt **PB1970**; *of Spye Park* **LG1952**
SPILLING *of Aldborough Hall* **LG1906**
SPILMAN **DFUSA**
SPINKS *of Brenley House* **LG1898**
SPITTY *of Billericay* **LG1898**
SPODE *of Hawkesyard* **LG1886**
SPOFFORTH *of Eastthorpe Hall* **LG1863**; **FR**
SPOKES *formerly of Wallingford* **LG1952**
SPOONER (*see* Inge-Innes-Lillingston)
SPOOR *of Whitburn* **LG1879**
SPOTTISWOOD (*now* MILBURN) *of Muiresk* **LG1952**
SPOTTISWOODE *formerly of Spottiswoode* **LG1952**
SPRAGUE **DFUSA**
SPRATT *of Pencil Hill* **LGI1912**
SPRIGG **DFUSA**
SPRIGNELL, Bt **EDD**
SPRING, Bt **EDB**; *of Castlemayne* **LG1879**
SPRINGFIELD *of Alburgh* **LG1937**
SPROAT *of Knowlands* **LG1969**
SPROSTON *of Sproston* **LG1886**
SPROT, Bt **PB1929**; *of Riddell* **LG1952**; *of Garnkirk* **LG1914**; **FR**
SPROWLS *formerly of Gurtmaoaooa Castle* **DFUSA**
SPRY *of Place* **LG1863**
ROLLESTON-SPUNNER (*see* Rolleston)
SPURRIER *of Marston-on-Dove* **LG1969**; *of Trafalgar* **LG1969**
SPURWAY *of Spurway and Oakford* **LG1972**
SPYNIE (*see* Lindsay)
SQUIBB *formerly of Belfield House* **LG1969**
SQUIRE *of Barton Place* **LG1875**
STABLE *of Plas Llwyn Owen* **LG1952**
STACEY *of Knaphill Manor* **LG1952**
STACK *of Ned Sherry, co Fermangh* **LGI1912**
STACPOOLE **IFR1976**; (*see also* de Stacpoole)
STAFFORD (Buckingham, D) **DEP**; (Devon, E) **DEP**; (Stafford, B) **DEP**; (Stafford, of Clinton, B) **DEP**; (Wiltshire, E) **DEP**; *of Finkley* **LG1952**; *of*

Blatherwycke Park **LG1894**; *of Maine* **LGI1912**; **CG**; (*see also* FitzHerbert; and Howard)
STAIEN *of Beaupré and Llanquian* **LG1952**
STAINTHORPE *of Sunnyfield House* **LG1952**
STAINTON (*formerly* ARBUTHNOT-LESLIE) *of Warthill* **LG1972**
GILLESPIE-STAINTON *of Bitteswell House* **LG1921**
STAIR (*see* Dalrymple)
STALBRIDGE (*see* Grosvenor)
STALLYBRASS *of Oakhill* **LG1952**
STAMER, Bt **PB1970**; *of Bath* **HI**
STAMFORD (*see* Grey)
STAMFORDHAM (*see* Bigge)
STAMP, B **PB1970**
STANBRIDGE *of Daylesford and Clare* **CG**
STANCLIFFE *formerly of Sion Hill* **LG1952**
STANCOMB *formerly of Blount's Court* **LG1952**
STANDISH, Bt **EDB**; *formerly of Standish and Scaleby* **LG1972**; *of Duxbury* **LG1894**
TOWNELEY-STANDISH (*see* Towneley)
STANDLEY **DFUSA**
STANFORD **LGI1958**
FANE-BENETT-STANFORD *of Pythouse* **LG1937**
THOMAS-STANFORD, Bt **PB1932**
STANHOPE (Harrington, E) **PB1970**; (Chesterfield and Stanhope, E) **PB1967**; (Weardale, B) **PB1923**; B **DEP**; (*see also* Roddam)
SPENCER-STANHOPE *of Canon Hall* **LG1952**
STANIER, Bt **PB1970**; *of Peplow* **LG1914**
STANLEY (Derby, E) **PB1970**; (Sheffield, B) **PB1970**; (Ashfield, B) **PB1940**; (Monteagle, B) **DEP**; (Stanley, B) **DEP**; Bt **EDB**; *of Dalegarth and Ponsonby Hall* **LG1952**; *of Cross Hall* **LG1937**; *of Furze Hill* **LG1921**; **DFUSA**; (*see also* Errington)
MASSEY-STANLEY (*see* Errington)
SLOANE-STANLEY *formerly of Paultons* **LG1972**
WENTWORTH-STANLEY *of High Wych* **LG1965**
STANMORE (*see* Hamilton-Gordon)
STANNARD **FR**; (*see also* Bancroft)
ST CLAIR-STANNARD (*see* Sinclair)
STANNUS **IFR1976**; **AA**
STANSFELD *of Dunninald* **LG1972**

CROMPTON-STANSFIELD   (*now* CROMPTON) *formerly of Esholt Hall* **LG1952**

STANSGATE (*see* Wedgwood Benn)

STANTON *of Snelston Hall* **LG1969**; *formerly of The Thrupp and Armscote* **LG1969**; **DFUSA**

STANYFORTH *of Kirk Hammerton Hall* **LG1952**

STAPLES, Bt **PB1970**; *of Ashman's Hall* **LG1921**; (*see also* Staples-Browne)

STAPLETON, Bt **PB1970**; B **DEP**; **IFR1976**; *of Sands* **LG1952**

STAPLEY, Bt **EDB**

STAPYLTON, Bt *of Carlton* **EDB**; Bt *of Myton* **EDB**; *of Myton* **LG1937**

CHETWYND-STAPYLTON *formerly of Wighill* **LG1952**

STAREY *of Milton Ernest* **LG1937**

STARK *of Troqueer, Holm* **AA**

STARKE *of Laugharne Castle* **LG1937**

HAMILTON-STARKE *of Troqueer Holm* **LG1906**

STARKEY, Bt **PB1970**; *of Radway Grange* **LG1952**; *of Wrenbury Hall* **LG1937**; *of Norwood Park* **LG1921**; *of Wakefield* **HI**

BARBER-STARKEY *formerly of Darley Dale* **LG1952**

STARKIE *of Huntroyde* **LG1952**; *of Twiston* **LG1847**

STARKY *of Bromham* **LG1863**

STARTIN *of Wyndlawn and Linley Hall* **LG1937**

STATHERS *formerly of Ryhill* **DFUSA**

STAUFFER (*see* Taylor)

STAUNTON, Bt **PB1859**; *of Staunton* **LG1969**; *late of Longbridge* **LG1937**; *of Eynesbury* **CG**

LYNCH-STAUNTON *of Clydagh* **LGI1912**

STAVELEY *of North Staveley Hall* **LG1972**

PEPPER-STAVELEY *of Woldhurstlea* **LG1937**

STAVERT *of Hoscote* **LG1972**

STAWEL, B **DEP**

STAWELL *of Rhyll House, co Devon* **LG1850/3**; *of Coolmain and of Kilbrittain and Lisnegar, co Cork* **LGI1912**; *of Crobeg* **LGI1912**

ALOCK-STAWELL (*see* Stawell)

STEADE (*see* Craven-Smith-Milnes)

STEARNES *formerly of Nayland* **DFUSA**

STEBBINS *formerly of Stebbing* **DFUSA**

STEDALL *of Billington Manor* **LG1952**

STEEL, Bt **PB1904**; *of Philiphaugh* **LG1937**; **CG**

COKE-STEEL *of Trusley* **LG1972**

STRANG STEEL, Bt **PB1970**

STEELE *of Rathbride* **LG1886**; *of Carlton* **CG**

STEEN *of Mountsandel* **LGI1958**

STEERE **CG**

KEMMIS-STEINMAN (*see* Kemmis)

STEINTHAL *of Bradford* **AA**

STENHOUSE *of Comox* **CG**

STEPHEN, Bt **PB1970**; (Mount Stephen, B) **PB1921**; *of Cleughearn Lodge* **LG1952**; *of Sydney* **CG**

STEPHENS, Bt **EDB**; *of Church House* **LG1952**; *formerly of Eastington* **LG1952**; *formerly of Llechryd* **LG1952**; *of Stedcombe Manor* **LG1937**; *of Bentworth Lodge* **LG1914**; *of Llananno* **LG1875**; *of Tregenna* **LG1875**; **PromFUSA**; *of Manchester* **AA**; *of Trewornan* (*see* Darell); (*see also* Sneyd *of Coldrenick*)

STEPHENSON, Bt **PB1970**; *formerly of Park Grange* **LG1952**; *of Hassop Hall* **LG1937**; **FR**; (*see also* Standish *formerly of Standish*)

STEPNEY, Bt **EDB**; (*see also* Stepney-Gulston)

COWELL-STEPNEY *of Llanelly* **LG1863**; **AA**

HERBERT-STEPNEY (*formerly* RAWSON) *formerly of Durrow Abbey and Abingdon Park* **LGI1958**

HOWARD-STEPNEY (*see* Fitzalan-Howard)

STERN (Michelham, B) **PB1970**; Bt *of Chertsey* **PB1933**; (Wandsworth, B) **PB1912**; *of Highdown Tower* **LG1952**

STERNDALE (*see* Pickford)

STERRY **FR**

VON STETTIN (*formerly* YOUNG) **DFUSA**

STEUART, Bt **PB1851**; *formerly of Ballechin* **LG1952**; *of Down* **LG1937**; *of Steuart Hall* **LG1921**; *of Tanachie and Auchlunkart* (*see* Gordon); (*see also* Steuart-Menzies *of Culdares*; and Shaw-Stewart)

DUCKETT-STEUART (*see* Eustace-Duckett)

DURRANT-STEUART *of Dalguise* **LG1898**

SETON-STEUART (*see* Macdonald *of Clanranald*)

STEVENS *of Dingle Bank* **LG1969**; *formerly of Caversham* **DFUSA**

MOORE-STEVENS *of Winscott* **LG1921**
STEWART-STEVENS *(formerly* STEW-
ART) *of Balnakeilly* **LG1972**
STEVENSON, B **PB1917**; *of Bolton Old
Hall, formerly of Westoe* **LG1972**; *of
Balladoole* **LG1952**; *late of Foxlease*
LG1937; *late of Playford Mount*
LG1937; *of Braidwood* **LG1921**; *of
Uffington* **LG1886**; **IFR1976**; *(Aus-
tralia)* **CG**
STUART-STEVENSON *(see* Stevenson
Hamilton)
STEWARD *of Gowthorpe Manor*
LG1952; *of Crawfordsburn* **LG1937**
Supp; *of Newton Manor* **LG1886**; *of
Nottington House* **LG1898**; *of Blunder-
ston* **LG1875**
STEWART (Galloway, E) **PB1970**; Bt *of
Athenree* **PB1970**; Bt *of Balgownie*
PB1970; Bt *of Fingask* **PB1970**; Bt *of
Ramelton* **PB1970**; Bt *of Stewartby*
PB1970; Bt *of Strathgarry* **PB1970**; Bt
of South Kensington **PB1949**; Bt *of
Allanbrook* **PB1849**; (Albany, D) **DEP**;
(Lennox, D) **DEP**; (Richmond, D) **DEP**;
(Ross, D) **DEP**; (Arran, E) **DEP**;
(Athol, E) **DEP**; (Atholl, E) **DEP**;
(Blesington, E) **DEP**; (Buchan, E) **DEP**;
(Carrick, E) **DEP**; (Mar, E) **DEP**; (Mar
and Garioch, E) **DEP**; (Orkney, E)
DEP; (Pittenweem, E) **DEP**; (Avon-
dale, Lord) **DEP**; (Bothwell, Lord) **DEP**;
(Methven, Lord) **DEP**; (Ochiltree, Lord)
DEP; (St Colme, Lord) **DEP**; Bt **EDB**;
Bt of Burray **EDB**; *of Appin* **LG1972**;
of Ardvorlich **LG1972**; *of Achnacone*
LG1952; *formerly of Alltyrodyn*
LG1952; *formerly of Ardpatrick*
LG1952; *formerly of Blackhouse*
LG1952; *of Cairnsmore* **LG1952**; *of
Banchory-Devenick* **LG1952**; *of Kin-
lochmoidart* **LG1952**; *of Lochbrae
House* **LG1952**; *of Murdostoun*
LG1952; *of Shambellie* **LG1952**; *of
Coll* **LG1937**; *of Garvochs* **LG1886**; *of
St Fort* **LG1886**; *of Urrard* **LG1886**;
formerly of Horn Head **LGI1958**; *of
Ballymena* **LGI1912**; *of Summerhill*
LGI1912; *(New Zealand)* **CG**; **DFUSA**;
formerly of Londonderry **DFUSA**; *for-
merly of Moneyrea* **DFUSA**; *of Murdos-
toun, co Lanark* **AA**; *of Craigiehall* **VF**;
of Binny (see Falconer-Stewart)
CUMBRAE-STEWART *of Montrose and
Wildernesse* **CG**
DRUMMOND-STEWART, Bt **PB1890**

FALCONAR-STEWART *of Feddal*
LG1952
HENDERSON-STEWART, Bt **PB1970**
JOHNSTON STEWART *of Physgill*
LG1952; *(formerly* CORSE-SCOTT)
of Synton **LG1952**
McTAGGART-STEWART, Bt **PB1940**
MURRAY-STEWART *(see* Galloway)
POYNTZ-STEWART *of Chesfield*
LG1937
SHAW-STEWART, Bt **PB1970**
VANE-TEMPEST-STEWART (London-
derry, M) **PB1970**
STILL *of Walreddon Manor* **LG1937**
STILLINGFLEET *of How Caple, co
Hereford* **LG1850/3**
STILWELL *formerly of Hilfield* **LG1952**
STINSON **DFUSA**
STIRLING, Bt **PB1970**; Bt *of Faskine*
PB1934; Bt *of Mansfield* **PB1844**; Bt *of
Ardoch* **EDB**; *formerly of Cadder and
Muiravonside* **LG1972**; *of Garden*
LG1972; *of Gargunnock* **LG1972**; *of
Fairburn* **LG1965**; *late of Larbert*
LG1937; (1) & (2) **DFUSA**; *of Auchyle
(see* Sheppard *of Rednock)*; *of Kippen-
davie (see* Stirling-Aird)
GRAHAM-STIRLING *of Dalginross*
LG1937
STISTED *of Egerton* **LG1937**
STOBART *of Farlam Ghyll* **LG1965**; *of
Headlam Hall* **LG1965**; *of Helme Park
formerly of Harperley Park* **LG1952**; *of
Pepper Arden* **LG1900**
STOCKDALE, Bt **PB1970**; *of Mears
Ashby Hall* **LG1900**
STOCKENSTROM, Bt **PB1956**
STOCKER *formerly of North Lands*
LG1952; *of Alvara House* **LG1937**
STOCKS, B **PB1970**; *formerly of Upper
Shibden* **LG1952**
STOCKTON *of St John* **CG**
STODART *of Kailzie and Ormiston*
LG1850/3
TWEEDIE-STODART *of Oliver* **LG1952**
STODDARD **PromFUSA**
STOFFOLD *(see* Godwin-Austen)
STOKER, Bt **PB1912**
STOKES; B **PB1970**; Bt **PB1916**; *St
Botolphs* **LG1937**; **IFR1976**; *of Mount-
hawk* **LGI1912**; **DFUSA**
STONE *formerly of Scyborwen* **LG1952**;
late of Erdington **LG1921**; **IFR1976**; *of
Kirby Firth Hall* **LG1921**; *late of Lea
Park* **LG1894**; *of Streatley House*
LG1886; *formerly of King's Bromley*
DFUSA; **FR**; *(see also* Bellyse Baker)

WARRY-STONE *of Badbury* **LG1937**
STONEHAVEN (*see* Baird)
STONESTREET *of Stondon* **LG1875**
STONEY **IFR1976**
BUTLER-STONEY *formerly of Portland Park* **LGI1958**
STONHAM (*see* Collins)
STONHOUSE, Bt **PB1970**; Bt **EDB**
STONOR (Camoys, B) **PB1970**
STOPFORD (Courtown, E) **PB1970**; (Stopford of Fallowfield, B) **PB1959**
STOPHAM (*see* Dawson *of Weston*)
JACKSON-STOPS *of Wood Burcote Court* **LG1952**
STORER (*now* EVANS) *of Purley Park* **LG1921**; *of Combe Court* **LG1875**
STOREY (Buckton, B) **PB1970**; *of Burton Hill House* **LG1937**; *formerly of Newcastle-on-Tyne* **DFUSA**
STORIE *of Camberwell, co Surrey* **LG1850/3**
STORRS *of Cusworth* **LG1969**; *formerly of Sutton-cum-Lound* **DFUSA**
STORY *of Lockington* **LG1875**; **IFR1976**
STOTHERT *of Cargen* **LG1863**
STOTT, Bt **PB1970**; *of Craigdun* **LG1937Supp**; *of Oldham and Stanton* **LG1914**
STOUGHTON, Bt **EDB**; *of Owlpen* **LGI1912**
STOURTON (Mowbray, Segrave and Stourton, B) **PB1970**
STOUT **DFUSA**; **CG**
STOW *of Hessle* **LG1952**
PHILIPSON-STOW, Bt **PB1970**; *of Blackdown House* **LG1906**
STOWELL *formerly of Bath* **DFUSA**; (*see also* Scott)
STOW HILL (*see* Soskice)
STRABOLGI (*see* Kenworthy)
STRACEY, Bt **PB1970**
STRACHAN, Bt **EDB**; *of Heacham Hall* **LG1937**
STRACHEY (O'Hagan, B) **PB1970**; (Strachie, B) **PB1970**
STRACHIE (*see* Strachey)
STRADBROKE (*see* Rous)
STRADLING, Bt **EDB**
STRAFFORD (*see* Byng; and Wentworth)
STRAKER *of Stagshaw* **LG1965**
STRANG, B **PB1970**
STRANGE (Strange, of Blackmere, B) **DEP**; (Strange, of Ellesmere, B) **DEP**; (Strange, of Knokyn, B) **DEP**; (*Alberta, Canada*) **CG**; (*Ontario, Canada*) **CG**
STRANGE OF KNOKIN (*see* Philipps)
STRANGFORD (*see* Smythe)

SWAINSTON-STRANGWAYES *of Alne* **LG1921**
STRANGWAYS *of Shapwick* **LG1906**
FOX-STRANGWAYS (Ilchester, E) **PB1970**
STRATFORD (Aldborough, E) **DEP**; *of Farmcote and of Sapperton Manor* **LG1914**
MORGAN-STRATFORD **FR**
WINGFIELD-STRATFORD (*see* Powerscourt)
STRATFORD DE REDCLIFFE (*see* Canning)
STRATHALMOND (*see* Fraser)
STRATHBOGIE (Athol, E) **DEP**
STRATHCARRON (*see* Macpherson)
STRATHCLYDE (*see* Galbraith; and Ure)
STRATHCONA AND MOUNT ROYAL (*see* Howard; and Smith)
STRATHEDEN AND CAMPBELL (*see* Campbell)
STRATHERN (*see* Graham; and Malise)
STRATHMORE AND KINGHORNE (*see* Bowes-Lyon)
STRATHNAIRN (*see* Rose)
STRATHSPEY (*see* Grant of Grant; and Ogilvie Grant)
STRATHY (*Canada*) **CG**
STRATTON *of Turweston* **LG1921**
VAN STRAUBENZEE (*see sub* VAN)
STRAUSS (Conesford, B) **PB1970**
STREATFEILD *formerly of Chiddingstone* **LG1972**; (*see also* Streatfeild-Moore)
SCARLETT-STREATFEILD *of The Rocks* **LG1969**
STRELLEY *of Oakethorpe* **LG1863**
STRETCH (*Australia*) **CG**
STRETTELL **LG1965**
STRICKLAND, B **PB1970**; *of Apperley Court* **LG1921**; *of Cokethorpe Park* **LG1879**; (*see also* Marriott)
HORNYOLD-STRICKLAND *of Sizergh* **LG1972**
CHETHAM-STRODE *of Southhill* **LG1894**
GRIGGS-STRODE *of Newnham Park* **LG1952**
STRONG *formerly of Thorpe Hall* **LG1952**; *of Nether Stronge now of The Chase* **LG1898**; **DFUSA**; (*see also* Gilchrist)
STRONGE, Bt **PB1970**
STROTHER *of Killinghall* **LG1937**; *of Eastfield, Northumberland* **AA**
STROYAN *of Lanrick* **LG1952**

STRUTT (Belper, B) **PB1970**; (Rayleigh, B) **PB1970**; Bt **EDB**; *of Belper* **LG1952**
STRYVELIN, B **DEP**
STUART (Castle Stewart, E) **PB1970**; (Moray, E) **PB1970**; (Stuart of Findhorn, V) **PB1970**; Bt **PB1970**; (Cambridge, D) **DEP**; (Gloucester, D) **DEP**; (Kendal, D) **DEP**; (York, D) **DEP**; (Traquair, E) **DEP**; (Stuart de Rothesay, B) **DEP;** (*see also* Stuart-Wortley); *of Inchbreck* **LG1921**; *of Kishorn* **LG1921**; *of Tempsford Hall* **LG1921**; *of Ballyhivistock* **LGI1958**; (*House of*) **RL**; *formerly of Ballydougherty* **DFUSA**; **FR**; *of Sydney* **CG**; (*see also* Corbett *of Peniarth Ucha*; and Stuart *of Wortley*)
BURNETT-STUART *of Ardmeallie* **LG1972**
CRICHTON-STUART (Bute, M) **PB1970**
CONSTABLE - MAXWELL - STUART (*see* Norfolk)
MOODY-STUART *of Annat* **LG1937**
CRAWFURD-STIRLING-STUART (*see* Stirling *of Gardon*)
VILLIERS-STUART (Stuart de Decies, B) **PB1874**; **IFR1976**; (*see also* Bute)
VILLIERS - STUART (*formerly* FIELDEN) *of Beachamwell* **LG1952**
HAMILTON STUBBER **IFR1976**; (*see also* Hamilton (*co Leix*))
STUBBS *of Danby* **LG1937Supp**; *of Wigwell Grange* **LG1898**; *of Cannock* **LG1863**; *of Fort William and Ballyboden* **LGI1912**
STUBLEY *formerly of Wiggerhall St Mary's* **LG1937**
STUCKEY *of Hill House* **LG1898**; (*New Zealand*) **CG**
STUCLEY, Bt **PB1970**
STUDD, Bt **PB1970**; *formerly of Exeleigh* **LG1952**
STUDDERT **IFR1976**
STUDDY *formerly of Waddeton Court* **LG1952**; **AA**
STUDHOLME, Bt **PB1970**; *of Perridge House* **LG1952**; *of Ballyeighan* **LGI1912**; **CG**
STUKELEY, Bt **EDB**
STUMP (*see* Haldane)
STURDEE, Bt **PB1970**
STURDY *of Trigon* **LG1952**
STURGES *of Stewkley House* **LG1952**; *formerly of Clipston* **DFUSA**
GRANT-STURGIS (*formerly* GRANT) *of Hillersdon House* **LG1952**
STURT (Alington, B) **PB1940**; *of Lower Churn* **LG1972**; (*Australia*) **CG**

STYCH, Bt **EDB**
STYDOLF, Bt **EDB**
STYLE, Bt **PB1970**; Bt **EDB**; *of Bicester House* **LG1863**
STYLEMAN (*see* Le Strange)
SUCKLING *of Barsham* **LG1952**
SUDBURY *of Wonersh Park* **LG1921**
SUDELEY, B **DEP**; (*see also* Hanbury-Tracy)
SUFFIELD (*see* Harbord-Hamond)
SUFFOLK (*see* Grey; Pole; and Ufford)
SUFFOLK AND BERKSHIRE (*see* Howard)
SUGDEN (St Leonards, B) **PB1970**
SUGRUE *of Fermoyle* **LGI1958**
SULLIVAN, Bt **PB1970**; Bt *of Garryduff* **PB1937**; **IFR1976**; *of Tullileas* **LGI1912**; *of Curramore* **LGI1912**; **PromFUSA**
SULLIVAN (*or* O'SULLIVAN) *formerly of Arden Castle* **DFUSA**
SUMMERS, Bt **PB1970**; *of Burnham House* **LG1952**
SUMMERSKILL, B **PB1970**
SUMMERSON *of Coatham Mundeville formerly of Haughton-le-Skerne* **LG1952**
SUMNER *of Ashfield House* **LG1937**; *of Park Hall* **LG1921**; *of Puttenham Priory* **LG1898**; *of Milton House* **LG1906**; **PromFUSA**; **FR**; (*see also* Hamilton)
SUNDERLAND **DFUSA**; (*see also* Scrope)
SUNDERLIN (*see* Malone)
SUNDON (*see* Clayton)
SUNLIGHT *of Hallside* **LG1937**
SURMAN *of Swindon Hall* **LG1879**
SURREY (*see* Holland; and Warren)
SURTEES *formerly of Dinsdale-on-Tees* **LG1969**; *formerly of Redworth* **LG1965**; (*see also* Altham)
SUSSEX (*see* Guelph; Lennard; Ratcliffe; Savile; and Yelverton)
SUTCLIFFE *of May Royd* **LG1952**
SUTER (*New Zealand*) **CG**
SUTHERLAND, Bt **PB1970**; (Duffus, Lord) **PB1875**; *of Noith Slipperfield, Ferniehaugh and Medwynhead* **LG1972**; *of Forse* **LG1937**; *late of Skibo Castle* **LG1914**; (*see also* Egerton; and Janson)
GRANT-SUTTIE, Bt **PB1970**
SUTTON, Bt **PB1970**; Bt *of Castle House* **PB1940**; Bt *of Beckenhem* **PB1934**; (Dudley, B) **DEP**; (Lexington, B) **DEP**; (Sutton, B) **DEP**; Bt *of Moulson* **EDB**; *of Elton* **LG1863**; *of*

Rossway **LG1863**; (1) & (2) **DFUSA**;
formerly of Yarndon **DFUSA**; **FR**
BLAND-SUTTON, Bt **PB1936**
MANNERS-SUTTON (Canterbury,
V) **PB1940**
SUTTOR (*Australia*) **CG**
SWABEY *of Langley Marish* **LG1952**
SWAINE *of Wisbech* **LG1850/3**
SWAINSON *formerly of Wistanstow*
LG1952
SWALE, Bt **EDB**
SWAN, Bt **EDB**; *of Boxford House*
LG1969; *of Baldwintown* **LG1886**; *of
Ardeelan* **LGI1958**; **FR**
SWANBOROUGH (*see* Isaacs)
SWANN, Bt **PB1970**; *late of Askham
Hall* **LG1898**; *formerly of Bedlington*
DFUSA
SWANSEA (*see* Vivian)
SWANSON *of Wergs Hall* **LG1952**
SWANZY **FR**
SWAYNE *formerly of Midleton* **LGI1958**;
FR
SWAYTHLING (*see* Montagu)
SWEDEN (*Royal House of*) **RL**
SWEET **DFUSA**
SWEETMAN **IFR1976**
SWETENHAM *formerly of Somerford
Booths* **LG1969**
WARREN-SWETTENHAM *of Swetten-
ham* **LG1921**
SWIFT (Carlingford, V) **DEP;** *formerly
of Rotherham* **DFUSA**; (*see also*
Swifte)
SWIFTE **IFR1976**
SWILLINGTON, B **DEP**
SWINBURNE *of Pontop Hall* **LG1952**
SWINFEN *of Swinfen* **LG1875**; (*see also*
Eady)
SWINLEY *of Broughtons* **LG1972**
SWINTON *of that Ilk* **LG1972**; *of
Kimmerghame* **LG1965**; (*see also*
Cunliffe-Lister)
SWIRE *of Hubbards Hall, formerly of
Hillingdon House* **LG1965**; *of Orbost,
formerly of Cononlay, Hartwith and
Littlethorpe* **LG1965**
SWITHINBANK *formerly of Denham
Court* **LG1972**
SWITZER **IFR1976**
SWORD (*formerly* ERNST) *of West-
combe* **LG1952**
DENNISTOUN SWORD *formerly of
Glottenham* **LG1972**
SWYFTE (*see* Swifte)
SWYNNERTON, B **DEP**

SYDENHAM, Bt **EDB**; (*see also*
Clarke and Thomson)
SYDNEY (Leicester, E) **DEP**; (Romney,
E) **DEP**; *of The Bourne* **LG1863**;
(*see also* Cosby; and Townshend)
BUCHAN-SYDSERFF *formerly of
Ruchlaw* **LG1952**
SYKES, Bt *of Basildon* **PB1970**; Bt *of
Kingsknowes* **PB1970**; Bt *of Sledmere*
PB1970; Bt *of Cheadle* **PB1940**; *of
Norrington* **LG1972**; *of Ball's Grove*
LG1952; **DFUSA**
SYLYARD, Bt **EDB**
SYME **DFUSA**
SYMES (*see* Sims; and Symes-Bullen)
SYMINGTON *formerly of Dalkeith*
DFUSA; *formerly of Paisley* **DFUSA**
SYMONDS *of Pengethly* **LG1937**;
DFUSA; **CG**
LODER-SYMONDS *formerly of Hinton
Waldrist* **LG1952**
SOLTAU-SYMONDS *of Chaddlewood*
LG1937
SYMONS, Bt **EDB**; *of Hatt* **LG1952**;
of Mynde Park **LG1921**
SYNGE, Bt **PB1970**; **IFR1976**
HART-SYNNOT **IFR1976**
SYNNOTT **IFR1976**
SYNOT (*see* Synnott)
SYSONBY (*see* Ponsonby)
TAAFFE, V **PB1917**; (Carlingford, E)
DEP; IFR1976
TABOR *of Little Codham Hall* **LG1972**;
of Bull's Green **LG1965**; *of Beech House*
LG1952
TABRIA, B **TNBE1956**
TACON *of Eye* **LG1952**
TADDY *of Caldecott* **LG1937**
TAFF **DFUSA**
TAFT **PresFUSA**
TAGART *of Northcote Manor* **LG1921**
TAILBY *of Skeffington* **LG1914**; *of
Quenby Hall* **LG1863**
RENNY-TAILYOUR *of Borrowfield*
LG1952
TAIT *of Milrigg* **LG1921**
TALBOT (Talbot de Malahide, B)
PB1970; Bt *of Belfast* **PB1850**;
(Furnival, B) **PB1849**; (Shrewsbury, D)
DEP; (Tyrconnel, D) **DEP**; (L'Isle, V)
DEP; Bt *of Carton* **EDB**; *of Lacock*
LG1937; *of Margam* **LG1900**; (*see*
Crosbie; and O'Reilly (*cos Dublin,
Kildare, Longford and Wexford*)
CHETWYND-TALBOT (Shrewsbury and
Waterford, E) **PB1970**
TALBOYS, B **DEP**

TALCOTT *formerly of Braintree* **DFUSA**
MACKAY-TALLACK *of Bicknor Park* **LG1952**
TALLMADGE **DFUSA**
TAMLYN *of Barnston* **LG1952**
TANCRED *of Weens* **LG1921**
LAWSON-TANCRED, Bt **PB1970**
TANGLEY (*see* Herbert)
TANGYE, Bt **PB1970**
TANKERVILLE (*see* Bennet; and Grey)
TANNER *of King's Nympton Park* **LG1952**; *of Hawson Court* **LG1921**
TAPPER *of Invercargill* **CG**
TARA (*see* Preston)
TARBELL **DFUSA**
TARDREW *of Aunery House* **LG1863**
TARDY *of The Grove* **LG1863**
TARLETON, Bt **EDB**; *of Breakspears* **LG1937**; *formerly of Killeigh Abbey* **LG1937Supp**
TARLTON *of Glenelg, Stirling East, and Adelaide* **CG**
TARRAS (*see* Scott)
TARRATT (*now* ROGERS) *of Ellary* **LG1937**
TASBOROUGH (*see* Anne)
TATE, Bt **PB1970**; *of Cheam Hall* **LG1879**; *formerly of Londonderry* **DFUSA**
TATEM (Glanely, B) **PB1940**
TATHAM *of Summerfield House* **LG1863**; (*see also* Bickersteth)
TATTERSALL *of Charlton Place* **LG1937**; **FR**
TATTESHALL, B **DEP**
TATTON (*formerly* TOWNLEY-PARKER) *of Cuerden* **LG1952**; *formerly of Wythenshawe* **LG1952**
FRY-GOLDIE-TAUBMAN *of The Nunnery* **LG1952**
TAUNTON *of Freeland Lodge* **LG1875**; (*see also* Labouchere)
TAYLEUR *late of Buntingsdale* **LG1937**
TAYLOR, B **PB1970**; (Taylor of Mansfield, B) **PB1970**; (Taylor of Gryfe, B) **PB1970**; Bt *of Cawthorne* **PB1970**; Bt *of Kennington* **PB1970**; (Maenan, B) **PB1949**; Bt *of Hollycombe* **PB1876**; Bt *of Lysson Hall* **EDB**; Bt *of Park House* **EDB**; *of Chipchase Castle* **LG1969**; *of Dodworth and Scaftworth* **LG1969**; *of Starston* **LG1969**; *of North Aston* **LG1965**; *formerly of Birkdault* **LG1952**; *of Dunmore* **LG1952**; *of Grassington* **LG1952**; *of Middlewood Hall* **LG1952**; *of Strensham* **LG1937**; *of Barnet* **LG1921**; *of Carshalton*

Park **LG1921**; *of Rendcomb Park* **LG1921**; *of Sherfield Manor* **LG1921**; *of Stanbury and Baysgarth Park* **LG1921**; *late of Tyn Llwyn* **LG1898**; *of Radcliffe-on-Trent* **LG1894**; *of Aston Rowant* **LG1875**; *of Burnham Manor* **LG1875**; *of Beaconfield late of Ogwell* **LG1875**; *of Todmorden Hall* **LG1875**; *of Ballinure* **LG11912**; **RFFK**; **PresFUSA**; **DFUSA**; *formerly of Carlisle* **DFUSA**; *formerly of Chediston* **DFUSA**; *formerly of Dudley Port* **DFUSA**; *formerly of Smethwick* **DFUSA**; *formerly of Tunbridge Wells* **DFUSA**; (1) (2) & (3) **FR**; *of Moreton Hall* **AA**; *of Strensham* **AA**; *of Todmorden Hall* **AA**; *of Penmaenucha* (*see* Wylie-Jones); (*see also* Granchester; and Taylor-Smith)
CHATFIELD-TAYLOR **DFUSA**
CLOUGH-TAYLOR *of Firby Hall* **LG1921**
KIRWAN-TAYLOR (*see* Grantchester)
ODDIN-TAYLOR *of Hardingham Grove* **LG1952**
PRINGLE-TAYLOR *of Pennington* **LG1898**
SHAWE-TAYLOR **IFR1976**
SUENSON-TAYLOR (Grantchester, B) **PB1970**
WATSON-TAYLOR *formerly of Erlestoke Park and Urchfont* **LG1952**
WORSLEY-TAYLOR, Bt **PB1956**; *of Moreton Hall* **LG1914**
TAYLOUR (Headfort, M) **PB1970**
TAYSIDE (*see* Urquhart)
TCHKOTOUA **DFUSA**
TEACKLE **DFUSA**
TEALE *of Leeds* **AA**
TEBBETT *of Rickling Hall* **LG1952**
TEDDER, B **PB1970**
TEELING (*formerly* BURKE) *formerly of Ower* **LG1958**
TEIGNMOUTH (*see* Shore)
TEMPEST, Bt *of Broughton Hall* **PB1865**; Bt *of Stella* **EDB**; Bt *of Tong* **EDB**; *of Broughton* **LG1972**; **FR**
PLUMBE TEMPEST (*see* Tempest)
TEMPLE, Bt **PB1970**; (Palmerston, V) **DEP**; Bt **EDB**; *formerly of Bishopstrow* **LG1952**; *of Dale House* **LG1952**; *formerly of East Knoyle* **LG1952**; **PromFUSA**
TEMPLE OF STOWE (*see* Temple-Gore-Langton)
TEMPLEMORE (*see* Chichester)
TEMPLER *late of Lindridge* **LG1937**;

of Stover **LG1863**; *formerly of Loughgall* **LG11958**
TEMPLETOWN (*see* Upton)
TEMPLEWOOD (*see* Hoare)
TENBY (*see* Lloyd George)
TENCH, Bt **EDB**; *of Ballyhaly* **LG1875**
TENISON *formerly of Rock Hall and Portnelligan* **LGI1958**; (*Tasmania*; **CG**; *of Lough Bawn* (*see* Hanbury-Tenison)
HANBURY-TENISON **IFR1976**
KING-TENISON (Kingston, E) **PB1970**
TENNANT (Glenconner, B) **PB1970**; *of The Eades formerly of St Anne's Manor* **LG1952**; *of Arncliffe Cote late of Chapel House* **LG1937**; **FR**
COOMBE TENNANT *of Cadoxton* **LG1952**
EMERSON-TENNENT, Bt **PB1876**; *of Tempo* **LG1863**
TOVEY-TENNENT *of Pynnacles and Poole Castle* **LG1863**
TENNYSON, B **PB1970**
TENTERDEN (*see* Abbott)
TERRINGTON (*see* Woodhouse)
TERRY **LG1972**; *formerly of Burvale* **LG1952**
IMBERT-TERRY, Bt **PB1970**
TESCHEMAKER *of Taipo Hill and Kauro Hill* **CG**
TESHMAKER (*see* Busk)
TEVIOT (*see* Kerr; Livingston; Rutherford; and Spencer)
TEW *formerly of Moorlands and Rawcliffe* **LG1972**
TEYNHAM (*see* Roper-Curzon)
THACKERAY **FR**
THACKWELL *formerly of Wilton Place* **LG1952**; *of Aghada Hall* **LGI1912**
PENROSE-THACKWELL (*see* Uniacke)
THANET (*see* Tufton)
THANKERTON (*see* Watson)
THARP *of Chippenham Park* **LG1952**
THELLUSSON (Rendlesham, B) **PB1970**; (*see also* Grant-Dalton)
THELWALL *of Llanbedr, co Denbigh* **LG1850/3**
THESIGER (Chelmsford, B) **PB1970**
THICKNESSE **LG1969**; *of Beech Hill* **AA**
THISTLETHWAYTE **LG1965**; (*see also* Borthwick-Norton)
THOMAS, Bt *of Garreglwyd* **PB1970**; Bt *of Wenvoe* **PB1970**; Bt *of Yapton* **PB1970**; Bt *of Ynyshir* **PB1970**; (Cilcennin, V) **PB1959**; (Rhondda, V) **PB1956**; (Pontypridd, B) **PB1927**; Bt *of Folkington* **EDB**; Bt *of Mitchelstown*

EDB; *of Southwick* **LG1972**; *formerly of The Poolfold* **LG1969**; *of Buckland* **LG1952**; *of Cefndyrys* (*formerly Welfield*) **LG1952**; *of Cockerton Hall* **LG1952**; *of Silver Ridge* **LG1952**; *of Kilvrough* **LG1937**; *of Ystrad Mynach and Llanbradach* **LG1937**; *Belmont* **LG1937Supp**; *of Trevor* **LG1898**; *of Brooklands* **LG1886**; *of Pwllywrach* **LG1863**; (1) & (2) **DFUSA**; **PromFUSA**; (*see also* Macthomas; and Pritchard)
BEAUMONT-THOMAS *of Great Brampton* **LG1937**
DE VISME THOMAS *of Eyhorne House* **LG1952**
EVAN-THOMAS *of Llwyn Madoc* **LG1952**
FREEMAN-THOMAS (Willingdon, M) **PB1970**; *of Ratton* **LG1906**
GORING-THOMAS *of Gellywernen formerly of Plâs Llannon* **LG1952**
HAMBLEN-THOMAS *of Caister Castle* **LG1952**
PATTEN-THOMAS (*see* Thomas *of Southwick*)
SKYRING THOMAS (*see* Thomas *of Southwick*)
VOSPER-THOMAS (*see* Vosper)
THOMOND (*see* O'Brien; and Wyndham-O'Brien)
THOMPSON, Bt, *of Guiseley* **PB1970**; Bt *of Hartsbourne Manor* **PB1970**; Bt *of Reculver* **PB1970**; Bt *of Walton-on-the-Hill* **PB1970**; Bt *of Wimpole Street* **PB1940**; Bt *of Virkes* **PB1868**; (Haversham, B) **DEP**; Bt **EDB**; Bt *of Haversham* **EDB**; *formerly of Clements* **LG1952**; *of East Bolton* **LG1952**; *of Gatacre Park* **LG1952**; *of Nunwick Hall* **LG1952**; *of Cranberry Portage* **LG1952Supp**; *of Newcastle Court* **LG1937**; *of Ashdown Park* **LG1914**; *of Sheriff Hutton* **LG1879**; *of Kirby Hall* **LG1875**; *of Rathnally* **LGI1958**; *of Triermore House* **LGI1958**; *of Clonfin* **LGI1912**; *of Kilcoke* **LGI1912**; *of Altnaveigh* **LGI1912**; *of Muckamore Abbey* **LGI1899**; (*see also* Sandford)
THOMPSON (*formerly* BIBBY) *of Sansaw* **LG1952Supp**
HOWARD THOMPSON *of Coton Hall* **LG1952**
MEYSEY-THOMPSON, Bt **PB1970**; (Knaresborough, B) **PB1929**
PEARSE-THOMPSON *of Kilham* **LG1898**

YOUNG-THOMPSON (*late* GREEN THOMPSON) *of Bridekirk* LG1937
THOMS *of Aberlemno* LG1952; FR
THOMSON (Thomson of Fleet, B) **PB1970;** Bt *of Glendarroch* **PB1970;** Bt *of Old Nunthorpe* **PB1970;** B **PB1930;** (Kelvin, B) **PB1907;** (Sydenham B) **DEP;** *of Corstorphine* LG1969; *of Duntrune* LG1952; *of Milton Brodie formerly of Muckairn* LG1952; *of Woodperry* LG1952; *of Banchory* LG1879; *of Castleton* LG1879; *of Treveryan* LG1863; *of Kenfield* LG1863; *formerly of Strantner* **DFUSA;** *of Lennel* **CG;** *of Charleton* **AA**
ANSTRUTHER-THOMSON   (*now* BONDE) *of Charleton* LG1952
CHARTERIS-THOMSON (*see* Charteris *of Armisfield*)
COURTAULD-THOMSON, B **PB1953**
MITCHELL-THOMSON (Selsdon, B) **PB1970**
WHITE-THOMSON *formerly of Broomford Manor* LG1972
THORBURN *formerly of Craigerne* LG1972
THORNE *of Knowl Hill House* LG1969
THORNELY *of Dodworth Hall* LG1863
THORNEWILL *of Dove Cliff* LG1875
THORNEYCROFT, B **PB1970;** *of Tettenhall Wood* **AA**
THORNHILL, Bt **EDB;** *of Fixby, Boxworth and Diddington* LG1972; *of Woodleys* LG1863
DAVIE-THORNHILL *of Stanton* LG1972
THORNHURST, Bt **EDB**
THORNICROFT, Bt **EDB**
THORNTON *formerly of Birkin* LG1969; *of Brockhall* LG1969; *of High Cross* LG1937; *of Ewell* LG1900; *of Grenville* LG1858; (Cassilhas, Count) **FT1939; FR; CG;** *of Sydney* **CG**
TODD-THORNTON *of Westbrook* **LGI1912**
THORNYCROFT *formerly of Thornycroft Hall* LG1969
THOROLD, Bt **PB1970;** Bt *of Harmeston* **EDB;** Bt *of The Haugh* **EDB**
GRANT-THOROLD *formerly of Weelsby House* LG1965
THOROTON (*see* Hildyard *of Flintham Hall*)
THORP *of Alnwick* LG1952; *of Headingley* LG1863; *of Ryton* LG1863; (*see also* Cobham)

THORPE, B **DEP;** *formerly of Coddington* LG1952; *late of Choisi* LG1937
THOYTS *formerly of Sulhamstead* LG1972
THRASH **DFUSA**
THREIPLAND, Bt **PB1882**
MURRAY THREIPLAND *of Dale and Toftinghall and Fingask* LG1972
THRELFALL *formerly of Grug Hill and Threlfall-in-the-Fylde* LG1952
THRING, Bt **PB1907;** *of Alford House* LG1972
THROCKMORTON, Bt **PB1970;** Bt **EDB; PromFUSA**
THRUSTON (*now* AUSTEN-LEIGH) *of Pennal* LG1952; (*see also* Mott-Radclyffe)
THUNDER *formerly of Lagore* LG1958
THURBURN LG1969
THURLOW (*see* Hovell-Thurlow-Cumming Bruce)
IM THURN *of Stainforth* LG1952
THURSBY, Bt **PB1940;** *of Culverlands* **LC1952**
THURSO (*see* Sinclair)
THURSTON *of Glebe Court* LG1952; **CG**
THWAITES *of Barley End* LG1937
THWENG, B **DEP;** LG1833/7
THYNNE (Bath, M) **PB1970;** (Carteret, B) **DEP**
TIARKS *formerly of Foxbury* LG1965
TIBBITS *of Barton Seagrave and Rothwell Grange* LG1898; (*see also* Maunsell)
TIBEAUDO *of Portnehinch, Queen's co* LG1850/3
TIBETOT (Tibetot, B) **DEP;** (Worcester, E) **DEP**
TICHBORNE (Ferrard, B) **DEP;** Bt **EDB**
DOUGHTY-TICHBORNE, Bt **PB1967**
TICKELL *formerly of Carnalway* **LGI1958**
TIDSWELL *formerly of Haresfield Court* LG1952; FR
TIDY (*see* Manbey)
TIERNEY, Bt **PB1860**
TIGHE *of Tegg Down* LG1972; **IFR1976**
TILDESLEY *of Kingslow Hall* LG1952 **Supp**
TILGHMAN *formerly of Holloway Court* **DFUSA; PromFUSA**
TILLARD *formerly of The Holme* LG1972; *of The Hooke* LG1972
TILLEY *of Duncreggan House* **LGI1912; CG**
TILNEY *of Sutton Bonington* LG1952

TIMPSON *formerly of Appleton Manor* LG1969
TINDAL *of Hanningfield* LG1879; *of Chelmsford* LG1863; *(Australia)* CG; *(see also* Tindal-Carrill-Worsley)
TINKER *of Meal Hill* LG1952
TINNE FR
TIPPETTS DFUSA
TIPPING, Bt EDB
GARTSIDE-TIPPING *(now* RICHARDSON) *of Bolton* LG1937
TISDALL *of Boughton Hall* LG1937; IFR1976
MAITLAND-TITTERTON *of Landmore* LGI1958
TITTLE *of Farm Hill* LG1863
TODD B PB1970; (1) & (2) DFUSA; *(Australia)* CG; *of Halnaby Hall* AA; *(see also* Madison)
STUART TODD *of Woodstock House formerly Clent Grove* LG1952
WILSON-TODD, Bt *of Eaton Place* PB1926; Bt *of Halnaby Hall* PB1925; *of Tranby Park Halnaby* LG1898
TODHUNTER *formerly of Kingsmoor House* LG1969
TOKE *of Bucksford formerly of Godington* LG1952; *of Godington* HI
TOLCHER FR
TOLER *of Swettenham Hall* LG1937
GRAHAM-TOLER (Norbury, E) PB1970
TOLHURST FR
TOLL *of Strete* LG1937
TOLLEMACHE, B PB1970; Bt PB1970; Bt EDB
TOLLET *of Betley Hall* LG1850/3
TOLSON *of Bridekirke* LG1850/3
TOMKINS *of Londonderry* LG1863
TOMKINSON *of Willington Hall* LG1972; *formerly of Franche Hall* LG1952
TOMLIN, B PB1935
TOMLIN *(now* PHARO-TOMLIN) *of Dane Court* LG1937
PRETYMAN TOMLINE *(see* Pretyman *of Orwell Park)*
TOMLINSON, Bt PB1912
PAGET-TOMLINSON *of The Biggins* LG1952
TOMPSON *of Woodston* LG1937; *of Witchingham Hall* LG1875
TONGE *(now* ADDINGTON) *of Highway* LG1937
TONI, B DEP
TONSON (Riversdale, B) DEP; *(see also* Tonson-Rye)

TOOKE *of Hurston Clays, Sussex* AA; *of Russell Square* HI; *(see also* Tooke-Hales; and Padwick)
TOOKER, Bt EDB; *of Norton Hall* LG1850/3
TOOLE *of Curracloe House* LGI1958
TOOTH *of Swifts, Cranbrook, co Kent* AA
LUCAS-TOOTH, Bt *of Queens Gate* PB1917
MUNRO-LUCAS-TOOTH, Bt PB1970
TOPHAM *of Cockerton Hall* LG1906; *of Middleham (see* Crewe-Smith-Milnes)
HARRISON-TOPHAM *of Caldbergh* LG1972
TOPP, Bt EDB; *of Whitton* LG1879
TORBOCK *of Crossrigg Hall* LG1952
TORKINGTON *of Great Stukeley* LG1879
TORPICHEN *(see* Sandilands)
TORR *formerly of Riby and Carlett Park* LG1965
TORRE *of Snydale* LG1921
TORRENCE DFUSA
TORRENS *of Rosstulla* LGI1912; *of Edenmore* LGI1912; *of Somerset* LGI1912
TORRINGTON *(see* Byng; Herbert; and Newport)
TOTTENHAM (Ely, M) PB1970; IFR1976
TOUCHE, Bt *of Dorking* PB1970; Bt *of Westcott* PB1970
TOUCHET (Castlehaven, E) DEP; (Audley, B) DEP; B DEP
TOULMIN *formerly of Hackney* LG1952; *of The Prè* LG1921
TOULSON *(see* Parker *of Browsholme)*
TOVEY, B PB1970
TOWER *formerly of Weald Hall* LG1965; *of Philadelphia* DFUSA; *PromFUSA; (see also* Baker *of Sedbury Hall)*
TOWERS *of Bushy Park* LG1850/3
TOWNELEY *of Dyneley* LG1965; *(see also* O'Hagan)
TOWNLEY *of Fulbourn* LG1972
TOWNSEND *of Honington Hall* LG1906; *of Downhills and Walpole* LG1886; *of Clifton Manor* LG1900; *(see also* Hughes; Roscoe; and Townshend)
TOWNSHEND, M PB1970; (Sydney, B) PB1890; (Bayning of Foxley, B) DEP; (Greenwich, B) DEP; *formerly of Caldecote* LG1952; *formerly of*

Trevallyn **LG1921; IFR1976;** (*Canada*) **CG**; (*see also* Brooke *of Haughton Hall*; Duncan *of Wincham*; and Ferrers)

TOWNSHEND (*or* TOWNSEND) *formerly of Bracon Ash* **DFUSA**

TOWNSHEND (*formerly* BLACK-BURNE) *of Tankardstown* **LGI1958**

MARSHAM-TOWNSHEND *of Scadbury Park* **LG1937**

TOYNBEE *of Fawke Wood* **LG1952**

TRACTON (*see* Dennis)

TRACY (Tracy of Rathcoole, V) **DEP**; Bt **EDB**

HANBURY-TRACY (Sudeley, B) **PB1970**

TRAFFORD *of Hill Court* **LG1972**; *of Wroxham* **LG1972**; *of Oughtrington* **LG1863**; *of Trafford* **LG1833/7**; **DFUSA**

TRAFFORD (*formerly* MOFFATT) *of Goodrich Court* **LG1952**

TRAGETT *of Awbridge Danes* **LG1879**

TRAHERNE *of Coedarhydyglyn* **LG1969**

TRAIL (*see* Traill)

TRAILL *formerly of Rattar* **LG1952**; **IFR1976**

TRANGMAR *of Burswood* **CG**

TRANT, Bt **EDB**; *formerly of Dovea* **LGI1958**

TRAPPES (*see* Trappes-Lomax)

TRAQUAIR (*see* Stuart)

TRASENSTER *of Coombe Place* **LG1952**

TRAVERS, Bt **PB1926; IFR1976;** (*see also* Hone)

HONE-TRAVERS (*see* Hone)

TREBY *of Goodamoor and Plympton House* **LG1875**

TREDCROFT *of Glen Ancrum* **LG1937**

TREDEGAR (*see* Morgan)

TREDENNICK *of Camlin* **LGI1912**

TREE *formerly of Dytchley Park* **LG1969**

TREFFRY *of Place* **LG1965**

TREFGARNE, B **PB1970**

TREFUSIS (Clinton B) **PB1970**

TREGONING *of Landue* **LG1969**

TREGONWELL *of Anderson* **LG1906**; *of Cranborne Lodge* **HI**

TREGOZ, B **DEP**

TREGOZE (*see* St John)

TREHERNE *of Downash and Bowley* **LG1952**

TREJAGO **LG1850/3**

TRELAWNY *of Shotwick* **LG1921**; *of Ham* (*see* Trelawny-Ross); *of Coldrenick* (*see* Sneyd)

SALUSBURY-TRELAWNY, Bt **PB1970**

TRELOAR, Bt **PB1923**

TREMAINE **DFUSA**

TREMAYNE *of Heligan and Sydenham* **LG1952**; *of Morval* **LG1937**

TREMENHEERE (*now* MONRO) *of Tremenheere* **LG1937**

TREMLETT *formerly of Sandford* **LG1965**; *of Littleham Cross* **LG1952**

TRENCH (Ashtown, B) **PB1970; IFR1976;** *formerly of Clonfert* **LGI1958;** (*see also* Fox *of Penjerrick*)

LE POER TRENCH (Clancarty, E) **PB1970**

TRENCHARD, B **PB1970; PromFUSA**

ASHFORDBY-TRENCHARD (*see* Masters *of Stanton Fitzwarren*)

DILLON-TRENCHARD *of Lytchett House* **LG1937**

TRENHOLM *formerly of Allerston* **DFUSA**

TRENOWTH **1850/3**

TRENT (*see* Boot)

TREOWEN (*see* Herbert)

TRESHAM, Bt **EDB**

TRESWELL, Bt **EDB**

TREVANION late of *Caerhayes* **LG1863**

TREVELYAN, B **PB1970;** Bt *of Nettlecombe* **PB1970;** Bt *of Wallington* **PB1970;** B *of Netherwitton* **LG1900**

TREVES, Bt **PB1923**

TREVETHIN AND OAKSEY (*see* Lawrence)

CELY TREVILIAN *of Midelney* **LG1969**

TREVILLION (*see* Cely-Trevilian)

TREVOR (Dungannon, V) **DEP**; (Hampden, V) **DEP**; Bt **EDB**; *of Trawscoed* **LG1952**; *of Trevallyn* **LG1850/3**; *formerly of Upton-on-Severn* **DFUSA**; (*see also* Buchan)

HILL-TREVOR (Trevor, B) **PB1970**

TRIBLE *formerly of Luffincott* **DFUSA**

TRICKETT (*see* Dent *of Ribston Hall*)

TRIMLESTOWN (*see* Barnewall)

TRINGHAM *of Nerquis Hall* **LG1952**

TRIPP *formerly of Sampford Brett and of Huntspill* **LG1952**; *of Otari Gorge* **CG**

TRIPPE **DFUSA**

TRIPPE (*formerly* ROSE) **DFUSA**

TRIST *of Tristford* **LG1937; AA**

TRISTRAM *formerly of Belbroughton* **LG1952**

TRITTON, Bt **PB1970**

TROLLOPE, Bt **PB1970**; (Kesteven, B) **PB1915**
TROTT, Bt **EDB**
TROTTER *of Brin, formerly of The Bush and Dryden* **LG1965**; *of Byers Green Hall* **LG1965**; *of Mells Park, formerly of Dyrham* **LG1965**; *of Mortonhall* **LG1965**; *of Barton Hartshorne* **LG1952**; *of Horton Manor* **LG1894**; *of Quansborough* **LG1863**; **DFUSA**; **CG**; *of Quansborough, co Galway* **AA**; (*see also* Lindsay; and Otway-Ruthven)
TROTTER (*now* STEAD) *of Ballindean* **LG1937**
TROUBRIDGE, Bt **PB1970**
TROUGHTON *of Walton Hall* **LG1863**
TROUP *of Dunbennan* **LG1965**
TROUTON (*Australia*) **CG**
TROWER *of Stanstead Bury* **LG1972**
ACLAND TROYTE *of Huntsham Court* **LG1937**
TRUELL *of Clonmannon* **LGI1912**
TRUEMAN *of Beacon Hall* **LG1952**
TRUITT **DFUSA**
TRUMAN **PresFUSA**; **PromFUSA**
TRURO (*see* Wilde)
TRUSCOTT, Bt **PB1970**
TRUSS *of Coleford* **AA**
TRUSSEL, B **DEP**
TRYDELL **LGI1958**
TRYE *formerly of Hartshill, Hardwicke, and Leckhampton* **LG1972**
TRYON, B **PB1970**; Bt **EDB**
TUBBS, Bt **PB1940**; **DFUSA**; (*see also* Mainwaring-Burton)
TUCK, Bt **PB1970**; *of Blofield Hall* **LG1898**; *of Cherry Hinton, co Cambridge* **LG1850/3**
TUCKER, B **PB1970**; *formerly of Coryton Park* **LG1952**; *of Beech Hill* **LG1937**; *of Collett Hall* **LG1937**; *of Trematon Castle* **LG1863**
SUTTON-SCOTT-TUCKER *of Bowden* **LG1972**
TUCKETT *of Cann House* **LG1952**
TUCKWELL *of Berthorpe* **LG1952**
TUDOR (Bedford, D) **DEP**; (Somerset, D) **DEP**; (York, D) **DEP**; (Richmond, E) **DEP**; *formerly of Lyndwood* **LG1952**
TUDWAY *of Wells* **LG1952**
TUFNELL *of Langleys* **LG1965**
TUFTON (Hothfield, B) **PB1970**; (Thanet, E) **DEP**
TUITE, Bt **PB1970**; *formerly of Kileen*

and Cloone **LGI1958**; *of Sonna* **LG1879**
TUKE, Bt **EDB**; *formerly of Borden* **LG1952**; *formerly of Walden Place* **LG1937**
TULIP *of Fallowfield* (*see* Mewburn-Watson)
TULL *of Crookham* **LG1952**
TULLOCH (*Australia*) **CG**
ARMSTRONG - LUSHINGTON - TULLOCH *of Shanboland* **LGI1958**
TULLY *of Newton Hall* **LG1937**
TULPE, Bt **EDB**
TUNNARD *formerly of Frampton House* **LG1952**
TUPPER, Bt **PB1970**; *of Guernsey* **LG1921**; *of Leyrath* **LGI1958**; **CG**
TURBERVILLE *of Ewenny Priory* **LG1952**; *of Coyty Castle* **LG1850/3**
TURBUTT *of Ogston* **LG1952**
TURING, Bt **PB1970**
TURNBULL *of Fitzroy House* **LG1952**; **DFUSA**; (*New Zealand*) **CG**
TURNER (Netherthorpe, B) **PB1970**; Bt *of Kirkleatham* **EDB**; Bt *of Warham* **EDB**; *formerly of Mulbarton* **LG1965**; *of Barnston Hall and Newland* **LG1952**; *of Kinharrachie formerly of Turnerhall* **LG1952**; *of Sylfaen formerly of Pentraheylin* **LG1952**; *of Thurstaston Hall* **LG1952**; *of Willington Hall formerly of Stanleigh House* **LG1952**; *of Menie* **LG1906**; **DFUSA**; (*Australia*) **CG**; *of Highfield* **CG**; (*see also* Frewen; and Marwood)
PAGE-TURNER *of Ambrosden* **LG1969**
POLHILL-TURNER (*see* Polhill *of Howbury*)
TURNLEY **AA**
TURNLY **IFR1976**; *of Drumnasole, co Antrim* **AA**
TURNOR *of Foxley Manor* **LG1952**; *of Stoke Rochford* **LG1952**
TURNOUR (Winterton, E) **PB1970**; B **PB1959**
TURPIN *of Greystones* **LGI1958**
TURTON, Bt *of Upsall* **PB1929**; Bt *of Starborough Castle* **PB1854**; *of Kildale and Upsall* **LG1965**
TURVILE *of Bosworth Hall* **LG1863**
TUTHILL *of Owenstown* **LGI1958**
TWEEDDALE (*see* Hay)
TWEEDIE *formerly of Oliver, Quarter, Rachan, and of Rawlinson* **LG1952**
TWEEDMOUTH (*see* Marjoribanks)
TWEEDSMUIR (*see* Buchan)
TWEEDY *of Widmore Lodge* **LG1921**;

of Cloonamahon **LGI1912**
TWEMLOW (*now* EMRYS-EVANS) *of Peatswood* **LG1937**; *of Hatherton* **LG1833/7**; **AA**
D'OYLY-TWEMLOW **FR**
FLETCHER-TWEMLOW (*see* Royds)
TWENTYMAN *formerly of Codsall* **LG1952**
TWIGG *formerly of Thorndale* **LGI1912**
TWINING, B **PB1967**; *of The Haywards* **LG1972**; (*Canada*) **CG**
TWISDEN, Bt *of Bradbourn* **PB1937**; Bt *of Roydon Hall* **EDB**
TWISS *of Birdhill* **LG1937Supp**; *of Hoseley, co Flint, and of Parkside and Allington, co Denbigh* **LG1850/3**; **DFUSA**
TWISTLETON, Bt **EDB**
O'BRIEN-TWOHIG *formerly of Dunowen House* **LGI1958**
TYE, B **DEP**
TYLDEN *of Milsted* **LG1937**; (*see also* Tylden-Wright)
TYLEE *of The Chantry* **LC1952**
TYLER, Bt **PB1907**; *formerly of Cottrell* **LG1969**; *of Tygwyn* **LG1952**; *of Newtownlimavady* **LG1875**; **Pres FUSA**; (1) & (2) **DFUSA**; (*Australia*) **CG**
TYLNEY (*see* Child)
TYNDALE (*see* Tyndale-Biscoe)
TYNDALL *of Oaklands* **LG1952Supp**; *of Ballyanne* **LGI1912**
TYNDELL **DFUSA**
TYNTE, Bt *of Dunlaven* **EDB**; Bt *of Halsewell* Bt **EDB**; (*see also* Tynte-Irvine)
KEMEYS-TYNTE *of Halsewell and Cefn Mably* **LG1914**; (*see also* Vintcent)
TYRAWLEY (*see* Cuff)
TYRAWLY (*see* O'Hara)
TYRCONNEL (*see* Brownlow; Carpenter; and Fitz-William)
TYRCONNELL (*see* O'Donnell; and Talbot)
TYRELL, Bt **PB1877**; *of Plashwood Haughley* **LG1886**
TUFNELL-TYRELL (*see* Tufnell)
TYRINGHAM *formerly of Tyringham* **LG1969**
TYRONE (*see* O'Neill; and Power)
TYRRELL (Tyrrell of Avon, B) **PB1940**; Bt *of Hanslape* **EDB**; Bt *of Lynn* **EDB**; Bt *of Springfield* **EDB**; Bt *of Thornton* **EDB**; *of Grange Castle* **LG1875**; *formerly of Grange Castle* **DFUSA**

TYRWHITT, Bt **PB1970**; Bt **EDB**; *of Nantyr* **CG**
TYSER *of Oakfield* **LG1921**
TYSSEN *of Petertavy Lodge* **LG1952**
FRASER-TYTLER *formerly of Woodhouselee* **LG1952**; *of Aldourie* **LG1937**
UDNY *of Udny* **LG1921**
UFFORD (Suffolk, E) **DEP**; (Ufford, B) **DEP**
UGHTRED, B **DEP**
ULLSWATER (*see* Lowther)
ULSTER (*see* de Burgh; and de Courcy)
ULYATE *of Hatfield Estate* **LG1952Supp**
UMFRAVILL (Angus, E) **DEP**
UMPLEBY *formerly of Felliscliffe* **DFUSA**
UNDERHILL **DFUSA**
UNDERWOOD (Inverness, D) **DEP**; *of Glanafon* **LG1952**
UNETT *formerly of Tittensor* **LG1972**; *of Woodlands* **LC1863**; *of Freen's Court* **LG1863**; **FR**
UNIACKE **IFR1976**
UNTHANK *of Intwood Hall* **LG1952**
UNWIN *formerly of Steeple Bumpstead* **LG1952**
UPCHER *of Sheringham* **LG1972**
UPJOHN, B **PB1970**; *formerly of Shaftesbury* **DFUSA**
UPPERMAN **DFUSA**
UPPER OSSORY (*see* Fitz-Patrick)
UPPLEBY *of Barrow Hall* **LG1937**; *of Wootton House* **HI**
UPTON (Templeton, V) **PB1970**; *of Hotham House and Coptfold* **LG1972**; *formerly of Ingmire Hall* **LG1972**; *of Langton House* **LG1937**; *of Glyde Court* **LG1894**; *of Coolatore* **LGI1912**
URE (Strathclyde, B) **PB1928**
URMSTON *formerly of Glen Morven* **LG1952**
URQUHART (Tayside, B) **PB1970**; *of That Ilk* **LG1969**; *of Meldrum and Byth* **LG1900**; *of New Abbey* **LGI1958**
POLLARD-URQUHART *formerly of Castlepollard* **LGI1958**
USBORNE *formerly of Writtle* **LG1972**
USHER, Bt **PB1970**
MURRAY-USHER *of Broughton and Cally* **LG1952**
USSHER **IFR1976**
NOWELL-USTICKE *of Polsue Philleigh* **LG1952**
UTHWATT, B **PB1949**; *of Maids Moreton Manor* **LG1921**
UVEDALE OF NORTH END (*see* Woodall)

UXBRIDGE (see Paget)
LAMPARD-VACHELL formerly of Lansdown Park LG1952
VAIL (Canada) CG
VAIZEY of Halstead LG1952
VALCKENBURGH, Bt EDB
MARTINDALE-VALE of Coddington Court LG1914
VALENCE (Pembroke, E) DEP
VALENTIA (see Annesley; and Power)
VALPY FR
VANACKER, Bt EDB
VAN BUREN PresFUSA
VAN CLIEF (see Carroll)
VAN CORTLANDT LG1850/3
VAN CUTSEM LG1965
VANDELEUR IFR1976
BAYLY-VANDELEUR (see Paget; and Vandeleur)
VANDEPUT, Bt EDB
VANDER-BRANDE, Bt EDB
VANDERSTEGEN (see Drake of Inshriach)
VAN DE WEYER formerly of New Lodge LG1965
VANE (Barnard, B) PB1970; V DEP; Bt EDB; of Sutton Bassett AA
FLETCHER-VANE (Inglewood, B) PB1970; Bt PB1934
VAN FRIESENDORF, Bt EDB
VAN KOUGHNET (Canada) CG
VANLORE, Bt EDB
VAN MONS (see Moens)
VANNECK (Huntingfield, B) PB1970
VANS of Barnbarroch LG1969
VANSITTART, B PB1956; (Bexley, B) DEP; (see also Vansittart-Neale)
VAN STRAUBENZEE of Spennithorne LG1965
VAN TROMP, Bt EDB
VARDON of Goldstone Hall LG1952
VARNUM formerly of Vernham Dean DFUSA; PromFUSA
VASSALL of Milford LG1850/3
VAUGHAN (Lisburne, E) PB1970; (Carbery, E) DEP; Bt of Nannau PB1859; of Courtfield LG1972; of Showborough House LG1969; of Humphreston LG1952; of Nannau LG1952; formerly of Rheola LG1952; of Burlton Hall LG1937; of The Castle, Builth LG1937; of Pen-y-Craig formerly of Brynog LG1937; of Quilly LGI1912; of Hallowell, Maine, formerly of Ballyboe DFUSA; of Cynghordy AA; (see also Vaughan-Jenkins; and Price of Greenstead Hall)

VAUGHAN formerly of Leicester (formerly HALFORD Bt of Wistow Hall) LG1952
LLOYD-VAUGHAN of Golden Grove LGI1912
ST ANDREW-VAUGHAN LG1921
WILLIAMS-VAUGHAN formerly of The Skreen LG1952
VAUX of Moulton Manor LG1972; DFUSA
VAUX OF HARROWDEN (see Gilbey)
VAVASOR, Bt of Copmanthorpe EDB; Bt of Haslewood EDB; Bt of Killingthorpe EDB
VAVASOUR, Bt PB1970; B DEP; (see also Dawson of Weston Hall)
DE JERSEY-VAVASSOUR formerly of Eaton Place LG1952
VAWDREY of Crill House LG1952; of Tushingham LG1937; (see also Worthington)
VEALE of Clifford House LG1952
MALET-VEALE formerly of Passaford LG1952
VEASEY DFUSA
VEATCH formerly of Muirdean DFUSA
VEITCH late of Eliock LG1914
VENABLE PromFUSA
VENABLES formerly of Aston House LG1937; (see Dillwyn-Venables-Llewellyn of Llysdinan Hall)
WHYTE-VENABLES of Redhills LGI1958
VENN of Freston Lodge LG1850/3
VENTRY (see Eveleigh de Moleyns)
VERDIN, Bt PB1917; of Stoke Hall and Garnstone LG1969
VERDON, B DEP; of Melbourne and Upper Macedon CG
VERE (Ireland, D) DEP; (Vere, B) DEP; (Vere, of Tilbury, B) DEP; of Carlton LG1875; (see also Broke)
HOPE-VERE formerly of Craigie Hall LG1952
VEREKER (Gort, V) PB1970
VERELST formerly of Aston Hall LG1952
VEREY of Barnsley LG1969
VERNATE, Bt EDB
VERNER, Bt PB1970
VERNEY (Willoughby de Broke, B) PB1970; Bt of Claydon House PB1970; Bt of Eaton House PB1970; E DEP; Bt EDB
VERNON (Lyveden, B) PB1970; (Vernon, B) PB1970; Bt of Hanbury Hall PB1940; (Shipbrook, E) DEP; Bt of Hodnet

EDB; *formerly of Hilton Park* **LG1969**; *of Stoke Bruerne* **LG1921**; *of Wyborne Gate* **LG1906**; *of Clontarf Castle* **LGI1912**; *of Coldstream* **CG**

VERNON (*now* DEWAR-MURRAY) *of Toddington Manor* **LG1921**

HARCOURT-VERNON *of Grove Hall* **LG1937**

VERRILL **DFUSA**

VERSCHOYLE **IFR1976**

VERTUE (*see* Mott-Radclyffe)

VERULAM (*see* Grimston)

VESCI, B **DEP**

VESCY (*see* Bromflete)

VESEY (De Vesci, V) **PB1970**; (De Vesci, B) **PB1903**; *of Derrabard* **LGI1912**; (*see also* Cramsie)

VESTEY, B **PB1970**; Bt **PB1970**; *of Assynt* **LG1937**

VICARY *of Scorhill* **LG1952**

VICK **LG1969**

VICKERMAN *of St Issells* **LG1952**

VICKERS *formerly of Tulloch* **LG1972**; *of Uffley Grove and Criggion* **LG1952**

VIGNE (*S Africa*) **CG**

VIGNOLES *of Cornahir* **LG1879**; **CG**; (*see also* Grey)

VIGORS **IFR1976**

VILAS **PromFUSA**

VILLIERS (Clarendon, E) **PB1970**; (Buckingham, D) **DEP**; (Anglesey, E) **DEP**; (Buckingham, E) **DEP**; (Grandison, E) **DEP**; (Purbeck, V) **DEP**; Bt **EDB**; (*see* Smith-Barry)

CHILD-VILLIERS (Jersey, E) **PB1970**

MASON-VILLIERS (*see* Villiers-Stuart)

VINCENT, Bt **PB1970**; (D'Abernon, V) **PB1940**; *formerly of Abbey Lodge* **LGI1958**; *of Summerhill* **LGI1912**; *of Boston Lodge* **LG1898**

INNES-VINE (*see* Mitchell-Innes)

VINER, Bt **EDB**; *of Week and Chapman-slade* **LG1833/7**

ELLIS-VINER *of Badgeworth* **LG1886**

VINTCENT (Wharton, B) **PB1970**

VINTON **PromFUSA**

VIPAN *of Sutton* **LG1875**; **FR**

VITUS, Bt **EDB**

VIVIAN, B **PB1970**; (Swansea, B) **PB1970**; *of Bosahan* **LG1921**; (*see also* Vivian-Neal)

COLBORNE-VIVIAN (Seaton, B) **PB1953**

GRAHAM-VIVIAN (*see* Graham)

RINGROSE-VOASE *formerly of Alanby House, Yorks* **LG1969**

VOGEL (*New Zealand*) **CG**

VON KALLENBRUNNEN (*see* Calburn)

VON MUELLER (*Australia*) **CG**

VON ROCHEID (*see* Kinloch)

VON SCHRÖDER, B **FT1917**

VON SCHUNCK (*see* Darnton)

VON STIEGLITZ *of Brisbane* **CG**

VOSPER (Runcorn, B) **PB1967**; *formerly of Trewoofe* **LG1972**

VOWE *of Hallaton* **LG1850/3**

VOWLER (*see* Vowler-Simcoe)

VYNER *of Gantby* **LG1900**; (*see also* Compton (*formerly* Vyner) *of Newby*; and Northampton)

HOWARD-VYSE *of Langton* **LG1965**; *formerly of Stoke* **LG1965**

VYVYAN, Bt **PB1970**

WACE **LG1952**

WADDELL *of Ardsloy* **LG1937**; *of Easter Moffat* **LG1850/3**; *of Beech House* **HI**

WADDILOVE *of Woodhorne* **LG1937**

WADDINGHAM (*now* RICHARDSON) *of Guiting Grange* **LG1937**

WADDINGTON *of Ely Grange and Waddington Old Hall* **LG1937**; *of Cavenham* **LG1914**; **IFR1976**

WADDY *of Clougheast* **LG1886**

WADE, B **PB1970**; *of Honiley Hall* **LG1952**; **IFR1976**; **DFUSA**; (*see also* Daniell; Wade-Gery; and Hyde)

WADSWORTH **PromFUSA**

WAECHTER, Bt **PB1970**

WAGNER **LG1965**

WAGSTAFF *of Manor Park* **LG1894**; *formerly of Daventry* **DFUSA**

WAHULL (de Wahull, B) **DEP**

WAILES (*see* Wailes-Fairbairn)

WAIT *of Woodborough* **LG1863**

WAITHMAN *of Moyne* **LGI1912**; *of Merlin Park* **LG1894**

WAKE, Bt **PB1970**; B **DEP**

WAKEFIELD, Bt **PB1970**; B **PB1940**; **DFUSA**; **FR**; (Wakefield of Kendal, B) **PB1970**

WAKEHURST (*see* Loder)

WAKELEY, Bt **PB1970**

WAKELY *of Ballyburly* **LGI1912**

WAKEMAN, Bt **PB1970**; *of Graig House* **LG1863**

WALBANKE (*see* Childers)

WALBRIDGE **DFUSA**

WALCHER (Northumberland, E) **DEP**

WALCOT *late of Bitterley Court* **LG1937**; *of Winkton* **LG1875**

WALCOTT **DFUSA**

WALDECK AND PYRMONT (*Princes of*) **RL**

WALDEGRAVE, E **PB1970**; (Radstock, B) **PB1953**
WALDEN **DFUSA**
WALDIE of Hendersyde Park **VSA**
MEADE-WALDO of Stonewall Park and Hever **LG1952**
WALDRON of Helen Park **LGI1912**
WALDY of Green Park **LG1952**; of Egglescliffe **HI**
WALE of Shelford **LG1937**
WALES (Kings and Princes of) **RL**
WALEYS, B **DEP**
WALFORD of Wolverton, formerly of Walford and Astley **LG1965**; formerly of Arle Bury **LG1952**; of Foxburrow **LG1921**; of Ruyton Towers **LG1921**; of St Vincent, Isle of Wight **LG1850/3**
WALKER, Bt of Oakley House **PB1970**; Bt of Pembroke House **PB1970**; Bt of Sand Hutton **PB1970**; (Wavertree, B) **PB1933**; Bt **EDB**; formerly of St John **LG1969**; of Pitlair **LG1965**; of Sutton Veny **LG1965**; of Churchill Court formerly of Boyne Hill House, Chapelthorpe **LG1952**; of Morrington formerly of Crawfordton **LG1952**; of Norton Court **LG1952**; formerly of Teignmouth **LG1952**; of Warden Court **LG1952**; late of Berkswell Hall **LG1937**; of Bewell **LG1937**; of Tykillan **LG1937 Supp**; late of Bowland **LG1914**; of The Priory, Bathwick **LG1894**; of Aberarder **LG1875**; of The Grange **LG1875**; of Redland **LG1875**; of Fonthill Abbey **LGI1958**; **RFFK**; (1) & (2) **DFUSA**; formerly of Wimbledon **DFUSA**; of Four Peales **CG**; of Ryde **CG**; of Windsor **CG**; (see also Blandy; Walker-Heneage; and Legh)
WALKER (now ROBERTSON-LUX-FORD) of Dalry **LG1914**
FAURE WALKER of Sandon Bury **LG1972**
FORESTIER-WALKER, Bt **PB1970**
KERRICH-WALKER of Newker House **LG1937**
ROBERTSON-WALKER of Gilgarran **LG1952**
WALKEY formerly of Alphington **LG1952**
WALL of Worthy Park **LG1875**
WALLACE, B **DEP**; Bt of Studham **PB1940**; Bt of Terreglestown **PB1940**; of Bagnor Manor **LG1972**; of Candacraig **LG1969**; of that Ilk **LG1969**; of Bursay Moor **LG1952**; formerly of Glassingall **LG1952**; of Asholme,

Knaresdale and Featherstone Castle **LG1875**; of Ardnamona **LGI1912**; of Ravarn **LGI1912**; of Myra Castle **LGI1912**; (1) & (2) **DFUSA**; **PromFUSA**; of Worthing, Sussex **AA**; (see also Hamilton of Elderslie)
WALLACE (formerly MACPHERSON) of Little Wyrley Hall **LG1952**
HOPE-WALLACE (see Linlithgow)
STEWART-WALLACE formerly of Edenderry **LG1969**
WALLER, Bt of Braywick Lodge **PB1970**; Bt of Newport **PB1970**; of Pen Park **LG1969**; (cos Kerry and Limerick) **IFR1976**; (co Tipperary) **IFR1976**; formerly of Speldhurst and Newport Pagnell **DFUSA**; of Spring Grove, Hounslow **AA**; (see also Waller-Bridge)
CRAIG WALLER formerly of Allenstown (see Waller (cos Kerry and Limerick))
WALLINGTON formerly of Dursley **LG1952**; **AA**
WALLIS of Eastington House **LG1952**; formerly of Elvendon Priory **LG1952**; **IFR1976**; of Curryglass (see also Wallis-Wright)
WALLOP (Portsmouth, E) **PB1970**
WALLSCOURT (see Blake)
WALMESLEY formerly of Westwood and Inglewood **LG1972**; of Bartle Hall **LG1952**; of Pilgrim's Hall **LG1914**; of The Hall of Ince **LG1898**; of Sholley **LG1863**; **DFUSA**
WALMODEN (Yarmouth, E) **DEP**
WALPOLE, B **PB1970**; (Orford, E) **PB1931**; (Orford, E) **DEP**
WALROND of Thorne Court **LG1972**
WALSH (Ormathwaite, B) **PB1970**; Bt of Ballykilcavan **PB1953**; formerly of Burningfold Hall **LG1952**; formerly of Grimblethorpe **LG1937**; **IFR1976**; formerly of Laragh **LGI1958**; of Mul Hussey **LGI1912**; of Fanningstown **LGI1912**; formerly of Clonmel **DFUSA**; (see also Walsh-Kemmis)
WALSH (formerly WILSON-SLATOR) of White Hill **LGI1958**
PAKENHAM-WALSH of Rowner Glebe **LG1952**
WALSHAM, Bt **PB1970**
WALSHE **IFR1976**
WALSINGHAM (see de Grey; and Schulenberg)
WALSTON, B **PB1970**
WALTER, Bt **EDB**; formerly of Bear Wood **LG1965**; of Churston Manor

LG1937; *of Clifton, co Gloucester* **AA**
WALTER (*formerly* ORDE) *of Hopton* **LG1952**
CAMPBELL-WALTER (*see* Campbell *of Airds Bay*)
WALTERS (*see* Palliser)
WALTHALL *formerly of Alton Manor and Wistaston Hall* **LG1952**; (*see also* Broughton)
WALTHAM (*see* Olmins)
WALTON, Bt **PB1923**; *of The Chantry* **LG1952**; *of Maperton House* **LG1914**
WALWYN *formerly of Longford* **LG1972**
WANDESFORDE, E **DEP**; Bt **EDB**
PRIOR-WANDESFORDE *of Castlecomer* **LGI1958**
WANDSWORTH (*see* Stern)
WANTAGE (*see* Lloyd-Lindsay)
WARBURTON, Bt **EDB**; *formerly of Garryhinch* **LGI1958**; (*Canada*) **CG**
EGERTON-WARBURTON *of Grafton Hall, formerly of Warburton* **LG1969**; (*Australia*) **CG**
WARD (Dudley, E) **PB1970**; (Bangor, V) **PB1970**; (Ward of Witley, V) **PB1970**; Bt *of Wellington* **PB1970**; Bt *of Wilbraham Place* **PB1970**; Bt *of Blyth* **PB1956**; (Dudley, B) **DEP**; Bt **EDB**; *formerly of Stramshall* **LG1972**; *of Northwood Park* **LG1952**; *formerly of St Peter's-in-Thanet* **LG1952**; *of Salhouse* **LG1952**; *late of Rodbaston* **LG1937**; *of Calverley* **LG1914**; *of Willey* **LG1863**; *of Ogbourne St Andrew* **LC1863**; **IFR1976**; (1) (2) (3) & (4) **DFUSA; PromFUSA**; *of Wanganui* **CG**
CRESWELL-WARD *late Neasham Hill* **LG1937**
NELSON-WARD *formerly Killamarsh* **LG1952**
WARDALE **LG1952**
WARDE (de la Warde, B) **DEP**; Bt *of Barham Court* **PB1937**; *of Squerryes Court* **LG1972**; *of Clopton House* **LG1863**; (*see also* Warde-Adam)
WARDELL *of Hengwrt* **LG1952**; *of Old Abbey* **LG1937Supp** (*see also* Potts and Wardell-Yerburgh)
WARDEN **LG1937Supp**
WARDINGTON (*see* Pease)
WARDLAW, Bt **PB1970**; *of Gogarmount and Dalchosnie* **LG1952**; (*see also* Wardlay-Ramsay)
MARK-WARDLAW *of Alyscroft* **LG1952**
WARDROP *of Bridge House* **LG1863**
WARE *of Tilford House* **LG1937**; *of Woodfort* **LG1886**

CUMBERLEGE-WARE *of Stanwell House* **LG1952**
WARGRAVE (*see* Goulding)
WARING, Bt **PB1970**; B **PB1940**; *formerly of Hewitts* **LG1952**; *of Beenham House* **LG1914**; *of Waringstown* **LGI1958**; (*Fiji*) **CG**; *of Lennel* (*see* Sitwell)
SCOTT-WARING (*see* Scott *of Lasborough, formerly of Betton*)
WARMINGTON, Bt **PB1970**
WARNEFORD *formerly of Warneford Place* **LG1952**
WARNER, Bt **PB1970**; Bt **EDB**; *formerly of Framlingham* **LG1965**; *late of Quorn Hall* **LG1921**; *of Walthamstow, Essex* **AA**; *of Ardeer* (*see* Roche); (*see also* Nicol)
LEE-WARNER *formerly of Walsingham and Abbey and Tyberton* **LG1972**
WARRAND *of Ormidale* **LG1952**
WARRE, Bt **EDB**; *formerly of Gledfield* **LG1965**; **FR**
WARRE (*now* MURRAY-SMITH) *of Westcliff* **LG1921**
WARREN, Bt **PB1970**; (Surrey, E) **DEP**; Bt **EDB**; *of The Hyde* **LG1972**; *of Handcross* **LG1937**; *of Rathfarnham Park* **LGI1912**; *late of Lodge Park* **LGI1912**, *of Ancoats, Manchester* **AA**; *of Hopton, Suffolk* **AA**; *of Mespil, co Dublin* **AA**
COURBOULD-WARREN *of Caystor Hall* **LG1952**
LEICESTER WARREN (*formerly* DAVENPORT) *of Davenport* **LG1952**
WARRENDER (Bruntisfield, B) **PB1970**
WARRINER *of Conock House* **LG1850/3**
WARRINGTON (Warrington of Clyffe, B) **PB1937**; (*see* Booth; and Grey)
WARRY *of Shapwick House* **LG1952**
WARTER *of Cruck Meole* **LG1952**; *and Eastcourt Manor* **LG1952**
TATHAM-WARTER (*see* Warter)
WARTNABY *of Clipston* **LG1952**
WARWICK *formerly of Balderton Hall and Upton Hall* **LG1952**; (*see also* Beauchamp; Dudley; Greville; Newburgh; Plessets; and Rich)
WASBROUGH *of Stockham* **LG1972**
WASHBURN *formerly of Little Washbourne and Wichenford* **DFUSA**; *of Brockworth* **CG**
WASHINGTON **PresFUSA**
WASTNEYS, Bt **EDB**
WATERFORD (*see* De La Poer Beresford)
WATERHOUSE *of Middleton* **LG1969**;

of Yattendon **LG1952**; *of Well Head* **LG1914**
WATERLOW, Bt *of Harrow Weald* **PB1970**; Bt *of London* **PB1970**
WATERPARK (*see* Cavendish)
WATERS *late of Sarnau* **LG1937**
WATERTON *formerly of Deeping Waterton*
WATHEN *of Bolwick Hall, formerly of Beckenham Lodge* **LG1969**
WATKIN, Bt **PB1914**; *of Danebank* **LG1937**; **DFUSA**
WATKINS *of Badby House* **LG1898**; *of Woodfield* **LG1894**
STRANG-WATKINS *of Shotton* **LG1921**
WATKINSON, V **PB1970**
PERRY-WATLINGTON *of Moor Hall* **LG1879**
WATNEY *of Cornbury Park* **LG1965**
WATSON (Manton, B) **PB1970**; (Thankerton, B) **PB1940**; Bt *of London* **PB1970**; Bt *of Sulhamstead* **PB1970**; Bt *of Newport* **PB1959**; (Thankerton, B) **PB1940**; Bt *of Fulmer* **PB1904**; B **PB1899**; (Rockingham, M) **DEP**; Bt **EDB**; *formerly of Ardgrain* **LG1952**; *formerly of Castle Carrock* **LG1952**; *formerly of Chadwick Manor* **LG1952**; *of Dinton* **LG1952**; *of Llansannor Court* **LG1937**; *of Adderstone Hall* **LG1921**; *of Ayton* **LG1921**; *of Calgarth Park* **LG1921**; *of Shirecliffe Hall* **LG1898**; *of Berwick House* **LG1894**; **IFR1976**; *of Glanworth* **CG**; *of Kilmanahan Castle* **AA**; (*see also* Calhoun; and Watson-Armstrong)
GRAHAM WATSON *of Lofts Hall* **LG1965**
GRANT-WATSON (*see* Watson-Gandy-Brandreth)
INGLEFIELD-WATSON, Bt **PB1970**
MEWBURN-WATSON *formerly of Langley House and of Acomb* **LG1952**
MILNE-WATSON, Bt **PB1970**
RICHMOND-WATSON *of Brightwell Park* **LG1952**
SCOTT-WATSON *of Burnhead* **LG1952**
WATT *of Robertland* **LG1952**; *of Gunthorpe* **LG1937**; *of Speke Hall* **LG1914**; *of Carrablagh, formerly of Thorn Hill* **LGI1958**; (*Australia*) **CG**; (*see also* Scarth)
WATT (*formerly* WHITEWAY) *of Hemingford Grey House* **LG1952**
GIBSON WATT *of Doldowlod* **LG1969**
HALL WATT *of Bishop Burton and formerly of Carrhead* **LG1952**

HARVIE-WATT, Bt **PB1970**
WATTERS (WATERS) *formerly of Middleham* **DFUSA**
WATTS *of Abney Hall* **LG1952**; *of Hawkesdale Hall* **LG1875**; **AA**
POORE - SAURIN - WATTS (*formerly* WATTS) *of Hanslope Park* **LG1952**
WAUCHOPE *of Niddrie Marischal* **LG1937**; (*see also* Eveleigh de Moleyns)
DON-WAUCHOPE, Bt **PB1970**
WAUD *of Manston Hall* **LG1894**
WAUGH *of Piers Court* **LG1952**
WAVELL, E **PB1953**
WAVENEY (*see* Adair)
WAVERLEY (*see* Anderson)
WAVERTREE (*see* Walker)
WAY, Bt **PB1916**; *of Denham* **LG1969**; *of Montefiore* **CG**
WAYER (Norfolk and Suffolk, E) **DEP**
WAYNE *of Eisg-Brachaidh and Stansted* **LG1972**; **CG**
WAYTE *of Colston Bassett* **LG1965**
WEARDALE (*see* Stanhope)
WEARE *of Hampton House* **LG1921**
WEARING *of Hipping Hall* **LG1937**
WEBB (Passfield, B) **PB1940**; Bt *of Llwynarthen* **PB1940**; *of The Brownsend* **LG1952**; *formerly of Odstock* **LG1952**; *of Elford House* **LG1937**; *of The Berrow* **LG1879**; *of Knocktoran* **LGI1958**; *formerly of Webbsborough* **LGI1958**; *of Kilmore* **LGI1912**; **DFUSA**; **FR**; *of Hathrop* **CG**; *of Harrow* **AA**; (*see also* Edge)
WESTON-WEBB *late of Gedling* **LG1937**
WEBBER *of Mathern Lodge* **LG1952**; **IFR1976**; **FR**
INCLEDON-WEBBER *of Buckland* **LG1965**
WEBLEY (*see* Webley-Parry-Pryse)
WEBSTER (Alverstone, V) **PB1915**; Bt *of Copthall* **PB1923**; *of Unthank Hall* **LG1952**; *late of The Penns* **LG1879**; *of Pallion* **LG1900**; **DFUSA**
BULLOCK-WEBSTER *of Higher Hisley* **LG1972**
RIDDELL-WEBSTER *of Lintrose House* **LG1952**
VASSAL-WEBSTER (*see* Webster)
WEDDALL *formerly of Barlby and Selby* **LG1972**
WEDDERBURN (Loughborough, B) **DEP**; (*see also* Halkett)
OGILVY-WEDDERBURN, Bt **PB1970**
SCRYMGEOUR-WEDDERBURN (Dundee, E) **PB1970**

WEDGEWOOD *of Etruria and Barlaston Lea* **LG1937**
WEDGWOOD, B **PB1970**; Bt **PB1970**
WEEKES *formerly of Hurstpierpoint* **LG1952**
WEEKS, B **PB1959**; *of Thirston House* **LG1952**; (1) & (2) **DFUSA**
WEIGALL, Bt **PB1949**
WEIR, V **PB1970**; (Inverforth, B) **PB1970**; Bt **EDB**; *formerly of Craig Hall* **LGI1958**
WELBY, Bt **PB1970**; B **PB1915**
WELCII, Bt **PB1970**; (*now* DENNE) *of Arle House* **LG1937**; **DFUSA**
KEMP-WELCH *formerly of Broadlands* **LG1969**
WELCHMAN *of Manaton* **LG1965**
WELD *of Chideock* **LG1965**; *of Lulworth* **LG1965**
BERKELEY WELD (*see* Berkeley *of Spetchley*)
CORNWALL - BRADY - HART-STONGE-WELD *of Rahinbawn and Myshall House* **LGI1912**
WELDON, Bt **PB1970**
WELFITT (*see* Need)
WELLBELOVED (*see* Scott *of Great Barr*)
WELLES (Welles, B) **DEP**; (Welles, V) **DEP**; *of Grebby Hall* **LG1863**
WELLESLEY (Cowley, F) **PD1970**; (Wellington, D) **PB1970**; M **DEP**; (Maryborough, B) **DEP**
WELLINGTON (*see* Wellesley)
WELLMAN **DFUSA**
WELLS, Bt **PB1970**; Bt *of Hove* **PB1956**; Bt *of Upper Grosvenor Street* **PB1906**; *of Mere House and Marlands* **LG1972**; *formerly of Bickley Hall and Holmewood* **LG1965**; **DFUSA**; (*see also* Fortescue-Brickdale; Dymoke; and Parker (*formerly* Wells) *of Houghton Lodge*)
COLLINGS-WELLS *formerly of Cuddington Hall* **LG1952**
GRENVILLE WELLS (*see* Wells *formerly of Brickley Hall and Holmewood*)
WELMAN *of Trewarthenick formerly of Poundisford Park and Norton Manor* **LG1952**
WELSTEAD (*now* Compton) *formerly of Kimbolton* **LG1952**
PENROSE-WELSTED *formerly of Shandangon and Ballywalter* **LGI1958**
MACONOCHIE-WELWOOD *of Kirknewton and Garvock* **LG1952**
WEMYS (Burntisland, Lord) **DEP**; *of*

Danesfort **LG1863**
WEMYSS (Wester Wemyss, B) **PB1933**; *of Carphin* **LG1952**; *of Trefechan* **LG1921**
WEMYSS AND MARCH (*see* Charteris)
COLCHESTER-WEMYSS *formerly of Westbury Court* **LG1952**
WENGER *of Trentham Priory* **LG1952**
WENLOCK, B **DEP**; (*see also* Lawley)
WENMAN (Wenman, V) **DEP**; Bt **EDB**; (*see also* Wykeham)
WENSLEYDALE (*see* Parke)
WENTGES (*formerly* WOODS) *of Milverton Hall* **LGI1958**
WENTWORTH, Bt *of Parlut* **PB1844**; (Rockingham, M) **DEP**; (Cleveland, E) **DEP**; (Strafford, E) **DEP**; Bt *of Brelton* **EDB**; Bt *of Gosfield* **EDB**; Bt *of North Emsal* **EDB**; Bt *of Wentworth Woodhouse* **EDB**; *of Woolley* **LG1937**; **CG**
VERNON-WENTWORTH *of Wentworth Castle* **LG1952**
WERDEN, Bt **EDB**
WERE *of Wellington* **LG1850/3**
WERNHER, Bt **PB1970**
WESLEY (*see* Wellesley)
WEST *formerly of White Park* **LGI1958**; (*see also* West-Erskine; and De Wend Fenton)
GRANVILLE-WEST, B **PB1970**
ALSTON-ROBERTS-WEST *of Alscot Park* **LG1972**
SACKVILLE-WEST (Sackville, D) **PB1970**
WESTBURY (*see* Bethell)
WESTBY **IFR1976**; *of Mowbreck* **VSA**; **AA**
WESTCAR *of Mascalls* **LG1875**
WESTCOMBE, Bt **EDB**
WESTENRA (Rossmore, B) **PB1970**
WESTERMAN *of Castle Grove* **VSA**; **AA**
WESTERN, B **DEP**; *of Tatingstone Place and Felix Hall* **LG1863**
BROWN-WESTHEAD **FR**
WESTMEATH (*see* Nugent)
WESTMINSTER (*see* Grosvenor)
WESTMORELAND (*see* Nevill)
WESTMORLAND (*see* Fane)
WESTON (Portland, E) **DEP**; Bt **PB1926**; *of Bente* **LG1952**; *formerly of West Horsley* **LG1952**; *of Lane House* **LG1900**; (*see also* Weston-Webb)
HUNTER-WESTON (*see* Hunter *of Hunterston*)
WESTHORPE (*see* Westropp)
WESTROPP *of Melford Place* **LG1952**; **IFR1976**

O'CALLAGHAN - WESTROPP (*see* O'Callaghan)
WESTWOOD, B **PB1970**
WETHERALL *of Astley Hall* **LG1898**
WETHERED *of Remnantz* **LG1969**
WETHERELL *formerly of Pashley* **LG1972**
WETHERILL **PromFUSA**
WETMORE **PromFUSA**
WETTENHALL (*see* Mainwaring)
HUME-WEYGAND (*formerly* HUME) *of Humewood* **LGI1958**
WEYLAND *of Woodeaton* **LG1937**
WHAITES (*see* Back)
WHALLEY (*see* Gardiner)
WHARNCLIFFE (*see* Montagu-Stuart-Wortley-Mackenzie)
WHARTON, D **DEP**; Bt **EDB**; **CG**; (*see also* Wharton-Duff; and Vintcent)
WHARTON (*now* DARWIN) *of Dryburn* **LG1921**
RINGROSE-WHARTON (*see* Ringrose-Voase)
WHATELEY *of Midford Castle formerly of Laurel Lodge* **LG1952**
WHATMAN *of Walsham Hall* **LG1952**
WHEATE, Bt **EDB**
WHEATLEY *of Berkswell Hall* **LG1937**; *of Gwersyllt Park* **LG1937**
WHEBLE *of Bulmershe Court* **LG1921**
WHEELER, Bt **PB1970**; *formerly in Dublin* **LG1952**; *of Bitterley Court and Newnham Court* **LG1937**; *of Bromwich House* **LG1921**; *of Kyrewood House* **LG1863**; (1) & (2) **DFUSA**; *formerly of Cranfield* **DFUSA**
DE COURCY-WHEELER **IFR1976**
WHELER, Bt **PB1970**; Bt *of Otterden* **PB1927**; *of Otterden Place* **LG1952**
WHETHAM *of Cadhay and Hilfield St. Nicholas* **LG1921**
BODDAM-WHETHAM *formerly of Kirklington Hall* **LG1952**
WHICHCOTE, Bt **PB1949**; (*see also* Playne)
WHIELDON *of Springfield House* **LG1898**; **VSA**
WHILE (*see* Richards)
WHIPPY *of Lee Place* **LG1863**
WHISTLER *formerly of Goring* **DFUSA**
WHITACRE *of Woodhouse* **LG1863**
WHITAKER, Bt **PB1970**; *of Pylewell Park* **LG1965**; *of Totterton Hall* **LG1965**; *of Balkholme Manor and Everthorpe* **LG1906**; *of Hesley Hall* **LG1900**; *of Symonstone* **LG1863**; **FR**
WHITAKER (*now* KAYE) *of Winsley Hall*

LG1965
MASTER-WHITAKER *of The Holme* **LG1914**
WHITBREAD *of Southill* **LG1965**; *of Loudham Park* **LG1914**
WHITBURGH (*see* Borthwick)
WHITBURN *formerly of Amport St Mary's* **LG1952**
WHITBY *of Symondsbury House* **LG1937**; *of Bishton Hall and Colwich formerly of Creswell* **LG1894**
WHITCOMBE *of Lake* **LG1969**
WHITE (Annaly, B) **PB1970**; Bt *of Boulge Hall* **PB1970**; Bt *of Bristol* **PB1970**; Bt *of Salle Park* **PB1970**; Bt *of Walling Wells* **PB1970**; (Overtown, B) **PB1908**; *formerly of Redheugh and Charlton* **LG1969**; *of Aspley Guise* **LG1952**; *formerly of Lough Eske Castle* **LG1952**; *of Boulge Hall* **LG1937**; *of Bredfield House* **LG1937**; *of Castor* **LG1921**; *of Kellerstain* **LG1921**; *of Salle Park* **LG1921**; *of Durham* **LG1906**; *of Congeloe Park* **LG1906**; *of Clement's Hall* **LG1875**; (co Limerick) **IFR1976**; (cos Tipperary and Limerick) **IFR1976**; *of Charleville* **LGI1912**; *of Cloone Grange* **LGI1912**; *of White Hall* **LGI1912**; *of Lough Eske Castle* **LGI1912**; *of Gracefield* **LGI1912**; *of Mount Sion* **LGI1912**; (1) (2) (3) (4) (5) (6) & (7) **DFUSA**; **FR**; (*NSW, Australia*) **CG**; (*see also* Popham; and White-Thomson)
BARRINGTON-WHITE *of Temple Dinsley and Orange Hill* **LGI1912**
BAZLEY-WHITE *of Gennings* **LG1898**
BROOMAN-WHITE *of Arddarroch* **LG1952**
DALRYMPLE-WHITE, Bt **PB1970**
ESMONDE-WHITE *formerly of Newlands* **LG1937Supp**
GROVE-WHITE **IFR1976**
HEDGES-WHITE (Bantry, E) **PB1891**
JERVIS-WHITE *of Ferns* **LGI1912**
SHELSWELL-WHITE **IFR1976**
WHITEFOORD, Bt **EDB**; *formerly of Blairquahan* **LG1972**
WHITEGREAVE *formerly of Stockerston Hall* **LG1952**
WHITEHEAD, Bt **PB1970**; *formerly of Deighton Grove* **LG1952**; *of Barming House* **LG1914**; *of Amberley Court* **LG1875**
WHITEHOUSE *formerly of Swan Village* **DFUSA**
WHITEHURST *of The Mount* **HI**

WHITELAW *of Gartshore* **LG1965**
WHITELEY (Marchamley, B) **PB1970**
HUNTINGTON - WHITELEY, Bt **PB1970**
WHITELOCKE *of Bulstrode* **VF**
WHITEWAY (*now* WATT) *of Hemingford Grey House* **LG1937**; *of Weston* **LG1898**
WHITFELD *of Hamsey* **LG1921**
WHITFIELD (Kenswood, B) **PB1970**
WHITGREAVE *of Moseley* **LG1900**
WHITHAM *formerly of Addingham* **DFUSA**
WHITING **DFUSA**; *formerly of Elton* **DFUSA**
WHITLA *of Beneadan* **LGI1912**; **DFUSA**
WHITLE *of Halton Hall* **LG1879**
WHITLEY *formerly of Alvanley* **LG1952**; (*see also* Wheatley-Hubbard and Bower)
WHITMORE, Bt **PB1970**; Bt **EDB**; *of Orsett Hall* **LG1952**
WOLRYCHE-WHITMORE *of Dudmaston* **LG1952**
WHITNEY *of Merton* **LG1863**; *of Brayfort* **LGI1912**; *formerly of Isleworth* **DFUSA**; **PromFUSA**
WHITON **PromFUSA**
FETHERSTONHAUGH - WHITNEY *of New Pass* **LGI1912**
HAWKINS-WHITSHED, Bt **PB1871**; (*see also* Hawkins)
WHITTAKER *of Walton-le-Dale* **LG1937**; *of Newcastle Court* **LG1863**
WHITTALL *of Liverpool* **AA**
WHITTELL *of Weston* **LG1863**
WHITTER *of Ashurst* **LG1863**
WHITTING *of Sandcroft House* **LG1863**; **AA**
WHITTINGHAM *of Potton* **LG1850/3**
FEARNLEY-WHITTINGSTALL *formerly of Watford and Hawkswick* **LG1969**
WHITTUCK *of Stoke Lodge* **LG1952**
WHITTWELL **PromFUSA**; **FR**
WHITWORTH, E **DEP**; B **DEP**; *of Wootton* **LG1952**
WHYTE **IFR1976**; *of Newtown Manor* **LG1937Supp**
WHYTEHEAD *late of Crayke* **LG1937**
WICKERSHAM *formerly of Horsham* **DFUSA**
WICKHAM *of Shoddesden Manor* **LG1952**; *late of Horsington* **LG1937**; *of Chestnut Grove* **LG1900**; *of Fronwnion* **LG1900**; *of Lightcliffe* **LG1850/3**; (*see also* Wickham-Boynton)

WICKHAM (*now* BONHAM-CARTER) *of Binsted Wyck* **LG1952**
WICKLOW (*see* Howard)
WICKSTED *of Shakenhurst* **LG1914**
WIDDRINGTON, B **DEP**; Bt *of Cartington* Bt **EDB**; Bt *of Widdrington* **EDB**; *of Newton Hall* **LG1952**
WIDVILE (Rivers, E) **DEP**; **VF**
WIENER *of Stoneleigh* **LG1921**
WIGAN, Bt **PB1970**; *of Drewitts* **LG1972**; *of Farthings* **LG1952**
GRAHAM-WIGAN (*now* BLOMEFIELD) *of Duntrune* **LG1937**
WIGG, B **PB1970**
WIGGETT (*see* Chute *of The Vyne*)
WIGGIN, Bt **PB1970**
WIGGINS (*see* Mowbray)
WIGGLESWORTH **DFUSA**
WIGHT *of Braboeuf Manor* **LG1863**; (*see also* Wight-Boycott)
WIGHTMAN *formerly of Burton-on-Trent* **DFUSA**
SETON-WIGHTMAN (*see* Macalpine-Downie)
WIGNALL *of Cambusmore* **LG1952**
WIGRAM, B **PB1970**; Bt **PB1970**
WIGTON (*see* Fleming)
WILBERFORCE, B **PB1970**; *of Markington* **LG1972**
WILBERFOSS (*see* Wilberforce)
WILBRAHAM, Bt **EDB**; *formerly of Delamere* **LG1965**
BAKER WILBRAHAM, Bt **PB1970**
BOOTLE-WILBRAHAM (Skelmersdale, B) **PB1970**; (Lathom, E) **PB1930**
WILBUR **DFUSA**
WILBY *of Westfield House* **LG1921**
WILCOX (*now* HOFFGAARD) *of Brandon and Wolston* **LG1937**; (1) & (2) **DFUSA**
WILCOX (*or* WILCOXSON) *sometime of Cossal* **DFUSA**
WILD *formerly of South Ash* **LG1952**; *formerly of High Wycombe* **DFUSA**
BAGNALL-WILD *of Costock* **LG1952**
WILDE (Penzance, B) **PB1899**; (Truro, B) **PB1899**; Bt **EDB**
WILDE (*now* HOLLAND) **IFR1976**
WILDER *of Purley Hall and Sulham* **LG1952**; **DFUSA**; *formerly of Shiplake* **DFUSA**
WILDING *of Penbryn* **LG1921**
WILDMAN (*see* Wildman-Lushington)
WILKES *of Elmdon Bury* **LG1952**
WILKIE *formerly of Ormiston* **LG1952**; *of Foulden* **LG1914**; *of Ellington House* **LG1898**

WILKIN *formerly of Carrickreagh*
LGI1958
WILKINS (*see* De Winton *of Maesllwch
Castle*)
WILKINSON, Bt **PB1970**; *of Mill House*
LG1969; *formerly of Sheraton*
LG1952; *formerly of Potterton Hall*
LG1937; *of Newall Hall and Winterburn Hall* **LG1921**; *of Upper Hare Park*
LG1894; *of Rose Dene* **LG1900**;
of White Webbs **LG1863**; *of Hilcote
Hall* **LG1850/3**; *of Glebe Point* **CG**;
of White Webbs Park **AA**; *of Helme
Park and of Harperley Park* (*see also*
Stobart)
KING-WILKINSON *of Slaidburn*
LG1952
WILKS, Bt **PB1911**
WILLANS *of Dolforgan* **LG1952**
WILLARD *formerly of Horsmonden*
DFUSA
WILLCOX *formerly of Bury St Edmunds*
DFUSA
WILLERT **LG1952**
WILLES *formerly of Newbold Comyn*
LG1969
WILLETS *formerly of Barley* **DFUSA**
WILLETTS **DFUSA**
WILLEY (Barnby, B) **PB1970**
WILLIAMS (Berners, B) **PB1970**; Bt
of Bodelwyddan **PB1970**; Bt *of Bridehead* **PB1970**; Bt *of Cilgeraint* **PB1970**;
Bt *of Deudraeth* **PB1970**; Bt *of
Tregullow* **PB1970**; (Williams of
Barnburgh, B) **PB1967**; B **PB1963**;
Bt *of Park* **PB1938**; Bt *of London*
PB1926; Bt of *Llwyny Wormwood*
PB1878; Bt *of Clovelly* **PB1861**;
(Williams of Thame, B) **DEP**; Bt
of Clapton **EDB**; Bt *of Edwinsford*
EDB; Bt *of Eltham* **EDB**; Bt *of
Gwernevet* **EDB**; Bt *of Llangibby*
EDB; Bt *of Marnhull* **EDB**; Bt *of
Minster* **EDB**; Bt *of Vaynol* **EDB**; *of
Crockham House* **LG1972**; *of Werrington and Caerhays* **LG1969**; *of
Aberpergwym* **LG1965**; *of Aspenden
House* **LG1952**; *of East Burnham
Park* **LG1952**; *of Herringston* **LG1952**;
of Llanrumney House **LG1952**;
Shernfold Park **LG1952**; *of Stock Hill*
LG1952; *formerly of Treffos* **LG1952**;
of Trwylan **LG1952**; *of Woolland
House* **LG1952**; *of Bryn Hyfryd*
LG1937; *of Dromenagh* **LG1937**; *late
of Pendley Manor* **LG1937**; *of Bryntirion* **LG1921**; *of Temple House*

LG1921; *of Warpool Court* **LG1921**;
of Bridehead **LG1914**; *of Napleton*
LG1914; *late of Wallog* **LG1914**; *of
Gnaton* **LG1898**; *of Malvern* **LG1894**;
Tre-Castell **LG1894**; **DFUSA**;
formerly of Crewe **DFUSA**; *formerly of
Norwich* **DFUSA**; **FR**; **CG**; *of
Pakaraka* **CG**; *of St Leonards* **CG**;
of Scorrier House and Cerhayes
AA; *of Gwernyfed* (*see* Wood); (*see also*
Murray *of Penpont*; and Williams-
Freeman)
ADDAMS-WILLIAMS *of Llangibby*
LG1952
CRAWSHAY-WILLIAMS *of Coed-y-
Mwstwr* **LG1952**
DUDLEY-WILLIAMS, Bt **PB1970**
FRANCIS-WILLIAMS, B **PB1970**
GARNONS WILLIAMS *of Abercamlais*
LG1972
GRESWOLDE-WILLIAMS *of Bredenbury Court* **LG1921**
GRIFFITH-WILLIAMS (*see* Noel)
GUEST-WILLIAMS *of Christleton Old
Hall and of Rackery Hall* **LG1952**
HANBURY-WILLIAMS *formerly of
Nant Oer and Coldbrook Park*
LG1972
HUME-WILLIAMS, Bt **PB1970**
LLOYD-WILLIAMS *of Gwernant*
LG1937
LOWSLEY WILLIAMS (*formerly
HOOLE and HOOLE-LOWSLEY-
WILLIAMS*) *of Chavenage* **LG1972**
REES-WILLIAMS (Ogmore, B) **PB1970**
RHYS WILLIAMS, Bt **PB1970**
SIMS WILLIAMS *of Temple Grove,
Windlesham* **LG1952**
WILLIAMSON (Forres, B) **PB1970**;
B **PB1970**; Bt **PB1970**; (Ashton, B)
PB1930; *formerly of Waggon Hill
and Kumra Lodge* **LG1972**; *late of
Lawers* **LG1937**; *late of Whickham*
LG1937; *of Cardrona* **LG1921**
WILLINGDON (*see* Freeman-Thomas)
WILLINGTON, B **DEP**; *formerly of St
Kierans* **LGI1958**; *of Tamworth* **AA**
WILLINK, Bt **PB1970**; *formerly of Hillfields* **LG1952**
WILLIS, B **PB1970**; *formerly of Fineshade
and Halsnead* **LG1969**; *of Atherfield*
LG1952; *of Monk's Barn* **LG1952**;
of Halsnead Park **AA**; (*see also*
Willis-Bund)
D'ANYERS WILLIS (*see* Willis *formerly
of Fineshade and Halsnead*)

WILLISON of Trentishoe Manor LG1952
WILLOUGHBY (Middleton, B) PB1970; B DEP; Bt of Risley EDB; Bt of Selston EDB; DFUSA; formerly of Portsmouth DFUSA
WILLOUGHBY DE BROKE (see Verney)
HEATHCOTE - DRUMMOND - WILLOUGHBY (Ancaster, E) PB1970
WILLS (Dulverton, B) PB1970; Bt of Blagdon PB1970; Bt of Hazelwood PB1970; (Winterstoke, B) PB1911; of Barley Wood LG1969; DFUSA
WILLSHIRE, Bt PB1940
WILLSON of Kenward LG1952; of Dulwich AA; (see also Cracroft-Arncotts; of Hackthorn)
WILLYAMS of Carnanton LG1952
WILLYS, Bt EDB; Bt of Fen Ditton EDB
WILMER (see Gossip; and Thomson-Moore)
WILMINGTON (see Compton)
WILMOT, Bt PB1970; (Wilmot of Selmeston, B) PB1963; (Rochester, E) DEP; Bt EDB; (see also Horton)
EARDLEY-WILMOT, Bt PB1970
WILSHERE of The Frythe LG1952
WILSON (Moran, B) PB1970; (Nunburnholme, B) PB1970; (Wilson, B) PB1970; (Wilson of Langside, B) PB1970; Bt of Airdrie PB1970; Bt of Carbeth PB1970; Bt of Eshton Hall PB1970; Bt of Currygane PB1922; Bt of Archer House PB1907; Bt of Killenure EDB; of Ashmore LG1972; of Jerusalem Hill LG1972; formerly of Coole Lane and Sandbach LG1972; of Cliffe Hall LG1965; of The Manor, Aston Somerville LG1952; of Greenock LG1952; formerly of Hexgreave LG1952; of Kilham and formerly of Crofton LG1952; of Rigmaden LG1952; of Thornthwaite Grange LG1952; of Waldershaigh LG1952; of Woodcock Hall LG1952; of Marton LG1937; of Stowlangtoft LG1937; of The Grove LG1921; of Ercildoune. LG1886; of Eshton Hall LG1875; of Knowle Hall LG1875; IFR1976; of Maryville LGI1912; PresFUSA; formerly of Cupar DFUSA; formerly of Fintona DFUSA; formerly of Hull DFUSA; (1) & (2) FR; of Bulls CG; of Ereildoune CG; of

Maryborough CG; (Tasmania) CG; of Wilcelyn CG; of Woodlands CG; of Stowlangtoft Hall AA; (see also Maitland Heriot (formerly Wilson Wood) formerly of Thursby Manor; and Luxmoore of Crackenthorpe
WILSON (formerly GODDARD) of Clyffe Pypard LG1952
WILSON (now WILSON-FILMER) formerly of Tranby Croft LG1952
BROMLEY-WILSON of Dallam Tower LG1898
CARUS-WILSON formerly of Casterton LG1952
HOLT-WILSON of Snape Hill LG1972
MARYON WILSON, Bt PB1970
RIMINGTON-WILSON of Broomhead LG1952
STEWART-WILSON (see Stewart-Stevens)
WILTES (see Scrope)
WILTON (see Egerton)
WILTSHIRE (see Butler; and Stafford)
WIMBERLEY formerly of Bitchfield LG1965
WIMDERLY DFUSA
WIMBLEDON (see Cecil)
WIMBORNE (see Guest)
WIMBROW DFUSA
WINCH, Bt EDB
WINCHCOMBE, Bt EDB
WINCHELL DFUSA
WINCHESTER formerly of Cranbrook DFUSA; (see also Bruges; Despencer; Paulet; and Quincy)
WINCHILSEA AND NOTTINGHAM (see Finch Hatton)
WINDERANK, Bt EDB
CORBETT-WINDER of Vaynor Park LG1972
WINDEYER CG
WINDHAM formerly of Waghen LG1969
SMIJTH-WINDHAM (see Windham formerly of Waghen)
WINDLESHAM (see Hennessy)
WINDSOR (Connaught and Strathearn, D) PB1940; (Plymouth, E) DEP; V DEP; (House of) RL
WINDSORE, B DEP
WINFORD, Bt EDB
WINFREY of Castor House LG1952
STAUNTON-WING of Fitzhead Court LG1937
WINGATE, Bt PB1970
WINGFIELD (Powerscourt, V) PB1970; Bt EDB; of Onslow LG1952; (see also

Wingfield-Digby)
PARRY-WINGFIELD *of Tickencote*
LG1952
WINLOCK **DFUSA**
WINMARLEIGH (*see* Wilson Patten)
WINN (Headley, B) **PB1970**; (St Oswald,
B) **PB1970**; *of Nostell Priory* **LG1879**;
(*see also* Ritchie)
WINNINGTON, Bt **PB1970**
WINSLOW **PromFUSA**
WINSTANLEY *formerly of Braunston*
LG1952; *formerly of Cuerden Hall*
LG1952
WINSTER (*see* Fletcher)
WINSTON **DFUSA**
WINTER *of Agher* **LGI1912**; (*New
Guinea*) **CG**
PURDON-WINTER (*see* Purdon)
WEST-WINTER **DFUSA**
WINTERBOTTOM, B **PB1970**
WINTERSTOKE (*see* Wills)
WINTHROP (*see* Bence-Jones)
WINTON *of Scremby* **LG1937**
WINTOUN (*see* Seton)
WINTOUR, Bt **EDB**
WINTRINGHAM, Bt **EDB**; *of Grimsby*
LG1937
WINWOOD *of Holworth* **LG1921**
WISE (*now* SKIRVING) *of Leamington*
LG1937; *of Clayton* **LG1921**; *of Hill-
bank and Rostellan Castle* **LG1886**;
of Woodcote **LG1863**; *of Manby* **CG**
WISEMAN, Bt **PB1970**; Bt *of Rivenhall*
EDB; Bt *of Thundersley* **EDB**
WISHARD **DFUSA**
WITHAM *of Sutton Place* **LG1914**
MAXWELL-WITHAM *of Kirkconnell*
LG1937
WITHERSPOON **DFUSA**; *formerly of
Haddington* **DFUSA**; (*see also*
Ransom)
WITHINGTON *formerly of Culcheth*
LG1952
WITTENHAM (*see* Faber)
WITTEWRONG, Bt **EDB**
WITTS *of Upper Slaughter* **LG1952**
WODDROP *of Dalmarnock* **LG1879**
WODEHOUSE (Kimberley, E) **PB1970**;
late of Woolmers Park **LG1937**
WOLCOTT *of Knowle House* **LG1879**;
formerly of Tolland **DFUSA**; **Prom
FUSA**
WOLFE (Kilwarden, V) **DEP**; *of Leighon*
LG1898; *of Wood Hall* **LG1894**;
IFR1976; (*Australia*) **CG**
PIPE-WOLFERSTAN *of Statfold*
LG1972

WOLFF, Bt **EDB**
WOLFSON, Bt **PB1970**
WOLLASTON, Bt **EDB**; *of Shenton*
LG1965; (*Australia*) **CG**
WOLLEY *of Allen Hill* **LG1863**; **HI**
WOLRICH, Bt **EDB**
WOLSELEY, Bt *of Mount Wolseley*
PB1970; Bt *of Wolseley* **PB1970**; V
PB1913
WOLSTENHOLME, Bt **EDB**
WOLVERHAMPTON (*see* Fowler)
WOLVERTON (*see* Glyn)
WOMBWELL, Bt **PB1970**
WOMBWELL (*formerly* MENZIES)
formerly of Hallyburton **LG1952**
WOMERSLEY, Bt **PB1970**
WOOD (Halifax, E) **PB1970**; Bt *of
Hatherley House* **PB1970**; Bt *of
Hengrave* **PB1970**; Bt *of Hermitage*
PB1940; (Hatherley, B) **PB1881**;
Bt *of Gatton* **EDB**; *of Belswardyne Hall*
LG1952; *formerly of Bruern Abbey*
LG1952; *of Dene Court* **LG1952**; *of
Henley Hall, Gollanfield and Seabridge
Hall* **LG1952**; *formerly of Hetton*
LG1952; *of Whitehouse* **LG1952**; *of
Brixworth Hall* **LG1937**; *of Pant Glas*
LG1937; *of Shalden Manor formerly of
Thedden Grange* **LG1937**; *formerly of
Singleton Lodge* **LG1937**; *of Arundel
House* **LG1921**; *of Bodlandeb* **LG1921**;
late of Freeland **LG1921**; *of Holnicote*
LG1921; *of Hengrave* **LG1914**; *of
Stouthall* **LG1898**; *of Hawnby*
LG1898; *of Rokeby Grange* **LG1898**;
of Sudbourne Hall **LG1898**; *of Driffield
and Robin Hood's Bay* **LG1898**; *of
Woolley Moor and Harrogate*
LG1894; *of Hollyhurst* **LG1894**;
(1) (2) & (3) **DFUSA**; (1) & (2) **FR**; *of
Riccarton* **CG**; (*see also* Anderson
(*formerly* Wood) *of Bilton Park and
Efford Park*; *and Craster*)
WOOD (*now* HORE RUTHVEN) *of
Gwernyfed* **LG1952**
WOOD (*now* BRADHURST) *of Wakes
Hall* **LG1937**
WOOD (*now* EDWARDS) *of Osmington*
LG1914
BOYNTON-WOOD *of Hollin Hall and
Copmanthorpe*
BRODIE-WOOD *of Keithick* **LG1937**
BURKE WOOD *late of Moreton Hall*
LG1921
COLLINS-WOOD (*see* Brodie-Wood)
HILL-WOOD, Bt **PB1970**

MACONCHIE-WOOD *of Kirknewton* **LG1972**
SMYTHE-WOOD **IFR1976**
WILSON-WOOD (*see* Maitland-Heriot)
WOODALL (Uvedale of North End, B) **PB1970**; *of Waverley Hill* **LG1952**
WOODBRIDGE (*see* Churchman)
WOODBURNE **FR**
WOODBURY *formerly of Burlescombe* **LG1969**; **DFUSA**
WOODCOCK *of Thrussington House* **LG1921**; *of Rearsby House* **LG1900**; *of Bolnore* **LG1900**
WOODD *formerly of Shynewood* **LG1969**
WOODFORD, Bt **EDB**
WOODFORDE *late of Ansford* **LG1921**
WOODGATE (*see* Davidson-Houston *of Pembury*)
WOODHOUSE (Terrington, B) **PB1970**; *of West Lodge* **LG1969**; *of Flamborough* **LG1952**; *formerly of Norley Hall* **LG1952**; *of Omeath Park* **LG1886**
WOODHULL **PromFUSA**
WOODIWISS *of Bath* **LG1921**
WOODLEY *of Halshanger* **LG1921**; **IFR1976**
WOODMAN (*see* Woodman-Hastings)
WOODMASS *of Compstall* **LG1898**
WOODROFFE **FR**
WOODS *of Warnford Park* **LG1937**; *of Milverton Hall* **LG1937Supp**; *of Wigan* **LG1850/3**; **DFUSA**; **PromFUSA**; **FR**; (*see also* Smythe-Wood)
WOODSIDE *of Carnsampson* **LGI1958**
WOODWARD *of Arley Castle* **LG1952**; *of Hopton Court* **LG1952**; *of Drumbarrow* **LG1875**; **DFUSA** (*see also* Lee-Warner)
WOODYEARE *of Crookhill* **LG1875**; **HI**
WOOLAVINGTON (*see* Buchanan)
WOOLLAM **FR**
WOOLLARD *formerly of Wood Ditton* **DFUSA**
WOOLLCOMBE *formerly of Ashbury and of Hemerdon* **LG1965**; **CG**
WOOLLEY, B **PB1970**; **DFUSA**; (1) & (2) **FR**
WOOLRYCH *formerly of Croxley* **LG1972**
WOOLSEY (*see* Barrow)
WOOLTON (*see* Marquis)
WOOLVERTON *formerly of Wolverhampton* **DFUSA**

WOOSNAM *of Cefnllysgwynne* **LG1952**
WOOTEN **DFUSA**
WOOTON (*see* Thomas *of Southwick*)
WOOTTEN **LG1952**
WOOTTON OF ABINGER (*see* Wright)
WORCESTER *formerly of Chedington* **DFUSA**; (*see also* Percy; and Tibetot)
WORDSWORTH *of The Glen* **LG1952**; *of Sockbridge* **LG1875**
WORLEY, Bt **PB1937**
WORMALD *of Heathfield* **LG1972**; *formerly of Sawley Hall* **LG1952**
WORNACK *of Norwich* **VSA**
WORSALD (*see* Lloyd-Oswald)
WORSFOLD, Bt **PB1936**; *of Mitcham* **LG1921**
WORSLEY, Bt **PB1970**; Bt **EDB**; (*see also* Worsley-Taylor)
CARILL-WORSLEY (*see* Tindal-Carill-Worsley)
TINDAL-CARILL-WORSLEY *formerly of East Carleton and Platt* **LG1972**
WORSTHORNE (*see* Koch de Gooreynd; and Towneley)
WORTHAM *formerly of Kneesworth Hall* **LG1952**
WORTHINGTON *of Kingston Russell* **LG1972**; *of Alderley Edge* **LG1952**; *of Moorhill* **LG1952**; *of The Bryn* **LG1875**; *of Maple Hayes* **LG1900**; *of Sandiway Bank* **LG1850/3**; **DFUSA**; **FR**
WORTHINGTON (*formerly* VAWDREY) *of Tushingham* **LG1952**
WORTLEY, Bt **EDB**
STUART-WORTLEY (Stuart of Wortley, B) **PB1926**
MONTAGU - STUART - WORTLEY (*see* Montagu - Stuart - Wortley Mackenzie)
WOTTON (Chesterfield, E) **DEP**; B **DEP**
WOULFE *of Tiermaclane* **LGI1912**
WRAGG *of Bretby and Swadlincote* **LG1972**
WRANGHAM *of Neswick Hall* **LG1937**
WRAXALL, Bt **PB1970**; (*see also* Gibbs)
WRAY, Bt *of Ashby* **EDB**; Bt *of Glentworth* **EDB**; *of Castle Wray* **LG1863**; *of Kelfield* **LG1850/3**; *of Glentworth* **LG1833/7**; (New Zealand) **CG**
WRENBURY (*see* Buckley)
WRENCH *of The Mill House* **LG1952**; *of Killacoona* **LGI1912**
WREY, Bt **PB1970**; *formerly of Thorntoun* **LG1952**
WRIGHT (Wootton of Abinger, B)

PB1970; (Wright of Ashton under
Lyne, B) **PB1970**; Bt *of Swansea*
PB1949; Bt **EDB**; *of Brightwell
Baldwin* **LG1972**; *formerly of Saxton*
LG1972; *of Auchinellan* **LG1969**;
formerly of Yeldersley **LG1965**; *of
Bolton Hall* **LG1952**; *of Brattleby Hall*
LG1952; *formerly of Butterley Hall*
LG1952; *of Wold Newton* **LG1952**;
of Wootton Court **LG1952**; *formerly of
Hawside* **LG1937**; *of West Bank and
Highfield* **LG1898**; *late of Hinton Blewitt*
LG1898; *of Kelvedon* **LG1894**; *of Castle
Park* **LG1894**; *of Halston* **LG1894**;
of Sigglesthorne Hall **LG1894**;
of Kilnacloy **LGI1912**; (1) (2) & (3)
DFUSA; *formerly of Kelvedon*
DFUSA; (1) & (2) **FR**; *of Perth* **CG**;
(Tasmania) **CG**; *of Wellington* **CG**;
of Guayaquil, South America **AA**; *of
Hatfield Priory (see* Luard); *of
Mapperley (see* Osmaston)
WRIGHT (*now* WALLIS-WRIGHT) *of
Mottram Hall* **LG1921**
WRIGHT (*now* WOOD-WRIGHT) *of
Golagh* **LG1879**
WRIGHT (*now* ERDMANN) **DFUSA**
CORY-WRIGHT, Bt **PB1970**
MONCRIEFF WRIGHT (*see* Moncrieff
of Kinmonth)
TYLDEN-WRIGHT **LG1952**; **FR**
WILSON-WRIGHT **IFR1976**
WRIGHTE, Bt **EDB**
WRIGHTSON, Bt **PB1970**; **FR**
BATTIE-WRIGHTSON *of Cusworth*
LG1937
WRIGLEY *of Overchess* **LG1952**; *of
Timberhurst* **LG1886**
WRIOTHESLEY (Chichester, E) **DEP**
WRIXON **CG**
WROTH, Bt **EDB**
WROTTESLEY, B **PB1970**
WROUGHTON *of Woolley Park*
LG1972; *of Ibstone Park* **LG1850/3**;
(*see also* Puxley)
WROUT (*see* Nightingale)
WURTS **DFUSA**
WÜRTTEMBERG (*Royal House of*) **RL**
WYATT *of Hurst Barton Manor*
LG1972; *of Cissbury* **LG1952**; *of
Austin Canons* **LG1937**; **DFUSA**;
(*see also* Wyatt-Edgell)
WYBERGH *of Borran's Hill formerly of
Clifton Hall* **LG1952**
WYCHE, Bt **EDB**; *of Holcombe Manor*
LG1921; *formerly of Davenham*
DFUSA

WYDEVILE (*see* Widvile)
WYFOLD (*see* Hermon-Hodge)
WYKEHAM (Wenman, B) **DEP**;
formerly of Tythrop **LG1972**; (*see also*
Wykeham-Musgrave; and Wykeham-
Martin)
WYLDE *of Southwell* **LG1875**
BOISSIER-WYLES (*see* Boissier)
WYLIE, Bt **PB1854**
DOUGHTY-WYLIE (*formerly*
DOUGHTY) *formerly of Theberton
Hall* **LG1952**
WYMAN *formerly of West Mill* **DFUSA**
WYMAN (*now* LIBBY) *formerly
of Westmill* **DFUSA**
WYNDHAM (Egremont and Leconfield,
B) **PB1970**; (Egremont, E) **DEP**; B
DEP; Bt *of Pilsden Court* **EDB**; Bt
of Trent **EDB**; *of Orchard Wyndham*
LG1965; *of Leconfield* **CG**
WYNELL (*see* Wynell-Mayow)
WYNFORD (*see* Best)
WYNN (Newborough, B) **PB1970**
WILLIAMS-WYNN, Bt **PB1970**
WYNNE, Bt, *of Gwedir* **EDB**; Bt *of
Leeswood* **EDB**; *of Voelas* **LG1875**;
IFR1976; *of Rosbrien* **LGI1912**; *of
Dyffrin Aled* (*see* Yorke); *of Llwyn* (*see*
Tringham *of Nerquis Hall*)
WYNNE (*now* BRODRICK) *of Coed Coch*
LG1937
WILLIAMS-WYNNE *of Peniarth*
LG1952; (*see also* Williams-Wynn)
WYNNIATT *late of Dymock Grange*
LG1894
WYRLEY (*see* Birch-Reynardson)
BONAPARTE WYSE **IFR1976**
WYTHAM, Bt **EDB**
WYTHES *formerly of Copped Hall*
LG1952
WYVILL, Bt **EDB**; *of Constable Burton*
LG1969
XIMENES *late of Bear Place* **LG1914**
YALD *of Blackdown* **LG1875**
YALE *formerly of Plas-yn-lâll* **LG1969**
YARBOROUGH (*see* Pelham)
COOKE-YARBOROUGH *of Camps-
mount* **LG1952**
YARKER **FR**
DUNN-YARKER *of Leyburn Hall*
LG1972
YARMOUTH (*see* Paston; and Wal-
moden)
YARROW, Bt **PB1970**
YATE, Bt *of Madeley Hall* **PB1940**; Bt *of
Buckland* **EDB**
YATES **DFUSA**

PARK-YATES *of Ince Hall* **LG1921**
YATMAN (*now* GUN) *of Winscombe*
LG1952; *of Wellesbourne* **AA**
YEA, Bt **PB1864**
YEAMAN *of Kilfinichen* **LG1952**
YEAMANS, Bt, *of Bristol* **EDB**; Bt *of*
Redland **EDB**
YEATMAN *of Stock Gaylard* **LG1965**;
of Stock House **HI**
YEATS **IFR1976**
YELVERTON (Avonmore, B) **PB1910**;
(Sussex, E) **DEP**; Bt *of Easton Munduit*
EDB; Bt *of Rougham* **EDB**
YEO (*now* BAIRD) *of Fremington*
LG1921
YEOMAN *of Woodlands* **LG1937**
YEOMANS **DFUSA**
YERBURGH (Alvingham, B) **PB1970**; *of*
Woodfold Park **LG1921**
WARDELL-YERBURGH *of Conkwell*
Grange **LG1952**
YONGE, Bt **EDB**; *of Puslinch* **LG1952**;
of Charnes Hall **LG1914**
YORK *of Long Marston* **LG1969**; *of*
Hutton Hall **LG1900**; *of Wighill Park*
LG1833/7; (*see also* Guelph; Planta-
genet; Stuart; and Tudor)
YORKE (Hardwicke, E) **PB1970**; Bt
EDD; *of Hatton Place, formerly of*
Beverley **LG1965**; *of Erthig* **LG1952**; *of*
Forthampton Court **LG1937**
DALLAS-YORKE *of Walmsgate* **LG1914**
WYNNE-YORKE *formerly of Dyffryn*
Aled **LG1952Supp**
CARTHEW-YORSTOUN *formerly of*
East Tinwald **LG1969**
YOUNG (Kennet, B) **PB1970**; Bt *of*
Bailieborough **PB1970**; Bt *of Formosa*
Place **PB1970**; Bt *of North Dean*

PB1970; Bt *of Partick* **PB1970**; (Lisgar
of Lisgar, B) **DEP**; Bt **EDB**; *formerly of*
Kingerby **LG1972**; *of Spring House*
LG1952; *of Stanhill Court* **LG1914**;
of Orlingbury **LG1894**; *of Cleish*
LG1894; *of Culdaff House* **LGI1958**;
of Fenaghy **LGI1958**; *of Coolkeiragh*
LGI1912; *of Harristown* **LGI1912**; *of*
Brockley Park **LGI1912**; *of Galgorm*
LGI1912; (1) (2) & (3) **DFUSA**; *formerly*
of Bristol **DFUSA**; *of Symmons Plains*
CG; (*Tasmania*) **CG**; (*see also* Chi-
chister, Parker (*formerly* Wells) *Lineage*
of De Latour; and von Stettin)
YOUNG (*formerly* HARRIS) *of Thornton*
Hall **LG1952**
HUGHES-YOUNG (St Helens, B)
PB1970; (*see also* Chichester)
KEAYS-YOUNG *of Eylesden* **LG1952**
YOUNGER (Younger of Leckie, V)
PB1970; Bt *of Auchen Castle* **PB1970**;
Bt *of Fountainbridge* **PB1970**; (Blanes-
borough, B) **PB1940**; *of Benmore*
LG1952; *of Auchen Castle* **LG1900**
YOUNGHUSBAND *formerly of Priory*
House **LG1972**
YPRES (*see* French)
YSTWYTH (*see* Davies)
YUGOSLAVIA (*Royal House of*) **RL**
YUILLE *of Darleith* **LG1898**
YULE, Bt **PB1928**
ZEAL *of Clovelly* **CG**
ZETLAND (*see* Dundas)
ZINOVIEFF *of Hillsboro* **LG1952**
ZOLLNER (*see* Allison)
ZOUCHE (Zouche, *of Ashby*, B) **DEP**,
(Zouche, *of Mortimer*, B) **DEP**; (*see*
also Frankland)